The Nature of Love

Other works of Dietrich von Hildebrand
available from St. Augustine's Press

The Heart: An Analysis of Human and Divine Affectivity

The Dietrich von Hildebrand LifeGuide™

The Nature of Love

Dietrich von Hildebrand

Translated by
John F. Crosby with John Henry Crosby

Introductory Study by John F. Crosby

Preface by Kenneth L. Schmitz

ST. AUGUSTINE'S PRESS
South Bend, Indiana

in association with the Dietrich von Hildebrand Legacy Project
www.hildebrandlegacy.org

Manufactured in the United States of America.

2 3 4 5 6   16 15 14 13 12 11 10

Library of Congress Cataloging in Publication Data
Von Hildebrand, Dietrich, 1889–1977.
[Wesen der Liebe. English]
The nature of love / Dietrich von Hildebrand;
translated by John F. Crosby with John Henry Crosby;
introductory study by John F. Crosby; preface by Kenneth L. Schmitz.
p. cm.
Includes bibliographical references and index.
ISBN-13: 978-1-58731-560-2 (hardcover: alk. paper)
ISBN-10: 1-58731-560-2 (hardcover: alk. paper)
1. Love. I. Title.
B3359.V63W4 2009
177'.7 – dc22   2009002019

ST. AUGUSTINE'S PRESS
www.staugustine.net

Suavissimae ac dilectissimae conjugi Lily

"Che sola a me par donna"
– Petrarch

Table of Contents

Acknowledgments

My work on this translation began in 2000 with a generous grant to me from Ave Maria University. Special thanks are due to Mr. Nicholas Healy, Jr., president of Ave Maria University. All of the other expenses of making and publishing the translation were covered by the Dietrich von Hildebrand Legacy Project, which for its part received support for this translation from several foundations, including the Dan Murphy Foundation, Our Sunday Visitor Institute, the Papal Foundation, and the Raskob Foundation for Catholic Activities. We also received support from individual donors, including Frank and Patricia Lynch, Michael and Suzanne Doherty, Lee and Margaret Matherne, Robert Luddy, Jules and Kathleen van Schaijik, and Robert and Joan Smith. My warmest thanks to all of them.

Towards the end of my translating labors, my university, Franciscan University of Steubenville—more exactly Dr. Max Bonilla, Vice-President for Academic Affairs, and Dr. Mark Roberts, Director of M.A. Philosophy—helped me by reducing my teaching load in the fall of 2006 and by funding a student assistant in the person of Stephen Phelan. My thanks to my university for this support.

Besides thanking Mr. Phelan I also want to thank two other students of mine. Some of the early chapters were drafted by dictation, and Christina Lorin patiently transcribed the dictation. At the very end of this project, John Tutuska ably produced the index and did the work of proofreading the text.

I consulted with various persons on difficult points of translation, including my wife Pia Crosby, Alice von Hildebrand, Josef Seifert, Fritz Wenisch, and Stephen Schwarz. The translation has been improved in many ways by their counsel, and I thank each of them. Pia Crosby and Josef Seifert also provided helpful comments on my introductory study.

The cover jacket was attractively designed by Anthony C. Gualandri and Katharina Seifert. Prof. Kenneth Schmitz has enhanced the volume with a prefatory word, for which we are especially grateful.

Thanks of a different kind are due to our publisher, Mr. Bruce Fingerhut of St. Augustine Press, whose patience I taxed in an unusual way by making innumerable changes in the translation even after the typesetting process had begun. Though he had, he said, never worked with such a fickle author before, he bore with me.

I also acknowledge Alice von Hildebrand, the widow of the author and the person to whom this work is dedicated. She never lost an opportunity to give me encouragement, and in this way to give impetus to my work of translation. She could not quite understood why the translation was so long in coming, but she never stopped hoping that, as she said, she would live to hold the finished book in her hands.

But there is one person whose help deserves special mention and who in fact almost merits the title of co-translator. My son, John Henry Crosby, the founder of the Dietrich von Hildebrand Legacy Project, has not only provided through the Legacy Project much of the funding of this translation project; he also drafted for me the translation of the last three chapters, which form almost a third of the work. In addition he reviewed down to the last detail and with great precision my draft of the first chapters of the work and he made innumerable improvements. He has a keen sense of German—he spoke German before he spoke English—and he understands from within the philosophical world of von Hildebrand. But I have had the final responsibility for making the translation, and so all criticisms of it should be brought directly to me.

John F. Crosby
July 17, 2008

Preface

Kenneth L. Schmitz
University of Toronto

Among Catholic philosophers in the past century, there arose a remarkable set of diverse thinkers who shared in the new explorations in phenomenology and yet reunited these with the more traditional concern for metaphysics. One thinks of such varied philosophers as Edith Stein, Gabriel Marcel, and Karol Wojtyla. Among them, Dietrich von Hildebrand is distinguished by the breadth and intensity of his reflections on the affective dimension of our human nature. His works on the subject are manifold, but they come together in this present volume on the essence of love. Having noted the radical difference between the subjectively satisfying and the other modalities of value, he has presented a subtle reflection on the diverse forms of value-response. In a way that is unprecedented in philosophical literature in its depth and clarity, von Hildebrand spells out the affective character of value that transcends our humanity, and calls for a value-response by which we are raised above our own capability in the realization of the very essence of love. Yet, while this carries us beyond ourselves, our experience with value does not end there. In his instructive introduction, Professor John F. Crosby draws our attention to a further relation that completes our experience of value. It is that whereby "a certain interior dimension of personal self-possession...comes to light," and that constitutes "the objective good for a person," and with it the fulfillment of the person in and through love. This recovery of the value of the person in and through love discloses a third kind of importance in the domain of love, a kind which is neither simply subjectively satisfying, nor important exclusively in itself, but a love that is the flourishing of the person in the supremely transcendent value of love.

In this work, von Hildebrand has given us what—in my view—is an unprecedented reflection upon the role of love in its several forms, with especial attention to the love of man and woman. The several deformations of authentic love, such as purely selfless love and its opposite, self-centered love, are treated with understanding as forms that fail to realize ourselves as persons.

No doubt, in the long history of philosophical reflection on love the distinction between good for us and good in itself has been addressed, but I do not think that it has received such explicit and enlightening attention in other philosophers. In addition to its own intrinsic value as—in my judgment—the most significant contribution of the past century to the thematic of love, the present work with its helpful introduction may be taken as an invitation to further discussion with other philosophical traditions, such as those of Kantian, Augustinian and Thomistic provenance.

Toronto, Canada
July 24, 2008

Introductory Study

John F. Crosby

Relatively late in life, beginning around 1958, Dietrich von Hildebrand (1889–1977) began working on a book that had been growing in him all his life, a phenomenological study of love. Already in the 1920's he had received a great deal of attention in the Catholic world for his writings on man and woman, the love between them, and Christian marriage. He had caught the attention of the Catholic world by his exalted vision of the love between man and woman.[1] Through his meditation on this love he was led to argue—in fact he was one of the first Catholic writers to argue—that the marital act has a dual meaning, it has not only a procreative but also a unitive meaning, in other words, it not only transmits life but also expresses conjugal love. It is now generally acknowledged that von Hildebrand was a pioneer of the teaching on the dual meaning of the marital act that was articulated at Vatican II in the chapter on Christian marriage in *Gaudium et spes*. But what he envisioned later in life was a more comprehensive phenomenological study of love in all of its categories and not just in the category of conjugal love. When his book, *Das Wesen der Liebe*, appeared in 1971, it was arguably the most important phenomenological contribution to the subject since Max Scheler's treatment of love in his 1913 book, *Wesen und Formen der Sympathie (The Nature of Sympathy)*.

Coming as it did at the end of a lifetime of philosophical research and writing, this treatise is embedded in his previous work in philosophy, and can be fully understood only on the background of this previous work. And so the first purpose of this introduction is to supply that background. Those who already know von Hildebrand's previous writings may find the following discussion to be of interest insofar as it makes a contribution towards placing *The Nature of Love* within the whole of his work. The second purpose of this introduction is to relate von Hildebrand's treatise to some recent phenomenological work on love, especially the work of Jean-Luc Marion.

---

1   He expressed this vision in his books *Reinheit und Jungfräulichkeit* (1927) and *Die Ehe* (1929). The former has been translated as *Purity* and the latter as *Marriage*. The full bibliographical reference for these and for all works of von Hildebrand cited by me in this introduction or by von Hildebrand himself in *The Nature of Love* can be found in the bibliography placed at the end of this book.

1. Value and value-response

The first writings of von Hildebrand are in ethics, and this is in fact the area in which he made his most significant contributions to philosophy. In his ethical works he starts from Scheler's value philosophy and develops an original concept of good and bad; he explores the structure of motivation, moral value and disvalue, moral virtue and vice, and moral obligation. He also explores the structure of the human person, especially the self-transcendence that persons achieve in their moral existence; the Christian personalism that has been ascribed to von Hildebrand is established in large part in the ethical writings. My purpose here is not to survey the whole of the von Hildebrandian ethics, but simply to present those themes in it that are essential for understanding his work on love. We begin with the concept of *value* and the related concept of *value-response*: these are foundational for everything in von Hildebrand, including his philosophy of love.

It is often said that the term *value* expresses something entirely subjective, something relative to the person who places a value on a thing. While it is true that many do use value in this subjectivistic sense, the term (just like *Wert* in German) is capable of being used in a deeper and richer sense, as one can see from this occurrence of the term in Shakespeare:

> But value dwells not in particular will;
> It holds his estimate and dignity
> As well where in 'tis precious of itself
> As in the prizer. (*Troilus and Cressida*, II, 1)

Even in our time value can readily mean something like "precious of itself," as when Oscar Wilde defines the cynic as "the person who knows the price of everything and the value of nothing," or as when C. S. Lewis writing in *The Abolition of Man* embraces what he calls "the doctrine of objective value." Now von Hildebrand's use of value is situated within this rich potential of the word.

Take the character of Socrates; as we get acquainted with his wisdom, his irony, his courage, his passion for truth, we experience value in him. The value does not depend on us the prizers, but we experience it as altogether independent of us and our prizing; we experience in Socrates something "precious of itself." We are filled with admiration and veneration, and we understand why Plato and others could have venerated him as they did. Now in order to throw value into relief von Hildebrand brings in for contrast what he calls "the importance of the subjectively satisfying." Consider the importance that another cigarette has for a heavy smoker; the cigarette does not present itself to him as "precious of itself" but is rather important for him simply because it satisfies his craving. If the cigarette did not provide him with satisfaction he would pass it by in complete indifference; he detects no intrinsic excellence in it that would sustain his interest in it in the absence of any subjective satisfaction. He takes another cigarette to consume it, not to revere it.

There is for von Hildebrand not only value but also disvalue, which would be that which is "odious of itself" and not just subjectively dissatisfying. When we condemn some violent and cruel crime, we do not just find it dissatisfying; we find that it is wicked with a wickedness that is entirely independent of our subjective dissatisfaction.

We can go deeper into von Hildebrand's understanding of value when we understand why it is that all value bears beauty. It is not that he thinks that all value is specifically aesthetic value; on the contrary, in the first chapters of his *Aesthetik I* he distinguishes aesthetic values with precision from other value domains. But he means that even non-aesthetic value, such as the value we find in Socrates, is marked by a certain beauty. This is why the deep intuitive experience of a value always confers some delight on the experiencing person; it is the delight that only the beautiful can give. Recall the way in which Alcibiades was fascinated by Socrates; it must have been a value-based fascination, for he mentions the beauty that he saw in Socrates (a beauty that was not an aesthetic quality but rather a certain radiance of the character of Socrates). By contrast, I find no beauty in that which appeals to me as merely subjectively satisfying. When my subjective satisfaction is the sole determinant of the importance that something takes on for me, then that importance, much as it makes the thing attractive to me, is unable to make the thing radiant with beauty.

Von Hildebrand was convinced that—to vary the famous utterance of Thales—the world is full of values. He thinks that we have to do with value in more ways than we can count, and that our world, especially in its deepest dimensions, would be disfigured beyond recognition if we bracketed all value out of it. The expression, *die Welt der Werte*, or the world of values, expresses for him all the depth and plenitude of being, as well as the hierarchical structure that makes our world a cosmos. Value also has a religious dimension for him; the values of things reflect in different ways the divine glory, which for its part is also a value concept. Thus *value* for von Hildebrand was as metaphysically potent as *being*. He knew nothing of the Heideggerian aversion for value and value philosophy. Whereas Heidegger could conceive of value only as something subjectivistically superimposed on being, von Hildebrand conceived of value as nothing other than being in all its dignity, nobility, and beauty.[2]

But we are here concerned with the ethical and personalist use that von

---

2   I have written against this Heideggerian condemnation of value, giving special attention to the particular mode of inherence that is found in the relation of value to being. See my studies, "The Idea of Value and the Reform of the Traditional Metaphysics of *Bonum*" in *Aletheia* I no 2 (1978): 221–336, and "Are Good and Being Really Convertible?" in *The New Scholasticism* 57 no. 4 (1983): 465–500.

Hildebrand makes of value. For this we have to explore a certain very revealing relation in which value stands to persons who know about it: every thing of value is worthy of a right response in virtue of its value. Thus Socrates is worthy of admiration and veneration; persons are worthy of respect; being is worthy of reverence; God is worthy of adoration. In each case some right response is due to a valuable being, or is merited by it; an elementary justice is fulfilled when the being that is in some way "precious of itself" receives the due response. Whoever admires a Socrates has the consciousness of Socrates being worthy of admiration, has the consciousness of one's admiration not just being a psychological fact but the fulfillment of an ought. With the importance of the subjectively satisfying, by contrast, we have no consciousness of the important thing being worthy of any response. The cigarette is not experienced as worthy of the interest of the smoker.

The full personalist significance of what von Hildebrand calls value-response shows itself if we consider value-response not only from the side of value, which merits the response, but also from the side of the human person, who gives the response. Von Hildebrand often marvels at the way in which a person *transcends himself* in giving a value-response, and in fact throughout his ethical writings he holds that the real "signature" of the human person lies in this self-transcendence achieved in value-response. He speaks of self-transcendence because a person who is caught up in the value of something is stepping beyond his own needs and, instead of seeing the world only from the point of view of satisfying them, he sees it for what it is in its own right, according to its own value, and he approaches it with reverence, responding to it with a response that it is proportioned to and measured by the value. By contrast, in pursuing something as subjectively satisfying we bend the thing to the satisfaction of our needs, seeing it only under the aspect of satisfying our needs, taking no interest in what it is in its own right. In this we precisely do not transcend ourselves but remain locked in our immanence, and so we give less evidence of existing as persons.

Von Hildebrand does not just contrast *individual acts* of value-response with *individual acts* of being motivated by the subjectively satisfying; he also contrasts *two kinds of persons*. The one kind of person lives primarily by value-response; this person never lets his interest in the subjectively satisfying interfere with or curtail his reverence towards the world of value. He is still quite capable of experiencing things subjectively satisfying and of desiring them, but he never pursues them at the expense of the call of value. The other kind of person lives primarily for the subjectively satisfying; in the end he ceases even to care about what is "precious of itself." Here for von Hildebrand lies the fundamental moral freedom of persons; here is the most radical self-determination of which we are capable, for here we choose between radically opposed forms of moral existence. Von Hildebrand offers here a value-based way of thinking about the two great loves distinguished by St. Augustine: the love of God that leads even to the contempt of self,[3] and the love of self that leads even to the contempt of God.

But von Hildebrand attempts to achieve greater precision regarding the two loves. He argues that it is a certain kind of value-response that stands at the center of the moral existence of the first kind of person. In speaking just now of the beauty of value we were taking value in its power of drawing and attracting us; but value sometimes also has the power, or rather authority, to bind me in the manner of moral obligation. If I am tempted to do some wrong, such as cast suspicion for a crime onto someone whom I know did not commit it, and if I am convicted in my conscience that I must not do this, then I experience certain values of the innocent person exercising this binding function. The values that exercise this function get a special name in the ethics of von Hildebrand; he calls them "morally relevant values," a term that the reader will often encounter in the present work. He contrasts them with "morally irrelevant values," which are things that indeed form a full contrast with the importance of the merely subjectively satisfying, but are not such as to bind me with obligation. A tree, for example, has von Hildebrandian value, a value that in fact, when strongly experienced, commands reverence; but if I want to cut one down for my use I do not find myself morally bound to let it stand. The tree is something "precious of itself," but it does not the power to bind that is the defining note of the morally relevant values.

Von Hildebrand takes very seriously this imperative power of the morally relevant values, for he thinks of it, just as Cardinal Newman thought of it, as being full of intimations of God. Only if this call is ultimately grounded in God, he says, can we make sense of the way in which these values pierce me with their unconditional call and energize my deepest freedom and elicit a kind of obedience from me in my response to them. In chapter 4 of the present work von Hildebrand explores further (beyond the previous ethical writings) the special transcendence that is achieved in relation to morally relevant values. He argues that the transcendence proper to all value-response is raised to a higher power in the case of the value-response given to morally relevant values. Here the implicit encounter with God calls me out of my immanence in a far more radical way. It follows that a more precise statement of the two opposite kinds of person and of the two opposite kinds of love would go like this: the one person gives absolute priority to all morally relevant values, never letting his interest in the subjectively satisfying divert him from the imperative call of these values, whereas the other person is willing to scorn even morally relevant values in the pursuit of his subjective satisfaction.

---

3   By appropriating this Augustinian formula von Hildebrand in no way means to deny the existence of a well-ordered self-love that coheres entirely with the love for God.

2. Value in relation to that which is objectively good for a person

The reader may be puzzled at the fact that in his ethical works as well as in the work on love von Hildebrand is frequently in debate with Thomistic philosophy. This is puzzling, since the Hildebrandian ethics as so far outlined would not seem to be controversial for Christian philosophers; it does not seem to say anything that they do not all say. But there is a reason for von Hildebrand's polemic, and it will come to light as soon as we see why he distinguishes a third kind of good, one different from either value or the importance of the subjectively satisfying.

Von Hildebrand thinks that a good such as being healthy, or being educated, is not just important for a person as a result of being subjectively satisfying for that person. When I take an interest in my education, and realize the importance of it, I quite understand that my subjective satisfaction is not the principle or cause of the importance; I understand that some other, stronger kind of importance is at stake. This is why I acknowledge a real moral fault in myself if, at some earlier time in my life, I neglected my education. If I *ought* to take an interest in my education—if in other words it is morally relevant—then there is more to the importance of education than its being just subjectively satisfying for me. But Hildebrand thinks that this more-than-subjective importance of my education is also not the importance of value, for my education is important *for me* in the sense that it is important for me *by being beneficial for me.* Thus the fact that it is my education and not yours enters into the importance that it has for me. But when some thing of value, such as the nobility of a generous person, has importance in my eyes, then I take an interest in it without having any thought of receiving a benefit. If I am filled with admiration for the generous person, I have no least thought of being enhanced in my being as a result of admiring him. The nobility of his character is important for me under the aspect of being good in its own right and not just beneficial for me. Thus the importance exemplified in the good of my education is importance of a third kind, reducible neither to the importance of the merely subjectively satisfying nor to the importance of value; von Hildebrand calls it the "objective good for the person," or the beneficial good, against which stands, in the negative, all that is objectively harmful for the person.

There is a remarkable passage in Plato's *Gorgias* that lets us see the difference between the objective good for the person and value. Early on Socrates is trying to convince Polus that it is worse for a human being to commit injustice than to be the victim of it. What he means is that it is incomparably harmful for a human being to commit injustice; he is in effect making a claim in terms of von Hildebrand's third kind of good/bad. Since he is having little success in persuading Polus about this supreme harmfulness of wrongdoing, he decides to take a different approach; he asks Polus whether wrongdoing is not *uglier* than suffering it. By taking wrongdoing under a certain aesthetic aspect, Socrates takes it precisely as a disvalue in von Hildebrand's sense. Socrates must have switched to a different aspect of good/bad, for now Polus agrees with him. It is easy to transpose this result into the positive; then we get the thesis that doing the just thing is supremely beneficial to the one who does it, and that, in addition, accomplishing justice also has its own beauty. In von Hildebrand's language: accomplishing justice is not only good for the person who accomplishes it, but also has value.

Now von Hildebrand thinks that the *bonum* of Thomistic philosophy centers largely around this third kind of good and does not take sufficient account of value and of value-response. He has in mind the Thomistic teaching that each being has a natural desire (*appetitus*) for the fullness of being proper to its kind, or in other words for the full actualization or perfection of its being, and that *bonum* or good simply expresses this perfection or actualization considered as desirable. *Bonum* thus seems to von Hildebrand to be defined in a way that is equivalent to his third kind of good—it seems to be good understood as that which is beneficial or fulfilling for some person. But if good is defined in this way, then little place is left for value and value-response. As a result, he says, the Thomistic ethics[4] cannot do full justice to the transcendence that really characterizes the moral life; in place of a life centered around giving things of value their due and obeying the call of morally relevant values, we now have a life centered around the full flourishing of myself. And although such a life is never to be confused with a life centered around the merely subjectively satisfying,[5] it is still deficient with respect to transcen-

---

4   Michael Waldstein has recently questioned this von Hildebrandian interpretation of Thomism in his study "Dietrich von Hildebrand and St. Thomas Aquinas on Goodness and Happiness," in *Nova et Vetera* I, no. 2 (2003): 403–464. Waldstein is, I think, right in saying that St. Thomas himself does not have to be interpreted as holding the position summarized in this paragraph. Von Hildebrand was basing himself on what he often heard certain Thomists say and he stopped short of ascribing to St. Thomas himself this conception of good and *appetitus*. Waldstein suggests that the real target of von Hildebrand is not St. Thomas but a degenerate form of Thomism that Waldstein dubs "entelechial Thomism." On the other hand, it can hardly be claimed, and Waldstein does not claim, that St. Thomas had the concept of value and of value-response and that he used these concepts, or equivalent concepts, at the level of his theoretical discourse on good and happiness. This means that St. Thomas does not capture the moment of transcendence in moral action with the precision with which von Hildebrand captures it.

5   Waldstein, *op. cit.*, especially pp. 404–414, does not avoid this confusion entirely. He speaks as if von Hildebrand were alleging that in Thomism the moral life is led at the level of the subjectively satisfying. In fact, von Hildebrand never thought that Thomism, or any school of Thomism, however degenerate, was inclined to an ethics based on the subjectively satisfying. He thought that he discerned, it is true, a defect of transcendence in the Thomistic account of the striving for good and for happiness, but he took this defect to derive from the place that the objective good for the person occupies in Thomism, which to his mind was a defect very different—utterly different—from the defect of advocating a life abandoned to the merely subjectively satisfying.

dence. Whenever von Hildebrand deplores *eudaemonism* in ethics, he is deploring a concern with my flourishing that compromises the spirit of value-response in which I ought to live.

When, for example, I defend an innocently accused person, I do so in the consciousness that I owe this in justice to the other; the thought that I flourish by defending the other is entirely in the background. Von Hildebrand is fiercely insistent on the fact that I defend the other for his or her sake, and not first of all for my sake. Of course I flourish and become happy as a result of defending the other, and in fact happy in a way in which people who do not live by value-response cannot be happy, but this experience of my flourishing for von Hildebrand flows superabundantly from my value-responding commitment to the other and functions as an entirely secondary motive, a motive entirely subordinate to the value-response to the other. Von Hildebrand makes a similar argument at the level of our religious existence. While we often approach God under the aspect of being supremely beneficial for us, as when we invoke Him as savior, protector, rock of refuge, comforter, we also approach Him under the aspect of value, as when we adore Him in the consciousness that He is worthy of adoration, or praise Him as one who is worthy of all praise. Our religious existence, he argues, becomes cramped if we always only approach Him in the first way; it has to be permeated by the transcendence that is achieved in value-responding adoration and praise.

In no way, however, does von Hildebrand aim at keeping out of the moral life all interest in things that are beneficial for me, as if the moral life were led exclusively in and through value-response and as if any interest in what is beneficial for me were an interest that falls outside of the moral life. He thinks in fact that objective goods for myself are frequently morally relevant for me (as we just saw in the example of neglecting my education) and that objective goods for other persons, so far as I am in a position to provide them for others, are always morally relevant for me. What distinguishes his ethics is the idea that the interest in objective goods for persons cannot be the whole of the moral life but must be situated within value-responding affirmations of value. In fact he makes a stronger claim: value-response should have a certain priority over all interest in what is beneficial for persons. Thus I should be more concerned that the innocent person be vindicated by my intervention than that I flourish and become happy by intervening on behalf of him or her. And I should be more concerned that God be exalted and praised than that I be blessed by Him and happy in Him.

But von Hildebrand also explores the interconnection, indeed interpenetration of the two kinds of interest, as when he claims that this priority of value-response is necessary for certain beneficial goods to be experienced in all of their beneficence for me. The act of intervening on the behalf of the innocent person is able fully to benefit me only if the will to be benefited is subordinate to the will to vindicate the innocent person. I can only be happy in God if I know how to adore Him and praise Him all for His own sake; if I do not know Him as one who is worthy of adoration, then my union with Him will not confer all the beatitude of which it is capable. So in the end his objection to what he took to be the Thomistic ethics is not that it takes *bonum* seriously but that it lacks the idea of good in itself, and of serving what is good in itself for its own sake. This means that this ethics cannot do full justice to the transcendence proper to the moral life, and it means, in addition, that it cannot unlock all those goods for persons that depend on value and that can be sought only in conjunction with value-response.

We are about to see another aspect of this interpenetration of the two kinds of interest; we will see how for von Hildebrand the transcendence of value-response can be raised to a higher power when it is joined with a certain concern for objective goods for the person.

We have now surveyed the three kinds or categories of good/bad that von Hildebrand distinguishes: the importance of the subjectively satisfying/dissatisfying; the objective good/evil for a person; and value/disvalue. He gives his fullest account of these three categories in chapters 1–3 of his *Ethics*; these chapters form a kind of cornerstone of the entire philosophy of von Hildebrand. It presents a theory of value and of human motivation that structures the treatise of love from beginning to end.

3. Love as a value-response

If readers know no more about von Hildebrand's ethics than we have just sketched out, they will not be at all surprised at the first chapter of *The Nature of Love*; they could have almost predicted that he would open this work with a chapter on "Love as Value-Response." The first chapter of this work is in fact entirely devoted to showing that love is a value-response to the beloved person as beautiful. The Platonic account of love in the *Symposium,* 199c–204c, is exactly the kind of account that von Hildebrand wants to overcome. I do not, as Plato thought, love out of need, and I am not drawn to the beloved under the aspect of one who can fulfill my need. I am drawn to the beloved as one who is lovable in his or her own right, and I love the other for his or her own sake. Von Hildebrand fights against eudaemonism in the theory of love no less than in his ethics.

He considers the objection that my love is often awakened by the good that a person does for me, and that this seems to show that I after all love the other under the aspect of being good for me rather than under the aspect of value. Von Hildebrand responds that when the other is good to me, she shows me something good and beautiful in her person; it is this beauty—a genuine datum of value—that engenders my love, and not the fact that the other has done good to me. The way the other turns to me doing good to me, reveals to me the goodness of the other, but this is a goodness that is not reducible to being good to me, but it is something worthy and splendid in its own right; the person, thus revealed, stands before me as radiant and beautiful, and so awakens in me a value-responding love for her.

Von Hildebrand takes care to avoid the idea that the beloved person is just a specimen of some excellence or value, and is lovable only on the basis of instantiating some excellence or value. If this were so, I would love the value more than the person. So love is not just any value-response, but it is a very particular one in which the value to which I respond is one with the unrepeatable person of the other. It is a value in which the beloved person is, as he says, altogether "thematic" as this individual person. Only in this way can I really love the other for his or her own sake. The richest insights of von Hildebrand into the unrepeatable individuality of a person are to be found right here in chapter 3 of the present work, where he discusses the *Wertgegebenheit* that enkindles love. It is understandable that the study of love would draw him more deeply into the unrepeatable individuality of persons than the study of ethical existence did. When I intervene to protect the unjustly accused person, I need not be aware of or respond to the person as *this individual*, for I should be ready to intervene on behalf of any other similarly accused person: but if I love that person—love of neighbor is a separate case—I must be aware of and respond to him or her as this unrepeatable person and no other.

Von Hildebrand also deals with the objection that would reverse the relation between my love and the value of the beloved. According to this objection, I first love, and then I invest the other with all kinds of noble qualities; far from being grounded in the value that I have experienced in the other, my love is in fact the source of such value. Von Hildebrand argues that it is in fact other attitudes mixed in with but really foreign to love that lead me to endow the other with value. For instance, in the love between man and woman sexual desire can lead to value illusions; in the love of parents for their children, a certain parental pride can lead to illusions about the superiority of one's own children over other people's children. Once these attitudes are distinguished from love, he argues, it becomes apparent that love, while it sensitizes me to the value of the beloved person, is characterized by a deep reverence that inhibits value illusions.

Von Hildebrand also examines the fact that each person has a deep need to love and to be loved; this is why it is so deeply fulfilling to love and why a loveless existence is a crippled existence. This significant fact may incline us to think that the beloved person is loved under the aspect of fulfilling this need. But then love would after all be no real value-response. Von Hildebrand responds that there are many different kinds of needs, and some of them actually have a value-responding structure. Why should there not be a need to love another for his or her own sake? a need to be captivated in a value-responding way by the beauty of another?[6] When Aristotle speaks of the natural desire of

6   I take "need" here in a broader sense than von Hildebrand usually takes it; whereas he usually means with this term something that arises in us on its own and bends to itself that which satisfies it, I use it here to mean anything in the human person that provides the basis for "fulfillment."

all human beings to know, he means of course to know things as they really are; only knowledge in this sense could fulfill the desire. Why then should it be surprising that the need to love can only be fulfilled when I am moved by the inner splendor, the real worthiness and value of a person?[7]

The first thing we want to show, then, is that von Hildebrand in his treatise on love continues along the line of his earlier ethical work. Self-transcending value-response is in its own way just as important for his account of love as it was for his account of moral action and moral virtues. The resolute opposition to eudaemonism that began in his ethical works continues here in his treatise on love. We could say, using language that is not von Hildebrand's, that he wants the beloved person to appear in all his or her otherness; any intrusion of me and my needs and my desire for happiness must be excluded if I am to encounter the other so as really to love him or her.

4. Love as a "super value-response"

But at the same time von Hildebrand notices that the transcendence that he had studied in ethics is modified in the case of some kinds of love. As a master phenomenologist he would never simply transfer to love all the patterns of transcendence found in the moral life. He observes that the imperative moment that he studied in connection with morally relevant values is not found in the love between friends nor is it found in the love between man and woman, which he regards as the most eminent kind of love. For it is never a matter of strict moral obligation to enter into friendship with a certain person or to enter into a man-woman love relation with a certain person. The imperative moment is indeed found in two kinds of love, namely in love of neighbor and in love for God, but it is not found in the other categories of love. Thus a certain power of moral transcendence is not proper to them. On the other hand, these loves have certain perfections of transcendence that are not found in the moral life. In this book von Hildebrand is always tracking the ways in which persons transcend themselves and is always examining how the transcendence of love is both like and unlike the transcendence achieved in a well-ordered moral existence.

Thus he argues, building on his earlier study of human affectivity,[8] that in loving another I take an *affective delight* in the other. If I exercise only my will, but not my heart, then however favorable to the other my willing may be, however beneficent, I do not really love the other. For this affective energy proper to all love—and he says that no other response is affective in the way that love is—lets me be fully present in my love, present with my whole self, with my real self, my intimate self; as a result it lets me give myself to the other in a way in which, exercising the will alone, I cannot give myself, and so it lets me

---

7   This train of thought, clearly, lends itself to serving as a bridge between the Thomistic ethics and the Hildebrandian ethics.

8   Dietrich von Hildebrand, *The Heart*, especially Part I, chapter 8.

transcend myself towards the other in a new way. This rich vein of thought on the affectivity of love is based in von Hildebrand on his value theory. For value, especially considered under the aspect of the beauty that it gives off, delights; value is revealed as value precisely through its capacity to delight, to affect, to move the heart. Thus the beloved person, appearing radiant with value, awakens my love by moving me affectively. Above we distinguished between the power of value to *attract or draw* a person, and the power of (morally relevant) value to *bind or oblige* a person. In love it is above all the former power that is at work. When value exercises its binding function, giving rise to an obligatory action, then it addresses my will; but insofar as it draws me to another in love, it addresses my heart. And though the will that bows before the obligation achieves a unique kind of transcendence, as we saw, the person who loves with affective plenitude achieves a different kind of transcendence towards the beloved person.

Von Hildebrand considers another form of transcendence that is proper to love; he gives it a special name, "super value-response," a term that appears here for the first time in von Hildebrand's corpus. It cannot be my goal here to offer a full discussion of "super value-response," but simply—in accordance with the limited purpose of this introduction—to show how von Hildebrand employs the categories of his ethics in order to form this new concept.

Let us go back to good in the sense of that which is objectively good for some person. Good in this sense can be reduced neither to value nor to the importance of the merely subjectively satisfying, as we saw. This kind of good plays a major role in raising love from the status of value-response to the status of a "super value-response." This seems surprising at first glance, since we explained value-response *in distinction to* an interest in what is beneficial for me: how then can this interest serve to raise value-response to a higher power of value-response?

I enter into a relation of love with someone. It would not be a relation of love if I did not stand in a value-responding relation to the other, as we saw, but my transcendence towards the other is not limited to value-response. For I am happy in loving the other and in being loved by the other—happy in the sense not just of being subjectively satisfied, but rather of being deeply, gratefully happy. This means that the beloved person, and our relationship, is an eminent case of something objectively good for me. At the same time I become something objectively good for the beloved person, who finds her happiness in her relation to me. Now von Hildebrand argues that I give myself to the beloved person in a unique way by willing to be the source of her happiness; he also argues that I give myself to the other by willing to receive from her my own deepest happiness. But this self-giving, though based on what is objectively good for a person, is a dimension of transcendence towards the other all its own; it is a transcendence that goes beyond the transcendence of value-response; it is that which makes love a "super value-response."

It is true that, in the abstract, to take an interest in something objectively good for me lacks the transcendence of a value-responding affirmation of something in it own right. But if the objective good for me *is embedded in value-response*, as it is in the case of love, then my interest in this good can join with my value-response in such a way as to effect a self-giving that surpasses the value-response alone and that qualifies as a "super value-response." The reader should give the closest attention to all that von Hildebrand writes about this embeddedness; he offers here a real dialectical feast of things interpenetrating each other despite the appearance of excluding each other.

It follows that even though love (apart from love of neighbor and love for God) lacks the transcendence achieved in relation to morally relevant values, it has its own singular transcendence, a transcendence that becomes intelligible, surprisingly, when we consider how the one who loves finds his own good and happiness in the beloved person.

5. The requital of love

But in his treatise on love von Hildebrand makes still more use of his concept of that which is objectively good for a person. He argues that the interest of the lover in what is good for himself not only enhances his love; von Hildebrand also argues that if the lover lacks this interest in his good—an interest always embedded in value-response, it goes without saying—then his love becomes disfigured, and in the end depersonalized in a certain way.

Let us suppose that someone is zealous for the selflessness and other-centeredness that characterize love, and that this person proceeds to propound a radically altruistic account of love, and to propound it in the terms of von Hildebrand's ethics. Such a person might begin by saying that love should be lived exclusively as value-response—"exclusively" in the sense that the lover should renounce any and every interest in his own good and his own happiness. This altruist might add that one can, in presenting the altruistic ideal of love, also make use of von Hildebrand's concept of the objective good for a person, but only in this way: the lover is concerned with all that is good for the beloved person, that is, he seeks out things for the other precisely under the aspect of them being good for the beloved person.[9] But the good for himself that arises from loving—this he renounces. So his love is radically other-centered in two von Hildebrandian ways: he stands in a value-responding relation to the beloved person and he is committed to all that is good for him or her.

---

9 In chapter 7 of the present work von Hildebrand explores with precision and subtlety this "for the good of the other" that is proper to love. In the previous chapters he had explained (in connection with "super value-response") how the other becomes an objective good for the one who loves; in chapter 7 he explains how the one who loves so enters into what is good for the other that this good becomes "indirectly" good for the one who loves.

The altruist thinks that by loving without any interest in acquiring some good or happiness for himself, he perfects this other-centered direction of love, and so perfects love itself.

We already know what one of von Hildebrand's responses to this altruistic proposal would be; he would say that it compromises the transcendence of love as "super value-response" and that it interferes with the self-giving proper to love. Let us now add another response that he would make; he would say that this interference leads to a caricature of love, as we can see if we imagine a man saying to a woman: "I love you for what you are, for your own sake, but whether you love me in return I don't care, and I don't care if our love is mutual and is a source of happiness for me; I want nothing for myself, I just want your good and your happiness." Such a man knows nothing about the love between man and woman; and far from raising his love to a high pitch of selflessness, he in fact insults the woman, as von Hildebrand observes. Thus altruism, while it poses as supreme love, in fact makes a mockery of love. It turns out, then, that the interest of the lover in his own happiness is not just an optional enhancement of love, but is an indispensable ingredient of love, without which love becomes severely deformed.

In his book von Hildebrand tries to explain why this deformation results. He takes very seriously this fact about the "genius" of love: in loving another I want to be loved in return by the other. This is obvious in the case of the love between man and woman, but it is hardly less obvious in the love between friends, or between parents and children. In all of these kinds, or categories, of love, I remain painfully "exposed" if I offer love to someone who does not return my love; I cannot fail to be disappointed by non-requital. If the other does return my love, then I am happy in being loved, and happy in the bond of mutual love that arises between us. So if I love the other I want this happiness of being united with the other; I cannot not want it. Von Hildebrand thus acknowledges that the issue of my happiness comes up in a different and more prominent way here in the case of love than it does in the case of moral action, and that as a result the debate with eudaemonism takes a different form with love than with moral action.

Now it is a huge mistake, von Hildebrand says, to see as in any way selfish this will to be loved in return and this will to be happy by being united with the beloved person: and it is just the mirror image of this mistake to think that my love is particularly selfless when I renounce any interest in being loved in return and when I renounce any interest in being happy in a mutual love, as if love became more truly love by taking on the altruistic form just described. Of course, if my offer of love were in some way conditional on the other person requiting my love—if I were proposing to the beloved person a kind of contract or exchange—then we would understandably detect something selfish in my will to be loved in return. But in fact nothing prevents me from loving the other unconditionally, even though I hope for a requital of my love. The altruist who wants to suppress all interest in his happiness is trying to live beyond the reciprocity that belongs essentially to love, and for this reason he produces a deformation of love.

Von Hildebrand identifies one reason that draws us into the altruistic mistake. He examines throughout his book the various "categories" or kinds of love, such as the love between man and woman, the love between friends, the love of children for their parents, or parents for their children. Among these categories is love of neighbor, as exemplified by the Good Samaritan. Now love of neighbor seems to be rather different from the other categories of love with respect to the desire for a return of love. The Good Samaritan does not seem to be waiting for the injured man whom he helped to love him in return, nor will he go away disappointed if his love is not returned, or at least not go away disappointed in the way in which I am disappointed if someone to whom I offer friendship does not want to be my friend. It belongs to this category of love that the issue of my happiness, so prominent in the other categories, recedes into the background. This category of love really is other-centered in a special way. Now if we take love of neighbor as the pattern of all love, then we move towards the altruistic conception of love. Von Hildebrand argues that we should not take it as the pattern of all love; we should see it as one category of love among others. The love between friends, categorially very different from love of neighbor, is also love; it has the value-responding structure proper to all love; but it can be the kind of love that it is only if each friend is concerned with a return of the other's love and with the happiness of being united with the other.

But if we are really to understand the disorder of the altruistic ideal of love, and to understand why it is indispensable for the lover to take an interest in his own happiness in loving, we have to follow von Hildebrand to a deeper level of analysis.

6. Love and *Eigenleben*

Von Hildebrand holds that the person who tries to love in this "selfless" way depersonalizes himself. He does not take himself seriously as person; he does not remain entirely intact as person as a result of his way of centering exclusively on the beloved person. Since von Hildebrand, as we saw, thinks of the person so much in terms of transcendence and value-response, it is natural to ask whether this selfless person seems to us depersonalized because of some defect of transcendence. But no sooner do we ask this than we see that it is not a defect of this transcendence at all; on the contrary, in this person we see self-transcendence grown monstrous. No, he is depersonalized as a result of an entirely different defect, namely a deficient relation to himself. This means that a human being is constituted as person not just in the moment of self-transcendence, but also in the moment of relating to himself. It is, then, a certain interior dimension of personal self-possession that comes to light at this point in von Hildebrand's treatise on love and that completes all that he had said in his ethical writings about the self-transcending, "ecstatic" capacity of the person in value-response.

Von Hildebrand explores this interior dimension under the name of *Eigenleben,* a new term that appears here for the first time in his corpus. No German word in this work presented a greater challenge to me as translator than the word *Eigenleben.* I settled in the end for "subjectivity,"[10] but sometimes I just keep the German term, and I will keep it in the present discussion. Of particular interest for us is that von Hildebrand characterizes *Eigenleben* in terms of good in the sense of the objective good for a person: "The defining trait of *Eigenleben* is the realm of all those things that are of concern to me as this unrepeatable individual, that stand in some relation to my happiness, that address me—this in contrast to all that belongs to the *Eigenleben* of another person whom I do not know" (203). If in transcending myself in value-response I give myself over to what is other than myself, in my *Eigenleben* I have to do with what is my own. The pronouns I and me and mine belong to my *Eigenleben.*

It is important for us to consider with von Hildebrand how central the place of *Eigenleben* is in the existence of a person. He says: "To have an *Eigenleben* in this sense . . . is a deeply significant characteristic of the human being as spiritual person and is profoundly associated with human dignity and with the metaphysical condition of human beings" (201). And in the following he contrasts this aspect of the dignity of persons with that other aspect that, as we saw above, is disclosed in the capacity for value-responding self-transcendence:

> Whoever does not acknowledge the transcendence of human beings [in value-response] fails to understand what distinguishes them as persons from all impersonal creatures. But whoever smells something egocentric in the fact that I desire an objective good for myself, whoever thinks that the ideal of human life is for me to lose all interest in things good for myself, fails to understand the character of the human person as subject. Such a one fails to see the mysterious center to which everything in my life as person is referred, the center that is addressed by beneficial goods and that is inseparably bound up with the dignity of a person. If the first error locks me in myself and in this way distorts my ultimate relation to the world . . . the second error deprives me of my character as a full self. The first error reduces me to the biological, taking me according to the model of a plant or animal. The second error robs me of my character as a full subject and

---

10　For my justification of this translation, see my note at the beginning of chapter 9, p. 200.

destroys the personal in me by exaggerating the objective to the point
of dissolving that which makes me subject (206).

This depreciation of the *Eigenleben* of the human person is for von
Hildebrand the root of the extreme altruistic ideal of love. In renouncing all
interest in being loved and in being happy by being loved, the altruist neglects
this mysterious center in himself, neglects himself as subject, and for this reason he neglects his dignity as person. Von Hildebrand gives many interesting
examples of what he calls "withered" *Eigenleben*, and some of them represent
vintage altruism. Thus in one place he speaks of "a type of person who lives
with a family as an old servant of the lady of the house, or perhaps as a friend
of hers, and who shares the life of the family and has her whole life in caring
for the children and the household. These are usually persons who do not feel
up to having a full *Eigenleben* of their own, whose aspirations for happiness
are weak and modest, whose primary relation to the great goods of life is weak
and who therefore incline to attach themselves to the lives of others . . . " (204)
This altruistic person does not in the first place lack transcendence, for she
may be extremely devoted to the family members; but she lacks *Eigenleben*;
she lacks the desire for her own happiness that belongs to being a fully awakened person. It is of course also true that her transcendence towards the members of the family is impaired; she would be able to turn to them in a more radically other-centered way if she acquired a stronger *Eigenleben*. But von
Hildebrand does not think of *Eigenleben* as existing exclusively for the sake of
enhancing transcendence; it has a meaning of its own, existing also for the
sake of the person whose *Eigenleben* it is.

Von Hildebrand is also well aware that there is a way of invoking religion
to discredit the *Eigenleben* of persons and to present self-transcendence as the
only thing that really matters before God. In the following he considers this
religiously driven altruism and then he rejects it:

> Now one might think that the possession of *Eigenleben* in our earthly
> existence belongs to the things that are *allowed*, but that it is more
> perfect to give it up in the sense of desiring no personal objective good
> for myself and remaining in an exclusively value-responding attitude.
> Is not the attitude of seeking *only* the kingdom of God simply an aug-
> mentation of the attitude of seeking *first* the kingdom of God? . . . By
> no means. *Eigenleben* belongs to the nature of the human person.. . . .
> This becomes clear in thinking about the sacred humanity of Christ.
> Even the Son of Man wept at the death of Lazarus. . . . We cannot
> stress this enough: *Eigenleben* belongs to the meaning and nature of
> a human being . . . (215)

In a much earlier work (*Transformation in Christ*) von Hildebrand dealt with
the structure of Christian humility, in the course of which he distinguished

certain forms of pseudo-humility, such as thinking of oneself in terms of a quantitative smallness, as if each human being were just an insignificant speck in an immense universe. If he had had *Eigenleben* on his mind when he wrote that earlier work, he would certainly have identified the religiously motivated depreciation of *Eigenleben* as a form of pseudo-humility, and he would have argued that even before God, or rather *most of all* before God, my *Eigenleben* is something important and refuses to be relativized into insignificance.

Von Hildebrand acknowledges, then, that the objective good for a person plays a different and larger role in love than in moral action. It not only underlies that new dimension of transcendence in love that he calls "super value-response," as we saw above; it also underlies an interior dimension of personal existence—*Eigenleben*—that shows itself in love in an eminent way. Von Hildebrand's image of the human person is fundamentally enlarged in this work; the earlier stress on transcendence is here developed into a polarity of transcendence and *Eigenleben*. And the category of the objective good for the person is the basic conceptual tool by which von Hildebrand thinks through this enlargement of his personalism.

Von Hildebrand often uses these results to bring clarity to the question of what counts as the *selflessness* that we admire in love, and what counts as the *selfishness* that disfigures love. Thus he argues that it is not selfish to want to have an *Eigenleben*; it is not selfish to want to be loved in return; it is not selfish to want to be happy in loving—as long, of course, as these desires are embedded in the value-responding affirmation of the beloved person. In other words, selflessness does not require indifference to one's *Eigenleben*, indifference to being loved in return, or indifference to being happy in loving. Far from promoting a morally admirable selflessness, such indifference undermines one's dignity as a personal self. What is condemned as selfish is commonly nothing other than the care of one's *Eigenleben,* which in itself is morally praiseworthy.

The reader will notice that these important distinctions can hardly be made if one does not distinguish with von Hildebrand between the merely subjectively satisfying and the objective good for a person. If one collapses the latter into the former, then one is sure to think of a strong *Eigenleben* in terms of selfishness. And one will never attain to the concept of a "super value-response," since one will have depreciated the very factor—the well-ordered concern for one's own happiness—that makes for a "super value-response."

7. Von Hildebrand and recent phenomenological work on love

I said above that a second purpose of this introduction is to set von Hildebrand in relation to some recent phenomenological work on the nature of love.

If von Hildebrand were alive today and were to examine this recent work, he would be struck by the fact that eudaemonism in the philosophy of love is no longer strongly represented, whereas altruism is dominant. He would see to his surprise that the task is not so much to refute eudaemonism as rather to defend against extreme forms of altruism the interest of the lover in being loved, and in being happy in being loved. This altruism is perhaps nowhere so much in evidence as in the work of Emmanuel Levinas. Here we encounter the contrast between love that fulfills the need of the lover, also called concupiscence and sometimes eros, and love that is based on the imperious claim of my neighbor, the "absolutely Other," also called love without concupiscence, and sometimes agape.[11] This latter love is presented in radically other-centered terms—so radical that it seems to many of Levinas's critics to be impossible to achieve in action. Thus John Caputo calls Levinasian love of neighbor "an impossible dream."[12]

Certainly von Hildebrand would welcome the anti-eudaemonism that is found in Levinas's account of love of neighbor. Levinas for his part, one would think, would welcome the strong stress on "for the sake of the other" found in von Hildebrand. He would presumably also welcome much that von Hildebrand says about the transcendence proper to the moral life. But von Hildebrand would wonder whether the other-centeredness of the one who loves is allowed by Levinas to be penetrated by the interest that this person might take in his own good and happiness. He would wonder whether Levinas acknowledges a self-giving that is precisely enhanced by the way in which the good of the lover enters into the self-giving; whether Levinas is open to the polarity of *Eigenleben* and transcendence; whether Levinas has what von Hildebrand regards as the true concept of selfishness/selflessness. He would look closely to see whether Levinas saw the need of moving *beyond both eudaemonism and altruism*. These questions coming from von Hildebrand reach into the heart of what Levinas has been doing. They show that the two philosophers have much to say to each other and many ways of challenging each other.

The encounter between von Hildebrand and Levinas is a project waiting to be carried out. Another such project is the encounter between von Hildebrand and Karol Wojtyla. One could focus this project not around the altruism/eudaemonism issue, but around the role of affectivity in love. Following Max Scheler, von Hildebrand lays great stress on the *affective character* of love, as we saw. If one does not take delight in the other, he says, one does not love the other. Perhaps no one has ever explored and affirmed the affectivity of loving in the way von Hildebrand has. Now Wojtyla, too, is greatly indebted to Scheler, and his work shows many of the excellences of phenomenology; but in his account of love Wojtyla seems to make more of the will than von Hildebrand does. If one comes from reading what von Hildebrand

---

11 On these two kinds of love in Levinas, see Corey Beals, *Levinas and the Wisdom of Love* (Waco, TX: Baylor University Press, 2007), chapters 2 and 3.

12 John Caputo, *Against Ethics* (Bloomington: Indiana University Press, 1993), 82.

writes on love as the most affective of all value-responses (see especially chapters 2, 4, and 10), one is bound to be perplexed on reading this in Wojtyla: "The emotions themselves [of sympathy and liking for the other] can commit the will, but only in a passive and somewhat superficial fashion, with a certain admixture of subjectivism. Friendship, however, demands a sincere commitment of the will with the fullest possible objective justification."[13] The question to be explored is whether the two thinkers are focusing on different aspects of the one truth about love, or whether there is a debate between them that needs to be worked through.

I turn now to a project that I do not just propose to others but actually try to initiate myself. I turn to Jean-Luc Marion and to his recent book, *The Erotic Phenomenon.* Marion gives us here a rich phenomenology of love that has many points of contact with von Hildebrand's work. And while there are many respects in which Marion and von Hildebrand converge, I would like to call attention to an apparent point of tension between them, not so as to be quarrelsome but so as to give an example of the fruitful dialogue that is possible between von Hildebrand and contemporary phenomenologists writing on love.

Von Hildebrand claims that love is a value-response, as we saw. Now Marion posits a relation between love and knowledge that puts into question the response-character of love. He writes in one place: "Properly speaking, she (the lover) does not know that which she loves, because what one loves does not appear before one loves it. It is up to the lover to make visible what is at issue—the other as beloved . . . . Knowledge does not make love possible, because knowledge flows from love. The lover makes visible what she loves and, without this love, nothing would appear to her. Thus, strictly speaking, the lover does not know what she loves—except insofar as she loves it."[14] Marion does not mean, of course, that the lover *invests* the beloved with a splendor that the beloved does not really have; he seems to mean that the lover *reveals* the splendor really there in the beloved. But on his view the lover does not begin to love by responding to the splendor of the beloved person, for it is his love that first makes the beloved person appear in all her splendor.

Von Hildebrand holds that the lover loves because he has caught a glimpse of the beauty of the beloved. This beauty affects the lover and fascinates him in such a way as to awaken his love. As a result he holds that the love initiated by the lover is responsive to some beauty in the beloved person. He would certainly have invoked the unforgettable account of love in the middle of Plato's *Phaedrus.* For von Hildebrand, as for Plato, it is the sight of beauty in the beloved person that stirs up the "madness" of love in the lover. But Marion

---

13   Karol Wojtyla, *Love and Responsibility* (New York: Farrar, Straus, & Giroux Inc., 1981), 92.

14   Jean-Luc Marion, *The Erotic Phenomenon*, trans. Stephen Lewis (Chicago: University of Chicago Press, 2007), 87.

seems to exclude from his account of love this engendering power of the beauty glimpsed by the lover in the beloved person, for he wants love to precede all that one apprehends in the beloved person, and to bring it to light for the first time. This is why, as I understand him, he introduces the "principle of insufficient reason" in explaining the initiative of the lover. Since the lover loves without the support of any apprehended beauty in the beloved person, he loves without sufficient reason.

Of course, von Hildebrand would grant that the beauty of a person does not show itself equally to every kind of looking. Marion speaks several times of the act of "sizing up" a person's qualities, the strong and weak points of the person, and he says quite rightly that this "objective" way of looking cannot lead me to love this person. For this is a kind of looking at another that yields only an object, a composite of qualities, and not a beloved person. It is not difficult to understand that it takes a loving way of looking at another in order to catch sight of the beauty of the person. This means that love does indeed in some sense precede and make possible the appearance of the other as beautiful and lovable, just as Marion says.

But von Hildebrand would say that the relation between love and knowledge is a mutual relation. He would say that once the beauty of the other is disclosed to the lover by virtue of his loving approach to the other, this beauty engenders love in the lover and motivates him to love the other. In other words, the priority of love over knowledge would seem quickly to yield to a certain priority of knowledge over love. Of course, once his love is engendered by apprehended beauty, the lover would seem to be empowered thereby to see more deeply into the beauty of the beloved. So the priority of love over knowledge would reassert itself—only to yield again to the priority of the now more visible beauty over the love that it elicits now more deeply than before. The principle at work in this mutuality is familiar to every student of the Aristotelian account of virtue. On the one hand, virtuous character is built up by morally worthy actions, but on the other hand, virtuous character also facilitates these actions. Virtuous character is, in relation to action, both cause and effect. This would mean that Marion's statement, just cited, "Knowledge does not make love possible, because knowledge flows from love," captures only part of the truth about knowledge and love as they exist in the one who initiates love. This would also mean that the lover is not as lacking in some "sufficient reason" for his initiative of love as Marion says.

Let us try to understand Marion's position better by inquiring into his reason for holding it. If I read him correctly, his position is based on his conception of love as gift. Marion claims, echoing Derrida as well as his own earlier analysis of the structure of the gift, that the one who loves steps out of any and every framework of exchange and commercial reciprocity. The lover does not love *on the condition that* he receive something in return from the beloved person, but rather loves unconditionally; he loves whether he is loved in return or hated in return. It is in the course of zealously contending for this unconditionality of the lover's initiative that Marion affirms his principle of the priority of love over knowledge. He fears perhaps that if love is awakened by something about the beloved, if love constitutes itself as love through the experience of and in response to the beloved person, then the lover may start seeking some *quid pro quo* in loving and may thus lose the unconditionality that makes love to be love. He may see his fear confirmed by the fact that von Hildebrand lays great stress on the lover hoping for some requital of his love. So Marion is trying to secure this unconditionality by affirming the principle of insufficient reason for the lover and by making the love of the lover always only precede the knowledge of the beloved person but never follow upon this knowledge.

To this von Hildebrand would respond that there is no good reason why the lover, just by being drawn by the beauty of the beloved person, has to fall away from his love into some kind of justice-based exchange. It all depends on the concept of value that is brought to your phenomenological examination of the beloved. If you think, in the vein of the Aristotelian-Thomistic doctrine of *bonum*, that whatever attracts me attracts me under the aspect of perfecting me and actualizing my nature, then there is indeed some cause for concern; I may really forfeit the unconditionality that is so important to Marion if a concern for my perfection controls my interest in the other. If Marion sees no alternative to such an interest, then we understand entirely the move he makes, namely holding that love arises independently of and prior to any acquaintance with and attraction to the beloved person. But what if there is an alternative? What if von Hildebrand is right that the beauty that engenders love is a beauty born of value, and that the lover is first of all drawn to the beloved not as one who is "beneficial for me" or "perfective of me" but rather of "worthy in herself" or "precious of herself"? In this case my value-based interest in the other coheres entirely with a radically other-centered approach to the other. Von Hildebrandian value-response is just as foreign to the economy of *quid pro quo* as anything that Marion says about the advance of the lover.

As for the concern that Marion would likely have regarding von Hildebrand's strong stress on desiring requital, we have already tried to explain why the lover desiring requital does not have to make receiving requital a condition for his loving.

But perhaps Marion will say that by stressing the response-character of love we conceive of love as too reactive. Even if the love of the lover does not decline into some kind of *quid pro quo*, it is still deprived of its gesture of taking the initiative and giving a gift; for now it simply registers what is given in the beloved and reacts in proportion to the excellence of the beloved. It is as if the lover by loving just gives to the beloved what is due to her in justice. We can capture the freedom of the lover's gift, Marion will say, only if we cut the advance of the lover loose from any beauty that elicits his love, only if we place the entire source of his advance in his free initiative.

In response, von Hildebrand acknowledges that the beauty seen in the beloved person does not have the effect of strictly obliging the lover to love the beloved, as we saw; his initiative to love remains a free spontaneous act, beyond all obligation. But why should beauty not awaken love and motivate love without interfering with the free initiative to love? Consider this parallel, taken indeed from an entirely different order of being, yet relevant to our question. It seems that the goodness of creation in some way motivated God to create, for He repeatedly says (*Genesis* 1) as He goes through the days of creation that the works of His hands are good, very good. And yet His initiative to create was absolutely free. So a motive of value or beauty need not interfere with the free initiative of the act that is motivated.

But there is another reservation that Marion possibly has about invoking value for the purpose of understanding the initiative of the lover. Perhaps he would say that this recourse to value is entirely inappropriate to what he calls the "phenomenality" of the beloved, who after all appears to the lover as unsubstitutable, unrepeatable. The idea behind this response is that if one invokes value for thinking about the beloved, then the beloved becomes a mere instance or specimen of the value invoked; but in becoming a mere instance the beloved is lost as unsubstitutable and so is lost as beloved, and the lover ends up loving the value more than the person.

Marion is absolutely right about the beloved appearing as unsubstitutable, and in fact he expresses this important truth forcefully and convincingly in his book, especially when he develops the contrast between the unsubstitutable beloved and the anonymous other as encountered in transactions of commercial exchange.[15] On this point von Hildebrand is in complete agreement with him. We have already examined his idea, developed in chapter 3 of the present work, that the value to which love responds must be a value in which the beloved person is entirely "thematic"; in other words, it must be a value that the beloved person has *as this unrepeatable person.* Von Hildebrand would respond to Marion's concern by asking: what is the difficulty here? Why does a value have to begin as some general quality, so that a valuable being only instantiates the value? Why should not the radiance of value and beauty found in the beloved person be unsubstitutable just as the beloved person is unsubstitutable?

Let us return to Marion's claim that the lover has no sufficient reason for loving. Von Hildebrand might also acknowledge a certain kind of insufficient reason for loving, but he would explain it in terms of the ineffability of the beauty of the beloved person. For von Hildebrand the insufficiency would be an insufficiency of reasons that the lover can formulate for loving this person, but it would not be an insufficiency of beauty appearing in the beloved person and eliciting the love of the lover. Von Hildebrand's insufficiency is, then,

---

15   *Ibid.* pp. 77–78

different from, and less than, Marion's. And if von Hildebrand were asked to explain the way in which the lover chooses the beloved without making comparisons with other possible recipients of love, he would say that this mysterious choosing or "election" of the beloved is not made understandable by the absence of any knowledge of the beloved, but by the presence of a kind of knowledge of the incommunicable preciousness of the beloved. At the level of incommunicable persons, comparisons cannot be meaningfully made; at this level persons are incommensurable with each other and so are incomparable with each other. Thus the knowledge on the basis of which the lover loves cannot be gained or enhanced by making comparisons with other persons—but a kind of knowledge it really is, and a kind of reason for loving it really is.

We conclude by observing that it would seem to be of no little importance for the phenomenology of love to acknowledge with von Hildebrand this role of the beauty of the beloved in awakening love. For one could well wonder if the beloved person will really feel loved if the lover advances towards her entirely on his own initiative and is already fully constituted as lover prior to being drawn by her. Will she not feel that his love shoots over her head, as it were, and is not sufficiently a love *for her*? Will she not feel somehow ignored as person if she provides no part of the reason for the advance of the lover? It is one thing for the Good Samaritan to approach the wounded man knowing nothing about him, to take an initiative of love without knowing anything about him beyond the fact of his being injured and in urgent need of help. But it is something else, and something far more problematic, for man and woman, or for friends, to love each other without knowing each other and without being drawn to each other by what they know. If, on the other hand, von Hildebrand is right about love being engendered by the beauty of the beloved person, then there is no danger of the beloved person feeling bypassed by the lover.

And this leads to another question. As Marion shows convincingly, I am empowered to love myself only by being loved. Left to myself I end in self-hatred, he argues. But if I am loved entirely on the initiative of the lover, providing through myself nothing that might awaken his love, does his love, von Hildebrand would ask, have the power to enable me to love even myself? Can his love really mediate to me the goodness of my existence if his love arises without in any way being motivated by the goodness of my existence?

We do not mean to offer here a finished von Hildebrandian critique of Marion. After all, we have not dealt with Marion's philosophical project as a whole. Marion might well make some response that would continue the dialogue. We have only wanted to start the dialogue with Marion so as to show the great fruitfulness of von Hildebrand's treatise on love. We have wanted to show that von Hildebrand addresses the concerns of philosophers and theologians like Levinas, Wojtyla, and Marion, and challenges them in various ways. He speaks with a powerful and original voice that has been neglected for too long in the discussions and debates of our time about the nature of love.

Introduction

The way to an adequate knowledge of the essence of love is usually obstructed by prejudices of a general philosophical nature.

Unfounded distrust of the personal act of love—dangerous analogies

The first prejudice is the notion that one abandons the metaphysical plane and loses oneself in mere "psychology" when, in order to understand the essence of love, the personal act of love is taken as a starting point. It is even thought that one thereby withdraws into a region of immanence and considers a purely subjective aspect of love, and that in so doing one cuts oneself off from the great world of elementary and objective realities.

This is an entirely unfounded prejudice. If this were true, it would also not be permissible to start the analysis of knowledge or of the will from the personal act of knowing or willing. No one has thought, however, of regarding the consideration of these personal acts as trailing off into mere "psychology," as a retreat to a merely subjective aspect of knowing, or as remaining in the confines of the immanent.

At the root of this prejudice is also the erroneous conception that impersonal being is somehow more objective than personal being. One fails to recognize that personal being stands incomparably higher than all impersonal being, and that in doing justice to the distinctive character of personal being, one penetrates much deeper into the realm of being and of metaphysics.

In the case of beings that exist as *conscious* beings, it is obviously nonsensical to regard the consideration of consciousness as trailing off into psychology. Acts such as willing, loving, rejoicing, mourning, and repenting can never be known in their essence if one starts only from more or less remote analogies, instead of starting from these acts taken in the literal and proper sense and taken as they are given to us immediately. If we want to know the essence of the will there is no point in starting from analogous phenomena such as the instinctive striving in an animal or even the incomparably more distantly analogous "striving" in the plant world. One has rather to start with man, and, what is more, even here not with merely instinctive striving but with personal action in the full sense, where the will is clearly given to us in its specific nature. There is no point in thinking of analogies until the essence of the will has already been analyzed as it is itself given to us—unless one draws upon them in order to throw into relief the specific difference between real willing and all these analogous things. To start with analogies and to treat these, as it were, as the genus that comprises the will, in the hope of understanding the will on a more general and therefore "more metaphysical" plane, is sure to obscure from the outset the essence of the will and to distort its specific character.

But the same is *a fortiori* true of love. We are from the very start blocked from understanding the essence of love if wholly analogous meanings of the word love, such as the striving for self-development and perfection that is also to be found in impersonal beings, are taken as the point of departure instead of the fundamental personal datum of love, which plays such a central role in man's life and which constitutes one of the main themes of the literature of all ages and countries. Not until one has come to know the essence of love where it is clearly given to us in the literal sense can one decide to what extent these phenomena of a much more general nature really represent something analogous. Indeed, in the case of love it is not permissible even to begin with self-love, for here too the term love has an analogous meaning, as we shall see later. One has to start with the love for other persons; this is the love that possesses all those elements of which we think when we speak of love, such as self-donation, delight in the other person, the happiness of love, and so on.

It must be clearly understood how completely dogmatic the thesis is that love in the literal sense is a species within quite general phenomena, such as the striving for self-perfection, or a movement towards an end (*finis*). Even if love is represented not as a species, but as a subjective "aspect" of these general strivings, one is still making a purely dogmatic assertion. In order not to leave the metaphysical plane—on which one is erroneously thought to remain by clinging to something completely abstract—it is dogmatically declared that love is in reality a subspecies of these general phenomena, which must therefore be taken as the point of departure if one wants to grasp the true essence and deeper meaning of love. Nobody takes the trouble to establish through an analysis of love in the literal sense that love is indeed a sub-species of these general phenomena, or whether there is even a genuine analogy between love and these phenomena. This attempt has a certain irony about it from an epistemological point of view; rather than starting from something that is unequivocally given to us, such as the personal act of love for another person, one clings to things which as such are not actually given but are more a fruit of speculation, as, for example, the striving for perfection in every being.

But even when it is a case of true analogies, and of analogies that are just as clearly given as love itself, it is still not to the point to choose analogies as the starting point of the investigation of a personal act such as love.

The eminent significance of drawing upon analogies in the knowledge of a given datum is by no means thereby denied. Whenever we investigate personal and spiritual entities we are compelled to avail ourselves of analogies from the physical sphere, and our language does this constantly. We speak, for example, of the insight into a necessary essence, employing for this purely spiritual act a word that is taken from the sphere of sense perception. Thus it is entirely legitimate and even indispensable to revert to analogies in elaborating the essence of personal, spiritual data. In the first place, however, these analogies must never serve as the starting point. One must look to the datum itself that one wants to investigate; analogies can only be used for the sake of illustrating certain characteristic features of the object to be investigated. Second, the analogous data that are used must be at least as clearly given as the object being investigated. Third, the analogous datum to which one reverts must above all be a genuine and valid analogy of the object under investigation. Finally, one has to guard against "clinging," as it were, to the analogy, and drawing upon it for more than is admissible. One cannot be cautious enough in this respect. The history of philosophy provides sufficient examples of how the analogous phenomenon that was drawn upon as an illustration becomes a prison; and one begins to derive consequences from this phenomenon for the object to be investigated—consequences which by no means really exist since they follow precisely from those points to which the analogy does not apply.

There are, however, also invalid analogies or at least such vague analogies that to have recourse to them runs the risk of failing to recognize the essence of the object of investigation.[1] Some very vague analogy is indeed to be found everywhere. But just as there are false similarities[2] to which unintelligent people cling, so there are analogies which mislead us into seeing something in a false light.

---

1   That is, for example, what happens when one seeks to illustrate the relation between individual and species by way of a vague analogy with the relation of part to whole. We obviously have here two completely different relationships. The relation of a single ship to the fleet can be characterized as that of part to whole – but the relation of the concrete ship to the species "ship" is plainly a totally different one. The individual ship is something concrete and real, just as the whole of which it is a part, namely the fleet, is concrete and individual. The individual ship and the species "ship," on the other hand, do not lie in the same order of being; the species "ship" is clearly neither individual nor in the same sense real. Therefore, having recourse to the vague analogy between both does not lead to a clarification of the relation of the individual to the species, but to a misunderstanding of this relation.

2   We can sometimes find between two people a certain quite superficial similarity that goes hand in hand with such a radical and profound difference that it can justifiably be spoken of as a "false" similarity. To take these two people to be similar is a sign of extraordinary naiveté, indeed, it is stupidity, a clinging to wholly unessential things, and it is a failure to understand that what is in certain ways similar in both, has in each such a different function that to regard the two as similar amounts to a specific misunderstanding of both. Something analogous can also be the case with melodies, and it constitutes a specific misunderstanding of a great and noble melody if it is considered, owing to quite superficial commonalties, to be similar to a completely trivial melody. To draw upon such "similarities" amounts to seeing both in a false light.

This is especially the case when one and the same term is used for two things, and the two analogous data are treated almost like two species of one and the same genus.[3] When it is said, on the other hand, that in love there is a spiritual movement towards the beloved, the purely analogous character of "movement" is fully understood, but the well-known and clearly given phenomenon of spatial or physical movement helps us to point out an important characteristic of love. It would not occur to anyone to hold that in order to study the essence of love one must start from an analysis of motion. Only if one concentrates entirely on love in the literal sense, if one looks to this datum and then, conscious of the analogous intention, cites a well-known phenomenon from a completely different sphere, can the analogy be a help to the understanding of what is being investigated. If one thinks, however, that it is permissible to use as a starting point something that possesses only a certain analogy and is not[4] rooted in the same sphere of being, and if one concentrates first on this analogous thing in order to bring its characteristics to bear upon that which is actually to be investigated, the danger is great that one thereby obstructs the way to the knowledge that one seeks. From the outset one sees the datum to be explored in the light of this analogy and one transfers to this datum precisely those characteristics that decisively distinguish the analogous thing from the primary datum.

Unfortunate distrust of what is given in experience— "explanation" instead of essential analysis

A further prejudice which blocks the path to an adequate investigation of love is the distrust of what is given in experience, the tendency not to take it seriously, and the belief that what is more real and valid is to be sought "behind" it. This prejudice is doubtless also at work in those who, as we saw, for fear of leaving the metaphysical plane, start in the philosophical analysis of love from vague impersonal "analogies" that are not immediately given to us, instead of starting from the personal act of love which is given to us immediately as such. They, too, are not free from the distrust of the immediately given, particularly in the sphere of personal experiences. The ignoring of the given, however, is above all to be found with those who have no interest whatsoever in metaphysics, who in fact, like Sigmund Freud, regard metaphysics as impossible and absurd. One abandons here any attempt at listening to the voice of being and starts from an arbitrary theory, to which love is reduced in the spirit of the famous saying that "this thing is in reality something totally different."

---

3   Teilhard de Chardin, for example, speaks in this way of material and mental energy as two species of the genus energy, although the two realities that are designated here with the same term "energy" are radically different; it is only a remote analogy that justifies our using this term for both.

4   [This "not" is missing in the German text, but the sense of the passage clearly calls for it. Trans.]

A typical example of this way of using "explanation" instead of essential analysis, of closing one's eyes to all that is given in experience, is Freud's attempt to construe love as a sublimated sexual drive. Freud dispenses with any phenomenological analysis of the sexual sphere. This sphere, as we will see later, discloses its true essence only if it is viewed in the light of love, and in fact of a special kind of love.

Though we can say that ice is in reality only water in another state, or that diamond is in reality coal, it is impossible and nonsensical to say, for example, that justice is in reality a mere product of the *ressentiment* of the weak. It may well be that with certain people the appeal to justice is motivated by *ressentiment*, but this changes nothing of the essence of justice. Indeed, we sometimes rebuke someone precisely by saying that his interest in justice is not sincere because he is really only interested in protecting himself against someone stronger than he is. We surely presuppose thereby the distinction between justice and *ressentiment*. But to say that justice is in reality nothing else but a product of the *ressentiment* of the weak, is equivalent to saying that the number 3 is at bottom nothing but the number 5. We called this widespread danger the "nothing but" method in the Prolegomena to our *Ethics*. Since we have spoken at length about it there as well as in *What is Philosophy?* we need only to comment on it briefly here. An example of this "nothing but" method is also Freud's thesis, just mentioned, that love in reality is nothing other than a sublimated sexual drive. Here, too, the "in reality" is meaningless, for love and sexual drive are in their essence two unequivocally different data, of which the one can no more be reduced to the other than the color red can be to the color green. The error which comes to light here, however, arises not only from illegitimately taking a method that is admissible in the natural sciences and employing it with respect to intelligible essences; this error also betrays the conviction that one attains to serious reality only if one looks behind the given, which one thinks can only be an "appearance," for something else—if everything immediately experienced is taken to be a "symbol" for something else. (Here we need only to think of the role of "symbols" in Freudian psychoanalysis.)

This tendency is likewise to be found with those who perceive in all the givens of experience merely a kind of secret code for other things, as is especially the case in many Eastern religions. This debasement and symbolization of what is given can take different forms; it can reduce the given to something lower, as in Freud, or to something higher, as in the Eastern religions, or take the given as a vague, abstract analogy for something else—but it is always disastrous for philosophical analysis. For our work in this book it obstructs the path leading into an understanding of the essence of love.

Erroneous derivation of love from union and self-love

Here we would like to call attention to a particular error that stems from this reluctance to take seriously personal and spiritual acts as experienced, and to discover in them their meaning and value. I refer to the notion that love is a kind of symptom of unity, a subjective manifestation of unity. It is thought that love can be derived from the union with other persons. Since it is frequently assumed that self-love is the origin of all love, and that the solidarity that one has with oneself is the expression of this love, it is therefore thought permissible to conclude that love is grounded in union. One loves oneself because one is identical with oneself, and love extends naturally to everything that in some way belongs to me, that constitutes a unity with me. It is thought evident that one loves oneself, and that self-love is fully intelligible, and indeed precisely on account of the unity with oneself. This unity is the root and source of love, and it proceeds—so one says—from the fact that I love the country to which I belong, that I love *my* family, *my* relatives, and so on. Everywhere it is unity, the belonging to me, that founds love, since after all love for others is merely an extension of self-love.

Or it is maintained that the part loves the whole precisely because it is united with the whole. What is more, it is even claimed that the part loves the whole even more than itself, or that this follows necessarily from self-love. It is self-love, according to this conception, that forces me to love the whole to which I belong more than I love myself. Here, too, it is considered indubitable that unity is the root and ground of love. Just because this is the case, it is thought that the part must love the whole, and—still in conformity with this thesis—it is thought that, because love is an expression of unity, that is, a subjective manifestation of unity, the ontological superiority of the whole over the part necessarily entails the part loving the whole more than itself.

In truth, however, it is not at all evident that union founds love. On the contrary, the genuine and true union between human persons is only established by mutual love, and every love contains an element of longing for union with the beloved. The union between persons is not the *source of love*, not the reason for love, but usually a consequence of love, an achievement of love.[5]

One could object that there are nevertheless cases in which the union between persons comes about without love and in which love is a result of this union. One thinks, for example, of the relationship of the child to its parents and to older brothers and sisters. The child is united with the parents and brothers and sisters even before it loves them. It discovers itself as belonging to this family, as sheltered in these surroundings. A union exists objectively with the parents through descent, with the brothers and sisters through consanguinity, even before the child becomes aware of it. A union of lived community comes about, and the child gradually becomes aware of it; this consciousness of belonging is the foundation of the love of the child for its parents and brothers

---

5   We will see later that it is equally wrong to regard love only as a means to union, to strip it thus of its own being and meaning in itself and to reduce its true *raison d'être* to bringing about unity.

and sisters. The child loves them because it belongs to them. Thus, union can indeed precede love and even be the reason for love.

We say in reply that it is false to hold that the consciousness of belonging together in the family is the *ground* of the love of the child for its parents and brothers and sisters. This experienced union goes instead hand in hand with the budding love. We will come back to this later and see that union or belonging is not the source of love, but only goes hand in hand with it.

In the attempt to derive love from unity, a further danger asserts itself as well, namely, the tendency to take a cheap plausibility as the ideal of philosophical intelligibility.

Pseudo-obviousness instead of evidence

There is a danger in philosophy of resorting to shallow plausibility in explaining away something clearly given (in fact such explanation merely seems to make something more understandable). Instead of venturing to be caught up in real philosophical wonder, in the readiness to acknowledge a mystery, one wants to evade going too deep, and so one tries to explain away the essence of a being and to reduce it to something that only seems plausible, with the result that the specific essence of the being is ignored.[6]

That is the case with all attempts to derive love from self-love. In doing this one overlooks the specifically transcendent dimension of love, the ability to take an interest in someone because he is so beautiful, so precious, that is, the value-responding character of love. One thinks that, in order to understand the essence of love, one has to have recourse to an instinctive solidarity, to the inevitable "interest" that we take in ourselves.

It is true that in every human being there is an instinctive and even inevitable solidarity with oneself. This expresses itself in the most various ways. Naturally, I am concerned about the pain in *my* leg because *I* feel it; *I* am touched, of course, by an uncharitable, humiliating, offensive attitude towards me because I am "one" with myself. I am interested in my happiness and shun unhappiness. This naturally given solidarity is not a result of love, however; it is not a bond that grows out of a love for myself but is given prior to all loving, given with the unity of our personal nature.

Out of the desire to start from a cheap plausibility, or rather to arrive at it, one thinks that in the case of love one has to derive the interest in the other per-

---

6   This is, for example, typical of all attempts to rob knowing of its transcendent character and to postulate that the object of knowing must somehow become a part of me in order to be known. One circumvents thereby the unique nature of knowing, its transcendence, the fact that the relation here between the intellect of the person and the object known distinguishes itself precisely from the relation of being-the-part-of-a-whole as well as from the self-consciousness of the person. The "miracle" of knowledge appears to be more understandable if it is reduced to the familiarity with something that is oneself. In truth, self-consciousness is no less a marvel than the consciousness of something that is not oneself.

son and the solidarity with him from "self-love," from the naturally given solidarity with oneself. This seems more plausible, more understandable. This is a typical case of evading a datum, of avoiding philosophical wonder, and of taking refuge in a cheap plausibility. Without penetrating into the essence of the datum, without learning something from it, one thinks one has found an explanation for it.

In truth the essence of love consists in being able to take an interest in another person in such a way that a solidarity with the other arises that is similar to what I have with myself. What in the case of love for another is really a consequence or an "achievement" of love, is in the case of oneself wrongly thought to be the basis and source of self-love. Solidarity with oneself is neither a result of nor a basis for love but is something essentially rooted in the nature of the human person. This solidarity with oneself can only be called "love" in a completely analogous sense, by seeing in it an implicit element of love.[7]

The impossibility of deriving love for another person from "self-love," that is, from the solidarity with oneself, becomes especially evident when we compare real love for another with that solidarity with another that is really just an extension of the solidarity with oneself. A typical case of this is the attitude of the husband who, although he does not really love his wife and perhaps even mistreats her, is extremely sensitive to any humiliating treatment of his wife by others, because he looks upon her as a part of himself. The fact that she is *his* wife draws her into the sphere of his solidarity with himself. He experiences an attack upon her as directed against himself—not because he loves her but because he regards her as an extension of his ego. We find the same thing with the master who mistreats, abuses, and in no way loves his servants, but considers it an insult to his person when someone else acts offensively towards these servants.

This solidarity clearly differs from that which is grounded in love. In the first place, it does not manifest itself in the I-Thou-relation to the other person. That is why this husband mistreats his wife and this master his servants. There is no interest whatsoever to be found here in the well-being and happiness of the other persons. This solidarity revives only when it is a question of the behavior of a third party towards the wife or the servants, in which case there is a mere "we-community" with the wife and the servants. But this "we-community" is, in contradistinction to many other we-communities, simply an extension of the ego; it is an extension of a dimension of self-love. This aspect of the wife and servants as an extension of the ego is restricted naturally to the situations in which they encounter a third person, and is thus restricted to the

---

7   We will see later that one can speak still in quite another sense of self-love, and here the expression love is much more adequately employed. This meaning of self-love does no need to be taken into consideration here since it is neither the presupposition for the solidarity with oneself nor the result of this solidarity.

we-dimension; it falls away, however, as soon as they are looked upon as a Thou.

The solidarity which is a fruit of love, by contrast, manifests itself primarily in the I-Thou-situation, in the confrontation with the other person. Here the other person is by no means looked upon as an extension of the ego; his Thou-character is fully thematic. And the we that grows out of love, and in which the same solidarity that is found in the I-Thou-situation lives on, is obviously just as little an extension of the ego.

In the second place, the solidarity which springs from an extension of the ego is lacking in all commitment, in all benevolence—elements which characterize precisely that solidarity which is a fruit of love.

It is not difficult to see that the solidarity with other persons that results exclusively from viewing them as an extension of one's own person, as a part of one's self, is radically different from the solidarity arising from love, where the lover says: Everything that delights you makes me happy too, and everything that causes you to suffer, grieves me. Just this comparison of a solidarity that grows out of viewing the other person as a part of me with the glorious and noble solidarity that springs from love shows us clearly how impossible it is to trace the loving interest for the person back to the solidarity with oneself.

It seems so plausible to say that the belonging to ourselves that we have by nature is the necessary basis for taking an interest in ourselves; and that, consequently, the key to taking a loving interest in other persons must also lie in this belonging to ourselves, in being a part of us. But this is a fallacy. The solidarity with ourselves is something naturally given, indeed unavoidable; and besides it cannot be an "explanation" for the love for another person, if only because it does not give rise to love in the genuine sense even in the case of one's own person.

As soon as the data are examined more closely, namely, love on the one hand and the solidarity with oneself on the other, one sees clearly that the attempt to derive love and its inherent interest in the other person from "self-love" is altogether impossible and in no way makes the love for other persons more intelligible. One circumvents the mystery of love, but at the same time one attains thereby only an *apparent* rational explanation for the interest inherent in love.

It is difficult to grasp why in the analysis of love one turns away from the clearly given phenomenon of love for another person and takes refuge in the merely analogous phenomenon of self-love. The only thing that throws some light on this is the general human tendency to circumvent philosophical wonder and to resort to an "explanation" that is plausible and that can be reached without delving into the essence of the thing itself.[8]

---

8 Not until the essence of love has been thoroughly examined can one investigate issues such as the following: the sense in which self-love can be spoken of, what

Metaphysical inferiority as the norm for certitude?

Closely connected with the search for a cheap plausibility is a further preju-dice that frequently obstructs the way to the adequate investigation of love. It is the notion that one has to proceed from that which is ontologically lower to that which is higher in order to understand the higher. I have called attention elsewhere to the tendency that asserts itself in recent philosophy to consider something as all the more indubitable the lower it stands ontologically. An instinct appears to these thinkers much more reliably and indubitably given than a spiritual act like joy, love, conviction, etc. Corporeal things appear to them more indisputable than anything mental. Instead of making the certitude of the existence of something dependent on how unambiguously and immedi-ately it is given and how intelligible it is, they think it justifiable to take onto-logical inferiority as the measure for the certitude of the existence of some-thing.[9]

Even thinkers, however, who do not fall into this error, who on the con-trary consider things that stand ontologically higher to be equally certain, often believe that one has to start from analogies based on what is ontologically lower in order to understand that which is higher. This error, which is much older than the one mentioned above, is widespread in all periods of philoso-phy. One tacitly presupposes thereby that that which stands lower can more easily be known than that which stands higher, and that for this reason it offers us the key to the higher—in the event there is an analogy.[10]

That is, however, not at all the case. While we do not want to go as far as Theodor Haecker, who maintains that everything lower can only be understood from the point of view of the higher, there are doubtless such cases. Thus for example, as I said in my book *Purity*, the essence of the sexual sphere, of sen-suality, can only be understood if it is analyzed in the light of love. There are also cases, however, in which advancing from the lower is the proper way, pro-vided that it is really more immediately given and is more intelligible than the higher. For the analysis of the essence of love, however, the notion that one has to start from something ontologically lower is disastrous. Unfortunately, thinkers have often proceeded in just this way. There is no need whatsoever for it, since love is given to us immediately and is much more intelligible than any instinct.

---

kinds of self-love there are, the difference between using this concept only analo-gously and using it in a stricter sense.

9   This error is identified and ably refuted by Denis de Rougemont, *L'Amour et L'Occident* (Paris, 1939), 49.

10   The reason why this ascent through analogies seems to some thinkers to be the epistemologically correct way is certainly that, when it comes to the knowledge of God, such a way of proceeding is the only possible way. But one forgets that this is a unique case, first because God is not given in our natural experience, and sec-ond because He is the creator of the world and possesses the fullness of being.

The fundamental datum of love is experienced in 1) understanding the love of others, 2) in being loved, and 3) in my own loving

If we want to start here in our analysis of love from the personal act of love for another person, this by no means implies that we want to confine ourselves to our own experience of loving. It is a widespread, profound error to believe that personal attitudes are given to us only in our own experiencing and not also given to us in other persons. It was rightly pointed out by Max Scheler and argued by us in an earlier book (*Die Metaphysik der Gemeinschaft* [The Metaphysics of Community]) that it is always untenable to try to derive the knowledge of other persons and their behavior by making an inference on the basis of an analogy with one's self, or by reducing this knowledge to an empathy with the other person, or however the projection may be conceived. There is a primordial and unmediated grasp of the attitude of other persons, of their anger, their joy, their love, their hatred; we grasp their conscious life in their facial expression, in their demeanor, as well as in the conscious and explicit declarations [*Verlautbarung*[11]] that they make of their acts.

Virtues are in fact primarily given to us in other persons. What humility is can only be grasped in another person; kindness is primarily given to us in others. Let us just think of the entirely new moral attitudes that are disclosed to us in a saint, of how we grasp in the saint new and hitherto unknown dimensions of personal attitudes; in this way we will comprehend the absurdity that lies in the notion that everything that we know of the attitudes of other persons is only a projection of our own experiences. This is another typical example of that approach in which one wants to explain away a mysterious datum instead of acknowledging it with genuine philosophical wonder and attempting to penetrate more deeply into it. One simply denies it by trying to reduce it to something that possesses a shallow plausibility and cheap intelligibility, which is after all only an apparent intelligibility. We spoke above at some length about this tendency. We are not able here to inquire in greater detail into this important epistemological problem of how other persons and their attitudes are given to us in experience; it is enough to call attention to it. For our purposes the important thing is to see that the essence of love is not only given to us when we ourselves love; it is also given to us immediately and primordially in the love of others.

It is above all given when another person encounters me with love, when the other turns to me in love. In the experience of being loved, the love of the other person is given to us; the experience of being loved presupposes this givenness. We need not enter here into a detailed account of such givenness; we need not examine how the love of the other manifests itself to me in looks, in actions, in being declared. It is enough to point out the fact that love is given

---

11   We have examined the structure of *Verlautbarung* in our *Die Metaphysik der Gemeinschaft*, 26–32.

here immediately in its distinctive character, and that the beauty of love and the immeasurable gift of love unfold before our mind's eye. Here is another reason for the impossibility of maintaining that the love of the other person can only be grasped through an analogy to one's own love: often people who have known no love of neighbor in themselves were deeply impressed and transformed when they were touched and embraced by the charity of a saint. And how often has someone who was never in love been awakened to such a love by the spousal love of another person for him.[12] This is why there are many people who, although they themselves have never loved, nevertheless know what love is and can be edified by the love of other people.

The love in others is not only given to us in our being loved, however, even if this is a unique form of the givenness of love in others. The love of another person for a third person can also be given to us immediately, be it the charity of a saint, the love of two friends for each other, or the love of a mother for her child. Here, too, love can so manifest itself that the essence of love *and* of the particular category of a given love is clearly given to us. Even in this form of the givenness of love, which compared with being loved is less intimate, the love of others can deeply stir, edify and move us; it, too, can stand before us intuitively alive and disclose to us new qualities and characteristic features of love.

We must go still further. We can also grasp the essence of love in works of art; above all, naturally, in literature when love is so portrayed as it is, for example, in Tolstoy's *Anna Karenina* or in Natasha's falling in love in *War and Peace* or in Shakespeare's *Romeo and Juliet*. The essence of love and its special atmosphere can also be given, however, in poetry and even in music.

Here too some feel for love is presupposed; a dry, unemotional type of person who has no understanding of love will of course also not grasp and comprehend anything of love when he reads such literature. What concerns us here, however, is not that someone must possess a sense for love in order to *grasp* love in other persons or in works of art, but the fact that love is not given to us exclusively in our own loving, but can also be grasped in another person; and that it is not a case here of a projection or a conclusion drawn from an analogy based on our own experience of loving.

---

12 The fact that someone can say, I do not know what love is because I have never loved, is no objection to the fact that love can be given to us in another person and that when it is we are not inferring from the analogy with our own experiences. For someone who says, I cannot conceive what love would be since I have never loved, is in fact lacking not only in the personal experience of love, but also in the receptivity and appreciation for love; that is why he will not understand love in others. This inability to grasp certain things, which we find, for example, in the value blindness in relation to artistic values, or in the lack of understanding of many higher data of a spiritual nature, is after all a deficiency within a capacity to grasp something and not only a lack of having experienced something.

It must be emphasized, however, that certain aspects of love disclose themselves to us only in our own experience of them, that is, in our lateral consciousness of performing them, whereas other aspects reveal themselves only in the love of other persons. For all personal acts have, as it were, an inner and outer side. Both belong essentially to the act, both are fully valid; the one is not a mere appearance of the other, nor is the outer side merely extrinsic to the inner side. When, for example, Scheler says about moral values that they are found on the "back" of the act, he is thereby clearly referring to the "outer side" of the act. The moral value of an act of the will, of a love, of a joy is given on the "outer side," not the inner side. It inheres in the act, however, on account of its inner side; that which happens in the inner side is essential for the moral value, which is itself, however, in the outer side of the act. We realize the expression "inner and outer side" is altogether inadequate, but there is no better one at our disposal for these essential realities. It is not the case, however, that in other persons only the outer side of the act of love is given and in our own experience only the inner side. But it is certain that many aspects of the outer side, such as, for example, the value of the act, are given only in other persons, and many aspects of the inner side only in our own experience.

In our context it is above all important to stress that love has an inner and outer side and that *both* must be fully taken into consideration if one wants to do justice to the nature of love. We will therefore take both the givenness of love in other persons as well as our own experience of loving as the basis and starting point for our analysis of love.

When we speak about or think of love, a whole world truly stands before our eyes, without our having thereby to think at all of analogous meanings of this word. We are thinking of the love of David for Absalom, or of the love of St. Monica for St. Augustine, of the love of a Leonore for Florestan in Beethoven's *Fidelio*, of a Romeo for Juliet, of the love of Tristan for Isolde in Wagner's opera. In short, we are speaking of all nuances and kinds of love, of that unique act that is the source of the most profound happiness in man's life. We mean the love of which Leonardo da Vinci says: "The greater the man, the deeper his love."

The goal of the following investigations

Thus we want first to try to grasp the nature of love in the place where it is intuitively given to us in all its fullness. We want then to try to examine carefully all the distinctions that come up, such as the distinction between *eros* and *agape*, or between *amor concupiscentiae* and *amor benevolentiae*, or between *amour egoiste* and *amour destineresse*, as well as the distinction between physical and ecstatic love (physical is a Scholastic term that does not mean bodily). We want to examine these distinctions in rigorous confrontation with reality, with the nature of love as intuitively given to us. Many problems, many alternatives, many difficulties that have been historically important will show themselves to be pseudo-problems and pseudo-alternatives. In this way we hope that our investigation of love will clear the way for a philosophical understanding of love that does more justice to this most centrally important and sublime act of the person.

CHAPTER ONE

Love as Value-Response

Love in the most proper and most immediate sense is love for *another* person, whether it be the love of a mother for her child, the love of a child for its parents, the love between friends, the love between man and woman, the love for God, or the love of neighbor. Love for non-personal things, such as the love for a nation or a homeland or a country or a work of art or a house, bears only a certain analogy to love. But it is much closer to love in the proper sense than is self-love.

The false analogy between love and "being-attached" to something merely subjectively satisfying

All ways of "being attached" to things like food, drink, money, etc. cannot be called love even in an analogous sense, for they are precisely distinguished from love in the most important point. The heavy drinker does not love alcohol, the greedy man does not love money. They are no doubt attached to these things and are under the power of them; these things have an indescribable attractive power for such people. But being attached, something which is also found in love, is here so different in kind, the power of attraction is in both cases so different, that we have a misleading analogy. In the introduction to this work we have already pointed out the danger of such analogies.

Thus the nature of love is necessarily misunderstood by starting from the phenomenon of "being attached" to something. The distinctive character of love, its specific nature implies precisely the contrast with all these other forms of "being attached" to something. The difference which is here at stake is the same fundamental difference which runs through the entire affective sphere and analogously through the sphere of the will: the difference between value-response and the response to something merely agreeable. We have elaborated this distinction in our *Ethics*, and so it suffices to refer to this earlier work.[1]

---

1   I want to avoid all misunderstandings by emphatically saying that the term value in my works has nothing at all to do with the value philosophy of Heinrich Rickert. It is even different from what Scheler understands by value. Although in Scheler's notion of value as well as in mine, there is a contrast to neutral, indifferent being,

But here our task is to refer again to the fundamental difference between the delightfulness that is rooted in value and the delightfulness that is not rooted in value. An example of the first is the delight I experience dwelling in a beautiful landscape. It is attractive and gives me joy because of its beauty, which is a kind of value. An example of the delightfulness not rooted in value is the pleasant character of a warm bath or the entertaining quality of playing cards. Here it is not a value meriting an appropriate response from me but rather the quality of the agreeable (we assume that the warm bath is agreeable for me, playing cards is enjoyable for me) that makes the agreeable thing an objective good for me. All "being-attached" that is based on this kind of good, that is, based on goods that are in the broadest sense of the word agreeable without themselves having value and that are in any case not delightful on the basis of some value, is radically different from all being attached to objective goods which are delightful on the basis of their value.[2]

---

it has to be emphatically stressed the real nature of value in my sense is not understood as long as the category of importance that I call the merely subjectively satisfying as well as the category that I call the objective good for the person, are not clearly distinguished from the category of value.

Above all we have to warn against two further misunderstandings. Some thinkers connect the term value with the turning away from concrete individual goods toward the sphere of the abstract. I want to affirm clearly that my concept of value has nothing to do with any such flight into the abstract. Other authors regard values as abstract principles that are supposed to be a substitute for the real command of the living God. No, values in my sense, and most especially the qualitative values, are a ray of light, a reflection of the infinite glory of the living God; they are a message from God in all created goods and exist as an ultimate reality in God Himself, who is, after all, Justice itself, Goodness itself, Love itself.

2   The interest in beautiful music and the desire to hear it, is in its structure entirely different from the interest in the merely agreeable and the subjectively satisfying. This deep difference in the kind of delightfulness is not, however, primarily a difference in the object. What matters is our attitude to the good. It is entirely possible to approach goods of great value in such a way that they are desired only from the point of view of subjectively satisfying. An example of this is found in the radical aesthete in his relation to beauty. This is of course a complete perversion because beauty clearly calls us to a value-responding attitude and the aesthete can never really grasp the value of beauty; though he has all the understanding of the connoisseur, he remains blind to the real depth of beauty in art and in nature. There are also goods in relation to which both attitudes are possible without any real perversion. We can take pleasure in smelling a flower that has a splendid aroma and in doing so we can think only of the agreeability of the aroma. But we can also grasp the nobility, the preciousness of the flower, the sublimity of its aroma, and can take a contemplative delight that is entirely based upon the value-responding attitude. In this case, the delightfulness is an outgrowth or gift of value, whereas in the first case it is something merely subjectively satisfying. We mention this case to show that in order to understand the fundamental difference between the

This is why it is necessary to point out the very great danger of investigating the nature of love by bringing in analogies from a sphere where the delightfulness is not rooted in value and where our stance toward the good is a fundamentally different one. For the specific mark of love is, as we shall see, its character of self-donation, indeed its transcendence.

Love is a value-response

It is essential for every kind of love that the beloved person stands before me as precious, beautiful, lovable. As long as someone is just useful for me, as long as I can just use him, the basis for love is missing. The self-giving and commitment proper to every kind of love, be it love for my parents, love for my child, the love between friends, the love between man and woman, is necessarily based on the fact that the beloved person stands before me as beautiful, precious, as objectively worthy of being loved. *Love exists as a value-response.*

Already Aristotle saw that true friendship is only possible when it is embedded in the good, because only then are we interested in the other person as person; this throws clearly into relief the fact that love is a value-response. The interest that I have for another when I love him is an interest in the other as person; his existence and his whole being are fully thematic for me. As long as the other person is only useful for me or a source of entertainment or amusement for me, he is not fully thematic as such, but is just of interest to me as a means for something else.

As long as someone is just useful for me, I do not have to be attracted at all by him. I can even find him repulsive but remain in contact with him because I need him for certain goals or projects. The usefulness is not even a basis for any kind of delightfulness. Besides, the other person in this case is in no way thematic as such, but is just of interest to me as a means for something else.

This kind of interest is as far removed from love as could be. Of course, the person who is at first of interest to me only as a means can go beyond the qualities underlying his usefulness, qualities like efficiency, being influential, being wealthy, and can manifest personal values like reliability, honesty, faithfulness, and the like, which can then indeed become the basis for a love of him. But then it is these personal values which awaken the love, and these have to be clearly distinguished from mere usefulness.

two kinds of delightfulness, or in other words, between the two kinds of *fruitio*, we do not have to think primarily in terms of the object, of the nature of the good that we encounter. This fundamental difference also shows itself in the fact that in the one case a good is desired because it functions as a means for our subjective satisfaction, whereas in the other case a good is aspired to on the basis of its value. In this latter case, the good is not at all considered as a means for my pleasure or my happiness but rather as something important in itself that we want to participate in because of its value and because of the happiness that flows superabundantly from our contact with its inner preciousness and dignity.

But it is not only the usefulness of a person which does not suffice to awaken love in us. Even if a person is a source of amusement for me, this kind of delightfulness is not sufficient to awaken love. Suppose that someone is funny without even intending it and makes us laugh simply by his manner. We can enjoy his company even though he is not at all attractive; he can be silly or even tasteless, but he can amuse us greatly by the way in which he is funny without intending it (this is what happens in the poems of Friedericke Kemptner). That which is comical can even be rooted in disvalue, in which case we have a delightfulness that is clearly not rooted in the values of this person. It is not difficult to see that this delightfulness of being funny and amusing is incapable of being the basis for love.[3] The person is not as such thematic; we enjoy the comical quality in which the person, so to speak, functions as an object. The person is in fact no more thematic as person here than in the case where someone interests me only by being useful to me.

The value foundation of love: the full thematicity of the beloved person as person

But let us suppose that someone amuses us by being funny not unintentionally but quite deliberately, as the "fools" in the courts of princes in earlier times: even this is not as such a basis for loving the other.[4] It is true that the delightfulness in this case is rooted in values and that the person is rather more thematic than in the two above-mentioned cases, but the value of the entertaining person and the delightfulness rooted in it has to be distinguished in principle from the value found in every love. In love the value and its delightfulness must be of such a kind that it is united with the full thematicity of the person as person. As long as someone just amuses us through his wittiness or his social graces, so that his company is pleasant and agreeable for us, we may find him to be likable, but we still do not love him. We merely like such a person under a certain point of view, but this attractiveness of the other does not suffice to make him fully thematic as person and to invest him as person with the radiance of value that is proper to the beloved person in all the forms of love. As long as the other simply serves to entertain me, he remains somehow a mere means and is not fully thematic as person. Thus in the case of love, the values in question and their delightfulness must be of such a kind that they form a unity with the person as person, and that the person is fully thematic in them.

Take someone whose being is full of poetical charm, whose rhythm of life has something enchanting: this value is clearly of such a kind as to make this

---

3   This is not to say that this comical quality is not a value. But it is in no way a personal value, it is an aesthetic value all its own; it is constituted "outside" of the person who is comical and it does not enhance the person.

4   A special case is given with actors who excel in portraying comical figures. Here we have in addition to the value of the comical also the value of talented acting. This latter value is one degree closer to the person than in the case of the court fool.

person precious and beautiful as person, and in the delightfulness of these values the person remains fully thematic. This is all the more the case when the value belongs to a lofty spiritual world which the person radiates in such a way as to charm and attract me. Any and every attempt to think of a person as a mere means for enjoying this spiritual world is condemned to failure, for our delight in this world would thereby break up. This value datum is so united with the person that it ennobles the person as such, making him precious; it makes the person fully thematic and lets our delight be a delight in this person. This holds all the more with moral and religious values. When another attracts me by his generosity, purity, goodness, or by his deep piety, his love for Christ, these values are so centrally united with this person that in being attracted by them, my attention is concentrated in a particular way on the personhood of the other.

Love in all its forms always involves this consciousness of the preciousness of the beloved person, and of a value datum so closely united with the person that the person stands before me as valuable, beautiful in himself, deriving all his attractive power and delightfulness from his preciousness and beauty.

It is not enough to stress that love is a value-response and thus is essentially different from all responses motivated by the merely subjectively satisfying. It has also to be stressed that love is grounded in a value so closely united with the person that the person as such, that is, this individual and unique person taken as subject, stands before me as valuable, precious, lovable, and is fully thematic for me. The value basis of love is such that it elevates and ennobles the person as person and completely excludes any possibility of looking upon the beloved person as a means for my happiness and delight.

Indeed, as we will later show in detail, the beloved person is, for the one who loves him, not just a bearer of values, not just a fortunate instantiation of genuine values, but is fully thematic in his beauty and his preciousness, which he embodies in his own unique way.

So we have to say that while every love is a value-response, something more is required for love than is required for value-responses such as enthusiasm, admiration, or joy. First of all, for love a certain kind of value must be given, namely, a value which invests a human being as a whole with a certain splendor, and secondly, the values of a beloved person must belong to him in a particular way.[5]

Reasons for overlooking that love is a value-response

1. *Confusing love with attitudes that are different from it or even opposed to it.* One often overlooks the fact that love is a value-response, because often in our

---

5   In the next chapter, when we discuss the difference between love and other value-responses, we will bring up many other things that belong to love over and above the value of the beloved person. Here it is simply our task to show that love is a value-response.

concrete relation to a beloved person various other attitudes that are very different in nature from love get closely connected with our love for the other. Some of these attitudes, though fundamentally different from love in motivation, structure, and quality, are not incompatible with love. They may be in themselves quite legitimate and in fact sometimes have a high value; their coexistence with love in no way does violence to love as long as they do not aim at substituting for it. But there are other attitudes which are not only essentially different from love but in fact contradict love in its ethos. They are attitudes which pollute and compromise love to the extent that they are present.

An example of the first kind of attitude—the one coexisting with love while being essentially different from it, yet without being opposed to it—is feeling strengthened and sheltered by the abundant vitality and cheerfulness of another person. His presence takes away from us the feeling of uncertainty and gives us courage to face life. Legitimate as this attitude towards the other is, it should not be confused with love for this person. It neither necessarily includes love for him nor does love for its part necessarily include such a relation of being sheltered. We will later come to speak about these attitudes in some detail and will show how they differ essentially from love.

An example of the second kind of attitude—the one opposed to the "genius" of love—is being proud of another person, for instance a child or spouse, on the grounds that one considers the other as a part of one's self and feels his excellences as an extension of one's own ego. This attitude can coexist with genuine love in a person, but it is not only essentially different from love, it also contradicts the very genius of love, polluting and compromising love to the extent that it predominates.

We will later examine in detail these accompaniments of love. We mention both of them here simply because they often prevent one from understanding the value-response character of love. Because one does not take the trouble to let love as such appear in our spiritual range of vision and to look at its *eidos* or essence, one confuses it with these accompaniments that are foreign to it by nature and one uses these as a proof of the fact that love is not essentially different from the desire for some pleasure-giving good or at least from an *appetitus*[6] that seeks satisfaction. This is why we want to call attention right now to the necessary task of distinguishing love clearly from all those elements that can coexist with it in a concrete case. Coexistence should never mislead us to identify the coexisting things.

2. *The awakening of love by conferring benefits on someone, and how this confirms that love is a value-response.* There is also another misunderstanding

---

6   [Von Hildebrand frequently uses this Latin term, *appetitus*, which he takes from neo-Scholastic philosophy. Since he does not translate it into German, we will not try to translate it into English, even though sometimes the English "appetite" would come close to rendering his meaning. Trans.]

that has to be countered. One could object that love is not really a value-response because it is often awakened through special benefits conferred on the one who loves. The child loves the person who always gives him candies and attractive toys. An adult often loves someone because this person has conferred so many benefits on him. One could try to prove from this that the motive of love is not the beauty and preciousness that the other has in himself, but is rather beneficial goods that the other confers. This is a point of view expressed in a banal way by the saying, "Love goes through the stomach."

One could also try to deduce from this that the beloved person is only a means for such benefits and that the interest shown in him is rooted in the fact that we have received and continue to receive benefits from him.

All of this is obviously a complete misunderstanding. One overlooks the fact that in cases where a love begins with benefits received from someone, it is the qualities of the person revealed and manifested in the conferring of the benefits that really motivate the love. Conferring the benefits normally comes from a friendly and kind attitude and as such they "speak" a word of kindness, as long as there are no signs in the behavior of the benefactor that contradict the presence of such an attitude. In the kind attitude there is revealed a quality of the person, his generosity, his goodness, his warm-heartedness, his capacity for love. It is in reality these personal qualities which awaken feeling for another and love for him or her; it is not at all simply the advantage, taken by itself, of receiving a beneficial good from the other. For the primitive mentality of a child, a kind attitude is revealed in the one who gives candies or toys. In the act of giving, the giver is revealed as "good" and "dear" and it is these qualities that the love of a child responds to. As soon as the giver seems to the child to be sinister, as soon as his behavior indicates qualities opposed to kindness, then the activity of giving is deprived of its character of revealing kindness, and all love in the child ceases.

This holds analogously for all those cases in which adults begin to love after receiving benefits. It is always the person's character that is revealed through its goodness to me; the person makes himself felt in a particular way when turning to me. To take an impersonal beneficial good and, as it were, to isolate it and to come to think of it as only causally connected with the giver, is an entirely primitive misconception of personal relations and an overlooking of what is revealed in an act addressed to me from another person. The primary experience in receiving gifts from another is the kind, friendly attitude of the other; of course not only friendly in itself, but also friendly to me. But the act of being kind to me is not separable in the other person from the quality of being kind as such.

We will return later to an extensive discussion of how being loved by another person, taken in the most general sense of the term, awakens my love for him. There is no question but that the loving and friendly attitude of another person toward me affects my stance toward him, but we can easily see from the following consideration that his friendly stance toward me cannot ground a really authentic love for him if I lose sight of the character of the other person as person.

That such friendliness is not the decisive basis for love is evident from the fact that often I can love another even though the other has never conferred any benefits upon me, indeed has not even shown any signs of a friendly stance toward me. Above all, we have to consider the following elements in those cases in which a friendly and loving attitude of a person is the point of departure for love for that person. First of all, the friendly attitude toward me that is manifested in the kind deed reveals a personal quality of goodness which the other has in himself, and this is what is able to engender love. Secondly, this value quality of a person reveals itself in a particular way to us when the kindness of the other is directed to me instead of to another. A person and his qualities present themselves to me in an entirely unique way when he addresses me in an other-directed act and declares to me his feeling for me. I can, of course, grasp the kindness of a person in his acting towards some third person, that is, when this person stands before me as "he" or "she," but it is a new and unique way of experiencing the person's goodness when it is revealed in a stance that addresses me.[7] The friendly and kind attitude that refers to me is not just something that I grasp, rather I feel it, it warms me with its breath, it touches my heart. Yet the goodness of another is given to me in an incomparable way when the other stands before me as a "you." Of course, the goodness that addresses some third person can deeply strike us and affect us. But this goodness is more expressive, more intimate, more personally given when another turns to me, and for this reason if for no other, the value of a person that presents itself in this way is even more capable of awakening love and providing the basis for a friendly and love-like way of turning to the person. And so we see that the fact that benefits conferred on me can awaken love in me for the giver in no way amounts to an objection to the fact that love is a value-response.

3. *The inability to indicate the reasons for loving someone and how this only serves to point out the deeper and more individual value datum that we call the "overall beauty" [Gesamtschönheit] of a person.* We should not doubt that love is a value-response simply because when asked why we love someone, we cannot indicate the value qualities that motivate our love in the same way that we can indicate them in explaining, say, our esteem for another person.

First of all, the value qualities in the world far exceed the value concepts that we human beings have. And the kinds of values exceed even more the names that we have for them. But more important is the fact that love has to do with the overall beauty [*Gesamtschönheit*] and preciousness of this individuality, which is a fundamental value datum; and while this value is nourished by many vital, spiritual, and moral values, it can never be completely analyzed

---

7   We have already referred to this in the introduction to this work.

into these nor can it be directly formulated as these can be. The overall beauty of this individuality is not able to be classified. In the love for a friend and even more in a spousal love, we see with particular clarity the central place of this value, the preciousness of this unique individuality. What grounds and engenders our love for the other person is the beauty and preciousness of this unique personality as a whole. One could perhaps say that it is the beauty of the particular "invention" of God which this individual embodies. It is certainly true that the particular preciousness of this individual is, as we said, nourished by vital, intellectual, moral, and many other personal values such as strength of personality and stature (what the French call *envergure*), or from all of these taken together. But as long as we are only talking about individual excellences, we do not yet have the specific foundation for love.

The individuality of the whole personality stands before us as precious and beautiful; only in this way can the person awaken love in us. The fact that we cannot easily point out as the basis of our love things like the reliability or the honesty or the intelligence or the spiritual awaked-ness of the other, proves nothing against the value-response character of love, but only shows us what a deep and central value datum love presupposes, or, as we could as well say, it reveals to us in a particular way the value-response character of love by turning our attention to the kind of value datum that is present in love.

4. *The idea that the overall beauty [Gesamtschönheit] of the person is a result of and not the basis for love.* We come now to another kind of misunderstanding that has to be avoided. One could think that the radiance of value that the beloved person undeniably has in all love is not the basis for but rather the result of love. One could object as follows: "Let us grant that the beloved person stands before me as precious and beautiful and not just as subjectively satisfying or agreeable. Nevertheless, this value is a correlate of love in the sense that the other person gets invested with this radiance of value through my love. Because I love the other, he stands before me as beautiful and precious; I do not love him because he first stands before me as beautiful and precious."

The priority of love over the value datum can be interpreted in different ways. It can mean that love is presupposed for understanding the other person in his beauty. In this case a great truth is expressed, namely that turning lovingly to someone opens our eyes and lets us grasp all the values that one would never see as long as one lived in an indifferent attitude. We have here a special case of the general relation between love and knowledge.

The priority of love over the value datum can also be meant in an opposite sense: love causes us invest the beloved person with all kinds of values. Whereas in the first case love opens our eyes to value and enables us to recognize what is really there, love plunges us into illusions according to this view. Love would thus be the reason why we see the beloved as radiant with value; love makes the beloved person appear in this deceptive light; we adorn him with value only because we love him.

Finally, the priority of love can be understood in a completely different sense: love actualizes new values in the beloved person. Here we have to do with the effect of love on the development of the person which is analogous to the effect of love on the one who loves. New levels of depth in the person are actualized in loving and in being loved. This is a great and important subject to which we will return for a more extensive discussion. Gabriel Marcel has brought to light in a convincing way this effect of being loved on the actualization of the person as person. We do not have to explore this problem here because this last conception of the priority of love to value clearly stands in no contradiction at all to the value-response character of love. That love has an energizing effect on the one who is loved, that being loved lets new values flourish in the one who is loved, in no way contradicts the fact that love is engendered by the beauty of the personality of the one who is loved. On the contrary, it is thereby confirmed, as we will later see.

a) The paradox of love presupposing value knowledge while at the same time empowering us to see value more clearly. The first priority of love to the apprehension of value is affirmed to a certain degree in Scheler's conception of love. But true as it is that love sharpens our vision of value, so that when we approach someone lovingly we grasp values in him that we did not see as long as we approached him indifferently, still it would be false to deny that love itself presupposes an apprehension of values and that it by its very nature responds to these values or is engendered by them. We have here a reciprocal process, as I have shown in my earlier work, *Sittlichkeit und ethische Werterkenntnis* (Morality and Ethical Value Knowledge).

Some apprehension of value is presupposed for the awakening of love, but love enables us to reach a new and deeper apprehension of value, which in turn grounds a new and deeper love, which in turn grounds a new and deeper apprehension of value. So it is quite right to point out the eminent value of love for the apprehension of value, but it would be a great mistake not to see that a certain level of value apprehension is already presupposed by love. When Romeo sees Juliet at the ball and his heart burns with love, her beauty first discloses itself to him along with her loveliness, purity, and preciousness, and then follows the response of love. Romeo was, after all, in love with another girl at the time of the ball at the Capulets.

Let us take another completely different kind of love, the love of veneration, such as we find it in the love of Lucia for Fr. Christoforo in the novel of Manzoni, *I Promessi Sposi*. Her love is clearly a response to his goodness, piety, and to the radiance of sanctity that suffuses his person.

One simply cannot say that no value is disclosed in a person whom we do not already love. One simply cannot deny that in the basic gesture of love one is related to the beauty and preciousness of the beloved person, and that love cannot be detached from the consciousness that the other is lovable and is worthy of love. Every attempt to deprive love of its character as value-response leads either to conceiving of love as arbitrary and entirely irrational or to artificially constructing other explanations of it. We will return to this problem later in some detail. For now it suffices to see the following: the fact that love opens our eyes to values in no way contradicts the other fact that our love presupposes some apprehension of value and is engendered by the radiance of the value of the other person. As long as one is only saying that love has a priority for a certain apprehension of value, there is no contradiction whatsoever with the value-response character of love. At the origin of love, however, there stands an apprehension of value that is presupposed by love and which in fact awakens it.

b) The attitudes other than love that lead to the illusory radiance of value and to value blindness. What concerns us at present is the thesis of the priority of love that says that love leads us to an illusion, as if the other were good, beautiful, noble only because I love him. This thesis tries to explain away the undeniable phenomenon that the beloved stands in my presence as beautiful and precious, thus mistaking what is really the *principium* (cause) for the *principiatum* (effect). In addition, the "effect" of loving is portrayed as an illusion. One assumes that in loving I project values into the beloved person, values that this person in no way possesses.

Love is seen here as resembling the state of mind produced by a "love potion," which sometimes appears in literature. We are not thinking here of the love potion in Wagner's opera *Tristan und Isolde*, where it after all does not cause the love but only serves to remove the hindrances for the two to declare their already existing love. We are rather thinking of something like the love potion in *A Midsummer Night's Dream* or the potion that Mephistopheles gives to Faust saying, "With this potion in your body, each woman will appear to you like another Helen." One treats love as an urge, as a desire that is in us quite independent of any motivating object, like a mere instinct. This is surely the most radical misconception of the nature of love. This view not only denies love its character as value-response, but even its character as an intentional act.

For our purposes it does not make much difference whether one reduces love to the sexual drive as Freud did, or whether one presents it as a higher spiritual drive (even though of course the theory of love as a sublimated sexual drive is in one respect a vastly more shallow error and a much more superstitious construction). Every view of love as an immanent movement of the soul, as a need in contrast to a response, every view that presents the value datum in the beloved person as a creation of this need, as an illusion, like seeing everything yellow after eating santonine, is a typical example of the dreadful reductionistic tendency we spoke of in the introduction to this work. I mean the tendency to pass over that which is unmistakably given and to think that one gets closer to reality by going behind the given and explaining the given in the sense of reducing it to something else. This way of proceeding has something in common with superstition. One thinks that one is more intelligent and more probing when one scorns the immediately given in its intelligibility and takes something fundamentally opposed to the given as the authentic reality. Love is unmistakably given as response. Every unprejudiced look at the essence of love shows unmistakably its intentional character, that is, the meaningful relation existing between the beauty and preciousness of the other person and the word of love spoken to the other.

We want now to encounter these attempts to reduce love to something radically opposed to its essence by examining those things to which is reduced. It is always the best procedure in dealing with these reductionistic theories to examine the cases that really correspond to the theory and that are mistakenly applied to something else. Thus in dealing with the view that reduces all kinds of mental phenomena to a process of association, we can do no better than to examine cases of real association in order to show the absurdity of this reduction. So now we want to consider those cases in which my stance toward another person really does lead to investing him with values that he does not have, or to falling into illusions about him.

Sensual desire. Sensual desire can put a man in a frame of mind where he thinks the women whom he encounters are more attractive and more beautiful than they are in reality. Here it is really a certain factor in our nature, a need, that makes us see someone in a certain light, and so there is a real possibility of seeing another in a light that does not correspond to reality. Here the saying of Mephistopheles, already quoted, fits well: "With this potion in your body, each woman will appear to you like another Helen."

But when we compare this case with authentic love, we cannot possibly overlook the absolute difference of the two. Love is characterized by a commitment [*Hingabe*] to the other person, by an affirmation of the other in his existence, by a unique kind of solidarity with him. There is none of all this in the case of a mere isolated sensual desire. The other may attract me, please me, but he is never thematic as person. I remain enclosed in my immanence, making no gesture of commitment, having no consciousness of the lovableness of the other or of the fact that the other merits my love.

Pride. It is certainly possible to be deceived about persons whom we really love, but such deception is not the fruit of love but rather of coexisting factors. It is often as a result of pride that one falls into illusions about another person. Besides loving their children, parents often also see them as a kind of extended ego and so are inclined to project many values into their children simply on the grounds that this satisfies their pride. Many parents have thought to themselves, "My children must be very talented, they are of course in every respect extraordinary because they are my children." But such a saying does not derive from love but from pride and from extended self-love. Because the other is seen as a part of us, our pride "colors" the child with all kinds of values that the child in no way really possesses. Indeed, one really thinks that one's child is more outstanding than he really is.

It is understandable that one might mistakenly take this illusion as a product of love, because the same parents who think of their children as an extended ego and as a part of themselves really do also love their children. Though love for another has nothing to do with the solidarity with another that comes from experiencing the other as an extended ego, the two can nevertheless coexist. Of course, the presence of this outgrowth of pride has an extremely negative influence on the love, compromising it and polluting it, but it need not destroy the love. This coexistence of pride and love leads to the erroneous theory that makes love responsible for such illusions.

Disordered yearning for happiness. Another case of investing a person whom one loves with valuable qualities is found in the one who has a naïve yearning for happiness and wants to think of himself as having won the great lottery of life. Here we do not have the pride just discussed, namely, the solidarity with others who are taken as an extended ego. It is the same disordered yearning for happiness that makes me talk myself into my love for someone; I want to love fully and unconditionally because this is a splendid thing to do and because it is a source of happiness. Thus I want to be able to see in the beloved person the epitome of all perfections, so that I can think of this love as a uniquely great love and think of myself as the happiest person in the world. I also do not want to seem to be any less successful than others in becoming happy, whether in respect of marriage or of children. The social image that I have of myself can also play a role: it becomes so important to think of myself as winning the great lottery of life that I would rather flee into illusions than to admit that I have not yet found the ideal that I long for.

Talking myself into love is indeed always a sign that a real love has not yet been granted. For if I truly love and am loved in return, I am simply happy and do not have to talk myself into my love. I will never use my love as a means for my happiness, rather I give my love to the beloved person in the consciousness that it is deserved and that I cannot help loving the other. I see the true beauty of the beloved so clearly that I do not have to project values into him or her that are not really there. And I no longer measure my happiness against the happiness of others; this rivalry with others plays no role, for it is precisely a distinguishing mark of genuine love that I am so focused on the beloved person and am so "filled" with him that a comparison with others is no longer an issue.

Thus this way of idealizing a person whom I love and want to love is also not a result of love as such but rather of a disordered desire for happiness, which is in fact an attitude directly opposed to love, even if it can coexist with a given love.

Naiveté on the part of the one who loves. There is also a trait proper to love which, as we will later see, often misleads one into thinking that love is blind. In contrast to mere esteem or admiration, which always refers to another person under the aspect of certain qualities, love always refers to the whole person. It presupposes the value-givenness of the individual person as a whole, but it also belongs to the response of love to give the other a kind of credit that surpasses all the beauty that one has already perceived in detail.

This act of "drawing out the line" of the beauty and preciousness of the other person is neither a yielding to illusions, nor a producing of a mirage, nor can it be detached from the value-response character of love. It is a trait proper to love, which is always a value-response; it has to do with the absoluteness of love. The value which flashes up in another person pierces my heart and engenders love for him. In being pierced, I experience the value that I have grasped as radiating throughout the other person as a whole. He stands before me not only adorned with certain values but he has become through and through beautiful and precious as a whole—as this individual. But love turns to the other in such a way as to, as it were, draw out this line of perfection into all the corners of the being of the other and to do this without necessarily falling into illusions. We say "not necessarily" because there are naïve persons who are just as naïve in their love as in their trust, in their gullibility, and in their way of knowing. This naiveté is a general trait of a person and shows itself throughout the life of the person, including in his way of loving. Just as this person easily believes everything which he is told, so he also assumes that, for example, a girl with whom he has fallen in love because of her beauty and charm must be an angel, a being endowed with all possible virtues. Such people draw out the line of perfection in a naïve way. A relatively peripheral value datum suffices to make the whole person appear as beautiful and precious, although they have not had the opportunity to really get to know the personality of the other.

It would clearly be false to ascribe to love as such, or to being in love as such, this possibility of being deceived and to think that it is a necessary result of love to invest the beloved person with all kinds of values. Such illusions are a result of the naiveté of certain people who fall into illusions and let themselves be deceived even apart from their loves. They take everybody at their word and they take for granted without asking any questions that everybody has only the best intentions.

The crucial point for us is the fact that love as such is always a value-response and that it requires some givenness of value in order to arise. A person has to stand before me as precious and beautiful to be able to engender my love for him. This is the decisive point. It is absolutely erroneous to say that love, instead of responding to the value of the other, generates an illusion that makes the beloved person appear to be beautiful and lovable. Love as such is not blind.

The interpretation of love as the aptitude for satisfying an immanent appetitus

1. *The distinction between appetitus and value-response.* But there is still another misunderstanding that we have to clear away. It is a radical distortion

of love to think that it is an appetitus or an urge and that love is in the realm of the spiritual what an instinct like thirst is in the realm of the bodily. On this view, the beauty of the beloved person and his attractiveness are not indeed presented as an illusion or as a mirage produced by love, but this beauty is wrongly reduced to the capacity of the beloved person to satisfy a yearning. And this error is not just an error about love, but about all kinds of taking an interest in things, it is an error about the nature of value-response in general and indeed about value itself. I have spoken about this error at length in my *Ethics* (especially in chapters 3, 8, 16, 17).

There are inclinations rooted in the human subject the fulfillment of which can be explained in terms of the dispositions and the needs of man. Examples are the bodily need to quench one's thirst, the spiritual need to develop one's talents, or the psychological need for the company of others. These needs play a great role in our life, but what defines them is that they are not engendered by the object and its importance but spontaneously arise in a personal subject and cause one to search out the object that can satisfy the need.

In all responses, by contrast, and most especially in all value-responses, it is the object and its importance which call into being the corresponding stance of the person. In all needs the desire is the *principium* (cause) and the object the *principiatum* (effect), whereas in all responses the object is the *principium* and the inclination that arises in man the *principiatum*. All needs are grounded in the nature of man and the object becomes important because this need already exists quite independently of the importance that the object possesses of itself. Its importance for man is grounded in the ability of the object to be able to satisfy a need. If the need, the drive, the appetitus were not already alive, the same object that is now so attractive would not be attractive at all and would not stand before us as important. Because we are thirsty, we look for water. The thirst is clearly no response to the water.

The decisive difference between an appetite and a value-response lies first of all in the fact that with a value-response the importance of the object does not derive from satisfying some subjective or objective need of the person: rather the object is important in itself. In the value-response, the value of a good is thematic, whereas with an appetitus, the satisfaction of the need, or perhaps the development of the subject, for which some thing is needed, is thematic. Secondly, in value-response, interest in the object is based on the value. The person is interested in some good because of its value, because of its importance in itself, which it has independently of the interest of the person. The value-response is motivated by value, it is called into being by the value of the object. Appetitus, on the other hand, arises in human beings on the basis of their makeup and it turns towards the object because the object has the ability to satisfy the need, because they need it, because it is an objective good for them on the basis of this satisfaction and not on the basis of its value.

2. *Forms of the legitimate coexistence of drive and value-response.* This fundamental difference does not mean that something cannot attract and move us by its value and at the same time satisfy an appetitus. In other words, it is entirely possible that an appetitus and a value-response coexist in a certain behavior or in a certain activity. Take the person who has a great talent for teaching and who thus has a need to develop this talent; this person may nonetheless, in his activity of teaching, be entirely directed to the value of mediating the truth to others in some area of knowledge. Let us suppose that this person teaches philosophy: although he feels a need to teach and develop this talent of his, he may be entirely motivated by the value of truth itself and of truth entering into the minds of other persons. That is the real theme for him when he teaches. We have to see that although appetitus and value-response are essentially different, they can still coexist in an organic way, and indeed that the value-response is not necessarily purer simply through the absence of the appetitus. The value-response would be compromised in its purity only if the urge to teach were to become the primary theme, replacing the value-response, or if this urge became the whole reason for teaching and eliminated the value-response. It belongs to the essence of value to be the primary theme; this is why our relation to a value-bearing good should refer primarily to the good insofar as it is valuable. As soon as the development of pedagogical talent becomes the primary theme of a teacher of philosophy, the value-response is compromised in its purity and a serious perversion results.

The fact that the desire for or need of something makes us more capable of seeing and appreciating the value of that thing, should not be used as an argument for denying the essential difference between a value-response and an appetitus.

It is true that if I have been alone for a long time and am "starved" for the company of other human beings, I see the value of even mere contact with others more clearly than ever when I finally encounter some other person. Of course, here we have primarily to do with a beneficial good that I have long been deprived of. Its importance and gift-character is thrown into relief by the fact that I have gone without it for a long time. But it would obviously be false to reduce this importance to the mere satisfaction of a desire for companionship. It can also happen that not only the importance of some beneficial good becomes clearer when it is already desired, but that such a desire can make me more sensitive to value. When I have not heard beautiful music for such a long time that I am "starved" for it, I acquire a disposition that lets the value of some piece of music stand forth in a particular way and that heightens my receptivity for it.

But this in no way means that beauty can be interpreted as the mere satisfaction of a desire: just the contrary is the case. We have to do here with the general fact that we are often more receptive for the value of something and more capable of taking it in just at the time that we have long been deprived of it. It is a weakness of our nature that we become insensitive to the value of the things that we are used to. But this neither transforms the importance of value in itself into a mere satisfaction nor does it transform our contemplative delight into a mere satisfaction of desire.

When one longs for beautiful music and when as a result its value stands out all the more, it is clear that the beauty of the music cannot be reduced to the satisfaction of the desire, because already this yearning is itself a value-response and is not an appetitus.

Even if a real appetitus should make us more receptive, it would still be completely wrong to think that one can find in the appetitus the source of the importance of the good, that is, to think that one can reduce value to the satisfaction of an appetitus. It cannot be denied that there is a certain bodily vitality [*Sinnlichkeit*] and an indefinite yearning rooted in this vitality that makes us more alive for many genuine values. The unique poetry of spring is more fully grasped by the one who is filled with this yearning than by a completely sober person lacking in this bodily vitality. We touch here upon the fact that Hans Sachs in Wagner's *Die Meistersinger* expresses when he says, "My friend, in the wonderful time of our youth when the heart swelled with powerful drives toward the blessed experience of first love . . ." And this yearning certainly makes us more alive for many values in the other sex, it predisposes us to perceive and notice the charm and beauty in the other sex, to recognize it and be impressed by it. But this function of a vital appetitus should not be used as an argument either for the reduction of these values to the mere satisfaction of a yearning, or for an identification of value-response—in this case it is the value-response of love—with this vital appetitus. We have already seen that both can coexist in an organic relation without thereby abolishing the fundamental distinction between value-response and appetitus. In this case, the connection of the two is such that the appetitus has an emphatically auxiliary function in relation to the value-response. This vital appetitus has the purpose of making us more capable of a certain kind of love, making us more awake and receptive for certain personal values and thus more capable of the value-response of love. It is an auxiliary function analogous to that which the whole sensual sphere possesses in relation to the love between man and woman, even if the "service" is here different as a result of the fact that this sphere is a particular field of expression and fulfillment for the union desired in this love. We have discussed all of this at some length in various earlier publications, including the books *Purity* and *Man and Woman*. Here we have just wanted to refer to these earlier discussions to show how false it is to doubt the value-response character of love on the basis of the auxiliary function that an appetitus can have in its coexistence with love.

There are two other ways of seeing how impossible it is to deny that love is a value-response and to interpret it as an appetitus because of the way in which an appetitus can serve a certain kind of love. First of all, this serving function is found only in the case of a love between man and woman and by no means in all the different categories of love. Secondly, this serving function is by no means an indispensable condition for love. Above all, we have only to think of those cases in which the appetitus loses its serving function and seeks only isolated satisfaction: this shows clearly the abyss separating the isolated sexual drive and the love between man and woman. The comparison also shows us what a perversion it is to isolate this drive and to abandon its function of serving love; this is to betray its real purpose.

3. *Analysis of the "yearning" for love and of the "fulfillment" of this yearning.* It is no objection to the value-response character of love that many people yearn for love. It cannot be denied that people can feel themselves to be capable of loving before they have ever in fact loved. It may happen that they feel and understand the beauty of love so strongly that they yearn to be able to love. It can happen that such people never do love because they never meet or find the right person who could awaken love in them. It can happen that they do find such a person and really love that person. But the yearning for love is essentially different from love itself and love can never be understood as the mere satisfaction of this yearning. The yearning for love is one thing and what happens when the yearning person finds someone to love is something entirely new. In the case of an attitude that is a real appetitus and corresponds on the spiritual level to thirst on the bodily level, the satisfaction and fulfillment of the yearning, like the satisfaction of thirst by means of drinking, does not involve the emergence of a new act. What we find here is that someone is thirsty and seeks a good capable of satisfying this desire. But the experience of the one yearning for love and finally finding someone who engenders love in him is in no way primarily the experience of satisfying his yearning nor is it just an experience of happiness over the fact that his yearning no longer disturbs him in its state of being unfulfilled. He is rather entirely directed towards the beloved person and his love is in response to the beauty of the beloved; it is a commitment to that person. An entirely new yearning for union with the beloved arises, what we will call the *intentio unionis*, which is essentially different from the previous yearning for love. The happiness of love has in no way the character of mere satisfaction of the yearning for love, but it is the happiness over the fact that a person such as the beloved exists. There is also the immanent happiness of loving of which we will later speak in some detail. Precisely the entirely new reality of love, as distinct from the yearning for love, shows us all the more clearly that love is not an appetitus.

To take love as an appetitus simply because there in human nature a yearning for love is just as mistaken as taking the yearning for religious faith found in certain people (as when they say "would that I could believe, it must be a beautiful thing to be able to believe") as a proof for the fact that belief in God is the fulfillment of an appetitus, in which God has only the function of satisfying the appetitus. Or it is as if some one were to say that knowledge of truth and the subsequent conviction about truth is nothing but the satisfaction of an *appetitus*, namely, of the yearning for truth that lives in man.

Love is never the direct continuation of the yearning for love in the way in which the development of a talent is a direct continuation of the yearning for this development. If, for example, someone has a great talent for acting on the stage and feels a drive to develop this talent, the development of the talent is dominated by the same theme as the drive itself. There is one "line of meaning" leading from the drive to the development of the talent. But this is in no way the case with authentic love. We do not deny that such elements often creep in to love, but they contradict the nature and genius of love and so they have the effect of cramping love and depriving it of its true beauty. This is why we sense something oppressive about those people for whom a beloved person just presents an occasion for indulging their drive to care for people. All such living out of my needs and making the other an object for my satisfaction seems discordant to us and seems to contradict the nature and genius of love: this fact shows all the more clearly that love can never be interpreted as an *appetitus*.

This will become clearer still if we now examine more closely the yearning for love. For there are two different kinds of yearning for love (we prescind here entirely from the elementary yearning to be loved and to receive love, which is something entirely different). We have to distinguish two different forms of the yearning for love in the sense of being able to love, and especially to love in the sense of the love between man and woman.

The first comes from understanding how beautiful and deep love is and what a source of happiness for me it must be, and also from realizing that I have a great potential for love, that I am quite capable of loving, indeed am made for loving. This yearning is no *appetitus*, it has neither the character of a need like the need for companionship, nor does it have the character of an overflowing inner strength that is driven to develop itself, like the drive to develop one's talents. It is rather partly a value-response to the beauty of love, to the great objective good for the person that love is, and partly it comes from the ordination of man to happiness and from the consciousness of being destined to and ordained to loving. The relation between this yearning, which is no *appetitus*, and the real love that is engendered by the personality of another, is not exclusively the relation of desire and fulfillment, and even less is it the relation of a drive and satisfaction of the drive.

The second form of yearning for love has less the character of a genuine yearning; it is not a response to the beauty of love but is rather a state of mind in which one is always looking out for an opportunity to love, with an element of sensual desire mixed in. It is the attitude typical of adolescence. One cannot even speak of an orientation toward true love, for it is a very peripheral love which is sought here, and it is mixed up with various other elements, above all sensuality and the desire for the elevated temperature of the soul that goes with being in love. This type of urge to love can appear in an appealing form, as in the character of Cerubino in Mozart's opera, *The Marriage of Figaro*. He is in a state of mind in which he is so starved for romance that he falls in love with every girl who comes along.

This type of urge to love is really an *appetitus* in contrast to the above mentioned yearning. But if I, animated by such an urge, really come to the point of loving, my love is in no way the direct fulfillment of this urge. This urge, which involves only a response to the charm of the other sex, potentially refers to any woman or any man. When I find an object, it is not really love that results. The fulfillment of the urge is the finding of an object for its satisfaction. But if the other is a personality capable of engendering authentic love in the love-hungry person, then this love is something entirely new and is not experienced as the fulfillment of this urge but rather unmasks the urge as something childish, unworthy of love.

Genuine love disavows this adolescent hankering after love, and is no mere fulfillment of it; the state of being deeply in love is instead experienced as an awakening out of an earlier and now surpassed condition. This makes it all the clearer that this readiness to fall in love is no proof for love being an *appetitus*.

One might object as follows: do not other traits of love show that it is after all an *appetitus*, and in fact a spiritual *appetitus*? Does one not often experience in love and especially in the love between man and woman a fulfillment that makes us want to say: You are the one for whom I have hoped, for whom I have yearned, you fulfill all that has lived in my yearnings! Is this not a sign that at least the love between man and woman has the character of spiritual *appetitus*? This love is a yearning that already existed in the person, a desire that is rooted in his or her nature; and the role of the beloved person consists in simply satisfying this yearning and desire by means of his or her particular personality.

We respond that this phenomenon of "fulfillment" is indeed characteristic of the love between man and woman, especially of a particularly deep and happy love; the beloved person is experienced as the fulfillment of all that one had longed for.[8] But in no way does it follow from this experience of fulfillment that love is an *appetitus*. First of all, the experience of fulfillment is found in the domain of value-response no less than in the domain of *appetitus*, even if the fulfillment is in each case very different in accordance with the fundamental difference between the two. Secondly, it is, as we saw, entirely possible for us to turn to some good both by way of appetite and by way of value-

---

8   Thus Kierkegaard writes someplace in his diaries: "Oh, can I really believe the stories of the poets, who say that when one sees the beloved for the first time one has the impression that one has already seen her long ago, and that all love is recollection, just as knowledge is?"

response. Thus the fact that some good can satisfy an appetitus is no proof that our interest in the good is only an appetitus.

It is, moreover, not difficult to see that the fulfillment of all previous yearning in the case of spousal love has an entirely different character from the mere satisfaction of a desire. The fulfillment is a very special kind of addition, but it is not the central focus of the experience, as one can see from the fact that it is not indispensable, not even for the love between man and woman. And the one who loves is happy in a way that far surpasses the satisfaction of the yearning. The fulfillment in the case of an appetitus, as for example a thirsty person experiences it, is after all merely a satisfaction or a quenching of a desire. The fulfillment in the case of love has nothing to do with the quenching of the desire. We are not thinking here of the fulfillment that consists in the requital of our love but rather of the fulfillment that consists in finding the person who through his beauty and preciousness has all that we have ever yearned for. For love is not a satisfaction, it is not yearning that has come to an end; it is something entirely new that has its meaning and its theme independent of this fulfillment. That which in the case of an appetitus entirely determines the importance of the object, in no way determines the importance of the object in the case of love and is in fact only a superabundant addition. The fulfillment in the case of love represents a particular intensification of love, whereas in the case of appetitus it simply "silences" our interest in and our inner movement towards an object.

This all becomes more understandable when one considers that this yearning is itself a value-response and not an appetitus. It is a kind of value-response that goes hand in hand with a certain way of being ordained to something [*Zuordnung*]. Just as there is a value-responding way of receiving intimations [*Ahnung*], so there is a value-responding yearning. The yearning fulfilled in love is not a desire for something that we need and that is only important because it satisfies this desire; rather this yearning is directed to something important in itself, to a world of goods, and to that happiness possible only in and through values. That which we yearn for can stand quite indefinitely before us, but it is always given as something valuable and important in itself and not as something needed as a matter of necessity.

Being-ordained-to [*Zuordnung*] in the realm of immanent drives and in the realm of value-responses

This kind of value-response, however, presupposes that the person is ordained to certain goods. But it would be a great mistake to think that every objective being-ordained-to has to have the character of a need for something and thus can be taken as showing that any act rooted in this being-ordained-to must be an appetitus. In fact, an appetitus is not even rooted in a being-ordained-to in the proper sense of that word. We need water or oxygen for our bodily existence, but we are not ordained to them in the proper sense. Real being-ordained-to is rather found in the relation to a good and its value; indeed, being-ordained-to is for the sake of the value. We will later return to the nature of being-ordained-to. For now it suffices to point out that being-ordained-to in no way entitles us to take an attitude grounded in it as an appetitus.

If one uses the term being-ordained-to in an analogous sense, then we have to stress that there are two kinds of it: the one found in the case of appetitus, whether it has the character of a need or of an urge, and the other found in value-response. When we say that man is ordained to a world of moral values, this means, first of all, that he is capable of understanding moral values and taking moral stances; but it means above all that he is objectively destined [bestimmt] to be morally good, that this belongs to his very reason for being.

This need not manifest itself in an experienced yearning. But there can be such an experience of being-ordained-to, a kind of a priori orientation to the world of morality from one's earliest youth. It is not difficult to see that the destiny [Bestimmung] to become morally good cannot be identified with an unconscious drive towards self-perfection, nor is it difficult to see that the a priori experience of being oriented to the world of moral values has nothing to do with an appetitus. For in both cases the theme is the moral world of value and our conformity with it, and not an unconscious and objective desire or a conscious desire, on the one hand, and the satisfaction of the desire, on the other. The decisive difference between an appetitus and a value-response, which we have already mentioned, also shows itself here clearly. In the appetitus, my desire, my need, is the theme and the object is important insofar as it satisfies this desire or contributes to my life and perfection. In the value-response, the object and its importance is itself the theme; I ought to give it an adequate response for its own sake. The same holds for being ordained to values and for experiencing the a priori yearning for them; the center of gravity, the meaning, the theme remains on the side of the object, and the object remains the principium. The importance of the object in no way consists in the satisfaction of a desire, not even in its significance for me and for the development of my nature, but in the value that the object as such possesses. We are ordained for it because it is valuable, rather than that it is valuable because we are ordained for it.

This kind of being ordained reaches its highest point in the ordination of man to God, which St. Augustine expressed in the words, "You have made us for yourself, O Lord."

Person and object are ordered to each other in an essential way. This connection does not deprive the person at all of transcendence, but rather reveals it in a particular way. It would be just as false to take the central value-responses as merely "accidental" responses, as it is to interpret them as an immanent appetitus. Love for God, the value-response to all moral and morally relevant values, as well as the value-response to truth, are certainly not the same kind of value-response that we give to the charm of a country that we happen to pass through on a trip.

There are so many surprising situations in life. Even if as Christians we are convinced that the providence of God rules throughout our lives, there yet remains a clear difference between those situations in which we respond to something to which we are not particularly ordained and those other situations in which we respond to something to which we are objectively ordained and in which we therefore have a sense of fulfillment. An example of this latter situation is the encounter with a person who engenders a deep love in us and seems to us to be the fulfillment of all that we have yearned for. An example of the former is the encounter with a person whom we find interesting and whom we appreciate in various ways but without in any way thinking that we "had" to meet the person, or that something is being fulfilled in meeting him.

Thus the division of attitudes into those that are rooted in the nature of man and those that are freely chosen is misleading. One sets the freely chosen attitudes in opposition to those rooted in an objective being-ordained-to. Then one says that only those attitudes having the character of an *appetitus* involve an objective being-ordained-to.

Against this conception we have to affirm, first of all, that freedom as such is not clearly understood here. Ontological freedom is far from excluding the consciousness of being obligated to decide in a certain way; in fact it is never greater than in the case of obedience to a moral imperative. There are of course cases in which the choice, morally speaking, between two possibilities is left up to us. If at a dinner we are given the choice between two different dishes, it is left up to us to choose which one we want. This freedom, involving the absence of any moral imperative or moral call, has to be sharply distinguished from the ontological freedom that consists in not being coerced or forced by any factor. The relative arbitrariness of our choosing in such cases is entirely distinct from the ontological freedom that is proper to every act of the will. Of course, ontological freedom is present even in this arbitrariness, but it is also present, and in fact far more properly present, when we follow the call of morally relevant values, when we obey the moral law, when we use our freedom in the way ordained by God, for in these cases we exercise moral freedom as well as ontological freedom.

The accidental character that the freely chosen acts have in contrast to those rooted in an objective being-ordained-to is only found in those cases where it is morally speaking left to us how we decide. Only this case can be taken as an opposite to an objective being-ordained-to. Those free acts in which we obey the moral imperative, in which we decide as we objectively ought to decide, have nothing accidental about them and are in no way incompatible with an objective being-ordained-to. We are objectively ordered to God, we are objectively made to attain beatitude, to attain eternal communion with God, to become holy, but all this is only possible if we freely say "yes" to these things and give a value-response to God, to His commands, and to the world of morally relevant goods. In spite of being objectively ordained, God has subjected it to our free responses whether we attain that for which we are objectively destined. The full depth that this free "yes" possesses, and the opposite that it forms to all things accidental, cannot be overlooked.

Besides, it is a false alternative [either freely chosen acts or appetitus], for one thereby overlooks the meaningful responses, especially the affective value-responses, which are not indeed free like the will is free[9] but which all the same are not therefore an appetitus or an unavoidable drive of our nature like an instinct. The joy over the conversion of a sinner, for example, is indeed not free in the sense in which the will and actions are free, but it is not for that reason an appetitus; it is rather an affective value-response.

Being-ordained-to not limited to the realm of teleological striving

It is another mistake to understand being-ordained-to according to the pattern of certain instincts. We can say of hunger and thirst that their real meaning consists in providing the body with the necessary food and drink. One can say that they are means for achieving this end. Their real meaning lies outside of hunger or thirst. But when we have to do with personal acts, with meaningful value-responses like veneration, enthusiasm, love, repentance, then the situation is entirely different. Here we cannot look outside of these acts for their real meaning or treat them as a means for something lying beyond the experience. Thus the being-ordained-to takes on there an entirely different character. It means that we are ordained to goods and values in the sense that we ought to give the response appropriate to these things. It may also sometimes mean that I as this individual have a particular affinity for the good, but in this case the being-ordained-to always shows itself precisely in the value-response, in the capacity of giving this response. The meaning does not lie behind and beyond the conscious personal act but in the act itself. We are objectively called to give this value-response.

Unfortunately, one often identifies the being-ordained-to with a teleological inclination that bypasses our personal center, as is really the case with all instincts. One thinks that one enters into a greater depth by going behind the conscious sphere and interpreting certain experiences as a mere means teleologically serving some objective end. Just as one interprets hunger as a mere means that serves the end of nourishing the organism, with the result that its meaning is not found in the experience of hunger but rather behind this experience, so one thinks that with regard to all spiritual conscious experiences the deeper objective meaning is to be sought behind them and not in them. As soon as one speaks of an objective being-ordained-to, one thinks that one has to abandon the conscious sphere and concentrate on the "tendency" or "power" and teleological (or entelechial) striving that lies beneath consciousness. There

---

9   [Von Hildebrand develops this contrast between affective and volitional responses in his *Ethics*, chapter 17. Trans.]

is in reality an objective being-ordained-to which refers precisely to the capacity to give a value-response and is fulfilled in value-response; in this ordination value-response has in no way the character of a mere means for the attainment of an end. A teleological inclination is, after all, only one case of being-ordained-to and is in no way identical with being-ordained-to as such. It is not even the most typical case of being-ordained-to[10] and it is certainly not the deepest.

Conclusion

By working out the difference between value-response and appetitus in general, we have cleared the way for seeing that love is a value-response and not an appetitus. Real interest in another person, solidarity with his well-being and his suffering, joy in his very being, being enchanted by him: all of this is clearly a response to a certain person and the beauty of his personality. It would clearly be a very artificial construction to say that one can love a person without first coming to know him, and that getting to know him only has the function of satisfying the love. Love is always in the first place not a desiring but a response to a person and a response to this very particular person. This is clearly shown in the fact that the inner movement of love, its fire, is not extinguished but rather keeps growing once we have found the other person.

We have seen that the character of love as value-response is not put into question either by the phenomenon of fulfillment as found in the love between man and woman, or the phenomenon of being objectively ordained whether to love itself or to some particular person.

One could object that if love is a value-response then Plato was right in conceiving of love as exclusively a response of a lower being to a higher being. But that would be a complete mistake, because this conception of love does not come from seeing love as a value-response but rather from identifying it with a yearning for perfection. It is a conception of love as the drive to grow, and to grow in a way that presupposes the superiority of the beloved person over the one who loves. Value-response by contrast in no way presupposes this. The higher someone stands, the more capable he is of seeing values and the more ready he is to give the proper value-response. Although a human being ranks vastly higher than an animal, he can nevertheless give a full value-response to the animal and love the animal. For example, he experiences an intelligent, faithful dog as something touching, something lovable, deserving a value-response. The higher he stands morally, the more sensitive he becomes for all

10 [Though here we have translated *Zuordnung* as "ordination and "being-ordained-to," later the context will require a different translation. When *Zuordnung* is said of human persons standing in some relation of love, we will say "affinity" or the "ordering" of persons to each other. Trans.]

goods having a genuine value, and in fact he discovers value in places where a morally inferior person passes thoughtlessly by. One can see that the value-response character of love in no way presupposes that only the lower can love the higher.

We have now become acquainted with the first decisive trait of love, its value-response character. Only the value given in another person explains love with its unique way of turning to the other, as well as the solidarity with the other that comes from love. Every attempt to find any other explanation leads unavoidably to a distortion of the nature of love.

CHAPTER TWO

Love in Distinction to Other Value-Responses

Is love a response of the will or an affective value-response?

As we set out to distinguish the specific character of love from all other value-responses, we first encounter the decisive question: does love belong to the volitional value-responses such as the morally good will, or does it belong to the affective value-responses such as veneration or enthusiasm? In traditional philosophy, love is reckoned to the volitional stances of the person; indeed, it is often called an act of the will. This is said especially of the love of God and love of neighbor. One must consider, however, that the term "will" in traditional philosophy is taken extremely broadly and in fact is often used analogically. Some have called by the name of will all conscious stances that were sharply distinguished from knowledge. Thus the traditional assertion that love is an act of the will should not be understood in the sense of identifying love with the will in the strict sense as found, for instance, in Kant. When Augustine exclaims, "Give me a lover and he will understand what I am saying," he is obviously aiming with the term love not at the will in the strict sense. Since a clear distinction between volitional and affective value-responses had not yet been carried out in traditional philosophy, we cannot take the thesis that love is an act of the will as an answer to our question.

In my *Ethics* I developed the distinction between volitional and affective responses. Here it will have to suffice to remind the reader of the main points which reveal the distinction between the two. The will in the positive sense of the word is always directed to some state of affairs that is not yet real but can be realized. I cannot will things or persons but only a state of affairs. My will is always that something come to be or that something not be. If the state of affairs is already real, it can no longer become the object of my willing. On the other hand, the not yet realized state of affairs must be in principle realizable if it is to become the object of my willing, as Aristotle pointed out in the *Nicomachean Ethics*. But we have to take another step: the state of affairs must not only be realizable in principle, it must also be realizable by me or by my cooperation. As long as we are dealing with a state of affairs over which I have no influence at all, I can only wish for it, but cannot will it.

In willing something, I say, as it were, to a state of affairs that is not yet real but is realizable through me: "You should and will become real, and become real through me." The theme of willing is a state of affairs becoming real, and being realized through me. This is what distinguishes willing from wishing, which also refers to a state of affairs becoming real. But will is furthermore characterized by freedom; only the will is free in the full sense of the word. Finally, the will has the unique power of commanding actions, a power that makes it the king and master of actions. We have only to think of these essential traits of willing in order to see that love cannot be interpreted as an act of the will. The object of love is not a state of affairs nor is its theme the realization of something not yet real. Love does not say: You ought to and will exist. Nor is love free in the same sense as the will. On the other hand, love has a fullness and warmth that the will does not possess. Love is clearly an affective response. When we say that love is not free in the same sense as the will, this does not mean that love, and especially the love of neighbor, is altogether beyond the reach of freedom. Freedom has here an important task, of which we will later speak. Here it suffices to affirm decisively that love is an affective value-response.

Differences within the affective value-responses

Within the affective value-responses there are very great differences, the examination of which is necessary for understanding the nature of love. Among the affective value-responses—taking affective in the broadest sense of the term—we first find those that are predominantly appreciative in character. Respect is a typically appreciative value-response. Such a response is minimally affective. The heart is much less involved here than in other value-responses, such as enthusiasm. Esteem is an affective value-response insofar as it is not a volitional stance and certainly not a theoretical one like conviction. The conviction that someone is a noble and morally worthy person goes indeed hand in hand with respect; but clearly respect is an affective response in comparison with the conviction and all the more with the assertion that expresses this conviction. In showing respect, we do not merely take the stance with intellect, we rather turn to the other person with our whole being in a certain way, which is why we have to reckon respect to the affective value-responses. On the other hand, respect is limited to an affective acknowledgement. It is much less affective than, for example, veneration, which is not only a much stronger response than respect but also one whose word and content are different in kind. What above all interests us here is the fact that veneration goes beyond acknowledging and appreciating and is thus a much more affective response than respect. In showing respect one keeps a certain distance to the other person; there is something specifically objective about respect. It is, as it were, the affective counterpart to a value judgment.

But this objectivity should in no way be interpreted as if it meant that respect is objectively more justified. True objectivity consists in the adequacy of a response. It depends on whether a response in its quality and degree corresponds to the value of the good on the object side and not on how far the heart is involved in the response, or how affective the response is. The so-called objectivity of respect does not make respect more objective than admiration or veneration even though it is less affective, cooler, more distanced, and limited to an appreciation.

In distinction to respect, we find both in veneration and in admiration something entirely new, a much more personal involvement, a much more affective note. The subject is here engaged in a stronger way, investing much more of himself in the veneration or admiration than in respect. This is reflected in the fact that while one can speak of greater or lesser respect, deeper or less deep respect, one cannot speak of an ardent respect, whereas one can perfectly well speak of ardent veneration and over-flowing admiration. For our purposes it suffices to show within the affective value-responses—affective taken in the broadest sense of the word—the distinction between merely appreciative value-responses such as respect, on the one hand, and the real affective responses—affective in the strict sense—such as veneration and admiration, on the other hand. We can contrast these latter responses, which are affective in a new and more proper sense, with the appreciative responses.

Great as the differences may be within this group of affective responses in respect to the involvement of the heart, and also in other respects, it suffices for our purposes to contrast all of them as a whole with the appreciative responses.

Essential traits of love

1. *Love as the most affective value-response.* Love presents itself as something entirely new in relation to all these affective value-responses, for it is incomparably more affective than all of these, and not just in the sense of a difference of degree but rather of an entirely new involvement of the heart. It is as far removed as could be from respect in the sense of being the most subjective value-response (in an entirely positive sense of the term subjective, which forms no contrast at all to true objectivity): it is a response in which the subject is involved in quite a new way. Later on in chapter 3 we will discuss at length this decisive trait of love.

2. *Love as essentially superactual in the proper sense.* We have discussed in various other books the distinction between actual and superactual experiences and stances.[1] There are experiences like pain in my finger that really exist only as long as they are felt. When the pain stops, it no longer exists, and if tomorrow exactly the same pain begins again, it is as experience not identi-

---

1   See my work *Sittlichkeit und ethische Werterkenntnis* (Morality and Ethical Value Knowledge), my *Ethics*, chapter 17, and my book *What is Philosophy?*, 28ff.

cal with the one of yesterday; it is a new individual entity even if the physiological causes, the quality, and the place where the pain is felt are exactly the same. But the veneration which I have for someone does not cease to exist when I am taken up with other things; when I encounter this person it is identically the same veneration that is actualized again. It endures as a personal reality even if I am not actualizing it at the moment. It lives on superactually. It is not just that the effects of veneration continue to be felt in the soul; the act of veneration itself endures. It is actualized from time to time.

Now we have to go further and distinguish two forms of the superactual. There are stances that are inherently superactual in the sense that the position that they take toward their object is valid beyond the present moment and that the motivating object continues in being. Thus the respect that I have for someone who plays no particular role in my life is superactual in the sense that it is not just a momentary stance like the irritation over someone's remark or like the fear felt in a dangerous situation that passes as soon as the situation passes, however many effects of the fear remain. As soon as I approach someone with respect, I take a position toward him which by its nature lasts, which does not lose its validity and meaning simply because it is no longer being consciously performed by me. This is *one* meaning of superactual, or one kind of superactuality. It is the continued validity of the "word" spoken in the attitude of respect; once this attitude has been taken toward another it continues as long as it is not explicitly renounced, even if one no longer thinks of the person whom one respects and even if that person plays no role in our lives.

In general, superactuality presupposes an object that as such continues to exist unchanged, such as persons, works of art, or countries, or events whose meaning does not fade, as for example the death of a beloved person. This superactuality of the object is here presupposed.

The continued validity of the stance is analogous to the continued binding force arising from the act of promising, which lasts until the promise is fulfilled. Of course this is only an analogy, for the two experiences are radically different; promising is a social act, whereas respect is a stance or attitude. What is important is to distinguish this superactuality not only from all the effects of the stance, but also from the pure potency for taking the stance. Many experiences that are in no sense of the word superactual leave behind lasting effects. A great fright or shock can have far reaching psychological effects, although a fright exists only in being experienced. We clearly have something entirely different in the case of respect. It is not the effect of it that lasts—the respect may in some cases have no effect at all on my psychological life—but the word spoken in respect retains its validity even when I no longer think of it. Respect is in its nature and meaning never limited to the present experience. Respect needs to have no particular effects in order to last in its validity. Fright, by contrast, can very easily have effects, even though it has no superactual validity.

The superactuality which lies in lasting validity is also not a mere potency like the capacity for walking, which I have even while I am sitting. This capacity is indeed something habitual and superactual, but it is not walking itself, but rather only the capacity for walking that is superactual. In the case of respect it is not just a capacity for showing respect that lasts. Of course, I can actualize the respect again and again when I think of the other or encounter him, but the continued validity is obviously something quite different from the mere capacity to actualize a respect again and again. On the other hand, this capacity for walking plays a much greater role in my consciousness. I carry this capacity around with me all the time. It is a part of the consciousness of my bodily existence.

For our purposes it is above all important to distinguish this superactuality based on validity from a far more authentic kind of superactuality, where not only the validity endures but where the act itself continues with full reality at a deeper level of ourselves. In this sense, a great love for another is superactual, as is a living faith in God and Christ. The new thing here is that not only does the word spoken by love endure in its validity, and that not only does a stance taken toward the other endure, but that this attitude itself endures in my soul, coloring and modifying all the real situations in which I live. The attitude of love remains fully alive in the soul as this identical psychological and spiritual reality, modifying the whole structure of our experiencing. When it ceases to exist, as in the case of falling away from the faith, when the faith in God and Christ dies away in us, or in the case where a great love ceases, dies, passes away, all of our conscious experiencing becomes different. The difference between this full-bodied superactuality and the superactuality based on mere continued validity stands out now in all clarity. Not only does our position remain intact, not only is the word spoken valid above and beyond the conscious performance of love, but the attitude of love itself fully lives on and is not interrupted by the fact that it does not fill our actual consciousness in every moment and is not always consciously performed by us. In addition, love has by its full superactual existence the character of an "antiphon" for all that we consciously live through as well as the character of a background against which everything in our conscious lives unfolds.

It belongs to the depth proper to these value-responses that they not only have a validity extending beyond their actual performance, but also occupy a deep level of the soul and there endure in their full reality and identity, casting a light on all of our conscious experiencing. Finally, this proper actuality is characterized by the tendency of the superactual stance to actualize itself again and again. If we love someone with spousal love, we are strongly inclined to return again and again to the full actualization of this love. If we are forced to concentrate on other things—to tend to our work, to speak with other persons—afterwards we are strongly inclined to turn with full actual consciousness to the beloved person, to think of him, to speak silently with him, or simply let the stream of our love reach him. It would obviously be nonsensical to interpret this superactuality as a mere potency.

But we have also to warn against the misunderstanding of confusing the superactual with the sphere of the unconscious that plays so great a role in psychoanalysis. We are fully conscious of our superactual stances in the sense that we know about them and are acquainted with them. Even if at a given moment they do not thematically fill our actual consciousness, still they eminently belong to the luminously conscious experiences and stand in sharp contrast to the subconscious or even repressed experiences that exercise their negative influence in a kind of twilight. The relation of the superactual experiences to the actual is not that of something hidden to a symbol, but rather that of an entirely conscious background. Whereas the unconscious or the repressed disturbs the meaningful flow of actual experiences, often introducing an irrational element into them, the superactual in no way disturbs the meaningful flow of actual experiences; in no way is it hidden behind them, interfering with the integrity of these experiences, but it remains in the case of love an animating background that is a source of happiness. Of course, love can still take such hold of our attention that it makes us distracted in performing some present task. It may happen that we can hardly pay attention to someone with whom we are speaking because we think of the beloved person, or that we can make a mistake in adding or subtracting as a result of being strongly present to the beloved person. But in these cases, love is, as it were, actualized at the wrong time and is precisely not limited to its superactual existence. This disturbance of the actual flow of consciousness is by no means an essential characteristic of the superactuality of stances or value-responses; it has rather to do with the intensity of certain value-responses and their strong inclination to be actualized even when something else is thematic.

We see now clearly that the superactual existence of stances and attitudes has nothing to do with the sphere of the unconscious. The level in our soul where the superactual experiences are situated is entirely different from the sphere of the unconscious; one could rather speak of the sphere of the "superconscious."

Let us return to the point of importance for this study, namely, the essential difference between the two kinds of superactuality, that is, between the superactuality based on enduring validity and the superactuality based on the real superactual existence of some stance of the person. This distinction is not so much a distinction between different stances or responses, but it concerns instead the different ways in which a stance, sometimes one and the same stance, can play a role in our lives and in our soul. Thus veneration can possess now the one, now the other form of superactuality, or more correctly expressed, it can possess only the first superactuality, or it can possess the second as well, for the second and more proper superactuality includes the first. If we encounter a person who impresses us with his moral stature so that we respond to him with veneration but never see him again and seldom ever think of him, this veneration has only the first kind of superactuality. But if it is the veneration of a disciple for his master, as found, for instance, in the disciple of a saint, then the veneration has the second form of superactuality.

But there are stances which, if they are really serious and deep, necessarily possess the second kind of superactuality. That is, for example, the case with every real spousal love or eminently the case with faith in God and love for Christ. It is important for us to understand that love, in contrast to other value-responses, always possesses a superactuality of the second kind. In love, provided that it is a real full love, there is always a deep involvement which brings with it a superactual existence in the soul. For we must not forget that the role played by a stance in our conscious lives admits of many degrees and that a stance does not have to dominate our conscious lives completely in order to have superactuality in the second and more proper sense.

The question of how central an experience is, of how great its lasting role is in our life, is surely related with superactuality in the proper sense, but it is not identical with it. Of course, a certain lasting role in our life is always presupposed for this superactuality, but there can still be very various degrees of the role played by stances that are all superactual. This will now become clearer still as we proceed to distinguish two kinds of role that are here in question.

On the one hand, the role played by a stance can mean how much it influences our life, what place it has in our soul or heart, and how much it fills the consciousness of a person. This kind of role is closely related to how strong the desire is to actualize the superactual stance, to perform it again and again in full actuality. This is obviously the case with a great love and quite clearly with a spousal love. On the other hand, one can refer with the talk of "playing a role in our lives" to the structural importance of a stance in the soul of a person. There are certain stances which are important for the foundation of our conscious life. They are more of a basis that is taken for granted; they do not constantly incline us, like love does, to actualize them. They are not so much themselves a full theme but have rather the specific character of an unproblematical basis. Take, for instance, the unconditional trust that a child has in its mother. Its life rests and unfolds on this basis. This trust typically lives in a superactual way in a child; it is naturally also actualized from time to time, according to the situation. But there is no tendency, no desire to make this trust a full theme, to actualize it explicitly again and again. It rather has its proper place as a foundation or basis. It has a great influence on the whole of our conscious life, but its specific function is more that of a basis. The superactual form of existence is the typical, the characteristic form of existence for this stance. With love, by contrast, the intention fully and thematically to actualize love is called for. It endures superactually by its very nature, but not in the sense of functioning as a mere basis.

And so we see that there are two ways in which something can play an important role in our lives. We could call the one the material role, and the other the formal role. A great and deep love plays a decisive role both in a formal and in a material respect, but there are stances which play only a formal role. The extent of the role, whether the formal or the material role, can, as we have said, vary within the superactual stances; it of course depends for the most part on the weight of a stance and its quality of depth. But superactuality in the full sense of a stance or a value-response really enduring superactually, always includes both a formal and a material role of the stance. Love is, as we have said, always superactual in this full sense; the deeper and fuller a love, the greater its material and formal role in the whole inner life of a person.

3. *Being delighted [Entzücktsein] by the beloved person.* One has often been misled into missing the value-response character of love by the specifically delightful character that the values of the beloved person have for the one who loves. This is why some have erroneously interpreted love in terms of a delight, a delight based on the merely subjectively satisfying. In reality, the importance of delightfulness in love only goes to show that love involves a very deep givenness of value; in loving one goes deep enough for the beauty of the value of the beloved person and the delightfulness of this value to unfold fully before our minds and to reveal itself to us.

The mere fact that love presupposes a value experienced as delightful has kept philosophers from distinguishing adequately between the love between man and woman, and a mere desire [Begehren]. After all, taking delight in someone is common to both cases. The beauty and loveliness of a woman may awaken mere desire in a Don Juan and it may awaken love in another person. This is what betrays us into assuming that the delight that the lover takes in the beloved is based on mere pleasure and is distinguished only in degree from the desire of a Don Juan, which is, after all, also built on pleasure and in many cases pleasure in the same qualities, for instance, beauty, loveliness, charm, and flourishing life.

But this is a great mistake; precisely a comparison of these two cases in which the same person in virtue of the same qualities attracts others, shows us clearly the difference between love as a value-response and mere desire that is not a value-response. The Don Juan type does not understand feminine charm or the beauty of feminine loveliness as values. He sees these only as things attracting him and pleasing him, that is, as subjectively satisfying for him. This is why his response is simply the will to possess and to enjoy without any element of self-giving [Hingabe] on his part, without any looking up to the other as something intrinsically precious, without any understanding of beauty, loveliness, and feminine charm as values. Besides, this type of person isolates these qualities, he cannot see in them any expression of the whole personality of the woman; he does not see the woman as noble, good, but rather only as attractive on the basis of her physical beauty, without taking any account of her as a whole person. This is why his response has the character of mere desire, why he wants to enjoy these attractive qualities, and why he wants to appropriate them for himself.

But these qualities are understood as values by the one who loves. They raise the other up, making her intrinsically precious; the woman stands as lovable before the man and he looks up to this preciousness. These qualities never remain isolated for him, they are—whether he is deceived or not does not matter here—the expression of a general preciousness, of a nobility of the whole individuality. He sees in this beauty, in this loveliness, in this feminine charm the radiance of an inner dignity, of a sublime noblesse. His response is one of real self-donation, of commitment for the beloved, of a real solidarity with her and the yearning for a lasting union, that is the union of a loving I-Thou encounter.

Of course, even the Don Juan type can desire the love of the other, and this is in fact characteristic for a Don Juan in contrast to other kinds of pure desire. But it is in no way the union that is constituted in mutual love that he desires, but rather the inability to resist him that makes the other a conquest. He does not really love and this is why he does not desire any real union. But the possession that he desires is not simply a physical possession of the woman; raping her would not suffice for him. He wants to enjoy the conquest, the success, his own irresistibility, and so he is driven by pride no less than by concupiscence. We can now clearly see how love as a value-response is sharply distinguished from all kinds of mere desire, even if it is the same qualities in a woman that motivate interest in her, that is, if it is objectively the same qualities that are understood in very different ways.

We find something analogous in the distinction between the aesthete, who enjoys works of art like a good wine, and the value-responding, reverent enjoying of the artistically sensitive person. The aesthete grasps indeed the beauty but without understanding it as value, he rather enjoys it as merely subjectively satisfying. He feels no reverence, he remains the center; his enjoyment is the important thing and the work of art is a means for his enjoyment. The truly artistic person, by contrast, grasps fully the value character of the artistic beauty, its inner dignity, its call to approach in reverence and to receive gratefully the delight superabundantly flowing from the artistic value.

And so we see that the value givenness presupposed for love not only has a distinctive content, namely the overall beauty of the individual, but also a distinctive mode of givenness; it has to be given as delightful. Related to this is the fact that the value of the overall beauty of the other must be intuitively [*anschaulich*] given; the image of the other person as a whole must not just be grasped as valuable but must be intuitively given. We contrast intuitive givenness with all those forms of knowledge in which we experience something indirectly, as by an inference or by being informed.[2] This intuitive givenness forms no contrast at all to rational knowledge; on the contrary, it is the high-

---

2   We have discussed in detail the nature of intuition in *What is Philosophy?*, 214ff.

est form of rational knowledge. It is distinguished from other forms of knowledge only by the immediate contact with the object, by being immediately given to the mind. All self-evident states of affairs are intuitively given whenever I immediately understand them. In our context it is a further mark of intuitive givenness that must be pointed out, namely, that which distinguishes an immediate seeing from a mere "knowing that something is the case." There is obviously a great difference between the case in which the beauty of a landscape stands before us—we not only directly perceive the landscape but also its beauty—and the case in which we learn from another person that the landscape is very beautiful. Here the intuitive givenness implies that the object unfolds in its qualitative character before my mind, in contrast to the mere understanding of a concept. Such understanding allows indeed for a tremendously precise rational contact with the object, but without this qualitative unfolding of the object.

Now love not only requires that the beauty of an individual as a whole be intuitively given to us, but in addition to this that this beauty affectively touch us, that its delightfulness touch our heart, that we not only clearly recognize it but that we are also delighted by it and affectively moved by it. In chapter 4 we will explore in detail these characteristics of the givenness of value that love presupposes. Here we simply wanted to mention it in connection with the distinction between love and the other affective value-responses.

Now love is distinguished from all other friendly affective value-responses, such as veneration, above all by two fundamental essential traits: the *intentio unionis* (striving for union with the beloved person) and the *intentio benevolentiae* (striving to benefit the beloved person). We now turn to the intentio unionis.

4. *Intentio unionis.* Whoever loves also desires a spiritual union with the beloved person. He desires not only the presence of the other, not only knowledge of his life, his joys, his sufferings, but above all else a union of hearts that only mutual love can grant.

Even if this yearning for the union of hearts is given in a unique way in spousal love, both in regard to the desired unity as well as in regard to the yearning for this unity, this intentio unionis is nevertheless found in some form in every love. For love always desires a requital or a return of love. Even in the case of love of neighbor, I wish that the other might be filled with love of neighbor for me, that I might be united with him in the great community of love in Christ. In every love I move toward the other in a spiritual way, in every love there is this gesture of hastening to the other.

Love not only has this intentio unionis; the unity desired is also accomplished at least by the one who loves. Of course, the full *unio* comes into being only if the love is returned and if the beloved person hastens to me just as I to him. All the same, my love is an essential factor in the constitution of the unity. Love has not only the intentio unionis but also a *virtus unitiva* (unitive power).

Love yearns for the *unio* that only the requital of love can give, but it also, as far as it lies in the power of love, constitutes something of this *unio*. This double aspect of love is of great importance.[3] The role of love for bringing about the *unio* not only consists in hastening to the beloved person but also in the fact that only in love does one disclose oneself and turn with one's spiritual face to the other. In love we "lift the mask" which otherwise covers and protects our intimate inner life. In love and only in love does one turn to another in such a way that one gives oneself and in fact gives one's most intimate being. This element is eminently characteristic of spousal love, but it is found analogously in every love, even if in very different ways according to the particular kind of love.

We will revisit this subject in much more detail in chapter 6. For now it suffices to affirm that the intentio unionis and the *virtus unitiva* of love clearly distinguish it from all other affective responses. Neither admiration nor enthusiasm nor even veneration include an intentio unionis nor do they possess the *virtus unitiva*.

5. *Intentio benevolentiae.* Intentio benevolentiae consists in the desire to make the other happy; it is above all else a real interest in the happiness, the well-being, and the salvation of the other. We find here in the nature of love a unique sharing in the other person, in the other's happiness and destiny. Of course, this mark of love also is found in a particular way in spousal love and it expresses itself there in the wish to confer benefits unceasingly on the beloved person. But in some form or other the intentio benevolentiae is an essential trait of every love.

The fact that we desire happiness for ourselves is not the result of self-love; it is rather an obvious trait of any human being, an unavoidable desire. But that we are concerned with the happiness of another is by no means obvious; it is rather a consequence of love. This solidarity is a fruit of love, which is not an effect existing apart from love but is rather something that arises in love and inheres in it. Indeed this deep interest for the happiness of the other cannot be separated from love.

But the intentio benevolentiae is far more than the desire to make the beloved person happy; it is far more than a deep interest in his well-being and happiness. It is a certain goodness felt toward the other, the breath of goodness [*Güte*]. Thus we find here something analogous to what we found with the intentio unionis. We saw that the intentio unionis is not only a yearning for union with the other, but is at the same time already a first step towards establishing this union, since one spiritually hastens to the other in love. In a similar way, the intentio benevolentiae is not only a desire to make the other happy, not only an interest in his well-being, but it is itself a breath of goodness that

---

3   Cf. my books *Die Metaphysik der Gemeinschaft* (The Metaphysics of Community) and *Purity*.

confers happiness, giving the other a unique and indeed irreplaceable gift. The intentio benevolentiae is also something found only in love and serves clearly to distinguish love from esteem, admiration, or veneration.

We must, however, acknowledge the fact that there is often an element of love in other positive affective responses to persons, even though these are to be distinguished from love in various ways. There is an element of love in every positive friendly attention given to another person that takes him seriously as person. Love is the epitome of all kinds of friendly attitudes to another; thus one can detect an element of love in every friendly attitude. There is an element of love in every value-responding joy over another person, every act of being enthused about him, in every deep admiration for him. There is even a certain element of love in all respect. But we have to distinguish clearly between love in the proper sense, as found in all kinds of love, and the element of love found in all positive affective value-responses to persons. In our analysis of the specific character of love, we should not lose sight of the essential difference between love and these other value-responses simply because of the element of love that they contain, or simply because of the way in which they are often connected with real love.

We should also not confuse wishing others well, which characterizes all positive affective value-responses to persons, with the intentio benevolentiae that is essential to love. This wishing others well is distinguished from the intentio benevolentiae by the fact that it involves no deep solidarity with them, no deep interest in and concern for their well-being, and no act of making their well-being our own concern. Nor is it a gift full of goodness, a stream of goodness surrounding the other, a spiritual embrace of the other with goodness.

We see then that love is distinguished from all other positive value-responses to persons by these two essential traits: the intentio unionis and the intentio benevolentiae.

6. *Self-donation* [*Selbstschenkung*]. There are various other traits of love closely related to the intentio unionis and the intentio benevolentiae. In every love there is a gesture of self-donation, which in the case of spousal love is so prominent that we can speak of a literal giving of one's self. In the case of love for God, the giving of one's self is lived out in quite another and much more real sense. But in every love there is at least some element of self-donation.

In order to understand better this element of self-donation, we want to begin again by considering spousal love. The word uttered by this love is, "I am yours." The giving of myself is deeply tied to the intentio unionis and above all to the hastening to the beloved that initiates the desired union. I want to belong to the beloved, I give myself to him or her spiritually in love, I give him or her my very heart. Naturally, this giving of myself should no more be thought of in terms of ontologically abandoning myself than the intentio unionis should be thought of in terms of a yearning for fusion with the other. The duality of two persons is preserved objectively in both cases, as is obvious and hardly needs to be said. Every person is essentially an individual and any conception of a fusion of one person with another person is intrinsically impossible and contradictory. The duality remains also on the subjective, that is, experiential, level, and in fact it is essential for the experience of giving oneself to another, just as it is for the experience of union. The lover who gives himself in love to the beloved in no way has the consciousness of giving up his very self. On the contrary, in this act of self-donation, he becomes himself more truly; he lives more fully and more authentically—his subjectivity is more awakened and he lives in a more existential way. The I-Thou consciousness is vividly preserved, indeed it reaches a certain unique thematicity, in this self-donation. In the word, "I am yours," there is no abandonment of one's self, because the whole gift that lies in "yours" presupposes that it is a full living person which belongs to the beloved. We will later return to this unique character of the self-donation contained in love and discuss it in more detail. Here it suffices to refer to this essential trait that presents itself so clearly in spousal love and that is in some way present in every love.[4]

Whether we think of the love for one's parents, the love for one's children, or the love for one's friend, we always find this element of giving one's heart. In all of these loves, I say to the other, "I am yours." Of course, we in no way want to obscure the deep difference that exists in respect of self-donation between spousal love and the other kinds of love. But different as this self-donation is in spousal love, being more properly and fully realized in it, something analogous to it is still found in all the other kinds of love. What concerns us here is that some element of self-donation is found in every love and serves to distinguish it from the other positive value-responses to persons. Neither in

---

4 One could object that this moment of self-donation cannot be found in love of neighbor. It is true that one cannot say, "I am yours," in the love of neighbor. One reason is that this love does not necessarily give rise to a superactual relation. And yet there is in true love of neighbor an element of self-donation, which we can see in the ardent interest for the well-being of the other, in the stream of goodness directed to the other, in the full thematicity of the neighbor. Even in this love, the neighbor becomes a real concern of mine; my heart belongs to him at least at the moment in which I turn to him, in which I am ready to make all kinds of sacrifices for him, in which my heart is filled with concern for his welfare and his salvation. It is true that the gesture of giving my heart is here furthest removed from the real giving of my heart that we find in spousal love. But this is balanced by the fact that another aspect of self-donation is especially strong in the love of neighbor. It is the flowing goodness, the readiness to sacrifice, the unique taking seriously of the other, the committing of oneself to the other—all elements that are closely connected with the intentio benevolentiae. This form of self-donation is foreign to esteem, admiration, and veneration, which lack this stream of goodness, this readiness to sacrifice, this commitment. This is why self-donation represents a distinct trait of love.

admiration nor in respect nor in veneration is this element of self-donation and of giving one's heart to be found. None of these responses contain the word, "I am yours."

7. *Extraordinary commitment to the beloved person; love and freedom.* Love is distinguished from all other positive affective value-responses by its commitment to the other. An incomparable commitment [*Einsatz*] of one's own person to the other is a mark of every love. It shows itself unmistakably and unsurpassably in spousal love with its element of decision and of binding oneself. But we have to repeat again that even if a particular kind of commitment is an essential trait of spousal love in contrast to the other kinds of love, in some way this commitment, this engagement, is to be found in every love, varying according to the character of the kind of the love. In the love of parents for their children there is a particular responsibility that gives the commitment a certain quality. In the love of children for their parents, the commitment is not so consciously lived, but it is implicit in the devotion, in the unproblematic shelteredness of this love, and in being anchored and rooted in it. In the love for a friend this moment of commitment has the different character of getting involved on behalf of the other, of standing by him, so that he can count on us. But in all the forms of love we find this commitment or engagement, this binding oneself to the beloved person.

In order to understand fully the element of self-donation in love, we have to take up again the relation between love and freedom. We have already stressed that love is an affective value-response and not a value-responding act of will. While this holds for every kind of love, it stands out most clearly in the case of spousal love.

If we compare the will in the proper sense of the word with the love of parents for their children, the love of children for their parents, or with the love between friends, or with spousal love, it cannot escape us that love is the voice of the heart, an affective response, indeed the most affective of all value-responses. Apart from any other differences, one cannot deny that love is not free in the same sense as the will is free. We cannot give ourselves love even if we want to. It is not in our power freely to posit such a response of the heart like we can posit a response of the will, nor is it in our power to command love like an action. Between the mere will to love someone and real love for that person there is an abyss. Whoever loves realizes that this love is not really returned as long as the other person only has the will to love him but without any involvement of the heart. If the other does not yearn for our presence and is not delighted by it and made happy by it, if his heart does not speak, then he does not love us, even if he makes the greatest effort of will to love.

The commitment of the heart that is proper to love is not a result of the will but a gift. It stands forth very clearly in spousal love. As long as this commitment of the heart is not a "necessity," that is, something stronger than we are, there is no real love. This is expressed wonderfully in Wagner's opera, *Die Meistersinger,* when Evchen says to Hans Sachs, comparing her stance towards him with her love for Walther: "If I had the choice, I would only choose you . . . but it was a necessity, it was a force compelling me." Even if this necessity is very strong in the case of spousal love, still every love has somehow this character of going beyond what is in my power, beyond what I can freely produce or command. St. Augustine pointed out in a wonderful way this phenomenon of "necessity" when he says of being drawn to Christ, "*Parum voluntate, etiam voluptate trahimur*."[5]

But true as it is that love is a pure gift, which we could never give ourselves, it would be false to think that the freedom of the person has no role to play. In chapter 25 of our *Ethics*, where we discuss "cooperative freedom," we explain at length that an affective value-response has the character of a valid stance of the person only if it is "sanctioned" by my free personal center. That of course holds eminently for love. On the one hand, the full giving of my heart in love requires that the love arise spontaneously with a kind of inner necessity, but on the other hand, this self-giving remains incomplete as long as the love is not sanctioned. There are, therefore, these two dimensions of self-giving: the voice of the heart and the "yes" spoken by the free personal center in the sanctioning of the love. And this sanction presupposes the pure gift of love. As long as the heart has not spoken, the free personal center has nothing to sanction. If the gift of love is not already present, then the free personal center could only activate the will to love, and this would be something entirely different from the sanction. The pure will to love by no means contains the dimension of self-giving that the sanctioned love possesses, nor does it contain a gesture of self-donation. It is a sad substitute for love. This is why we cannot separate the work of sanctioning from the affective response of love spontaneously arising in the person. Of course, the affective response of the heart can be detached from the sanction; that is, there are non-sanctioned ways of loving. It sometimes happens that someone struggles against a love, for instance, because he thinks that it is morally improper, whether because a vow or the faithfulness owed to another person obliges him to suppress this love, to fight against it and to disavow it. There may really be a moral duty to disavow a love, although one may wrongly think that one has to disavow a love. In this disavowed love there is indeed a dimension of self-donation in the voice of the heart, but the other dimension is clearly missing. Indeed, the disavowal acts against the self-donation that lies in the voice of the heart.[6]

---

5   "It is too little to be drawn by the will, we are also drawn by delight."

6   But there is a further distinction to be made. If it is a love that I feel to be morally wrong, if for instance I am just superficially attracted to someone and so tempted to be unfaithful to a real and deep love, then this love should be explicitly disavowed, that is, declared from within to be invalid. But if it is a deep love, perhaps even a much more authentic and deep love than any other in my life, but that is not allowed because of certain circumstances, it does not have to be disavowed in the same strong sense; it rather has to be opposed, suppressed, or transformed.

But it can also happen that a love is already present and that, although it has not yet been disavowed, it has also not yet been sanctioned. A girl, for instance, loves a man with spousal love, but she is not yet sure whether she is not called to enter a convent. As long as she is still testing this before God, she has not yet performed this giving of herself with her free personal center. Clearly in this case something essential is missing from the love. Here we do not have, as in the previous case, the heart and the free personal center saying opposite things, but the word of the free personal center has not been spoken. Here too, an essential dimension of self-donation is still missing, the dimension of the belonging to the other, but vastly more is here given to the other than when one only wills to love the other.[7]

And so we see that there are these two dimensions of self-donation. The first is purely affective in nature, having the character of a gift that we can never ourselves give; it is a pure voice of the heart. The second is the voice of our free personal center; it is the sanctioning of the gift of an affective response of love. Only when both are present does the self-donation of love take on its full character, as I have discussed in my book, *The Heart.*

8. *Love as the value-response that brings happiness like no other value-response.* A particular trait of love distinguishing it from all other affective value-responses is the unique happiness that love confers, or as we could as well say, that is deeply bound up with the act of loving.

The great theme of love and happiness will be discussed later in chapter 10. Here we simply want to point out briefly the unique source of happiness which distinguishes love from all other value-responses. Respect is not as such a source of happiness, admiration is somewhat more of such a source, and enthusiasm still more. But the happiness of loving is clearly incomparably greater. This follows already from the superactual character of love. Enthusiasm is not superactual in the same sense as love; it confers happiness only in actually being consciously lived through. But love even in its superactual form sheds a ray of happiness illuminating our life, even while we are occupied with entirely different things.

Of course, it makes one happy to be able to experience veneration; the very existence of someone who merits veneration makes us happy. And yet love confers vastly more happiness than veneration. This trait of love naturally varies greatly according to the kind of love. Spousal love is tied to a unique happiness, which cannot be compared with the happiness of the love between friends. But one clearly cannot fail to notice the happiness proper to the love of parents for their children or of children for their parents. Perhaps the meas-

---

7   This dimension of the definitive giving of myself and the sanctioning of the love is encountered in a wonderful way in the marital consent, which as such is considered to be the crowning of spousal love. Here we see clearly the great and decisive task that is entrusted to the free personal center, a task that extends far beyond the sanctioning of the love, reaching the point of creating a marriage.

ure of happiness in love is not so much the kind of love as rather the question of how great the love is, how unconditioned, how deep it is, what place it has in our life. It is clear that the happiness that goes with a deep ardent love of God surpasses every other happiness, as we can clearly see from the lives of the saints.

9. *Desire for a return of one's love.* A further trait of love is that it desires a return, or requital, of love. Thus we have here another source of happiness that is not in the same way to be found with the other value-responses given to persons. Neither admiration nor enthusiasm nor veneration has an intentio unionis that includes the yearning for a requital of our stance to the other. The one-sidedness of these responses is no cause for unhappiness. There is no such thing as an unhappy, unrequited admiration, enthusiasm, veneration as there is an unhappy, unrequited love. In chapter 10, which treats of love and happiness, we will return to this difference between love and all other value-responses addressed to persons.

Now all these essential traits of love and especially the quite new element of commitment, the *virtus unitiva* of love, and the self-donation of love show us that, although it is a value-response *par excellence*, nevertheless there is something "given" by the one who loves that surpasses all the other value-responses. The subject is more active here than in any other value-response. In our next chapter we will speak of this "gift" [*Gabe*] of love, for without understanding this we cannot hope to enter more deeply into the nature of love.

CHAPTER THREE

The "Gift"[1] of Love

In saying that love is essentially a value-response, we do not mean that the content of love, the word addressed by love to the beloved person, the gift inhering in love itself, arises exclusively from a participation in the value of the beloved person. That would amount to a misunderstanding both of value-response in general and of love in particular. First of all, no value-response can be thought of as a mere participation in the value of the object. Secondly, love distinguishes itself from all other value-responses, such as respect, enthusiasm, veneration, and admiration, precisely by the fact that the contribution made from the side of the subject, that is, from the side of the one who loves, is much greater than and different in kind from what is found in all other value-responses.

The contribution of the subject in every value-response goes beyond "participation" in the object

In every value-response it is the stance of a person to some good and its value that is of decisive importance. Our task here is to bring out what is new in the response of a person to a good and to its value, that is, what goes beyond a mere participation in the value of the object.

Whether St. Thomas stresses the participation of the knower in the thing known by interpreting knowing in the Aristotelian sense of an intentional becoming of the object, or whether St. Augustine sees in the love for something a communion with the thing that surpasses all knowing, what is at issue is the participation in an object and its value.[2] But a stance [*Stellungnahme*]

---

1   [*Gabe* in German. It means gift or offering, but von Hildebrand puts quotation marks around *Gabe* to alert the reader to a rather special sense that the term is supposed to bear in this chapter. He uses this term to express the fact that in loving another, I in a sense exceed or surpass all that it due to the other in virtue of his or her value, and that in this sense I give the other an unmerited gift. We had at first tried to translate *Gabe* as "excess," and then as "surplus," and though these translations had to be abandoned, they capture something of what von Hildebrand's "*Gabe*" means to express. Trans.]

2   St. Thomas, too, stresses this when he says: "Thus love has a greater unifying power than knowledge." *Summa Theologica*, I-II, q. 28, a. 1, ad 3.

has a meaning that differs from the participation in the value of the object. A person taking a conscious stance, especially a sanctioned value-response, creates something quite new over and above the mere participation in the value of the object. It is something all its own, which gives evidence of the new dimension of being that lies in personal existence. Something new arises over and above the value of the good on the object side. The word spoken by the subject, *his* word, is certainly motivated and given direction by the value of the object and it refers to the valuable being, but there is something new in the fact that a subject takes a stance to the valuable being; it is a qualitatively new contribution of the *subject*. This in no way contradicts the fact that the value of the object is the *principium* and the response of the subject the *principiatum*. It does not bring value-response any closer to an appetitus, for we are not saying that the value-response is a desire rooted in the subject independently of the object and is satisfied by the object and its value. On the contrary, it is the object and its value which represent the real theme, and we must start from them if we are to understand value-response; but the stance of the person adds something new. This is why the moral value of a value-response is not just a reflection of the value of the object, but rather (at least in those cases where the morally relevant value is not itself a moral value) is something qualitatively entirely new, that is, a moral value, which is an even *higher* type of value.

We will see this new element in a value-response more clearly by making the following comparison. Let us compare the relation that the value of a value-response has to the object responded to, with the relation between indirect and direct value.[3] A medicine is important thanks to its contribution to the health of a human being. Health is something of value and the medicine shares in this value by being a means to preserving or restoring health. As a means the medicine "borrows" something from the value of the end. By contrast, the moral value of some heroic life-saving action is emphatically not an indirect value. It is not a value that merely shares in the value of the life saved. The moral value of the life-saving action is qualitatively something entirely new over against the value of the life of the one who is saved. It is a grave error to confuse this moral value with the value that the life-saving action has as a

---

3 [Hildebrand introduces and explains in chapter 3 of his *Ethics* the terms "direct" and "indirect" as used here. He says that the direct importance of a being is the importance that it has when sought for its own sake, whereas the indirect importance of a being is the importance that it has when sought as an instrumental means for something else. Thus direct and indirect importance do not name, he says, kinds of importance but rather ways in which importance belongs to its bearer. In the case of indirect importance the importance of a means is "borrowed" from the importance of the end, whereas in the case of direct importance the importance is found in the important being itself and without any such borrowing. It is worth noting that in chapter 7 of the present work the terms "direct" and "indirect" are used in an entirely different sense. Trans.]

means for preserving life, as if the action of the life-saver were a mere instrument for bringing about the safety of the endangered person. We have only to compare these two cases with each other in order to recognize this serious error. Let us suppose that someone accidentally, without wanting to save anyone, comes on the scene in such a way as to make a murderer flee and thus saves the endangered person from the murderer: his coming on the scene is a purely objective cause of saving a life and in this way it becomes something important, something valuable. Perhaps we will say, "How fortunate that he came just at that moment," and then we are referring to the indirect value of his coming, to the value which his coming, through its causal connection with the rescue of a life, *borrows* from this rescue. There is obviously no moral value at stake in this case; his coming is not the bearer of a moral value. If, on the other hand, someone recognizes the danger in which another person finds himself and hastens to rescue him, then his action is not just a lucky event that causes the saving of the life of the other, but it is a personal stance and thus the bearer of a direct value that is quite different in kind—the bearer of a moral value.

We encounter here the fundamental error of every ethical utilitarianism. This position overlooks moral value and disvalue entirely and sees all human action only as indirectly valuable or disvaluable, that is, it sees only the value or disvalue which action has as a means for the realization of a good. Utilitarianism reduces, as it were, the moral value of all human action to the indirect value which human action and behavior can possess to the extent that it is a cause of the realization of extra-moral goods. It is the same indirect value which even a morally bad action can have when we speak of it as a *felix culpa* (a fortunate fault), although we are clearly aware that the moral disvalue of the action is not thereby taken away.

But here we are not so much concerned to show that the value of a response to some good is something qualitatively new over against the value of the good, but rather to show what is new in the word that is spoken in the stance taken towards the good. The value of the stance is, as Scheler put it, on the "back" of the act; it is not consciously experienced. But the "word" that is spoken in the stance taken towards the good, which constitutes the content of the value-response, *is* consciously performed. This word is the bearer of the value of the stance. It is, of course, conditioned by the value of the good and is even born of this value and largely determined in its quality by it. But it is the stance of a person to the good and so it is something altogether new over against the value of the good; it is situated in a different sphere of being and is something exclusively personal in its meaning and nature.

Now what makes this "word" something entirely new in relation to the object is not only the formal fact that it is the conscious stance of a person; the particular individual character of the responding person also has a significant influence on the character of this word. In a value-response there is a unique encounter of subject and object. The subject or person engages the good with its value and is conscious only of the good and its value. But at the same time, the person grows in a unique way in giving a value-response. The person thrives as person more than ever by giving himself to the good. The dignity of the person and the whole new dimension of being that only a person can have, is actualized in the value-response. But also the individual make-up of the person, his spiritual and moral status, is manifested in the word spoken in the stance, and manifested in the quality and depth, in the purity and the adequacy of the word. Here in value-response we find the deepest and most significant collaboration of subject and object—the specific unfolding of the person and of the transcendence that is proper to the person.

In spite of the difference between the conscious word of the value-response and the value that it has, a value that is not experienced in giving a response, the fact that the moral value is not just a participation in the value of the good that is responded to, throws an important light on all that is new in this word.

The entirely new contribution of the subject in love

But in the case of love we are further removed from a mere participation in the value of the object than we are with the other value-responses. The entirely new role of the subject is a distinctive mark of love, distinguishing it precisely from all other affective value-responses.[4] With love we not only find the subject manifesting itself in the "word" spoken in every value-response, but we also find a certain contribution [*Beitrag*] of the person, which we could call the "gift" [*Gabe*] of the one who loves. This "gift," too, has much to do with determining the value of a love.

To avoid all misunderstandings let us once again stress emphatically the value-response character of love as well as the decisive importance that the value of the beloved person has for the quality of the love.

If we speak of a primarily vital love and contrast it with a personal love, we are surely aiming at differences deriving from the kinds of value presenting themselves in the other person and affecting the heart of the one who loves. Whether my love is engendered primarily by the charm of the other or by the fascinating intellectual richness or by the goodness and purity of the other, naturally has a great influence on the quality of my love. Or perhaps we can say it better by asking: in what domain of value do I encounter the beloved person, in what domain of value is he situated for me, into what domain of value am I drawn by

---

4   In order to work out more clearly that element of love that does not grow out of the value-response character of love, we have to prescind for the time being from the love for God, for here we have to do with such a unique case on account of the absolute and ultimate value datum, that we can hardly speak of any content or value in our love that would go beyond a participation in the value of the beloved.

him, from which values is the radiance surrounding his personality nourished? The higher the realm of value, the more sublime the response of love.

But the personality of the one who loves has also a great influence on the quality of the love. The fact that there are different kinds of value that can awaken love in different persons shows the significant role of the subject in love. The personality you love is extremely characteristic for who you are. In the opera of Bizet, *Carmen*, it is very characteristic for José, for his whole personality, that he loves Carmen. Someone like Werther (in the novel of Goethe, *Die Lieden des Jungen Werther* [*The Sorrows of Young Werther*]) would never love the likes of Carmen. But what we are aiming at here is not how the subject influences the quality of love, for as we see this influence is found in every value-response. Each value-response, indeed each being-affected, presupposes in a person the depth and the sensitivity to value that enables the person to be affected by this value rather than another one, or to respond to this value rather than another one.[5]

By the way, even in all moral acts of the will we encounter the fact that the degree of commitment depends not only on the kind of good and on the rank of its value, but also on the personality of the one who wills. The whole moral status of a person is expressed in how far the person is willing to go to fulfill the demands of a particular situation. The point at which a person says, "It is impossible," and at which the obstacles seem insurmountable to him so that he feels excused in his conscience, is reached sooner by some and later by others. Many factors may be responsible for this difference, but a large factor is the degree of ardor in a value-response, the degree of interest and the resulting readiness to make sacrifices and to give of oneself.

This is particularly the case when there is no moral obligation but only the invitation of some morally relevant good. For instance, one person will go further in helping to relieve the need of someone than another person is willing to go, assuming that in both cases there is no obligation to help. We have to do here with a higher degree of value-responding commitment, with a "more" of value-response that has to be clearly distinguished from the "more" required by the hierarchy of goods—from the hierarchical "more," as we could call it. We showed in our *Ethics*, chapters 17 and 18, that to the higher values "more" of a value-response should be given. The higher good deserves more of a response than the lower good. But if the value of a good is fully understood, then this "more" in the affective value-responses arises by itself. Someone who fully understands the value of two works of art, one of which is much superior to the other, will necessarily take more delight in the more beautiful one. His delight will be qualitatively different, it will be deeper as well, but it will

---

5   Here we do not have to do with the aspect expressed as *secundum modum recipientis* ("according to the capacity of the recipient"), but with the particular abundance of love that the lover invests in the commitment of himself.

also contain this "more," expressing the fact that the one work of art is preferred to the other. Now from this hierarchical "more" we have to distinguish the "more" of delight and enthusiasm that one person possesses to a greater degree than another and that derives from his general personal structure, from his potential for discerning values and for giving himself to them.

In this connection we have to point out something else, namely, the overall relation of a person to the world of value as a whole. Apart from the understanding for particular kinds of value, such as aesthetic, intellectual, or vital values, and from the resulting difference in the value-response to these values, there is a general relation to the world of value as such that varies greatly from one person to another. Some people have a greater capacity than others to be affected by values, a greater capacity for ardor and awakedness in their responses to values. Their overall relation to the world of values, to the important in itself, to all that contains a message from above, is deeper, more alert, more intensive, more ardent. When this overall relation of a person to value is very deep, then the response of that person to particular values, such as aesthetic or artistic values, even if he has less of a sense for these than a connoisseur has, is still more adequate, assuming that the connoisseur has less of an overall relation to the world of values. In other words, the overall relation to the world of values is so decisive that in a particular case it can compensate for the defect of a particular value understanding (for example, in music) in the sense that the response, though perhaps less adequate in relation to the hierarchical "more," is still more reverent, deeper, more spiritually awakened than that of the connoisseur. Now from this role of the subject in all value-responses we have to distinguish the role of the subject in the "gift" of love, although that which holds for all value-responses holds especially for love.

Here is one way of seeing that in love the activity of the subject goes far beyond what we find in all other value-responses. In these, for example, in admiration, enthusiasm, or veneration, every inadequacy in the response is something distinctly negative, which compromises the value of the response. Indeed, if someone is enthused about something that objectively does not merit any enthusiasm, there is no longer any real value-response present at all. Elements foreign to value-response have insinuated themselves into the enthusiasm. Missing here is the real and undiluted act of turning to the value of the good, so that one is exclusively motivated by something important in itself. This is why St. Augustine says that he mainly wants to know *why* someone is enthusiastic, *what* it is that he loves, thereby implicitly expressing the fact that the purity and genuineness of a value-response depends upon the good to which it refers.

Of course, we are not thinking here of the case in which someone is deceived about another person. When Oronté in the play of Moliere, *Tartuffe,* reveres Tartuffe, wrongly taking him for a saint, his response is indeed objectively inadequate but not subjectively inadequate. It is inadequate because he is deceived about Tartuffe, because this man is not what he thinks. But given the image that he wrongly has of Tartuffe, his veneration is appropriate. This is why it is a genuine value-response. Regrettable is only the factual error but not the relation between the response and the perceived value, which is in this case the saintly piety that Tartuffe only apparently possesses.

Regrettable as this mere factual error is and much as we feel the desire to liberate the person from his error, it does not affect the genuineness and the purity of the value-response. But suppose that one person without committing any error excessively reveres another because of the other's superficial education, or his strong vitality, or the fact that he is a Nietzschean superman, then there is no real reverence, no pure value-response, because he is fascinated by illegitimate qualities and his stance to the other is nourished by factors other than values. But even if he has to do with a good endowed with genuine values and not an idol, the purity and genuineness of his value-response depends upon how much his reverence corresponds to the rank of the good. If the reverence is exaggerated, then we see it as something distinctly negative. The inappropriateness of this reverence or veneration offends against the hierarchy of values and proves conclusively that it cannot be an authentic value-response—assuming, of course, that the excessiveness of the response is not based on a mere factual error but on some value blindness.

But in the case of love not every inadequate love has to undermine the value and genuineness of love. If we continue to prescind from factual errors, that is, from those cases where the one who loves makes some mistake about the beloved person or is deceived about him, then we can say that an inadequate love does not necessarily have something negative about it. It often happens that one person ardently loves another, for instance, a woman loves a man or one friend another friend, even though the other is in every respect inferior to him. We say perhaps that this man or this friend is not worthy of such love, but the love remains still something touching, something beautiful and pure. Of course, there are cases where the inadequacy of the love compromises the quality of the love. This is especially found when the love has the character of an addictive dependency or when pride and the above-mentioned expansion of one's ego enter into the love. The inadequacy of love can undermine the character of a value-response, can be a symptom for the absence of a genuine and pure love and for the presence of a love with disvalue rather than with value. But the inadequacy of a love does not always *have to* mean this. There are many cases in which love goes far beyond what is required for adequacy from a pure value-response point of view and still retains something touching and beautiful. This fact shows that the contribution of the one who loves is much greater than in all other responses, since it goes beyond that which is motivated by the beauty of the beloved person.

When in chapter 12 we treat of the sources of the moral value of natural love, or in other words of the relation of love and morality, we will discuss extensively the role of this contribution of the one who loves in its relation to the moral value of love. Here we have only wanted to show that love goes beyond all other value-responses in its response, that the "gift" of love is greater than in any other value-response, and above all that it objectively[6] surpasses the value of the good that merits a response.

Love in contrast to arbitrariness, even though love is the least "appreciative" of all responses

With this we arrive at the following mark of love. It is in one respect the least "appreciative" of all responses. We spoke in chapter 2 of the purely appreciative value-responses like respect and the much more affective but still appreciative responses like enthusiasm, veneration, or admiration. Love is the most affective of all responses and is in a certain sense, as we said, the least appreciative. It does not imply so definite an objective value judgment as does, for example, veneration. It does not claim to have the same "objectivity" that admiration or veneration necessarily claim to have. But on the other hand, love grants a position to the beloved person which goes far beyond all other value-responses. Love "enthrones" the beloved person, as we are about to see. It gives him more than any of the other value-responses do. This holds above all for spousal love, but also for any and every great love, for any love in which one loves another "above all else." The other is then set on a unique kind of throne but without the appreciative character of veneration. If I say that I venerate this person more than all others, then I am implicitly ranking him objectively higher than the others. But when Rigoletto says of his daughter Gilda, "She is everything, everything for me in this world," there is no such value-response at stake. Walther von der Vogelweide says of his beloved in relation to other women, "Perhaps they are better, but you are good."

We have to understand that this element of "subjectivity" forms no contradiction to the value-response character of love. Above all, it would be entirely wrong to think that there is some element of arbitrariness in this subjectivity. Love is rather entirely opposed to the arbitrary. As soon as I really love, I enter, as it were, into a world in which there is no place for the arbitrary. When we say arbitrary, we are thinking of the attitude of a person who feels himself to be entirely his own master and who yields without any resistance to whatever he finds subjectively satisfying. We do not think of the person who feels himself to be his own master because he has learned to control himself, because he has himself in hand, but rather of the one who approaches life in the consciousness of being able to do or to omit whatever he likes, whose basic attitude can be expressed in the words, "for such is my pleasure."

---

6   With "objective" we mean here the response that is in reality required by the object, in contrast to the consciousness of the one who loves, who, as we will see, thinks that he never sufficiently responds to the other.

Genuine love is incompatible with this kind of arbitrary attitude, which is contradicted by the self-donation implied in every love, by the gesture of binding oneself that animates every love, by the promise of permanence that is intrinsic to every love. But above all it is the entrance of the lover into the deep rhythm of the realm of value, into the kingdom of what is important and serious, that implies a break with all arbitrariness. Of course, the one who loves can fall back into this attitude of arbitrariness after his love has come to an end. We do not say that the lover gives up this attitude once and for all. We only say that he comes out of this attitude as long as he loves, in so far as he loves, and to the degree that his love is a pure love.

Love is no less a value-response than veneration, but it unfolds in a different direction in that it is less appreciative while at the same time its word is a "contribution" of the loving person that is stronger than and goes farther than veneration. This is related to both the value datum which underlies the love as well as to the role of the particular affinity presupposed in all the natural categories of love.

Aspects of the "gift" of love

1. *Affirmation and "enthronement" of the beloved person.* We saw that it is always the beauty of a particular individual person which engenders love in us. This beauty has to present itself to us in some way. We spoke of the many conditions which determine that this beauty present itself to us in one person but not in another, even if objectively the one cannot be placed above the other.

The step from an individual value of the other to the overall beauty [*Gesamtschönheit*] of his individual being can be taken even before we love the other. But in the unique kind of affirmation of another person that belongs to love, there is a personal enacting of this step. It is analogous to the theoretical response of conviction, wherein we say "yes" to the existence of an object, thereby reenacting the independent being of the object of knowledge, the self-disclosure of itself as "existent."

In love we enthrone the beloved as a whole independently of whatever flaws and deficiencies he may have; he is as a whole not *made* to be precious, but is rather *declared* to be precious in love. As the value datum that founds love is always the overall beauty of this individual personality, so there is this enthronement in every love. It is quite a different enthronement from the one of a mere value judgment or of the one that is given in admiration or veneration. The difference of the enthronement of love from the one found in every value judgment is perfectly obvious; the value judgment remains in the theoretical sphere and as a purely theoretical affirmation is to be distinguished from the affective value-responses.

The enthronement found in affective value-responses like admiration or veneration is clearly different from that of love. First of all, the throne on which the beloved person is set, or the crown with which he is crowned, has an entirely different character. We stressed already the role of the delightfulness of value in love. Lacordaire says that the virtues can awaken love only when they have reached the perfection of showing forth their beauty. That holds in an analogous way for the throne on which the beloved person is set. The overall beauty of the other has to present itself to me if the response of love is to be awakened in me, and this beauty is not only a value datum but also a specifically delightful value datum, one that enchants me. The other emerges from the sphere of indifference not only into the sphere of the precious, the valuable, the estimable, but also into the sphere of the enchanting and of the delightful [*Beglückenden*]. Of course, this holds in a special way for spousal love or any great and deep love of some other kind, but there is something of this present whenever my heart is in any way conquered by another.

The value datum underlying love distinguishes itself, therefore, not only by the fact that it is the overall beauty of the individual rather than just individual valuable traits, as in the case of admiration and respect, but above all by the fact that it is always being a thing of beauty, a specifically delightful value datum, the value of the lovable [*Liebenswertheit*]. This distinction stands forth more clearly if we consider the act of declaring the other to be lovable, the subjective reenactment of this lovableness that already presents itself in knowledge and that we called enthronement. Here we really see that this enthronement is qualitatively very different from the one contained in veneration, which of course also refers to the other as a whole. The throne on which the other is set by the affirmation of love stands in quite another personal relation to me, affects me and my subjectivity in quite another way, makes an appeal to me in quite another way. It is the throne of delightfulness and of happiness, and the enthronement has quite a different warmth from the primarily appreciative gesture of veneration.

2. *The "credit" of love.* But we have now to distinguish between this enthronement and the credit given to the other by the one who loves; this latter represents a new moment of love. We are referring to the credit that one gives to a beloved person for those qualities in his being that one has not yet had the opportunity of getting to know. Love draws out the line of the beauty and preciousness of an individual being into all the individual traits of that being, including those which it has not yet been able to experience directly. Love believes the best about the beloved person; even when I hear something negative told about him, I will not at first believe that it is true or at least not believe that it has been adequately interpreted. I am referring to faith in the other, to the positive interpretation of the other and to assuming only good about the other as long as one has not unmistakably found some fault. Here we are not speaking of the step from some particular value of the other to the overall beauty of the other as individual, a step that precedes love, nor are we merely speaking about the subjective re-enactment of this step that we called enthronement. We are rather speaking about drawing out the line of the beauty of this individual

into all particular traits and situations. It is a credit which one gives the beloved person, going far beyond what one can observe in him.

And so there is in every love an element of faith; even that which has not yet been seen of the beauty of the other is believed on the basis of the beauty that one already knows. We are not here talking about trust in another person, the trust that normally goes hand in hand with love and is very characteristic for certain kinds of love, such as the love between friends, and the love of a child for its parents. The element of faith of which we here speak rather consists in drawing out the line from the overall beauty of the other into all the levels and areas of the beloved person that one does not yet know. We will return later to this element of faith and discuss it in detail. It is a distant reflection of what St. Paul says of charity: "Love believes all." It is found in all kinds of love, even in their "unbaptized" forms.

Interpreting another "from above"—the opposite of self-indulgent idealization of the other. This credit of faith is also a kind of enthronement, as one could call it, but at a new level, for it is something new in relation to the already-mentioned affirmation of the other. It is something more than just entering into what is given in the other is and re-enacting it, but it is a "gift" of love. Together with giving this credit there is also the readiness to interpret everything in the beloved from above, to interpret everything positively as long as it has not unmistakably shown itself to be negative. There are, after all, so many things in a human being that can be interpreted very differently, so many deeds, utterances, modes of behavior that in themselves are not unambiguously morally good or bad, beautiful or ugly, intelligent or foolish, but which take on their full meaning and character only on the background of the particular individual person. Whereas it is typical for suspicion and hatred to be always on the alert for the weaknesses of another and to interpret all aspects of the other in a negative light and from below, it is a basic element of love to hope that the other is treading the path of what is just, good and beautiful and to have the readiness to interpret in the best possible light everything that admits of various interpretations. This readiness to interpret the other from above is of course closely related with the credit of faith in the other.

But giving this credit of faith should not be confused with the idealization of the other that one finds in certain emotionally overwrought persons [*schwärmerische Menschen*]. These people do not have the generosity of love, which after all presupposes a corresponding value datum in the other that makes the generosity meaningful and justified; they show instead the need to experience the joy of encountering wonderful and extraordinary people. One wants to have this pleasure and so gives in to an unjustified idealization. Indeed, one enjoys raving [*Schwärmen*] about another person, and this person is more of an opportunity to indulge in this raving than someone really taken seriously in his own right. One sees clearly the distinction between the above-mentioned credit of faith that characterizes love and this unfounded assumption that everything must be splendid and grand in the other person, although one has not yet had the opportunity of knowing him well enough to experience this directly.

The credit of faith is contained in what we are calling the "gift" of love, which is itself a value-response. Even if it surpasses a pure value-response, it is nevertheless in no way a spontaneous need and it cannot be detached from the value-response character of love. But raving about another is a typical need and appetitus that strives to indulge itself and has nothing to do with a value-response. The credit of trust in love is closely connected with the self-donation of love; the one who loves is in no way seeking his own gratification by means of this credit; he is entirely directed to the other and this credit of faith has entirely the character of "for the sake of the other." It contains no element of enjoying oneself. But the raving about another is relished as such and it is not lived for the sake of the other but for the sake of the one who indulges in the raving.

There is nothing overly spiritual about the credit of faith and in fact it goes together with the consciousness that human beings are frail and that even a noble person is exposed to all kinds of dangers. This credit reckons with the possibility that even where one interprets everything positively some weakness or fault could be present. But this does not change the love, which always interprets weaknesses and faults as something inauthentic and transitory. The credit of faith does not exist in a thin and unreal space, but rather in a fully real space, in an atmosphere of noble sobriety.

The radical difference between the credit of faith and an illusion born of self-indulgent idealization is not reduced by the fact that even in an authentic love I can be deceived and my credit of faith can at some point be disappointed. It is not the possibility of deception that characterizes the gesture of self-indulgent idealization, but rather the absence of authentic love, the gratification of an urge, the thin and unreal, indeed ungenuine atmosphere. We could say it like this: the one who loves can be deceived, but the one who gives in to self-indulgent idealization deceives himself.

The way we approach the faults of a beloved person. Finally, it is an essential mark of all love that all the worthy traits of the other are seen as the authentic other, as that which makes up the real self of the other, whereas his faults are interpreted as a *lack of faithfulness* to his true being. It is typical of love to deal with the bad qualities of another by saying, "That is not the way he really is." For one who does not love another, both the qualitative strengths and weaknesses of the other seem to belong to the other in the same way; but it is typical for love, which after all includes a response to the beauty of the whole person, that it sees everything negative in the beloved person as uncharacteristic, indeed as being unfaithful to his real being.

But the loving attitude toward the faults of the beloved person varies according to the kind of fault. There are many faults that are, as it were, the back side of good qualities. We pointed out in our *Ethics* something about the virtues that stand in a certain polar opposition to each other; only in the saints can these virtues so interpenetrate as to be able to cohere in one and the same person, for example, meekness and a great and ardent zeal for the good, or humility and forcefulness in fighting for the good, or humility and the ability to exercise authority with great energy. It follows that a strong personality filled with burning zeal for the good can easily become violent. Such violence is, as it were, a wart or a welt on a great and noble quality, and it can only be avoided or overcome in Christ. The meek and humble person can under certain circumstances be too compliant and in some situations act with too little of the strength and energy that is morally required. Now as long as the one who loves is dealing with qualities that are the "back sides" of great and noble excellences, he will indeed regret these faults, but he will see them in the light of those excellences of which they are the back sides and he will recognize in the faults the lovable capacities that are being misused. He will wish that the beloved person would overcome these faults, but he sees them as a kind of derailment of lovable and noble traits of character. These traits, in their positive forms, are characteristic for the beloved person, whereas the derailment of them is seen as something provisional and temporary.

Other faults, by contrast, are not simply the back sides of good qualities, but are the sheer flowering of pride and concupiscence, for example, envy, greed, or impurity. In loving another I see these traits of character as a betrayal of the real being of the beloved person. These are the faults of which I say, "That is not his true being"; I perceive these faults as an infidelity committed against the authentic being of the one whom I love.

We have here an essential mark that distinguishes all kinds of love from a neutral, so-called objective, attitude towards persons. A supposedly objective observer or a judge will consider both the positive and the negative qualities of the person as equally characteristic for him, as belonging equally to him. The one who loves takes the good qualities as authentic, as that which belongs in truth to the beloved person, and takes the bad qualities as infidelity, falling away, betrayal, and denial of his true being. That is the unheard-of credit that love and only love gives.

This credit presents itself to us quite unambiguously in love of neighbor. Since this love responds to the ontological value of a human being and not to his qualitative values, since it responds to the *imago Dei* in the other and sees him in the light of the *similitudo Dei* that he is destined to achieve, this love sees qualitative disvalues as a contradiction to the *imago Dei*, as a falling away from it, as inauthentic.

This credit has nothing to do with the question how many faults I find in a person, nor with the question how clearly I see these faults. The fact that I consider the faults of a beloved friend as not belonging to him and as not characteristic for him in the way in which his good qualities belong to him and are characteristic for him, does not mean that I am inclined to overlook his faults or to explain them away, nor that I see them less clearly and distinctly. Love makes me more sensitive to the faults of a beloved person, because the beauty of the person as a whole has been revealed to me and because I am concerned that he remain faithful to his own most proper being and fully develop his true self. It is entirely false to think that love makes blind—on the contrary, love makes me see more clearly. But the pride that is often mixed in with love does indeed make blind. The mother who considers her child as an extension of her ego thinks that *her* child can have no faults at all. This is in no way a result of love, but rather of pride.

Of course, my stance toward the faults of a beloved person is different from my stance toward the faults of a person whom I do not love. The faults of one to whom I am more or less indifferent irritate me, they anger me and produce in me a reaction against the other person. They are not seen on the background of the beauty of the person as a whole, they are seen in isolation from the person and are taken to be just as characteristic of him as his good qualities. But with a beloved person the faults do not irritate me, I am not angry at him, but I am unhappy about them; I am unhappy for the beloved. Out of our deep solidarity with him I am sad about this infidelity committed against his true being.[7] Conscious of my own weakness and fragility, and mindful how unfaithful I have been to my own God-given self, I trace lovingly the emergence of the faults of the other, I understand empathetically all of his dangers and weaknesses, and out of solidarity with him I reject the faults. The view I have of the faults of another is much more objective, in the true sense of that word, when I love the other than when I do not love him. I do more justice to reality by seeing the faults in the light of the person as a whole, by understanding them from within, and by being sad about them for the sake of the beloved person. I suffer under them for his sake and not because they are a burden for me, and so in loving I am much less inclined to overlook faults, because I am much more concerned with the growth of the other for his own sake and with his perfection than when I do not love him.

And so we see that love neither makes me overlook faults nor makes me see them less clearly. Only that pride that expresses itself in extended self-love makes me overlook faults or explain them away or trivialize them. The fact that in loving I do not consider the faults as really belonging to the true image of the other does not at all incline me to overlook those faults.

This credit given by love has a specific nobility. Here we encounter the particular generosity of love. This credit also contains an element of hope,

---

7   St. Augustine expressed this in speaking of the brotherly spirit of love and in referring to those "who approve of what they see good in me and disapprove of what they see bad in me, but whether they see good or ill still love me." *Confessions*, X, 4.

which is a particular gift for the beloved person, as is the generosity contained in the "gift" of love. This element of hope also belongs to the "gift" of love.

Let us summarize as follows. First of all, love assumes the best as long as it has no basis for acknowledging a fault. In giving this credit, love interprets "from above" those things which are not unambiguous. Secondly, the faults that love clearly sees are taken by love as a betrayal of or an infidelity committed against the true being of the beloved person. And thirdly, love does not see faults as being just as characteristic for the beloved person as his good qualities are. That is the three-fold credit that love and *only* love gives to the beloved person.

This three-fold credit undoubtedly has a particular value, indeed a moral value. This value grows not out of the pure value-responding character of love but is rather rooted in the "gift" of love.

3. *Love always refers to an individual and unique person as this individual being.* It is a further essential trait of love that its word is always spoken to the individual person as a whole. The goodness and warmth of its breath surrounds the whole individual person, the "gift" of love refers to the person as a whole. Although it is the beauty of this individual that wounds my heart, in the act of love I am entirely directed to the person himself and in fact to the whole person. After all, I do not love the beauty of this person but the person himself.

We have to distinguish between that which motivates our love and that to which our love refers. Here we encounter a specific mark of love distinguishing it from the other value-responses. Of course, it holds for all value-responses that my response refers to the good and not the value; it refers to the good *on the basis of* the value.[8] I take delight in Mozart's opera *Figaro*, *because of* its beauty. The beauty motivates my delight, which however refers to the bearer of this beauty. I marvel at some heroic moral action. The moral value grounds my marveling, this is what motivates it, it affects my heart and engenders my marveling: but the word of marveling is spoken to the concrete real deed and refers to it. What I utter in the marveling *refers to* the deed; it is spoken to the deed on the basis of its moral value.

This distinction between that which motivates my value-response and that to which my response refers is a distinction valid in general for all value-responses, but it takes on a new character in the case of love. In the context of love for human persons, for instance, for a friend or bride, it is something entirely new to say that love refers to the whole person and not just to the values of the person. It means that we give our heart to this individual person, that we enter into solidarity with this real individual. And the way in which the beauty of this individual is united with the person is radically different from

---

8   [Von Hildebrand inserts here a long footnote in which he discusses the distinction that he makes in his value philosophy between "value" and "good"; because of its length and its significance it has been placed as an appendix to this chapter.]

what is found in other value-responses. The difference stands out most clearly by comparing love with joy. We hear of some heroic life-saving action. We rejoice that such a thing has happened and that moral value has been realized and that this realization of value glorifies God. But in the case of a beloved person, things are quite different. Here we have to do, as we have already seen, not with values like faithfulness, humility, intellectual depth, physical beauty, etc., but rather with an entirely individual unique value quality inhering in this individual. The idea of the realization of some general value does not come into question here. The idea of participating in some value in general makes no sense here. The beauty of the individual as a whole, or, as we could say, of the unique unrepeatable idea of God[9] embodied in this person, is after all no general value type, but already as a quality it is something entirely individual and unique. Of course, it is nourished by many general values, as we saw, but important as these general values may be as a point of departure for love, love itself is always motivated by the overall beauty [*Gesamtschönheit*]. The role of the different general values consists here primarily in building up the overall beauty of this individual and not in realizing the general value types, as in the case of moral action.

But the distinction between love and the other value-responses goes still further. It is not only the overall beauty of this individual that motivates love, but the person is here in no way a mere bearer of this overall beauty. For a person embodies this overall beauty in such a way that love refers to the person himself, not only in the sense in which all value-responses refer to the bearer of value, but rather in a quite new sense, which brings us back to the "gift" of love. Love does not just respond to the beloved person on the basis of his overall beauty, but rather encompasses his real person as such. The one who loves gives his heart to the beloved person; he decides for the other as a whole being. The "gift" of warmth, of goodness, of ultimate concern, of solidarity refers entirely to this real person in such a way that it would be impossible to take this person simply as the bearer of typical values like moral, aesthetic, or vital values, and to rejoice primarily over the realization of these values. This

---

9   This expression is not to be taken in a theological sense. It would of course be very daring to say that we can recognize the idea of God that is embodied (in the strict sense of the word) in human beings. With this expression we are only referring to the more proper and deeper being of a human being, of his particular individuality, including that which he could be and ought to be. What we are expressing is that the one who truly loves searches more deeply and reaches the point of finding that particular "invention" which an individual human being embodies. I am not here speaking of an abstract theoretical insight into all the possibilities and talents of a person, but rather of the organic intuitively-grasped total image of the other, in which we can sharply distinguish the essential from the inessential, the valid from the invalid; it is an image that is not restricted to that which has been realized but includes all that the beloved person is destined to become.

unique trait of love, which sets love apart from all other value-responses, will become clearer still when we distinguish it from that which is proper to all value-responses to persons (in contrast to value-responses directed to impersonal objects).

Those value-responses that are directed to persons give rise to a situation that is in many ways entirely new. This direction to another person gives value-responses an entirely new character. This holds both for those value-responses that are necessarily directed only to other persons as well as for those that can be directed either to persons or to non-personal beings. Veneration and respect are necessarily directed to another person, and the same holds for admiration and love in the proper sense; but enthusiasm can be directed either to persons or non-persons. A value-response, however, always takes on a new character by referring to a person, to a conscious subject, to a "you." The entirely new dimension of reality possessed by persons confers upon the value-response a new dimension of reality. An entirely new situation is created by the fact that the content of a value-response can reach its object in quite another way, that the object here is precisely not an object but a subject who can in principle understand and receive our value-response. The word spoken in a value-response can penetrate his mind and heart, affecting him with the content of a value-response. And when we also consider that this affecting of the other person is not only possible but is always somehow intended, that every such value-response by its nature tends to declare itself to the other (even if for certain reasons this declaration is explicitly omitted), then we see more clearly than ever the new gesture proper to all value-responses referring to persons.[10]

In our context it is above all important to see that the relation between the bearer of a value and the value itself is one thing in the case of all value-responses directed to persons (whether this personal direction be essential or accidental to the response), and it is something else in the case of those value-responses referring to non-persons. We have already mentioned the distinction in general between that which motivates a response and that to which a response refers. Now this distinction takes on a new significance with all value-responses directed to other persons. For with persons there is a union of a value with the particular good that is different from impersonal goods. Qualities like generosity, goodness, intelligence, charm, the stature of a personality, all belong to

---

10   We prescind here from the case in which my value-response refers to a deceased person. Here there is a particular modification; though the value-response is directed to a person, this person is withdrawn from the reach of my response, at least as far as our natural human experience is concerned. Admiration for a great artist who died a long time ago, or for a Socrates, naturally lacks many of the traits of a value-response directed to a living person, who may even be present to me. Yet the value-response is even here different from the response directed to a non-person. But as soon as we turn to the deceased person in the perspective of faith [and realize that he is still alive], the situation is again different.

a person in such a way as to incline us to stop speaking of a *bearing* of values, or of the person as the *bearer* of values. In admiring someone for their genius, or their goodness, or their generosity, we find a certain "embodiment" of values in the person, which is more than just a realization of values but is, as it were, a coming alive of values. I am here thinking not of enthusiasm about some deed, but of a value-response referring to and thus motivated by enduring value qualities of the person, even if they also show themselves in a particular deed. Now the essential trait of love discussed above clearly distinguishes itself as something quite new in relation to this characteristic of all value-responses directed to other persons. Of course, all that characterizes the value-responses directed to persons (in contrast to those directed to non-persons) is also found with love. But love goes in various ways far beyond this.

For here, far more than with the other value-responses directed to persons, the beauty of this unique individual is woven together with its "bearer." This is expressed in the fact that the response, besides referring entirely to the person and not just to some value of the person—this is the case with all value-responses directed to other persons—is such that this "referring" to a person takes on a new character. The person who is loved is much less the *bearer* of value than with the other value-responses directed to persons. The theme of love is altogether the other person. Of course, this person is taken in her unique beauty, which in the case of spousal love is even the embodiment of the world of value, being a kind of door opening on to this world; but this individual real person taken as a whole still remains the theme.[11]

Here is a way of seeing quite clearly this thematicity of the person as something unique and unrepeatable. Let us suppose two persons both endowed with exactly the same values, let us say with the same goodness and purity. I

---

11   We have to stress again and again that we would be well advised, in searching for the essence of some attitude, some act, some value or quality, to start with cases in which the thing sought is given in a very characteristic and intense way. This is why when studying the nature of love we take our bearings from cases of great and deep and intense love, from love that is centrally important in the life of the one who loves. Take, for instance, the love between friends; we find an eminent example of this love in the love of a David for Jonathan, or an Arestes for Pylades, where we see a word of love spoken to *the* friend *par excellence*. If we take the love of parents for their child, we might think of the love of St. Monica for St. Augustine, or the love of St. Thomas More for his daughter Margaret. It is advisable to think of a love, of whatever category, which is centrally important in the life of the lover or perhaps even the central love in his life. This is why we often start from spousal love, which among the natural kinds of love is in many ways the most typical love; even though it has its own distinctive character, many traits of love in general are presented nowhere so clearly as in spousal love. Thus in working out the nature of love, we will choose to start with spousal love, even if some of its characteristic features are found only analogously in the other categories of love.

first get to know one of them and my heart is touched by the goodness and purity of that person; I come to love her and to give her my heart. Now I get to know the second one and I see that she is very similar to the one I love and I am impressed with her goodness and purity. But I love only the first one with spousal love, for I love this unique, definite, unsubstitutable individual. It does not even occur to me that I could just as well love the other simply because she is similar to the first and has the same goodness and purity.

Now one could object that this results from the obvious fact that love, and most especially spousal love, responds to the overall beauty [*Gesamtschönheit*] of the individual and for this reason, if for no other, could never let the beloved person be replaced by some other, not even if the other had exactly the same moral values that serve to initiate my love. This objection is perfectly correct. But let us make the assumption, even if it is an intrinsically impossible assumption, that the other person possesses qualitatively the same individuality, that she possesses qualitatively the same overall beauty: surely this person could never replace the one I love, and I who love could never have the feeling that I could just as well love the other person, as if it made no difference whether the one or the other person returned my love. It remains this real, unique, unrepeatable individual whom I love and by whom I desire to be loved in return. This fiction helps us to see how it is that in love the other real person is altogether and entirely thematic as person.

An apparent "antimony" of love

We encounter here an apparent antimony. On the one hand, all love is in a unique way a value-response, as we see most clearly in the case of spousal love. It is not enough to say that the overall beauty of this individual engenders love, nor enough to say that love is experienced as insufficient in comparison to the love that the other would deserve; in addition, love is in a mysterious way also connected with the whole world of value, as we have seen and are about to see more exactly. On the other hand, love refers to the individual person; this is the theme of love, and though I love the other for his beauty and lovableness, I do not just love him insofar as he realizes these values. And in addition, love goes beyond a pure value-response in that it involves a highly personal commitment that is not obligatory and that gives "something" that transcends all value-responses. We have to examine more closely this apparent antimony of love, which is no real antimony but which rather illuminates the mystery of love.

Love is the deepest and most radical value-response, as we have said. This is seen in the fact that with love the value, the overall beauty of the individual, affects us more deeply than does value in the case of any other value-response. We are of course thinking here of value-responses that presuppose some being-affected, such as enthusiasm, and are not thinking of merely appreciative responses such as respect, which presuppose no being-affected, for in this latter case, the very possibility of a comparison with love is excluded. Being affected by value in the process of the engendering of love goes further and is *more intense* than in the analogous case of enthusiasm. The fact that the delightfulness of value is found here in a unique way, that value enchants us more and more deeply than in the other affective value-responses, is not an indication that love is any less of a real value-response. For the delightfulness flows right out of the value and is in no way the delightfulness of the merely agreeable, as we have already seen. It also does not run parallel to value, but grows out of the overall beauty of the individual person and cannot be separated from the *value* as value. We will understand all of this better when we later explore the relation between this delightfulness and the inner aspect or the material aspect of values. But the value-response character of love is not limited to the fact that love is based upon the deepest possible being-affected by value and its delightfulness.

When a person loves—and this is once again eminently the case with spousal love—he discovers a whole new world of goodness; he becomes alert to an aspect of the world that had before not intuitively revealed itself to him, he becomes alert to a new dimension of beauty and depth in the universe. The contact with the world of values that is achieved in love reaches far beyond the value-response to the beloved person. In loving I awaken to a deeper view of all values and to a new and deeper relationship to them; in experiencing the happiness immanent in the act of loving, the happiness conferred by loving as such, I also experience happiness over this new aspect of the cosmos, over this new contact with the world of values. There is here a reciprocal rhythmic movement. On the one hand, love is awakened by the overall beauty of the individuality of the other person; in loving I discover "how beautiful the world really is." On the other hand, I respond to this whole aspect of the world and of human existence that is disclosed to me as if for the first time.

A new door into the world of values is opened to me when I love. In loving I walk through this door and I respond to this new light. There exists a profound relation between this new contact with the world of the good and the beautiful that grows out of loving, and a certain "embodiment" of this world in the beloved person.

The "gift" of love as value-response and as "super value-response"

Finally, love is a value-response, for the "gift" of love, though not exclusively born out of the response to the overall beauty of the beloved person, as we have seen, still grows out of the response to the world of values and ultimately to God. The "best" in ourselves that we show to the beloved person cannot itself be detached from our overall response to the world of values. The "best" that we give in love, a gift that we have received, is of course latent in us before this love awakens; but it is profoundly nourished by all the value-responses that we have given, especially by all the superactual ones. For all these reasons, love is a value-response *par excellence* and is connected in the most various ways with the world of values, in spite of the fact that it, at least in its natural categories, is not morally obligatory and is not limited to morally relevant values, and in fact it is not even obligatory in the sense in which enthusiasm or veneration for a noble person is.

On the other hand, love is distinguished from all other value-responses by the fact that the "word" of love, or as we have called it, the "gift" of love does not derive exclusively from our response to the beauty of the beloved person and is thus in some ways more dependent on the nature of the lover than on the nature of the beloved. Love distinguishes itself, furthermore, from all deep value-responses by the fact that the beloved person is thematic as a whole person, that love refers to this person, and that the place of values in the overall beauty of the individual, great as it was in motivating love, recedes behind the person as such. Of course, the beloved person is resplendent with values and especially with his overall beauty, but love aims at him so much as this individual that our love could never be shaken by acknowledging that some other person may rank much higher in value. Indeed, even the fiction of some person possessing qualitatively the same overall beauty would not keep us from loving this unique individual, for whom no other person can be substituted.

Furthermore, in every one of the natural categories of love there is always, in addition to the value-response, a consciousness of a special affinity, of being made for one another, of having to do with one another—it is as if a special word were spoken by God between the two. This factor is not only decisive for coming to apprehend the overall beauty of the other, for being capable of the value-response of love, but it is also, apart from this function in love, an important factor in its own right, which is experienced as such even after love has come into being.

This becomes particularly clear when we consider, as mentioned above, that love goes far beyond all other value-responses. It contains a decision for the other, a kind of self-donation, which is not obligatory in the setting of the natural categories of love. Much as respect, admiration, enthusiasm, and veneration are required as due responses, this is not in the same way the case with love. We see this clearly in bringing in the duty of love of neighbor for comparison. Every human being as an image of God merits love of neighbor; and all the beauty, goodness, and value that we find in an individual person merits a corresponding esteem, veneration, and admiration. But the giving of one's heart in the case of love goes beyond that which is due in response to these values. It is evident from the fact, as we have already seen, that I can know many other persons who are equally worthy and yet can love only one of them with spousal love and love only a few as friends. Indeed, if in love I were strictly required to give value its adequate response, then it would be wrong for me to love a person spousally when there is someone else whom I revere even more, or to love someone as a friend when I revere this other more. This "independence" of love from the rank of the value is related to the fact that a particular affinity must be given, that God must have spoke, as it were, a particular word between the two. In all these natural categories of love there is an element of a "vocation" to love.

What we have said holds for the external aspect of love, that which belongs to its essence when looked at "from without."[12] But in loving I must have the consciousness that the other person deserves far more love than I can give. This is an example of how the internal and external aspects, the duality of which is so important for the essence of a response, as we said in the Introduction, seem to contradict each other. But this difference of aspects belongs to the nature of love. The "gift" of love goes beyond the due and required value-response, even if subjectively I have the consciousness of not doing justice to the call of value.

In conclusion, we want to stress that this going beyond the required response to values that we find in love does not really deviate from value-response, nor is it based on any factors opposed to value-response or on any that are just out of harmony with it. It rather grows so organically out of value-response that this "going beyond" represents an "super value-response." We will discuss this in greater detail in the next chapter.

Appendix on "value" and "good"

We can avoid all misunderstandings by once again discussing the relation of the concept of good and the concept of value, or at least the meaning that the two terms have in the present work and in my other works. By a good I understand any being having importance and capable of motivating an act of the will or an affective response according to one of the three categories of importance (the merely subjectively satisfying, the objective good for the person, and value). From this broad sense of good we have to distinguish the other sense according to which a good has value, or in other words has an importance that rests in itself. For our purposes it is important to bring out this latter concept of good in its relation to the concept of value. Value is that which makes these goods to be goods. A good by contrast is the whole real being in its value. An act of love of neighbor is a good on the basis of the special moral value that it embodies. A beautiful landscape is a good on the basis of the fact that it is beautiful. The beauty itself is a value. In a good, a value finds its realization.

The relation of a value to the good embodying it can vary greatly, as we have shown in our *Ethics*, chapter 10, where we distinguished between ontological and qualitative values. And within the qualitative values there is a great difference between the way in which visible and audible things bear aesthetic values and the way in which the acts of persons bear moral values, a difference

---

12 Cf. the introduction, p. 13, where I introduced the concepts of the external and internal aspect of acts.

to which we have referred in various essays, especially in our essay, "Beauty in the Light of the Redemption."[13] This difference is so great that the expression "bear" is used only analogously in these two cases. And so we see that we have to distinguish between good in the narrower sense, that is, good as a bearer of value, and the value itself.

Only in God, the *bonum absolutum*, is this difference transcended. God is the epitome of all value and is at the same time the absolute good. God is not only just, He is Justice itself; He is not only good, He is Goodness.

But it has to be above all affirmed that with this distinction between value and good we are in no way denying the foundation of value in the nature of the underlying goods. (We prescind here from the aesthetic values of visible and audible things, where a very special relation of grounding presents itself.) Both the ontological values as well as the qualitative values are grounded in the nature or character of the underlying being; the ontological in the enduring essence of a being, the qualitative in particular attitudes and qualities and the like. The sublime qualitative value of a deep love is grounded in the nature of this act, the qualitative value of purity is grounded in a certain way of acting on the part of a person. This intelligible relation of grounding has to be clearly distinguished from the question of the realization of values in a concrete case. For it is even found between a value and some behavior of a fictional person in a novel, although here there is no realization in the proper sense of the word. It is even found when I contemplate the nature of love in general and on this basis apprehend its distinctive value. It exists between the nature of a being and its value. But the realization that a value undergoes by an individual person acting in a certain way under certain circumstances, is something quite different from the general relation of some value being grounded in the nature of a good. This realization enriches the real world with something, it fulfills a requirement growing out of an ought. People ought to behave morally and when this happens in a particular case, there is a new value, a glorification of God, a fulfillment of what ought to be.

Value-responses, for the most part, refer to realized values, that is, to concrete goods. They are motivated by the value but they refer (in very different ways) to the good. But sometimes the fact that a value has been realized plays a decisive role for our motivation; sometimes this wonderful enrichment of the real world of history is responded to, as well as the specific value of the fulfillment of what ought to be.

But there is also a kind of value-response that refers to a not yet realized value. In meditating on love in general, we can not only be affected by its beauty, but can also respond to it. We can not only be touched by it, we can be enthused about it. The grounding of value in the good is, however, always presupposed. I cannot grasp the beauty of love without looking at love; I cannot

13   In our *The New Tower of Babel*.

contemplate justice without considering some just behavior, not indeed some concrete behavior, but rather the behavior that in general grounds justice.

The misunderstanding of values as forming a separate world of ideas derives from mistaking the distinction between value and good for a separation, and also from thinking that the grounding of value in the character of the underlying goods is being denied. And besides one confuses the essential relation of grounding with the concrete realization. The very fundamental importance of realization is in no way denied by the fact that we can give a value-response to values that are not yet real, nor by the fact that one acknowledges the "ideal existence" of values. The statement that justice is morally good remains valid and true independent of the question whether justice is realized in the world.

If in my works I frequently speak of "the world of values" rather than "the world of goods," this is not because we are referring to a world of mere ideas. We use the term "world of values" in order to point out that we are referring not only to values but to all possible future realizations of values and indeed even to the mode of being that values have independently of all realization. For there is such a thing as justice, even if no just person exists. The distinction between just and unjust would in this case not be eliminated, and the imperative to be just would remain valid. And this justice has its ultimate foundation in the infinite justice of God. The term "world of values" is therefore broader than the concept "world of goods," even if we only designate as a good that which bears some value.

A value-response always refers to some good. Though it is motivated by the value of the good, it refers to the good. But in the present context it is important to stress that it is motivated by the value realized in this good. Thus the moral imperative often issues from the morally relevant value realized in a concrete good.

But it would be false to say that a value-response can only respond to some concretely realized value of a good. Even if this is usually the case, there are yet certain value-responses motivated by a general value and without any thought of a concrete good. For a moral call issues from a not-yet-realized value, which of course is grounded in a good. The moral imperative to eliminate some evil, for instance, to put a stop to the bad influence of a person on someone else and to bring this other into an environment where he will be exposed to good influences, is grounded in the disvalue of bad influence and the value of good influence. Of course, the good which is not yet realized but will be realized, is built into reality; it links up with real people, a real situation, a real evil. But the good that I am supposed to realize is not yet real and all the same the imperative to realize it issues from its value.

Now there are also value-responses that neither respond to a real morally relevant good nor link up with one, but are rather motivated by the general value itself. Someone contemplating the nature of justice or purity can respond with reverence to its beauty and with joy to the fact that these values exist at all. Of course here the value-response presupposes that I in some way count on the metaphysical validity of the message qualitatively contained in these values and count on them having the last word in relation to all evil and all neutral powers of the world. A radical metaphysical pessimist would, on contemplating these values, find that the tragic aspect of the world is enlarged and so he would experience not joy but sadness and despair.

But when we speak of the ability to see value and of value blindness, we are thinking of apprehending the value itself and not of apprehending a good. Of course, insofar as a value is grounded in the nature of a good and insofar as it is a matter of ontological values, the understanding of value presupposes an understanding of the nature of the good. In order to understand the ontological value of a human being, we have to understand the nature of human beings as persons.

But when we think of the superactual general value-responses that underlie virtues,[14] then we have to do with the response to a general value type, to the value characterizing a whole domain. Of course even here a value is not *separable* from the goods corresponding to the values, but the response does not refer here to any concrete individual good.

14   See my *Ethics*, chapter 27.

CHAPTER FOUR

Love and Transcendence

The different dimensions of transcendence and of commitment
[*Hingabe*] within the sphere of value-response

If we are to understand in what sense love surpasses all other value-responses and takes on the character of a super value-response, we must first distinguish various dimensions of value-response in general. For the "more" that sets one kind of value-response above another can go in very different directions. As we have seen, veneration goes farther than admiration in appreciating a person; it represents a "more" in the sphere of value-response. But that is only *one* dimension of "more." We prescind here from the augmentation of a value-response that comes from the rank of the value of some good. The more sublime work of art, assuming that it is understood for what it really is, awakens a greater enthusiasm than some lesser work of art. This greater enthusiasm is a higher degree of enthusiasm, and in addition the "word" spoken in it is a qualitatively "higher" word. We prescind from these forms of "more" in a value-response, whether it be within the response of enthusiasm, admiration, veneration, or something else. What interests us is only the way in which a *type* of value-response can be more than some other *type*; for this is the kind of "more" that distinguishes love and that we have in mind when we call love a super value-response.

We want now to list briefly these dimensions of "more" and the different perfections that one kind of value-response has over against another kind; we will then offer a brief discussion of each dimension.

There is first of all a degree of commitment [*Hingabe*] and transcendence that is possessed only by responses to morally relevant goods and to moral values. The way in which the value-responses belonging to the moral sphere surpass all other value-responses is one important dimension of "more." It concerns the kind of transcendence and commitment. We will treat of this in a separate chapter. This is incumbent upon us since this "more" of commitment and transcendence that characterizes the moral value-responses is found only in love for God and in love of neighbor and not in the various natural categories of love.[1] This is a completely different "more" than the one that lets us call love

---

1   We will see in chapter 11 that the transcendence of a moral value-response in the setting of love of neighbor is not quite the same as in the case of moral value-

a super value-response. So as to clear the way for understanding the nature of love and the way it surpasses other value-responses, we will have first to elaborate this quite different dimension of "more" of commitment and transcendence that only value-responses in the moral sphere possess and that is possessed in the highest form in the love for God.

A second and quite different dimension of "more" in value-response is given when it is not only the will but also the heart that responds to the value. This "more" goes in the direction of the totality of the response; it is the dimension of involvement of the whole person. When we say "whole person," this should not be taken to mean that the value-response of the will is in some way only conditional and not a full value-response—this is by no means the case. It is precisely a special mark of the will that it can commit the whole person in a unique way. The fullness of commitment that comes with the involvement of the heart goes in quite a different direction. The "more" that is here at stake does not mean being more unconditional but rather being more complete. The opposite of this fullness is not a conditional commitment; rather, it is less fullness and warmth. This dimension of value-response is unfolded in love in a unique way, as we will see; love is the response of the heart *par excellence*. It contains an element of self-donation and in this way surpasses all other value-responses, even all other affective value-responses. We have already spoken of this in mentioning the "gift" of love. This dimension also belongs to the character of love as super value-response, but, as we are about to see, there are also many other dimensions of the "more" of love. We will come back to this dimension in a section of its own, even if only briefly, since we have already spoken about it more than once.

A third dimension of "more" in a value-response comes to light when the value, or rather the valuable good, confers some deep happiness on me. This dimension is related in various ways with the second one (the involvement of one's heart), and yet it is a dimension all its own. It touches upon the central problem of the relation between value and happiness, a problem to which we devote all of the following chapter. When is happiness thematic in a value-response or in being affected by the value of some good? Does the fact that happiness is a theme in all love (except in the case of love of neighbor) imply that the value-response character of love has been compromised? In the history of philosophy, we find quite opposed theories about the relation of value and happiness (as far as one can speak of value in these theories, for they lack any clear conception of value). Though we will treat this dimension above all with respect to love, there are still some general questions to be treated in this connection, as for example the role of the various value data in the sphere of value-response and being affected by values, and the various kinds of role that happiness can play here.

---

responses apart from love of neighbor. In chapter 12 we will see that analogies to this transcendence can be found even in the natural categories of love.

We will deal with a new and fourth dimension of "more" in the value-response of love when we see how a good on the basis of its value becomes an objective good for me in the full sense of the word. Only then do we reach the point at which love discloses itself as a super value-response.

Finally, a fifth and highly significant dimension of the "more" of the value-response of love is the intentio unionis, or desire for union with the beloved person, which involves a still deeper commitment to the value. This dimension is profoundly characteristic for love and in fact is strictly speaking found only in love. In general it is possible only in relation to certain goods, and properly speaking only in relation to persons. It is something of special significance when our interest in the value of a good goes so far that we desire union with it. This union is a theme of its own; it has its own value, and the yearning for it is inseparable from the movement toward the beloved person that we discussed above. The most important thing about this dimension of commitment, that is, of the value-responding interest embodied in the intentio unionis, is that this union is sought for the sake of the beauty and preciousness of the beloved person and not just for the sake of the incomparable happiness that it grants. This union is a theme all its own. We will devote an entire chapter to this dimension, that is, to the intentio unionis, because the "more" of value-response proper to it has often not been acknowledged, and because the desire for union was thought to involve some selfish disfigurement of the value-responding commitment of love. In this misunderstanding of the intentio unionis, we touch upon the source of some grievous errors about the nature of love.

The incomparable transcendence of moral value-response

The specifically moral value-response occupies a position all its own within the sphere of value-responses. By a moral value-response we will mean above all the response of the will to morally relevant goods, especially the response that fulfils an obligation to deal with morally relevant goods and to conform to them. The commitment and transcendence of a moral response appears in a particular way whenever a moral obligation is present either to prevent some evil by actively intervening, or to eliminate some already existing evil, or deliberately to omit the act of realizing some morally relevant evil. Here the response of the will involves a definite submission, indeed an element of obedience. This element of submission is related in a particular way to the nature of the morally relevant values, that is, to the moral relevance of these goods and the obligation resulting from them. We about to see this more clearly.

The commitment and transcendence of the moral value-response is intimately connected with the special relation existing between moral values, indeed the whole moral sphere, and God. Only moral evil offends God; intellectual disvalues like stupidity or superficiality do not offend Him, nor do the aesthetic disvalues of the ugliness or triviality of a work of art. Only in this sphere are there commands in the full sense of the word. A human being objectively obeys God in obeying these commands even if, being ignorant of the existence of God, he does not know that it is the voice of God that here speaks to him. Through this unique relation of moral values and disvalues to God—we see it in the glorification of God and in the offense given to God and in the divine imperative to do the morally right thing—the response of the will to morally relevant goods takes on a specific character of submission and obedience that is absent in all extra-moral value-responses, for instance, in the response of enthusiasm over a great work of art.

This form of commitment found in submission and obedience has to be clearly distinguished from the due relation [*Gebührenzbeziehung*] found with all values; it is discussed by us extensively in our *Ethics*, chapters 17 and 18. An adequate response is due to every good bearing value. In being enthused about some great work of art, we realize that our response is due to it and that whoever is insensitive to the work of art or thinks that it is bad, brings about, in addition to his personal failing, an objective disharmony by not fulfilling the due relation. But the consciousness that enthusiasm is due to this work of art, that it merits this response, is clearly different from the apprehension of a moral obligation. There is no *command* at work here. The incomparable seriousness of the moral sphere is missing; the voice of God does not speak imperatively from the work of art. That does not mean that the beauty of the work of art or the beauty of nature does not contain a message of God. This beauty, like all authentic values, is a reflection of the infinite glory of God. It, too, announces God and gives Him praise in a particular way. But just as this praise is distinct from the *glorification* of God, so this reflection of God in beauty is distinguished from the command of God in the moral sphere. We can now understand why the moral value-response possesses a commitment and a kind of transcendence that is missing in any extra-moral value-response. What surpasses the transcendence of being motivated by some value is the unique submission and the following of the divine imperative. What we find here and only here is the acceptance of the yoke, the actualization of the *similitudo Dei*. God speaks not only as the epitome of holiness and beauty, but He also speaks to us as the absolute Lord.

Does this hold for all morally good responses of the will or only for the obligatory ones? This is the question that we have now to ask, and the answer is: yes, it holds for all of them. The particular relation of the moral sphere to God remains here the same. Moral relevance remains fully intact even in the absence of any obligation. The meritorious and heroic actions that go beyond all obligation could never take on the character of a merely spontaneous "inclination" without losing their true moral character. If I rescue someone whose life is in danger, thereby risking my own life, it is only out of compassion that I can act for the other. In this case my action is of course morally good. We will return in some detail later to this motivation expressed by "for the other" and its moral importance. But if the question of moral relevance plays no role at all in my motivation, then the moral value of my life-saving action would be seriously weakened. Even though risking my own life keeps the life-saving action from being obligatory, I still have to act in the consciousness of doing what is morally right and good, and if I am a believer, of following an invitation of God.

With the heroic and meritorious acts of the saints, we find that the primacy of value over the objective good for the person is so strong that the very question whether something is obligatory or only meritorious does not even arise. It is typical for them to ask simply, is it pleasing to God? This is particularly clear in the case of the vow that St. Teresa of Avila made always to choose the more perfect course of action. In making such a vow one does not act with the motivation proper to love of neighbor, namely, the concern "for the other." But it is a typical expression of the love for God; it is an outpouring of the love that does not stop with fulfilling strict obligations or with avoiding the sin of omitting what is morally required. Just doing what one is obliged to do seems to the one who loves like an ungenerous way of acting, indeed like a thriftiness that borders on greed. But this does not blur the distinction between moral obligation and morally good but non-obligatory action, nor does it imply that moral relevance plays no role with the meritorious but non-obligatory actions. And so we can say that the unique nature of the moral value-response can even be found in the absence of any strict obligation; in this case, too, a value-response retains its special transcendence.

The involvement of the heart as an enhancement of the commitment within the moral value-response. We touch already here on the second main kind of "more" in a value-response, namely, the involvement of the heart. We will discuss it below, but here we treat of it mainly with a view to showing that the cooperation of the heart does not compromise the transcendence and commitment that is proper to the moral value-response. Of course, we are also referring here to the "more" and to the particular perfection that this cooperation of the heart can confer on the moral value-response. We are not yet talking about the intensification that a value-response always undergoes through the involvement of the heart and that is not limited to the moral sphere. We are restricting ourselves to the moral value-response. We mention this new dimension of "more" in a moral value-response, namely, the involvement of the heart, only to distinguish it from the "more" of transcendence and commitment that is proper to the moral value-response.[2] But by showing the additional excellence that the involvement of the heart brings to the moral value-response, we clear the way for understanding the dimension of totality and fullness as such.

---

2 Although this affective involvement is not being discussed at present as an intensification of value-response as such—of the value-response that is not limited to the moral sphere and that therefore has to be distinguished from the new dimension of "more" found in the moral value-responses with their characteristic transcendence and commitment—we see here clearly how this affective involvement enhances value-response as such.

If we are to understand rightly the specific kind of commitment of value-responses within the moral sphere we have to free ourselves from various traditional misunderstandings.

Kant's mistake of identifying moral obedience with the struggle against illegitimate hindrances. The first misunderstanding is the erroneous identification of the gesture of submission, the element of obedience, with the effort of struggling against the moral hindrances set up in our nature by pride and concupiscence. This was one of the great mistakes in the ethics of Kant. He rightly affirms the ultimate seriousness of morality, the gesture of submission, of obedience, the consciousness of a unique kind of obligation; but he identifies all of this with the overcoming of the moral hindrances of our nature. He regarded the effortlessness of virtuous action as incompatible with this commitment. According to him spontaneity and morality exclude each other. All spontaneity is taken as inclination and is set over against duty. Inclination is seen in the light of some unfree tendency of our nature and this tendency is in turn identified with the desire for pleasure—with the desire for the satisfaction of our instincts, with appetitus, with the desire for the subjectively satisfying; and such spontaneity is for Kant incompatible with freedom, even if this is less stressed by him.

Aristotle's confusion of the effortlessness of virtue with that of habit. Aristotle rightly stressed the effortlessness of the good action of a virtuous person and acknowledged the particular value of this effortlessness, but he confused it with the almost automatic character proper to actions performed out of habit and routine. He compares a virtuous person with a good harp player who plays his piece without effort and without having to think explicitly about it, who has practiced so much that his fingers almost play by themselves. That is a serious error. As I showed in my *Ethics*, effortlessly performed good action is the very opposite of an activity done by habit. A virtuous action is always a fully consciously motivated and freely willed action; the effortlessness of it is only a result of the fundamental attitude of moral value-response victoriously overcoming by free moral striving all the hindrances of pride and concupiscence. Not only are the two kinds of effortlessness entirely different in their origin, they are also qualitatively altogether different from each other. The spontaneity has an entirely different character in both cases, indeed the term "effortlessness" means something entirely different in these two cases. If a virtuous person could perform objectively good actions out of habit, as it were automatically, in the way in which he almost automatically winds his watch in the evening—we are assuming of course an intrinsically *impossible* fiction—then such action would be completely deprived of its moral value and we would have to draw the paradoxical conclusion that being virtuous deprives a person of the possibility of performing morally good actions, that is, actions that enrich the person with moral values. But this conclusion was drawn neither by Aristotle nor by St. Thomas, since they, despite their wrong interpretation of the effortlessness of virtuous action, did not consistently think of it as an almost unconscious and automatic event.

The confusion of the effortlessness of virtue with extra-moral motives for right action. But even prescinding from the Aristotelian confusion of moral effortlessness with the automatic character that certain activities acquire as a result of habit, the concept of effortlessness can vary considerably. If the effortlessness comes from the fact that someone is motivated by extramoral reasons to do an objectively good action, then he clearly destroys the moral value of his action. Suppose that someone courageously stands up for an innocent person, because he hopes to be mentioned in the newspapers and perhaps by means of his good reputation to win an election. Then clearly the courageous act of standing up for the innocent person, in itself morally good, is deprived of its moral motivation; it ceases to be a value-response and becomes instead a self-centered desire by which the person simply uses as a means an objectively good moral action. If Kant in speaking of inclination were thinking of such cases, then he would be quite right to say that only those actions done not from inclination but from duty have moral value. But the ease with which a virtuous person performs a morally obligatory action in no way derives from the intrusion of motives foreign to the morally relevant value. This ease is rather a victory of the fundamental moral attitude (which is a superactual value-response to all that is morally relevant) over all the hindrances deriving from pride and concupiscence. The reason for this ease is that the entire person has been penetrated by the primacy of morally relevant values over all other goods and above all over all that is merely subjectively satisfying for him. In the case of a religious person we have to do with a victory of the love of God over everything else. This effortlessness is an intensification of the moral value and is in no way a diminishment of it. It is in no way based on the intrusion of other motives that would compromise the value-response; on the contrary, the effortlessness arises from the habitual superactual moral value-response penetrating the whole person.

Confusing virtue with what makes it easily observable by others. Of course, if we perform a moral action by first overcoming with our will a great moral hindrance, it is easier to observe that our motivation was free of extra-moral motives and of an interest in the merely agreeable. But this ease in observing virtuous actions is not something that objectively makes for moral value. Objectively, the only decisive thing is being motivated simply by the morally relevant value. As long as this is intact, then from the moral point of view the effortlessness is entirely positive. But it should also be said that this holds only for the effortlessness that derives from virtue.

The "ease" of virtue and the "difficulty" involved in making a sacrifice: two different dimensions of moral commitment. For there is another possible reason for effortlessness in acting besides virtue or the presence of extra-moral motives, or even being just motivated by the merely subjectively satisfying.

There are certain temperamental dispositions, in themselves morally neutral, that can make the performance of a moral action more or less difficult. It is obviously more difficult for a shy person to challenge publicly some injustice than it is for one who is not shy. The situation, for example, of being morally obliged to expose publicly some slanderer, is more difficult for the shy person than for the person who is in no way shy. The effortlessness of one who is not shy is in no way a moral excellence. The moral motivation can be equally pure with or without having to overcome some such temperamental hindrance. But the same action performed by the shy person has a somewhat greater moral value insofar as it is a sign for the degree of one's commitment to morality. Here we touch upon an entirely new point of view that is important for the moral value of an action: the degree of commitment to the moral imperative and ultimately to God, the unconditional character of this commitment. The point at which a person says, "It is impossible," is in general very characteristic for that person. For example, someone may be willing enough to resist some injustice, but only as long as his resistance does not really endanger him. An essential criterion for the rank of moral value is the unconditioned-ness of the will, the strength of commitment, the absolute primacy of morality over everything else. We have already discussed this in our *Ethics*.

The degree of a person's commitment shows itself above all in the sacrifices that he is willing to make in following the moral imperative. Here we have to take care to understand the term sacrifice in its full and authentic meaning. A sacrifice is only the voluntary renunciation of some legitimate good for myself or the voluntary taking on of some objective evil for myself. So to fight against pride and concupiscence in ourselves is no real sacrifice, for here we have to do with something morally negative that I ought to give up on account of its negativity. It is a real sacrifice if a missionary gives up all comfort in life in order to win souls for Christ. It is a real sacrifice if I give up or renounce some great objective good for myself, even to the point of risking my own life, in order to save another person or to give my life as a martyr for Christ. In some cases a particular deed is no longer morally obligatory if it can only be performed at the expense of sacrificing my life, or at least of risking the loss of it. But in other cases, I am obliged even to the point of sacrificing my own life. If, for example, someone tries to coerce me with threats to my life to commit a sin (a case that often enough occurred in Communist countries or in Nazi Germany), then I am obliged to lose my life rather than commit the sin.

But performing a moral action that includes some real sacrifice, some renunciation of a legitimate good, always serves to increase the moral value of the action, because it clearly actualizes an unconditional and unbounded commitment and is a sign for the degree of the commitment.[3]

---

3   Of course this commitment can be present in the absence of any opportunity of

Of course, the subjective attachment (we are thinking of a rightly ordered attachment) to the legitimate good that is freely given away in the sacrifice is also an important factor. For example, cutting one's sleep back to a minimum is subjectively a much greater sacrifice for one individual than it is for another.

As we have already mentioned, the degree of one's commitment can be seen by considering which obstacles in my individual makeup have to be overcome when I do what is morally required, or even what is not strictly required but is still morally good. We mentioned the shy person. This is not a case of a typical sacrifice, but it has something in common with the readiness to make a real sacrifice in doing the morally good thing: that which has to be overcome is not in itself morally bad, but is only a temperamental disposition that is neither morally good nor bad. Here too we find that the same action that costs the shy person a great effort and costs the person who is not shy no such effort, is a sign of greater commitment when performed by the shy person and is also an actualization of a greater commitment and is thus more meritorious.

But how can the effortlessness of virtue follow from a greater degree of commitment to the good and from love for the good if in the case of sacrifice or the above-mentioned temperamental disposition the overcoming of hindrances is a sign of and an actualization of a more unconditional commitment to and love for the good? This is at first glance surprising. How can first the difficulty and then the ease and effortlessness be a sign of and actualization of the unconditional commitment to the morally good? The paradox is resolved as soon as we realize that we have here two different dimensions of commitment. In the one case we have to do with the primacy of value and of moral obligation within the sphere of individual actions, and here the action requiring some sacrifice gives evidence *ceteris paribus* of a greater commitment than does the action requiring no such sacrifice. We find something analogous when the purely temperamental dispositions make the morally good action more difficult. Now the victory that is expressed in the ease of virtue consists in the removal of all obstacles to a pure value-response; it is the full penetration of the whole person with the moral value-response, or better, with the love for God. If I do something for God's sake that I find difficult to do either for neutral reasons or for quite legitimate ones, so that in doing it I give evidence of the degree of my moral commitment, this commitment is different from the commitment in which I have no more illegitimate obstacles to overcome and in which the love of God can unfold without

—————————————

    making a great sacrifice in the performance of some good action; a St. Francis of Assisi loves God no less than a martyr does.

4   St. Thomas Aquinas expresses something similar in a wonderful way: "To love one's enemy is better than to love one's friend, because it shows a greater love of God. But if we consider both of those acts in themselves, it is better to love the friend than the enemy and it is better to love God than one's friend. It is not the

impediment.[4] This latter fullness of commitment is shown in the fact that not only the will but also the heart gives the moral value-response to God. Both dimensions work together as the climax of unconditional commitment, even if the sacrifice that I make—which should pain me and to which I should not become insensitive—is gladly accepted, as with the martyrs. Then we see raised to the highest power the unconditional commitment and the general victory of love for God.

We have seen that the ease of the virtuous person in performing a good action in no way diminishes the moral value of the action but rather increases it. To show this we had first to distinguish this ease both from the "facility" deriving from habit and enabling some activity to be performed almost by itself, automatically, as well as from all inclination deriving from the interference of extra-moral motives. We have also seen that a particular value accrues to a moral action that is performed with an unconditional commitment as a result of some sacrifice made by the person performing the action. But we have seen that this is no argument against the fact that authentic effortlessness enhances the moral value of an action. We have here two different dimensions of the unconditionality of value-responding commitment and of the victory of moral value-response.

The involvement of the heart as further enhancement of value-response

We now turn to the second dimension of "more" in a value-response: the involvement of the heart. We will limit ourselves for now to the importance of this dimension in the moral sphere.

The affective moral value-response as a new dimension of the morally good. Consider the victory of the attitude of moral value-response over pride and concupiscence, over all that impedes a full moral commitment to the morally good, a victory that is won to a degree by the virtuous person and is won fully by the saint. It is clear that this victory includes the full involvement of the heart. The virtuous person not only wants the good, he also loves it; he rejoices over the good prevailing, whether this comes about by his fulfilling his moral obligation, or by having the opportunity to do meritorious deeds, or even by other persons acting morally well. Already Aristotle saw this when he said in his *Nicomachean Ethics* that the good man not only wants the good but also rejoices over it. And St. Augustine expresses the same thing at a much higher level when he says of following the commands of God: "*Parum voluntate,*

---

difficulty of loving one's enemy that makes it meritorious, but the perfection of love is made manifest by prevailing over this difficulty. If therefore love were so perfect as to eliminate completely the difficulty, it would be even more meritorious." *Questiones disputatae de caritate*, 8, ad 17. And in another place St. Thomas says, "The essence of virtue lies more in the good than in the difficult." *Summa Theologica*, II-II, q. 123, a. 12, ad 2.

etiam voluptate trahimur" ("It is not enough for us to be moved by the will, we must also be moved by delight").[5]

But we have to distinguish the commitment of the will from the involvement of the heart as soon as we are dealing not with the whole person of the virtuous man who has achieved the effortlessness of doing good, but are dealing only with an individual moral action. There are persons who have a strong will and a great sense of duty and who prefer to make any sacrifice rather than not fulfill their moral duty. Such persons are particularly conscientious. This is certainly a great moral value. Let us compare two persons. One of them is ready to do what is morally required and even what is morally desirable but not required, no matter how great the sacrifice. The other, by contrast, is ready to do the same things but only up to a certain point, that is, as long as he does not have to make any serious sacrifice. The greater and more unconditional commitment in the will of the first does not necessarily include the involvement of the heart. There are extremely conscientious persons who have with their will a great unconditional commitment to morality but who do not have full love and joy, or who do not give any affective value-response. In the religious sphere, too, there is the type of person who obeys God with great conscientiousness and who does this with a great force of the will, but who still does not have a full love for God such as we find it in the saints.

In dealing with an individual action and not with the whole person, we have to distinguish between the unconditional commitment of the will and the involvement of the heart. The fullness of the commitment of the will is decisive for the moral value of an action and the moral status of a person; but the victory evidenced in the involvement of the heart is a still further step, a new dimension augmenting and elevating in a significant way the moral value of the action and above all the moral value of the whole person.

Heart and freedom—Kant's confusion of affective moral value-response with extra-moral inclination. We encounter here a further error of Kant's. When he confuses effort with pure motivation, as we saw, he regards every involvement of the heart, which he takes to be mere inclination, as incompatible with being motivated by moral duty (we would say, motivated by the morally relevant good).

But the affective value-responses to moral values differ from the response of the will in that they do not lie in the realm of our direct freedom and control. Only the will has this unique perfection; only it is free in the sense of directly positing the act and in the sense of its power of initiating a new causal chain. The affective responses do not have this perfection. They arise spontaneously; they can neither be called into being by us, as the will can be, nor can they be commanded by our will in the way in which bodily movement or the activity of speaking can be commanded. This spontaneity of joy, of

---

5   St. Augustine, *Tractate 26 on the Gospel of St. John.*

enthusiasm, of sadness, of compassion makes for a significant contrast with the freedom of the will. But as we showed in our *Ethics*, this spontaneity in no way implies an antithesis to freedom, as causation does. The way in which, for example, one idea evokes another by association, or in which mental exertion brings about exhaustion, is directly opposed to freedom, for here the meaningful conscious relation to an object implied by free will is missing; when we freely decide to do something on the grounds that it is morally required and good, this meaningful conscious relation to an object that is based on some knowledge is present. In the case of pure causation, this meaningful relation is missing. Furthermore, one thing being causally produced by another forms a radical contrast to the absolutely new initiation of a causal chain through our will, a contrast to the capacity of the will to act through itself.

The spontaneity of the affective value-responses, by contrast, forms an antithesis to freedom insofar as it lacks the control and the acting through one's self that characterizes the will. But the affective value-responses share with the will the conscious meaningful relation to the object, the motivation by value. In addition, they are never beyond our freedom in the manner of physiological and psychological causal connections that unfold by themselves, for the affective responses can be sanctioned by our free personal center, indeed they call for this and they lie in the realm of our indirect freedom. Thus we are responsible for their absence; not as if we could indirectly command them, as with certain causal physiological events, for example, the removal of a headache by taking aspirin, but we can gradually and indirectly remove the obstacles to them in a manner that is analogous to the acquisition of virtues, which after all are also not subject to our direct control. We have spoken about all of this not only in our *Ethics*, but also in our book *The Heart*. The important thing here is to remember that the spontaneity of the affective value-responses, different as it is from the freedom that is proper to the will, does not deprive them of their capacity for having moral values. On the contrary, in the case of a good action joyfully performed, the joy, assuming that it is a real value-response, joins organically together with the response of the will, and the spontaneity of this affective value-response, far from diminishing the freedom of a response of the will, augments the moral value. The superactual free response of the will in which the decision for the good and for God is made—this free fundamental direction of the person to God—makes itself felt not only in the actual response of the will but also in the value-response of the heart. Thus we can say of the joyful response of the will: *even* his heart belongs to God, and he is directed to God even in a spontaneous way.

This spontaneity is, in the final analysis, a fruit of freedom, even though it is at the same time also a gift; it is a fruit of freedom insofar as it is based upon triumph of the free fundamental attitude of the person over all the obstacles to the love for God.

For our purposes, however, the important thing is that the unique commitment and transcendence proper to the moral value-response does not extend only to the moral response of the will but also to the affective moral value-response. Even the affective value-response is performed with full awareness of the incomparable seriousness of the moral sphere and of all the traits of this sphere which we discussed above. The affective value-response exists in the realm of moral imperatives, of the glorification of God, of the act of submitting one's self to God, and of the consciousness of how dreadful sin is. For in these affective moral responses, which in the actions are united with the will, the element of obedience is in no way absent; the spontaneity involves no shaking off of the "yoke" of the moral ought. The love for God does not eliminate the obedience to God but rather perfects it in a quite particular way. It goes beyond obedience but does not extinguish it; it contains it *per eminentiam.*

Contemplative affective value-responses. But does this hold even for the affective value-responses that do not accompany the will in some action and that we have called the contemplative value-responses? For there is undoubtedly a great difference between an action, a decision of the will, and the contemplative situation of the affective value-responses. It is a special kind of situation when I am challenged to intervene with an action and to make some decision of the will. And this is not limited to positive actions but is found as well in a conscious and deliberate act of omission. The appeal issued to my direct freedom by the morally relevant goods and evils, whether the appeal be in the form of an obligation or only of an invitation, is not present in the same way when I hear of the morally heroic deed of some other person, which merits a response of joy and enthusiasm. When an action is required, I am personally engaged in a unique way. I am called upon in conscience to do the morally good thing and even more to omit what is bad and evil. Here there is a unique kind of confrontation with God; we mentioned already the voice of God in the moral imperative. Now, is this personal engagement, this same kind of appeal to my conscience found also in the contemplative situations in which I ought to give the due affective response to the moral values in the actions of other persons and also to the triumph of the good in its many forms? Here the appeal is made to my heart and not directly to my will.

Of course, in the case of the response to God's infinite holiness and goodness, the different ways of responding to creaturely values is transcended. In the love for God that is required of us, the appeal is directed to the whole man, will and heart, and so is the personal engagement. So we limit ourselves here to the response to moral and morally relevant values within the finite world and within our earthly situation. We mean by this our situation *in statu viae* (as earthly pilgrims), for in the situation of eternity of which St. Augustine says, "Behold we will rest and we will see," all intervention by way of actions is surpassed and there remains only the contemplative situation. But let us return to the distinction as it is found here on earth in the world known to us by experience, the distinction between appealing to our will and appealing to our heart. We want to limit ourselves here to pure value-responses and to set aside for now the morally so important motivation based on sharing in the life of another person and entering in to what some event means for the other. We will later discuss in detail this dimension of love, which represents a kind of transcendence all its own.

Let us compare these two cases. One person hears about the action of Sister Maria in Auschwitz and is deeply moved by this action and is filled with admiration for its moral greatness. This being moved and being filled with admiration is itself a morally worthy way of acting. Another person hears about it and remains insensitive and indifferent; this person betrays an amoral attitude and his or her conduct is morally regrettable. But in hearing about the deed of Sister Maria no one is challenged to make a decision. The one who is gripped by the action of Sister Maria and who admires it, despite the tragic circumstances, rejoices that so heroic a deed was performed; this person surely has the awareness that an affective response is due to this deed and that he would behave in a shabby way if he were just to ignore it and move on to the next item of business. He is aware of the appeal made to his heart, an appeal issuing from God. But it is not an appeal to make a decision, for *him* to make a decision. And the one who does not react as he feels he should react will regret and disavow his present insensitivity. But a situation calling for a decision is not given. The person whose character is morally insensitive will not experience any call, he will notice nothing; whereas if he is called to a response of the will, he at least notices that he is challenged to make a decision.

But in spite of the essential difference between the contemplative value-responses and the responses of the will that belong to actions, the unique commitment and transcendence proper to all value-responses given to moral or morally relevant goods, are also to be found with the contemplative responses to these goods. We have already seen that this commitment and transcendence are found in the affective value-responses that accompany an action. Now we have to understand that such commitment and transcendence are also found in the affective contemplative value-responses, even if in a modified form. Even if some characteristics of an action are missing, such as the imperative in the strict sense, being personally challenged, the full burden of responsibility, still the appeal that is made here to our heart has a distinctly moral character and distinguishes itself from the general requirement to give a due value-response to all those goods that have value. Here too the majesty of morality and its unique relationship with God is grasped, here too one "looks upwards" in a particular way. Of course, the character of a "yoke" and of a specific obedience recedes here, but not the gesture of submission and not the unique commitment and transcendence. We have only to compare enthusiasm over some great work of art with enthusiasm for the moral behavior of a person, and then we see that even this contemplative affective value-response to the moral value possesses the incomparable commitment and transcendence, even if not in the same way as the moral action.

Commitment in the extra-moral value-responses. Now that we have seen that the unique commitment and transcendence of morality is found both in the moral responses of the will and in the moral affective responses (this despite the difference between them), we have now to turn to the kind of commitment contained in all extra-moral value responses.

We have already pointed out the difference between the due relation that exists with everything of value, on the one hand, and the imperative that issues only from the morally relevant values and from the moral values, on the other. We now have to see that when the yoke of obligation, of the moral imperative drops away, there remains a kind of spontaneity that clearly differs from the spontaneity of affective moral value-responses. The will is not centrally important here, even if these responses do not thereby lie outside the reach of our freedom. Think of the admiration for a great work of art or the admiration for some great thinker (we are assuming that the work of art and the thinker objectively merit this response). There is a certain acknowledgement, a purely appreciative value-response that is in a way within the realm of my freedom, assuming that the value of the work of art and the greatness of the thinker have been disclosed to me, which in turn presupposes certain gifts in me (for the absence of which I am not responsible). But if I have this talent and clearly see the value, then it does lie in my freedom to give the due response[6] and not to evade it on the grounds that I do not feel like recollecting myself deeply, or on the grounds that I would rather just deal with things that are entertaining in a superficial way, or simply gratify my craving for the sensational. For all great aesthetic values appeal to the depth in myself; at the least they call upon me to free myself from my preoccupation with the merely subjectively satisfying and with my own interests, as well as from the tension of a pragmatic attitude. And if I respond with admiration to this beauty, being mindful of the value and the due relation that are at stake and letting myself be motivated by that which is important in itself, then I achieve a noble *objectivity* that represents a definite form of transcendence. There is a certain looking up in reverence, a certain commitment in acknowledging and responding to this beauty, but the factors of submission and obedience, which in some form or other penetrate the entire moral sphere, are here missing.

We have to distinguish here two types of response to extra-moral values. There are persons who are very objective and have the ability to take a deep interest in all goods with genuine value, and this even when these goods stand

---

6   The role of freedom stands out with particular clarity if the great thinker or artist is a rival of mine or if he is for whatever reason an enemy of mine.

in no relation to the satisfaction of their needs. In all the areas in which these people have the corresponding organ of cognition, they are impressed by value-bearing goods; they turn to them giving them the due response. This value-response is motivated by the intrinsic importance of the good and so has the character of transcending a merely immanent concern with what they need or with what they find pleasing. They may have great understanding for the values in many different areas, as for the beauty of nature and art, for the depth and truth of an insight, or for the great stature of some thinker. Within this type there are many differences in regard to reverence and to one's stance towards the whole word of values. But the relation of a thorough-going aesthete to some work of art, the beauty of which he enjoys like a good wine, falls outside of real value-response. Though he is a connoisseur and registers subtle differences, he misunderstands the intrinsic importance of values. This is why we prescind here entirely from him, for he obviously lacks any and every form of transcendence and commitment.

But there are also persons who penetrate to the message of God lying in the extra-moral values. We are thinking of persons who find in all great natural truth a message of Him who is the Truth, of persons who in the profound insights found in a dialogue like the *Phaedo* of Plato are overwhelmed by the radiance of a world above us and are deeply moved by the nobility of truth. In the same way, there are persons who penetrate to the solemn mystery of the beauty of nature and of the great works of art, finding in them a reflection of the eternal absolute beauty of God. These persons reach the point at which the extra-moral qualitative values reveal their kinship with moral values, the point at which the deep inner connection of beauty, truth, and goodness is made manifest. The value-response of these persons to extra-moral values clearly possesses quite another degree of commitment and transcendence than we found in the first type of person. Such value-response is still to be distinguished from the commitment and transcendence of a moral value-response, and yet admiration, joy, as well as being affected and touched take on here the character of reverence, of humility, of looking upwards, and so are invested with a great dignity. Here the due relation is fully developed, here the *mirandum* (something worthy of being marveled at) and *admirandum* (something worthy of being admired) organically calls us to the praise of God and makes us aware of the silent praise of God coming from these natural goods. "*Quam magnificata sunt opera tua, Domine!*" ("How wonderful are your works, O Lord!")

As we said, the spontaneity proper to the affective value-responses to extra-moral values forms no antithesis at all to the consciousness of giving value its due. Just as the understanding of these values (this often presupposes some particular organ of cognition, as we said) is a gift, so the affective response arises by itself once the values have been grasped and is not a result of our will, not even of the freedom proper to the will. Of course, we can turn away from the value-bearing beings; our pride, our superficiality, our laziness can make us closed to values. This is why we can, as we said above, be responsible for not fulfilling the due relation. But once the value is grasped, then assuming the absence of any impediments for which we are responsible, the value-response as well as the being affected comes by itself; it is a gift, indeed a being overwhelmed by value, so that one cannot do otherwise than respond to it. This spontaneity forms, therefore, an extreme antithesis to the response of the will that fulfills the moral imperative *à contre cœur*. But it forms just as sharp a contrast to all arbitrariness, to all letting one's self be carried away by passions, or to the spontaneity of instinct.

We will see later that value-response in the various categories of natural love, in contrast to the love for God, is an extra-moral value-response and stands much closer to the response to extra-moral values, notwithstanding its various relations to morality.

The involvement of the heart in love as a new dimension of commitment. We have seen that the particular transcendence of value-response in the moral sphere is not proper to the natural categories of love (love for one's parents, for one's children, for one's friend, for one's siblings, spousal love). But as for the second dimension of "more," the augmentation of value-response deriving from the involvement of the heart, it is nowhere so developed as in love, and in fact in every category of love. We saw above that love goes much further than admiration or veneration. It "gives" incomparably more, and in this unique self-giving, this incomparable turning to another person, the dimension of "more" based on the heart is all-important. Only in love is there a giving of the heart, though this varies very much according to the degree and category of love. But this giving away of the heart clearly goes much further than that involvement of the heart of which we spoke in the previous chapter in connection with the joy found within the moral sphere.

We saw above that the effortlessness and the spontaneity of the virtuous person in performing moral actions make for an augmentation of the value-response in a certain way and are the bearers of a high value. We also saw that this spontaneity forms no contrast to freedom. In addition we spoke of the spontaneity of the affective moral value-response and of the fact that it does not lie in our direct control, that affective value-responses do not have that freedom that the will has, but that this does not mean that they fall completely outside our freedom. But with love this spontaneity, with its gift character, this arising on its own, takes on a particular meaning. The more this is the case, the more authentic is love and the greater is the gift given in love to the beloved person. Of course, the free sanction of this love belongs necessarily to the full self-donation. But this does not change the fact that love itself does not arise from a free choice, but arises on its own as a gift, as Eva says in a wonderful way in Wagner's opera *Die Meistersinger*, "I had to love, I was forced to it."

In Part I of my book, *The Heart*, in chapter 8, I pointed out that in certain domains of life, as in the moral domain, the will is the real and valid self; but in other domains it is the heart that is the real self. Now in love it is the word of the heart that expresses the unique self-donation.

And here the "more" of value-response is clearly given that distinguishes love from all other affective responses and also from the response of the will. It is the dimension of "more" that lies in the fact that the *heart* gives the value-response in a unique way. This dimension does not characterize a whole sphere, like the above mentioned submission that is found only in the moral sphere, but it is an augmentation that occurs in all spheres of value-response. It reaches its high point in the love for God, where this dimension is joined with all the others.

For us it suffices here to see clearly that love, though distinguished in all its forms by a unique spontaneity and characterized by a donation of the heart, is not thereby deprived of its character as value-response.

Although natural love, in contrast to love for God, does not possess that dimension of commitment and transcendence proper only to value-responses in the moral sphere, it possesses a unique perfection with respect to totality and fullness. It is in respect of the involvement of the heart the queen of value-responses, and this dimension of "more" is one of the factors constituting love as a super value-response.

CHAPTER FIVE

Value and Happiness

Above we recognized that a value-response becomes "more" in a certain way when the good to which I respond confers happiness on me by its value, or more precisely when my happiness is thematic in my relation to the good, even if in a secondary way. In the history of philosophy we sometimes encounter the view that my love is no longer selfless and no longer a thing of real self-donation as soon as my happiness becomes important. It is well known that Kant thought that any concern with happiness in the moral life diminishes moral value. On the other hand, happiness is granted the decisive and central place in all forms of eudaemonism. It is not our task here to subject these two opposite views to a thorough critical analysis. But in order to see that happiness, when it becomes thematic in love, does not destroy the value-response character of love but rather enhances it, we have briefly to explore the general relation between happiness and value.

The confusion of self-centered happiness with authentic happiness

There is a disastrous error that must be avoided right from the beginning, namely, failing to acknowledge the fundamental difference between pleasurable goods and those goods that are the source of deep happiness. We have already mentioned this in chapter 1, where we showed how one thereby obstructs from the outset any understanding of the nature of love; one does this, as we showed, by taking the desire for some good food, or the attachment to merely subjectively satisfying goods, as a primitive analogy for love. We encounter again and again in the history of philosophy this way of proceeding. The failure to distinguish the two radically different kinds of happiness, self-centered happiness and authentic happiness, renders impossible any understanding of the true relation between value and happiness that concerns us here. For the equivocal use of the term "happiness" leads inevitably either to thinking that the happiness flowing from value is a kind of pollution of the value-response attitude—and this view would be justified if this happiness were a self-centered happiness—or else it leads, as in the many forms of eudaemonism, to granting too much of a place to self-centered happiness in ethics.

Furthermore, this equivocation leads to regarding the value-bearing good as a means to happiness, a view that is justified with merely subjectively satisfying goods, which really are only a means for attaining to self-centered happiness. With this one lends support to the disastrous idea that in love the beloved person functions only as a means for my happiness, an idea that has unfortunately been often accepted, even though it represents perhaps the most radical of all misconceptions of love. It is especially important for us in our examination of the nature of love to understand this consequence flowing from the equivocal use of the term happiness and of the term good, and also from the failure to understand the radical difference between value-bearing goods and goods that are merely subjectively satisfying. As a consequence of these equivocations one radically misconceives the true nature of love by saying that the beloved person is a means to the end of my happiness.

When should happiness play a role?

But our subject here is the issue of the manifold relations between happiness and value. We can formulate the question of the relation of value and happiness like this: when is happiness, in the sense of authentic happiness, which includes joy, when is it in any way thematic in our relation to value-bearing goods? And when we say "thematic," we mean this: when does happiness objectively belong to the meaning of our relation to values, when may and should it play some role?

1. *The existence of goods as objectively gladdening [erfreulich].* First of all, the existence of everything having value, the existence of all value-bearing goods is objectively gladdening, just as the existence of all evils, of all that has disvalue, is objectively saddening [*traurig*], that is, the opposite of gladdening. For example, the existence of a noble person or the fact that someone performs a morally worthy action, such as an act of generous forgiveness, is objectively gladdening. It is also objectively gladdening when someone converts to the true faith, whereas it is objectively saddening when he falls away from the true faith, or when someone does something morally bad. It is objectively gladdening that there exist great works of art, such as The Slaves of Michelangelo, the Palazzo Farnese, Beethoven's *Fidelio*, or Shakespeare's *King Lear*.

One could object that this quality of the objectively gladdening even in the mentioned examples is only something potentially gladdening *for persons*. The existence of great works of art, for example, is an objective gift for us. The character of being objectively gladdening is therefore nothing other than an expression of the fact that these value-bearing goods are, on the basis of their value, also objective goods for the person and that they have the capacity to confer happiness on whoever understands them. The objectively gladdening, according to this objection, has only the objectivity that an objective good for the person has in contrast to the merely subjectively satisfying. It is not something inhering in a state of affairs without any reference to a person, like the *value*, the importance in itself of a state of affairs.

This objection is surely valid in many of the cases in which we speak of gladdening and saddening events. If we say that the recovery of a woman is gladdening for the husband who loves her, we are surely aiming at the objective importance that this event has for the husband. But in no way does that mean that there is not also an entirely objective quality of gladdening and saddening in events; in thinking about this quality we are not thinking about the importance that the same event can have as an objective good or evil for the person. An event can be, given its values, gladdening in itself (or given its disvalues, saddening in itself), and then the relation to the person lies only in the fact that joy is the required and due response to it, that the event is a *gaudendum* (something worthy of rejoicing).

It goes without saying that all objective goods for the person are objectively gladdening *for* them. That is almost an analytic proposition. The very concept of an objective good for a person includes some relation to the person's interest, advantage, or happiness. We say of this gift character of the objective goods for the person that these are objectively gladdening for the person, and not that they always have to gladden persons. For it happens all too often that people chase after illegitimately subjectively satisfying goods, goods appealing to the negative centers of pride and concupiscence, and that they fail entirely to appreciate the true objective goods for the person. What makes some good an objective good for the person does not depend on how much persons find it to be gladdening, but above all on what it objectively means for their happiness and salvation, what kind of objective good for them it is.

What concerns us here is the question: is there only the objective gladdening quality that a state of affairs possesses as an objective good for a person, or can the state of affairs be objectively gladdening *in itself* and not just *for someone*? Let us think of the case of someone converting to God. This fact is surely a great objective good for the one who converts. It is therefore objectively gladdening *for* him. But if we call this event gladdening in the case of someone not particularly close to us and not loved by us, of someone who is a stranger, then we are clearly aiming primarily not at what is gladdening *for* him, or, in other words, at the objective good that the conversion is for him, but rather at a quality that this state of affairs has in itself.[1] Its importance in itself makes it gladden-

---

1   The difference between the objectively gladdening quality of a state of affairs in itself and the objectively gladdening quality of a state of affairs *for* someone stands out clearly in the case where one and the same state of affairs is objectively gladdening for one person and objectively saddening for another. That is expressed by the saying, "One man's meat is another man's poison." This saying refers unambiguously to objective goods for the person and not to their being gladdening or saddening on the basis of their value or disvalue. It goes without saying that in a war the victor is glad and the vanquished is sad. But that is independent of the question of the objective value that this victory has; it can objectively be a blessing or a catastrophe, and this is independent of the question whether the victor or the vanquished find it to be gladdening or saddening. We are here only thinking of cases where the gladdening quality is an objective character of an

ing not only for the convert. In addition to this quality of being gladdening for someone there is also the quality of being gladdening in itself; this is found whenever a state of affairs is gladdening *in itself* on the basis of its value.

In this quality of being objectively gladdening in itself, which is proper to all value-bearing states of affairs, the first fundamental relation between value and happiness emerges. (This quality of being gladdening in itself has a certain analogy to that which objectively ought to be, which is also proper to the existence of all that has value.) This relation is not yet the relation between value and the happiness of the human person. It is a relation between value and this ultimate datum, the quality of the objectively gladdening, this particular kind of light, of being fundamentally positive. This relation distinguishes happiness from its opposite, unhappiness (this is like the opposition of value and disvalue). It is also a reflection of the fact that God, the epitome of all values and of all holiness, is at the same time the infinitely blessed One. We cannot explore this deep phenomenon of the union of the objectively gladdening and value as much as the depth of this mysterious relation deserves; we can only make reference to it. What above all concerns us here is *the fact that everything objectively gladdening ought to give us happiness and calls for a response of joy from us.* We already mentioned that every valuable state of affairs is a *gaudendum* and that it merits a response of joy. A response of joy is due to all objectively valuable states of affairs and facts that are objectively gladdening. Joy is here the classical value-response that is appropriate. When we said that objectively gladdening facts are a *gaudendum*, we said this because they call us to joy, because we ought to rejoice over them, and because joy is here the specific value-response, and in many cases is the only possible one.

There is a deeply meaningful and intelligible relation between the particular content of a given value-response and the value-bearing good on the object side. In chapter 17 of my *Ethics*, I have spoken at length about this relation and about the fact that a value-response should correspond in its quality, degree, and depth to the nature of the given good or evil, or rather to its value and disvalue. A good having great value merits a value-response qualitatively

---

event rooted exclusively in its value, and here the above-mentioned saying is not applicable. It is obvious that if someone gets a good position that he had applied for, with the result that some other applicant does not get the position, the winner is glad and the loser is sad. Here the point of view of an objective good for the person clearly predominates. Among objective goods for the person there are those which cannot simultaneously benefit several persons; one person possessing one of them excludes another from possessing it at the same time. In this case, the character of gladdening and saddening legitimately varies from one person to another. In other words, the same event that is an objective good for one person is an objective evil for another. But this kind of gladdening character is clearly distinguished from that gladdening character rooted exclusively in the value of an event.

different from a good having a more modest value. The same holds for the degree and depth of the value-response. But in addition the kind of value (whether a moral or aesthetic or intellectual value) can have an influence on the nature of the value-response. Thus veneration responds only to some moral value, whereas admiration can also respond to intellectual values. The important thing is to see that the kind of value and also the ontological make-up of the good play a decisive role in determining what the appropriate value-response is. There are various stances that are only possible as directed toward persons, such as veneration, scorn, envy, jealousy, forgiveness, revenge, love and hate in the proper sense of the term, and adoration (this last mentioned value-response is by its very nature possible only as directed toward the Absolute Person, God). But the role of the ontological make-up of the good that determines which value-responses are appropriate, is not limited to this distinction between persons and non-persons.

It makes a great difference whether the bearer of value is a state of affairs,[2] such as an event, or whether it is a person, an act of a person, a community (such as a nation, a family, a religious order, or the church), or just works of art, landscapes, animals, etc. Certain kinds of value-responses are only possible towards states of affairs, whereas many other value-responses are not possible as responses to states of affairs. The ontological and structural difference between states of affairs and all these other things, different as they are among themselves, is in one respect particularly radical. While love in the strict sense can only refer to persons, one can still meaningfully speak in an analogous sense of love for a community, for a landscape, for a city, for a work of art. But one can never speak of love for some state of affairs or for some event. On the other hand, the response of the will can be directed to states of affairs. We can never will a person or a work of art or a city or an animal. We can only will to be together with a person or to see a work of art or to possess an animal, etc. Besides, our response always refers to the realization of a state of affairs. The object of the will must not only be a state of affairs but also a not-yet-realized state of affairs, a point to which we are about to return.

What above all concerns us here is to see that "joy over" [*Freude über*]

---

2 ["State of affairs" translates the German *Sachverhalt*. This term is sometimes also translated as "fact," but we follow here the rendering of *Sachverhalt* found in von Hildebrand's other English works. We refer to a state of affairs in speaking of "the fact that Thomas died last year." But Thomas himself is not a state of affairs; no person exists as a state of affairs, nor does any non-personal thing ever exist as a state of affairs. Von Hildebrand proceeds in the text to contrast "joy over" with "joy in" by showing that the former always refers to some state of affairs, whereas the latter never refers to a state of affairs. For a fuller account of *Sachverhalt* in von Hildebrand's sense see the discussion of the concept in the study of his teacher Adolf Reinach, "The Theory of the Negative Judgment," *Aletheia 2* (1981): esp. 32–41. Trans.]

can only refer to states of affairs. It is a typical value-response given to valuable, objectively gladdening states of affairs. With other goods, such as a person, or the virtue of a person, or a work of art, such a "joy over" is out of the question. It can only refer to the existence of goods, to the fact that some noble man exists, to the fact that this great work of art exists or that someone acts in such and such a way. Whereas the "joy over" can only refer to states of affairs, the "joy in" [*Freude an*] can direct itself to persons and works of art. We can have great joy in a person, a work of art, a landscape, a house. But clearly "joy over" and "joy in" are formally different kinds of stances, even if they are qualitatively quite close to each other and share the decisive element of engendering happiness.

But the "joy over" is a more of a response than the "joy in." The "joy in" has a contemplative element missing in the "joy over"; it is closer to a *frui*[3] than is the "joy over." But above all the "joy in" is not a response to the quality of being objectively gladdening. It refers not to states of affairs and to their objectively gladdening character, but refers to objects and persons and their values. We can have joy in the beauty of a house that we inhabit. We can have a joy in the development of a child, in its mind, its conscientious efforts, its alertness, etc. We can have joy in the possession of a dog. We can also speak of joy in some thing in the sense that that thing is in general attractive to us and that we have a feel for it. "Do you take joy in music?" When someone asks us this, he means to ask whether we love music, whether we have an ear for it. If we limit ourselves here to the "joy in" that has the character of a value-response, the question can be intended to ask whether we are capable of grasping the beauty of music and appreciating it, and appreciating it to the point of being made happy by it. But with the "joy over," such a question is not possible, for such joy refers clearly to the concrete state of affairs and does not have the potential character that the "joy in" can have.

For the present study it is above all important that the "joy over" is the natural response to states of affairs that are objectively gladdening, that it is the "joy over" that is due as a response to the objectively gladdening character of states of affairs. As long as we are talking about already existing valuable states of affairs, the "joy over" is in a certain sense *the* response. When we hear of a state of affairs that is objectively gladdening on the basis of its value, for instance that someone has converted, that someone has overcome some vice, or that an innocent person has been acquitted, the "joy over" is the proper and appropriate response.[4]

---

3   [The author expects that the reader will be aware of the contrast between the Latin terms *frui* (taking delight in) and *uti* (making some use of); he uses *frui* to express the idea of taking contemplative delight in some good. *Fruitio*, which also occurs occasionally in the following pages, is simply a noun-form of *frui*. Trans.]

4   Kant completely overlooked the existence of such a value-responding joy. This is

In all these cases where joy and sadness are the meaningful and the objectively required value-responses, no reasonable person could possibly think that such joy stands in contrast to value-response. For here the joy or the sadness is the appropriate meaningful value-response; if this response is not given, then we have a typical absence of value-response that often consists in a bad and unworthy indifference. And if we respond with regret or annoyance at that which is objectively gladdening, then our response forms a specific opposite to value-response.

And so we see that "joy over" is the typical value-response to valuable, objectively gladdening states of affairs.

2. *The unthematic joy that we ought to feel at the realization of value-bearing states of affairs.* But if the states of affairs are not yet real, if we are in a situation in which a value-bearing state of affairs ought to be realized, then it is not joy but rather the will to realize it that is the appropriate and required value-response. For here the theme is the realization of some value and, as a result, the response of the will is the indispensable and required response. I am called upon to intervene with an action. We saw in the previous chapter that when joy is added to an action, when a good action is joyfully performed, the moral value can be augmented, and we examined the condition under which this happens: when joy is motivated purely by the value that also motivates my will. We need not explore this any further here. But what must be stressed is that joy or being made happy is in no way the theme. Joy is indeed called for; it is better and more appropriate if the joy is there, but it is not indispensable, as we saw, and hence it is not thematic.

The distinction in the relation between value and happiness in these two cases is clear. If we are dealing with valuable states of affairs that have already been realized, then it is the "joy over" that is the appropriate response to the objectively gladdening states of affairs. If they are not yet realized and can be

---

not surprising, for he acknowledged neither the existence of values nor a response to them. But that he did not see the existence of a morally worthy and in fact morally required joy, this is more difficult to understand. The source of this failure is that he not only conflated joy, happiness, and pleasure, but also thought that everything affective was motivated only in a hedonistic way. What kept him from acknowledging the moral value of such a joy was the fact that this joy is not free in the sense in which a will is free, that is it is not within our power to generate this joy as it is to posit an act of willing. But as I have shown in my *Ethics*, this joy does not fall entirely outside the reach of our freedom. It is within the reach of indirect freedom and it can be freely sanctioned. Even if the phenomenon of indirect freedom and of the fully free sanction and disavowal was not known to Kant, it still remains surprising that he did not notice the difference between a noble joy and a sadistic joy and did not consider the possibility of an affective moral act, of a response that is just as "objectively" motivated as the will that follows what he called the categorical imperative.

realized by me, then the response of the will is the appropriate value-response. If joy accompanies the action, if we are filled with happiness in performing it, this is a particular value and, as we saw, has nothing to do with sullying the moral value of the action. In this case, too, we have to do with a relation between happiness and value, but it is a case in which happiness is definitely not thematic. It is, in contrast, quite different in the case of already real valuable states of affairs. Here joy as the appropriate response is thematic and being made happy by the worthy event, or by the existence of some value, is most definitely thematic. But this is not the only case in which the relation of value and happiness is such that happiness is thematic.

3. *The superabundant happiness engendered by values in all* frui; *happiness as a secondary theme.* Let us now consider the many cases in which a bearer of values confers happiness on us superabundantly, whether this happens by the presence of a great and noble personality filling my soul with happiness, or by the beauty of a work of art that I can fully appreciate touching me and letting happiness flow into my soul. I am thinking above all of the cases in which a *fruitio* arises in me from some more intimate contact with a value, which then confers happiness on mé in a superabundant way. We will deal here mainly with this third form of the relation of value and happiness, where happiness is indeed thematic but in a definitely secondary way. The main theme is the value of the good.

We will enter more deeply into the relation of value and happiness by showing how the first case, in which the objectively gladdening character of all valuable states of affairs calls for joy, differs from the third case, being made happy by some valuable good. It will above all let us understand better the way in which happiness is thematic in love.

This third form of the relation between value and happiness emerges especially in those cases in which some valuable good affects us, deeply moving us, whether it be some great work of art, the beauty of a landscape, the moral greatness of an action, or the goodness and nobility of a person. This being-affected that engenders happiness is distinguished from the above-mentioned cases in which joy and sadness are the meaningfully required value-responses. Of course, in these cases, too, joy is thematic, in contrast to the active character of an action. In them the happiness that comes from being penetrated by the event forms an organic unity with our value-responding joy. But there is missing here a contemplative opening of myself to value and drinking it in by way of *frui*. In being affected, by contrast, something entirely different happens in that I am purely receptive and my happiness becomes thematic in a new way.

At this point, we touch upon another problem that is closely related to being-affected: the difference within value-bearing goods that concerns the levels of relation to them that are allowed by their structure. We want, first of all, to consider different kinds of being-affected that are conditioned by the different types of goods and their values. We saw that a certain kind of being-affected is found in all those cases in which some event makes us deeply happy, this happiness forming an intimate union with the value-response of joy. Someone once told me of the overwhelming moment of venturing out of a cellar into a street after an intense bombardment in Florence and suddenly seeing an English jeep coming around the corner, a sign of being liberated from the Nazis. The wonderful fact of being free, finally liberated, was so moving that he broke out into tears, and the people who experienced this together embraced each other with deep emotion and gratitude. Of course, the "joy over" this fact, the value-response, organically grew out of this being-affected and resonated for a long time, filling all everyday situations with light. But still the being-affected, the being-filled with the importance of the event stands out as a kind of experience all its own. But it must be said that this being-affected is a special case, a particular type of authentic being-affected, which is entirely different from the happiness wrought by the object in the case of *fruitio*.

This deep being-affected, this being deeply moved by a great event has a dramatic and not a contemplative character. This difference clearly does not concern the degree, the intensity, or the depth of happiness. No, it is quite another kind of difference, which we refer to with the expressions "dramatic" and "contemplative"; it stands forth clearly as soon as we realize that there would be no sense in speaking here of a *frui* in relation to some good. If we compare the case of being absorbed in the beauty of the landscape or of hearing some splendid music, so that this beauty deeply moves us and flows into the soul causing great happiness, then it is clear that we can speak here of a *frui* that is not in the same sense possible in the just-mentioned event of liberation. We are about to return to this distinction below.

In the first relation of value and happiness, we have to do with a typical response, whereas in the third relation we have above all to do with being-affected. The formal difference between response and being-affected is very important for the kind of thematicity that happiness has. The affective value-responses do not have the same active character that the will and action have. In contrast with actions, they have a relatively contemplative character. Some of them are more contemplative than others. For example, joy is more contemplative than enthusiasm, but they all lack the distinctly active and dramatic character that distinguishes the response of the will and of the action. But they are not receptive in the way in which being affected is. They are not receptive in the eminent way in which, for example, being touched or being edified are receptive. They are rather distinctly spontaneous; each of them is a response, a word spoken by the person to the object. In being-affected there is a receiving of a particular kind, a taking in; the object "speaks" to us and its value touches the soul.

There is another point to be made, one closely related to the distinction between value-response and being-affected by values. In the value-response of joy over states of affairs that are objectively gladdening on the basis of their values, the relation of value and happiness is given already in the object, and the responding joy is my participation in the objectively gladdening quality, it is the response required of me. Here the themes of value and happiness are woven together in the object itself. Of course, the value is the predominant theme and the theme of happiness is entirely dependent on it. But my joy is primarily a participation in the objectively gladdening states of affairs, and in my act of responding my happiness is not thematic. By contrast, I receive a gift when happiness flows into the soul through experiencing the beauty of some great work of art or the company of some noble personality or in the experience of being moved by the nobility of someone's moral behavior. Here we have a happiness that dwells in the soul. My happiness here is distinctly thematic, even though it is a secondary theme. The first and decisive theme is the value. But the union of value and happiness is in this case the value in the object and the happiness in the person; they are two distinct themes, even if the happiness is exclusively an overflow of the value and is as a theme entirely secondary.

When we spoke of the "joy over" as the typical value-response to states of affairs that are objectively gladdening on the basis of their values, we did not mean to say that states of affairs cannot also affect us with deep happiness. We were only saying that this kind of value-response does not comprise all value-responses; for instance, it does not comprise responses directed to other persons. States of affairs, too, such as events, can deeply move us; they can affect us with joy and touch us to the point of tears or affect us painfully, eliciting tears of sadness. Here we do not mean the above-mentioned kind of being-affected, which is so closely connected with the response of joy or sadness that it is hardly experienced as such and is not thrown into relief as a kind of experience all its own. No, we mean that states of affairs, such as events, deeply affect us, whether positively or negatively; we mean that it is their content that penetrates the soul making it either happy or sad, and that we can speak of an "effect" of this event. Of course, we do not mean effect in the sense of real causality, for it is an intelligible and deeply meaningful relation that is given in being affected, separated by an abyss from the real causal relation that is at stake when I burn my finger by touching something hot and feeling physical pain as the effect. But we must again stress that in speaking of a typical case of being-affected by events, a case in which the experience of being-affected clearly stands out as a distinct experience, we are not saying that the response of joy is not also joined with it.[5]

---

5   One could object as follows. Granted that stances and responses are a different kind of experience than being-affected, they are both nevertheless found so closely linked together that it is questionable whether one can mention them as two different kinds of the relation between value and happiness, or in other words whether the distinction between response and being-affected really has an impor-

We will understand better this third kind of relation of value and happiness if we bring out now a further structural distinction within goods. In the case of certain goods, for example, events, the mere knowing about their existence, about their becoming real, is already the closest contact possible with them; but with other goods, for example, a human person, a work of art, a landscape, many levels of contact are possible, and a whole hierarchy of possible union presents itself.

But we should not exaggerate this distinction between events as bearers of values, and objects or things as bearers of values. Very important here is the kind of event and its significance; also important is whether one stresses the event as a state of affairs or stresses the event as event, that is, as the sudden becoming real of a state of affairs. Great as this difference is between the state of affairs, on the one hand, and an object or a person, on the other hand, states of affairs can be contemplatively experienced and their value can affect us in a way that comes very close to a *frui*. States of affairs are everywhere; that is, to every good there corresponds the state of affairs *that it exists*. In addition, goods often function as "members" of states of affairs.[6] The distinction that concerns us here consists rather in the fact that sometimes the mere existence of a good makes us happy, whereas at other times this state of affairs that it exists is only a beginning, beyond which many levels of being-affected with happiness are possible.

The fact that a war has come to an end and peace has been restored, or that someone has performed some noble deed, is not only a motive for our value-response of joy, it also fills me with happiness, touches and moves me, pour-

---

tant influence on the kind of relation existing between value and happiness. We would answer by saying that it is certainly correct to affirm that a certain being-affected usually goes together with a response, but that it makes a great difference whether the being-affected is the essential thing and the theme, or whether the response is. There is of course the being-affected that is often so linked together with the motivation of the value-response that it does not stand forth as something of its own, as when I learn that an unjustly imprisoned person has been liberated and my being-gladdened by the news and my response of joy over it are woven closely together. From such a case, we have to distinguish those cases in which something moves me deeply, as in hearing some splendid music and being filled with peace and happiness. We will later distinguish within being-affected various further forms, including those involving a *frui*. But in all the cases in which we contrast being made happy by a value with giving the value-response of joy as two different types of the relation of value and happiness, we are not thinking of the being-affected that is organically woven together with the value response, but rather of the one that distinguishes itself clearly as a receptive experience all its own from the value-response of joy, even if, as we said, many kinds and levels can still be discriminated within this being-affected. We are about to say more about this.

6   [For example, the fact that one good ranks higher than another. Trans.]

ing light and happiness into the soul. But over and above the existence of this good, of this event, there is no possible augmentation apart from the decisive factor of our disposition, our readiness to take in deep things. But when it is some noble and splendid person of whose existence I hear, this is a state of affairs that moves me and fills me with happiness. This state of affairs is a source of happiness and can affect the soul joyfully. But at the same time, we wish to get to know this person and to be able to dwell in his presence and if possible to enter into some closer contact with him. If that is granted to us, then we really have a source of happiness that goes far beyond the mere knowledge of the existence of such a person. An entirely new form of being joyfully affected is now possible; we might meaningfully express it by saying that we have enjoyed being together with him, that his presence is a great gift. Here we have a fully developed *frui*.

This difference stands out more clearly when we think of aesthetic values. There is indeed some reason for joy in learning that a splendid country exists somewhere in the world, that some great work of art exists, such as the Ninth Symphony of Beethoven, the St. Matthew Passion of Bach, or the Dying Slave of Michelangelo. When we hear such things described we are gladdened to know that they exist, that the world contains such treasures, but the main experience here is the longing to get to know them, to be able to see or hear them. We go decisively beyond knowing about their existence when we see photographs of the country or of a work of art and the opera or symphony or quartet is played for us on the piano. Here is the decisive step from merely knowing that there exists something beautiful to entering into contact with the quality of the beautiful thing by *perceiving* it. That of course makes possible a radically new kind of being-affected. The mere fact that there exists somewhere something beautiful cannot touch and move us. A joy over this fact can of course arise in us, but here the being-affected, being-gladdened, being-impressed is just something preliminary. But when one can perceive the beauty and not just abstractly know that there exists something beautiful, something entirely new occurs: being joyfully affected, being touched and moved. Beauty enters into us here so as to make us happy and to elevate us. A *frui* is entirely possible. But even then one longs for a closer contact that would make possible a higher level of *frui*: one wants to hear the music fully realized in a performance, one wants to dwell in the beautiful country, one wants to see the work of art *itself* and not just a reproduction of it.

When we hear about a noble deed, the quality of the moral value is perceived, and far more is conveyed to us than just a knowledge of its existence; whereas with aesthetic values the mere fact that something beautiful exists does not yet convey to us any perception of beauty. We normally do not even get acquainted with the quality of the beauty of the work of art or of a landscape on the basis of merely being informed about it. This is in itself a significant and intriguing problem, which is related to the way in which moral values are given in distinction to the way in which the beauty of visible and audible things is given to us. We can only refer to this problem.[7]

Since our subject here is the relation between happiness and value, as well as the different ways in which this relation shows itself, the main distinction for us is the one between those goods that allow us to go beyond just knowing of their existence and to encounter them more intimately, thus experiencing them as *fruenda* (things in which I take delight), and on the other hand those goods that do not allow any such closer contact. And here we can draw a sharp line: on the one hand, facts that make me deeply happy by their real existence but in no further way, and on the other hand all those goods that have value over and above their existence and that make the soul happy, assuming that a particular and more intimate encounter with them has been granted to me. The first is some happy event, such as a person being liberated from the communists or a war ending or a plague stopping or someone performing a noble heroic deed, etc. The second, as found, for example, in some noble extraordinary personality or in some great work of art or some splendid landscape, is at the same time a *fruendum* (something in which I take delight), whereas the first is more of a *gaudendum* (something I am glad about).

So as to avoid all misunderstandings let us stress that in the case of *events* both the value in question and also our behavior toward the value is very important. The facts that have an absolute and incomparable significance, such as the existence of an infinitely holy God, or the redemption of the world by Christ, are not only the superactual basis of our deepest happiness, but they constantly illuminate our whole life with happiness. A distant analogy to this is found in spousal love when the beloved person requites my love: this requital is an inexhaustible source of happiness and of being joyfully affected. This does not hold for many of the above-mentioned facts; it does not hold for typical events. Besides, the case of a requital of love is a strong objective good for the person; although built on values it represents a unique case to which we will later return. This state of affairs is so far removed from a mere event because the act of requiting love is the fundamental reality and is itself something entirely different from a state of affairs. This holds even more for the person of the beloved. We prescind in our present discussion, however, from this kind of states of affairs.

There is of course also a way of becoming contemplatively absorbed in

---

7   Clearly we have in mind the distinction between merely knowing that there exists something beautiful and the perception of this beauty; we do not have in mind the case in which the beauty of a country is conveyed to us by means of a vivid description. From a certain vivid description of the particular quality of the beauty of this country, an intuitive contact, a knowing of the quality of the beauty, can be conveyed to us. Interesting as these distinctions are, we will not examine them more closely here; they belong to an analysis of aesthetic problems.

states of affairs of ultimate importance, which gives a more intimate contact with the values than just learning of their existence. We hear about some noble deed. It touches us, making us happy, and we rejoice over the realization of this moral value. That is the normal case of which we have already spoken. We saw that in the case of moral values there is not just an indirect knowledge of some morally good behavior, but a perception of a moral value. The difference between witnessing this noble action and just reading about it or hearing about it, is relatively unimportant. I can achieve a closer contact with this moral event, or rather with the moral value realized in it, by contemplatively being absorbed in it, by making a point of meditating on the moral beauty of the action. Then it can happen, but it need not, that the moral value raises up my soul by its beauty. This takes on a particular importance when we meditate on the extraordinary deeds in the life of some saint, for example, when we contemplatively immerse ourselves in the martyrdom of St. Stephen. Its high point is the contemplation of the words of Jesus Christ. But in all of the being-affected that is here intended, our happiness is not the theme, nor is there any question of a real *frui*. All these states of affairs bearing great values or even the greatest values, allow for many levels of awareness of their existence, all the way up to the contemplative absorption in them. These levels of awareness exist analogously in our way of relating to some objective good for us.

If I am going to do full justice to some value, I have to become explicitly aware of it. After someone who loves me has assured me of his love, I may have the need to keep this fact constantly in mind: he or she loves me. But all these levels of a more explicit awareness of some state of affairs of great value (whether it involves some action, some attitude, or some fact) must be distinguished from the more intimate contact possible only with certain goods and leading to a *frui*. If the love of a beloved person penetrates me in a loving personal encounter with that person, then the conditions for a full *frui* are fulfilled.

We limit ourselves for now to moral values. Suppose we read of the sacrifice made by Sr. Maria in Auschwitz or of the attitude of St. Maria Goretti toward her murderer; this touches us and moves us. We come more closely into contact with the value by giving more attention to it and achieving a greater consciousness of it, as when we realize more that such a thing really happened, or immerse ourselves more in this victory over the world and even over human nature. But this is and remains something very different from the levels of real contact of which we spoke above: knowing of a great personality, dwelling in his presence, and entering into some closer and more personal communion with him.

How being happy enhances self-giving;
how happiness is destroyed when it is made the primary theme

We see here a new way of being affected by the values of this personality, and this opens the possibility of a new dimension of happiness; only now does a *frui* come into question. The decisive issue for us is this: does this *frui* and the thematicity of happiness lying in *frui* imply some departure from value-responding transcendence, some abandonment of or even opposition to the attitude of value-response?

We have already seen that this is not the case with the value-responding joy over objectively gladdening events, which we designated as the first kind of relation between value and happiness. The happiness that comes from being affected by such value clearly has nothing to do with abandoning the attitude of value-response. But there is no question here of any *frui*. How is it, then, in those cases where a genuine *frui* is indeed given, that is, in the most pronounced kind of relation between value and happiness that we designated as the third kind?

We have to say as decisively as possible that not even this case involves as such any departure from value-response. The *frui* in no way interferes with the thematicity of value, with our interest both in the capacity of moral value to glorify God as well as in the silent praise of God in all authentic beauty and in all deep truth—it does not interfere with this as long as the happiness of *frui* remains the *second* theme with the value remaining the first. As soon as the disorder occurs of making the happiness granted by the *frui* into the first and most important theme, the attitude of value-response would indeed be radically abandoned, but along with it the authentic *frui* would also be destroyed. In observing this we are in no way denying the fact that this paradoxical danger exists in human nature. But in our present discussion we are not dealing with possible perversions, even if the danger of them is great, but with the question whether the *frui* as such and the thematicity of happiness that goes with it imply falling out of the attitude of value-response and out of the transcendence of value-response. The question is whether the pure thematicity of value is reduced by the secondary thematicity of happiness, or whether, on the contrary, the secondary thematicity of happiness grows organically out of value and even represents an enhancement of the thematicity of value.

Let us first take a look at the case which occurs in the sphere of moral goods and values. We saw that here value-response has a unique and incomparable transcendence and commitment. We saw that this commitment is found not only in the case of moral action but also in all contemplative responses to moral values. It is the commitment that finds its high point in the love for God. But here we see fully and distinctly that the yearning for the closest contact with God and the greatest *frui* of Him belongs to the love of God, in which the glorification of God is the first theme. This is expressed unambiguously in the fundamental truth that the *similitudo Dei* (likeness to God) (and the *glorificatio Dei* [glorification of God] contained in it) is the *finis primarius ultimus* (primary ultimate end) of man, and that the *beatitudo* (blessedness) (the *fruitio* of the *visio beatifica* [beatific vision]) is the *finis secundarius ultimus* (secondary ultimate end) of man.

The thematicity of happiness does not imply
any separability of happiness from value

This shows us unmistakably that at the highest level of being there is no antithesis or incompatibility of value and happiness, but that both of them form a deep and indissoluble unity. The primacy of value is here clearly expressed, and true happiness could never amount to something separable from it, never be an independent theme of its own; it essentially presupposes value as the superior reality and can only grow out of value. Every form of eudaemonism in which this order is reversed, which means that value would be derived from happiness, is inherently contradictory; one distorts the true essence of happiness and is compelled to replace true happiness with the purely immanent and contingent happiness that is ultimately condemned to dissolution—even if this is opposed to one's conscious intention.

This is why we have to say of the happiness that comes with the highest kind of *frui*: the thematicity of happiness does not mean that it is in any way or in any sense a separable theme. It would be false to think that happiness is indeed a secondary theme but at the same time is a theme of its own in the same sense as value. No, happiness depends so profoundly and indissolubly on the triumphant thematicity of value, it flows out of value in a superabundant way, it is a dimension of the radiant splendor of value; it can never be sought for its own sake without being falsified. If we speak here of the thematicity of happiness, we do so only in the sense that happiness should be fully experienced, that it would be wrong and indeed insane not to acknowledge the overwhelming significance of this happiness flowing organically from value and the *fruitio* of the good. If we speak of the thematicity of happiness and the *frui* of great goods, in contrast to those cases in which a *frui* is not in the same way given, that only means that happiness here *ought* to be, that something would be lacking without happiness, that happiness ought to be fully experienced and appreciated.

But even in the case of being affected by extramoral values, where the value-response does not have the same transcendence that is proper to the moral value-responses, being made happy through the *frui* of some good is by no means an abandonment of the attitude of value-response or a lapse into immanence. We saw that in our response to the beauty of nature and art we do not achieve the same transcendence and commitment that we achieve in the moral value-responses. But in spite of this important difference, these value-responses possess after all a strong transcendence and are absolutely centered on value. And yet in many of these cases the *frui* is particularly prominent. The yearning for a deeper contact with the good and for the full *frui* belongs to these value-responses. In contrast to those goods lacking in value that are objective goods for the person only because they are pleasant and pleasurable for the person, the extra-moral goods of which we speak are *fruenda* only on the basis of their *value*. Their value is the main thing, and the existence of a good bearing this value is something in itself gladdening. But they are never-theless specifically delightful, as all beauty is, and they are in a particular way *fruenda*. The *frui* cannot be detached from a value or in any way made inde-pendent or turned into a theme all its own. But in spite of this dependency, the *frui* has here quite another thematicity than it has within the moral domain; the good appeals to the *frui* and, as it were, requires it. The goods that contain a word of God, such as the beauty of nature or works of art (that often speak of God in a way that surpasses all that the artist consciously intended), have to be experienced in the form of *frui* if the word is to be understood.

The value of a moral deed or the moral values of some personality are not only a word of God, a reflection of His infinite goodness and glory, but also a word spoken to God, and they retain their fulfillment even if they were never to be seen by any human being. But all beauty, and especially the beauty of the visible and the audible, is not only a word of God in the sense of being a reflec-tion of His infinite beauty, it is not only a dew descending from above (just like all moral value), it is also a kind of incense ascending to God as a silent hymn of praise. And it is also a word spoken *to* man. Those things where beauty is the main theme, such as works of art, are objectively destined to be perceived and enjoyed.

But does the fact that the *frui* is here more thematic than elsewhere, that it belongs to the very meaning of these goods that they should be enjoyed, that these goods are specifically delightful—does this fact mean that the *frui* here involves some loss of the attitude of value-response, some lapse from transcen-dence into immanence, even if in an innocent way? This should be emphatical-ly denied. There is no question of any such thing happening. When we "drink in" beauty and are made happy by the value, we entirely remain in the attitude of transcendence and commitment. The absolute primacy of value and its the-maticity remains here entirely untouched, and happiness is never a theme of its own. When we say "never" we mean, of course: as long as no perversions arise. In the aesthete we see precisely the perversion of making pleasure the end and the work of art a mere means. As a result the aesthete achieves neither true happiness nor an authentic *frui*; he replaces these things with a purely immanent satisfaction on the model of merely pleasurable goods. And so we see that even here in the *frui* of extraordinarily great goods, the being-affected and the happiness represent no departure from the attitude of value-response and of its transcendence.

On the background of this general relation of value and happiness, we can understand why happiness, though it is so important in love and in the union desired by love, involves no departure from the attitude of value-response, no diminishment of the pure thematicity of value. On the contrary, my interest in value is increased in a unique way when the beloved person becomes the source of my happiness. We will understand this when we proceed now to explore the cases in which some good becomes an objective good for me on the basis of its values. But already this analysis of the relation of value and happiness lets us understand that the thematicity of happiness in love in no way deprives love of its self-donation and transcendence; in all the categories of love, in the love of God as well as in the natural kinds of love, with the exception of love of neighbor, my happiness must play a decisive role.

Love as super value-response:
the beloved person becomes an objective good for the one who loves

We enter a new dimension that goes beyond the thematicity of happiness when the bearer of value becomes an objective good for me and becomes this on the basis of its value. This dimension is closely related to the dimension of happiness but it goes beyond it as well. We are referring here to certain goods that are first understood and responded to in their value and *then become objective goods for me*. This happens on the basis of their value, but something new occurs when they, besides eliciting a value-response, reach into my subjectivity and take on a specifically personal meaning by becoming objective goods for me. This is a specifically new phase in encountering the delightfulness of their value. Once again the all-important thing to understand is that this new phase is an organic continuation of value-response and not a distortion of it, not, as it were, a transition from one theme to another, and certainly not a reduction of the transcendence of the underlying value-response. We are thinking here mainly of those things which we not only appreciate, for which we not only occasionally feel enthusiasm, but which we love, to which we have developed a very personal relation, such as certain works of art or the works of certain philosophers, or certain countries and cities which mean so much to us that they play a permanent role in our lives as a source of joy and happiness, becoming objective goods for us in the full sense of the word.[8]

As we already have said, this love, this personal relation grows organically out of value-response. Of course, in most cases it requires some special affinity, but such affinity simply enables us to continue in a certain direction or even to intensify the value-responding engagement with the good and its

---

8   One can speak of an objective good for me in a broader and in a more narrow sense. In the broader sense everything that engenders happiness is an objective good for me. All beauty of nature and art, for example, is an objective good for me as soon as it makes me happy. As soon as I am filled with happiness over such things they become a gift for me on the basis of their value. But from this we must distinguish the narrower sense of an objective good for me. Here an object plays a permanent role in my life because of its value and becomes a lasting source of happiness for me. This occurs, for example, with works of art that I love in a special way and that then become a part of the cultural world in which I live and move. The same holds for landscapes or countries that I particularly love because of their beauty.

value. This is expressed in an entirely new way in the love for a person (love taken in the strict sense). In every kind of love, with the exception of love of neighbor, the beloved person becomes an objective good for the one who loves, though this character of the objective good varies with the category of love and above all with the intensity and depth of the love. Perhaps I respect some person, perhaps I appreciate him and admire him—but I do not yet love him. He is not yet my friend, I have not granted him a place in my heart, he has not yet become a source of happiness for me.

We have to understand that there is even here no compromise of value-response in the fact that a person is an objective good for me as a result of my loving him as friend or loving her with spousal love, which involves loving in a fuller and qualitatively new way. It is not as if this becoming an objective good for me just stands next to the value-response without diminishing it; it rather grows out of value-response, indeed the other person becoming the source of my personal happiness involves a fuller appreciation of that person's values. We have here a new dimension of self-giving; it is a giving of my subjectivity, taking "subjective" in the most positive sense of the word. And this goes hand in hand with the new dimension of value-response. This is why we can say that in love there is a "super value-response" [*Überwertantwort*], a value-response that goes so far that the beloved person becomes a central objective good for the one who loves, indeed sometimes even the source of his or her most personal happiness. This element of love emerges strongly in the intentio unionis, though not only there, but also in the way in which the beloved person makes me happy and in the role that he or she plays in my life. This involves a new dimension of engaging the good. We could say that it is a victory of value that reaches all the way into the subjective sphere; we have here the point at which the subjective and the objective encounter each other in a unique way and interpenetrate.

Beatitude and the love for God

This is nowhere so clearly and perfectly in evidence as in the love for God. This is the value-response *par excellence*, the most transcendent act of a person and the most objective. But when God is not only the absolute good in itself but also the absolute good for me, there is a new dimension of self-giving and an even more personal commitment.

It would be a great error to think that my stance toward God is less committed and less value-responding simply because God is also my supreme objective good and the source of my beatitude. This would only be the case if the value-response to God's infinite holiness, glory, and majesty, if the unconditional commitment to God and His holy will, and if zeal for God's honor and glorification, did not have for me the first place, did not have the primacy. But the response to God as the absolute objective good for me, which grows out of the response to God's infinite holiness and beauty, is as such an enhanced commitment of a certain kind. It is so great an interest in the infinite glory of God that he becomes the source of my beatitude. It is so moving an encounter with the glory of God as to affect my most personal subjectivity down to the deepest depth and to be profoundly "subjective" on the basis of the objective infinite beauty of God.

Of course, there are so many aspects of the relation of man to God that many other attitudes besides love are involved. There is, for example, the response to the absolute ontological dependency on God, the absolute belonging to Him from whom we have received existence and by whom we are constantly preserved in being, on whose protection and help we are entirely dependent, in whose hands are our life and death and above all our eternal destiny. In addition, there is the absolute personal subordination to the absolute Lord, and many other religious stances.

These facts, too, make God an absolute objective good for us, as does the fact that we can receive supernatural life only from Him and can attain eternal life only through Him. But these things are not the foundation for the love for God. This love is rather rooted in the pure value-response to God's infinite holiness and beauty, and God emerges as my absolute good as a result of this value-response.

These two reasons for God being the absolute good for the person must not be confused. According to the first reason, this fact is grounded in the relation of Creator to creature, of the absolute Lord to his servant; it is grounded in the ontological ordination to God, in the absolute dependency on Him. According to the second reason—this has to be clearly distinguished from the first—God is the absolute good for the person on the basis of His infinite glory and His infinite worthiness of being loved. And this is personally experienced only in consciously loving God and only to the degree that one loves God. Here God becomes the absolute objective good for me, not only objectively, but also experientially. By loving Him, the value-response to God's infinite beauty goes so deep that He is also experienced as my absolute good, so deep that I desire eternal union with Him above all other things.

As soon as one fails to distinguish these two reasons for the fact that God is the absolute objective good for me, one misunderstands the love of God and its value-response character. One then thinks in terms of objective goods for the person that are not grounded in values but that are needed as the basis for my existence; one thinks that this is the way in which God is my objective good. But in this way value-response is completely forgotten. And thus one identifies the love for God with the desire for perfection or with the ultimate dependency on God. Though one can indeed think along these lines in dealing with many other aspects of our relation to God, it is impossible to think this way about the love of God. For love is by its essence a value-response and the fact that God is the absolute good for me and the source of my experienced personal happiness has here an entirely different ground, which cannot be understood as long as one fails to acknowledge love as a value-response. St. Thomas Aquinas seems to run this risk when he says that we could not love God if He were only the absolute good in itself and were not also our absolute good.[9] He is of course right that being our absolute good belongs essentially to the full love for God; but unfortunately he takes as the basis of love what is in reality the consequence of it. God need not be understood as objective good for me in order to ground our love for Him; rather love as a value-response to God as the absolute good in itself lets Him be experienced as the absolute good for me. The value-response here goes so far, the participation in the divine glory goes so far, that in my love for Him He is experienced as my absolute objective good. In this sense, St. Augustine says: God is the absolute good in itself and He is my absolute good.

God is also our absolute good insofar as our eternal happiness depends on Him; only through Him and His will can we attain to eternal blessedness. Here the relation between happiness and God lies in the fact that only *He* can choose us for beatitude. But this is the opposite of what we find in the *love* for God: He not only preserves us from eternal suffering and calls us to happiness, but our love responds to the infinite holiness that He has in Himself. This holiness becomes the source of our happiness and we find this happiness fully only in eternal union with Him.

It goes without saying that everything is unique in the love for God. No particular affinity is presupposed for this most objective of all value-responses; God is the epitome of all values; the value-response to Him is the heart of all morality and is morally obligatory: in these respects the love of God cannot be compared with any other love. Unique also is the way in which the absolute good for me grows out of the pure value-response of love. But the fact that the beloved person becomes an objective good for me, takes on the character of a super value-response even in the other categories of love. In the love between friends or in the love between man and woman, the beloved person is also an objective good for me. This implies a further step in participating in the value of the other, a step that goes beyond all those cases where there is a value-response without the good becoming an objective good for me. In the case of a response motivated by the value of justice, or of a response to the value of a person, as when we show respect for the freedom of another, the good responded to does not become an objective good for me. Even if the value-response is joy, as over the conversion of a sinner, this event does not become an objective good for me in the strict sense of the word. The love between friends or the love between man and woman are indeed value-responses, even if they as such are not necessarily moral responses in the precise sense of the word. They are value-responses that presuppose, in addition to the value apprehended in the beloved person, also a particular affinity between the persons.

---

9   St. Thomas Aquinas, *Summa Theologica*, II-II, q. 26, a. 13, ad 3.

But the important point is this: the fact that a person moves me so deeply by his value and so enchants me that he becomes an objective good for me—we could say that my value-response of love installs him or her in my subjectivity as my objective good—this fact does not imply any compromise or abandonment of the value-responding attitude and its transcendence, but rather implies an extension of my self-giving [*Hingabe*], a greater participation in the value. It is a personal self-giving, a giving of myself as subject, of my subjectivity, and as such it is a super value-response. This enhancement of the value-response does not constitute any enhancement of the *moral* value of the self-giving—except in the love for God—but is rather an enhancement that confers on the beloved person, assuming he or she requites the love, the specific happiness of the gift of love.

We cannot say that this super value-response is more selfless than any other value-response. The "more" of self-giving does not mean a greater selflessness. But it would be entirely wrong to think that there is some selfish element in the super value-response and that the self-giving of the person in it is disrupted and deprived of its transcendence. The "more" of self-giving goes in a different direction than the issue of selflessness; it goes in the direction of totality of self-giving, of belonging to the other, of giving one's heart; it goes in the direction of taking the other person and his or her subjectivity into my subjectivity.

Only through this "more" of self-giving that distinguishes love as super value-response from all other value-responses, do I come to belong to the other; only here can it be said, "I am yours," and can the beloved person say, "He is mine" or "She is mine." Indeed, in this love the beloved person already becomes mine even apart from returning my love. All this will become clearer in chapter 8 when we analyze in some detail the various kinds of "mine."

CHAPTER SIX

Intentio Unionis

Widespread misunderstandings of the intentio unionis

There is perhaps no other element of love that has been more often misunderstood than the intentio unionis [desire for union with the beloved person]. Already in the *Symposium* of Plato, where the importance of the values on the object side, that is in the beloved person, is so strongly stressed, the intentio unionis is interpreted as a will to grow by participating in the values of the beloved person. Love is thus only a demi-god, the son of *Poros* (Plenty) and *Penia* (Neediness); for it presupposes the relative imperfection of the one who loves, who needs to grow through participation in the values of the beloved person. And so while love is a response to the beauty of the beloved, it is for Plato no real value-response; in particular the intentio unionis is interpreted by him as a longing born of a need, a longing for the perfection of one's own person. The intentio unionis is not understood as an element of a value-response, but rather as an appetitus. The inner movement of love is not seen as a value-response, as something the source of which is value, as an act of self-donation having a strongly transcendent character, but rather as something that is indeed engendered by the beauty of the other but that in the final analysis turns to the beloved out of an immanent yearning for perfection. This holds all the more for the intentio unionis, which in Plato completely overshadows the intentio benevolentiae.

Later in the history of philosophy, one often encounters the vastly more superficial interpretation of love and its intentio unionis according to which the interest in the other person is a *means* for my happiness. In this case, the value-response character of love is more radically misunderstood. Philosophers have put the yearning for happiness in the place of the noble yearning for self-perfection, for being lifted to a higher level, and have degraded the other person to a mere means. They have developed this idea precisely with a view to the intentio unionis, which they contrast with the selfless love that they think is found only in the intentio benevolentiae. In making this contrast they see in the intentio unionis some kind of selfish interest, which they set against the selfless love found in the love of neighbor, which is supposed to be pure self-donation since it completely lacks the intentio unionis and is completely dominated by the intentio benevolentiae. Sometimes the intentio unionis is presented as a mark of spousal love, especially of being in love, which is then presented as *amor concupiscentiae* and contrasted with the *amor benevolentiae*, which supposedly encompasses the love between friends and the love of parents for their children. One overlooks that these loves too have their own intentio unionis, even if it is less intense. In making the contrast between eros and agape, one also sometimes saw the intentio unionis as the decisive mark of eros, which is thought to give it a selfish character in distinction to agape. In chapter 11 we will discuss in detail the true and highly significant distinction between eros and agape.

The intentio unionis as an enhancement of the transcendence and commitment of love

Our main concern here is to work out the true nature of the intentio unionis, which is an organic component of love as value-response and which is so far from imparting a selfish character to love that it is much rather an element that in a certain respect strengthens the value-response and represents more rather than less commitment.

One of the reasons that has promoted the misunderstanding of the intentio unionis is the fact that this union is a specific source of happiness. Indeed, it presents itself to me as a source of happiness whenever I love. From this fact one may erroneously conclude that the intentio unionis is nothing other than the yearning and desiring of my happiness. Since the union with the beloved person is thought of as a mere means for my happiness, the intentio unionis is thought to derive not from commitment but from a selfishness that contradicts all true commitment. One concludes that when I desire union with another, I am thinking not of the happiness of the beloved but only of my own happiness. Indeed, I do not even take the beloved fully as person in desiring union with him, for not only the union with him but even the beloved himself is treated as a means to my happiness.

This conception is entirely false and misconceives the nature of the intentio unionis in various respects. This will become quite clear once we have examined more closely the essence of the union desired in love.

The nature of union between persons

In the previous chapter we picked out within the value-bearing goods those which allow of various levels of contact. We also saw that the full happiness conferred by these goods presupposes a certain level of close contact, and that we desire as intimate a contact as possible with them. We must now clarify the basic distinction between the contact with non-personal goods and with persons. The contact among persons surpasses in a formal respect not only all possible union that non-personal things are capable of, but even all kinds of contact that persons can have with non-personal goods. The union among non-personal things is so different from the union among persons that one can use the term "union" only in a very analogous sense.

1. *The error of taking the fusion of non-personal beings as the model of personal union.* Starting with unification and bonding and union as it exists in the realm of non-personal things, one erroneously takes the most radical form of union, namely the fusion of two individual things into *one* individual, as the ideal of union in general. In my book, *Die Metaphysik der Gemeinschaft* (The Metaphysics of Community), I pointed out that such amalgamation is in reality an incomparably weaker form of union than the union possible to persons. The metal balls that are melted down into one new one are, first of all, not united, because at the moment of their union they no longer exist as individual things, and secondly, because they have no consciousness of their union. The conscious union, the encounter in mutual love that includes some acquaintance and familiarity with the other and involves some spiritual movement of the persons towards each other, is an incomparably superior union to any and every amalgamation. Indeed, union as it occurs among persons, who are individuals in an entirely new sense and could never give up their individuality without being annihilated, completely surpasses all the union that is possible in the non-personal world, although amalgamation is out of the question for persons. The union of persons is all the deeper for the very reason that as persons they cannot lose their individual existence, and for the reason that their union, far from involving any loss of individual existence, lets both persons stand forth more fully and properly in their own individual existence. It is also much deeper because it is a conscious experience of union, whereas all union in the non-personal world and especially in the purely material world is a non-conscious and non-experienced union. This is connected with the incomparable superiority of persons and with their new dimension of existence. What is important for our purposes is not so much this distinction but rather another one.

2. *The distinction between the conscious union of a person with non-personal goods, and the conscious union of a person with other persons.* We need to recognize the entirely new dimension of union that comes from the fact that the union is no longer one-sided, as when subject and object stand over and against each other, but is mutual, the two subjects facing each other in an I-Thou situation. This mutuality and the fact that instead of dealing with an non-personal object I am dealing with a person, makes possible an entirely different and incomparably more real and authentic union. This new union essentially presupposes that I encounter the other as person and treat the other as person, never approaching him or her as an object.[1]

Even the deep union that we can enter into with a beautiful landscape by dwelling in it—not only becoming contemplatively absorbed in it and drinking

---

1   [Here von Hildebrand inserts a long and significant footnote on the subject-object relation. I have taken the liberty of moving it from the notes to the text at the end of this chapter and calling it "Excursus on the subject-object difference and on the problem of objectifying persons." Trans.]

in its beauty but also living in it so that it becomes a part of our lives—is in a formal respect profoundly different from the union that one person can achieve with another person. For in spite of its depth, the relation of a person to a landscape is one-sided. Of course, we can in an analogous way speak of a dialogue even with the landscape or with a work of art or with profound truths or the insight into them. The object "speaks" to us, discloses itself to us, affects us, and we understand and receive what the object discloses, deeply cooperating in the way of real receptivity: all of this contains a certain duality and above all a real transcendence. But compared with the dialogue with another person or with the encounter of souls, this union is still unilateral. An entirely new dimension of union is given when the subject-object situation gives way to the I-Thou situation, when two persons encounter each other, when two conscious acts interpenetrate, when the same kind of conscious receiving and responding is found in both persons. We prescind for now from the depth of the experience and think only of the purely formal nature of the contact that is possible in the union of persons; one simply cannot overlook the tremendous superiority of the contact between persons qua contact. Even if the one-sided, silent dialogue with nature, with a work of art, with some profound truth, can be and usually is far richer and deeper than a dialogue or an encounter with a human being, and in many cases even richer and deeper than union with him, still it remains only *my* experience, and there is no experience on the side of nature, or the work of art, or the truth; they remain in the position of mere object.

3. *The full union of persons is possible only through the interpenetration of looks [Ineinanderblick] that is proper to love.* More important than this new formal possibility of the union between persons is the fact that a real union between two persons can come about only in the interpenetration of looks that is proper to love.[2] The depth of union depends on the category of love, on the quality and depth and greatness of the love, and above all, on the depth[3] of the persons who love each other. But the important point for us here is that the desired union, the union aimed at in the intentio unionis, can only come into being through a requital of love; indeed, mutual love is the only possible way for achieving the full union of two persons. As long as the beloved person does not return our love, we do not reach the desired union.[4]

2　I am thinking here of the union formed by two persons and not of the kind of union that comes merely from two people being both members of the same community—of the same family, for example, or of the same nation, or of mankind.

3　The depth that we have in mind here is above all *specific depth*, that is the "weight" that is essentially linked with the rank of a value, and also *qualitative depth*, that is the "purity" with which an act (in our case the act of love) is performed by a person. Cf. the detailed analysis of seven kinds of depth within the person in my book, *Sittlichkeit und ethische Werterkenntnis* (Morality and Ethical Value Knowledge).

4　In some categories of love the requital of love must be of the same kind as the love

4. *Relations between love and community, and differences between them.* Here it is necessary to stress emphatically that the union of which we are speaking in connection with the intentio unionis is not the same as community. Even if union represents the highest form of personal community, still there are many communities that have a very different character. One would therefore completely misunderstand what we are saying about union being constituted only in mutual love, if one were to draw the conclusion that mutual love or requited love is the only foundation for a community. That is by no means the case.

In my book, *Die Metaphysik der Gemeinschaft*, I distinguished two kinds of community, the material and the formal communities. Let us take the exclusively formal community of an association [*Verein*]. One enters the association through a social act, love for the members being in no way required. What unites the members of the association is the goal of it, the good and the value that it serves. Without the conscious act of entering the association (which is a definite social act such as promising or entering into a contract) one can never belong to this community. But clearly this kind of community and being-together is entirely different from the union aimed at by love.

But not only in the case of the exclusively formal communities is the membership in the community independent of love. The solidarity that is found in a state, in a nation, and in mankind not only does not presuppose love, but does not presuppose any explicit social act, any conscious act of entering. One belongs to the community of mankind in virtue of sharing a common destiny, of sharing the same meaning of life, valid for every human being; these causes of belonging to mankind are independent from all of our conscious stances. We cannot leave this community, just as we do not have to enter it by means of some particular conscious act. We can be born into a state or into a nation. This holds as well for the children in a family; they find themselves as members of this community. In all of these cases, one sees clearly that it is the objective theme of these communities, or some objective realm of goods and values, which builds up the community from within, holding its members together and uniting them.[5] This kind of community is clearly quite different from the union aimed at by the love for some individual person and by the intentio unionis of that love.

We saw in chapter 1 that it is false to derive love from community. This error, which is analogous to the error of deriving love from self-love, is expressed in the thesis that the part loves the whole, a thesis that is erroneously thought to be exemplified in the family. One says that a child loves its par-

---

which comes first and seeks requital, for example, friendship and above all spousal love; but in other categories of love, the requital is different in kind, as in love of parents for their children and of children for their parents, though such love is equal in quality and in intensity.

5   Cf. my book, *Die Metaphysik der Gemeinschaft*, Part I, chapters 6–8; Part II, chapter 4.

ents and siblings because it feels itself united with them from the beginning, because it discovers itself as a part of the family and belongs to the family. We also saw that this interpretation of the love of children for their parents and siblings turns out, on closer inspection, to be false, just as false as the assertion that the love of parents for their children is an extended self-love, as if parents loved their children as part of themselves. But here we have to stress that love and community are not the same thing; even if the union aimed at by the intentio unionis represents a deep community, and in fact in the case of marriage the deepest natural community, it is nevertheless the case that community is not the source of all love nor is love always the basis for belonging to a community.

The depth of solidarity in a community depends on the nature and rank of the unifying realm of value. Certain goods and domains of value appeal more than others to the love of the members of a community for each other. The family is a community in which love is much more closely bound up with the unifying realm of value than in the case of the state. Love is a central theme in a family, even if the family does not grow out of the love but is rather constituted by an objective domain of goods and values. But the question of how far the love of the members for each other is required by the meaning and nature of a community, has to be distinguished from the question whether this love is constitutive for the community. A family in which there is little love does not cease to be a family even though it is a very imperfect family, one which does not do justice to its meaning or purpose. But if in a state the members do not love each other, the state remains untouched in its meaning and purpose, as long as the laws of the state are just and wise and the citizens respect the laws and submit to the authority of the state.

The important thing here is to distinguish between love and the consciousness of community, and also to distinguish between the union aimed at by love from the solidarity that in many communities is built up from other sources. Even if we prescind from the objective belonging to a community and think of the experience of belonging together in the community, of the lived we-solidarity, the difference remains evident between love, which is always a definite response to a Thou (even in relations in which the we predominates), and a mere we-solidarity.

The experience of the we-solidarity in certain communities like nation, state, or church is an experience all its own. It is a we-solidarity, a belonging together, that extends far beyond all those persons whom one knows. In certain situations, when, for example, the state to which one belongs is attacked by another country or when for whatever reason a war breaks out, the solidarity with all the citizens of the state is experienced strongly, indeed something of this is experienced whenever the state is endangered. The solidarity that is actualized for many people at the playing of the national anthem (in fact the anthem explicitly appeals to and tries to awaken this solidarity), along with the loyalty to the state and along with the experience of belonging to the whole: this experience of the solidarity that encompasses everyone in the state including the many whom we do not know, is something fundamentally different from love. In spite of the friendly element that is found in this kind of we-solidarity and that at certain decisive moments is experienced as a bond with the members of the group to which one belongs oneself, this solidarity is fundamentally different from love in all its kinds.

The experience of this solidarity is different from love in a purely formal respect: it involves no *response* to an individual person. It is feeling myself to be in solidarity with many persons, both those known to me and those not known to me; it is a certain kind of solidarity that is defined by the fact that one is a member of the community to which the others also belong. It does not have the act-character of love; it lacks the character of a definite stance taken toward other persons. It is, of course, not merely a non-intentional state of mind, for it is not lacking a certain transcendence, but this is not the transcendence of love. Furthermore, it is not a value-response as love is. There is lacking here the specific word of love, namely the self-donation to a Thou, the thematicity of the other person. We will return to this subject in chapter 8, which is devoted to the various kinds of "mine."

We want to make a point here of adding the following thought. Love for an individual Thou and the union with the other that is desired are indeed different from this solidarity both objectively and in all that concerns the experience of solidarity; but they can of course coexist. I can be a friend of a fellow party member or with someone belonging to the same nation; in relation to this person, I feel both the solidarity born of love and in addition the very differently structured solidarity that he has as fellow member of the party, or as a member of the same nation and the same state. But this co-existence does not eliminate the difference between love and the union sought by love, on the one hand, and the other kind of belonging together, on the other hand. In fact, as we have already mentioned, the theme of certain communities appeals to the love of the members, and does so according to the kind and rank of the theme of the community.

Finally, we want to stress that for every love it is important that persons encounter each other in certain realms of goods and values, a fact that we have discussed extensively in our work, *Die Metaphysik der Gemeinschaft*. But this encounter in some realm of goods and values, to which already Aristotle pointed in Books VIII and IX of his *Nicomachean Ethics* as a central mark of friendship, is clearly very different from the objective solidarity that persons have as members of a community and that can exist without any love; it is also different from the experience of this objective solidarity.

5. *The levels of union between persons who love each other.* Only in love do I disclose to another person the face of my being and turn to him; only in

love do I hasten spiritually to him, as we have seen above. But I really reach the beloved person, I encounter him in a shared "here," only if he returns my love, only if he turns his spiritual face to me, hastening toward me. The first level is that my love penetrates the soul of the other, fills the other with happiness, and is fully received by him or her. But only if, over and above all of this, the other returns my love, filling my soul with happiness, indeed only in the interpenetration of loving looks between us, is the desired union established. This stands out with particular clarity in spousal love, in which a union is desired that surpasses all the other natural kinds of love; but it holds analogously for every union between two persons. However important many other things may be for the union, such as the presence of the beloved person, the possibility of speaking with him, sharing in his thoughts and in his life, all this does not lead to the desired union if the beloved person does not return my love. Even the identification of our exterior lives in marriage, along with all the tenderness and even the becoming one flesh in marriage, all of this fails to establish a true inner personal union as long as the interpenetration of loving looks is missing.[6] One never reaches the beloved person in the way that is desired by spousal love. But the interpenetration of loving looks or the mutual love establishes a profound union, even if everything else is missing: it is a true encounter of persons in a shared "here." Only on the basis of this unity can all the other elements, such as presence, dialogue, living together, and in the case of marriage, tenderness, and above all the becoming one flesh, unfold their unifying power, and only then can they confer the fulfilling happiness of union, which varies according to the love and the kind of union desired in it.

---

6   This in no way puts into question the formal unity that comes about through the act of marrying and that is as such independent of the inner union of love; I am referring to the indissoluble bond of marriage. I pointed out in many earlier writings that the act of marrying ought to emerge organically out of the unity born of mutual love, that in the case of mutual spousal love one necessarily aims at marrying, that this act is the specific expression of this love, and that the inner union here calls for this new formal unity that can come about only through the act of marrying. I have also discussed how the mutual self-donation in the marital act presupposes according to its very meaning not only the mutual love but also the marriage bond. The fact that only a mutual spousal love can establish the inner personal union desired in spousal love, is no objection to the fact that the act of marrying itself (although there is some abuse in performing the act of marrying without any love) establishes a highly significant formal unity, namely the marital bond that imposes certain duties and that even has the character of a sacrament. There is an analogy with the case of a valid priestly ordination of someone who is not really called to this office. He possesses through his ordination the power of confecting the sacrament and he is obliged to celibacy, even if he lacks a full faith and lacks a real love for Christ.

The yearning for unity as a kind of self-donation; the incompatibility of egoism with the real union of love

After all that was shown in the previous chapter on the relation of value and happiness, and after clarifying the nature of the union intended in the intentio unionis and also clarifying the conditions under which the union can come into being, we are in the position to see clearly how wrong the conception is that the intentio unionis interferes with the true commitment of love and has a self-ish character. By considering the following points we can overcome the misconception of the intentio unionis that culminates in the idea that another person is just being used as a means to our happiness in the intentio unionis; we can also overcome all the consequences that are drawn from this idea.

1. *The intentio unionis as an essential element of the self-donation of love and as an irreplaceable gift for the beloved person.* First of all, the intentio unionis is a fundamental gesture of love, an essential part of the word and the "gifts" of love. We have already seen how in responding to the beauty and preciousness of the beloved person, I hasten spiritually to him. It is precisely in recognizing his preciousness, in being deeply impressed by him and drawn to him, in giving the specific value-response of love, that I long to share in his life. In love I open the arms of my soul so as to surround the soul of the beloved person. The intentio unionis is an essential element of love, even apart from all the happiness that flows from union. There is a deep, ultimate bond between love and union, even if it is quite wrong, as we saw in chapter 1, to think that love is based on some already existing union. The bond rather shows itself in the fact that love yearns for union, and that union has a value all its own for the one who loves. The central importance of union stands forth very clearly as soon as we realize that the intentio unionis is an essential component of the incomparable gift that the surplus of love involves. The gift that is given to me when I am loved by another consists precisely in the great interest that the other takes in me, an interest that goes so far as not only to wish me well, but also to desire union with me. It is precisely the intentio unionis that explains why the act of turning toward the other is tremendously increased in the case of love, so that this act serves to distinguish love from all compassion, all admiration, all esteem. A person can give me no greater gift than desiring union with me and longing for the return of my love. If he is only generous and kind to me but I clearly see that he does not desire my presence or seek out any union with me, then, for all of my gratitude to him for his kindness, I do not experience the special and irreplaceable happiness that his love with its intentio unionis can confer on me.

In stressing the fact that union has its own proper meaning and value in itself and that the intentio unionis, even prior to all consideration of our happiness, is a basic gesture of love, we certainly do not mean thereby to deny that happiness is objectively inseparable from union. A union that conferred no happiness would be deprived of its very soul. No one could possibly say: I desire indeed union with another, although this union does not present itself to me as a source of happiness.

We see this with particular clarity in thinking, as we did above, of the gift that the intentio unionis is for the beloved person. It belongs precisely to this gift that I am a source of happiness for the one who loves me, that the union with me makes the one who loves me happy.

And with this we come to a further important point. Just as the yearning for union, the gesture of hastening to the beloved person, implies an increase of the value-response, so does the fact that this union presents itself to me as a source of happiness (varying according to the intensity, depth, and category of love), and in the case of union with God, as the source of beatitude.

We saw in the previous chapter that being made happy by value-bearing goods in no way entitles us to speak of a means-end relation. Such goods are in no way a means for my happiness; it is rather the case that I am made happy in a superabundant way by giving myself to them and letting their intrinsic value stand at the center of my attention. Thus the fact that some good makes me happy by its values, that in being affected by their splendor and beauty happiness streams into my soul, in no way interferes with the value-response and with the thematicity of value; it is rather the case that our relation to that good grows, indeed that a greater place is granted to the good in my soul. This holds in a particular way for union in the sense of the intentio unionis. To infer from the fact that union with the beloved person makes me happy, to the conclusion that intentio unionis desires union only as a means for one's happiness, is based on a two-fold error. First of all, true happiness and its gift-character are confused with self-centered happiness, with mere satisfaction, or even with mere pleasure; secondly, the relation of the superabundance obtaining between union and happiness is wrongly construed as a means-end relation.

2. *The priority that the happiness of the beloved person has over my own happiness deriving from union with him.* Above all, we should not forget that the interest and the happiness and ultimate well-being of the beloved person always has a priority over our union with him and the happiness flowing from that. But the fact that the intentio benevolentiae has a priority over the intentio unionis in no way implies that the intentio unionis is not an element of self-donation all its own that can be replaced by nothing else.

3. *Union is by its very nature equally sought as a source of my own and of the other person's happiness.* But it becomes clearer than ever that there is nothing selfish in the intentio unionis as soon as we consider that the union, being mutual, presupposes that both persons are made happy by it. We saw that the primary and decisive union is established only in the interpenetration of loving looks. The real intentio unionis is thus primarily a yearning for a return of love. As long as the beloved person does not return my love, my intentio unionis is inseparable from the hope that he might yet return it. The happiness

of union by its essence is mutual, that is, it would not be union if it were not a source of happiness for the beloved person as well as for myself; or as we could also put it, the requital of love brings with it an intentio unionis on the part of the beloved person, who must desire the union just as truly as I desire it. The reason why I am made happy by the return of his love is precisely because the other desires this union for my sake, that he finds his happiness in it, as we have seen. Thus in every real intentio unionis the union is necessarily seen as a source of the other person's happiness just as much as of my own. And so it becomes even clearer that there is no least shadow of selfishness in the intentio unionis as such.

We repeat: a mutual love includes a mutual intentio unionis, and this implies in turn that the union is a source of happiness for both persons. If the union is not desired by both, if it is not a source of happiness for both, then there is no mutual love and union cannot come into being. And union not only implies that it is a source of happiness for both, but also that each knows that it is a source of happiness for the other. Neither of them can desire union without being consciously directed to the happiness of the beloved other.

Essential as it is that the union be a source of happiness for the beloved person, I cannot desire this exclusively under the aspect of my own happiness. If I were interested only in my own happiness and not also in that of the other, I would no longer seek and desire real union. The yearning for union cannot be detached from the yearning for a return of love, and the happiness conferred by union necessarily presupposes that union is a source of happiness for the other. My own happiness and the happiness of the beloved person are inseparably woven together in the union of love. Thus in the intentio unionis I desire *our* happiness; retreating into my own happiness and being indifferent to the happiness of the beloved person is profoundly incompatible not only with love but also with the authentic intentio unionis.

We said that union does not come about apart from some return of love. But that should not be taken to mean that the love has to be equally great on both sides and has to belong to the same category of love. There are in fact many relations where the category of love differs from one side to the other. The love of children for their parents is categorically different from the love of parents for their children, and the highest union is here achieved in the interpenetration of two categorially different loves, assuming that they are the same in their depth and degree of love. Something similar holds for the relation between master and disciple, or even for certain friendships. The union intended by spousal love, by contrast, requires that the categorically same love is given on both sides. But what must be stressed here is that, even if the ideal union always presupposes the same degree of love in both persons, a union can still come about even when the degree of love differs from one person to another. We should not forget that the capacity for loving [*Liebespotential*] varies greatly from one person to another. A union can come about even between persons who are very different in their capacity for loving. But even apart from this difference (which expresses itself above all in how central a role the love plays in the life of a person) it can happen that one person is more attracted by another than vice versa. There are many friendships in which one person loves more deeply than the other but in which a personal union comes about just the same. The greater the difference between the love of the one and the love of the other, the less the union, and the less is the intentio unionis fulfilled in the one who loves more. But as long as there is some return of love, there can be some union.

The same thing holds in the case of spousal love. If a man loves a woman more—more deeply, more ardently—than he is loved by her, or the other way around, a certain union can still come about. I may enter into marriage with another even knowing that the marriage does not mean as much for the other as it means for me, and that the intentio unionis is not as ardent on the part of the other as on my part, and that the marriage is not the same source of happiness for the other as it is for me. I may receive the gift of the other with happiness and gratitude, realizing that I cannot expect the same degree of love that I give. But I must at least assume that the other loves me and desires this union, even if not in the same measure as I desire it.

Suppose that the other does not love me and yet for whatever reason marries me. I can accept this only if I hope that I will eventually win the heart of the other, that is, if I hope that the other will eventually love me and will find happiness in being united with me. If I cannot seriously hope for this, then I cannot enter the marriage as long as I really love the other. We are not speaking here of what I ought to do, but rather of an inner impossibility. If I really love and have a real intentio unionis, then I understand that, in the absence of any intentio unionis on the part of the other and in the absence of any prospect of it in the future, the desired union can never come about and marriage cannot represent any fulfillment of my love. A man would not really love who would, instead of marrying on the basis of this hope, marry without it. But even if he did marry without it, one could still not say that union was being placed above the happiness of the other; and this is a kind of limit case, because the man who loves will hardly enter a marriage as long as the consent of the woman is felt by him to be nothing but a sacrifice. If he has any hope of having his love requited, he will postpone the marriage until it is requited, because he understands that the marital community, by its very nature, becomes, in the complete absence of love, a terrible imposition. Every person who is unhappy in love aims with his intentio unionis primarily at the return of his love. This is what he yearns for and hopes for; and included in this is the hope that the union will be as great a source of happiness for the other as it is for him.

If we realize that the union desired in the intentio unionis is necessarily desired as a source of happiness for the other, then we see clearly that the intentio unionis forms a contrast with a selfish attitude, and that it rather represents an unsurpassable self-donation to the beloved person. This is why it is an essential element in love considered as a super value-response.

4. *If union with another person is desired exclusively under the aspect of one's own happiness, love is replaced by the "will to possess."* As soon as a union is desired that is not built on a return of love and thus is not desired equally for the happiness of both, then there is no real intentio unionis. What is desired is no longer a personal union but rather some kind of possessing; and such desire is emphatically self-centered. It is no longer authentic love.

With this we touch upon a further source of confusion about the intentio unionis: one fails to distinguish clearly between union and possession. Possession or ownership is a relation that objectively can exist only between a person and a non-person. Only persons can possess something in the full sense[7]; only they can be the owners of something. And only an impersonal thing can be validly possessed, that is, can serve as the property of the person. The ancient Romans sensed this when they denied personality to the slaves and regarded each of them as a mere *res*, a mere thing.[8] That is of course an absurd fiction, for persons remain truly persons and can never become things. But it shows some understanding for the fact that only non-personal beings can be validly owned as property.

The union established between a person and the object he possesses is a union all its own; it has to be sharply distinguished from the union that is achieved in the full *frui* of some great good. This latter union is, first of all, of a much deeper and more spiritual nature. Secondly, in this union there is no subordination of the good to the person, even though here a person stands over against a non-personal good endowed with great value.[9] On the contrary, as person I give myself to the beauty in which I delight, approaching it with reverence and seeing in it something superior to which I look up. In spite of the

---

7   I prescind here from the distinction made by the jurists between possession and property. We are thinking of the curious legally valid relation that obviously includes having legitimate dominion over some object and being the owner of it.

8   In saying that only persons can possess something or be the real owners of something, we are not denying that animals show an instinctive gesture of possessing that is analogous to personal possessing. Especially the gesture of excluding others from the use of a thing, "staking a claim" to it, and defending it against any other who wants to contest it, is found in the dog who growls at other dogs and at human beings when he is chewing on a bone, or when the dog will not tolerate as a fellow occupant of the house another dog that is new to the house. But there is clearly here only a vague possessive feeling that in no way entitles us to say that the dog could objectively be the owner of something. The collar that one puts around his neck is indeed meant for him but it does not belong to him in a real sense.

9   This distinction no longer holds with goods that are only subjectively satisfying; but even then this *frui* is a relation quite different from possession.

ontological superiority of a person, this union has the character of a commitment of the person to the good and its values. But the union established by possession or ownership clearly puts the person in a superior position as possessor in relation to the possessed. For the relation of possession as such, it does not matter whether the thing possessed is a distinguished palace of great artistic value or just some neutral object.

The bond with some good that one owns is in itself an entirely legitimate and noble bond.[10] But all these dangers of owning do not amount to an objection to the objective justification and dignity of this relation. It is a God-given reality and a primary right of man. To take away this right from the outside, as for instance in the communist state, is to commit a great injustice. It is a classic way of being related to impersonal goods, and it is the basis for the need, growing spontaneously out of love, to give something to a beloved person. By giving someone something, one not only helps him to an enjoyment of the good, whether it is a book that he can read whenever he wants to or whether it is a house in which he can live, etc.; by giving there arises the further fact that the thing given is made to be the property of the other.

---

10   This is in no way to deny that there are certain classic dangers in possession and in owning. Gabriel Marcel has said some deep things about this. He points out that an owner can easily become the slave of his property. Although it belongs to the nature of possession that the owner occupies a position of dominion toward the object, he is easily led by avarice to be so anxious about his property that he becomes the slave of it. His thoughts center around the security of his possession, and being an owner becomes in an exaggerated way the main source of satisfaction for him. His life becomes dependent on his property. He is like the capitalist so brilliantly described by Sombart; this capitalist never gets around to enjoying his wealth because he is completely dominated by the immanent logic of his factory or organization. He becomes even more of a slave of it than the workers whom he exploits, and he keeps on working even when the workers take time for rest. But this enslavement to one's possession, to one's property shows itself above all in the greedy person, as so wonderfully presented by Molière in his play *Avare*.

A second main danger of property pointed out by Gabriel Marcel is the defensive attitude toward other persons that grows out of the experience of something as mine, of "belonging to me and not to you." I then am always on the alert to see to it that others do not get too close to me and endanger my property. I close myself off against other persons, fortify myself in myself, falling into an almost hostile attitude towards my neighbor; at the least I approach the other in a potential defensive attitude.

We can add to these dangers pointed out by Marcel yet another one, which however is not in the same way rooted in the nature of possession: feeling myself to be important and superior because of what I possess or, as we could also say, making of my property a source of respectability, dignity, of a claim to be important. This is especially clearly given in the type of *nouveau riche* wonderfully characterized by Fritz Reuter and others.

The main point here is to distinguish resolutely between the union of persons naturally desired by love from any and every possession of the beloved person. We mentioned above that it is not objectively possible for persons to be possessed; even if one treats a person like a thing and acts as if the person were one's property, a valid relation of possession would objectively never come into being.

To consider a person as property is not only an illusion, not only a pure "as if," but it is also, in contrast to the possessing of things, profoundly immoral. Although every attempt to own persons is invalid and rests on a fiction, the attempt has nevertheless often been made to treat people like property. Just think of slavery in the ancient world, of the owner of a harem, or of totalitarian states like Nazi Germany or Soviet Russia or Communist China, in which the citizens function as property of the state. But these are drastic cases of treating people as property; it is more important for our purposes to notice those cases in which elements of the mentality of an owner creep into the relation to a beloved person.

This danger is often found in the relation of parents to their children. Parents often have the feeling that children "belong" to them. The position of superiority that parents have in relation to their children, as well as the legitimate authority that obliges them to command and to forbid certain things to their children, facilitates the intrusion of a partial distortion of their relation to their children in the direction of possession. This is especially the case when parents illegitimately see in their children an extension of their own ego. Then the deep personal union of the family, in which children are entrusted in a unique way to the parents by God, is turned into a property relation—of course not theoretically, but in the practice of parents.[11] But also in the relation of man and woman in marriage, the category of possession can creep in, especially on the part of the man. He lays claim to his wife, who belongs to him as if a piece of property.

But this is wrong and incompatible with the genius of love, even if, as with many other elements opposed to the genius of love, it can creep into a love, compromising the love and making it less authentic, although without completely eliminating the love. But above all, and this is what concerns us most of all here, this "pseudo-possession" does not imply any union; by laying claim to the other as if to some property no real personal union is achieved, but rather this "as if" possession undermines all true union.

Mutuality, or reciprocity, is the soul of personal union; the one-sidedness that necessarily lies in the relation of possession or owning stands, therefore,

---

11   In the course of history, the idea of children as property has had dreadful consequences. In Roman law a father had the right to decide about the life and death of his children. Even into the modern period parents have presumed to determine whom their children should marry.

in sharp contrast to all personal union. Much as possession involves a specific union in relation to non-personal goods, even if it does not represent the closest possible union with them in many cases, it would form no union with persons, even if it could legitimately exist in relation to them. And thus all attempts to treat another as property and to desire the possession of the other, quite apart from their objective invalidity, are a way of searching for union in a completely wrong place, in a place where true personal union is impossible. Thus the dreadful statement of Aristippus, who when asked whether he loved his concubine answered, "If I eat a fish, I don't ask if the fish enjoys being eaten," is the extreme opposite of love, surely just as opposed to love as hatred is, even if in a different way. In love one gives oneself to another and this is the very opposite of possession. But it would be false to interpret this self-giving as if one wanted to make the other person the owner of oneself. The self-giving aims at quite a different relation from that of being possessed; "I am yours" is something utterly different, possible only between persons.[12]

As soon as one confuses union with possession, and the intentio unionis with the will to possess, then the intentio unionis seems to be something that compromises the pure value-response and to be incompatible with authentic self-donation. But as soon as one understands what this union really is, one also sees that the intentio unionis flows organically out of the basic gesture of love, out of the value-responding affirmation of the beloved person; instead of spoiling the self-donation with an egocentric element, it represents the very summit of self-donation, the supreme form of ultimate interest in the beloved person.

The error of thinking that the absence of the intentio unionis in love of neighbor is the source of its moral selflessness

We turn now to another source of misinterpretation concerning the intentio unionis; it involves a much more subtle confusion than the confusion of possession and union. We are referring to the fact that one often takes the love of neighbor as the model of all pure and selfless love. Sublime as this love undoubtedly is, we would be wrong to think that its sublime character comes from the fact that, in accordance with the particular theme of this love, the intentio unionis is overshadowed by the intentio benevolentiae. The sublime

---

12 We will discuss this in some detail later and will distinguish the relation that the spouses in marriage have to each other's body (the right to one's own body that is granted in the act of marrying, as well as all that is expressed in the words, "I am yours," or "I belong to you") from the relation of possessing in the true sense. At present it is enough to see that the intentio unionis inherent in love has nothing to do with the will to possess the other and that personal union, in that it is by its nature a mutual self-donation, constitutes the very opposite of a relation of possession.

character of this love derives rather from its inherently supernatural foundation, from its bond with Christ and the love for Christ. The intentio unionis
recedes in this love exclusively because of its specific theme; the same thing
that makes here for supremely selfless love would be a deficiency of love in
the setting of friendship or of spousal love, or even of the love for God, for in
each of these the theme is a very different one.

1. *Two kinds of commitment.* It is not correct to say that in the love for my
neighbor only an intentio benevolentiae is found and that the intentio unionis
is entirely absent; union and love are intrinsically connected, as we have
already said. But it is true that the intentio unionis shows itself in the love of
neighbor only in the yearning to be united with my neighbor in the kingdom
of Christ. Here too a return of love is desired, but here this means that I desire
that my neighbor approaches me in the attitude of love of neighbor, or, to say
it better, that the love of neighbor reigns in his heart. The union that arises in
mutual love of neighbor cannot be compared with the union desired in all the
other categories of love. It has a different character, deriving as it does from
the incorporation of both into the kingdom of Christ.

The exclusive "for the other's sake," the removal of my own person, my
own happiness and subjectivity [*Eigenleben*], represents in this kind of love
the fullness of pure self-donation, of victoriously flowing love. But in spousal
love an exclusive "for the other's sake" and a removal of my own person would
in no way represent the fullness of spousal love. On the contrary, a man who
would say to a woman, "I want to marry you only for the sake of your happiness, so that you might be happy—my own happiness is not important," would
obviously not love her at all with spousal love, and he would by such an attitude withhold from her the great gift that makes the spousally beloved person
so deeply happy. Indeed, in such an utterance there would be a definite insult
given to the woman. This "selflessness" would be the sign of a pharisaical
pride and would represent something shameless. The important point for us is
to see that in the case of spousal love such an attitude would withhold from the
other precisely the great gift that confers happiness. This gift is nothing other
than the intentio unionis, the fact that I desire the marriage not only for the
beloved person, not only for the sake of her happiness, but also for my sake,
that I myself see in this union the greatest source of my earthly happiness. The
intentio unionis and the happiness flowing from it belong to the meaning and
theme of this love; far from reducing the spousal self-donation in any way, they
involve a kind of self-donation not found in love of neighbor. The very thing
that makes for the greatest self-donation in spousal love is not only absent in
the love of neighbor—this accords with the theme and the categorical difference of these two loves—but in fact this absence is constitutive of the excellence of the self-donation found in the love of neighbor.

When in chapter 11 we explore in detail the nature of love of neighbor,
we will understand better why the "only for the other's sake and for the

sake of his happiness" of this love, in accordance with its particular theme, makes for the fullness of selfless self-donation. Here it suffices to see that it is wrong to take traits of the love of neighbor that derive from its particular categorical identity and to make them into conditions for real and authentic self-donation in love as such, and so to regard as selfish all those kinds of love that lack these traits.

2. *The ambiguity of the terms "selfish" and "selfless."* There is clearly an equivocation at work here with the terms "selfless" and "selfish." On the one hand, with "selfless" one means that in the love of neighbor I step out of my subjectivity, and that my neighbor does not represent an objective good for me. One uses "selfless" in the sense of "independent from my subjectivity." One should not present "selfless" in this sense as the opposite of egoism. Of course, this selflessness is incompatible with egoism, but it does not imply an antithesis to egoism, because what we are here calling "self" has nothing at all to do with egoism. That which is not "selfless" in this sense is not therefore egoistic, indeed it is not necessarily even any closer to egoism. The fact that in the natural categories of love there is a possibility of egoism that does not exist in the love of neighbor, does not entitle us to call these loves egoistic simply because they are not "selfless" in this sense.

We find an analogy to this in speaking of the innocence of a small child. Here we have something in mind that is incompatible with moral badness, and yet innocence is not the specific antithesis to moral badness. Not every adult who lacks this innocence is therefore morally bad, or even any closer to being morally bad. It does not matter that there is the possibility for an adult to become morally guilty that does not exist in the child, who can not make any use of its free will. The true opposite to the morally bad is the morally good and not innocence. In the same way, "selflessness" in the present sense is not the antithesis to egoism, although it is incompatible with egoism. This meaning of "selfless" is not a primarily moral meaning; its specific difference refers to something that is not moral but rather has a structural character.

On the other hand, the term "selfless" is used in quite another sense and this time we do indeed have to do with a purely moral sense. Here one means the absence of egoism, the opposite of the moral disvalue that one is aiming at with the term egoism. Let us just think, for example, of a person who looks at everything from the point of view of the subjectively satisfying, who thinks only of what is pleasurable for him. This equivocation is facilitated by the fact that love of neighbor is selfless in this sense too, indeed, represents an eminent form of selflessness in this moral sense. This makes it all the more important to avoid the equivocation. The reason why love of neighbor is selfless in the first and formal or categorical sense is very different from the reason for it being the epitome of selflessness in the moral sense. A love of neighbor is selfless in the formal or categorical sense because in it one steps beyond one's own subjectivity. It is selfless in the moral sense, is indeed a supreme form of moral selflessness, because it is filled with charity, with this entirely new supernatural love that is constituted in the love of God. We will speak later of this in chapter 11.

But it does not suffice to see that the intentio unionis implies no lapse from the attitude of value-response, that it is not incompatible with the commitment of love; one must also see that the intentio unionis makes for a particular kind of commitment in all the categories of love with the exception of love of neighbor. The intentio unionis belongs to the elements that make love a super value-response. This is particularly evident in our love for God.

3. *Fenelon's ideal of* amour desinteressé *(disinterested love).* In Fenelon's idea of *amour desinteressé* the intentio unionis is misunderstood in a particular way. It is a great error to think that the yearning for eternal union with God, does not belong necessarily to the love for God. The *amour desinteressé* of Fenelon is not only impossible for man; even if it were possible it would in no way be a more sublime love but would rather be an inferior love.

A very personal and deep commitment to another implies that I wholeheartedly yearn for union with the beloved person, that this union is the supreme source of my happiness. If I attempt to exclude the intentio unionis from the love of God, I achieve not the selflessness of love of neighbor, but rather the annihilation of my own person. An *amour desinteressé* in relation to God is in reality less love, for the absence of the intentio unionis, as expressed in the words, "My happiness is not important," would, just as in the case of spousal love, amount to a standing apart with myself and my subjectivity and failing really to give myself. And not only that, it would even amount to a throwing away of my own self, a dissolution of my own subjectivity; for here I have to do with my absolute and ultimate happiness, so that indifference to my eternal union with God amounts to a dissolution of my own self, an annihilation of my personal existence. Besides, it would not at all be a sublime moral selflessness, as in the case of love of neighbor, but rather a sham heroism; for God wants this union with us. This attitude would be a refusal to appreciate the gift that God offers in His infinite love for us. Given the fact that we are created for God and are called by His love to eternal beatitude, and given that we have here to do with the infinitely holy and absolute Lord, it follows that a gesture that in love of neighbor is heroic and sublime becomes something extremely arrogant, the very opposite of true commitment, a kind of sham heroism.[13]

---

13 We will later see that certain well-known statements of St. Theresa of Avila or of St. Francis Xavier in no way contradict what we have just said about *amour desinteressé*. [Von Hildebrand refers here to prayers written by these saints, such as this one from St. Francis Xavier: "Then why, O blessed Jesus Christ, should I not love Thee well: Not for the sake of winning Heaven, or of escaping Hell; Not with the hope of gaining aught, not seeking a reward; But, as Thyself hast loved me, O

The idea of an *amour desinteressé* is understandable as a reaction against the view that derives all love from self-love, thus depriving it of its self-transcending character of commitment. Here the character of love as value-response, along with the transcendence of love, is completely misunderstood. Love is taken as an immanent striving, as presupposing that the beloved person presents himself as an objective good for me. We could express it more exactly like this: the other person is not taken as objectively valuable, precious, beautiful, and it is not the intrinsic importance of the other that grounds my love and awakens it; it is rather the fact that the other has the character of an objective good for me. One says that union with the beloved person is an objective good for me not because of the beauty and worth of that person, but because the other is able to satisfy my *appetitus* (for fulfillment). The love for God is thought to be a consequence of the striving for perfection. Of course, despite the immanence of this love, it should not be seen as egocentric. The *intentio unionis* is also in no way thought of as egocentric or as in any way imperfect. But in accordance with this general conception of love, the *intentio unionis* is deprived of its real character, that is, of its commitment and transcendence. This conception of love provokes the wish to find some place for a love with a transcendent and heroic character, and one thinks one finds this in the love of neighbor. One wrongly thinks that it is the absence of the *intentio unionis* that gives this love its heroic character. This is why one tries in the love for God to achieve something similar by way of an *amour desinteressé*.

But this leads, as we saw, not to some supreme heroic commitment, but to a self-contradictory love and a pseudo-heroism. The correction of this view of love can come only by establishing the true nature of the *intentio unionis* and not by trying to liberate love from immanence and sometimes from a selfish note by removing the *intentio unionis* even from those kinds of love to which it naturally belongs. Neither a conception of the love for God that has been deprived of its transcendence and commitment, nor the conception of *amour desinteressé* is able to do justice to the true nature of the love for God.

A further misunderstanding underlying the *amour desinteressé* is the failure to understand the intentional and transcendent character of true happiness,

---

ever-loving Lord?"] They are referring to the inner order of every true love, mainly the priority that the beloved person and his well-being has in relation to my union with him; we could also say, the priority of the *intentio benevolentiae* over the *intentio unionis*. This means, in the case of the love of God, the priority of the glorification of God, the honor of God, His holy will, over the question of our eternal salvation. We will understand this better once we have analyzed the alternative that one usually presupposes. Besides, the famous statements of the saints, as is often the case with mystics and saints, have to be understood as exclamations of overflowing love; one cannot take them as a formulation of the enduring nature of their love. This is why they cannot be cited as constituting proof for the sublimity of *amour desinteressé*.

which we have discussed in the previous chapter. As soon as one takes happiness to be something self-contained and separates it from the good out of whose value it superabundantly grows, one is already on the wrong track. If one presents happiness as if it were primarily a certain state of my own soul that can be abstracted from the good conferring happiness on me and grounding my happiness, one thereby necessarily restricts oneself to the inauthentic self-centered happiness.[14]

This detachment of happiness from its source leads necessarily to a merely self-centered happiness; it becomes grotesque if applied to God and eternity. If one speaks of beatitude as if it were something that could be detached from the beatific vision, one has unavoidably falsified entirely the nature of beatitude and deprived it of its dimension of eternity. This is the grotesque conception that can be found in certain critics of Christian ethics who object that this ethics is locked into a pure eudaemonism. Thus Kant subsumes the heavenly reward of the Christian under the category of pleasure [*Lust*], and we can often encounter the view that Christians only act well for the sake of securing a good and safe place for themselves in eternity. Here one takes a self-centered happiness that not only has a purely earthly and contingent character, but even in the perspective of earthly happiness belongs to a lower, secondary, superficial sphere; one then projects this into eternity and affirms that this happiness is the beatitude promised in Christian ethics as a heavenly reward. Unfortunately, the impossibility of detaching beatitude from the eternal union with God has not always been sufficiently seen by Catholic writers in their treatment of beatitude. Insofar as beatitude is the absolute absence of suffering, one could possibly aim at it without basing oneself on the union of God. But even here one cannot mean the absence of all suffering, for only the union with God can take away that suffering that comes from a lack of fulfillment in the soul. St. Augustine spoke of it when he said, "You have made us for Yourself, O Lord, and our heart is restless until it rests in You." This holds all the more for the suffering that arises when the intentio unionis of our love for God remains unfulfilled, for the intentio unionis is the basis for achieving beatitude.[15]

---

14 *This* happiness plays no role at all in true love and has no place in it. There is in this striving for a self-centered happiness, as we already said, nothing morally negative, but also nothing morally good, and in fact it is not even the bearer of an extra-moral value, as we saw. But it right away becomes something egoistic if it comes between me and the call of a morally relevant value so as to prevent me from responding to this call, or if it in some way creeps into my love as a foreign body that compromises it.

15 This unfulfilled love is expressed in the splendid hymn of St. Thomas Aquinas:
Jesu, quem velatum nunc aspicio,
Oro, fiat illud, quod tam sitio:
Ut, te revelata cernens facie,

But as soon as we come to the positive meaning of beatitude, which after all infinitely surpasses the mere absence of suffering, including the suffering of unfulfilled longing for God, we find it quite impossible to detach beatitude in any way at all from the beatific vision, from the eternal and indestructible union of love with God, and to treat it in any way as being a self-contained state of the soul. Beatitude presupposes love for God, just as a reward presupposes the deed that merits the reward; not only that, but since beatitude consists in a union of love with God, it can really be beatitude only for the one who loves God and yearns for Him.

In conclusion, we affirm that the intentio unionis belongs essentially to love; and in all the categories of love, with the exception of love of neighbor, it constitutes the fullness of commitment and value-response.

The unfulfilled character of desire does not belong necessarily to the intentio unionis

But if, as we saw, the intentio unionis belongs essentially to love, this does not mean that the ardor of love can be reduced to the tension proper to all kinds of unsatisfied desire. The interest in union makes itself felt as a yearning for union as long as union has not yet been achieved, and when it has been achieved this interest makes itself felt as happiness. Whereas in all forms of appetitus the ardor and thrust of desire derive from the tension of unsatisfied desire, the satisfaction of which brings about a state of full rest, this is in no way the case with love understood as a genuine value-response. The ardor and fire of love are rather a fruit of the beauty of the beloved person and they in no way decrease, any more than the love itself decreases, once the union with the beloved person is achieved. Plato made this mistake when in the *Symposium* he called love the son of *Poros* (Plenty) and *Penia* (Neediness).[16] Our expression *intentio* could perhaps awaken the idea that an unsatisfied yearning is essential to the intentio unionis But that is in no way the case. The essential trait that we are pointing out in all love is found just as much in the joy and happiness of fulfilled union as in the yearning for a not-yet-achieved union.

Summary on love as a super value-response

Let us summarize as follows: even if the natural love for creatures does not have the commitment and transcendence that is only proper to moral value-responses, still it possesses in another respect a unique commitment and

---

Visu sim beatus tuae gloriae.

O Jesus, who are at present veiled to my gaze,

I pray and thirst to see you unveiled, face to face,

So that I might be blessed in the vision of your glory.

16 *Symposium* 203a ff. *Penia* is according to the myth told here by Plato the poor and ignorant mother of *Eros*, which means love, and the god *Poros* is the wise and rich father of *Eros*.

transcendence, which gives us the occasion to speak of a "super value-response."

First of all, love is a super value-response because the beloved person is a source of happiness for the one who loves. We saw in chapter 5 that in the value-response of love happiness is a secondary theme, that it does not deprive the value-response of its character of commitment and transcendence, but rather, on the contrary, makes for an intensification of the value-responding interest. Secondly, love is a super value-response because the interest in the beloved person goes so far that he becomes on the basis of his value an objective good for me in the strict sense of the word. Finally, love is a super value-response because of its intentio unionis, this interest in the beloved person that surpasses all other value-responses.

But even these three elements constituting love as a super value-response do not exhaust the extraordinary self-donation and transcendence of love. These three elements are profoundly interrelated and really represent *one* dimension of super value-response; but there is another entirely different dimension of self-donation and transcendence constituting love as a super value-response, and it is the subject of the following chapter.

*   *   *

Excursus on the subject-object difference
and on the problem of objectifying persons

The terms "object" and "objective" have taken on a negative sense as a result of existentialist philosophy. One sees the object in the light of an illicit objectification, of making a thing out of beings that are not thing-like. In this sense, a French thinker has rightly warned against making the human person into a thing—something he has called "chosisme" ("thing-ism"). Gabriel Marcel, Martin Buber and many others have again and again pointed to the difference between relating to another as person, as Thou, and relating to another as "he" or "she," or even as an impersonal object.

However true and important this is, it would nevertheless be quite false to overlook the place and importance of the fundamental datum which is the subject-object situation. The term "object" can have two entirely different meanings. On the one hand, one can use it to characterize the nature of the being, and in doing so one to some extent thinks of an object on the model of a *thing*. On the other hand, one can use the term to express the position that a being occupies in relation to the I. We can start from the fundamental datum of subject and object, from the fundamental situation given in all authentic apprehension of beings, in the consciousness of the world that surrounds us. Object in this sense is everything that stands over against us, that presents itself in front of us, in contrast to all that we ourselves consciously are, for example, in contrast to the stances that we consciously live in.

But it would be entirely wrong to think that the object position, that is, the fact that something is over against me and that I look at it, necessarily implies that this being is an object in the ontological sense of the word, that one has turned it into a thing. Making something into a thing can rightly be called objectification. But the fact that something is over against me, is there on the object side, is not the result of any activity or stance of a person that one could call objectification, but it is a primary datum that is given to me. And in fact it is found in an eminent way in the I-Thou situation. Even in the interpenetration of looks that expresses love, this duality has a central position; the consciousness of my own self and of the other person to whom I am directed, to whom my love refers, to whom I look and to whom I give myself, is in a purely formal respect a subject-object situation, different as it may be from other subject-object situations. Instead of denying that we have here a subject facing an object and that in this very formal sense the Thou is my object, one should instead elaborate the radical ontological difference of persons from non-persons and also the fundamental difference of the I-Thou relation from all other subject-object relations. The I-Thou relation is the very opposite of any objectification. With this we come to a further significant problem with the terms "object" and "objective."

One includes in the subject-object situation an attitude that suggests the model of scientific research and makes us think of what it is to be an object in a laboratory. One thinks that if something is an object for us then it must be something neutral, something that leaves us personally uninvolved. It is put at a distance, like putting it on a table, and in this way we detach it from the living solidarity with ourselves; we neutralize it. This is the neutralizing attitude that Kierkegaard fought against. Many authors contrast it rightly with the more authentic situation in which the object has for us its full, real, living significance and in which we live a "committed" existence in relation to it. One contrasts the existential solidarity of subject and object with an abstract, neutralizing attitude, with objectification taken in a certain sense. With this contrast, one points out something extremely important: in the antithesis to this kind of objectification, something fundamentally important is seen and affirmed. But as soon as one takes this neutralization as an essential mark of the formal subject-object situation, as soon as one thinks that the quite formal subject-object situation or even the distinction of subject and object is the product of this neutralizing kind of objectification, one falls into a great error. Not only that, but this attempt to make the fundamental subject-object situation into something artificially devised by us leads to absurdity, to the undermining of all knowledge. The fundamental and pervasive subject-object situation in no way includes this note of anti-existential and artificial objectification; and even less should the expression "objective" be identified with "neutral."

CHAPTER SEVEN

Intentio Benevolentiae, Value-Response, and Super Value-Response

As we saw, love is not compromised as a value-response by the fact that the beloved person becomes an objective good for me; this fact (which occurs in all love except love of neighbor) rather raises love to the level of a super value-response. But since the beloved person is an objective good for me, since his existence is a source of happiness, much that affects him—this holds to the degree that the love is great and deep—becomes an objective good for me. His health is not only an objective good for him but also for me. In the same way his intelligence and moral virtues are a gift for me. We can say: all his valuable qualities are a gift for the one who loves him; they give the lover joy and delight.

From this we have to distinguish another essential trait of love proper to all the categories of love between human beings. When I love I consider all that happens to the beloved person not only under the aspect of value and not only under the aspect of the objective good for me, but also under the aspect of the objective good or evil for the beloved person. And I do not just *consider* it under this aspect; everything *affects* me under the aspect of the objective good or evil for the beloved person. I who love rejoice because the other experiences something that is gladdening for him, and I suffer when the other suffers. That seems at first glance to be so obvious that the reader may wonder why it is here introduced as a distinct mark of love. One is perhaps inclined to say: it is obvious that when I love someone, I am concerned that he is happy and prospers. We all take it for granted that I am affected by the objective goods and evils for him.

But that is a deception. In reality this interest in all that befalls the beloved person under the aspect of the objective good or evil for him, is something extraordinary, an entirely new dimension of the transcendence of love, surpassing all the previously mentioned ones. It is altogether worthy of marveling, it is something we must approach with the wonder that is indispensable for the philosopher. This becomes clear if we first examine more closely the distinction between the aspect of value and the aspect of the objective good for the person, or the beneficial good, as we can as well say, and then establish the radical difference in point of view between the objective good for myself and the objective good for some other person.

The point of view of value contrasted with the point of view of the objective good for the beloved person

If a beloved person is, for example, treated unjustly, if others do him some wrong, we first of all reject this from the point of view of the disvalue involved. We are indignant at the injustice. But we can and should do this even if we do not love the unjustly treated person. As soon as we love him, we go beyond indignation and are sad over the fact that an injustice has been committed against him; we see the injustice under the aspect of an objective evil for him. Or go back to an example used earlier: if someone whom I love finds the true faith and converts, I am not only glad that God is glorified through this conversion, but I am also glad about the great objective good that this person thereby receives. The joy over the glorification of God is a pure value-response. When we consider this event simply from the value point of view, its value is identical with the glorification of God implied in the event, and this response under the aspect of value and under the aspect of the glorification of God must have the priority. We can also refer under the aspect of value to the fact that this conversion represents the greatest objective good for the person. For the fact that some great good is bestowed upon a person is always the bearer of a value. But we are not here thinking of the response to this value, that is, of the value responding stance to the fact that someone has received an objective good for himself; we are thinking of the response considered under the aspect of an objective good for him. For only this latter is a specific characteristic of love; only love gives birth to this kind of interest in the other person. The response to the objective good for the other under the aspect of value can be given even though we do not love the person in question, indeed do not even know him or her. But it is a characteristic of love to respond to this event also under the aspect of being an objective good for the other. This is an entirely different dimension of transcendence from the one involved in the moral value-response; but it is also different from the transcendence proper to love as a super value-response, that is, insofar as the beloved person is an objective good for the one who loves him.

In order to understand this, we have to consider how much the point of view of the objective good for the person refers to oneself, in contrast to the point of view of value. It is not surprising that I give the same value-response as someone else. In fact, we expect of each person who lives out of a fundamental attitude of value-response that he gives an adequate response to value-bearing goods. For value does not derive its importance from some relation to a person; a great work of art is not beautiful *for* someone, an action is not morally good *for* someone. As long as I just think of value and take an interest in some good under the aspect of value, as above all in every response to morally relevant goods and also to the moral values of another, we are dealing with the most objective stance that a person can possibly take. This is why, as long as value is the exclusive theme, it makes no difference whether the value is in me or in another; the pure value-response is the same in each case. The concern that God not be offended by sin or that He be glorified by some moral deed has, as value-response, the same character whether it is I or someone else who is acting. We prescind here from the significant difference arising from the fact that when I am the agent the action depends on my free will, making me responsible for it, whereas this responsibility is missing when it is another person who is acting. Important and decisive as this distinction is, it goes in a different direction; thus we can ignore it at present. The important thing for us is seen in the following. Compare my avoiding a situation that is morally dangerous for me, with my helping someone else avoid a situation that is morally dangerous for him: it would clearly be nonsensical to say that my concern with the moral danger for the other is more selfless or morally better.

But as soon as something is approached under the aspect of the objective good for someone, it makes a large difference whether the objective good is for me or for another. It is not as if my interest in objective goods for myself would necessarily have any kind of selfish character; we have already explained in detail why this is not the case. There can be no question of self-ishness, even though the character of my interest varies according to the different kinds of objective good for me. But it is true that the possibility of a selfish attitude arises here, and that there is a large difference between being interested in my own objective good and in being interested in that of another.

In a pure value-response our attention is turned to some good exclusively under the aspect of value. Each person transcends his own subjectivity, especially in a moral value-response. We will discuss this more in chapter 9, where we will treat of subjectivity and transcendence. What concerns us at present is to see that value as such, and especially morally relevant value, necessarily addresses each person in the same way. In a value-response one enters into an attitude that everyone ought to have; or, as we could as well say, value as the important in itself is by its very nature common to all, since it has to do with all in the same way. But as soon as I approach the world under the aspect of the objective good for the person, I am living out of a center of myself as person that is different in each person; it is not qualitatively but ontologically different, being based on the ontological distinctness of every single individual. Thus it makes a difference whether I am interested in my own objective good or in that of another; my attitude is in each case essentially different. The difference is like the difference between the pain I feel in my leg and the pain that someone else feels in his leg.

The difference between aiming at my own objective good and that of another stands out with particular clarity when we think of goods that are delightful on the basis of their value and that enable us to take a delight in them; here the interest in my own objective good does not have the same character as my interest in the other's objective good. The desire to enjoy such a good, for instance, to visit a beautiful country or to attend the performance of magnificent music, is certainly something entirely legitimate, indeed something noble and worthy. But this desire has a different character when I want someone whom I love to enjoy the good, for then my desire has an element of warmth and goodness that is not found in my desire to enjoy the good myself, however justified and noble this desire is. This difference is still greater in the case of elementary goods, by which we mean things that are objectively good for persons because related in some elementary way to their very life, such as having an indispensable minimum of food and drink, of security, or being in good health. Though it is justified and in fact, up to a certain point, obligatory for me to desire the elementary goods for myself, my desire that another person should have them clearly has a very different character; it has a moral radiance, a warmth, an element of goodness [*Güte*] that is missing in my desire to have the elementary goods myself. This difference (between myself and another) is greatest of all in the case of those objective goods that are only agreeable, that are objective goods on the basis of being agreeable (always assuming that they are not in any way illegitimate).[1]

Here we encounter an aspect of the extraordinary solidarity of love: all that affects the beloved person enters into the same intimate relation to me which my objective goods and evils have to me; all that affects him affects me "personally" and in my own subjectivity. Another aspect of this solidarity is given in the fact that we share in that level of the beloved person's self that is addressed by objective goods—that unique reference point that is each person's own. Thus I do not just ask what the value of something is, and not just what it means for me, but also what it means for the beloved person. Something becomes important for me for the very reason that it means something to him, even if it would have otherwise had no importance for me.

I have already discussed in my *Ethics* the distinction between the aspect of value and the aspect of the objective good for the person. Here I have wanted to take it *under a particular point of view*; I have wanted to stress that value in principle addresses every person in the same way, whereas the objective good for the person addresses in each case a particular person. This is why one and the same event can be an objective good for one person and an objective evil for another.

How love bridges the gap between my own objective good and that of another person

In emphasizing this difference we have already referred to the other significant difference between the point of view of the objective good for me and the point

---

1   [Von Hildebrand is here following the hierarchy of objective goods for the person that he lays out in his *Ethics*, chapter 7, and that he summarizes a few pages below in the present chapter. Trans.]

of view of the objective good for another. In grasping the value of a thing we understand something that is valid for everyone. But in grasping that something is an objective good for me I in no way know as yet whether for another person it is also an objective good or an objective evil, or whether it is entirely indifferent. The mere fact that I find that some event or thing is an objective good for me leaves the question entirely unanswered what the same event or thing means for another under the aspect of what is objectively good for that person. In the sphere of beneficial goods the objective good for myself is separated from the objective good for another by an abyss that is not present as long as we approach the world under the aspect of value alone.

Of course, there are cases in which an event affects many people in the same way under the aspect of beneficial goods and harmful evils. Starvation is an objective evil for the whole community affected by it, whether a city or a country or an entire continent. Bankruptcy may be a blow for many people, being driven from one's land and home may be a common evil for an entire family. After all, there are not just objective goods and evils for individuals, but also for communities. We will return to this point below. But apart from objective goods and evils for communities where each member is affected in more or less the same way, the difference between the point of view of the objective good for me and for some other is a radical difference, one that is surpassed only by the difference between what is merely subjectively satisfying for me and what is merely subjectively satisfying for another. The person who, like Aristippus, approaches everything only under the aspect of the subjectively satisfying is necessarily disinterested in the question whether something is subjectively satisfying for another. All attempts to pass from an individual hedonism to a social hedonism, that is, to build a bridge from the individual hedonism of Aristippus to the social hedonism of Bentham, are doomed from the very beginning.

Of course, we do not find this kind of gap within the category of the objective good for the person. But even here it is impossible—as long as I acknowledge no other category of importance but that of the beneficial good—to pass from the point of view of the objective good for me to an interest in the objective good for another. In other words, even here it is impossible to derive some motive for taking an interest in the objective good of another merely from the motive I have for taking an interest in my own objective good.

As soon as we realize this we can grasp the extraordinary "achievement" of love: the one who loves takes very seriously the point of view of the objective good of the other; the abyss separating the point of view of the objective good for myself and for the other is bridged. We now understand better why this "participation" in the other is a real marvel.

Direct and indirect objective goods for the person

We should clearly understand that it is one thing for objective goods and evils for me to affect me, and it is quite something else for the joys and sufferings of a beloved person to affect me as much as they do him—and to affect me more as my love for him becomes greater. All objective goods for me address themselves directly to me, including the objective good for me of the beloved person himself and all that makes him a gift for me and a source of my happiness. But here in this self-transcending sharing in the other, things become objective goods and evils for me *for the very reason* that they are so for the beloved person. We propose to call these goods and evils that grow out of a loving sharing in the other by the name of "indirect" objective goods and evils for me. The corresponding term "direct" is not supposed to express any superiority, as little as the term "indirect" expresses something secondary; these terms only mark the difference between that which directly affects me and that which affects me on account of the other. The indirectness at issue here consists in the fact that we share in the subjectivity of the beloved person, that the importance of certain things for me is motivated by what they mean for him.

This highly significant difference between direct and indirect objective goods for me will stand out all the more clearly once we have gotten acquainted with certain further differences within the point of view of the objective good for the person and once we have distinguished the specific character of this self-transcending "participation" from other phenomena based on a completely different kind of "having in common."

Another kind of fundamental difference between my way of relating to objective goods for myself and relating to objective goods for others

Apart from the essential difference in the direction of beneficial goods towards one's own person and towards other persons, there are still many differences within the way of relating to the objective goods for me, differences that vary according to the kind of objective good at stake.

To be virtuous is not only significant insofar as one realizes moral values and thereby glorifies God. Being virtuous is also a great objective good for the virtuous person; being virtuous is highly significant under the aspect of the category of importance that we call the beneficial good. But virtues are not something to be enjoyed and dwelt upon; they are not an objective good for the person that is meant to be experienced. Here the character of the objective good for the person is purely objective; it is a gift that is not as such experienced by the person. Of course, virtues are constituted on the basis of conscious, superactual value-responses and in no other way. But they are experienced by the virtuous person only as a certain kind of harmony, peace, and inner happiness, which make up the inwardness of being virtuous. These experiences presuppose that the person is virtuous, but they are not experiences in which the virtues that are possessed serve as a conscious source of joy and happiness, so that we rejoice over the fact that we possess them.

But when it is a question of the virtues of *another person*, then we have to do with something that can be enjoyed and dwelt upon, something that I should know about and experience gladly as a gift, of course always on the basis of giving a value-response to the virtues of the other. Here the virtues of the other are not a purely *objective* gift for me, as in the case of my own virtues; they are instead a beneficial good for me that is meant to be experienced, as the beauty of a landscape or of a work of art.

There are two formally distinct kinds of objective good for the person: the purely objective good and the good that exists only as experienced [*erlebniszugewandt*]. One and the same good can be for one person objective in the sense of not being meant to be experienced and can for another person be meant to be experienced. The virtues of a person are just such a good. His virtues can obviously never be a good for me in the same sense in which they are a good for him, for he alone possesses them. But they can be for me what they can never be for their possessor, namely, a good meant to be experienced, or an experiential good, as we could as well call it.

Here we have a typical case in which our stance towards one and the same thing varies according as it is our own or someone else's. The thing requires an entirely different response in each case, to the point that a response that is noble and appropriate when directed to the other, becomes morally quite negative and incompatible with humility when directed to oneself. The beneficial goods that are not meant to be experienced in oneself, such as all values possessed by persons and especially moral values, can only take on the character of something to be experienced and enjoyed when they are seen in another person.

We see that the category of the beneficial good comprises very different kinds of goods. I have elaborated the specific identity of this category in my *Ethics*. It is distinguished from the category of value by the fact that the importance includes a relation to a human person for whom the good is good, whereas value is importance in itself, which includes no such relation to a person. Note well that it is the value importance itself that is not "for" a person; that which lacks any relation to a person is this importance, not the being that has it. Thus a friendship can have a great value as well as be a great good for the two friends. We are not discussing here whether the bearer of a value or of a beneficial good includes a relation to another person, whether this bearer needs other persons in order to become real; we are only discussing the dimension of importance, the distinction between importance in itself and importance for someone. It is also the distinction between two different points of view, two different categories of importance.

The objective good for the person is also entirely different from the "for" of the merely subjectively satisfying. As we already saw, someone who, like Aristippus, considers the world merely from the point of view of what gives him pleasure, neither asks whether something is valuable in itself nor whether it is an objective gift for some person. He knows only one kind of importance: the merely subjectively satisfying.

The term "objective" in the expression, "the objective good for the person," is supposed to intimate that, although this category of importance includes a relation to a person for whom the good is good, the good has the character of an objective gift for the person, that it represents something objectively friendly for the person. This "for the person" is something objectively valid, independent of the reaction of the benefited person. This "for" does not have the relativizing character of the merely subjectively satisfying.

We refer here to these fundamental differences among the three categories of importance, which we elaborated in detail in our *Ethics*, so as to consider the main kinds of beneficial goods from a point of view that is important for our present discussion. The highest beneficial goods always presuppose value. Their gift-character is rooted in their value. The gift that comes to the virtuous person from possessing virtues is clearly based on the value of virtue, its importance in itself, its beauty. In the same way, the gift that a great work of art is for the viewer is based on the value of the work of art. This gift flows superabundantly from the value.

We already referred to the difference between these two kinds of beneficial good. Virtue is not an experiential beneficial good for the virtuous person, whereas the work of art is an experiential beneficial good. This important difference goes hand in hand with a difference that I analyzed in my essay, "The Three Modes of Participation in Values." The first basic mode that I distinguished there is *bearing or having* values, as when someone is good, pure, or intelligent. These values are realized in him and he is their "bearer" [*Träger*]. The second mode is coming into contact with goods and their values as given over against me. This contact ranges from knowing about the existence of something valuable all the way to the full delighting in the value. Here the values appear in my field of vision; I look at them and in various ways I come to a conscious possession, to a comprehension of them, to a being-affected by them, to a union with them in the form of a full contemplative delight in them.[2]

Four kinds of objective goods for the person

Analogous to these two fundamentally different types of personal contact with values—having values and coming into contact with the values of goods standing over against me, including the values of other persons, whether this contact takes the form of knowing values, being affected by them, taking delight in them, or responding to them—are two fundamentally different kinds of beneficial goods, the experiential and the non-experiential. The latter are beneficial goods on the basis of their value; the benefited person need not know

---

2   [Von Hildebrand is referring here to his essay, "The Three Modes of Participation in Value," in *International Philosophical Quarterly* 1 (1961): 58–84. By the way, the third mode of participation in values discussed by von Hildebrand in this essay is the producing of valuable things. Trans.]

about them or be consciously directed to them. The former are also beneficial goods on the basis of their value, but they have to be apprehended by me, they have to touch my soul consciously; they stand over against me and through their value enrich my soul, elevate it, give joy to it in a superabundant manner.

But that is not the way it is with all kinds of beneficial goods. There are also things that are beneficial goods not because of their value, but because of the elementary significance, the indispensability that they have for my existence. Food, housing, a minimum of money, health and the like have, as we showed in our *Ethics*, an entirely different character; it is not their value that makes them beneficial goods but rather the fact that they are the basis for living my life without too much suffering, or the basis just for surviving. They are not necessarily experiential goods; they need not be experienced in order to be constituted as beneficial goods, even though they usually reach into my sphere of experience. Neither knowing about them nor enjoying them is in any way negative.

Finally, there are also agreeable things that do not appeal to an illegitimate center in the person or that do not harm the person; things such as delicious meals and drinks, or comfort of all kinds, are also beneficial goods. Here too it is something quite different from value that establishes the "friendly" character, or the gift-character, of something "for" a person; here something is desirable not because of the superabundant overflow from a value but because of a capacity to confer pleasure. But its legitimate desirability confers on it the character of a beneficial good, of a gift.

How it is the individual person who is addressed by beneficial goods

For our purposes in this study it is important to understand that all four kinds of beneficial goods, assuming that I take them under the aspect of beneficial goods, address me in a particular way; they appeal to a center in me that is inseparable from my "I," from my existence as this individual person. Their importance as goods for me is objectively valid and in no way relative to my subjective reaction, and yet at the same time they address *me*. This is what distinguishes this category of importance from that of value, which is important entirely in itself.

The difference between co-experienced rejoicing and rejoicing over that which gladdens the beloved person

The self-transcendence that we achieve in taking an interest in those goods that benefit another for the very reason that they benefit the other, and in taking an interest in those evils that harm another for the very reason that they harm the other, is not the same thing as co-experienced joy or co-experienced pain. While it is true that grieving with another and rejoicing with another play a large role in love, it has to be sharply distinguished from rejoicing because the other rejoices and from grieving because the other grieves.

As we saw above, there are many events that address and affect a number of people in the same way. The ending of a war and the restoration of peace is an objective good for very many people. What we have here is a case in which, first of all, many people objectively experience the same thing, since it represents an objective good for many. Secondly, people share an experience of receiving a gift; the return of peace does not just affect them all in the same way, but it is expressly experienced as something that affects them in common, to the point that a we-solidarity is formed, encompassing even many people whom we do not know personally. This co-rejoicing and co-grieving take on quite a different character when the people sharing in these experiences are united by a bond of mutual love, especially by a bond of married love. Consider how parents rejoice together at the birth of a child or grieve together at the death of a child. Thanks to the deep "we" that is born of mutual love, the response to goods and evils that equally affect the parents takes on a shared character, a co-experienced character in a new and more proper sense. We see here with particular clarity the difference between parallel responses of different individuals to the same good or evil, and the shared, co-experienced response. The fact that it is commonly the same things and the same events that affect in the same way those who love each other is a particular sign of their objective unity. Everything addresses them as a couple. They like the same things, they have the same interests, a fact which expresses a particular objective affinity between them. They also form such a unity that all goods and evils address them as a couple. That is certainly a great sign of an unusual mutual love and of an exceptional mutual understanding.

But this co-experiencing is something entirely different from that defining note of all love that we are here exploring, namely, the unique participation in the other that comes from rejoicing because the other rejoices over something. I am moved only because something is desirable for the other. The difference is already evident in this: in the case of co-experienced pain or co-experienced joy the object moves and affects both persons *directly* and independently of the love that each has for the other. Thus both are directed to the same object in their response, even if their response is co-experienced in that special way that derives from mutual love. But in the case of my delight in that which is gladdening for the other, where my delight is motivated by the thing being gladdening for him, the beneficial good of the other does not affect me directly but is dependent on the other. It is not a shared beneficial good, which equally affects both persons; it is a beneficial good for the one person and only indirectly does it move me. Of course, we can say that for me too it is a beneficial good, but it is not a direct one; it comes from sharing in the subjectivity of the beloved person and is in that sense indirect. We have already examined in some detail the difference between direct and indirect beneficial goods.

Furthermore, the pain felt over the suffering of the beloved person is often qualitatively and ontologically quite different from his own suffering. We have already seen this. The pain I feel because the other suffers bodily torments is not itself a bodily torment; it belongs only to the soul and has quite a different quality.

Sharing in this way in the suffering or the joy of another is neither a co-experienced suffering nor a co-experienced joy; there is no one act that is performed by the two persons in common. The saying, "All your joys and sufferings are mine," can mean that a love is so great that all the beneficial goods and harmful evils of another person become indirect beneficial goods and harmful evils of my own, and in fact I can suffer more under the indirect good or evil than under the corresponding direct good or evil. Thus this saying can express the culmination of this dimension of love, the incomparable self-transcendence that includes a culmination of love itself. But the same saying could also refer to the fact that two people understand each other so well and have such an affinity of soul and such a unity of shared life that everything affects both in the same way, that everything affects them together. But it is not difficult to see that this saying primarily expresses the first meaning, the fact that all direct beneficial goods and harmful evils of the other become indirect goods and evils for me.

Reductionistic attempts at explaining this self-transcendence of love

At this point we have to consider certain incomparably lower phenomena that are often confused with this self-transcending dimension of love. Indeed, one has tried to reduce to these lower phenomena this essential trait of love, thereby radically distorting love, which is so obviously different from them. Let us consider, first of all, a way of being affected by the joys and fears of other persons that has nothing to do with love and can be found in a radical egoist no less than in a loving and selfless person. We find this way of being affected in its most primitive form in the shock felt at the sight of the physical sufferings of others, especially at the sight of wounds and flowing blood. This shock is nothing but an "effect" on us, which is radically different from an intentional or a motivated being-affected, or from an intentional stance taken to the other's sufferings. It is simply an expression of a certain impressionability that goes with delicate nerves. A completely insensitive, crude type of person is not impressionable in this way, neither is a sluggish type person, like the giant Fafner (a character in Wagner's opera, *Das Rheingold*). Only when he himself suffers pain does he take notice. But this impressionability is in no way a sign of real sharing in the lives of others. Of course, it can be joined with a genuine sharing, but it does not guarantee it.

We have something similar in the pleasant reaction to seeing friendly faces and to having an atmosphere of peripheral gladness, and even more in the unpleasant reaction that the depression and suffering of others can cause. First of all, it is only an effect and not a meaningful and intentional way of being affected; even less is it a stance taken towards the others. Secondly, this reaction affects me directly; without any real sharing in the other I have my pleasant and unpleasant reactions. It can be found in the greatest egoist as long as he is not thick-skinned. The well-known expression, "Throw the beggar out, his suffering breaks my heart," expresses this well. We said that we have here a mere effect on one of the sight of suffering and not a meaningful and intentional way of being affected. But all the same it is an effect that comes from the sight of suffering and is not a purely causal effect. Here is the decisive point of contrast with suffering because the other suffers: in reacting to the sight of suffering, the other person does not really count (and is not treated as person), all that counts is the sad and depressing impression. As soon as one no longer sees the suffering one is no longer depressed by it, one is completely indifferent to it. One simply feels the atmosphere of suffering to be depressing; the air is as it were filled with suffering and grief, all of which one finds unbearable. One remains indifferent to the other person.

In general the depressive effect of suffering plays a greater role in this kind of reaction than does the pleasant effect of the joy of others. But this pleasant effect involves no sharing in the other person; the atmosphere of joy, taken as an object, produces a pleasant and glad effect. Such people say, "I want to have happy people around me."

Very different from this effect is being infected by the anger, enthusiasm, etc. of others, such as occurs in large crowds. The fact that many are angry at or approving of what the speaker says, sweeps along many others in the crowd who could not even hear the speaker or understand what he said. This emotional infection is much further removed from all meaningful and intentional responses than the above-mentioned reaction. It lacks even that residue of a meaningful relation between subject and object that we find in being affected by the sight of other people's suffering. The emotionally infected man or woman is swept away by a dynamism that bypasses him or her as person. The infection is not the effect of something apprehended in front of me, as we found in that case of being-affected; it is rather a way of being swept away that is in some way akin to the way in which an easily suggestible person goes along with what is suggested to him.[3] It is not difficult to see the difference between feeling with a beloved person's joys and sufferings and being affected by an atmosphere of gladness or sadness as well as being infected by other people's feelings. Neither in this being affected nor in being infected can we find anything like love or the transcendence of love, which lets me share in the beneficial goods and harmful evils of the beloved person to the point that they become indirect goods and evils of my own.

Much more dangerous is the confusion of this transcendence of love with

---

3   I studied the phenomenon of suggestion in my earlier essays, "Über die Autorität" and "Legitime und illegitime Formen der Beeinflussung," both in my collection, *Die Menschheit am Scheideweg* (Mankind at the Crossroads).

the solidarity which comes about when another person becomes an extension of my ego. We could put it more correctly like this: more plausible and more widespread is the error that tries to reduce the transcendent sharing of love to making another a mere extension of my ego. We have already shown in chapter 1 the radical difference between the solidarity based on love and the solidarity based on extending my ego to another so that the other gets incorporated into my ego. We considered there the man who takes his wife and children as extensions of his ego: although he reacts to an insult to them as if it were directed to himself, he is nevertheless capable of treating them badly and of being indifferent to their happiness. If a given solidarity is based on an extension of someone's ego, that person need not be concerned at all with the beneficial goods and harmful evils of the other. The whole sharing in the subjectivity of the beloved person, the whole concern with goods and evils "for his sake," is here absent. All that affects the other can at the most become a direct beneficial good or harmful evil of the person with the extended ego, but it can never become an indirect good or evil in our special sense of indirect.[4] The solidarity based on an extended ego is opposed to the solidarity based on love. The self-transcending gesture of love, which is our subject here, is the very opposite of the gesture of the extended ego.

Another radical misunderstanding of the sharing proper to love is found in the sympathy theory of Hume and Adam Smith. Here the thing that is confused with love is not even a real phenomenon or psychic event, but is rather a typical abstract hypothesis, a fictional X, which is supposed to "explain" the unique transcendence of love, or to which love is supposed to be reduced. Hume's "sympathy" is a pure construction without any basis in experience. Hume and Smith assert that there is in human nature a way of resonating with other people's sufferings and joys that arises by itself, automatically. There is, therefore, no real stance taken by one person towards another person but rather only an inescapable being swept away by the affective experiences of others.

This transcendence of love not a merely theoretical knowledge or a kind of empathy

We have said that the beneficial goods address themselves to a person as individual and we have stressed the transcendence that lies in the fact that the beneficial goods of a beloved person affect me. But this should not be taken to mean that this special transcendence is achieved as soon as I merely empathize with another and recognize something as being objectively good for him. In

---

4   Note well that the terms "direct" and "indirect" have here an entirely different sense than they when we speak of direct and indirect importance in our *Ethics*, chapters 3–4, and in chapter 3 of the present book. [Direct importance refers in those places to the importance of that which is sought for its own sake, indirect to the importance of what is sought as an instrumental means. Trans.]

stressing that it belongs to the genius of love to take the well-being of the beloved person not only under the aspect of value but also under the aspect of the beneficial good, we are by no means thinking of some kind of theoretical knowledge or mere empathetic understanding. We rather mean that the well-being of the beloved person, all that he does and experiences, affects us not only from the point of view of value but also from the point of view of what is beneficial and harmful for him.

As long as one understands just theoretically what something means for another, as long as one just raises this question and answers it and takes some interest in the answer, there need not be any love or any of the transcendence that we have discussed. For example, I may want to know how something will be perceived by another, whether it is agreeable or disagreeable to him, because I want to make use of his reaction in deliberating over how to achieve my goals. Suppose that an employer gives an employee a job. The employee should have the energy needed for carrying out the job. The employer will calculate exactly whether the demands of the job exceed the energy of the employee. Being theoretically interested like this in whether a job is going to be too great a burden for another and thus going to be harmful for him, is in no way an expression of the transcendence of which we have spoken.

There is indeed an intellectual talent for being able to consider situations from the point of view of others instead of just unimaginatively considering them from my own point of view, as positive or negative for myself. But I can exercise this talent without in any way surpassing the limits of my selfish interests. A person obsessed with his ambition and locked in his own interests can possess this talent to a high degree.

The transcendence at which we are aiming is achieved only when I am so moved by something being beneficial or harmful for another that a beneficial good of his is *a source of my happiness* and a harmful evil of his is *a source of my unhappiness*. We grow out of our immanence only when our responses to the other are motivated not only from the point of view of value but also from that of his beneficial good. Thus this transcendence is only achieved when our acting involves a response to things beneficial or harmful to the other.

After all, hatred, though devoid of transcendence, is concerned with what is good or bad for another. Whoever hates wants to inflict some evil on the hated person; he wants to harm him and tries to strike him at his most vulnerable point. Though the question of value is completely indifferent to him, the question whether something is harmful for the other, indeed objectively harmful, is very important for him. The interest of the one who hates is the very opposite of a loving interest: he takes great satisfaction in some harm befalling the other and is angry at objective goods being given to him. Hatred makes a person very alert to the most vulnerable place in the soul of the other. The one who hates considers the well-being of the other under the aspect of what it means for that person, but in hating he remains entirely self-enclosed, since the well-being of the other affects him in a manner just the opposite of the manner in which it affects the one who loves. The direct beneficial good of the other does not become an indirect beneficial good of his own, and the direct harmful evil for the other does not become an indirect evil for himself: just the opposite happens. His satisfaction has nothing of the nobility that we find in rejoicing and grieving for the sake of the other, but it deviates from all other selfish satisfaction by being directly opposed to love; it is marked by a particular disvalue, by a malicious evil, which far surpasses the disvalue of mere selfishness.

The one who hates represents the most extreme opposite of the transcendence of love. Although he is concerned with what benefits and what harms the other, he is much more locked up in himself than is the most insensitive egoist, who is completely unconcerned with what benefits and what harms the other. For the one who hates not only remains in himself, but he contradicts the "for the sake of the other" and he performs a gesture that is the very opposite of the gesture of love. Hatred is the ultimate antithesis to value-response. It is not just the negative counterpart of love, a no instead of a yes. It does not have the same relation to love that indignation has to enthusiasm, or contempt to veneration, or sadness to joy. These are value-responses, some of them affirming a value and others negating a disvalue. By contrast, hatred is no more a value-response than envy or malicious joy at the suffering of another [*Schadenfreude*] is a value-response. Of course, we are not thinking here of the hatred of sin, of moral evil; this is a real value-response. We are rather thinking of the completely different kind of hatred that is found in hating an enemy or a rival; while such hatred is indeed a response, it is no value-response at all. In it there is no conforming to a value or a disvalue, to something positive or something negative on the object-side; it is rather an attitude originating in the subject and lacking the gesture of self-donation, or submitting, of *adequatio voluntatis et cordis ad valorem* (the correspondence of the will and the heart with value) that is proper to every value-response.

For our purposes it suffices to establish that transcendence does not consist in seeing whether something is beneficial or harmful for another, but in being affected by whether it is beneficial or harmful, and this in inner conformity with the other.

Now that we have seen that the dimension of love that we are studying in this chapter cannot be confused with the ability to empathize with another or with wanting to know what is beneficial or harmful for the other, let us continue the analysis of this dimension of love.

As long as I respond exclusively under the aspect of value, as in giving alms to a beggar on the grounds that I want to obey the moral law, that there is a disvalue in a human being living in extreme poverty, then an element of warmth is missing along with a deeply significant moral beauty. What is missing is precisely love, which implies that I consider something not only under the aspect of objective value but also of the beneficial good for the other, that I am moved for this reason and act for this reason. This "on account of the other"—not in the sense of some kind of yielding to or of being influenced by him, but rather in the sense that something is important for me on account of the importance that it has for him—this letting the other be for me what I am normally for myself, is a tremendous gift that love gives to the other.

The erroneous attempt to derive love from self-love

We are now in a position to understand how the dreadful error came about of trying to derive love from self-love. This participation of love in the other person is somewhat analogous to the solidarity in which I stand with myself, and this fact can mislead us into thinking that love, where we share in the intimate relation that beneficial goods and harmful evils have to another and where his fate and well-being affect me like my own fate and well-being, is simply a matter of me extending to the other the relation I have to myself. Those who think like this seek a confirmation of their view in the words of our Lord, "Love your neighbor as yourself." But the meaning of this statement is in no way an identification of self-love with love of neighbor; our Lord rather means that self-love provides a standard for the measure of solidarity with my neighbor, which should be just as great as the solidarity I have with myself. But this in no way means that the love of neighbor is to be derived from the solidarity I have with myself, called self-love. In fact, the abyss that separates the two kinds of solidarity—the unavoidable self-love that I have by nature, and the solidarity that is born of love and is an achievement of love—stands forth in this commandment in all clarity. On the one hand, there is a moral requirement to love one's neighbor, which is difficult to fulfill and is the backbone of most of morality; on the other hand, there is the solidarity with oneself, something so natural and normal that it can be taken as the standard for the moral requirement to love one's neighbor.

We have to realize again and again that the solidarity of love is, in its foundation, its quality, and its whole structure, entirely different from the solidarity with oneself. We saw above how radically the solidarity of love differs from the extended ego. This is what we now have to stress again. My participation in the other in love is not based on me taking the other as an extended ego; it is just the other way around: since I love him he becomes an *alter ego*, but not an extension of my ego. My participation in his life is a consequence of love and is not the basis of love.

The statement, "I experience all that affects you as if it affected me," expresses the greatest triumph of self-donation and love; it does not eliminate the distinction between what affects me directly and what affects me indirectly for the sake of the beloved person. To say, "as if it affected me," means that something affects me just as strongly, just as intimately as if it directly affected me, but it does not mean that the mode of being affected is identical in its quality in both cases. For in the "for his sake," which makes me experience something as if it directly affected me—in the fact that his joys and sufferings move me as if they were my own—we find the radiance of love and all the warmth, all the transcendence that is *not* involved in the inevitable experience that I have of my own well-being.

The beloved person as a direct beneficial good for the one who loves him

When we said that the eyes of love do not look at the world only from the point of view of value but also from the point of view of the beneficial good of the beloved person, we were referring to the fact that all that affects him becomes an indirect good or evil for me. But as we saw earlier, it also belongs essentially to love that many of the beneficial goods of the beloved person are *direct* beneficial goods of mine, since the beloved person himself has become an objective good for me. It characterizes all forms of love, including love of neighbor, that beneficial goods of the other become indirect beneficial goods of mine. But as for the beloved person and his beneficial goods becoming a direct beneficial good of mine, this characterizes all forms of love with the exception of love of neighbor. It is one thing to pass from taking the beloved person under the aspect of value to taking him and his beneficial goods under the aspect of my direct beneficial good, and it is quite something else to pass from taking him under the aspect of value to taking him under the aspect of his beneficial goods that become my indirect beneficial goods. In chapter 5 we spoke at length about the beloved person becoming a direct beneficial good of mine. Here we have a gift that flows superabundantly from value. We find something analogous whenever a city or a great work of art or the like becomes a beneficial good of mine in the full sense of the word. Just as such things can be loved in an analogous sense, so they can become beneficial goods in an analogous sense. But the step from the point of view of value to the point of view of the beneficial good of the other is very different in the other dimension of love, in the self-transcending sharing in the life of the other, where all beneficial goods of the other become indirect beneficial goods of mine. Here we do not have a gift growing organically and superabundantly out of value as a necessary and direct result of the value-response of love. Here we have a much more mysterious relation of this value-response to the experience of being affected by the beneficial goods of the other—being affected for the other's sake. It is a sharing in the subjectivity of the other. But here, too, value plays a decisive role.[5]

---

5   It should be pointed out here that many objective goods for the other can be both direct and indirect goods for me, just as many objective evils for him can be both direct and indirect evils for me. Of course, this in no way eliminates the fundamental difference between direct and indirect.

Value-response and the intentio benevolentiae

This apparent departure from a pure value-responding attitude, which seems to be a new "subjective" element of love, is in reality an element that has a particular moral value, and in fact it displays a particular glory of love. It is no departure at all from a value-responding attitude, no turning away in another direction, but it is rather a specific expression of love as the deepest and most central of all value-responses.

In the love for God, the purest value-response, the absolute value-response, there no longer exist the two aspects that we have distinguished; there is no difference between "God in Himself" and "for God's sake," or in other words, between the aspect of value and the aspect of the beloved person's beneficial good. When we say of moral evil that it "offends" God, this is equivalent to speaking of its moral disvalue. In God the subjective and the objective dimension coincide. We consider some human action exclusively under the aspect of value when we speak of it offending or glorifying God. In the love for God the two dimensions no longer exist; but this should not be understood as the absence of one of the dimensions, but as a transcending of the fact that they are two. Thus there is eminently contained in the love for God all the ardor, warmth, and goodness that love has in distinction to all other value-responses. The specific character of love that in all the other categories of love presupposes a twofold aspect—in addition to the aspect of value there is the aspect of "for his sake"—is given *per eminentiam* in the love for God. This emerges clearly when we compare love for God with mere obedience to God. Obedience alone is indeed a pure value-response but it lacks a giving of the heart. Thus it is no real super value-response. That element of love that leads us to call love a super value-response—the beloved person becomes a beneficial good of ours and a source of our happiness—is clearly present, as we saw above, in the love for God. For God is our absolute beneficial good, the absolute source of our happiness. The vision of God is beatitude. We can understand this without directly experiencing it; but in the love for God we do not just know this, but we experience God as the source of our happiness already here on earth, and we give Him our heart.

This comparison of mere obedience to God with the love for God shows clearly that the specific character of love, present in all the other categories of love in the form of "for the other's sake," is entirely present here too, even if the duality of points of view is here given only *per eminentiam*. For God is the supreme embodiment of the moral order; He is Goodness itself, He is the absolute Person. Thus the intimacy that is given in the relation of a beneficial good to myself is entirely contained in the love for God. We have only to think of the repentance of St. Peter after his denial of Jesus. His repentance refers to the sin he committed, which for its part was bound up with the betrayal of his love for Jesus. Here the two points of view, value and the beneficial good, flow together in such a way that they can no longer be taken as separate aspects.

Everything that is directed against a morally relevant good and has moral disvalue, everything that violates a moral command, wounds the most Sacred Heart of Jesus and is not just an explicit lack of love. But as we said, this coinciding is a surpassing of the two points of view and not a reduction of the two to the value point of view. And thus the love for God possesses in the highest degree all the warmth and ardor and intimacy that otherwise takes the form of "for his sake" and requires a distinct point of view. As we said, this fact stands out with particular clarity in the contrast between mere obedience to God and the love for God.

But it stands out even more clearly in the contrast between a value-response to morally relevant goods in the setting of a Platonic world and a value-response to morally relevant goods where the response is embedded in the love for God. If someone wills to suffer injustice rather than to commit it and is motivated by a pure value-response to the moral world of values, his act certainly has a high moral value. But if we compare him with the martyr who gives his life out of ardent love for Christ and God, then we see clearly that love is something utterly new in relation to all other value-responses. Only love possesses this incomparable radiance, this unique warmth, this giving of the heart.

We touch here on the point that is decisive for the newness of all of Christian ethics. I have discussed this in the concluding chapters of my three books, *Ethics, True Morality and Situation Ethics,* and *Graven Images.*

When we are dealing with the categories of love other than the love for God, then the point of view of value should predominate, even if the point of view of the beneficial good should not be missing. If a person loves God and so makes the value point of view merge with the love for God, then there will be nothing cool and distant about the predominance of the value point of view in his natural loves for created beings. This predominance is not only free of cool objectivity, but it unites itself so organically with the point of view of the beloved person's beneficial good that the warmth and goodness of this person become in this way incomparably greater.

Suppose that someone whom we love undergoes a religious conversion. We are glad because of the inner beauty of this act and because God is thereby glorified. We are *also* glad on account of the beloved person, because it is the greatest beneficial good that he could have; but the glorification of God naturally has the primacy. The joy over his beneficial good, however, is so organically united with this primacy that nothing is taken away from our love for the other person, nor is anything taken away from our love for God by this concern with the beneficial good of the other. The reason for this is that God loves the other person infinitely more than we can love him. This is why love for God necessarily requires that the point of view of what benefits someone should play a role in our stance towards creatures. If someone says, "I am glad that God is glorified, but I am indifferent to what it means for this person and his ultimate well-being," he would not really love God. He would at the most have an attitude of reverent obedience to God. He would be glad that what happens is objectively right and gives God His due. Although not morally negative, this attitude would still be morally imperfect because of its coldness. But as soon as someone really loves God, the aspect of "for his sake" becomes important in relation to every human being; it flows organically from the love for God and is a decisive factor in the love of neighbor (or charity) that is grounded in the love for God.

Now we should not be confused by the great moral value found in the self-transcending gesture of love through which the beneficial goods of the other become indirect beneficial goods of the one who loves; this moral value should not obscure for us the difference between the aspect of value and the aspect of the beneficial good.

Many actions directed to other persons have a moral value or disvalue. In all these actions the response to the *moral significance* of our acting towards the other person belongs essentially to the full moral value of the action. We have spoken at length about this in chapter 19 of our *Ethics*. If I encounter someone whose life is in danger, the call to save him should not be separated from the *moral* imperative. Of course, this call should also not be separated from the value of the human life that is at risk, for this value grounds the moral imperative. But the fact that I offend God by not saving him should play a larger role in my motivation than saving his life.

But things are different when it comes to the moral value of the self-transcending gesture of love. For it belongs essentially to love that I am completely filled by the point of view of the other's beneficial good. In contrast to all actions, it cannot be primarily for the sake of the moral value that I take a self-transcending interest in what affects the other. Of course, I can pray to be able to perform this gesture, especially as it is found in the love of neighbor; I can try to clear away the main obstacles blocking the flow of love, namely, pride and concupiscence. And in this freely chosen action of praying and working on myself I am motivated by the moral value of the action. Especially in the love of neighbor we should be motivated by the fact that it is pleasing to God, that it glorifies God, that we follow Christ by living this kind of love. But in performing an act of love of neighbor with the self-transcending gesture of being concerned with what something means for the other, I act from the point of view of the other's beneficial goods and harmful evils and am directed to the other. This gesture is not performed from the value point of view but from the point of view of "for the other." That is the nature of this gesture, and it is senseless to try to give the value aspect a decisive role in my motivation, as in the case of an action. Here the moral value arises from looking at something under the aspect of what it means to the other, it is letting the other's beneficial goods become my indirect beneficial goods. It is impossible to posit here a situation similar to what we found with actions in which I give a value-response to morally relevant goods, as, for instance, in saving my neighbor from a threat to his life. Such a love would be like a snake that bites itself in the tail.

And so we see: the fact that the self-transcending gesture of love has a great moral value does not imply that it is motivated by this value.[6] But on the other hand—and this is a point of great importance—it would be a disastrous error to think that the category of value importance is not objectively an indispensable condition for this gesture of "for the other" and to think that the thematicity of value is not present in all dimensions of love. To show this is our next task.

The thematicity of value in taking an interest in what something means for the beloved person

1. *How the value point of view can be obscured.* One is sometimes hindered from distinguishing the value point of view from the point of view of "for the other" by the fact that the bearer of the moral value[7] often consists in the act of doing good to another and the bearer of a moral disvalue often consists in the act of doing harm to another. Objectively it is often a beneficial good that I ought, morally speaking, to provide for the other, and it is a harmful evil that I morally should not inflict on him. I can consider from a pure value point of view my action of inflicting some harm on another, which means that I consider it as morally bad and offensive to God. In omitting the action, I can also consider it from this moral point of view. We have here a harmful evil that is morally relevant; we do not just have a value, which has nothing to do with acting towards another person. But this fact should not obscure in our minds the difference between the two points of view, namely, of value (or being pleasing to God) and of "for the other." In the same way, the fact, characteristic of love, that the interest in the good of the other has an eminent moral value and so glorifies God and ought to be present for God's sake, should not obscure in our minds the difference between the two points of view, namely, value-response and interest in the beneficial good of the other. We must distinguish unambiguously between the value point of view and the importance of "for the other person," in spite of their being woven together. In our chapter on charity we will see how the love for God, which always goes together with the morally

---

6   In chapter 11, which deals with charity, we will examine in some detail the way in which love of neighbor is deeply embedded in the love for God.

7   [The German that I translate here as "the bearer of the moral value" is "der Träger des sittlich bedeutsamen Wertes." But the entire context shows that von Hildebrand must have meant to write "der Träger des sittlichen Wertes." As the reader will have noticed by now, he distinguishes sharply between "der sittliche Wert" and "der sittlich bedeutsame Wert," and he can only have meant the former in this sentence. I discuss this distinction in my introduction. Trans.]

relevant value point of view, is organically joined with love of neighbor, which always has an interest in the good of the other.

2. *The value point of view in the case of a conflict between higher and lower objective goods for the beloved person.* In order to see the basic character of "for the other" in contrast to the pure value point of view, and also to see the interconnection of both, let us consider the following. One who loves another constantly deals with the conflict between higher and lower beneficial goods for the other. He has to deny the other some pleasure when it is harmful for him. For instance, he has to deny him wine if the health of the beloved person is harmed by it. He has to deny it to him out of love. But he has to be sorry to deny him some pleasure. If he is not sorry about this on the grounds that the real interest of the other is served by withholding something from him, then he does not really love the other. This conflict can repeat itself at all levels. Out of love one will inflict some pain on the beloved person because this is required by some higher beneficial good of his. Now with this kind of conflict the point of view of value is of decisive importance. We have to recur to the value point of view in order to determine the higher beneficial good of his. This is why in these cases there is no conflict between the value point of view and the point of view of the beneficial good, for these go together. In this sense, Socrates says that it is better to suffer injustice than to commit it.

But the important thing about love in contrast to morally correct behavior *without* love is that one suffers from having to cause some pain to the beloved person, even if this is done in his interest. One acts morally correctly when, in imposing something unpleasant or painful on him, one acts exclusively from the value point of view and in the interest of his greater objective good. But love requires that one not only act from the value point of view but also from the point of view of beneficial goods. In addition—and here we see clearly the distinctive character of the "for the other"—one should suffer from having to inflict on the other a lower negative experience, even though one does this out of love for him.

But when we say that we should be sorry about having to cause him some pain out of love, we are not thinking of a pain that comes from denying him something that is inherently bad. When I try to keep a beloved person from something inherently bad, say, from taking revenge on another by slander or from indulging his vanity by bragging, love does not require that I suffer from the pain I cause him in blocking the intrinsically negative thing that he wants. To suffer from this would be no sign of love. Here I should rather be sad that he desires such bad things; love makes me suffer from his wanting to get revenge or to satisfy his vanity.

3. *The inseparability of "for the beloved person" from the value-response to him or her.* But quite apart from the interconnection, just discussed, of the value point of view and the "for the other" point of view (which, as we saw, in no way effaces the difference between the two points of view), there is quite

another way in which value and value-response form the basis of the "for the other" that is proper to love. It is very important to recognize this. Here there is not so much an interpenetration of the two points of view as rather a radiation of value into the "for the other." The preciousness and beauty of the beloved person, which are the factors that give rise to love, decisively affect the "for the other." This latter cannot be separated from the preciousness of beauty of the other; it is always "for the sake of this precious, unique being that the other is." The value-response contained in love is always the basis. Value permeates the entire "for the other."

This becomes especially clear when we think of the entirely different "for the other" that exists in the solidarity resulting from an extended ego. Here value-response provides no basis at all; the interest in the other's beneficial good is born of this solidarity with him. We have already shown how all self-giving is clearly missing here, since the solidarity is not born of love. Now we have to add that it in no way depends on value, whether directly or indirectly. Take the concern of a husband that his wife, whom he does not love and whom he in fact mistreats, should be esteemed by others and not put at any disadvantage. This concern involves no real "for her sake," it is rather ultimately "for his sake," since the husband does not really enter into her as person. The mother who lives with her children in a kind of animal solidarity and loves them on the grounds that they are "of one piece with her" wishes them well and may even act ruthlessly to get good things for them; but there is no genuine love here, no value-response at the basis of her interest in her children. The value point of view is entirely missing and does not even indirectly permeate the "for them."

4. *Value and legitimately agreeable goods for the beloved person.* The point of view of "for the other" predominates, as we saw, in the case of merely agreeable goods for the other. It is "for his sake" that we have to give the beloved person a good meal, to make him comfortable, to give him joy. This kind of beneficial good is not seen under the aspect of value but exclusively under the aspect of his beneficial good. But even here value is indirectly present. First of all, the question whether some agreeable thing is really a beneficial good for him depends on the thing being legitimate, that is, being *morally unobjectionable*. That is clearly a pure value question; it can only be answered from the point of view of value. And there is something else that depends on the question of value; even if some agreeable good is morally unobjectionable, the question remains whether it is not harmful for the health of the beloved person or whether, given his character, it could not have dangerous consequences for him. The value aspect is present with all these agreeable goods in the form of a *licet* or a *nihil obstat*, which determines whether something can be taken as a beneficial good for the other. This is, of course, a negative aspect; something can and should be seen as a beneficial good and granted to the other only as long as it contains no disvalue (whether moral or morally relevant disvalue) that would make it harmful for him.

In addition to this there is, of course, the indirect role of value mentioned above (#2). It is very significant. In wanting to make the beloved person happy by means of such goods the preciousness of that person stands forth in all the radiance of his value; here too value permeates the entire "for him." As soon as the value-response is missing, there is no longer any real "for him" or "for the sake of the other."

Here we have to consider different cases. Consider the case of a disordered love that expresses itself by yielding in weakness to the beloved person. Here one makes so much of the question whether this person is subjectively satisfied that one is not in a position to deny him something even if it is objectively harmful for him. We are thinking of people who are quite capable of applying moral standards to their own wishes and who in principle want what is really beneficial for the beloved person; but they are just not able to deny him something when he wants it, nor are they able to insist on something that is disagreeable but beneficial for him. The "for him" is perverted here, because the distinction between the beneficial good and the merely subjectively satisfying is no longer resolutely made. Real love is necessarily ordered to the beneficial good of the other.

But there can be very different reasons for the subjectively satisfying winning out over the beneficial good of the other. First of all, it can be a matter of weakness, just not being able to say no, being good-natured in a wrong way. Such a person by no means ignores the difference between the beneficial and the merely subjectively satisfying, but he just cannot bring himself to deny something to the beloved person; he wants absolutely to spare the other every trouble, every disappointment, every displeasure. Thus he just cannot bring himself not to give a drink to an alcoholic or not to give another injection to a drug addict. He will always lend money to a gambler or give children candy, however harmful for them. This weakness often goes together with real love; it is not entirely incompatible with real love, even if it is at odds with the spirit of it. It can even co-exist with a great love, just as pride can coexist with love, as we saw. Of course, it contradicts the genius of love. It is not the case that this weak type of person is unacquainted with the category of the beneficial good, of that which is objectively beneficial for others, but he sees the subjectively satisfying for the other in the light of the beneficial good, even if it is in fact harmful for the other. In these cases he is confused and unhappy because of the conflict he faces between two things that appear to him as favorable to the other, for instance, the health of the other and the injection of morphine that he desires. He is also affected by the "advantage"—of course an illegitimate advantage—that the present moment has. He would prefer that the other would only want what is objectively better for him; but he cannot bring himself to cause the other pain and to see him suffer.

Very different is the case of someone who cannot even conceive of not giving the other agreeable things, who does not even distinguish in principle between the merely subjectively satisfying and the beneficial good. For this type of person the question of value does not even exist. He cannot really love. He is incapable of a real concern for another. He may have some kind of attachment to the other, whether he takes the other as an extension of his own ego or whether he has some sensual desire for the other—but he does not love the other. In the case of the extended ego the "for him" is replaced by a "for myself." One is concerned with the contentment and well-being of the other only because one takes the other as a part of oneself. The category of the importance of the merely subjectively satisfying refers ultimately to one's own person, as we saw; on this level one cannot take the step towards the other that makes for a real "for him." Whoever knows only this point of view and knows nothing of the point of view of the beneficial good or of value is incapable of any transcendence and necessarily remains shut up in himself. Only when the value-response of love has established the direction of transcendence am I able to share in that *subjective* center in the beloved person which the beneficial good addresses, and only in this way does a genuine "for him" arise in my motivation.

So we see: the essential trait of love that consists in approaching the other not only under the aspect of value but also under the aspect of his beneficial good, necessarily presupposes the value-response character of love as well as the manifold thematicity of value. The "for him" is not only compatible with the value-response character of love, it necessarily presupposes it and can only thrive on this basis, that is, as a result of this unique value-response, as a flowering of love. This again entitles us to designate love as a super value-response. We should not be deceived by the fact that the real "for him" that lies in love is often—even in the case of real love—overshadowed by the "for me." It goes with fallen human nature that even when I really love someone I can fall again and again into a selfish attitude. We will discuss this in detail in chapter 12.

Here we have to see that a person is incapable of love as long as he is incapable of value-response and sees everything under the aspect of his subjective satisfaction. Aristippus was not able to love, not without giving up his basic attitude. He cannot with this attitude turn to others in such a way as to take an interest in their beneficial good for their sakes—an interest that belongs essentially to love.[8]

---

8   There are of course cases in which a real love, however imperfect, can be found in a dangerous egoist, for instance, in Heathcliff in Bronte's *Wuthering Heights*. Heathcliff loves Catherine in spite of all his inconsiderate selfishness. Of course, this love is very imperfect, shot through with elements opposed to the spirit of true love, but one cannot deny that he passionately loves her. Though he is evil and vengeful and does dreadful things, Heathcliff is not incapable of all value-response; he is neither an Aristippus nor a Don Juan nor an Iago. He is very arrogant and embittered by the treatment he has received; he is also deeply wounded

We want to say by way of concluding that the merely subjectively satisfying addresses in principle only myself. As long as I see everything from the point of view of the subjectively satisfying, I am completely locked in my immanence. One and the same thing may be agreeable for several people at the same time, but as long as each of them approaches it only under the aspect of the subjectively satisfying, each remains isolated and each remains indifferent to what is subjectively satisfying for some other person. Of course, it is possible for me, without any love or any value interests, to be concerned with what is agreeable for another, as in desiring the "reaction" of a sexual partner. But in this case I am only interested in the reaction of the other, not for his or her sake, but because it is satisfying or attractive for me. (This is a dreadful abuse of the true meaning of spousal union, which by its very nature is a fulfillment of the intentio unionis of spousal love.) As long as someone only acknowledges the point of view of the merely subjectively satisfying he can never transcend himself and enter into the soul of the other. A real interest "for the other" is only possible if I see what is agreeable to the other in the light of his beneficial good.

In the previous chapter we called love a super value-response on the grounds that the beloved person becomes a beneficial good of mine. In the present chapter we have discovered a new dimension of love that requires us to speak of it as a super value-response, namely, the "for the sake of the other." All of the other's beneficial goods and harmful evils become important for me. This holds for all categories of love for creatures, including love of neighbor. But as we are about to see, all of the beloved person's beneficial goods become direct[9] beneficial goods of mine, just as the evils that harm him become direct harmful evils of mine. This is only found in the natural categories of love for creatures, but it is not found in the love of neighbor. We shall return to this subject, especially in chapter 11.

How direct goods and evils for the beloved person become direct goods and evils for the lover

Now we have to deal with something that has given rise to misunderstandings and especially to an erroneous concept of "selfless" love. We have already in chapters 5 and 6 spoken of various misunderstandings regarding selfless love. But here we have to point out something that is typical for all natural categories of love with the exception of love of neighbor.

---

by the marriage of Catherine, which he takes as a betrayal of their mutual love and also as superficial throwing away of herself. And all of this poisons his love. But before this poisoning occurred he was really concerned with Catherine's happiness and was capable of a real "for her sake."

9   [The two occurrences of "direct" in this sentence represent a correction of the German text, which says "indirekt." Von Hildebrand could have only meant "direkt." Trans.]

We saw that the beloved person is a beneficial good for the lover, and the greater the love the more this is the case. But there are many beneficial goods of the beloved person that become direct beneficial goods for the lover, and this as a logical consequence of the fact that the beloved person is a beneficial good for him. Through the power of love a person becomes a beneficial good of mine in an eminent sense; as a result, all of those qualities of his that awaken my love are beneficial goods of mine. The intelligence, the talents, the beauty, all the moral values of the beloved person are not just beneficial for him, they are also *directly* beneficial for me. They are sources of my happiness. They give me joy not only for his sake but for mine. They are a direct gift for me and are not indirect beneficial goods of mine, as is everything that affects me from the point of view of what is beneficial for the other. The same holds for the health of the beloved person. I do not just consider this from the point of view of what health means for this person, that is, how health is good for him and how the undermining of his health is harmful for him; I who love am also affected by the health of the beloved person under the aspect of a direct beneficial good. The death of a beloved person obviously affects me not just because of the evil for him of dying, but also because of the great loss for me. The same holds for every dangerous sickness of the beloved person, or even for the decline of his mental power or his moral commitments. All of these things must be direct evils for me. The same holds for the corresponding beneficial goods; the health of the beloved person, his mental and moral development must be direct beneficial goods of mine.

So we see the threefold role that the beneficial goods of the beloved person play for me. First, there is the pure value-response in the case of goods that glorify God by their value, such as the conversion of the beloved person, or his moral and religious growth. Second, many of the beneficial goods of the beloved person, such as his life, his health, his intellectual and moral development, as well as his being appreciated and loved by others, become important for me because they are a source of my happiness. Third, these objective goods of the beloved person become important for me on the grounds that they are important for the beloved person. The first and the third roles of beneficial goods are found in all categories of love for creatures, but the second, while it is found in all natural categories of love, is not found in the love of neighbor.

Some further distinctions

Now we have to draw here the decisive distinction between a beneficial good of mine that is independent of love, for instance, my own health or my own mental soundness, and a direct beneficial good of mine that is based on the good of the beloved person, such as his health or mental soundness. It is important to understand the distinctive character of these direct beneficial goods: they are goods of mine only in virtue of my love for the other.

The direct good which the beloved person is for me, has much in common with the impersonal goods that are good for me on the basis of their value, such as some great work of art or some beautiful city. I can say that I love them. That holds for much in the beloved person that is a direct beneficial good of mine (it is of course also a beneficial good of his). But since I love the other and am moved by all that is a beneficial good for him—something that has no place with impersonal goods, although I love them in an analogous sense—there is something different about my direct beneficial good that derives from the goodness, beauty, intelligence, talents, health, etc., of the other, something different from those impersonal goods that are beneficial for me simply on the basis of their value.

The unique warmth proper to love shows itself in my interest in all that is beneficial and harmful for the beloved person; it illumines all other dimensions of love. Everything about the other that is a direct beneficial good for me takes on a particular character that distinguishes it from direct impersonal goods for me, which do not admit of the whole dimension of the "for him," or, as we could as well say, of being indirect goods.

Which goods are directly important for me and not just indirectly important for me because of what they mean for the beloved person (we prescind here from love of neighbor)? It is especially those beneficial goods for the other that are not, strictly speaking, experiential [*erlebniszugewandt*] goods. These are the goods we had in mind when we said above that the health of the beloved person is not only important for that person but also important in the same direct way for the friend, mother, child who loves him.

A further equivocation with "selflessness"

But all these goods and evils of the beloved person move me in my love not only as direct goods and evils of my own but also for his sake, that is, as taken under the point of view of what they mean for him. In fact, many of the beneficial goods that are strongly experienced in their delightfulness move me only for the sake of the other; they move me only because they are fortunate or unfortunate for him, joyful or painful for him, pleasant or unpleasant for him. But as we will see later on, even though I am motivated for the sake of the other, these goods affect and move me very deeply and sometimes even more deeply than the same goods affect me when they are direct goods for me.

Two kinds of commitment to another person within love of neighbor

In the love of neighbor there are only two points of view under which we approach all that concerns the neighbor: the point of view of value and disvalue, and the point of view of what is objectively beneficial or harmful for the neighbor. All action inspired by the love of neighbor is performed from these two points of view, which cannot contradict each other, as we saw, and which always lead to the same result. But it is necessary for love of neighbor that we not approach a situation only from the value point of view but also from the point of view of what is objectively beneficial for the other. If we really love the other as our neighbor, we aim at his conversion or moral growth not only under the aspect of glorifying God but also under the aspect of what is objectively good for him.

But as we said, in love of neighbor the neighbor is not an objective good for me, and so it is not the case that certain beneficial goods of his, besides being of interest to me for his sake, also become direct beneficial goods of mine. Love of neighbor has a unique kind of selflessness as a result of the fact that my interest in the neighbor is motivated only by his happiness (apart from a value-responding interest in him), only by what is objectively good or bad for him. But something is lost here that in all the other categories of love makes for the particularly joyful abundance of love, as we have already seen more than once. In the love of neighbor the other is not a source of my happiness; the intentio unionis recedes here into the background, even if, as we saw, it is never entirely missing. If in the other categories of love, such as in the love between friends or in spousal love, the well-being of the other interested me only under those two points of view—value and the beneficial good of the other—this would not be a sign of selflessness but rather of a deficiency of love. If the beloved person is sick, the one who loves (with a love other than love of neighbor) must feel his sickness to be a direct evil of his own and not only be sad about the sickness as an evil for the other. (Of course, this direct evil will vary with the strength of the love.) But we should not forget that, as we have seen, there are many goods and evils which even in these other categories of love move the one who loves exclusively from the point of view of what is beneficial or harmful for the other, as when the other suffers a relatively harmless physical pain, or is deprived of something he particularly likes, such as playing a sport and enjoying merely agreeable goods, or is unfairly treated, to name only a few examples. In all these cases (which belong to the categories of natural love) the happiness or the suffering of the beloved person is not a direct objective good or evil for me, but it is an indirect objective good or evil for me. There is, however, no loss of transcendence when it sometimes happens in these cases that the objective good or evil for the other moves me with happiness or sadness not only because of what it means for him but at the same time because of what it *directly* means for me on the basis of my love for him.

If I love someone as a friend or with spousal love, there is something particularly delightful for me in experiencing with him great spiritual goods. But this is only delightful because I love the other. To travel to a beautiful place or to listen to beautiful music with someone for whom I feel only love of neighbor is not particularly delightful. It may sometimes be even more delightful to enjoy these things alone.[10] One must love the other if the *shared* enjoyment of beauty is going to be delightful. So we have here to do with a delightfulness

---

10   Apart from the pleasure of giving joy to the other, my delight in the trip can be severely limited by the presence of the other; his presence can be something negative for me.

that is based on some love other than love of neighbor and that is spontaneously desired by such love. Of course, it is taken for granted here that the beloved person is receptive to the beauty of a country and a work of music and that he takes it as a precious gift. And in fact, the other must also take the shared enjoyment as a distinct source of delightfulness. Here various points of view are interwoven. First of all, only on the basis of love (other than love of neighbor) is the shared enjoyment delightful. Secondly, the good, whatever it is, must be delightful for the beloved person. Thirdly, the shared enjoyment must also be delightful for him. Thus the shared enjoyment is for the one who loves not only a direct objective good for him that grows out of love but is also an indirect good that passes through the "for the other" and involves the point of view of what is delightful for him.

We have seen that in the natural categories of love all that is considered by me from the point of view of what is objectively beneficial or harmful for the beloved person is also indirectly beneficial or harmful for me. And the greater the love, the more this is the case. In the case of an ultimate love, the physical suffering of the beloved person is worse for me than my own suffering of the same kind. It is more important for me that the beloved person is successful, that he is treated well and considerately by others, than that I myself have these goods. An experiential benefit or harm of the other becomes my most intimate concern even more than when this benefit or harm affects me directly.[11] The fact that my interest in the "for the other" can have the same weight and sometimes an even greater weight, that this interest can reach in the most intimate way into my happiness or misery, is so certain a sign of love that the degree of my being intimately affected by what something means for the other is a sure criterion of the depth of my love.

One could object: can this kind of sharing in the other not reach a high degree in the love of neighbor? When St. Paul says, "Who weeps and I do not weep?" he seems to express clearly the importance that the suffering and joy of my neighbor has for me. But intense as this importance may be, it still has a different character in deep natural love. In love of neighbor it does not penetrate into my subjectivity, it does not become a part of my happiness or misery. If I am moved by love of neighbor to ask God to bear some suffering of my neighbor, if I want to bear it instead of my neighbor, this has a different ring from me asking God to let me bear some suffering instead of my friend bearing it. In this latter case the suffering of the beloved person has become a greater evil for me than my own suffering. My prayer is not exactly heroic but rather a sign of genuine and deep love. In the case of love of neighbor, by contrast, it is an outgrowth of goodness, it is an unambiguously moral act, an heroic act. In this sacrifice it is somehow the love of Christ that engenders

---

11 Of course, this does not hold for the highest of all beneficial goods, one's salvation.

the heroism. But in the case of the loving husband or friend there is not sacrifice but only a choosing of the lesser evil. And *that* it is the lesser evil is nothing but a fruit of love; this fact distinguishes this evil from all those evils that affect me without involving a relation to another person, such as some sickness of mine, or my own physical pains, or my own extreme poverty.

It would be a very great error to bring in here the argumentation of the Fable of the Bees of Mandeville.[12] It obviously does not apply to strictly moral value-responses. One would have to be blind to say that, in deciding for the point of view of morally relevant values rather than following the subjectively satisfying, one is simply choosing what one likes better. For there is no common denominator for these two points of view. But someone might think that the thesis of Mandeville holds at least for the present case where we are dealing with objective goods and evils, which are certainly what is at issue when I say, "It is more distressing for me if the beloved person suffers great pains than if I had them myself." Someone might think that here I prefer to suffer physical pains on the grounds that this is less painful for me, just as if I were to say, "It is less distressing for me to suffer physical pains than to lose money." But this would be a great mistake. The fact that the evil suffered by the beloved person is worse for me than my own suffering is a result of the value-response of love, of self-donation, of transcendence.

The point of view of the merely subjectively satisfying is no longer at stake here. There is a world of difference between being interested in a good because it is subjectively satisfying and being interested in it because it is a beneficial good on the basis of its value. After all, this latter interest presupposes a value-response. But the present case, where one's own suffering is preferred to the suffering of the beloved person, is only possible on the basis of love, of growing beyond oneself—of the whole glorious reality of love and its transcendence. The fact that the physical suffering of the beloved person becomes my suffering and that it even surpasses my own physical suffering, does not take the transcendence out of my preference and put it on a level with the avoidance of some evil that affects me directly; it is rather the case that this fact implies a particular triumph of love.

To see this clearly we have only to bring in the following case for comparison. Suppose someone were to say, "I would rather have a headache than my wife have one, because her complaining about hers is worse for me than having my own headache." In this case the husband remains exclusively in the realm of

---

12   [Von Hildebrand refers here to the work of Bernard Mandeville (1670–1733) entitled *The Fable of the Bees: or Private Vices, Publick Benefits*. It is enough for the reader to take note of the hedonism that von Hildebrand ascribes to Mandeville, and to see that von Hildebrand wants to show the impossibility of explaining hedonistically the way in which the goods and evils of another become indirect goods and evils for the one who loves the other. Trans.]

the agreeable and disagreeable and fails really to share in the suffering of his wife; completely missing is any "for the other," any love.[13] The distinction between this case and the one we are examining could not be clearer.

The fallacy at the basis of Mandeville's thesis emerges clearly. In the case in which I would rather endure pains than that the beloved person would endure them, the point of view of the merely subjectively satisfying is necessarily left behind entirely. We have already seen above that the joy and suffering of another person can have no importance for a consistent hedonist, that there can be for him no "for the sake of the other." The fact that I would rather suffer pain myself than see a beloved person suffer it can never be understood in terms of what "I like better" in the sense of the merely subjectively satisfying. This fact is only possible on the basis of value-response and of love along with the category of importance of the beneficial good for the other that is rooted in love.

So we see that the thesis of Mandeville is just as false in the case of being motivated by the beneficial good of the beloved person as it is in the case of being motivated by values.

Now the sufferings and joys that I experience when the beloved person suffers and rejoices are qualitatively different from those which directly affect me. This is clearest of all in the case of bodily pains; when I suffer because the other suffers bodily pains, my pain is of a psychic and indeed spiritual nature, in contrast with the pains felt by the other, which are bodily. But it is not only with pains that we see this difference; if, for example, I am insulted or humiliated, my pain is different in kind from what I suffer when a beloved person is insulted or humiliated. The disvalue of the action of insulting is in both cases the same, but the pain over the insult to the beloved person has a more pure and more noble quality than being affected by an insult to myself. Indeed, in the case of very great love I am more affected, more personally concerned, by the beloved person being unjustly treated than I am by being unjustly treated myself. But this being-more-personally-concerned goes in a different direction than the difference in quality, and therefore does not eliminate it. Here the value-response to the injustice plays a much larger role (than in the case of being unjustly treated myself). But even prescinding from this significant factor there remains the difference in the quality of being hurt by the unjust treatment.

This is even clearer in the case of states of consciousness [*Zustände*]. If the beloved person is depressed, I am sad, but this sadness is not a state of consciousness like depression; it is rather an intentional response. Perhaps we say, "Would that I could be depressed in his place." Out of love for him I would rather be depressed myself than see him depressed. But my sadness over his depression is not itself a depression but rather the intentionally motivated response of sadness.

---

13   We mean that this wish, this preference, is no expression of love, but this does not mean that someone who says such a thing could not after all really love the other.

But suppose that there is no such structural difference; suppose that I am happy because the beloved person is happy. This (indirect) happiness of mine is different from a happiness flowing from objective goods that address me directly and that lack this moment of "for the sake of the other."

In love of neighbor, by contrast, the well-being of my neighbor does not become in the same way an indirect good or evil for me. It does not reach into my subjectivity [*Eigenleben*], even though my sharing in the other can have the greatest intensity and make my heart overflow. But as we will later see with greater precision, in the love of neighbor I step beyond my subjectivity, betaking myself to the other without, as it were, bringing my subjectivity along.

Conclusion

For our purposes there are three dimensions of transcendence that are important. They are found in all *natural* categories of love, as we have seen. The first is the transcendence of value-response as such; love has this in common with other value-responses. The second consists in the beloved person becoming a beneficial good of mine. And the third consists in all of his beneficial goods becoming of concern to me for his sake, indeed becoming an indirect beneficial good of mine. The second dimension of transcendence makes love, as we saw, a super value-response, and the third also makes love, though in a *new* sense, a super value-response.

After elaborating this decisive trait of love we now turn to the various kinds of "mine" with a view to investigating more closely the unique interpenetration of self-donation and entering into the other, on the one hand, and the subjectivity of the one who loves, on the other.

CHAPTER EIGHT

The Different Kinds of "Mine"

The word "mine" can mean different things, even if a purely formal relation to one's own person recurs in all of the meanings. At present we are of course not concerned with listing all the ways in which the word "mine" can be used. For it only takes a fleeting relation between some thing and myself, a relation that has little basis in reality, for me to have a reason to call a thing mine, especially when this expression emphasizes the contrast to the relation in which the thing stands to some other person. For example, we can ask, "Is that my glass or yours?" Or we say, "My path goes to the right, does yours go in the same direction?" Or: "I have to leave because my flight is about to depart." "Mine" and "my" have indeed a meaning in all these cases, but the underlying relation to myself is so transitory and accidental that these meanings of "mine" are of no interest to us in the present context. We limit ourselves to the kinds of "mine" where a very definite experience of "mine" corresponds to some objective belonging. There are different classical kinds of significant objective belonging to me each of which underlies a certain experience of "mine"—a qualitative experience of "mine" that varies as the belonging varies. In the following we will analyze the different classical kinds of objective belonging to my own person, as well as the corresponding experiences of "mine," that is, the experiences in which I consciously live the objective belonging to myself by experiencing something as "mine." For it is one thing merely to know that something belongs to me and to point out this objective relation by calling it "mine," and it is something else to experience something as "mine," to experience the belonging and all that is implied in this experience.

And so in the following we will not examine all possible meaningful and legitimate uses of the term, "mine," but only those classical relations of belonging that correspond to an experience of "mine" and that play an important role in our lives. We will give particular attention to this experience of "mine." But we are above all concerned with elaborating the particular experience of "mine" that goes with love.

The "mine" of my belonging to myself as person

The first meaning of the word "mine" refers to the fundamental belonging of me to myself (which is usually taken for granted), as when we say *my* body, *my* health, *my* leg, *my* sleep, etc. Here the "mine" is not the result of a conscious stance to these things; they do not become mine on the basis of being particularly important to me. No, they are mine from the very beginning, like it or not, independently from all conscious stances. They are important to me in a fundamental way because they are mine. They are in fact mine before I am aware of them. This is not to deny that my health as such also has a particular value that I can appreciate more or less, but it is an elementary good for me as a result of being *my* health. The solidarity that I have with it does not flow from my appreciation of its value, but is taken for granted. We can see its value when we gratefully experience it as a gift of God.

The "mine" that goes with owning something

"Mine" takes on a second meaning when it expresses the relation of owning something.[1] In this case it need not, as with the first meaning, refer to a relation that is taken for granted and that is pre-given to us and is even inseparable from us, but it includes all those cases in which something becomes mine by becoming my property. In this sense we speak of my house, my dress, my money, my horse, my dog, etc. Although this meaning of "mine," as we said, differs from the first one in that the relation to me is not pre-given as an element of my fundamental constitution and so as inseparable from me, it is still like the first in that the "mine" is not the result of a conscious stance but rather has a merely objective and formal character. For the relation of possessing is either already there, as in the case of inheriting something, or it grows out of a social act[2] (such as buying). The "mine" of possessing has a certain legal character. Whether the thing possessed is itself beautiful or not beautiful, whether I appreciate its beauty or not, in no way affects the fact that it is mine and does not belong to anyone else. But the fact that it is mine invests it with an importance for me. The very fact of having something as my property establishes a certain solidarity between me and that thing. Something is important for me, it becomes an objective good for me, because it is mine, because I possess it. Of course, it can also happen that the thing possessed is something very dear to me, as a house is dear to me because of its beauty or because of the memories I have invested in it. And it often enough even happens that I buy something because I find it beautiful, that its purchase is motivated by its value; the fact that it is my property is then closely connected with the value-

---

1   Cf. our discussion in chapter 6 of a person possessing something.

2   ["Social act" is always used by von Hildebrand in the sense given to it by his teacher, Adolf Reinach, that is, in the sense of an act that has an addressee and that must be heard by the addressee in order to be complete. In his ground-breaking work, *The Apriori Foundations of the Civil Law* (translated by me in *Aletheia* 3 [1983]: 1–142) Reinach gave particular attention to the legally relevant social acts, and especially to the social act of promising. Trans.]

response. But the *formal, legal being-mine* that results from owning something should not be confused with the relation to me that comes from the fact that I am drawn to its beauty.

This latter is an entirely new bond that is supported by the value of the object and not by possessing it as such. Of course, if I am drawn to an object because it is beautiful and because my interest in it has the character of a value-response, then the fact that it is my property takes on an entirely new meaning. It makes me happy to have the new tie to something beautiful that comes with owning it. In this case there is the remarkable result that the relation, first established by the value-response, is fulfilled in a certain direction. Here the object does not take on importance because it is mine, but it is important on the basis of its value; the fact that it is mine makes me happy because I already love it on the basis of its value. Whereas in a pure relation of owning, the thing which is mine has the character of an extended ego, deriving its importance from the fact that it is mine, the "mine" that comes from owning something dear to me because of its value involves a more intimate relation of the thing to me. It is true that the thing comes, as it were, to me and becomes mine because it is my property, but the owning is important for me only because of the value of the object. In spite of the formal sameness of the "mine," which is in both cases rooted in the owning, it is only in the first case that the extension of the ego stands forth. In the second case it is the gift-character of the thing that stands forth, and the thing becomes even more of a gift through me owning it; it moves, as it were, towards me and is no extension of me. So we find two very different functions in the "mine" formally constituted through owning.

The "mine" deriving from being a part of something

A third type of "mine" stands in contrast to both of the previously mentioned types; indeed, it is in one sense the very opposite of them. It is based on belonging to something as a part of it. If I say, "my family," "my country," "my political party," I am dealing with something that is by no means a part of me, such as my leg, or with something that I own, such as my house. In this new "mine" I am instead a part of something that contains me; I belong to it.

But by itself the fact that I am a part of something and belong to it does not suffice to establish a "mine." Also required is the fact that the community to which I belong is not all-encompassing in the sense that all human beings belong to it. There would obviously be no sense in saying, "my mankind," since mankind encompasses everyone. For this kind of "mine," as indeed the previously discussed kinds as well, always implies some demarcation from "yours," some contrast between what stands in a special relation to me and what does not stand in this relation to me but rather stands in the same relation to others. If I speak of "my family," the implication is that there are families to which I do not belong. But this demarcation from the other does not include any hostile antithesis and should not be seen as setting one against the other.

Of course, perversion is possible with this "mine" of belonging to something, of being a part of something, just as perversions are possible with the "mine" of owning.[3] But the perversion goes in a different direction than in the case of owning. The family to which I belong can take on the character of an extended ego and become the source of my arrogance. The danger here is typical for the nationalist. The nation to which he belongs is the source which nourishes his arrogance. As long as he speaks as individual person he may give evidence of being modest. He might say, "Oh, I'm not very important, I'm in no way extraordinary, and some people are much superior to me." But as soon as he speaks of his nation he claims for it the first place among all nations. His arrogance is gratified by belonging to the nation that is supposedly the greatest and the most significant. His being a part of the nation does not exactly give rise to an extended ego, but to an enlarged and exalted ego; the ego becomes great and significant by being a part of something great.[4]

But this perversion should not be taken as characteristic for the third kind of "mine" as such. For in the essence of this "mine" there is no element of the enlarged and exalted ego. The patriot who says "my country" forms a contrast to the nationalist in that he does not think that his country is the greatest and the best one, and also in that he does not feel confirmed in his arrogance by belonging to his country. His "mine" is the expression of the fully experienced belonging to his country, through which he consciously lives his responsibility for it and his bond with it. There is in addition usually another, very different source of "mine" in this case, and we will deal with it directly below.

The point that concerns us here is to establish that the formal "mine" flowing from the objective fact of being a part of something is a type of "mine" all its own. To this objective belonging there corresponds an experience of belonging. In addition there can arise an entirely new experience of "mine" that is born of love for the community. We can even say that the formal "mine" is ordered to a love for the community, as we see clearly in the case of the family. But this does not prevent us from sharply distinguishing this formal "mine" as such from the "mine" deriving from love. After all, the formal "mine" can occur apart from any love.

The "mine" of some special belonging of one person to another

Another kind of "mine" is given whenever there is a special bond of belonging to a particular person. This can occur in three different directions: the belonging can be to someone placed above me, or to someone on my level, or

---

3   In chapter 6 we pointed out the dangers inherent in the relation of owning.

4   [In his polemical writings against German National Socialism from the 1930's von Hildebrand often explores this enlarged ego of the nationalist; see, for example, his essay from 1936, "Masse und Gemeinschaft," in *Memoiren und Aufsätze gegen den Nationalsozialismus* (Memoirs and Anti-Nazi Writings) (Grünewald, 1994). Trans.]

to someone placed below me. If a servant speaks of "my" master or a subject speaks of "my" emperor or a child of "my" mother or father, the "my" expresses being bound to and belonging to someone placed above the speaker. But if the master speaks of "my" servant or the mother of "my" child, then "my" expresses the relation of belonging to someone placed below the speaker. These relations are of course always reciprocal; the relation of belonging in which one person "looks up" to another, is a relation in which the other "looks down" to the first person. In fact, the reciprocal character goes so far that each of the two persons in his "mine" takes account not only of the direction of his belonging to the other but also of the direction of the other's belonging to him. We are thinking here, as above, of the "mine" resulting from mutual ordering of persons to each other [*Zuordnung*] and not yet of the "mine" resulting from love. This latter often unites with the other "mine," especially in the relations of children to their parents and parents to their children.

There are also relations of belonging among those on the same level, such as among comrades, colleagues, siblings who are close in age, and twins.

In all relations involving a tie to a person placed above me (my emperor, my lord, my mother, my father), the "my" is by no means the expression of an extended ego. For the elements of giving oneself, of looking up to the other, and of being in a subordinate position all serve to distinguish it clearly from both of the above-mentioned types of "my" and "mine," that is, from something being a part of me such as my leg, and from something being owned by me such as my house.

Of course, even here perversions can enter in. A child can experience the excellences and the stature of its father or mother as an elevation of its own ego, just as the nationalist can experience his belonging to his country as a source of arrogance. In this case we have not exactly an extended ego, but rather, as with the nationalist, an exalted, expanded ego.

There is also no extended ego in the "mine" constituted in the relation of a higher-placed person to a lower-placed person. Since the lower-placed person is a person, and since any and every owning is inappropriate and impossible in relation to persons, this "mine" is completely different in kind from the "mine" of something that is a part of me as well as from the "mine" of something owned by me. But the danger of taking the other as an extended ego is much greater here, since the one in the superior position is exposed to the danger of falling into this perversion. Thus a mother may consider her child as a part of herself, or a master may consider his servants as his property.

As for the "mine" that comes from belonging together with others at the same level (colleague, comrade, brother), the danger of taking these equals as an extended ego is much less, especially in the case of colleagues or comrades. But this perversion is never impossible.

The belonging together that is given in all these cases can also take on a formal character when it is, as it were, confirmed by a social act.

But there is also a "mine" that is based only on a formal unity of persons and grows exclusively out of certain social acts. If I form a partnership with someone, the "my" and "mine" express our belonging together. The nature of this belonging together has a definite we-character and lacks entirely the I-Thou dimension. It can sometimes happen that certain acts and decisions can only be carried out if I act together with my partner. In addition, it is a purely formal unity; as such it does not include any mutual love or friendship, but is entirely independent of any human bond. This "mine" is different from the one of the extended ego or of owning. Since my partner and I have equal rights and share common tasks, the "mine" has in no way the character of an extended ego, and it just as little comes from being a part of the other. It is a kind of unity in which both stand on the same level, the other being just as much my partner as I am his partner. This unity may sometimes deeply affect our daily lives. What above all concerns us is, first of all, the purely formal-juridical character of the "mine," and secondly, the emphatic we-form of unity, and thirdly, the respect for the rights of the other, which forms the basis of the unity. All kinds of human relations may be added, each of which gives rise to a new kind of "mine." We have wanted above all to point out the "mine" that builds on the belonging together that flows from a social act.

The primordial experience of "being at home," and the "mine" that is rooted in it

Now we have to examine another very significant "mine," which finds its typical expression in the experience of being at home [*Heimaterlebnis*] in the broad sense of this word. We are not thinking of the relation that results from the objective fact of being at home in some place, for this "mine" is contained in the belonging to something as a part of it and was discussed above. We are thinking of the specific experience of home; it presupposes all kinds of factors, but it amounts to a primordial datum, something *sui generis*. It presupposes a lived familiarity with some surroundings, a certain affinity for them, an experience of shelteredness in the surroundings, and in the case of a literal home one must have lived there for a long time and must have invested all kinds of experiences in the surroundings, especially the experiences of one's earliest youth. In the experience of home there is also necessarily an element of love. Whoever fully experiences a country, a city, a village as his home and strongly feels how his rootedness in it and rejoices in dwelling at home there, will also love this home. But we have to distinguish the "mine" that grows out this experience of home from the "mine" that is a result of love and that we will discuss in some detail later in this chapter. The difference between the two shows itself already in the fact that not every love for a place or a landscape involves an experience of home.

First of all, the element of familiarity is important. Familiarity is more than just an exact knowing of something and being used to it. We can understand the nature of familiarity more clearly by thinking about its opposite, "foreignness," or "strangeness." The phenomenon of foreignness is mainly characterized by feeling ourselves surrounded by that to which we have no access, which we cannot understand, and which thus does not speak to us. A typical case of this foreign experiencing is being in a country whose language one does not understand and whose customs one does not know. Being cut off and isolated, indeed, being "lost," is typical for real foreignness. One does not understand the people and they do not understand what we say; we no longer know our way or understand what is going on; we are cut off and cannot reach the others.

To get a better grasp of foreignness we have only to distinguish it from newness [*Neuheit*]. Something can be completely new to us and yet speak to us, can be understandable to us, accessible to us, and so in no way be foreign to us. Foreignness is depressing, but newness is not at all and in fact it can even be a source of gladness. One may lose sight of this fact by thinking of people who are so temperamentally conservative that whatever is unknown to them, whatever they are not used to, seems to them foreign or strange. For them everything new is foreign. But that is only the result of a particular disposition and does not eliminate the objective difference between newness and foreignness. These people are so constituted that they cannot deal with anything new; for them newness impedes understanding. Only by repeated contact with the new thing can they overcome this hindrance and let the thing begin to speak to them. This phenomenon can occur in certain areas even for people who do not have the specifically conservative attitude. For example, if they listen to a difficult piece of music they find that it remains for them after the first hearing like a sealed book. An easily understandable piece, by contrast, can fully speak to them when they first hear it. Whether something is foreign or not depends not on whether it is already known to me or is new to me, but on whether it is understandable for me, whether it speaks to me and is accessible to me.

The term foreign is applied even those cases where some content in no way resonates with me, so that I have no feel for it, even if I have known it for a long time. But here foreign is being used analogously. It now refers to what we might express better by saying that something is not my thing, not my cup of tea. Real foreignness is at stake only on the basis of the element of not getting into the thing, of being cut off from it.

As for all those things that present themselves to me as having disvalue on the basis of their objective content, it would be obviously inadequate to call them foreign or strange. It would be ridiculous to say of totalitarian systems like Hitler's National Socialism or Communism that they are foreign or strange to me. We go altogether beyond the foreign and the strange in condemning evil and untruth. First of all, foreignness is necessarily subjective; something is foreign or strange *to me* and need not be foreign to someone else. But to declare something to have a disvalue or to be false is to make an essentially objective statement that involves no relation to me or to any other subject. Secondly, the rejection that is called for by disvalue and untruth is far more radical and qualitatively different from the rejection motivated by foreignness.

But the things that we have no affinity for and that we do not like, though they share with foreignness the subjective element, do not constitute the specific experience of foreignness. People whom we have known for some time but do not like, may irritate and oppress us by their presence, but we do not feel "lost" as we do with people whose language we do not understand. In the experience of foreignness in the literal sense there is not even any aversion to the other, there is not primarily something that is disagreeable by "going against the grain," but rather a losing of the ground under one's feet. Foreignness engenders a feeling of anxiety, not of annoyance and antipathy.

The difference between what is foreign to me and what I dislike should not be overlooked on the grounds that, speaking in an analogous sense, I can say of an intellectual milieu or of a personality type which I dislike: it is foreign to me. It can also happen that, if I am suddenly forced to live together with people whom I have known for a long time but for whom I have a certain disliking and whose ways are not my ways, I can have a real experience of "exile," of being placed among strangers. That is then a true analogy to the literal experience of foreignness, because there is added the element of being uprooted. But the analogy is only given when I am encompassed by that which causes a certain disliking in me and am thereby separate from all that is congenial to me. A typical encounter with that for which I have some disliking does not engender a truly analogous feeling of the foreign.

That is very revealing, because the element of being lost, of being isolated, of being cut off, which in the case of foreignness in the literal sense comes from not understanding something and having no access to it, is here replaced by being cut off from one's usual congenial environment and by being handed over to disagreeable people. So we see: the foreignness that normally presupposes not understanding something and having no access to it, can be analogously brought about in the special case of being cast into an environment of people who, though not unknown to us, are disagreeable to us and are not our kind of people. In both cases we find the foreignness that has an element of being uprooted, of being lost, of losing the ground under one's feet.

But the difference that leads us to speak of an analogy is this: in the case of an environment that we dislike and find to be not our kind of thing we suffer mainly under the objective qualitative character of the environment, whereas in the case of literal foreignness the feeling of anxiety predominates. There is also this difference, that the literal foreignness can have a provisional character; we can think of it as something that will go away with time, since it is not rooted in the nature of the foreign thing. But in the case of that which, because of its qualitative makeup, is not my kind of thing, one does not have the impression that the foreignness is something provisional that will give way in time. But common to the two cases is the experience of being unsheltered [*Ungeborgenheit*].

Familiarity, the specific opposite of foreignness, emerges now more clearly in its distinctive character. We have here a subjective experience in the sense that something is always familiar *to* someone. It is also far more than just knowing something well, or just being used to something. Familiarity contains an element of delight; the familiar thing is congenial to me, resonates with me. It does not matter whether this congeniality is the result of getting used to something, of being formally embedded in my life, as with the specifically conservative type of person, or whether it also requires the particular quality of the thing, as with those who are not specifically conservative. The experience of familiarity as such always possesses, over and above the mere acquaintance with the thing, the element of the appealing, the comforting, the accessible.

But the comforting element of familiarity necessarily presupposes that the thing is embedded in my life, it presupposes a certain intimacy; the familiar thing has as it were a sweet sound, which also derives from the fact that something is reflected in it of the rhythm of the continuity of our life. The fact that something has spoken to me many times in the past makes of it a principle connecting the present with the past; it resounds intimately in my subjectivity, as if it were like an old friend. Of course, an appropriate content is always presupposed; something painful or depressing or offensive can never take on this character, even if it is well enough known and has accompanied me throughout life, for then it is more like an old enemy than an old friend.

In the case of a home—a place, a city, a country in which someone grew up and which he *experiences* as home—we mention first of all the element of familiarity. The phenomenon of a home includes in its positive meaning the familiarity of a place. Then there is the element of shelteredness, which, as one can easily see, surpasses that of familiarity. A home encompasses me lovingly; I am known to the people and to the community of the home, and I feel known and accepted by them. A home is not only familiar to us, but we also experience that we are familiar to it. The shelteredness extends even beyond the people of the community of the home. When I return home after a long time away I have the feeling, which is only a subjective impression that corresponds to no extra-mental reality, of being "greeted" by all the familiar mountains, trees, and meadows.[5]

---

5   In his *Aus dem Leben eines Taugenichts* (Ansbach, 1955), ch. 9, Eichendorff portrays this in a wonderful way:

   Die treuen Berg stehn auf der Wacht:
   "Wer streicht bei stiller Morgenzeit
   Da aus der Fremde durch die Heid?"
   Ich aber mir die Berg betracht
   Und lach ich mich vor grosser Lust
   Und rufe recht aus frischer Brust
   Parol und Feldgeschrei zugleich:

In the experience of being at home there is also, in addition to the shelteredness, a particular form of belonging-to [*dazugehören*], of our existence being rooted in a place. This being rooted is clearly a particular form of belonging-to. It is not only being a part of something, but also a "coming from there," a particular element of tradition. Being rooted also plays a decisive role in the belonging to a family. A family is usually, after all, an elementary home. But the experience of home that we have in the family is something different from being a part of something. This is why, as long as we were only speaking of the "mine" deriving from being a part of something, we did not yet mention this aspect of the family.

Being rooted in one's home means that it was here that one had all the basic experiences of life, that one awakened to the world, that one's life unfolded, that one as it were grew into life. It was here that nature revealed herself in her different faces, that the realm of Thou and We disclosed itself to us, that we experienced happiness, joy, and pain. Closely related to being rooted, where the element of awakening to the fullness of life is especially in evidence, is the element of investing something of ourselves in a place through our daily life in it. (By "daily" I do not mean the ordinary "everyday" [*alltäglich*] things but rather deep experiences that permeate our daily lives.) Here is the church where we went to daily mass, where we prayed, here is the place where we fell in love, where we experienced beauty in nature and in art. We invest in the space surrounding us all the experiences that we had there: in the house in which we lived, in the place where something took place. Notice that the successive unfolding of our life plays a role here, by which I mean frequently experiencing the same thing in the same place. Of course, a significant relation between some place and some important event is found even when a unique event invests a place with significance. This is the case with places where great historic events have taken place, such as Waterloo, the Milvian Bridge, Ponte Molle, Marathon, and in a much more real and significant way with places where some great supernatural events took place, giving rise to places of pilgrimage like Lourdes. But in the case of experiencing a place as home, what we find is continually investing in some place all our significant experiences, together with all that we experience along with them. While a place can be dear or venerable to us because of something special that we once experienced there, to experience a place as home requires a continual investing of our life in the place.

Vivat Östreich!
    Da kennt mich erst die ganze Rund,
Nun grüssen Bach und Vöglein zart
Und Wälder rings nach Landesart,
Die Donau blitzt aus tiefem Grund,
Der Stephansturm auch ganz von fern
Guckt überm Berg und säh mich gern,
Und ist ers nicht, so kommt er doch gleich,
Vivat Östreich! (pp. 75–76)

Now all of these elements contained in the experience of home constitute a very definite kind of "mine." If a love of my home is added to all of these, then we have yet another source of "mine," even though this love and those elements blend together organically in the experience of "my" home.

But it has to be emphatically said that "home" is not necessarily the place where I was born and grew up. First of all, a change can take place with regard to home; what was once our home can be replaced by another home. We might say, "This has now become my home."

We can, however, also speak of home in a sense that is both broader and deeper. Without wanting to depreciate the value and the depth of the experience of home in the literal sense, we have to say that there is a still deeper form of home. For Catholics the Church is the true home. This is because they are rooted in it in their supernatural existence in a new and much realer sense. For not only are they baptized in the Church, but their membership in the Church is inseparably connected with receiving the life of grace; only as members of the Church do they preserve their supernatural life. But we want to speak here of the experience of home that is had by believers when they experience the Church as the mother who lovingly surrounds them, as the true and supremely valid home, in which they are profoundly sheltered in their existence, and sheltered in a way that reaches beyond their earthly existence. If they know how really to "think with the Church" (*sentire cum ecclesia*), they will breathe the air of home immediately upon entering a church, or attending the holy sacrifice anywhere in the world, or hearing the Gregorian Chant.

To this spiritual home, which is home in the supreme and profoundest sense, there are many analogies, which, while they do not claim to be the true and ultimate home, represent a kind of spiritual home. The analogy to the supreme spiritual home lies in the fact that these experiences of home do not derive, as the literal home derives, from a continuous living in the home but from the objective makeup of the home and its deep affinity to us. Thus someone can, on coming for the first time into a cultural milieu, have the feeling that this is "my true home."

Perhaps a person grows over time into this spiritual and cultural home, or perhaps a person has to live for a long time in this "qualitative" home in order to take root in it. Thus Rome was home for Winckelmann and Vienna became home for Schlegel. When we call the experience of home a primordial reality [*Urphänomen*], we are referring not just to home in the literal sense, but to that which is common to the literal home and to the spiritual-cultural home: rootedness, familiarity, shelteredness. For being at home is grounded in the metaphysical situation of man. The need for being sheltered is grounded on the one hand in the creaturehood of man, and on the other hand in his existing as person. There are indeed attempts to live without shelteredness, but these are theoretical illusions. Without shelteredness there is no real happiness, no uncramped existence, and above all no life in the truth. There is a residue of truth in the person who experiences unsheltered existence as despair.

True and ultimate shelteredness is the shelteredness in God in His love. But there are many analogous kinds of shelteredness within the created world. The development of a human being from birth to relative independence shows the classical role and significance of shelteredness. Being sheltered is one of the primordial experiences of a child. Just as parents represent God through their authority, so they provide for their children whom they shelter a distant image of shelteredness in God. But not only is shelteredness a fundamental human reality, not only is the need for it grounded in the nature of man, but the experience of home, which as we saw includes shelteredness, also has the character of a fundamental human reality. It belongs to the nature of man to be rooted someplace, to be at home.

Even if a person has no home in the literal sense—perhaps his parents were always traveling and took him from one place to another and perhaps even in later life he lived in very different places—he still knows the experience of spiritual home. As I explained in my book, *Die Metaphysik der Gemeinschaft* (The Metaphysics of Community), every human being is incorporated in a certain realm of value and goods, just as all relations to other persons are primarily situated in a shared realm of value and goods; each finds his spiritual home, and breaths the air of home, in the realm in which he is primarily incorporated. For the scholar the world of knowledge is the primary home; here he feels himself at home, happily received and sheltered. The artist finds his home in the world of art. But this primary incorporation in a realm of value is not only found in the professions in which a person can fully fulfill himself and to which he can fully devote himself. Every human being is primarily incorporated in some such realm. It suffices that he is ordered in a special way to some realm of value and of goods and that he has a particular understanding for it.

The *homo religiosus* is the man who is primarily at home in the religious sphere of existence, and not just objectively—for objectively every human being is primarily ordained to this realm—but subjectively as well.

We hope that these remarks will suffice to show forth the classical significance of the experience of being at home. Man necessarily has a home, and the "mine" grounded in the experience of home is an authentic "mine" all its own. In this "mine" there is no danger of a perversion in the direction of an expanded or an enlarged ego, which we found in nationalism. On the contrary, in the experience of being at home and in the resulting "mine" there is an element of gratitude; there is an experienced contrast between my ego and a reality that encompasses me, but not in the sense of containing me as a part but in the sense of grounding me and sheltering me in it. For shelteredness is something opposed to arrogance, since there is in it—in contrast to all self-glorification and all feeling strong and secure in oneself—an acknowledgement of one's need for protection, for feeling secure through something beyond our-selves.

This "mine" based on the experience of home is, as is evident, different from the "mine" that comes from something being a part of myself, and also from the "mine" grounded in ownership. But it is also different from the "mine" of me being a part of something else, and also from that of belonging to someone, including someone who is in a position above me. Of course, it has more in common with these last two than with the first two, but it is some-thing new even in relation to those forms of "mine" that are relatively close to it. The fact that it often goes hand in hand with being a part of something should not obscure for us the difference between the two. We have already said, and more than once, that the fact that two things present themselves together and even form a kind of symbiosis does not eliminate the difference between the things. Willing is always connected with thinking, cannot occur without thinking; and yet these two things are, as is obvious, entirely different one from another. Even things opposed to each other can be strongly connected with each other, as when arrogance creeps into attitudes that are entirely opposed to arrogance. But even when things stand in no kind of essential opposition to each other but rather organically interpenetrate, they are not for that reason identical.

Thus the "mine" of parents, or the "mine" of belonging to a nation can interpenetrate the "mine" of being at home, and can do this in so organic a way that what results is one experienced "mine." And yet the "mine" deriving from being a part of a nation is different from the one deriving from the experience of being at home. To see this we have only to think of the cases in which the former occurs *without* the experience of being at home.

The "mine" that grows out of love

But now we have to turn to the "mine" that concerns us here in this book, namely, the "mine" that grows out of love, which represents something entire-ly new in relation to all the kinds of "mine" that we have examined so far. This "mine" derives exclusively from the fact that something becomes an objective good for me on the basis of its value and of its particular affinity with me, that it enters into my subjectivity.[6]

This "mine" is *radically* different from the first kind of "mine," the indis-soluble solidarity with myself that I take for granted. If I not only acknowledge in a value-responding way a country or a work of art or any good of great value, but also grant it a place in my heart on the basis of its beauty, if in other words I love it, then a certain "mine" is constituted by this love. Here we see clearly the opposite of the natural solidarity with myself. In this case

---

6   Cf. chapters 5 and 9.

something takes on importance because it is mine. But in the case of love something becomes mine because I love it for its value. This antithesis is also given in the case of the "mine" where something is important to me only because it is my property. Here we see the extended ego, whereas in the case of the "mine" flowing from love there is no extended ego, but rather a fruit of value-response.

It is of the greatest importance to draw a sharp distinction between the "mine" based on an extended ego and the "mine" based on love, for here we have one of the main sources of many errors, such as the derivation of love from self-love. The question why something belongs to my subjectivity, why and in what sense it is mine, is of decisive importance, especially if it is raised with respect to love taken in the more proper and typical sense, namely, the love for persons. As a result of loving someone, whether as friend or in a spousal way, the other becomes "mine" by becoming an objective good for me. This of course happens on the basis of his value, but in such a way that a unique personal relation arises that goes beyond my value-response; as a result of this relation the other finds a home in my subjectivity. Indeed, the other becomes mine only insofar as I have said to him, "I am yours." This "mine" is so opposed to the extended ego that it rather grows out of the commitment to the other.

The "mine" growing out of love is also distinguished sharply from all of the other kinds of "mine" that we discussed. This means that it is distinguished from the "mine" deriving from being a part of something else, from the qualitative "mine" deriving from some objective belonging to another person, and from the formal "mine" that is the result of a social act. But whereas the "mine" of the extended ego and also the "mine" deriving from ownership are incompatible with the "mine" of love and form a contrast to it, all the other forms of "mine" can not only co-exist with love but can be organically united with love. In fact we have already seen that some of them need to be filled with love, or are at least such as to be ordered to love, as in the case of "my mother" or "my child." We are about to discuss how this fulfillment of the "mine" of love works in marriage, which as such issues from a unique social act, the act of marrying.

We gave particular attention to the case of being at home in its different meanings and saw that the "mine" of shelteredness and of rootedness is normally united with love. But although many significant relations exist between love and the previously discussed forms of "mine"—apart from the extended ego of ownership—the "mine" that grows out of love is something altogether different. Here something becomes "mine" because it has affected my heart by its value, because it has become through its value an objective good for me, and above all because I love it. This "mine" is exclusively a fruit of love and is not conditioned by any other factor.

But there is another point that must be stressed. With persons there are entirely new possibilities of union, which is desired with the beloved person in every category of love, as we have seen, though differently in the different categories. Now this union, to which the intentio unionis is directed, comes about only through some return or requital of love, as we saw. With this union a completely new kind of "mine" is achieved. Whereas every value-responding love as such establishes a certain "mine," this is far from the "mine" that is intended in the intentio unionis. What I intend can only be given to me by the requital of my love. The other becomes mine in this new sense upon saying, "I am yours." But he becomes this only when his "I am yours" encounters my "I am yours," and when his "I am yours" is spoken into the "mine" that has already emerged from my "I am yours." Only then does there arise a mutual, entirely new "mine."

We have already explained in chapter 6 that this "mine" can in no way be taken as a form of possession or ownership, so we need not discuss this again. But it is important to understand that this new "mine," which is possible only with persons and which can result only from their mutual love, is not a source of happiness because it involves the extended ego. That would be the greatest possible misunderstanding. The happiness of union with the beloved person grows unmistakably out of the love; it is highly intelligible that this union with the other confers happiness on me because I love the other. Every attempt to derive this happiness from something else commits the philosophical mistake of searching for a cheap plausibility when high intelligibility is clearly granted to us; or, as we could also say, of searching for a further explanation of something that, if only one takes the trouble to look more closely at it, shows itself to be self-evident.

What we want to stress above all else is that the greatest possible union of persons in the mutuality of a deep spousal love grounded in Christ, where the two become one and in a way identify their subjectivities,[7] as I put it in my book, *Die Metaphysik der Gemeinschaft*, in no way means that the beloved person becomes an extension of my ego. For the basic gesture of this identification of subjectivities is expressed by saying, "Your life is my life"; it is commitment, self-donation; it is saying, "I am yours." Here giving oneself is truly finding oneself. Of course, the union does not grow only out of the force of self-donation, but out of the mutual self-gift. Being supported by the self-donation of both persons, it is the very opposite of the extended ego as well as of any appropriation of the other. This is evident from the fact that if someone loves me without me loving that person in return with the same kind of love, no real "mine" arises in me and certainly not the ultimate "mine" of true union.

---

7   [The German word is *Eigenleben*, a word about which I will say more in the first
     footnote of the next chapter, where the word appears in the chapter title and
     throughout the text of the chapter. Trans.]

The "mine" deriving from the act of marrying and the "mine" of love

We have to distinguish this "material" or qualitative personal union from the formal personal union resulting from the act of marrying. As such this latter union is meant to provide a new fulfillment of the qualitative union, which involves a kind of identification of the subjectivity of the man and the subjectivity of the woman. But the formal union of the marriage bond, which establishes the marital community, is as such something new and can even exist, however inadequately, in the absence of the qualitative union.

What concerns us at present is that this formal union also establishes a "mine." In saying "my husband" or "my wife," one is referring to this union. When this formal union is the fulfillment of qualitative love, the "mine" is not different from the "mine" that comes from mutual love (both are opposites of the "mine" of the extended ego). Then it is the expression of a new and joyful fulfillment of the intentio unionis of love (which occurs in all love except love of neighbor); it is then the "mine" that flows from the mutual "I am yours."

But when the act of marrying does not issue from the interchange of love, when it is motivated by practical considerations, then we are faced with the purely formal "mine," which, as mentioned above, grows out of a social act. The highest type of union that issues from a social act is of course marriage, constituted by the act of marrying. The meaning and the *raison d'être* of this act is incomparable with all other social acts. The act of marrying is a social act which, according to its meaning, has the purpose of completing the union desired in spousal love. But this act does not forfeit its validity and its formal efficacy when it is performed in the absence of mutual love, even if it is then very inadequate and, as it were, deprived of its soul. The act brings about marriage, even if it does not bring about the community of love, which is the soul of marriage and confers on it a sublime character.

What we want above all to stress is that the "mine" of a marriage that is devoid of any mutual love and that grows exclusively out of the social act of marrying, belongs to the type of "mine" that we encountered above in the case of forming a partnership. Of course, the union goes much farther here, since the extraordinary social act of marrying makes for a blending of the external lives of the two. But even if its real function is missing, namely, the function of being the significant external expression of the identification of subjectivities that grows out of mutual spousal love, what is brought into being is more than just a formal relationship, it is a formal community.[8]

And important as it is to emphasize that the "mine" of "my wife" or "my husband" is different from the "mine" of love, it is also essential to see that this "mine" is not to be confused with the "mine" of the extended ego or with that

---

8   [The author here contrasts *relationship* with *community* just as he had in his earlier work, *Die Metaphysik der Gemeinschaft* (Part II, ch. 1): the former exists *between* persons, the latter *encompasses* and even *contains* persons. Trans.]

of being a part of something. This "mine" of the formal marriage bond is filled with obligations towards the other, with responsibility for his or her well-being, and with respect for his or her rights. We have already mentioned more than once the type of solidarity with another where I consider the other as a part of myself, as when a husband who does not love his wife takes offense at her being treated impolitely because he himself feels offended thereby. We called the "mine" that is built only on this solidarity the "mine" of the extended ego. It is important to see that the "mine" deriving exclusively from the act of marrying (as in a "marriage of reason," which is entered without spousal love and in which no spousal love subsequently arises) is not to be identified with the "mine" of the extended ego. The person of the other is not seen here as a part of myself in the sense of the extended ego, but as a partner for leading a common life, as someone to whom I am just as obliged as that person is to me. What we have here is a formal "mine" which corresponds to a formal "yours," a formal "mine" of mutual duties, of rights to the other, of common interests, of a "we" in which the two stand on the same level.

The really important point is that in this case the other person concerns me, is dear to me, plays an important role for me, because the other is "my wife" or "my husband." The "mine" is not born of a value-response, but of a social act; the other is not mine because I love her and because this love is a response to her value, but she is important to me because she is mine.

In explaining the essential difference between these two kinds of "mine," we in no way mean to deny the danger that exits for our fallen human nature of occasionally lapsing into a "we" that has the character of an extended ego; this can happen even in a marriage that is the completion of a mutual love and that thus contains the "transcendent" mine. This danger is particularly great in the case of conflicts with third persons, especially with other married couples.

The relation between parents and children, and the "mine" of love

A far more difficult problem is the "mine" that we find in the love of parents for their children and in the love of children for their parents; for here we have obviously to do with a union of persons that is pre-given and is not constituted on the basis of love. The parents are objectively the child's parents, independent of any conscious stance of the child, and the child is the child of its parents, belonging to them prior to any value-response of theirs to the child and independent of their love for the child.

We have already referred to this kind of material or qualitative "mine" that is constituted by an objective ordering of persons to each other. We saw that it can not only co-exist with the "mine" of love but can often be organically united with this "mine," and indeed can even be fulfilled by love. In the case of the love of parents for their children and of the love of children for their parents we have first of all to examine the relation between this objective "mine" and the "mine" resulting from these loves. Then we will see clearly that these loves are not grounded in the objective "mine" of belonging and that they are not motivated by the union that comes from this belonging.

But the objective belonging, or objective union, is already established in the relation of children to their parents; they belong to their parents before becoming fully conscious. In the relation of parents to their children the objective belonging is not in the same way pre-given but is rather established by the fact of generating the child and is apart from any conscious stance towards the child. There is not only this objective belonging, but also the lived experience of it, the lived sense of "mine," and this in both of these kinds of love; but this lived belonging is also not grounded in love for one another. The child discovers the parents as *his* parents. As soon as the child is conscious of who his parents are, he experiences them as belonging to him. In the experience of parents their child belongs to *them*; already during pregnancy they await "their" child, apart from any value-response to the child as a particular individual personality. But as we have already seen, the love of parents for their children and the love of children for their parents are not grounded in any pre-existing unity. It is not the case that love is grounded in a unity which can be understood in terms of an extended ego. The "mine" that is given with parents and children is, in contrast to the "mine" of friendship or of spousal love, not the result of love. We cannot say there that the child is mine only because I love it with a value-responding love; it has not become mine only because it is so dear to me. But we also cannot simply say that the child is dear to me because it is mine.

This issue of the foundation of the love of parents for their children and of the love of children for their parents is much more complicated, and the foundation is not simply to be found in the pre-existing "mine." We hope to explain this in a second volume of this work in which these two kinds of love will be treated in a chapter of their own. But as we have already seen, it is quite wrong to think that the pre-existing unity that grounds the "mine" is the *motive* or the basis for love. There are many other factors that come into play here, such as parents and children being ordered to each other by God, the elementary entrustment of children to their parents, the relation to the love of the spouses, the value-response to the "naked" and still unwritten humanity of the child. In the case of the love of children for their parents some of the factors that come into play are, to name just two of them, being accepted and sheltered by the love of the parents and the function of the parents as benefactors.

What interests us here is precisely the fact that there is in the relation between parents and children an experienced "mine"; it is built on the purely objective ordering of them to each other and it has to be distinguished from the "mine" that is a fruit of love. Normally parents have an anticipatory love for their child. This love is grounded neither in the objective "mine" nor in the experience of this "mine"; it only goes hand in hand with the constitution of this "mine."

Parents usually begin to love a child as soon as they expect it, and they love it as their own child. We say "usually," because it may happen that they do not want to have a child and that they anticipate the birth with fright and the refusal to accept it. In this case we can hardly speak of an anticipatory love. But this is of no concern to us here, for we are dealing with the foundation of the *love* of parents for their children. This love is a response to the fact that God has granted them the opportunity to participate in the coming-to-be of a new human being, that this new human being is entrusted to them in so mysterious a way, and that it is the fruit of their mutual love. Once the child, so uniquely entrusted to them by God, is born and is there before them as an independent being, the anticipatory love becomes a value-response to the beauty of man as image of God. The preciousness and loveableness of a human being who is still unwritten and "blank" is, as it were, addressed in a special way to the parents. On the background of the fact that this child sees the light of day thanks to the parents, that it is entrusted to them by God in so mysterious a way, the preciousness of a human person flashes up in a particular way. Thus this love, even before it becomes a value-response to the *particular* beauty of the child as individual person, is from the beginning a value-response and thus it proceeds hand in hand with the objectively existing "mine" and with the experience of it. The objective "mine" and the "mine" of love interpenetrate from the outset. The way they go hand in hand differs from the "mine" of married persons, for whom in the ideal case of marriage the material "mine" of love leads to the formal "mine" of marriage—for whom, in other words, the latter is the fulfillment of the former.

But as we have already said, the "mine" of the objective ordering of parents and children to each other is not the basis for the love of children for their parents; this "mine" does not motivate or ground that love.[9] The true spiritual love of children for their parents is not motivated by the objective "mine," even though much that is related to the constitution of the formal "mine" is also involved in the motivation of love; they both proceed hand in hand, as we have said.

The fact that the objective "mine" is different from the "mine" of love is evident from the fact that the first can exist without the second. It is not only the objective relation that remains for parents and children in the absence of any love, but the experience of "mine" built on this objective relation remains

---

9   Some such grounding and motivation is found only in the quasi-animal love in which a mother considers her child as flesh of her flesh and is for this reason attached to it, or bound up with it in a primitive way. This attachment, certainly not negative in itself, is clearly not an authentic love. It is not a spiritual act, but an instinctual, elementary attachment, a primitive solidarity. In this kind of solidarity, the expression "my child" can indeed take on something of the extended ego. But there are many different factors at work here, and we will discuss them only in the second volume of this work when we treat in some detail of the love of children for their parents.

as well. It can especially happen with grown children that there is no love between them and their parents, yet even here an experience of "mine" remains that expresses the indestructible, objective belonging. The duties flowing from this objective relation also remain—not only the duties of parents towards their children but also the duties of children towards their parents.

The important point is to see that this objective "mine" is different from the one born of love, even if, as we have seen, they can be closely interconnected in the case of parents and children. Even without any love the "mine" of the objective ordering of persons to each other remains a reality of its own.

In conclusion we can say that the "mine" created by love, and especially by mutual love, has nothing to do with the extended ego, and also nothing to do with the "mine" of ownership. But it is also distinguished from all the other forms of "mine" that we have studied, that is, from the "mine" that derives from being a part of something, from the "mine" born of an objective ordering of persons to each other, or of a social act, and from the "mine" of being rooted and sheltered in something.

The "mine" of love also brings out clearly the essential element that makes love a super value-response. It confirms, as we have already seen, that this reaching into the subjectivity of persons, this way of going beyond the pure value-response, is not any kind of deviation from value-response, nor does it imply anything egocentric, but it rather imparts to love the character of a super value-response.

CHAPTER NINE

Eigenleben[1] and Transcendence

In the following we will try to clarify the relation between the subjectivity of each person and the transcendence that is proper to human persons. It often happens that my capacities for transcendence are thought to be incompatible with being my own self. But on closer examination we find that the two not only do not exclude each other but in fact complete each other. These elements interpenetrate in a kind of polarity, so that selfhood in its most significant and

---

1   [This German word, *Eigenleben*, has proved so difficult to translate that I leave it untranslated in the chapter title and will sometimes leave it untranslated in the text. My English translation of it is "subjectivity," and in fact whenever "subjectivity" is used in this chapter, it is *Eigenleben* that is being translated. I acknowledge that this is not an entirely satisfactory translation, but I cannot find a better one. It was pointed out to me that "subjective" often bears a negative connotation (as in von Hildebrand's own expression, "the merely subjectively satisfying") that is entirely foreign to *Eigenleben*. But this concern is dealt with by von Hildebrand himself when he writes in his work, *What is Philosophy?*: "The very term 'subjective' is unfortunate because of its inevitable [negative] epistemological flavor; *on the other hand, the term 'subjectivity' is much clearer and unambiguous and is easily understood as referring to the person as subject*" (p. 154; my italics). And I am encouraged in my use of "subjectivity" here in chapter 9 by the fact that elsewhere in the present book von Hildebrand sometimes says *Subjektivität* where he could just as well have said *Eigenleben*, as when he says in chapter 7, "Die Indirektheit besteht darin, dass wir an der Subjektivität des Geliebten teilnehmen, dass die Bedeutung dieser Dinge fuer mich durch das motiviert ist, was sie fuer ihn bedeuten" (p. 205). He could as well have written, "darin, dass wir an dem Eigenleben des Geliebten teilnehmen." Or consider this sentence from the present chapter: "Hoechste Objektivitaet und hoechste Subjektivität greifen hier ineinander" (p. 275). He could as well have written, using the language of the chapter title, "Hoechste Transzendenz und intensivstes Eigenleben greifen hier ineinander." By the way, even the adjectival *subjektiv* is often used in the present book in an entirely positive sense that is akin to *Eigenleben*, as for example in the first sentence on p. 230 of the German text. The main element of meaning in *Eigenleben* that is not entirely captured by "subjectivity" is the thought of "one's own" as opposed to "another's." I sometimes try to capture this by rendering *Eigenleben* as "my subjectivity." Trans.]

deepest manifestations would hardly be possible without transcendence, just as true transcendence would collapse if subjectivity were to be extinguished.

Eigenleben in the broader and in the narrower sense

Our first task is to clarify briefly our use of this term. One can speak of subjectivity in different senses. One can mean all the conscious experiencing of an individual person considered apart from the content that is experienced. Subjectivity is then equivalent to the conscious existence of a person. Some of the religions of India think of the dissolution of subjectivity in this sense as an ideal (in Buddhism it is a dissolution into Nirvana, in Hinduism a dissolution into the divinity). The dissolution of subjectivity in this sense is in reality identical with the annihilation of personal existence. In the following we will use this term in a narrower sense. Like every other person, I have a subjectivity in the sense that there are certain things that have to do with me and my concerns and that refer in particular to my happiness. In this sense subjectivity by no means encompasses all that a person consciously experiences but rather refers only to those things that concern him as individual person in a special way, to those things of which it can be said, *"Tua res agitur"* ("Your personal concern is at stake").

Eigenleben not egocentricity

We begin by declaring emphatically that subjectivity in this sense by no means refers to egocentric living, and that it should not be connected in any way with egoism. To have a subjectivity in this sense means instead something entirely positive; it is a deeply significant characteristic of man as a spiritual person and is profoundly associated with the dignity of man and with his metaphysical condition. The deepest part of this subjectivity is the dialogue between man and God, for here the *"tua res agitur"* eminently applies. Subjectivity confronts us with all the seriousness and greatness of the metaphysical situation of man.

Of course, this dialogue with God makes up the deepest level of our subjectivity. As we use the term subjectivity it also refers to all that grows out of the natural or instinctive solidarity that we have with ourselves and in this way it is ordered to the sphere of happiness. Subjectivity in this expanded sense (expanded beyond religious subjectivity) represents a significant and legitimate sense of subjectivity. This subjectivity encompasses my being, my life, my health, my welfare, my economic condition, etc. It also encompasses all bodily drives and spiritual strivings that are rooted in the nature of man, in other words, all those things that have been traditionally called by the name of appetitus.

True as it is that all of this belongs to personal subjectivity, it would be false to take as the essential trait of subjectivity the immanence that is proper to the sphere of drives, needs, and appetitus.

Eigenleben irreducible to the natural solidarity of a person with himself

A person's subjectivity should by no means be identified with the natural solidarity that we have with ourselves. This solidarity is neither morally good nor morally bad but belongs essentially to personal existence and is as such something good and valuable. Absolutely no category of love can be derived from this solidarity with oneself, or from self-love, as one sometimes calls it. The interest in the beloved person that belongs to value-response and to love is most certainly not rooted in self-love, and yet my friend, to say nothing of a spousally loved person, belongs to my subjectivity in an eminent sense. The concept of solidarity with oneself refers, as we saw, to the fact that I need no self-love in order to take an interest in my well-being. Whereas the well-being of another person does not necessarily affect me—except in the case in which I have a loving attitude towards the other—the interest in my own well-being arises as a result of a natural necessity. I feel pain in my leg independent of any stance that I take towards myself. I need no stance towards myself in order to be distressed at being treated unjustly. I prefer being happy to being unhappy, not because I love myself, but because I necessarily experience happiness and unhappiness in this way.

This solidarity is distinguished by the fact that it is almost a kind of truism. If we were to say that each person is interested in his own well-being and if we were to present this as something significant, one would respond that there is no need to make a point of saying this. There is here a kind of emptiness as in the case of analytic propositions in the sense of Kant; my proposition is a triviality that makes us want to say, "But of course, it goes without saying." There is no point in asking why. But there is, by contrast, nothing trivial at all about the statement that I am sad about the pain of *another* person and take great interest in the *other*. This interest does not have the unavoidable and natural character of the interest in my own well-being. We are right to ask why, and this interest becomes understandable only on the basis of the entirely new factor of love *for the other*. The same holds for all genuine value-responses and especially for the moral value-responses. It is not unavoidable that I commit myself to justice, or to suffering injustice rather than committing it; there is here none of the trivial intelligibility that we just noticed. We are right to ask why, and only by understanding the importance in itself of the morally relevant value and good do we understand why I can and ought to have this interest (in fact the intelligibility here is much deeper than in the case of taking an interest in my own well-being). This "ought" does not play the same role in my interest in my own well-being, since this interest is in any case present. Here we have a typical mistake that is often made: to reduce everything to this trivial plausibility or intelligibility, or to derive everything from it, thinking that one stands thereby on solid ground.[2]

---

2   We ask an entirely new question when we ask which free stance a person concretely performs, that is, when we ask what a person lets himself be motivated by. This

The sphere of solidarity with oneself, although it can as such in no way be characterized as egocentric, belongs to the sphere of immanence. But it would be a complete misunderstanding of subjectivity in the proper sense to take immanence as its essential trait. A person's subjectivity is by no means confined to the sphere of immanence. Even if the relation to my happiness is a very significant trait of my subjectivity, we can already discern in this relation an indication that subjectivity cannot be taken in a purely immanent sense, for the higher kinds of happiness can be granted to us only if we transcend the sphere of the immanent. Whoever remains in pure immanence cannot be truly happy. I become happy only in giving some value-response. The happiness that is superabundantly conferred on me by value-bearing goods is possible only if I am affected by these values *as values* and then respond to them, two stances in which the transcendence of human persons is actualized. The more important and significant part of my subjectivity is to be found precisely in relation to those goods that confer happiness in virtue of their values, and in relation to those great objective goods for the person that presuppose some value-response.

The defining trait of subjectivity is the realm of all those things that are of concern to me as this unrepeatable individual, that stand in some relation to my happiness, that address me—this in contrast to all that belongs to the subjectivity of another person whom I do not know. This will become clearer as we proceed now to identify that which does not belong to subjectivity and which forms some antithesis to it.

Eigenleben in contrast to exercising an office

All that a person does in exercising some office, such as the office of judge or of public official, does not belong to that person's subjectivity. We of course are thinking here of what a person does *only* in his capacity of exercising an office, of what flows from the logic of his office, or from the duties that go with the office. All of the work that flows from some official function—supervising the activities of others, praising and blaming others, giving them tasks, settling accounts—is as such no part of subjectivity in our sense. A correct and conscientious official does not do any of this as a private person. The rebukes that he is required by the rules of his office to issue, have nothing to do with any personal dissatisfaction or personal anger or irritation. He presents himself to me as official and not as this private person, not as Carl or John. Of course, some personal irritation may enter into his actions, some personal antipathy to others. But that would be an illegitimate overflow of his subjectivity into an area that by its nature and meaning does not belong to his subjectivity. But there is no need for

---

has nothing to do with the natural solidarity with oneself, which only means that a person's own well-being naturally affects and concerns that person. But I can freely decide either for that which so naturally interests me, or else for something valuable in itself, or for the well-being of another person whom I love.

us to discuss such cases. For the purpose of clearly distinguishing between sub-jectivity and all that is not subjectivity, we have only to think of cases in which I act in the name of some authority and do only what follows from this function, and then to contrast these cases with subjectivity in our sense.

One could raise the following objection. There are after all people who have a real passion for exercising an office, for instance, people who take a particular pleasure in dealing with the issues and tasks that go with being a judge. Is not this exercise of their office a part of their subjectivity? Is this activity, which they take delight in as private persons and which constitutes an important objective good in their lives, not also something that eminently belongs to their subjectivity? Do they not have a very personal relation to their beloved work? Here is how I would respond to the objection. Of course, both my personal relation to the office that I hold as well as the moral qualitites that I invest in the exercise of the office, such as faithfulness and conscientious-ness, belong to my subjectivity. After all, everything moral belongs eminently to my subjectivity, as we shall see. The case of a conflict between the imma-nent demands of the office and the laws of morality, belongs entirely to my subjectivity. And yet what I do within the activities of the office is not dictat-ed by considerations of my subjectivity but rather by the immanent logic of the office. However much I may take pleasure in doing the things that a judge does, what I decide in my capacity as judge is not determined by this pleasure but by the immanent logic of the relevant laws; as such my judicial decisions are not performed by me as private person, as this individual person, but as judge—except insofar as moral issues enter in. And so this objection does not do away with the fact that what I do as an official in the exercise of my office does not belong to my subjectivity, for I do not do it as the person I am but as exercising some authority. What is at stake is not what I personally like, not what is agreeable to me, not what inflames my heart and draws me by its value, not what moves me to act from love, but rather only what follows from the meaning, logic, and duty of the office.

Some antitheses to healthy Eigenleben

Suppose that someone holding an office (whether he is an official like a judge, or a statesman) is so completely taken over by the office that he ceases to have a life as this individual person: he no longer has any real subjectivity. Another case of a certain loss of subjectivity is found among those persons who attach themselves so closely to others and who live so completely for them that their own subjectivity withers. This is the type of person, for example, who lives with a family as an old servant of the lady of the house, or perhaps as a friend of hers, and who shares the life of the family and has her whole life in caring for the children and the household. These are usually persons who do not feel up to having a full subjectivity of their own, whose aspirations for happiness are weak and modest, whose primary relation to the great goods of life is weak and who therefore incline to attach themselves to the lives of others, and indeed strive to do just that. These are typical "background persons" in distinction to "center stage persons." There is a certain kind of caregiver who ought to be mentioned in this connection.

Of course, this withering of subjectivity in these persons does not involve the de-humanization that we find in the one who has made himself into a mere official. They are still capable of loving the family for which they live and can have preferences for one or the other of the children; their heart is not shut down as in the case of the mere official. But their overall stance towards life is such that they give up a full subjectivity of their own. They are distinguished by being very "modest" in relation to happiness and in relation to all that life has to offer. This attitude may even reach into their religious lives. While they may be believers, they are "modest" in their relation to God and to Christ and so they do not break through to a fully personal relation.

These winning, good-hearted, self-sacrificing persons are often wrongly presented as the highest representatives of love of neighbor. But this elimination of subjectivity has nothing to do with love of neighbor. It is rather an entirely natural drive that makes them so ready to serve and is by no means the conscious love of neighbor that is grounded in the love of God. It is true that the real love of neighbor as found in the saints involves stepping out of one's subjectivity, but subjectivity as such is found in them in the highest and most sublime form. They are eminently "center stage persons."

A still more radical loss of subjectivity is found in the suggestive type of person, who because of a constitutional weakness is incapable of taking an independent stance. I have discussed this type elsewhere.[3] These are the persons who both in their judgments about things and in their affective responses live from the impulse of other people's judgments and responses, living a kind of proxy life. In particular they live from the energy of dynamically stronger persons. They are not conscious of their dependency on these others. Their dependency has nothing to do with the conscious act of submitting to an authority. They do not realize that they just repeat what the stronger person forcefully says and do not notice that they would change their mind if someone came along energetically affirming the opposite. Such persons are all the more incapable of having real subjectivity, suffering as they do from a constitutional deficiency that blocks genuine contact with reality and that is present early on, even before subjectivity in the proper sense can emerge.

Two radical misunderstandings of Eigenleben: eudaemonism and altruism

There are two fundamental misunderstandings of man and of his nature and dignity as person. One of them goes in the direction of obscuring his

---

3   In my study, "Legitime und illegitime Formen der Beeinflussung," in *Die Menschheit am Scheideweg* (Mankind at the Crossroads), esp. 371–405.

transcendence, holding that man is in principle incapable of taking an interest in something having value in itself but that he can only be moved by something beneficial for himself. The opposite misunderstanding consists in thinking that man achieves his full destiny when he no longer has any beneficial goods for himself, when he has become indifferent to happiness and unhappiness to the point of living only by pure value-response. On this view, I am thought to remain locked in my immanence if I take an interest in something beneficial for myself, in fact I am thought to be selfish and to live at odds with every kind of transcendence.

Both conceptions are disastrous errors. Whoever does not acknowledge the transcendence of human beings fails to understand what distinguishes them as persons from all impersonal creatures. But whoever smells something egocentric in the fact that I desire an objective good for myself, whoever thinks that the ideal of human life is for me to lose all interest in beneficial goods for myself, fails to understand the character of man as subject. He fails to see the mysterious center to which everything in the life of a person is referred, the center that is addressed by beneficial goods and that is inseparably bound up with his dignity as person. If the first error locks persons in themselves and in this way distorts their ultimate relation to the world and to God, the second error deprives them of their character as full selves. The first error reduces man to the biological, taking him according to the model of a plant or animal. The second error robs him of his character as a full subject and destroys the personal in him by exaggerating the objective to the point of dissolving that which makes him a subject. We have to keep clear of both errors.

The interpenetration of Eigenleben and transcendence in the moral sphere

The way in which subjectivity and transcendence interpenetrate is nowhere so clear as in the moral sphere.

A moral call is addressed to a person to intervene in a certain situation; perhaps another is in danger, or perhaps some injustice has to be prevented, or perhaps that person has to refuse to do some evil which is asked of him. He grasps the morally relevant value, he understands its call, he is aware of the moral obligation, which appeals to his conscience. On the one hand, we have here a high-point of transcendence in the pure commitment to the morally relevant value. But on the other hand, this call, insofar as it is morally obligatory, pre-eminently contains the element of *"tua res agitur"* ("your personal concern is at stake"). In a certain sense this call is my most intimate and personal concern, in which I experience the uniqueness of my self. Supreme objectivity and supreme subjectivity interpenetrate here. One can even say that we have here the dramatic high-point of the *"tua res agitur"* in our earthly existence. On the one hand, I commit myself to something which in no way stands before me as merely an objective good for me, but rather as something which appeals to me as valuable in itself; but on the other hand, since what is at stake is my moral obligation in its unique impact, which is ultimately the call of God, my decision to follow the call or not to follow it reaches eminently into my own subjectivity. When the moral call is addressed to me and appeals to my conscience, then at the same time the question of my own salvation comes up. It is not just the objective issue which is at stake; I and my salvation are just as much at stake. The statement of Socrates that it is better for man to suffer injustice than to commit it, bears witness to this. For the believer this is an entirely understandable state of affairs, while for the non-believer the state of affairs is inexplicable and yet somehow experienced.

It is all-important to avoid interpreting any kind of instrumental relation into these facts. The moral call appeals to our obedience to the divine imperative, and the morally relevant value motivates our will. Absolutely wrong is the idea that the morally relevant value, or the action to which I am called, is only a *means* for my salvation. The moral call, or the obligation, has a clearly categorical character, and I am interested in the morally relevant good for its own sake. I completely misconstrue the nature of morality if I turn the morally relevant good into a mere opportunity for a morally good act and turn this act into a mere means for something else. I also thereby deprive morality of its meaning and its seriousness.

We have to understand that the issue of salvation is present to my consciousness without constituting the main motive of my action, that the destiny-determining character of moral obligation is only the radiation of the majesty and weight of morality, and that it, far from replacing the point of view of value, reveals the ultimate seriousness of value and the entirely personal call of moral obligation. Only by avoiding altogether any and every artificial projection of a means-end relation into morality can we do justice to the extraordinary interpenetration of supreme transcendence, as given in pure value-response, and the supreme subjectivity that is actualized along with it. We have to recognize that there are two "movements" here that, though closely woven together in reality, have to be clearly distinguished from one another. There is the exclusively object-directed movement of pure self-gift, and the complementary movement issuing from the morally relevant good (from its moral relevance, to say it with precision) that enters into me and calls me. We have to understand this unified whole in order to understand how it is that, in being morally obliged, supreme transcendence goes hand in hand with the actualization of the most vital and existential (in the deepest sense of that term) sphere of our subjectivity.

But even apart from this case of the interpenetration of supreme transcendence and supreme subjectivity, all deeper subjective life presupposes, as we have seen, value-response and thus also transcendence. All those things that are particularly dear to us and that we love, whether they be spiritual entities like works of art, or countries or persons that we love, belong to our subjectivity and concern us personally. All of this is in contrast to those things to which we turn exclusively in the way of value-response, that is, without them also becoming objective goods for us. Thus there is a realm of value-response which plays a role in our personal lives, and in fact a highly significant and very central role, but which does not as such belong to our subjectivity. We have now to make a point of characterizing this domain, even if only in a summary way.

Eigenleben and love of neighbor

It is important to affirm that, while having a subjectivity belongs essentially to being a person, so does the ability to transcend one's subjectivity. As we have seen, subjectivity is not restricted to the sphere of immanence, but it also comprises stances and attitudes having a definite transcendent character. Now we have to focus on the fact that human persons are not only capable of acts and attitudes in which they go beyond their immanence, but that they are also capable of stepping out of their (not merely immanent) subjectivity. This happens above all in the love of neighbor. We touch here on the dimension of transcendence that we examined in detail in chapter 7.[4] In contrast to a friend, a

---

4   We pointed out there the fact that in all the natural categories of love we find the moment of "for the beloved person," "for his sake," and that the joys and sufferings of the beloved person, all his objective goods and evils, become indirect goods and evils for the one who loves him. We have now to add something to the concept of an indirect objective good for a person. If the person whom I love suffers physical pains, this is for me an objective evil in the full sense of the word. It is not just pity that I feel, but this evil enters entirely into my subjectivity; it is my personal concern. It is distinguished from a direct objective evil for me only by the fact that it lacks the direct relation to me that is found in my own bodily pains; I feel only my own pains and not those of another. Only because of my love for the other does his pain become an objective evil for me. The previously discussed distinction between a direct and an indirect objective evil for me is obvious. But what we want to add now is that the indirect objective good and evil for me belongs just as much to my subjectivity as the direct does. It is important to understand this, since in the love of neighbor the moment of "for the other" and "for the sake of the other" plays an eminent role, even though the neighbor does not reach into my subjectivity, even though I step out of my subjectivity in love of neighbor, as we have already seen. The moment of "for the other" is eminently present in loving my neighbor; in being moved by love of neighbor I can be deeply moved by the pain of my neighbor and can be filled with compassion for him, and yet this "for him" does not belong to my subjectivity. We can express this in the following way: if the one whom I love has become a direct objective good for me, as happens in all natural love, then all the direct objective goods and evils for him become indirect objective goods and evils for me. All loves, with the exception of love of neighbor, grant to the beloved person such a place in my subjectivity that this has a decisive effect on the "for him," the "for his sake." As soon as someone is a direct objective good for me, all of the direct objective goods and evils for him become

brother, or a spouse, a neighbor does not reach into my subjectivity, and this despite the fact that in loving a neighbor I share in his life in an ultimate way. For my neighbor as neighbor is not a source of happiness for me; in contrast to all other categories of love my happiness is not thematic in my relation to my neighbor. Thus in love of neighbor I step out of my subjectivity in a specific way. It is necessary for subjectivity in the strict sense of the word that I in some way have to do with "my concerns," where I am addressed in my unique and individual personal being. There has to be some connection with my own happiness or unhappiness; in this sense subjectivity stands under the category of *tua res agitur*. As such my neighbor is not a person who is personally close to me. His well-being, his happiness, his fate do not as such reach into my subjectivity. I step out of my subjectivity when I share in my neighbor's well-being, when I have compassion with him and act for his good. Here I enter into the subjectivity of the other yet without that subjectivity becoming a part of what makes up my own world. We have here to do with a completely new kind of transcendence. It is not the transcendence which, as we saw above, underlies the higher levels of my subjectivity, and it is certainly not the transcendence that is given in every genuine love. What is here transcended is precisely my subjectivity.

But here two things have to be clearly distinguished. When we say that in loving my neighbor I step out of my subjectivity, this means that I turn away from my own concerns and turn towards the subjectivity of the other, towards his salvation, his life, his well-being (at all levels), and all this without any attention to myself. But this act of transcending my subjectivity is intrinsically a part of my subjectivity in an entirely new and very deep way. This is because of the caritas that lives within me and that moves me to turn to the subjectivity of the other with love of neighbor. For caritas, which is constituted in loving God, becomes in love of neighbor triumphant and holy goodness, and this love of neighbor is eminently my concern. The love of God makes up the most central and important part of my subjectivity, and when it is actualized as caritas it is inseparable from my subjectivity. The question whether caritas has begun to dwell in a person or not, is the central question of that person's subjectivity; here the *tua res agitur* applies eminently. And all that was said above about moral obligation applies fully to caritas. The command of the Lord to love my neighbor as myself penetrates my subjectivity in an incomparable way.

And yet it is true to say that in loving my neighbor I step out of my subjectivity, since my neighbor, unlike a friend, does not reach directly into my subjectivity. The type of transcendence here is something unique; it goes in a different direction than in the case of other moral obligations, in which I do not

---

indirect objective goods and evils for me. Great is the difference between love of neighbor and all the natural categories of love that are built on a value-response to the personality of the other person—so great, in fact, that the moment of "for the other," proper to all categories of love, shows itself differently in love of neighbor.

necessarily transcend my subjectivity. But here in the case of love of neighbor we have a unique situation because of the fact that my own happiness is in no way thematic, and the subjectivity of the other is exclusively thematic.

Stepping out of my Eigenleben in contrast to abandoning it

But when I step out of my subjectivity in loving my neighbor I am by no means abandoning my subjectivity, or losing interest in it, or dying to it. What is meant is only that the well-being of my neighbor, on which I am focused in loving him or her, has as such no relation to my subjectivity. Thus my subjectivity in no way ceases to exist. What occurs is rather a change of theme, not a dying to my subjectivity. We see this in those persons in whom love of neighbor is fully developed, in the saints. Although love of neighbor is so central to them, subjectivity takes on its fullest form in them. The personal relation to Christ that stands at the center of their lives amounts to a qualitative transfiguration of their subjectivity, which is such that only subjectivity tied to transcendence plays any role with them. But this transfiguration obviously does not imply any extinction of subjectivity. If we think of St. Francis of Assisi we see clearly that his life is the extreme opposite of the person who lives by Fenelon's ideal of *amour désintéressé* (extreme altruism), who radically strives to possess no subjectivity at all, who does not ardently yearn for his eternal salvation, and for whom there is no longer any *tua res agitur*. Or let us think of St. Louis of France, who showed in his deep and tender love for his wife how intense his subjectivity was.

"Crossing over" [*Überschreiten*] my Eigenleben in value-response

Though in loving my neighbor I step out of my subjectivity, there is in value-response, such as we find it throughout the liturgy, a different form of transcendence in relation to my subjectivity. Here we "cross over" our subjectivity, as it were. This is what happens when we pray in the Gloria, "We give you thanks for your great glory," or when we pray the first part of the Our Father. Here in adoration and in the pure re-enactment of what ought to be, of what is valuable in itself, we achieve a specific crossing over of our subjectivity, for here the relation to me and my salvation is in no way thematic and I share as it were in the rhythm of the absolute.

And so we see that, on the one hand, it belongs essentially to each human person to have subjectivity, but that, on the other hand, it is no less essential for each to be able either to step out of his or her subjectivity, or else to cross over it.

It is important to understand that such a crossing over of my subjectivity no more involves an abandonment of it, or a dying away of it, than in the case of stepping out of it in love of neighbor. Subjectivity and the act of reaching beyond it interpenetrate in an organic way. The Our Father in its first and second part shows us in the clearest possible way this organic interpenetration. I should take stances that belong to my subjectivity but I should also take stances in which I reach beyond it, according to the call of the situation. Both belong so essentially to the end of human existence that any attempt to restrict my life to only one of the two leads not only to a crippling of myself as a human person but also distorts both of them. It belongs to an authentic and especially to a qualitatively perfected subjectivity to be able to cross over it, just as this act of self-transcendence can only be fully valid and have an ardent character if it is performed by a person who has a well-developed and intense subjectivity.

Withered Eigenleben

We can see just how important this last point is by thinking of cases of withered subjectivity. In works of literature we often find descriptions of two types of withered subjectivity. The one is the official who is so absorbed in his official activities that he is in a way extinguished as a human being. He hardly exists any more as the individual person that he is, or in other words, to use a trivial expression, he has ceased to be a private person. He has no genuine relation to the sphere of objective goods for himself. He does not yearn for happiness. He is incapable of real friendship and even more incapable of spousal love. He can no longer really take personal stances. Personal inclinations and interests no longer exist in him. Indeed, he no longer takes any personal moral stances, nor does he experience any call of conscience, any appeal of morally relevant values: it is as official that he does whatever he does. His subjectivity has been dissolved into the function of his office, with the result that, at least at the level of his experience, there is no longer any *tua res agitur* for him. Even his relation to God is a part of his official function. We have here what I have elsewhere called the "metaphysical bureaucrat." Even if he is rarely found among real people in this radical form, there are many men and women whom our description largely fits. There is no doubt but that we have here a radical de-personalization and de-humanization.

The loss of subjectivity stands forth perhaps even more drastically in the ideal of the loyal citizen of a totalitarian state. This citizen is not supposed to acknowledge any duty except to the state; he has no room for moral laws, for love of neighbor, indeed even for his own happiness. He is considered to be only an instrumental means for the collectivity, and so his subjectivity is not acknowledged as having any justification at all. He can fulfill this totalitarian ideal only if he ceases to have or to desire a subjectivity in our sense of the term.

Making a gift of one's Eigenleben in love

We now turn to an examination of the relation between subjectivity and transcendence in those categories of love that in a certain sense make up the heart of our subjectivity.

In any great love, whether love for a child, a friend, or a spouse, there is a particular dimension of self-donation [*Hingabe*]. Deeply connected with my self-donation to a person is the fact that this person is a more or less decisive factor in my earthly happiness, and indeed is sometimes *the* decisive factor. This self-donation is a *gift* for the beloved person. Now it is very important to realize here that all such self-donation is characterized precisely by the fact that I do *not* step out of my subjectivity, but that I grant to the other a dominant place within my subjectivity. This represents an intimate personal self-donation that is not found in love of neighbor. Giving my heart away to another, my mysterious individual self, is a dimension of self-giving that precisely presupposes and includes the full actualization of my subjectivity. The opposite of this self-donation is the egocentricity that expresses itself in a person being never so happy as when he is independent of others and able to live out his desires without being bothered by them. In the case of love of neighbor, where I step out of my subjectivity, the antithesis to love is hardness of heart, egoism in the typical sense. But with the other categories of love the antithesis to self-donation consists in a laziness of heart that shrinks from the adventure of self-donation and that craves a selfish happiness that is not dependent on anyone. Laziness of heart is connected here with a proud drive for independence.

We have only to think of the typical bachelor-egoism and then we can, on the background of this opposite, clearly grasp the distinct character of this self-donation that is proper to love and especially to a great love for another person that dominates the life of the lover. In the opposite of the bachelor-egoism we see that in a great love the full actualization of subjectivity is what forms the antithesis to all egocentricity.

The priority of pure transcendence over my Eigenleben

It goes without saying that in these forms of love the happiness and salvation of the beloved person rank higher than the happiness of my union with him or her. But these two things can be combined in a very deep harmony.

There is something analogous at the highest level in the fact that God's honor and holy will have priority over our happiness and salvation. The first theme is our becoming like God, and the second is my beatitude. Only when God's honor has priority over the whole of my subjectivity, even the deepest and highest aspirations of it, does my subjectivity have the inner order that is proper to it; only then is it formed as it ought to be. In this act of reaching entirely beyond my subjectivity my transcendence is not only actualized to the fullest, but my subjectivity receives its authentic character, and this even in a qualitative respect.

This priority of pure transcendence over subjectivity involves absolutely no extinguishing of subjectivity; indeed, the ideal of such an extinguishing rests on a disastrous error, as we shall now see by comparing the following fundamental religious attitudes. The one attitude is found in persons who have definite wishes and hopes and who are alive to objective goods for themselves. They pray for all the things that they long for. In their prayers of petition they turn with confidence to the infinite mercy of God. But the holy will of God has for them the priority over all the things that they long for. Each of their prayers ends with the words of Jesus on the Mount of Olives: "Not my will but yours be done." This priority shows itself in the readiness that they constantly have to give up something, even something that gives them great happiness, if God asks this of them. They are intent on discerning the will of God in every situation. They will sacrifice something that is as such good and noble and a source of great happiness, for instance, an artistic experience, if they feel called to help someone in spiritual need. They possess a full subjectivity, but they are immediately ready to subordinate their subjectivity whether to the call of a morally relevant good or in response to the will of God speaking to them through particular circumstances.

The other attitude is found in the person who says, "I have no wishes, no hopes, I do not care what happens, whatever happens is God's will. I will not address any petitionary prayers to God, for He knows better what should happen and only His will really counts." We do not propose to raise the question whether such an attitude is possible at all, whether it can be lived at all. It suffices for us that there are people who think of this attitude as the ideal. Here one sees the abandonment of one's subjectivity as particularly perfect, as the summit of resignation to God and of selflessness. We easily see the difference between this attitude and the above-mentioned one. This unfortunate ideal, which stands in sharp contradiction to the liturgy and to the lives of the saints, can be lived in a more radical way and in a less radical way.

In the more radical way one fails to understand the nature of the person because one overlooks entirely the role that God has granted to man by giving him free will. One even denies (by thinking this attitude through to the end) that persons are capable of "hungering and thirsting for justice," and "seeking first the kingdom of God." One denies that persons are capable of praying for or hoping for something in a pure value-responding attitude; in the final analysis, one denies that they are capable of knowing values and especially morally relevant values and of making a personal commitment on their behalf. In order to give God everything, in order to do nothing other than perform unconditional obedience towards God, in order to let Him alone speak, one arrives at a position that dissolves the human person and denies that which distinguishes him from all impersonal creatures, negating his character as full subject, as the being to whom God speaks, whom He addresses, whom He engages in dialogue. And yet these are all elements that belong essentially to the image of God in man. An ill-considered zeal for stressing the commitment to God leads to a dissolution of man as person; instead of being seen as God-like, man is deprived of his soul, he is instrumentalized. This error goes far beyond the abandonment of subjectivity that was described above. The idea behind this error is a complete depersonalization and in the end a passive fatalism.

More important for us is the much less radical way in which this ideal of selflessness can be lived. In this case it does not lead to depersonalization but merely leads one to see a particular perfection in abandoning what we have called subjectivity. This is the case where one sees the ideal attitude as the one in which I give myself in pure moral value-responses and in the attitude of "hunger and thirst for the kingdom of God," but in which I make in myself no place for objective goods for myself. What results is not a radical depersonalization, but rather the loss of my subjectivity. Thus the comparison of this less radical attitude with the more radical one is instructive for our purposes. We have to recognize the difference between those persons who have personal wishes, hopes, and yearnings, but who are ready to set them aside when the will of God requires this,[5] and those persons who have given up their subjectivity, who have no wishes and hopes, for whom there are no objective goods for themselves, but who seek only that which is intrinsically valuable, the kingdom of God and His justice. But Christ said, "Seek first the kingdom of God and His justice," He did not say, "Seek *only* the kingdom of God." The first group of people adheres to the ideal of *amour désintéressé* or extreme altruism. Though such persons burn for the glory of God, they no longer have any capacity for personal happiness, not even for the sublime happiness of union with God in the beatific vision.

Eigenleben never too strong, only crippled or disordered

There is of course a false religious attitude that goes in the opposite direction. We are thinking of the attitude of those who are so set on objective goods for themselves that God has for them only the role of the absolute lord and governor of their destiny, but is not for them the supreme and unsurpassable good. These are the people who are indeed ready to obey God and not to violate His commands, and who know that they are entirely dependent on God; but God is not the greatest source of their happiness, they have no real love for God and do not yearn for Christ. They see in God above all the lord who governs their lives and whom they should obey. These people are not ruled by pride and concupiscence, nor are they pure egoists. They may be conscientious, but they lack the true relation to God. We mention this false attitude because it is in a certain way a revealing opposite of the attitude that wants to give up all subjectivity.

Now it would be a mistake to think that such persons have too much subjectivity and that persons of the opposite type have too little of it. Such an antithesis would in no way do justice to the real state of affairs. No, the deviation does not lie in subjectivity being too strong or too intensive, but in not

---

5   I encounter His will in the demands of values or when God works some mysterious providence in my life to which I am challenged to say "yes."

being qualitatively the way it ought to be. People who see in God only the lord and governor of their destiny have a crippled subjectivity because they lack the summit of subjectivity, which is the love for God. This is connected with the fact that they overlook the priority that the pure value-responding stance should have; this is why their subjectivity is not too strong but is rather deprived of its supreme fulfillment.

Now one might think that the possession of subjectivity in our earthly existence belongs to the things that are *allowed*, but that it is more perfect to give it up in the sense of desiring no personal objective good for myself and remaining in an exclusively value-responding attitude. Is not the attitude of seeking *only* the kingdom of God simply an augmentation of the attitude of seeking *first* the kingdom of God? Is it not therefore better and more pleasing to God? By no means. Subjectivity belongs to the nature of the human person; this is the way the human person is created and intended by God; it belongs to his perfection that he should possess a full subjectivity, even if his happiness stands in second place and not in first place, as we have seen. This becomes clear in thinking about the sacred humanity of Christ. Even the Son of Man wept at the death of Lazarus, wept over Jerusalem, and in Gethsemane prayed, "If it is possible let this cup pass from me." We cannot stress this enough: subjectivity belongs to the meaning and nature of man, and in fact to have it in fullness is a necessary basis for the ardor of value-response and for the ardent commitment to the will of God. Subjectivity takes on its fullest form in the personal love for Christ and in the yearning for eternal union with him. Much as eternity modifies the content of subjectivity, it also provides the highest fulfillment of it.

We have seen that holiness does not involve any loss of subjectivity but rather requires a certain *quality* of subjectivity. For the decisive question is *how* subjectivity is structured. As long as we are dealing with the nature of subjectivity as such we do not touch on the question of moral good and evil. Subjectivity can be dominated by pride and concupiscence, poisoned by ambition, envy, hatred; or it can be filled with the response to great objective goods for the person, and especially with love in its various categories, as with the love between friends, with the love of parents for children and of children for parents, or with spousal love. It can be superficial, filled with attachments to peripheral goods, or it can be deep and rich, penetrated by the yearning for goods of great value. It can be egoistic or at least egocentric as soon as I remain "stuck" in it (which can happen even with great goods that I desire). It can be perverted by standing in first place and usurping the primacy of moral value-response and obedience to the divine will.

The danger of remaining "stuck" in my Eigenleben

We have already pointed out the disvalue that lies in the withering of subjectivity: now we have to point out the opposite danger, which is the danger of remaining stuck in subjectivity. This is a definite distortion of subjectivity and it occurs when the priority of pure value-response over subjectivity is not preserved. It is not a subjectivity that has become too strong and intense, but is rather a cramped subjectivity, misshapen by the fact that reaching beyond subjectivity no longer has the due priority. We are not thinking here of the egoism of someone who is dominated by pride and concupiscence. To say that a Richard III suffers from remaining stuck in his subjectivity would obviously be an understatement, as if one were to classify murder as a kind of impoliteness. We are rather thinking of the people who are so caught in their subjectivity that they become incapable of setting it aside when they are called upon to do so. There are people who are so "stuck" in their subjectivity that they live in constant fear of something happening to their well-being and their legitimate interests. In all situations in which something happens to them their attitude is dominated by the concern with avoiding disruptions to their way of life. Whether it is the wishes and goals of a particular day or whether it is the general beneficial goods such as their own health or the health of beloved persons, or their own security or their own economic existence, the one dominant point of view is always whether one of these goods is endangered. If they are asked to do something or are given a task, or if they are challenged by a moral call in a certain situation, everything is apprehended by them from this one point of view. This does not mean that they cannot sometimes follow a moral call that is at odds with their subjectivity, even if they do so with a heavy heart. But their general attitude is such that everything is seen primarily from this *one* point of view. These people see the world through the lens of their own interests.

There are of course here great differences according to the content of their interests. The way these people remain stuck in their subjectivity has one definite quality if the interests are of an immanent nature, such as their own life and health, their own security, their own economic existence, the growth of their wealth, and all legitimately satisfying things, whereas remaining stuck in subjectivity has a different quality if the interests mainly concern the well-being of beloved persons such as one's own children, a beloved spouse, a friend, etc. These are all interests that presuppose transcendence. But what is common is being preoccupied with one's interests in all situations of life. These function like eyeglasses that one wears and through which one sees everything. The formal mistake of remaining stuck in one's subjectivity is the same, even if the moral character of the two cases is very different. There is no doubt but that the person locked into his concern with immanent goods is an egoist in quite another sense than the person preoccupied with his family's well-being. But all the same, and in spite of such differences, both are locked in their subjectivity, and this leads in both cases to a deep lack of freedom, to an oppressive being-cramped. We are referring to the loss, or at least the reduction, of the freedom that empowers us at every moment to respond to the call of God, to which we are admonished in the psalm which says, "If today you hear his voice, harden not your heart." Just as the hardening of the heart impedes us from following the call of God, so does the lack of freedom that comes from remaining stuck in one's subjectivity and being too preoccupied with one's interests. By being preoccupied like this, one cuts oneself off in a sense from the objective *logos*, from the rhythm of the world of values, and from one's neighbor—ultimately from God.

But however regrettable it is to be locked in one's subjectivity, it would be false to think that this comes simply from the intensity of one's subjectivity, or from the extent of one's love for creaturely objective goods for oneself. It comes rather from the fact that the objective hierarchy is disrupted, that the priority of pure value-response and of commitment to God's will is not present. It would be naïve to think that by dismantling subjectivity one can arrive at pure value-response, love of God, and love of neighbor. One arrives rather at a fatalism and a stoic indifference. On the contrary, the more the right order is preserved, the more intense and the more genuine is subjectivity.

By the way, there is also the type of person who even in the religious sphere remains stuck in his subjectivity. If a believer thinks only of the salvation of his soul, considering everything from the point of view of whether he might endanger his own eternal blessedness, instead of considering everything from the point of view of the glorification of God and the will of God, then he too remains stuck in his subjectivity. Of course, such an attitude involves a perverted understanding of blessedness and of the salvation of one's soul. Blessedness is detached from God by such a believer and made into something of its own; he no longer sees that here the greatest objective good for himself coincides with that which is valuable in itself, or flows into it, or in other words that here subjectivity coincides with what is valuable in itself. Such a person is inclined to look at all fellow human beings only from the point of view of whether they could endanger him in his salvation, whether they are useful or necessary for this. He also undermines real love of neighbor and cannot take an interest in the other and in the salvation of the other.

It is of course legitimate and even obligatory to be above all concerned with not offending God; the moral question always has the priority over everything else. "Even if we could free all the damned from hell by committing a single venial sin, we must not commit it," says St. Augustine. It is true that my salvation, since it cannot be objectively detached from the question of what pleases God and what is morally good, is my first concern and concerns me more immediately than the salvation of another. We spoke above of the unique *tua res agitur* contained in moral obligation. My salvation coincides with the "one thing needful," namely to avoid offending God and to walk in His paths. The salvation of a beloved person can and should be just as important to me as my own salvation. But I am directly responsible only for my own salvation; no one can relieve me of this task. But a person remains stuck in his subjectivity if he does not hold fast to the inner connection between achieving salvation and pleasing God, if he treats salvation as *his own* blessedness, as the fulfillment of *his own* subjectivity, and prefers it to the salvation of others in such a way that he sees everything through the glasses of his own salvation and holds back from any real commitment to his neighbor out of fear of jeopardizing his own salvation. We can even detect the danger of remaining stuck in one's religious subjectivity in the common expression: "God and my salvation are the only important things, everything else is only a means for glorifying God and saving my soul." This implies that my neighbor is only an instrumental means—an attitude that is completely incompatible with true love of neighbor and that as a result excludes real love for God. But this relatively sublime case of remaining stuck in one's religious subjectivity is not so easy to detect because it goes together with the primacy of God and of the commitment to God, or in other words with a definite transcendence.

But here too it would be a mistake to think that the reason for this remaining stuck in one's subjectivity is that one's subjectivity is too strong. The yearning for our eternal salvation, for the eternal union with God, can never be strong enough. But salvation must be rightly understood in its essential connection with the love for God, and the priority of the glorification of God must be preserved.

The legitimate preference given to goods belonging to my Eigenleben

We must now make the essential distinction between staying stuck in my subjectivity and legitimately preferring the great goods of my subjectivity to those not belonging to my subjectivity. This preference of course never extends to the demands made by morally relevant goods, but rather refers to the extramoral sphere. For instance, it is legitimate, as we have shown elsewhere, for me to be more concerned with the well-being of a friend than of someone whom I know only casually. It is legitimate for a mother to be more concerned for her children than for those of someone else, etc. Where is the border separating this legitimate preference from remaining stuck in my subjectivity? I clearly remain stuck whenever I inflict some positive harm on another in order to create some advantage for a beloved person. We say "positive harm" because there are indirect harms that are unavoidable and do not arise from any kind of loveless attitude towards the other. Let us think of the case in which several persons apply for a job. If one of them gets the job, this implies of course some harm for all the others who applied for it. If I support a friend applying for a position and if I am convinced that he objectively deserves it, then I am acting for something that implies some harm for the others. But that is not a positive harm that I inflict on them. A positive harm would be inflicted if I were to try to get someone fired so as to clear the way for my friend, and this without any objective motives, such as that my friend would be more capable in the job, or that the other is objectively not doing the job well.

This example is perhaps suited to showing the boundary that divides the legitimate preferring of those whom I love from remaining stuck in my subjectivity. As long as I give first place to objective standards, such as the question who can best fill the job in the case of jobs involving genuine goods (or who of the applicants most needs the job in the case of jobs not involving such goods), and as long as I do nothing morally dubious against any of the applicants, it is entirely legitimate to work for the success of the person whom I love and thus indirectly to work against the success of the others. But if I ignore the objective standards and if I work for my friend even though someone else is much better suited for the job and needs it much more, then I remain in some sense stuck in my subjectivity.

The objective significance of the job for the applicants plays a role here. If we consider that I in no way remain stuck in my subjectivity when I apply for a position in competition with other applicants, we see that this holds all the more for the help that I give to an applicant out of love for him or her. We assume here that this interest in the success of one of the applicants grows out of real love for that person and not out of the fact that I take him or her as an extended ego.

Here is another way of showing the boundary between remaining stuck in my subjectivity and granting a special place to beloved persons (and, analogously, to great goods for myself): in the former case I measure everything by its relation to my subjectivity, this is my first and instinctive reaction, even in the case of things that have nothing to do with my well-being. That shows a very definite lack of objectivity, an incapacity to enter into the given theme of a situation, to let myself be moved by it instead of just being concerned with whether it could be harmful or helpful for me or for the people whom I love. Suppose that I hear about some great success of a colleague of mine: my first reaction could be either joy over a success that I think my colleague really deserves, or it could be something like this, "Could this success interfere with my career or with the career of some friend of mine?" Or suppose that someone makes a request of me: instead of first of all taking an interest in his concern, I may perceive everything from this point of view, "Could this request harm me or some friend of mine?"

In these cases the content of the situation in which I am involved has no direct objective relation to my subjectivity, that is, to my well-being or to that of my loved ones. If the first question that I raise nevertheless concerns this relation, then I am a good example of someone stuck in his or her subjectivity. But if there is in the theme of the situation a direct relation to my subjectivity, it is legitimate for me to raise this question, provided that I do not close myself to the moral call that may arise for me from the situation. For example, if I hear about the outbreak of an epidemic, it is legitimate that I think first of all of the danger to those whom I love and to myself as well, for here in the theme of the situation a direct relation to my subjectivity is objectively given. The only way of remaining stuck in my subjectivity would be to fail to take any interest in all the others who might be endangered, as for instance by warning them when I have the opportunity to warn them. If I respond to the situation by saying in effect, "As long as nothing happens to me and my loved ones, the others are of no concern to me," then I remain stuck in my subjectivity and act in a very loveless way. But the fact that I ask first about the danger to my loved ones is not necessarily illegitimate and with this we come to the decisive point. As soon as the love for friends, children, spouse is formed from within by the spirit of Christ, the legitimate preference of these goes hand in hand with increased love of neighbor; the love for my own in no way closes me off against others but rather enables me to encounter every situation with a heart that is fuller, more open, more loving.

Love and Eigenleben

But now we have to point out the deep change that comes about in my subjectivity when a person whom I love (and not some impersonal good) stands at the center of my subjectivity. In the case of such a central love I *make a gift* as it were of my subjectivity to the beloved person. Rather than stepping out of my subjectivity, or crossing over it as I do in pure value-response, I unfold my subjectivity in a unique way in and through this self-gift. We can express this giving of my subjectivity and the incomparable self-donation that goes with it by saying that I make the beloved person the "lord" of my subjectivity; his or her subjectivity becomes mine insofar as my happiness depends on his or hers.

We find something analogous at a vastly higher level when we think of the love for Christ and through Christ for God. Here the giving of my subjectivity is far more authentic; Christ is in an entirely different sense the "king of my existence."

But there is quite another way of speaking about giving my subjectivity as a gift. There is also the gesture of handing myself over unconditionally to God by placing my subjectivity as it were back into His hands. Here we have to do not with a giving that produces a deep qualitative change in my subjectivity, but rather with a radical transcending of my subjectivity, indeed with *giving it away*. But this giving away does not aim at the final death of my subjectivity. It belongs to the meaning of this free self-emptying of my subjectivity that I receive it back from God purified and transfigured and at the same time tremendously enhanced and enriched. This gesture, in which the absolute primacy of God over myself is acknowledged, is a real dying to myself so as to rise anew in Christ, and so it stands in contrast with the ideal of making my subjectivity disappear. It holds for all value-bearing goods that they do not play less of a role in a subjectivity given back by God but rather play a new and transfigured role. This holds above all for beloved persons; the love for them becomes an *amare in Deo* (loving them in God). But it cannot be said emphatically enough that this *amare in Deo* in no way makes love less ardent; nothing is taken away from the categorial character of a human love, on the contrary, it comes to its fullest unfolding.

CHAPTER TEN

The Happiness of Love

Three ways of experiencing love: in loving, in being loved, and in the awareness of the love existing between two other persons

In order to understand the relation between love and happiness we want to recall briefly that love can disclose itself in very different ways. For the nature of love is given to us from different angles. The first way is learning what love is by loving someone. Here we have that unique source of experiencing that in other works we have called lateral experience and have contrasted with frontal experiencing, which involves the consciousness-of.[1] In performing certain acts we get acquainted with their character. This is eminently the case with affective responses such as joy, sadness, enthusiasm, indignation, love, and hatred. Here the term *experiencing* [*erleben*] finds its most authentic fulfillment. In loving we experience what love is, even though we are entirely directed to the beloved person.

The second way is finding love in other persons. We are sometimes witnesses of the love of one person for another, for instance, of two friends or of spouses. In this way we can come to know the nature of love, its particular quality, the commitment that it implies, the happiness proper to it, and other things as well. Here it is a frontal experience, a consciousness of someone's love, that discloses to us the reality and nature of love as object.

And then there is a third way in which the nature of love discloses itself to us. When I am loved by someone, when the light of his love shines in my soul, when his love encompasses me, then the nature of love shows itself in yet another way. This is neither a lateral nor a purely frontal experience. It is a way of being affected by the love of the other. The content and quality of the love encounters my soul and this involves a new kind of experience. Of course, in one respect it is more like the frontal experience, but in another respect it is altogether different insofar as it goes far beyond knowing and involves an experiencing. It is in general the case that being affected occupies a middle

---

1   [The most relevant of these "other works" is von Hildebrand's posthumously published lecture, "Das Cogito und die Erkenntnis der realen Welt," ed. Josef Seifert, in *Aletheia* 6 (1993–1994); see especially the discussion of the different meanings of *Bewusstseinsinhalt* (12–13). Trans.]

position between frontal and lateral experience. But in the case of being loved the reality of the other person, of the Thou, stands completely in the foreground.

Of course, there are in the experience of being loved many elements that go beyond the disclosure of the quality of love. The fact that the other turns *to me* with a love that is *for me*, this is in principle an element all its own. By its very nature love refers to someone, it is not only a value-response to another but is a word spoken to him and comes to its highest fulfillment when the love is declared. In being received and affected by the love of another for me the content of love is brought uniquely close to me, even though it comes from without. On the other hand, this moment of love whereby it "refers to me" can never be given in the frontal experience of the love that someone has for someone else. This "being breathed on" by love is an aspect of it that is only given in being loved. And it takes on a particular fullness when my being loved by someone is the requital of my love.

Three sources of happiness

We have already mentioned that it is characteristic for love to be the source of a particular happiness. This is one of the ways in which love is distinguished from the other positive affective value-responses. Of course, many of these make us happy, such as admiration, enthusiasm, or veneration. But love makes us happy with quite another fullness and in quite a different sense. We already saw that there is in all positive affective value-responses a source conferring happiness in the broadest sense of the word. The existence of the good that we respond to confers happiness all by itself. If we admire an actor, the fact that such a fine actor exists is felt to be something positive. We can put it like this: in our admiration there is always a certain joy over the existence of that which we admire, whether it be a person, a community such as a people or a state, or a work of art. The existence of a valuable being is always something positive that motivates happiness. This element can be found even in the purely appreciative value-response of esteem.

There is a being-affected by some good that goes hand in hand with certain affective value-responses, such as enthusiasm [*Begeisterung*]. This represents a new way of being made happy. Whereas I can esteem or even admire someone without being affected by his values, without being touched and moved by them, it is always required for enthusiasm that I be affected by the value of a work of art or of some good or person. Indeed, being affected by beauty, depth, greatness, nobility, goodness, and the like is in general one of the primary sources of happiness. In being-affected the delightfulness of value makes itself fully felt; here we also find the basis for all true and deep contemplative enjoyment (*fruitio*). This is why it is understandable that we are happy in all positive affective value-responses insofar as they involve some being-affected.

But there are also affective value-responses which confer happiness all on their own and apart from the being-affected that belongs to them. Enthusiasm is one such value-response. It makes me happy to be enthused, to be able to be enthused. It makes me happy to be lifted up in experiencing enthusiasm and to develop as a person in this ardent response. It is an exhilarating liberation to step out of myself, to grow beyond myself, to be able to give myself.

Two misunderstandings of happiness

There are two possible misunderstandings that we must at this point ward off. First of all, there is the view that the happiness that flows from enthusiasm is in some way the main theme of enthusiasm and that one experiences enthusiasm in order to enjoy this happiness. And there is, secondly, the view that the happiness of enthusiasm comes from the fulfillment of a drive to experience enthusiasm, rather like the way in which the development of a talent that one possesses is a source of satisfaction and happiness.

To the first misunderstanding we reply as follows. There is indeed the case in which someone seeks and intends the happiness of enthusiasm, but this is a typical perversion, which renders impossible any true enthusiasm. As soon as someone makes the happiness of enthusiasm the main theme, he or she can no longer experience genuine enthusiasm. If one tries to experience it instead of being directed entirely to the object and its value—if one makes enthusiasm itself the theme instead of some value-bearing good—no authentic enthusiasm can come about. One can try to work oneself up into a state of enthusiasm, but the result—if indeed anything results—is a state that may have an external resemblance with enthusiasm but that, in terms of both form and content, has in fact nothing to do with true enthusiasm. What results is a state of mind [*Zustand*] rather than a meaningful intentional response; the person does not grow beyond himself but is rather tossed about in a depersonalizing way, nor does he experience anything of the true happiness that enthusiasm can confer. For without being in touch with reality, without being entirely "possessed" by the good and its value, the quality proper to the experience of being lifted up cannot form itself in the soul. An enthusiasm that is sought for its own sake can at most have the character of a pseudo-enthusiasm such as we find in the case of the emotional infection that runs through a crowd. The happiness of enthusiasm is by its nature an epiphenomenon, it can never be the main theme. Significant as this happiness is, essential as it is to enthusiasm, it can never be the main point and even less can it be intended as the goal of enthusiasm.

To the second misunderstanding we reply as follows. It would be entirely wrong to take the happiness that belongs intrinsically to experiencing enthusiasm and to reduce it to the satisfaction of a drive or urge. There are in human beings many powers in the soul that "press" toward their full unfolding. These form a kind of analogy with bodily powers, for instance, the need of a child to move and jump around. We have spoken at length in chapter 1 about these experiences when we distinguished value-response from appetitus. Thus people have a drive to experience many things, to know things, or to achieve something, or to complete a task, which varies very much according to the particular ability of a person. To embrace these powers and to fulfill these drives is as such something satisfying.

In the case of special talents, for instance a talent for acting on the stage, for organizing, for teaching, or for creative artistic work, there are of course also other sources of happiness over and above the satisfaction that comes from developing a talent. What I am referring to is the realization of values, such as the service of the actor to the dramatic work that he "brings alive," or the value and meaning of all that we bring about by our power of organizing, or the service to the truth which the teacher is able to mediate to his students, or the value possessed by the diffusion of truth and the reception of it in the students, or the beauty of the work that the artist produces. Though it is entirely legitimate to take satisfaction in the development of one's human powers, and though it is entirely in order that this development of one's personality be experienced as a source of happiness, the good that one serves must remain the main theme. It must be the primary theme in the sense that it must be the main motive for our activity and also in the sense that the happiness that derives from being allowed to help to realize this good, from being allowed to serve it, must have priority over the happiness that comes from the mere development of our own powers and gifts.[2]

Now if, in the case of the development of talents, the satisfaction derived from fulfilling a drive has to take second place in relation to the happiness deriving from serving value, and if the happiness that goes with performing such activities can never be exclusively reduced to the fulfillment of some drive, this holds all the more for enthusiasm. For first of all enthusiasm is not an appetitus, a spiritual energy striving to unfold itself, but is rather a value-response in which, as we saw, the object and its value are the *principium*. Here the object is not just the primary theme, as it is in the case of those activities, but is the exclusive theme. If enthusiasm is nevertheless a source of happiness, this happiness can never be reduced to the mere fulfillment of a drive. Besides, the very idea of a felt drive to experience enthusiasm is something strange. There can at the most be a yearning to encounter goods the value of which is such as to merit the response of enthusiasm. But the yearning refers to the goods and not to the opportunity to experience enthusiasm. There would be something perverse about a drive that one would express in words like this, "It has been so long since I have felt enthusiasm, I yearn for an opportunity to experience it again."

2	All these issues will be thoroughly treated in a work I am planning on *Happiness and Morality*. Cf. also chapter 1 of the present work. [The work that von Hildebrand mentions here was never written. Trans.]

But it is correct to say that human beings are by their nature ordered to goods that merit enthusiasm, and that enthusiasm is the development of a specifically personal gift, that it is a participating in the world of values, that it involves spiritual awakedness and a strong inner life, and that this is the source of happiness. And yet it must be emphatically stressed that this happiness inherent in enthusiasm is in reality precisely the happiness of being able to transcend oneself, that it is the happiness of being able to grow beyond oneself, and that it is so united with the delightfulness of the good and its value that any attempt to isolate it leads to some perversion.

Now it is obvious that love represents an incomparably greater source of happiness than enthusiasm. This follows from the fact, discussed in chapter 5, that the beloved person becomes an objective good for me, something that does not necessarily happen in the case of enthusiasm. It also follows from the fact that love in the proper sense of the word is essentially superactual, whereas enthusiasm possesses only the superactuality of validity. In every love the beloved person plays a significant role in our subjectivity, a role that of course varies greatly according to the degree and category of love. But the fact that the beloved person is installed in my subjectivity as an objective good for me, shows clearly the entirely new role that happiness plays in love.

In the setting of the present discussion it is important to stress that with love the very fact that the beloved person exists is a source of happiness all its own. It is not hard to see that, as we have already said, the beloved person represents an objective good for me and is established in my subjectivity in a sense not found in other responses, so that his or her existence as such is a more intimate source of my happiness than in other responses.

The unique happiness of love that comes from being affected by the beloved person

The difference between love and all other positive affective value-responses with respect to happiness comes out still more clearly when we think of the second source of happiness distinguished above, namely, being affected by the beauty and preciousness of the beloved person. We saw at the beginning of this work that the beauty, the nobility, the preciousness of the beloved person has to unfold precisely in its delightfulness if love for that person is to be engendered in me. This is the basis for the specific source of happiness that the beloved person is—the person with his or her nature, presence, life, and my contact with and communion with him or her. The nature and the personality of the other enchants me, and this means that it confers happiness. The other affects my heart and wins it over and thus I am in a particular way made happy by the other. Of course, this varies greatly according to the degree of love and especially according to the category of love. It is given in spousal love in a special way and is given most fully in the experience of being in love.

The happiness flowing from being affected by the beauty and

preciousness of the beloved person is not only incomparably greater than in the case of any other affective value-response, it is also entirely different from any of them. It makes us happy to see a person for whom we feel enthusiasm, and to enjoy his nature and his distinctive personal manner by being in his presence and speaking with him and having a living relation with him. But this happiness is much less than in the case of love, assuming of course that we are dealing with an enthusiasm without any love. And the happiness of love is also qualitatively different, because it is much more intimate, because the other person as a source of happiness affects me personally far more than a person who is only appreciated, because there is a mysterious affinity between myself and the other, and because the experience of being enchanted is more deeply rooted in me, engaging me in quite another way and thus becoming a permanent factor in my life.

In love the other stands before me emphatically as a "thou" and never as a mere "he" or "she." This is significantly expressed in the way in which I am made happy by the beloved person and in which I am affected by his or her beauty and preciousness. This experience of being made happy is radically different from any and every "enjoying" that comes from immersing myself in the beauty of a person who remains in the position of "he" or "she." The being of the beloved person says, as it were, "thou" to the one who loves.

Love is distinguished from all other positive affective value-responses by the fact that the being-affected by the beauty of the beloved person is deeper, more lasting, more personal, more intimate. Some of these responses, such as esteem and admiration, presuppose no being-affected at all, but the contrast with enthusiasm and veneration, which do presuppose this, shows us what is new and distinctive about the being-affected that underlies love.

The beloved person enchants us and makes us happy by his or her very being and does so all the more when we love more. A child delights its mother with all the ways it expresses itself; it is a constant source of delight, of joy for her. As for the one who loves in a spousal way, the nature of the beloved person, the personal manner, the particular way of speaking, of laughing, the feel of life, the rhythm of life, all of this in the beloved person is a continuous source of happiness, enchanting the one who loves and affecting his or her heart with happiness.

In spousal love, if developed in its greatness and beauty, the whole world of values is embodied in the beloved person in a certain way; as a result, the happiness that comes from being affected takes on a special character. It is as if in the beloved person the whole world of values were to light up and were to be concretely realized in such a way as to pour its streams of happiness upon me. "You may hide yourself in a thousand ways, you most beloved one, but I always recognize you," Goethe says in *Westöstlichen Diwan* (*West-Eastern Divan*), giving a unique expression to this essential trait of love.

And we should not forget that even the radiance of values in the beloved person and the delightfulness of them is entirely different than it is in the case of persons towards whom we have affective value-responses other than love. There is a certain analogy to this in the way in which works of art or the beauty of nature confer happiness on us.

The incomparable happiness of loving

But the greatest difference with respect to happiness that we find between love and other responses comes to light when we consider how the act of loving as such makes us happy. This "immanent" source of happiness in the case of love cannot be compared with the "immanent" source of happiness in the case of enthusiasm or veneration. For to love, to be able to love, is a unique happiness. Of course, all that we mentioned in connection with enthusiasm—growing beyond oneself, transcending oneself, coming to oneself as a spiritual person—are given in the case of love in a vastly fuller way. But the transcendence of love is of a different kind on account of the literal self-giving [*Hingabe*] that is proper to love. We have already spoken in detail about self-giving. At present we need to understand that this self-giving is a specific source of happiness. First of all, the communion with value is here unique. Just as the being-affected that precedes love is unique, so the one who loves is made happy by the "participation" in the beloved person that comes with loving him—love is the response that, as we saw, goes further than all other value-responses—as well as by the union with the beloved person and with the beauty and preciousness of this person.

But in addition the act of loving involves a new and more authentic form of personal existence, an incomparable awakening, a coming to one's true self, and all of this is as such a principle of happiness. Here we want to pick out just one source of happiness and in doing so to distinguish various elements of it. There is first of all the state of soul in the one who loves; this person becomes awakened in relation to the whole world of values, and this is a source of happiness. Secondly, there is, as already noted, the new kind of awakedness in the performance of all acts. We are more awakened in taking our basic stances; these are as such a source of happiness, and they become much more so in virtue of this awakedness. A final source of happiness is coming to one's true self and achieving the fulfillment of oneself proper to love. Needless to say, all the moments are very different according to the degree of love and above all according to the category of love. To love in the sense of spousal love is of course a source of happiness that far surpasses all other natural categories of love; here the elements that we just distinguished in love as such, come out in an entirely new way. The sayings of Goethe apply here: "Only the soul which loves is happy," and, "Yet if I did not love you, Lili, where would I find my happiness?"

The first and second elements—the two dimensions of awakedness—are fully given only in spousal love. But the third element—finding oneself and coming to oneself—is found in every love, and found more as the love becomes greater. We can see this clearly by thinking of a person who loves no one, who is familiar neither with friendship nor with love for one's parents nor with love for one's children nor with spousal love. The inauthenticity of his existence, the emptiness of it, the state of being locked in himself so as never to come to his true self, show us the incomparable actualization of the person as person in love.

But the important thing is not to fall into the error of thinking of love as an appetitus, as an immanent unfolding of the person. It would be entirely false to take the fact that in loving I come to myself and achieve the fullness of my personal being, and to infer from this that love is nothing but the fulfillment of a drive for my full self-development and that this is the meaning and the nature of love. No, love is a value-response, its meaning is the beloved person, who merits this response; love is through and through self-giving and the beloved person is the only and the absolute theme of it. But since authentic personal being is actualized precisely in self-giving, since the human person is made for self-giving and finds fulfillment only in it—most of all in the love for God, of course—love is at the same time the full actualization of the person. This is not the theme of love, not its meaning, not its motive, for all of this lies in the beloved person and in his value. But it is a superabundant consequence, a gift that grows out of a love lived exclusively for the sake of the beloved person. In all love there is a reflection of what Christ says about the love for God: "Whoever loses his soul will save it."

The fact that we are made for transcendence does not make transcendence into something immanent. The fact that we are made for love, are destined and called to the act of loving, so that only in love can we come to full authentic personal existence, in no way makes love into a kind of drive for full self-fulfillment. We are made for the love of God because God deserves our love and not because we find ourselves through this love. We are made for this love because it glorifies God by its value. That we come through it into our own being is something added as a superabundant gift.

We must understand in this light all that has been said here. The happiness through which we find ourselves is a pure epiphenomenon, never the main theme, however great and significant this happiness is. The same holds even more for the happiness that comes from the existence of the beloved person and from being affected by the beauty and preciousness of the beloved person: the one who loves can never separate his happiness from the other who is the source of it.

We see now how the happiness of love, coming from the three sources of happiness distinguished above, is vastly greater and deeper than in any other affective value-response and that this extraordinary happiness belongs to the nature of happiness. But at the same time it has to be decisively reaffirmed that the primary theme of love is not my happiness but the beloved person, his happiness, his salvation, my union with him being secondary. It is important to understand that the greatness and importance of something does not necessarily involve being the main theme. There are many great and significant things that by their nature are not the primary theme but are rather a gift given "over and above." This being given as superabundant gift *in no way* implies that the content of what is given is not great, significant, and high in value, and even thematic in a secondary way. And so the expression "epiphenomenon" as we use it here should by no means suggest some kind of non-essential addition. Thus, for example, the beauty of a virtue or even of sanctity is not the main theme in the way in which the moral and religious value of virtue is. But from this it does not follow that this beauty is insignificant. And so it is here. The experience of an incomparable kind of happiness belongs essentially to love; a love that engendered no happiness would be no real love. And yet happiness is not the primary theme, and in fact not a theme at all in the strict sense of theme, as we saw in chapter 5.

There is a further source of the happiness of love, which shows itself mainly in spousal love: as a superactual value-response love illumines the whole of one's daily life and lights up every situation, even those situations which, considered in themselves, are neutral and which tend to dominate by their autonomous logic [*Eigengesetzlichkeit*] and sobriety those persons who do not love. There is a blessed melody that sounds throughout one's daily life, and it is a specific mark of spousal love and especially of being in love.

The "indwelling" of happiness in the one who loves

A particular characteristic of the role of happiness in those who love is the new kind of indwelling of happiness in them. Happiness has, as it were, made a dwelling for itself in them, and in fact in the very center of their beings and hearts. With happiness we find a centripetal movement that corresponds to the centrifugal happiness deriving from the beloved person who affects us deeply by his or her beauty. From the hearts of those who love there wells up, as it were, a source of happiness that fills all of their lives. I am not yet speaking here of the fact, so characteristic for love, that the one who loves speaks a word engendering happiness in the beloved person, who by his being makes the lover happy; that is, I am not yet speaking of the fact that the content of love, its very substance with its warmth and goodness, is meant to fill the beloved person with happiness; in other words, I am not yet speaking of what is at work in the intentio benevolentiae of love. But I speak of a stream of happiness in those who love; it pours itself out into situations of life and into the whole of their lives and in a way it has the character of an indwelling happiness in them.

The happiness that comes from the requital of love

But in love, and only in love, there is another dimension of happiness: I am made happy by being loved in return, by having my love requited, or, as we could also put it, by the union that love desires with the beloved person. We saw above that an intentio unionis is proper to every kind of love. We also saw that this intentio varies from one category of love to another and in fact varies in importance from one to another. Now every love desires a corresponding return of love, since it is only in the interpenetrating looks [*Ineinanderblick*] of the two who love each other that a true personal union can come about. The greater and the more intense the love, the more the return of love is desired. If my love is not returned, I am unhappy. This unhappiness becomes greater in proportion to the intensity and ardor of the love. A mother who loves her child above all else, suffers if she is not loved by the child; someone who loves another deeply as friend and does not receive a return of his love, is pained by this. The pain of unhappiness is greatest in unrequited spousal love, where the term "unhappy love" originates.

But this unhappiness does not eliminate the happiness that dwells in love. Happiness and unhappiness exist next to each other and interpenetrate, but not in such a way that the one who loves wishes that he did not love the other or had never met the other. We have to distinguish here different stages. At first the act of loving brings with it undiminished happiness, even in the absence of a return of love which there is every reason to hope for. As long as the beloved person does not in some way refuse the return of love, as long as the one who loves—whether a friend, a mother, someone in love—can hope for a return of love, his or her love is unimpeded in unfolding its power of making happy; the intentio unionis imparts happiness even if it is not yet fulfilled. If the return of love has been refused but the one who loves still hopes—perhaps hopes against hope—then the happiness is still stronger than the pain of non-requital. But if there is no prospect at all of requital, then the pain may be stronger than the happiness in certain categories of love such as spousal love. Then the unrequited love can indirectly become for this person the source of an unhappiness that poisons the rest of his or her life. What concerns us here is to focus on the specific happiness of receiving the return of love and to see it as a new dimension of happiness that is distinct from the happiness of loving. It is also distinct from the happiness that comes from the existence of the beloved person as well as from that which comes from being affected by his or her beauty.

So let us take the case of someone who loves with spousal love and who at first does not know whether his love will be returned but who has no reason not to hope for this. He will experience all the above-mentioned happiness that goes with loving. But if his love is requited, he receives in addition quite another happiness, which unites organically with the happiness of loving and builds on this happiness as its basis.

We saw that the union desired by love can only come about by the requital of love. The real union of persons can only be achieved through the interchange of looks that express love. Thus it is apparent what an unfathomable happiness is granted by requited love. The union with the beloved person is an immeasurable source of happiness that cannot be compared with any other earthly happiness.

But it would be entirely wrong to think that the union is a source of happiness only in the sense of fulfilling the intentio unionis, that is, as the satisfaction of a yearning. We have seen that love is in no way an appetitus and that its ardor and fire is not the result of a lack of fulfillment which yields to a satiated state as soon as the desired union is achieved. The intentio unionis is the interest in union that is experienced as yearning for union only as long as the union is not reached, and then is experienced as deep happiness over the union as soon as it is reached.

Further dimensions of the happiness of being loved

But the requital of love has many other dimensions of engendering love. In having my love returned, as in a deep spousal love, I experience it as a tremendous gift to be loved, since I am, as it were, given to myself by being loved. When the beloved person receives and shelters my being in love, giving me a unique confirmation of my individual existence, I experience almost a new birth of my self. I receive the greatest possible gift, irreplaceable by any other. I experience that I not only am but ought to be. My accidental and contingent existence is experienced as providential.

We hope in the second volume of this work to deal in some detail with the phenomenon of being loved and the way it reaches deep into the roots of our personal existence and is deeply characteristic of our metaphysical situation. In that connection we will explore more the happiness that comes from being loved. At present I want just to make a few points so that we can fully understand the influence that being loved has on the happiness of loving.

Even independent of our own love it is a great source of happiness to be loved, to be sheltered in the love of another person. We grasp the whole glory of the quality of love when a ray of someone's love penetrates my heart with its warmth and happiness. Let us just think of the experience of the child who feels itself sheltered in the love of its parents, or of the experience of someone who has never been loved before and now for the first time receives a love directed to himself. Splendid as it is to see the love between other persons, an entirely new dimension of experiencing the unique quality of love is given when the love is a love for me. It is a fundamental kind of encounter with the quality of love and it is in addition to the encounter that lies in performing the act of loving. Different as the experience of one's own loving is from the experience of being loved, in both of them the quality of *love* is given, in both of them one experiences what love is and in both one experiences the delightful sweetness of love, which presents itself in its unique power to engender happiness. In the extraordinary experience of being loved the quality of love is not just experienced like the beauty of nature, but it is instead imparted to us so as to *affect* us in a real and living way and to confer happiness on us.

What we have said holds for all the categories of love. But this happiness varies very much according to the quality of the love that is shown to us, according to the personality of the one who loves us, according to the category of love, and according to our stance towards that person. A genuine Christian love of neighbor is so sublime in its quality that it confers deep happiness on anyone who receives it—unless one were so distorted by pride and concupiscence as to misunderstand completely the quality of this love. The point is that the experience of being loved with Christian love of neighbor is a deep source of happiness for a normal person, even if the one who is loved does not know or love the one who approaches him with love of neighbor. Here we can measure the role of the quality of love for conferring happiness. The degree of love also plays a role in all other categories of love. The more one is loved, the greater one's happiness.

The "task" or "burden" that can grow out of being loved

Now my stance toward the one who loves me plays a decisive role. Only if the one who loves me is not disagreeable or embarrassing for me is being loved by him a source of happiness for me, otherwise it can instead be a burden.

But even if the other is not definitely disagreeable to me, the intensity of his or her love can be oppressive for me if I love that person much less, for I feel that the other is constantly expecting more from me than I can give him or her with my love. By his love for me the other appeals (not necessarily with words) for a full return of his love, and this can make it a burden for me to be loved by that person. But this is by no means the case when a friend asks for no other return of love than the one I give him, that is, when his love for me has a particular character and does not call for a return of love from me that is the same in strength and depth.

Thus the inequality of love in a relationship imposes particular duties on me when I am the one who loves more. I have to adapt to the love of the other (who loves less) the rhythm of the relationship, the demands to be together, and the expressions of love. The genius of the relationship requires in this case that the one who loves less sets the tone. The talk here of "more" and "less" love refers to the degree of love and to the role that someone plays in my life, that is, to the place that he occupies in my heart. It does not refer to the nobility of the love or to the caritas that may fill the love and so make it qualitatively higher.

The love that I receive can be a burden rather than a source of happiness most of all when the other loves me spousally and I love the other only as friend. If the other constantly hopes that I will approach him or her with a categorically different love, when the other wants to adapt the rhythm of the relationship to his or her love, then this love can become burdensome for me and I may wish that the other would stop loving me in this way. But what was just said above holds here too: the love of the other is burdensome for me only if it contains the implicit appeal to be loved with the same category of love.

How the requital of love augments all the sources of happiness in love

But we are thinking here above all of the happiness that comes with the requital of love, of the case in which my love is returned with an equal love. This happiness of fulfilling all that is desired by the *intentio unionis* occurs most of all in the case of spousal love.

Let us return to the happiness of requited love, which joins itself organically to the happiness that comes from the act of loving. Here we have to understand that my happiness over the existence of the beloved person, of which we spoke above, is immeasurably augmented by the fact that he loves me.

We have on various occasions mentioned that each person who loves turns his true face to the beloved person and reveals his true being. This of course happens in various ways, according to the greatness and depth of the love and also according to the category of love. It is most of all the case—at least among the natural kinds of love—with spousal love, but it is found in some way or other in every true love. We have only to compare the situation of meeting someone who is indifferent to me with the situation of meeting someone who loves me: we cannot fail to see that the other in loving me reveals himself to me in an entirely new way and grants me a glimpse of his real personality (it does not matter that the depth and intimacy of what is disclosed varies greatly, according to the kind of love at stake).

This becomes entirely understandable as soon as we consider that every person who truly loves actualizes his true self and turns in a unique way towards the beloved person. Thus the happiness that flows from the very existence of the beloved person is immeasurably augmented by his requital of my love. The beautiful and beloved being of the other becomes more visible to me; indeed, it is disclosed to me in an intimate way that is only possible when he turns his face to me in love. But the beloved person does not only disclose his being to me in a new way by requiting my love; he becomes objectively more beautiful and more loveable by loving. The wonderful statement of St. Augustine applies here: "The lover becomes himself more loveable by loving." In chapter 12, when we deal with the relation between natural love and morality, we will examine more closely how it is that every person who loves becomes thereby more awake, more heroic, more beautiful.

Here we simply want to point out the importance that this has for the happiness that flows from the requital of my love. For it is only when the other loves me that I discover entirely new aspects and treasures of his being. With some persons the difference between loving and not loving is so great that we are tempted to say that we do not really know them at all until they disclose themselves in love.

But there is something else to be considered here. We can grasp how a person becomes more beautiful by loving, even when we see love between two other persons. Suppose we know someone who has never really loved and suddenly is seized by a great and deep love. Even in this case we can clearly see how much more beautiful he becomes, how liberated from the chains of comfort and routine, how much greater he becomes, how much less mediocre, how much more humble, more heroic. Even as an uninvolved third party we can observe in someone who loves something of what is expressed in Goethe's poem, "Herz, mein Herz, was soll das geben," or in the noble words of Tristan in Wagner's opera, *Tristan und Isolde*, "How can I give a thought to Tristan's honor?" or in the words of the Song of Songs, "If a man should give away all of his wealth for the sake of love, he would esteem the loss as nothing at all." But what we are thinking of here—a certain way of disclosing a person's intimate being and the beauty that the person takes on by loving—goes far beyond all of this. It is a knowledge of the loving person that is only granted to the one to whom his or her love is addressed. It is a deeper and more intimate level that arises in the one who loves when he discloses himself to the beloved person. For this disclosure it is necessary that the face of the one who loves be completely turned towards the other, that the self-giving of love be directed to the other. Only then does the happiness over the existence of the beloved person get fully augmented. This particular source of happiness is only present in the requital of love and not in being loved as such.

The happiness that comes from the self-giving of the beloved person and from the union with him

But more important than the augmentation of happiness over the existence of the other is the happiness over the beloved person giving himself to me. Immeasurable is the happiness that can be expressed in the words: how beautiful you are, you who love me. First comes the whole preciousness of the beloved person that inflames my heart, first comes his existence and the intimate beauty that discloses itself to me in his love: and then comes the incomprehensible gift that he loves me and gives himself to me. The more precious and more beautiful the beloved person is, the more precious is the gift of self that goes with love and the greater the happiness.

There is in addition the blessedness of the union, the interchange of looks that expresses love. On the one hand, there is the full duality of I and Thou, the clear difference between them, the full consciousness of the Thou of the beloved person and his unique individuality; on the other hand, there is the ultimate unity that can only be granted by the interchange of looks that expresses love and by the mutual sharing in the being of each other.

Of course, all that we have said cannot adequately express the happiness of love and of the requital of love. This we leave to the poets. But we have had to make mention of the incomparable happiness of love, since it belongs to the nature of love; love now stands out more clearly in contrast to all other value-responses. But at the same time we have to affirm once again: happiness is neither the motive nor the goal of love, not even the primary theme of love: it is a superabundant gift flowing from love.

CHAPTER ELEVEN

Caritas

We have shown how impossible it is to see in the intentio unionis an element that compromises the purity of the self-giving and of the value-response character of love. We have also seen that the difference between selfish and selfless love depends on factors very different from the presence or absence of the intentio unionis. Furthermore, we have seen that one completely misunderstands the intentio unionis if one calls the love in which it is present by the name of *amor concupiscentiae* and calls the love in which it is absent by the name of *amor benevolentiae.*

Our question is this: what is it that makes love of neighbor a kind of agape in contrast to the eros that comprises the natural categories of love? If the answer is not the absence of the intentio unionis and the theme of happiness in the love of neighbor, then what is it? It is tempting to think of the tremendous theological superiority of agape to eros, as a result of which agape is a supernatural love whereas eros is only a natural one. But we have to prescind here from this fundamental theological difference, which is after all an object of faith and not a datum available to our natural experience. We will limit ourselves in the following to those differences between agape and the natural categories of love that are known to us in our natural experience.

Different relation to the moral sphere

A first and rather obvious difference between the two has to do with the way each is related to the moral sphere.

Christ says, "If you love those who love you, what merit do you have in that? Do not the pagans do as much?" We can obviously refer these words to all natural categories of love, such as the love between friends, parental love, love of children for their parents, or spousal love, in contrast to Christian love of neighbor. Even if these words refer primarily to the love for one's enemy as contrasted with love for those who do us good and wish us well, they also refer to the fundamental moral difference between Christian love of neighbor and the other natural categories of love. Christian love of neighbor is not only the bearer of the highest moral values, but together with the love for God it forms the axis of natural and supernatural morality.[1] The law and the prophets depend on these two loves. By contrast, the love of friends, parental love, love of children for their parents, and spousal love, whatever relations they might have to the world of morality, do not stand at the center of morality and do not belong to the heart of it in the way in which love of neighbor does. This difference is expressed as clearly as possible in the fact that love of neighbor is a command and that it is in fact, after the command to love God, the most important and central command, whereas all natural loves mainly have the character of a gift. These are all based on some special affinity between persons (whether the affinity be objective, as in the love between parents and children, or subjective, as in the love between friends or spouses). But the main point is that Christian love of neighbor centers around morality, whereas all the other kinds of love for a person have a different center, a center all its own. The natural categories of love are not the result of moral striving, but they are gifts.

This does not mean that the natural categories of love are not in many ways connected with the world of morality. On the contrary, parental love involves moral responsibility. The place of moral obedience in the love of children for their parents is obvious. The love of friends is based on persons encountering each other in the good, as Aristotle pointed out. And spousal love involves the eminent moral issue of faithfulness. Many other significant relations to the moral sphere might be shown in the categories of love, and we will discuss them later in detail. At present the point is simply to see that none of these categories of love as such is a mere outgrowth of the fundamental moral attitude, the fundamental will to walk in the paths of the Lord. They have a center of their own that is distinct from morality.

Though these categories of love are imperfect in the form in which pagans practice them, one cannot deny that even here we find genuine natural love.

If we want to do justice to this decisive difference between Christian love of neighbor and all the other natural categories of love, we have to consider the natural categories of love as they exist prior to being influenced by the love for God or transformed through Christ. The value-response in all of these loves arises naturally and effortlessly and does not require any particular moral consciousness in those who love. In fact it belongs essentially to the self-giving in these loves that it is not a result of the will but an impulse of the heart. In all of these loves I have the sense of "not being able to help myself" in loving the other, who is made deeply happy by this way of giving myself to him or her. For this is a giving of my heart and cannot be replaced by anything else.

In all responses to morally relevant values, the *center of our concern* is the

---

1   This should by no means be taken as implying that there is not a great and significant part of morality that falls outside of love of neighbor. Consider the attitudes commanded in the first three commandments of the Decalogue, the primordial sin of pride, and the incomparable virtue of humility.

moral world of value, its imperative character, and obedience to its call and ultimately to God. This is not the immediate center of concern in a love between friends, in a parental love, or in a spousal love. The value-response has here a different theme than that of moral importance. The beloved person is a great gift for me; giving myself to him or her is a personal theme, a giving of myself that is quite different from the self-giving that I perform in relation to morally relevant values. I give my heart in a way that varies with the kind and intensity of the love. This self-giving is not experienced as free, as if it were an act of the will, but rather as a gift, a being-drawn, and it is also not experienced as the fulfillment of a moral obligation. The lovableness of the other does not appeal to my conscience. On the other hand, none of these loves is in any way just arbitrary, as we saw. But there is as it were something proper to me as this particular individual and to my subjectivity that I am able to give to the other, and especially when I love the other spousally. That invests all of these loves with a character that, from a moral point of view, is different from the love of neighbor.

This fundamental moral difference stands out most clearly when we consider that Christian love of neighbor is necessarily built on the love for God, whereas the natural kinds of love are not. This difference is primarily a religious one, but one that obviously has very great consequences for all of morality. All other natural categories of love, such as the love between friends, parental love, or spousal love, do not necessarily require any belief in God and certainly none in Christian revelation. Our question here is not how these categories of love can be changed, deepened, or elevated by the belief in the God who reveals Himself in Christ, nor is it the question whether they do not come fully into their own only in Christ. At present we want only to affirm that they are possible even among pagans.

By contrast, Christian love of neighbor necessarily builds on Christian revelation and on faith in this revelation, even if we prescind from its supernatural character in the theological sense. There is a beauty and worth that inheres in every human person for as long as he lives, even if he is stained by the worst qualitative disvalues. If I am going to give the appropriate value-response to this beauty, then I have first to acknowledge each person as existing in the image of God, as created by God, and called to eternal communion with Him. As we will see later in more detail, real Christian love of neighbor sees neighbors in the light of the fact that they are infinitely loved by Christ, who died on the cross for them. Christian love of neighbor is inseparable from faith in the God who reveals Himself in Christ and from love for this God. But since love for God is the supreme value-response in which all moral value-responses culminate, we see clearly how deep the divide is between Christian love of neighbor and the natural kinds of love that are found even "among the pagans." At the same time this fact shows that the difference between Christian love of neighbor and all other natural categories of love reaches far beyond all natural morality, for in love of neighbor the glory of supernatural morality shines forth and a certain breath of holiness is felt.

But now the question arises: to what extent is this fundamental difference rooted in the categorial character of love of neighbor? Is the incomparable sublimity of Christian love of neighbor inseparable from the fact that in this love the intentio unionis recedes in importance and that the happiness of the one who loves is in no way a central concern? We have to answer emphatically in the negative, since the intentio unionis is fully developed in the love for God and since the theme of happiness is also eminently present there, if only in a secondary way. The decisive difference lies rather in the quality of the love that is found both in the love for God and in the love of neighbor, and this quality is not tied to the categorial character of love of neighbor. This will now become clearer as we explore the qualitative difference between Christian love of neighbor and the natural categories of love.

The qualitative difference between Christian love of neighbor and the natural categories of love

I can love someone deeply as a friend and at the same time hate someone else. An ardent spousal love in no way excludes hating someone else at the same time. But with Christian love of neighbor this is impossible. If I turn to someone with genuine Christian love of neighbor I cannot at the same time be filled with hatred for someone else. This throws a significant light on the deep qualitative difference between love of neighbor and all the "unbaptized" natural loves.

Let us just compare the intentio benevolentiae in the two kinds of love. In the natural categories of love we find in it three elements. There is the interest in the happiness of the beloved person; then there is the wish to make the beloved person happy, heaping one benefit after another on him or her (this second element varies according to the category of love—it is most prominent in spousal love and in the love for one's children); and finally there is the goodness and kindness[2] that I "breathe" into the soul of the beloved person, by which we refer to the way in which I "take hold" of the soul of the one whom I love, sheltering it and receiving it, so that the beloved person feels warmed and made happy by my love. (In the first element, which involves a great solidarity with the beloved person, we can discern the transcendence of which we spoke in chapter 7: I am moved by all that is an objective good or evil for the beloved person, and am moved for the very reason that his or her objective well-being is at stake.)

The important point at present is this: the entire intentio benevolentiae

---

2   [For the first time in this chapter the term *Güte* is used, and it is used repeatedly throughout the discussion of caritas. I will usually render it as "goodness and kindness," or some variant of this. Trans.]

flows from the value-responding affirmation of the other as this individual person; because the other so enchants me I want to be good to him or her. First of all, this being good to the other is grounded in the value-response to the other; secondly, I am good *to him* but not necessarily good with my whole being as a person. Though I show a face of goodness to the other and direct to him or her this stream of goodness, I can still hate someone else at the same time. Of course, there is in every natural love the tendency to love with one's whole being (more on this in chapter 12). But this tendency of every authentic natural love cannot be taken to mean that in loving I am completely filled with goodness, as if the reverent and loving center in me were entirely dominant, or as we could as well say, as if I dwelt in the realm of goodness.

But with Christian love of neighbor the intentio benevolentiae is not a result of affirming my neighbor in a value-responding way; it is rather an actualization of the goodness dwelling in the soul of the one who loves. Although this goodness can only be actualized in a value-response to my neighbor, it does not arise by taking delight in him or her. The one who loves another with love of neighbor is good to the other on the basis of the goodness and the fundamental attitude of love that reigns in him; he brings this to the encounter with the other. This is why the one who loves is never good just to this one person but is ready to be good to any and every neighbor. From this it follows that he cannot love one person and at the same time hate another.

The intentio benevolentiae has here an entirely different character and a new quality. For it is, apart from the above-mentioned elements of the intentio benevolentiae, not only a word of goodness for the other, but it involves directing to the other a "substantial" goodness, a holy goodness, which refers to him entirely as person and surpasses the word of goodness contained in the intentio benevolentiae of the natural categories of love.

In spite of the way Christian love of neighbor "anticipates" the other, this love takes full interest in the individual person who is loved; it refers entirely to this person; the neighbor is altogether at the center of my concern. It would be a complete misunderstanding to think that the goodness dwelling in the one who loves just overflows spontaneously and only by accident pours itself over this neighbor. For we should by no means think of the holy goodness and the superactual attitude of love as a kind of strength, a fullness of life, a potential; it is rather an intentional attitude founded in the love for God. The superactual character of this attitude makes the person who possesses it to be one-who-loves. The fact that in this case the love anticipates the encounter with the neighbor in no way interferes with the value-response character of this love and with giving full attention to the neighbor. The unique way of entering into the world of the neighbor is in no way mitigated by the fact the love has here this anticipatory character.

Love of neighbor is also distinguished by the fact that the typical I-Thou situation does not prevail in it. We can understand this only if we consider that the I-Thou relation can be spoken of in very various senses. 1) One can have in mind the basic dimension of communion with other persons that is contrasted with the we-solidarity of persons. It was in this sense that I spoke of I-Thou in my book, *Die Metaphysik der Gemeinschaft* (The Metaphysics of Community). 2) But one speaks of it in an entirely different sense in referring to the dialogical situation in which the other is taken entirely as subject and in no way as object. Then one is contrasting Thou with He or She. There is no real dialogical, person-to-person contact with another who is taken as He or She; instead of being taken as subject the other is put in the place where otherwise only impersonal things are found. Of course, one knows that the other is a person, knows that the other is a He or She and not an It. But one encounters the other formally as an object; the knowing about the other as person does not involve any actualization of personal contact with the other, of contact of a kind possible only with persons. Martin Buber gives special attention to Thou as it emerges from this contrast to He or She. 3) In the writings of Gabriel Marcel the I-Thou takes on a further meaning in addition to this second one: in his view my true "I" can only be actualized in the I-Thou situation. Thus he not only contrasts Thou with He or She, but he also contrasts *je* with *moi*. Only in giving myself to a Thou do I transcend my immanence and break out of the prison of my self-absorption and so liberate my real self. In this reading of the I-Thou, my true self, my I (*je*), is freed up by being centrally concerned with the Thou. Corresponding to the contrast of Thou and He or She is the contrast between *je* and *moi*, between the authentic, fully personal self and the egocentric pseudo-self. 4) We can also think of those forms of communion among persons in which the mutual love is the central concern and in which, as a result, the union of persons stands at the center of their relation. This is most of all the case in spousal love, where the two face each other in a special way. This I-Thou is not just the one emerging from the contrast with we-solidarity, it also involves the "we" of Gabriel Marcel; that is, the I-Thou union itself centrally concerns both the man and the woman.

Now love of neighbor stands in contrast to this last-mentioned I-Thou: though my neighbor is here a full Thou and is not He or She, my "I" is not as fully involved in the relation (as in the 4th I-Thou). It is my neighbor who stands at the center of my attention and not my personal union with him or her, not the mutual love between us, and even less the happiness flowing from personal union. It is rather the case that my neighbor is a kind of He or She in a sense entirely different from the impersonal He or She mentioned above. My neighbor is He or She in the sense of being exclusively thematic, in the sense that it is He or She as such and not our relation that stands in the foreground. In love of neighbor I do not aim at the interchange of loving looks with my neighbor, but I look at my neighbor as such. In speaking of my neighbor as He or She I am referring to a certain independence of the neighbor from myself.

It goes without saying that something of this is to be found in every real love. The primacy that the beloved person possesses as such, the priority of his happiness and salvation over my union with him, belongs essentially to every authentic love, as we saw. This is an inner hierarchy that comes to its fulfillment when love is penetrated by caritas. In this sense the beloved person is never exclusively a Thou, not even in spousal love, where the I-Thou is most fully developed. Even here love includes a certain silent thinking about the beloved person that is of the greatest importance. Since even here the primacy of the beloved person holds, the act of entrusting the beloved person to God plays a large role, as does approaching the beloved person in the consciousness of sharing in God's love for him or her. Even here there is a kind of monologue spoken by the one who loves, even though it is a monologue penetrated by the I-Thou relation.

But though it is true that in any love, spousal love included, the beloved person is never exclusively a Thou, it is also true that love of neighbor differs from all the natural categories of love by the fact that my neighbor is much more of a He or She (in the positive sense of the word) than a Thou. Perhaps we can say it more clearly like this: here the I-Thou situation gives way to the "for the other." Even though in the love of neighbor my neighbor is taken entirely as a person, even though I turn to him or her entirely as a person, the I-Thou situation is in a way weaker, since my neighbor is exclusively thematic. In the love of neighbor there is always a gesture of looking up to the absolute Thou of God. Thus in a certain sense my neighbor is taken as a person in an incomparable way: the ultimate seriousness and depth of the personality of the other stands forth in love of neighbor.

The difference between love of neighbor and caritas

The nature of Christian love of neighbor and the way in which it is distinguished from all natural love such as is possible among pagans becomes clearer for us once we distinguish the nature of caritas from the categorial character that it takes on in the case of love of neighbor. For some of the mentioned traits of love of neighbor are rooted in its categorial character and others are rooted in the unique quality of caritas.

In a categorial respect the love for God and the love of neighbor are obviously entirely different. The love for God is the purest value-response, the value-response *par excellence*. Love is here born and sustained by the infinite glory and holiness of the beloved, and this in a way that is not found in any other kind of love. There is no question here of the element of anticipation that goes with love of neighbor. The substantial goodness and kindness of the whole person, the actualization of the reverent and loving center in myself, my full participation in the kingdom of holy goodness, is here a fruit of the value-response to God. In addition, the intentio benevolentiae takes on a character completely different from what is found in all loves directed to a creaturely person (this includes love of neighbor): it has the character of burning for the honor of God; an absolute interest in the glorification of God forms here the unquestionably central concern. Very prominent is the adoring affirmation of God, along with the absolute giving of myself to Him. This is why the intentio unionis occupies a central place, as does happiness, even if in a secondary way.

Obviously none of this is found in the love of neighbor, which has an anticipatory character that is not born purely of the value of the beloved person. This holds all the more for the substantial goodness and kindness of the one who loves and for his participation in the kingdom of holy goodness. These are not the fruits of the value-response to my neighbor; it is rather the case that this value-response presupposes them. The value-response to my neighbor is a manifestation of the holy goodness that is born of the love for God. The intentio benevolentiae is present in its typical way, while the intentio unionis is only weakly present. And whereas the intentio unionis takes on its supreme form in the love for God, it takes on a different form in the love of neighbor, where it is no longer connected with the theme of happiness. With regard to the intentio unionis, then, the love for God has more categorial affinity with spousal love—of course in other respects it is radically different from this love—than with love of neighbor.[3] But with regard to the intentio benevolentiae the love of neighbor, directed as it is to a creaturely

---

3   The love for God cannot be compared with any other love. One of the many reasons for this is that this love refers to God, the absolute Lord, the almighty, omniscient, infinitely holy One. There is a unique connection of love for God with morality, as we can see from the fact that God is the personification of the moral order of the world, and from the fact that our love for God cannot be lived apart from obeying the commands of God and from striving to walk in His ways. Expressing our love for God is essentially connected with wanting to glorify God. The intentio benevolentiae in the other categories of love becomes in this one the glorification of God through our moral perfection and our holiness. Indeed, the morally good deed, the morally good behavior, the imitation of Christ is here the outgrowth of loving God; it is the way this love expresses itself. This does not mean that the moral life is the only focus of the love for God, for there is also a direct loving self-donation to God, a pure response of love for Christ, a pure value-response directed to Him that is filled by love. There is a danger of reducing the love for God to obedience; this would be a misunderstanding of the statement of Christ, "Whoever loves me will keep my commands." Just because this obedience is the indispensable criterion for the love for God as well as an essential expression of it, we should not lose sight of the adoring response of love and the blessed giving of my heart in love for God. Let us think of the response of St. Peter to the threefold question of Christ: "Simon Peter, do you love me?" or of his words at the washing of the feet. The love for God is, in spite of its ultimate bond with the moral theme, also the exemplary cause, or model, of all creaturely love; it is the purest, most expressive value-response of love, the ultimate, absolute, total giving of my heart, of my very self. Here the theme of love as such reaches its maximum, as we can see from the fact that the intentio unionis reaches here its maximum.

person, has much more categorial affinity with the natural categories of love than with love for God. So we see how different the love for God and the love of neighbor are from a categorial point of view.

We also see how senseless the frequently made statement is that love for God and love of neighbor are identical. Even the statement that love of neighbor is the only way to live our love for God is completely mistaken. The imitation of Christ does not occur only in love of neighbor but also in all the rest of morality, and especially in humility and purity. But the most important thing to say here is that there is also a direct love for Christ—we find it in all of the saints—that is an adoring value-response to the infinite holiness and beauty of Jesus and that expresses itself in an intimate interchange with Him. True as it is that Christian love of neighbor is a criterion for the genuineness of our love for Christ, it is nevertheless patently false to take love of neighbor as the only way of living our love for God. This has to be kept in mind when we now point out how closely conjoined the two loves are in the quality of caritas.

In both of them we find the entirely new supernatural kind of love that is called caritas, which is characterized by a holy goodness and kindness and by a blessed freedom. As a result caritas is the soul of supernatural morality and the soul of holiness. It is caritas that empowers those who are animated by it to enter the kingdom of holy goodness, and it is caritas that brings about the dominion of the humble, reverent, and loving center in them over the center of pride and concupiscence. It is caritas that comprises all of morality and of which Christ spoke in saying that all of the law and the prophets depend on it. It is all-important to see that, though the category of love of neighbor is possible only through caritas and lives entirely from caritas, we should in no way take the categorial traits of love of neighbor as necessary for caritas. Caritas is constituted in the love for God, and the love of neighbor is a fruit of caritas. Without love for God caritas could not take hold of us. Without caritas the Christian love of neighbor would not be possible. So we see that we have to distinguish clearly between caritas and the categorial character of love of neighbor.

In the experience of being loved, too, we can find the qualitative difference, deriving from caritas, between Christian love of neighbor and all natural categories of love.[4] In all of these categories the tremendous gift of being loved involves a confrontation with a goodness and kindness that refers to me. In elaborating the objective good for the person, we pointed out the friendly gesture towards the person, we pointed out the element of "in his favor" that distinguishes the objective good for the person from something merely

---

4   But we should never forget that the categorial identity of a love expresses itself significantly in the quality of the love. Only when we contrast the category of a love with the quality of a love and think of quality in terms of the depth, the spirituality, the sublimity of love, do we have in mind a sense of quality that allows us to say that it is independent from the categorial identity of a love.

subjectively satisfying. It is a solidarity with the true interest of the person, with the true benefit for the person. We are referring here to that aspect of the objective good for the person that allows us to consider it as a gift of God, as an outgrowth of His love and goodness. This gesture of friendliness that is present as it were objectified in all impersonal objective goods for the person, lends itself as a natural expression of the human intentio benevolentiae. The gifts that I want to give to a beloved person are always objective goods for the person. But in addition to the "in his favor" of the objective good there is also the personal gesture of affirmation, of friendliness. This gesture is still more literally, more really, to be found in the conscious act of love whereby I am moved to give to a beloved person an objective gift for him or her, or in other words provide him or her with some benefit. But this gesture of "in his favor" is above all to be found in the word of love itself, even apart from being expressed in the giving of some benefit. This is why in the love that someone shows to me this fundamental gesture is much more real and more articulated than it is in an impersonal objective good for me; indeed, the latter cannot even be compared with the former. In all objective goods for me, the affirmation of me, the friendly turning to me, is only indirectly given, but with love there is also the personal friendliness, the goodness referring to me, the act of being good to me on the part of the one who loves me. When I am loved, I experience as a great source of happiness the light of goodness that shines into me. But when I experience the caritas that refers to me, I am not only touched by the "in my favor," by the goodness referring to me that comes from the intentio benevolentiae, but I also have an encounter with the holy substantial goodness and kindness of the other. I experience the breath of holy goodness as it unfolds in the love spoken to me. Once again the difference between caritas and natural love, of which we spoke above, shows itself here clearly.

In a natural love such as is possible even among pagans it is a personal "in my favor" that is communicated to me; this does not just come to me through value as in the objective goods for me that are based on value, but as it were unmediated. It is the "for me" as such. It is goodness for me, the affirmation of my person, the tremendous gift of this unique interest in me. But in caritas it is the holy goodness and kindness as such that is turned to me. The "for me" is an outgrowth of goodness and love as such; we experience the overwhelming gift of being breathed upon by holy goodness. In a certain sense I experience an encounter with Christ when I am encompassed by someone's Christian love of neighbor. In the caritas that encompasses me I hear the voice of Christ, whereas in all unbaptized natural love I hear only the voice of the heart of some human being. As we saw, the Christian who loves his neighbor finds Christ and he sees his neighbor in the light of the redemption as one who is infinitely loved by Christ. "What you have done to the least of my brothers you have done to me." Even more does the one who receives caritas experience the encounter with Christ.

We saw in chapter 9 that in the love of neighbor I step out of my subjectivity whereas in the natural categories of love I grant to the beloved person an extraordinary place in my subjectivity (and in the case of spousal love I let the beloved person be the lord of my subjectivity). Thus from a purely categorial point of view, the gift of self made to the beloved person in a deep and ardent natural love (of whatever natural category) is greater than in Christian love of neighbor. This is why I am made happier by being loved with such a love than with love of neighbor. We are comparing here Christian love of neighbor with an "unbaptized" natural love, and doing so with respect to categorial identity.

But when we think of the experience of being moved by caritas, when we think of experiencing the light of substantial holy goodness and kindness pouring into me, we see that this is a tremendous gift and a unique experience. For then I am confronted with this substantial holy goodness, which is not just a matter of someone being good to me but of the world of holy goodness affecting me. In this goodness I in a certain sense encounter Christ, as we have said, and I hear his voice. This experience brings with it an entirely different dimension of happiness; it may liberate me in a deep way and awaken a *metanoia* (conversion) in me that no unbaptized natural love could awaken. So though Christian love of neighbor in one respect—the categorial respect—gives less than natural love, caritas involves a tremendous gift of its own. But of course the two dimensions of gift and happiness come together when a natural love is penetrated by caritas.

Love of neighbor in distinction to the mutual love of those united in Christ

In order to see that caritas is not limited to love of neighbor we have only to think of the love expressed in the words, "*Ubi caritas et amor, Deus ibi est*" ("Where charity and love prevail, there God is ever found"). And in the words, "*Congregavit nos in unum Christi amor*" ("The love of Christ has gathered us together"), we find a clear reference to the mutual love of persons in Christ and to their encounter with each other in Christ. This love presupposes the lived community in Christ, it responds to the other not only as image of God and as one beloved of Christ, but also as one who loves Christ.

This love is found in various forms. It can enter into all the natural categories of love, as when two persons encounter each other in Christ—when they are not just believers but have a relation that is situated in Christ. This can happen in the love between siblings, between friends, or in spousal love. But this love in Christ is also possible even towards persons to whom I have no particular natural love but of whom I know that they are believers and living members of the mystical body of Christ. In this case the union of love in Christ occurs "by itself." The two cases—a natural category of love receiving a new supernatural radiance by the encounter of two persons in Christ, and the bond between persons united in Christ but without the support of any natural love—

are of course profoundly different. We want to examine first the latter case; this will serve to bring out the difference between this love in Christ and love of neighbor.

First of all, the value responded to by the one who loves is different in each of these cases. Love of neighbor responds to the neighbor as image of God and as one who is redeemed and loved by Christ, whereas the love expressed in "*congregavit nos in unum*" responds to the other as one who loves Christ. Secondly, in love of neighbor the intentio unionis takes on a different character and remains more or less in the background of the relation. It does not involve joy over an already existing union; the union is not the central concern of the one who loves, nor is the happiness flowing from it. By contrast, in the love contained in the "*congregavit nos in unum Christi amor,*" the union is fully thematic and so is the happiness flowing from it; the union is not established by love but is rather presupposed by love. But this does not mean that the formal fact of a union as such engenders love (we have already seen that union as such is no foundation at all for love). It rather means that a union comes about through the shared love for Christ and through a supernatural bond in Christ in the kingdom of His love; this endows the other person with a new beauty and preciousness, making him or her loveable in a new way. We are about to return to the radical difference of this union, which precedes the love for another, from other ways of having something in common as well as from a mere ontological bond, such as that of part and whole. At present our aim is to work out still other differences between love of neighbor and love of persons in Christ.

Caritas is common to the two cases of love: both love of neighbor as well as the love of the "*congregavit nos in unum*" are fruits of caritas, being possible only through caritas. But we also find here significant differences. The anticipatory character of love of neighbor is not found in the same way in a love in Christ. Value-response is more prominent in this love. Besides, a different aspect of caritas stands out in each of the loves. With love of neighbor it is the holy substantial goodness and kindness of caritas, which gives an entirely new character to the intentio benevolentiae; with the love of the "*congregavit nos in unum*" it is the experience of the unifying power of the love of Christ, the transfigured harmony of charity, the blessedness of the holy union. Both are grounded in the love for God and are inseparable from the love for Christ. But whereas in love of neighbor Christ acts as it were in the soul of the one who loves and the neighbor is loved with Christ and through Christ, in the love of the "*congregavit nos in unum*" Christ is between us ("Christ is in our midst"), making for a love not only through Jesus but also *in* Jesus.[5]

---

5   Christian love of neighbor and a communion of love in Christ are not only different, but love of neighbor extends even to heretics, bad persons, enemies of God, with whom I should have no communion. Cf. the introduction to my book, *Celibacy and the Crisis of Faith.*

It follows that this latter love essentially presupposes mutuality. Being an encounter in Christ, it can only come about when the other experiences this communion with me. This is by no means necessarily the case with the love of neighbor. True as it is that the person filled with love of neighbor wishes for the neighbor to be drawn with him into the kingdom of the love of Christ, this is certainly not required for love of neighbor to come about, as we have seen.

In love of neighbor a definite I-Thou always predominates. I always face an individual Thou. The love of the *"congregavit nos in unum,"* by contrast, can refer to any number of others at the same time. It can refer to a community of many. It can even be realized in a we-solidarity, in a "we" that is gathered around Christ. But though it can, in contrast to love of neighbor, appear in this form, it need not; it can be fully realized in an I-Thou situation and in fact it reaches here its deepest and fullest unfolding.

This holy love in Jesus can appear in many different forms, as has already been said. First of all, it appears in the experience of the union that derives from Christ and is grounded in Him, and in the experience of the kingdom of Christ's love. That is the just-mentioned situation in which a number of people feel themselves to be united in the love of Christ. Here, too, each reaches out to the other with this holy love, which in its quality is saturated with the substantial goodness that, as we have seen, characterizes caritas.

But the encounter in Christ can be between only two persons meeting each other for the first time (recall the wonderful meeting of St. Louis of France with Blessed Aegidius). This love between two saints is an extraordinary case of the interchange of loving looks. Here we have a most excellent form of this love. Finally, there can be a lasting relationship of mutual love in Jesus, as we again find it in the lives of the saints, as for example the love between Blessed Jordan of Saxony and Blessed Diana, or the love between St. Francis de Sales and St. Jane Frances de Chantal. But for this of course there has to be some special religious ordination of the persons to each other and also an ultimate affinity of the two individualities. Here love implies a full response to the individuality of the other. It takes on an entirely new character as compared with love of neighbor; the love as love becomes much more thematic. Whereas in the previously-mentioned cases the harmonious union of hearts is the dominant theme, here it is love that is the main theme. What is common is the love *in* Jesus, encountering each other in Jesus. Here, too, it can be said, *"Congregavit nos in unum Christi amor. Et in medio nostri sit Christus Deus."*

Yet another and entirely different form of this holy love is found when it is joined with friendship or with spousal love. In these cases the love in Jesus forms as it were the crowning of the friendship (which as such may be situated in many other realms of value) or the crowning of the spousal love. We can also say that this holy love, this union in Jesus informs and transfigures the friendship or the spousal love. It always requires a special religious affinity of persons. Two friends may be deeply religious and yet their friendship need not include a love in Jesus. In the same way, a man and woman can love each other without their love being a love in Jesus, even though each of them is deeply religious. The more differentiated a relation between persons is, the greater must be their affinity in the religious sphere if a holy love in Jesus is to exist between them. On the other hand, we have to apply again what was said above about caritas penetrating all natural loves: only if persons encounter each other in Christ, transfiguring their natural love by a love in Jesus, does their love reach the unity to which it aspires.

We proceed now to ask how this holy love in Jesus stands in relation to caritas. We have already seen that it is clearly different in all its forms from love of neighbor, even when it is a love for a stranger. But it is no more to be identified with caritas than is the love of neighbor, for it has categorial elements that are not constitutive for caritas.[6] This follows from the fact that caritas is also found in the categorially very different love of neighbor as well as in the categorially still more different love for God. But the holy love in Jesus is inseparable from caritas and is a definite articulation of caritas. If I am to experience this union, this holy joy over my union with another in Jesus, my heart must be filled, at least at this moment, with the substantial goodness and kindness of caritas. As we said with regard to love of neighbor, so we say here: it is impossible really to experience this unity in Jesus, this *"congregavit nos in unum,"* while at the same time hating someone; to have the love for another in Jesus I must have entered into the kingdom of holy goodness, just as in the case of love of neighbor. But this does not mean that I cannot experience this love and then later fall out of this kingdom of goodness into an attitude of hatred for an enemy. What is impossible is only this: to live this holy love and at the same time to hate another.

This holy love in Jesus anticipates in a certain way our life in eternity, the love that fills the communion of saints. It is the love of which St. Augustine speaks in the conclusion of *The City of God*: "There we shall rest and see, see and love, love and praise. This is what shall be in the end without end."[7]

This holy love, categorially so different from love of neighbor, lives from caritas and has the qualitative characteristics of caritas; what St. Paul says about love in 1 Corinthians 13 holds for this love too. But whereas in the cat-

---

6   We cannot take this holy love in Jesus as a unified category of love all its own, for as we have seen it can appear in very various forms. A distinct category of love is found only in two of the above-mentioned forms, namely, in the individual holy love in Jesus that we find among saints, and in the case where this holy love embraces one or several persons with whom one has no lasting individual relation. We will limit ourselves to this latter case, in which the difference from love of neighbor becomes clearest, for this form of the holy love in Jesus is categorially rather closer to love of neighbor than the other forms of the holy love in Jesus.

7   St. Augustine, *The City of God*, trans. Dodds (New York: Random House, Inc., 1950), XXII, 30, p. 867.

egory of love of neighbor it is above all the intentio benevolentiae and not my happiness that is my central concern, in the category of the holy love, as we saw, my central concern is above all the union in Christ and the deep happiness flowing from it.

And it is not difficult to see how vast the difference is between this holy union in Christ and all natural ways of experiencing solidarity and community. We prescind here from all perversions of this experiencing, such as we find in nationalism or in family pride. We are thinking of the legitimate and morally unobjectionable experience of community, such as the joyful shelteredness in a family or the experience of solidarity with others in my nation, as when I return to it after being away for a long time, or as at great and significant moments in the life of my nation, such as being liberated from foreign rule. All these experiences of community have a we-character that lets us feel rooted together in the same soil and gives rise to a certain element of self-affirmation. But the experience of union in Christ as expressed in "*congregavit nos in unum*" has an entirely different character. This experience has something "hovering" [*schwebend*] about it; we are lifted out of any self-affirmation and are raised up into a holy unity that is not of this world. We experience ourselves as taken up into the kingdom of Christ, the kingdom of truth and holiness, into which we can enter only if caritas lives in us and fills us.

Love of neighbor and Christ's love for me

When we said that in receiving Christian love of neighbor we hear the voice of Christ and detect the breath of His holiness, we did not mean that the love of Christ for me has the character of love of neighbor. The love of Christ for each of us is categorially something entirely different; but it is caritas. One might be surprised to find us speaking of the love of Christ for me as if it were given in experience just like a saint's love of neighbor is given. But the love of Christ for me, in which every Christian believes and for which each yearns, has its own distinct categorial structure as a result of the fact that Christ is the God-man, the second person of the Trinity. The love that proceeds from the absolute Lord of heaven and earth, from the One who *is* Holiness, who *is* Goodness, who *is* Beauty, who *is* Love, as St. John says, has an all-encompassing character, which infinitely separates it in a categorial respect from any human love. It has been rightly said of God and of Christ that though He does not love all people equally He loves each one of them infinitely. Thus the turning to each human individual has one categorial character when it is God who loves and a entirely different one when it is a human being who loves a fellow human being with love of neighbor.[8] Even apart from the infinite superiority of God,

---

8   We have only to think of the relationships that the saintly Christian mystics had to Christ, and also of Christ's love for them, which they not only believed in but *experienced*: then we clearly see the categorial difference between Christ's love and Christian love of neighbor.

apart from the character of His merciful condescension, and of His movement down towards us, He turns to each individual in such a way that all the lack that we found in love of neighbor as compared to natural love, is abundantly given in Christ's love for me.

The categorial difference between His love for me, a divine love, and Christian love of neighbor stands out clearly as soon as we consider that in Christ's love for me the intentio unionis is fully developed, whereas it is restricted in the love of neighbor. To see this we have only to realize that in my love for God and for Christ the intentio unionis becomes a central concern. If I am asked what kind of return of love I yearn for, what kind of looking into the eyes of the other, then it is clear that, despite the infinite distance between my love for God and His love for me, some return of love is hoped for. This may seem paradoxical. On the one side there is the infinite love of the one who is Love itself, and on the other side there is the love of a human being for God that has all of the limitedness proper to a creature. How can one speak here of mutuality? But the point is not to assert any equality of human and divine love, but rather to show that God and man are here centrally concerned with the encounter of the two streams of love and hence also centrally concerned with the intentio unionis.

Even in the setting of the love between human beings there are cases in which the interlocking of categorially different loves forms the highest possible union. We have only to think of the love of parents for their children and of the love of children for their parents: the union that comes about here with the requital of love precisely presupposes the categorial difference between parental love and the love of children for their parents. These two kinds of love are such that the union desired in them can only be achieved by the interpenetration of categorially different loves. We find the same thing in the relation between disciple and master. The love of a Brother Leo for St. Francis had a different categorial character from the love of St. Francis for him, and yet in both of them the intentio unionis is fully given and the desired union comes about only through the interpenetration of categorially different loves. And so it is analogously with the absolute categorial difference of God's love for man and man's love for God. In saying "analogously" we mean of course that everything is utterly different in these two loves apart from the aspect of the fulfillment of the intentio unionis through the interpenetration of categorially different loves.

But our concern here is primarily to understand that the love of Christ for me—now as He sits at the right hand of the Father—does not have the categorial character of love of neighbor. For the union desired in the love of neighbor only concerns, as we saw, being united in the kingdom of Christ; it only concerns my neighbor responding to my love of neighbor for the sake of this union. Ardent as love of neighbor may be and much as it aims at the neighbor as unique individual, it does not establish any lasting personal union with him or her. Of course, a personal relation may develop where at first there was only love of neighbor, but for this to happen other factors must be at work. In love of neighbor as such this kind of relation is not sought or intended, but in Christ's love for me a full and lasting personal union is at stake. To see this we have only to ask what kind of union I desire in loving Christ, what requital of love I desire. Only Christ's love for me can fulfill my love with its intense intentio unionis. Despite the universality of His love, which extends to everyone, it responds to each individual in the most personal and intimate way, penetrating to the ultimate center of each individual's existence.

We said above that the love for God is categorially closer to spousal love than to love of neighbor; this throws a light on the categorial difference of love of neighbor and God's love for me. Infinitely different though the divine love for me is from spousal love, it must nevertheless possess all perfections of a categorial nature that love of neighbor lacks, and it must possess all that can fulfill the union desired by my love for God. We have only to posit for a moment the fiction that Christ's love for me is love of neighbor; then we will understand that this would not fulfill my yearning and my hope. If we think of the love of St. Peter for Jesus and of his words at the washing of the feet, we see the ultimate intensity of his intentio unionis and what a love he desires from Jesus. The *coincidentia oppositorum*, or union of apparent opposites,[9] that is found in God shows itself in the fact that God infinitely loves everyone and each one individually, and that God's love has nothing of the relative exclusivity of personal loves among human beings (and in the case of spousal love absolute exclusivity), even though He can enter into the deepest and most personal union with each of us.[10] It is no accident that in the Gospel God's love is so often compared with a wedding and that Christ is called the bridegroom of souls.

Great as the categorial difference is between Christ's love for me and Christian love of neighbor as practiced by human beings, still in both loves caritas is present. In Christ's love it is present with its infinite fullness, and in

---

9   We do not hold, as Nicholas of Cusa held, that we have here a coinciding of contradictory or contrary opposites; we speak instead only of polar opposites among certain values that exclude each other at a lower level of being. Cf. my *Ethics*, chapter 11.

10 We prescind here from the fact that the desired union with God infinitely surpasses all the kinds of union that are possible with creaturely persons. Entirely new dimensions of union are possible here and only here in relation to God, as we can see from the Christian belief in the indwelling of the Trinity in each baptized Christian, or in the Christian belief in the imparting of a new divine principle of life, sanctifying grace. And these beliefs refer only to our life on earth; the union with God that we hope for in eternity goes much further. But here we have pure mysteries of faith that cannot be the object of philosophical analysis, and so they fall outside of the focus of this work.

human love of neighbor it is present as a breath, a ray, so that we are entitled to say that we hear the voice of Christ in being encompassed by genuine Christian love of neighbor.

In love of neighbor, caritas takes the form of a diminished intentio unionis and it lacks the theme of happiness, but these traits result from the categorial characteristic of love of neighbor. They are in no way characteristic for caritas as such. For in our love for God, which is eminently caritas, we find the intentio unionis in its classical, typical form and we find as well a central concern with happiness.

The perfection of the natural categories of love through caritas

We have seen that caritas is not tied to the categorial character of love of neighbor, since love for God, categorially so different, is caritas *par excellence*. We can also see this independence of caritas from love of neighbor in this way: all the natural categories of love can and should be penetrated by caritas. As we have seen, this penetration by caritas does not involve any change of the given categorial identity. Neither spousal love nor parental love are deprived by caritas of their specific traits. On the contrary, it is only through this transformation in Christ that each of them can fully develop its "genius." The specific word of love that is uttered in each of them can reach its full and pure unfolding only if it is penetrated by caritas.

If we compare the "unbaptized" natural categories of love with those that have been penetrated by caritas, we see anew how wrong it is to identify caritas with love of neighbor, and at the same time a new light is thrown for us on the deep inner relation that essentially exists between natural love and caritas.

This penetration of the natural categories of love with caritas shows itself in the following way: the danger disappears of "egoism for the beloved person," which exists in all the "unbaptized" natural categories of love, where my love can betray me into harming some third person for the sake of securing a benefit for the beloved person.

I am, of course, justified in loving my own child more than someone else's child, and in loving only my own spouse with spousal love; there is no least trace of negative subjectivity in this, but rather a fully justified subjectivity, ordained by God. But it is regrettable if I put others at a disadvantage or am unkind towards them, for the sake of getting some good thing for the person whom I love. In the natural categories of love, I wish the beloved person well but do not enter into the kingdom of holy goodness and kindness so as to become, so to say, a universal lover, as we find it in Christian love of neighbor; as a result, it can happen that the special place that the beloved person naturally has in these categories is asserted without due restraint.

But this danger found in the natural categories of love is characteristic for them in a different way than the above-mentioned possibility of the co-existence of love for one person and hatred for another. For egoism for the beloved person follows from the inner logic of natural love; out of love for this person I tend to become egoistic in acting for him or her. But the hatred towards some third person has as such nothing at all to do with natural love; it does not follow from this love. It is just that love does not suffice to exclude hatred. This natural love in no way disposes us to hate a third person; on the contrary, the full actualization of natural love and the intentio benevolentiae towards the beloved person has rather a tendency that is opposed to any hatred. It is much more normal for hatred not to coexist with love, whereas the danger of egoism for the beloved normally grows out of the natural "unbaptized" loves.[11]

But this egoism for the beloved person is different from the other kinds of egoism. We saw above that in an egoistical love I remain stuck in myself, loving too little and giving myself incompletely. This egoism for the beloved person, this way of being unjust towards others as a result of being preoccupied with getting good things for the beloved person, cannot be called an egoistical love; it is rather an *egoism from love*. This is why it is by no means just an accidental distortion of love, whether in the sense of egoistical love or in the sense of other elements foreign to love that give love an egoistical note. It is a question of something that grows out of the inner logic of natural love when it is left to develop entirely on its own. The unique commitment to the beloved person, the interest I take in all objective goods for him or her, the self-transcendence of which we spoke in chapter 1, all result from my value-response to this individual person. The intentio benevolentiae is here a word spoken by me only to this person; my goodness and kindness is entirely embedded in the relation to him or her.

Thus this danger of egoism for the other can never be overcome by the intensity of love. On the contrary, the more ardent my love for another, the greater is this danger. As we will see later, it can only be eliminated by a strong moral consciousness or overcome from within by caritas.

The egoism for the beloved person that we have in mind must be sharply distinguished from the egoism for another that results from the other becoming an extension of my ego. In the case of the solidarity that grows out of being an extension of my ego we have an *égoisme à deux* (egoism shared by two people) or sometimes an *égoisme à plusieurs* (egoism shared by several people). It is pure egoism that makes a father use one standard for his own children and

---

11   There is, by contrast, a hatred that can grow out of a natural "unbaptized" love: if someone commits some great wrong against a person dear to me I may feel a hatred that is, as it were, a hatred "for the other," and in fact the more I love the other the more I will be inclined to hate the one who did wrong to him or her. This hatred, which cannot be separated in my motivation from my love, is clearly not just something that my love cannot prevent, as in the case of the above-mentioned hatred, but it follows from the inner logic of unbaptized love, just like the egoism for the beloved person.

another standard for other people's children and to seek advantages for his own that are at the expense of other people's. Those who act like this are egoists for themselves; the illegitimate preference for all those who are considered as an extension of their egos is really no real interest for the well-being of these others—it is nothing but an interest for themselves and for all that belongs to them. Although in many cases the result may seem to be very similar to the egoism for the beloved person that grows out of authentic natural love for him or her, these two egoists are in reality fundamentally different. The *égoisme à deux* is not different from the *égoisme à un* (egoism involving only one person). The egoist who sees another merely as an extension of his ego, extends his egoism to cover the other person. But in the case that we have called egoism for the beloved, the one who loves need not be egoistical for himself. As long as he does not love, he may consider very objectively and fairly the claims of others and be quite ready to make sacrifices for them, giving up his own advantage; but as soon as he ardently loves someone, he is so absorbed with providing good things for the other that he does not notice that he is imposing on third persons. The *egoist à deux* says, "My wife must have the better seat because she is my wife." The egoist for the beloved person says, "My wife should have the better seat because she is so good, so loveable, so precious." This latter egoism is not a consequence of everyday egoism, but is a way of being unfair out of love for someone; it is the intentio benevolentiae run amuck. It is obvious that this egoism for the other, though morally not in order, is morally much less bad than the *égoisme à deux*, for there is in it an element of genuine self-giving that is entirely missing in the latter.

But since attitudes that contradict each other can exist together in the same human being, which means that the solidarity with someone who is taken as an extension of my ego can co-exist with love for that person, the *égoisme à deux* and the egoism for the beloved person can co-exist in the same person. This happens most of all with parents, who often consider their children as an extension of their ego but at the same time really love them. But this always implies some defect of love, which, as we have already seen, necessarily involves a limitation of genuine love. But the possibility of a symbiosis of the two egoisms should not prevent us from seeing the fundamental difference between the two. At present we are mainly interested in the cases in which this egoism for the beloved person is only a consequence of the love for him or her. For this is the only case that can help us in working out the essential difference between "baptized" and "unbaptized" love.

The fact that egoism for the beloved person is incompatible with Christian love of neighbor may seem to be obscured by the fact that in some cases of apparent love of neighbor other people may be put at a disadvantage for the sake of the neighbor. We are thinking of cases in which I take on certain persons in a special way, such as crippled children, orphans, blind persons. It is not parental love or friendship that unites me with these people, but rather love of neighbor. But the fact that I work professionally with these groups of people, that my concern for them belongs to my work in life and even to my official work, makes their well-being my own concern. This is not, however, an outgrowth of pure love of neighbor. It can come from mere duty or from the particular significance of my God-given task. As long as the special attention that I show is only an outgrowth of the task entrusted to me by God and is experienced as such, it is not possible for me to put others at a disadvantage for the sake of a beloved person (which is not to deny that it is always possible for us human beings to fall out of a good attitude into a bad one). But it can easily happen that the mere fact of being committed to a good end makes me concentrate exclusively on it and thus makes me one-sided, so that I either see everything else from the point of view of this end or else entirely ignore everything else. This danger is found whenever I commit myself to some end; it is simply a consequence of human limitedness. I can avoid this danger only by going back again and again to Christ and by encountering Him in the depth of myself and so returning to the full freedom of love. But clearly the danger does not come from the solidarity of love of neighbor.

But the danger of egoism for my own task or project becomes great when something is my concern as a result of being taken into *my* professional work, so that, in addition to the formal commitment of myself to a project, I am involved in it to the point that it becomes a part, and perhaps even the most important part, of my own subjectivity [*Eigenleben*]. It is easy to see that this danger, even less than the previously mentioned one, in no way comes from love of neighbor as such, which perhaps played a large role in choosing the project and in carrying it out. This way of being inconsiderate towards all that falls outside the boundaries of my project—we can call it the egoism of the *idealist*—naturally has an entirely different character from everyday straightforward egoism. In the cases which we have in mind the egoism is penetrated by a value-responding commitment to some good bearing a great value. But since this commitment takes on further weight by being blended with *my own* work, there enters into my motivation an element of the extended ego. Thus in working on my project I push other people around and am unkind and inconsiderate towards whoever does not fit in with my project; I feel justified in using others ruthlessly in order to complete it. At present our goal is not so much to discuss this danger as an issue in its own right or to consider how it can be overcome, as rather to show that it is a failing that grows not out of love of neighbor but out of a distortion of our way of relating to our own projects. After all, the danger is just as real, indeed is still more real, in the case of a project or work that has nothing to do with love of neighbor, such as the work of an artist or statesman, or committing oneself to the triumph of some ideal.

And so we can rightly identify as a defining mark of love of neighbor in contrast to all other natural loves, which are possible even "among pagans," the fact that in the setting of these natural loves I can be inconsiderate towards others on the basis of love, whereas with love of neighbor this is excluded by caritas.

Even works undertaken only out of love of God and His honor can be undermined by being too narrowly thought of as *my* works and by being made the measure of everything else. For here too I may be unkind towards others and evaluate their destinies and wishes only from the point of view of what impact they can have on *my* work. This danger is particularly great since I wrongly think that it pleasing to God to act in this way; I think that I am acting for God's sake, that I am preferring God to everything else. But clearly this can never be taken as a danger that is intrinsic to the love for God. Illegitimately preferring those who have to do with my work is by no means a consequence of love for God. The immanent logic of genuine love for God—if we can even speak of "immanent logic" here—can never lead to an offense against love or to some injustice. We can apply to this love, which as we saw is a substantial goodness and kindness, the famous saying of St. Augustine, *"Ama et fac quod vis"* ("Love and do what you will"). When I yield to this danger I fall out of the attitude of love for God. Then it happens that a work undertaken for God's honor and chosen out of love for God, such as a missionary activity or founding a religious order, unconsciously becomes so much *my* work that it takes on a privileged position in relation to everything else, for I have made it my life's work. It is the immanent logic of the project to which we have dedicated ourselves and committed ourselves that leads to a lack of consideration for everything that does not belong to this work, and this is an attitude that precisely excludes true love for God.

The unloving behavior that seems to grow out of love for God

It is obviously still more impossible to think that I could become unkind and inconsiderate towards others out of the intensity of my love for God. This is impossible, first of all, because the absolute primacy of God in relation to creatures is such that any illegitimate preference is out of the question, and secondly, because God is infinite Love, so that the devotion to God can never make me less loving towards a creature.

But this fact is not inconsistent with the other fact that there are often people who are really harsh and unkind towards others and who think that they are acting from love for God. For in these cases there is in fact no genuine love for God, or at least the harshness does not stem from their love for God but from other elements of their nature which have led them to a false ideal of love for God. They may think that they are acting from love of God when in fact they are governed by completely different motives. We are thinking of cases in which religious people fall into fanaticism; in their fight for the kingdom of God, which they make into some kind of ideal, they are betrayed into a loveless severity (we might think here of Pope Paul IV, Caraffa). In such cases there is a genuine love for God, but that is not what elicits harshness and severity;

this is rather elicited by a kind of commitment to an ideal imposed by the massive pull of the zealots' fallen nature, by the cramp of their idealistic involvement. They forget that God is infinite love and they confuse fighting for God and His honor and His kingdom with a merely natural zeal, a zeal that treats God like an impersonal ideal. In these cases, though they fight *for God* they do not fight *from God*, they do not fight out of the spirit of love for God, nor are they filled with caritas.

Or think of all the cases in which I might advocate in a rigoristic spirit a false supernaturalism, thinking that I may, indeed should, set aside all human points of view and be concerned only with the salvation of my neighbor's soul, disdaining his earthly well-being as unworthy of my attention. Here too we have to repeat what was said in reference to love of neighbor: such a failure of love is not a result of the love for God; it has as such nothing to do with love itself, but is the consequence either of fanaticism or of rigorism, of making God into an ideal or of living by a false conception of God.

Although religious people are often affected by these distortions, we nevertheless see clearly the mentioned difference between love for God and all natural categories of love. These distortions are a danger rooted in fallen man but not a danger that is intrinsic to the love for God.

We now see clearly that neither in the case of the love for God nor in the case of Christian love of neighbor can there be the danger of illegitimate preference. For all the disordered attitudes that we have mentioned in connection with love for God and with love of neighbor are born not of the inner logic of these loves but rather born of some pseudo-love for God, or else of abandoning the love of neighbor and falling into some very different attitude. In Christian love of neighbor, as we have seen, each and every way of being good to the other is an outgrowth of being filled with holy goodness and kindness; all love of the other is an outgrowth of the fact that I have become a lover simply speaking and of the fact that love of neighbor is grounded in love for God and cannot be separated from it. And so it is right to say that it is caritas that excludes any and every egoism for my neighbor, even though the categorial character of love of neighbor also seems to exclude it. For the category of love that we call love of neighbor is possible only on the basis of caritas; it lives from caritas, even if caritas itself does not depend on the categorial character of love of neighbor.

But when we say that the love for Christ, and in Him the love for God, makes each person a lover simply speaking [*schlechtweg*], this should not be misunderstood in the sense of a false irenicism. Becoming this kind of lover means here only that I am not just good to one particular person but that the holy goodness and kindness dwells in me and that I approach all persons with this goodness and kindness. But this lover also hates everything evil and is even ready to take up the struggle against evil. True Christian love of neighbor is also distinguished by holy strength and is completely penetrated by zeal for

God's honor. Of course, it excludes the hatred (we spoke of it above) that is no value-response but only an outgrowth of pride and concupiscence.

We have to realize that hatred can mean many different things. There is first of all the bitter and hostile attitude that grows out of pride and concupiscence, which are in themselves evil and which make a person evil. Second, and radically different, there is the value-response that rejects disvalue, evil, untruth. This hatred is an eminently moral stance of a person, for it is a necessary consequence of loving God. We cannot love truth if we do not hate fundamentally false theories such as relativism, immanentism, or materialism. We cannot love virtue if we do not hate vice. We cannot love morality if we do not hate sin. We cannot love God if we do not hate the devil. Thirdly, there is a hatred that first appears as a value-response, thus distinguishing itself entirely from hatred in our first sense, but that becomes disordered because I reject evil in another person in such a way as to reject completely the whole person. We should hate all evil in the enemy of God and fight against his efforts at poisoning the souls of others, but we should at the same time persevere in loving the immortal soul of this person, who does not lose the beauty of the image of God as long as he lives. I have spoken at length about this in my book, *True Morality and Situation Ethics*.

For our purposes it is very important to see that true love for God and love of neighbor exclude hatred only in the first and third senses; hatred in the second sense is not only compatible with caritas, but is a necessary element of it.[12]

Two dimensions of the conquest of egoism for the beloved person

But one could object as follows. Granted that it is caritas that makes love of neighbor possible, it can still not be denied that the danger of egoism for a beloved person is mainly found in those loves having a strong intentio unionis and a strong presence of the concern for happiness. It is only when the other has become an objective good for me in the sense explained in chapter 5, it is only when love has the character of a super value-response, that the danger of egoism for the beloved person is really present. Even if it is right to say that Christian love of neighbor lives only from caritas, it may still be the case that the egoism for the beloved person is missing as a real danger in part because the beloved person does not occupy the special place that comes from being an objective good for me.

Of course, in a purely negative way the categorial identity of love of neighbor excludes the danger of egoism for the beloved person, for there is missing here the factor that gives rise to this danger, namely, the role that the beloved plays in my subjectivity in all the natural categories of love. But it is

---

12   Cf. the introduction to my book, *Celibacy and the Crisis of Faith*, and also my book, *The Trojan Horse in the City of God*.

caritas that in a positive way overcomes and excludes this danger by its very quality, by the holy goodness and kindness that essentially belongs to it. This is why this danger can be entirely overcome in every natural category of love insofar as each category is penetrated with caritas. Of course, the occasion for this danger, not to say the temptation to it, is not missing in these other categories of love as it is in love of neighbor.

We can see something analogous in the double meaning of "selfless," discussed above. Love of neighbor is "selfless" by its very categorial character, for in this love we in a sense step out of our subjectivity. In this sense "selfless" does not have a specifically moral meaning. But insofar as this love is filled with caritas and lives from it, insofar as it is selfless in its quality rather than in its categorial character, it is "selfless" in the moral sense of the word and forms an antithesis to all forms of egoism. So it is precisely the comparison between the "baptized" natural kinds of love and the "unbaptized" natural kinds of love that shows forth both the independence of caritas from the particular situation proper to love of neighbor, as well as the fact that only caritas lets the natural kinds of love fully unfold their genius.

We saw that it is entirely legitimate that the beloved person is a great objective good for me and that his happiness is my happiness; in fact, this is proper to the nature of love of children for their parents, of parental love, of love between friends, and above all of spousal love. It is entirely legitimate that the well-being of the beloved person concerns me more than that of others and engages me in a more elaborate and intensive way than that of others. It is right here in this legitimate preference for the beloved person that we find the possibility and danger of sliding into an illegitimate preference and of being inconsiderate and unkind towards third persons. It is very important to explain clearly the boundary dividing the illegitimate preference from the legitimate, or in other words to identify the moment at which the legitimate one gets derailed into an illegitimate one. For the present it suffices to show that a genuine love for someone, such as the love between friends, parental love, spousal love, does not exclude this derailing and can in fact easily end in this way as long as these loves are not transformed by Christ and penetrated by caritas.

The penetration of all other categories of love with this stream of caritas, with this entirely new kind of self-giving and goodness, is very organic; it brings to perfection the specific categorial character of a given love and confers on its intentio unionis and its intentio benevolentiae a vastly more genuine character, endowing it in fact with a completely new kind of sublimity.

This penetration of all other categories of love with the stream of caritas calls for the primacy of love for God in the soul of the one who loves. The love that is penetrated by the spirit of caritas is thereby in a unique way filled with the spirit expressed in the words of Christ: "Seek first the kingdom of God and His justice." The spirit of caritas establishes a human love so strongly in the world of moral values and of the divine law that everything morally bad is experienced as the enemy of the mutual love and its union. We saw above that love for God and love of neighbor include all morality and that the theme of this love cannot be detached from obedience to divine commands, from walking the paths of the Lord, from striving for holiness. "If someone loves me he will keep my words." The natural categories of love, as we saw, do not have this theme, but rather a different one. But now we have to add that even they, insofar as they are transformed in Christ and penetrated by the spirit of caritas, are so established in the moral world of value, so flooded with the breath of fear of God and love for God (though without ever giving up their particular theme), that they can never lead to doing wrong for the sake of the love. We mean that the dangers found in "unbaptized" love (much more about them in chapter 12) are not simply blocked from without in the given natural category of love but are uprooted from within. This holds both for the danger of setting aside a moral law for the sake of the happiness that comes from union with the beloved person, as well as for the danger of bestowing benefits on the beloved person at the expense of others, in other words, of acting unkindly towards others for the sake of the happiness of the beloved person.

The influence of caritas on natural love compared with the influence of moral conscientiousness

In order better to understand how these dangers in the natural categories of love can be uprooted by being penetrated with the spirit of caritas, we want to make the following comparison: we compare the way in which these dangers can be dealt with by a morally conscientious non-Christian, with the way in which they can be dealt with by the spirit of caritas entering into the natural loves. There are undoubtedly people who, even if they love someone very much, would, in the event of a conflict between the happiness of this love and a moral law, follow the moral law. These people understand the primacy of moral obligation over even the most noble earthly happiness. Their basic stance to life is completely formed by a fundamental moral attitude, by the will to do nothing that their conscience forbids on the grounds of it being morally wrong. The supreme case of this attitude is found in Socrates, who said, "It is better for man to suffer wrong than to commit it." Even if such people love a person to the point that he or she stands at the center of their lives and is the main source of their earthly happiness, they will, if the happiness of their love should conflict with a moral law, follow the call of the moral law. Thus if a beloved person were to require them to approve of something they take to be morally wrong, they would refuse, even at the risk of losing the love of that person. If their dearest friend were to require the advocacy of something involving a moral wrong, they would not do it, even if the friendship were to break up over this. They would not act like a mother who approves of some wrong done by her son so as not to lose his love.

But we cannot say of such people that their love is different from the love of those who do not acknowledge the same primacy of morality over earthly happiness. Their love does not show a new quality and is not a more genuine or a deeper love; it is just that they acknowledge the general primacy of morality.[13] In this way, a limit is set from without on their love. They say in effect, "I will gladly do anything for you and make any sacrifice for you, but I cannot act against my conscience." Their love is not as such established in the world of moral values; it remains qualitatively like any "unbaptized" love, but a protective wall is set up—the fundamental moral attitude that stands next to this love has the last word. And it has the last word not only for one's own behavior but also for the behavior of the beloved person. The one who loves will accept any sacrifice rather than allow the beloved person to go morally astray. And yet the love is not changed from within as in the case of "baptized" love.

We clearly see how this is different from the case of penetrating the natural categories of love with the spirit of caritas. Here the love for God, from which flows the primacy of morality in relation to earthly happiness, does not just stand next to these loves, imposing a limit on their tendencies in the event of a conflict, but here the natural love, as we see, is penetrated by the love for God and by the holy goodness and kindness of caritas; it is established in the world of God's holy law, formed from within, so that it takes on an entirely new quality.

First, in the case of spousal love, if it is filled with the spirit of caritas and is formed by love for God, I feel that any wrong to which my love could seduce me is not only an offense against the divine law but also is something opposed to the spirit of spousal love, something incompatible with it. Or if the beloved person should wish for something that I know to be morally wrong, the pain over not being able to fulfill his wish would be less than the pain over the beloved person wanting to do something wrong. I would realize the incompatibility of his wish with true union; I would feel all that separates us from God as being also a betrayal of the mutual love. The love of the morally conscious person, for whom the moral question has the last word, can be called an "ordered" love; but when a natural love is penetrated by the spirit of caritas it becomes an incomparably greater love, it becomes more love—more authentic love.

A second essential difference between the "baptized" love, the love transformed in Christ, and the love of the morally conscientious person is this: the unique quality of caritas is missing from the latter, the quality that brings each category of love to its true fulfillment. The more noble a man, the higher his

---

13 But in chapter 12, part 2, we will see that even the natural moral attitude of one who loves has an essential impact on the quality of his love. But this has nothing to do with the transfiguring, supernatural quality of caritas, nor does it suffice to take the external limit imposed by morality on love and to turn it into an inner transformation of the love as such.

position in the moral world, then the more noble and qualitatively higher will be his love, whether it is his spousal love or his friendship or some other love. But the sublime quality of caritas is in relation to all of this something entirely new. It involves entering into the kingdom of goodness and kindness, a breath of holy goodness and kindness, an entirely new fire.

Third, the protective wall erected by the fundamental moral attitude against the dangers of natural love does not extend nearly as far as the "redemption" of natural love from its dangers that comes from love being penetrated with the spirit of caritas. Even if the morally conscientious person, who has a sound fundamental moral attitude, follows the voice of his conscience in the case of an open conflict between his conscience and the supposed happiness of the beloved person, his conscience raises its voice only in relatively massive cases. He would not, like José (in the opera *Carmen*), desert, become a smuggler, and live with Carmen. A father would not consent to something dishonest, obviously wrong, in order to help his son out of some predicament or to secure his future. But that is, as it were, only the external fortress of the morally good. He is not protected by his fundamental moral attitude from yielding to jealousy, or from measuring the interests of the beloved person with a different standard than he uses for all other people. In saying that he yields to jealousy we do not mean that he inflicts harm on the beloved person out of jealousy or on third persons who cause the jealousy, but that he yields to bitterness and has an inner attitude towards third persons that is devoid of love.

Above all, he is not aware of the boundless dimension of selflessness that is found in a love in spite of its ardor; he has no idea of the dangers of creeping egoism, no idea that the way of becoming ever more selfless (without giving up the full intentio unionis and the theme of happiness in love) is as it were an infinite way, that each selfless step that is taken has to be followed by very many further such steps, or as we could as well say, that at each level of selflessness I can always find new hiding-places in which my egoism is lurking. The fundamental moral attitude of which we have spoken simply does not suffice to make us notice the dangers that result from wanting to give joy to a beloved person by giving him or her gifts but doing so in such a way as to seek my own happiness more than that of the beloved person. Only the spirit of caritas gives us eyes and ears for this and enables us to seek the happiness of the other ahead of our own, but of course without blocking out the interest in our own happiness. We can sum up by saying that the morally conscientious person is protected against the dangers of love only in the case in which love collides with the world of moral values; this protection does not amount to the moral transfiguration of love itself.

We want to make a point of saying that in overcoming all egoism through this moral transfiguration of love by means of caritas there is no question of giving up the concern with happiness that is immanent in all the natural categories of love. That would be to fall back into the mistake that the intentio unionis, and the yearning for the happiness that flows from it, are incompatible with selflessness. This error involves the equivocation that we already pointed out: one alternates between understanding the term selfless in the sense of stepping out of one's subjectivity, as we see it in the love of neighbor, and understanding it as the antithesis of all egoism.

We mentioned above the following form of hidden egoism: in wanting to make beloved persons happy, I seek mainly my own joy in making them happy. We want now to add that this does not mean there is any least trace of egoism in being happy by making the other happy. On the contrary, there would be no love at all without this, and certainly no spousal love, or love between friends, or parental love; nor would there be any increase in selflessness. The only thing that is egoistic is intending this happiness of mine in the place of the happiness of the beloved person. With all gifts that I give to the beloved person the happiness of this person must be the main motive and main concern. But my being made happy by doing good to the beloved person is absolutely essential if I am really to love him or her; I just have to see to it that my happiness is not my main motive. This is why the decisive question to be asked about a particular expression of my love is whether it really makes the beloved person happy at this moment. Maybe the thing I want to give her will not please her, or will even be a burden to her because of special circumstances of the moment, or maybe an expression of my love could be too much for her at a moment when she is exhausted. A spousal love penetrated by the spirit of caritas will not just yield to the urge to heap gifts and expressions of love on the beloved person but will listen closely to when and how and by what the beloved person can be made happy. But both the urge to give gifts to the other as well as the deep happiness that this imparts to me have nothing to do with egoism. These things belong to love, to its beauty, and also to making the beloved person happy; for it belongs to making him or her happy, in the case of a mutual love, that giving a gift makes the giver happy. The most precious thing about a gift is after all the expression of love, and this includes the giver being happy at being able to give. If the beloved person who receives the gift has the feeling that the giver is not made happy by giving, he would feel a kind of cold breath, a vacuum of love.

Let us return to our main subject, which is the difference between neutralizing the dangers of love by a fundamental moral attitude and overcoming them by the spirit of caritas. This deep and fundamental difference now stands forth clearly and it shows us the very special connection of all the natural categories of love with the world of moral values, a connection that comes about when they are penetrated by the spirit of caritas. The main element in caritas that brings this about is one that we have previously discussed: the *amare in Deo*, or establishing a love in the holy world of God and letting this love be penetrated by ultimate reverence for the holy law of God. What we are aiming at is the overall state of soul marked by goodness and kindness; it involves entering into the kingdom of the love of Christ and having a heart melted by Christ and His love. If this state of soul is realized—it could also be described as the dominance of the reverent and loving self—then a word full of goodness and kindness is spoken to the other; this breath of goodness and kindness is given to the other through love, penetrating the heart with joy and warmth.

If now a spousal love is penetrated by this spirit, if it arises from within a person who is full of goodness, if it flows from a heart melted by Christ's love, then this love takes on an entirely new quality, which is at the same time the crown and fulfillment of the intentio benevolentiae proper to every love; and the intentio unionis, far from being weakened in any way, becomes thereby deeper, purer, more complete, more sublime; it too can fully develop its own genius only through this quality of goodness.

The gift of love, the gift of myself, of my heart, becomes what it intends to be according to its genius only by way of this quality of goodness. If this quality penetrates spousal love, a real renunciation of all forms of egoism (more on this later) follows. And the renunciation of all egoism is not only towards the beloved person, but also towards other persons for the sake of the beloved person. This love then becomes such that any and every egoism towards other persons for the sake of the beloved person is felt to have a jarring sound, to be incompatible with the love because it is incompatible with Christ. This is not to deny that we have to be constantly on guard against falling into egoism and to be constantly beginning anew in resisting egoism. But this work consists precisely in letting our love be penetrated again and again by the love of Christ, in letting it be again and again permeated by the spirit of goodness and kindness.

But it is very important to see that the interest in the objective good for the beloved person reaches an entirely new level in caritas. To see this we have only to compare the love for a friend, for a brother, for parents, or for a spouse that is penetrated by caritas with the "unbaptized" love of the same category. First of all, the real objective good for the other person is discerned in each situation with a new kind of clarity. Caritas opens my eyes for what is really beneficial, because it sees everything in the light of God. The boundary dividing the true objective good from what is just intensely desired, the higher objective good from the lower, the lasting from the transitory, is given with full clarity only to the eyes of caritas. Secondly, the full transcendence involved in willing something "for the other" is present only in caritas. Only here can we really will that which makes the other happy while leaving intact the categorial identity of the natural love. Only this holy goodness enables us to live the commitment involved in the "for the other" while entirely preserving the categorial identity, the ardently desired intentio unionis, and the (secondary) concern with happiness. Once again we see the difference between caritas and the benevolence that flows from a serious moral attitude.

With this we come upon another trait of human love that is penetrated by caritas: in spite of the central role of the intentio unionis, the well-being, happiness, and salvation of the beloved person has an absolute priority over my union with him or her. We already spoke of this above when we were showing that the intentio unionis as such has no egoistical character, that egoism comes from reversing the inner order of love by putting my union with the other in the first and highest place. But at present we want to show how the love penetrated by goodness and kindness, which is a flowing goodness and kindness, contains as an essential element this primacy of the happiness of the beloved person. This moment is deeply connected with the self-giving of love, at least with one dimension of self-giving. To put my union with the other above the well-being, happiness, and salvation of the other is incompatible with this quality of caritas, with this holy goodness and kindness.

How caritas preserves and completes the *logos* of every natural category of love

We have to stress once again that the spirit of true love not only does not take away the categorial differences, but even makes us more alert and more sensitive to each kind of love. This spirit of love, far from leveling the different loves, requires that we do justice to the inner demands of each of them. This is in fact a specific fruit of caritas, a specific manifestation of it. It would be opposed to love not to give to the other that which corresponds to the *logos* of the relation, to the word of God spoken between us. This gentle listening to the *logos*, this alertness to its demands, belongs to the spirit of caritas. If I encounter a close friend in the same way I encounter a stranger whom I approach with love of neighbor, I obviously act in a loveless way; I deny to my friend the inner word that is due to him as friend and that I previously spoke to him as our friendship came into being. Thus there exists a deep link between the spirit of caritas, this flowing goodness and kindness, and the particular word of love that is proper to the different categories of love. Though this word as such is different from the quality of caritas, this quality, this spirit of love, still requires that I should utter to a beloved person that word of love that corresponds to the given category and logos of the individual relationship. It is not opposed to love if I do not enter into friendship with someone, if there is between us no particular word spoken by God. The same holds for spousal love. But if I have entered into a friendship, if this is granted to me, or if I receive another with spousal love, then the spirit of love prescribes to me a certain word as being due to the other, and it is opposed to love in the sense of violating the spirit of love for me to refuse the word to the other, or to love him or her only with love of neighbor. This holds both for the word of love itself as well as for all manifestations of it even in the sphere of volitional behavior. Thus what we have to understand here is that a way of acting that does not correspond to the particular demands of the *logos* of a relationship, not only involves a lack of faithfulness to the beloved person, but offends against the spirit of love, against caritas. This throws light on the particular link between caritas and each category of love.

Two forms of "natural love of neighbor" in contrast with Christian love of neighbor

Let us continue examining the difference between that which comes from the categorial character of love of neighbor and that which comes from caritas. It can happen on a purely natural level that I take an interest in some stranger who is neither my friend nor my brother or sister, and that I can open my heart to him or her. This is just as possible "among pagans" as friendship, parental love, or spousal love is possible for them. There are people with a distinctly good heart who approach everyone, and especially the needy, with a kind and sympathetic heart. This loving interest in everyone whom I encounter can also be the result of conscious moral striving. But this natural love of neighbor in both of its forms, though it seems to resemble Christian love of neighbor, is essentially different from it. Only Christian love of neighbor merits the name of love in the full sense. We will see this clearly by analyzing more closely the two forms of natural love of neighbor and comparing them with Christian love of neighbor.

Let us first examine the kind and benevolent person who on the basis not of his high moral consciousness but of his good heart approaches everyone with a friendly readiness to help. It is by no means necessary that he be a morally conscious person. Tom Jones in the novel of the same name by Fielding, though a typically morally unconscious person, has this kindness of heart that lets him approach every stranger with sympathy and readiness to help. Even though this type stands in contrast to the person whose benevolent attitude towards others is an expression of serious moral striving, his behavior is much closer to morality than is similar behavior in the other natural categories of love. For this benevolence is not morally indifferent; it has a certain moral value and is above all a loveable attitude. But its moral incompleteness stands out as soon as we consider that this benevolence—for it is no real love but a benevolence and a loving sympathy—easily puts me in a position in which I cannot say no to anyone, so that I yield to others where morally speaking I should not (which also fails to serve the real well-being of others).

This inability to say no should not make us run together this general benevolence with good-natured laziness. There is a type of good-natured person who wants to avoid conflict under all circumstances. These people want to live in an atmosphere of harmony with everyone, in part because of a certain laziness, and this is why they never say no. They dislike the "effort" of enduring disharmony and of having to disturb the peace more than they dislike the "effort" of performing a real service for others. They are specifically good-natured but lack the deep benevolence that entitles us to speak of a good and kind heart. They are friendly and ready to do anyone a favor, but they do not have the real readiness to serve that was discussed above. They would really rather be left in peace, but they are ready to help anyone who turns to them. They are more interested in a peaceful and quiet atmosphere than in the well-being of others. This is reflected in the way they take an interest in others: their interest awakens only when another appeals to them.

Even more do we have to distinguish the person possessing natural kindness from another type, namely, from persons who cannot say no simply because they are too weak to offer resistance. They lack any real benevolence and any real goodness. They give in out of weakness, letting themselves be used by everyone, because they have neither the strength nor the courage to resist.

Finally, the naturally benevolent person should not be confused with the person who is friendly and helpful to everyone because he enjoys having a certain social image. He enjoys himself in the role of one who is friendly to everyone and who is therefore loved by everyone. No, we are thinking of one who has real goodness of heart, who has truly selfless benevolence for all others and genuine sympathy with them.

But there is also the type, as we have already indicated, whose fundamental moral stance makes him concerned and ready to help even in relation to others with whom he has no special personal affinity and no kind of objective bond. He does not have to have a good heart, nor does he have to have the attractive kindness of heart that can go so far as to block the ability to say no. Rather, he is animated by the will to do the morally right thing. Such a person apprehends the moral significance of the just demands of strangers. We are thinking of the concern and the benevolence that a great moral personality like Socrates possessed. This benevolence born of a fundamental moral attitude is much more pronounced among certain people in our time who, though not Christian believers, have nevertheless taken over many Christian elements in their understanding of the moral universe; in this way the benevolence takes on a more universal character.

The attitude of the one whose good heart disposes him favorably to his neighbor is warmer; but the attitude of the one who acts in a morally conscientious way is more awakened, more consciously enacted, more a matter of principle. The attitude of the former is more human, the attitude of the latter is emphatically more moral.

We prescind here from the love of "mankind in general" that is born of a certain humanitarian ideal. This attitude of the philanthropist is the outgrowth of a certain abstract ideal and has nothing of the warmth or of the benevolence of the naturally good-hearted person. It is much farther removed from real love than the naturally good-hearted person is. The philanthropist is interested in the other not as this individual but as an instance of the human species. And he does not take the other fully as person but rather as an object of the benevolence that flows from his philanthropic ideal. Even all real transcendence is missing here, all real interest "for the sake of the other." One remains enclosed in oneself and in one's abstract ideal, and one's beneficent deeds have an almost professional character. As Dostoevsky puts it in *The Idiot*, "Abstract love of humanity is almost always self-love."

When we spoke of the *apparent* similarity of the natural love of neighbor and Christian love of neighbor, we wanted to say that both of these loves, although at first glance seeming to have some formal elements in common, are after all fundamentally different. For all that goes beyond these common formal elements is profoundly different, and not only that, but even the common formal elements reveal on closer inspection a significant difference. For these elements all have to do only with the categorial characteristic of love of neighbor and in no way with Christian love as caritas.

But first we want to survey all that these two loves—the natural and the Christian—have in common. 1) We find in both loves a relation to persons to whom one has no particular personal bond of the kind that we find in all the other natural categories of love; thus all the motives are missing that are otherwise found in a natural love. 2) The concern with my happiness, present in all other natural loves (even if only in a secondary way) is missing both in the natural and in the Christian love of neighbor. 3) The intentio benevolentiae whether of Christian or of natural love of neighbor does not derive from a value-response to the neighbor, but rather anticipates the encounter with the neighbor. Take the person with the warm heart: his interest in his neighbor is a result of his good heart, which precedes the encounter with the neighbor. This is even clearer in the other case of natural love of neighbor, the case of the morally conscientious person. Here the fundamental moral stance is the root of the kind attention to one's neighbor and not the value-response to this person's dignity and beauty, which touches the heart. The fundamental moral stance goes ahead of the encounter with the neighbor. 4) The moral theme is found in both kinds of natural love of neighbor, even if in different ways. Morality is much more thematic in them than in all the other natural categories of love; this, too, draws natural love of neighbor into the categorial proximity of Christian love of neighbor.

But the radical difference between these quasi-loves of neighbor and Christian love of neighbor stands out clearly when we consider that the former are not really love, whereas Christian love of neighbor constitutes a full and real love. We saw in chapter 2 (where we analyzed the essential traits common to all kinds of love) that love of neighbor, despite its categorial peculiarity, shows all the essential traits of genuine love: we now add that these are missing in both forms of natural benevolence. For both of these lack the full concern with the other person as this person, the value-response to the other, the specific word of love that is poured into the soul of the other, warming him or her with happiness. Both lack any and every kind of intentio unionis, and this in contrast to Christian love of neighbor. In the case of natural benevolence sprung from moral conscientiousness, the moral theme overshadows a real interest in the other as such. For the other is more someone-who-gives-rise-to-a-moral-obligation than this individual person as such. The value-response of the will in this case refers more to the need of the other, or to his or her rights, than to the other as person. The intentio benevolentiae does not have much of an affective character; it does not encompass the other as a whole. It does not include taking a special interest in the other as such. Not even the benevolence of the warm-hearted type of person constitutes real love, even if it has a warmer and more affective note, for it formally lacks the character of a response, lacks the specific response of love—the self-giving and the unique kind of interest taken in the other.

Now when we say that this natural kindness and benevolence formally lacks the character of a response, we do not mean to say that it does not have the structure of an intentional act. Someone sees another in need and responds to this need with compassion and the readiness to help. Or someone is asked by a stranger for something and he responds with a kindly interest and is ready to fulfill his request. The character of a response is missing from these benevolent acts in the sense that they are not a response to the particular beauty of one's neighbor. In contrast to the love between friends, to parental love, and especially to spousal love, these acts are not value-responses to the person of the other; and in contrast to love of neighbor these are not responses to the dignity that each human person has as image of God and as a being who is loved and redeemed by Christ. It is rather the warmheartedness as such, the capacity for sympathy that engenders this benevolence without letting it become a value-response. Of course, even in the case of love of neighbor, as we saw, the state of soul of the one who loves, the full actuality of the reverent and loving self, plays a decisive role. But love of neighbor also has the element of value-response, indeed it is necessarily realized only in a value-response. Every love of neighbor necessarily has the consciousness of the ontological dignity of one's neighbor, of the beauty that he has apart from his particular individuality and cannot lose as long as he lives.

Even if sympathy and concrete attention to another are not only intentional acts but value-responses to the need or happiness of another, the benevolence as such does not have the character of a value-response. But above all this benevolence is no real love; what is missing is the self-giving that is characteristic of love, the affirmation of the person of the neighbor that surrounds him with goodness and kindness, and raises him up. In every other natural love we find this self-giving, this affirmation of the beloved person, this gesture of surrounding and elevating the beloved person with the intentio benevolentiae, of course always joined with the intentio unionis.

The central difference between this benevolence and love is shown in the fact that in the love of neighbor the intentio unionis is not missing, but has a different character. It does not aim, as in the human loves, at union with the beloved person but rather at unity in the kingdom of Christ. But with the natural benevolence the intentio unionis is entirely missing, because there is no interest in the other person as a whole.

The supernatural basis of Christian love of neighbor

But the decisive difference is to be found in the nature of the substantial goodness and kindness that is proper to caritas, in the loving fundamental attitude that dwells in the one who is possessed of Christian love of neighbor. Since this love is caritas, it is separated by an abyss from the quasi-love of neighbor, which is something merely natural. The triumphant, transfigured goodness and kindness, in which strength and meekness interpenetrate, is missing entirely in the benevolence, winning though it may be. An analogous difference is the one between the agreeable modesty of someone who stays in the background because he realizes the superiority of others, and the glorious virtue of humility.

In Christian love of neighbor there is always a movement of rising up into the ultimate reality of the world of God, of breaking out of the prison of the purely earthly, everyday world. Whereas the natural benevolence remains confined within the limits of the earthly interpersonal sphere, there is a breath of triumphant freedom in Christian love of neighbor. As soon as we encounter an act of true Christian love of neighbor, it is as if heaven were to open, as if we were to be elevated into the world of the absolute, as if we were to feel the breath of the greatness of the infinite. We need only to think of the scene in the novel of Manzoni, *The Betrothed*, in which Cardinal Federigo Borromeo receives the unnamed man: this suffices to let us grasp clearly these essential features of Christian love of neighbor as caritas. This breath-taking greatness is closely related with the fact that the love of neighbor is based on the love for God, and on seeing the neighbor in the light of God, indeed in the light of Christ. The neighbor shines forth in the radiance of the fact that Christ loves him or her infinitely and died on the cross for him or her. Genuine Christian love of neighbor always contains within itself a victory over the world, a reaching out into the unbounded depth of the world of God. There is nothing of all of this in natural benevolence. There is in it no breath of the infinite, of ultimate greatness and freedom, of victory over the world, nor does it see the neighbor in this supernatural light. We said above that whoever is received by an act of Christian love of neighbor hears the voice of Christ. There is nothing of this when someone encounters me merely with natural benevolence. The substantial holy goodness and kindness of caritas is constituted, as we saw, in the love for God and cannot be separated from it. By contrast, the "good heart" of natural benevolence, as well as the fundamental moral stance of the other form of natural benevolence, are not grounded in the love for God; they can co-exist with love for God, but they do not flow precisely from it; they are not any actualization of the love for God.

Let us just consider what it takes to help us break through to love of neighbor in the case of a person who greatly disgusts us and angers us, such as an Iago, or a Father Karamazov. We have to get beyond all that this person has made of himself, beyond the entire atmosphere which he exudes and into which he wants to draw us, beyond the level on which he meets us, and we have to break through to the situation in which he stands before God. Even if he denies the existence of God, in reality God speaks even to him saying, "Adam, where are you?" In reality he too stands before God and awaits the judgment of God. Then suddenly the wretched, miserable, repulsive world in which he has placed himself drops away from view and we stand before the tragic greatness of a person who, created in the image of God, has given himself over to the devil. We penetrate to ultimate valid reality, to the way God sees things, and then our soul grows wings, wings for the merciful love which despite everything encompasses this person. We have only to think how greatly we are helped to break through to a real love of neighbor by having this view of the kingdom of God, and then we understand the inseparable bond between love of neighbor and love for God. And with this we understand how great the divide is between love of neighbor filled with caritas, and all merely natural benevolence.

Thus Christian love of neighbor extends not only to the foreigner, but also to my rival, my opponent, my enemy, indeed even to the enemy of God. But with the forms of natural benevolence the intentio benevolentiae is restricted to the stranger who is a kind of *tabula rasa*, but it does not extend to my rival, my opponent, my enemy, and certainly not to the enemy of God.

In Christian love of neighbor we find a *coincidentia oppositorum*, or union of apparent opposites, insofar as in loving the enemy of God I do not overlook or belittle his faults. Christian love of neighbor is organically linked with entirely rejecting the sin of the enemy of God. The natural benevolence in both of its forms stops as soon as I see clearly the hatefulness of the enemy of God and fully reject it.[14] This incompatibility of benevolence with clearly knowing and unambiguously rejecting the evil attitude of the enemy of God, shows itself differently in each of the two forms of natural benevolence. In the case of the person whose benevolence is a matter of moral conscientiousness, his rejection has the effect of limiting his love. The person who is benevolent because of his good heart has the tendency to back away from an unambiguous rejection of evil and to adopt instead a *laissez faire* attitude towards it.

Conclusion on natural and supernatural love

It is not our task here to give a full account of the quality of caritas. This has been done in 1 Corinthians 13 in a way that cannot be surpassed or even com-

---

14   "It is almost impossible to me sometimes to stand people *with* God; without God, it would have been impossible." Baron Friedrich von Hügel, *Letters to a Niece, xxv–xxvi.*

pleted. But if we now summarize what we have already said about the nature of caritas, the difference between it and all natural concern for my neighbor will stand out more clearly. First we have to distinguish between caritas as a quality of love and as the categorial characteristic of love of neighbor. This emerges from the fact that the quality of caritas is not only found in the love for God but can be constituted only in the response to God, even though the categorial characteristic of love for God is clearly different from that of love of neighbor.

We further saw that all natural categories of love can be filled and pene-trated with this caritas, and in fact that only in this way can they fully unfold their own proper genius. This is why the contrast of eros with agape, or of *amor concupiscentiae* with *amor benevolentiae* is misleading. We already saw in chapter 6 that it is false to call any love with an intentio unionis by the name of eros and to call love of neighbor, where the intentio unionis is much reduced, by the name of agape. We have to add that it is a major mistake to place the difference between eros and agape on the level of categorial charac-teristics. This also holds for spousal love, which is altogether different from all other natural kinds of love and which has a categorial structure that forms a contrast with love of neighbor: it would be entirely false to identify spousal love with eros (though this is suggested by the term eros) and thus to oppose it to agape. The real datum that one is aiming at with the distinction between eros and agape is to be found in the quality of love, in the spirit of caritas, which is essentially bound to love for God and love of neighbor. This quality of love is not only compatible with the categorial identity of the different kinds of love, but it is the principle of the perfection of each kind of love in its spe-cific genius.

And so if we gather together all natural kinds of love, which are possible even "among pagans," and call them eros, taking as the distinguishing mark of eros not the categorial identity of any one of them but rather the fact that they have not yet been transformed by Christ, that they are purely "natural," and if we contrast eros in this sense with agape understood as the spirit of caritas, the incomparable quality of caritas, then we are contrasting eros and agape in a way that is not only fully justified but that serves to point out something emi-nently important in the sphere of love.

But this difference is not an antithesis. With this we come to the decisive point of our investigation. If we take eros in the sense of the quality of the nat-ural kinds of love and contrast it with the quality of caritas—and this is the only correct way of distinguishing between eros and agape—then we have a significant difference, but not an antithesis. There is an analogy to the relation between natural and supernatural morality. Supernatural Christian morality, centered on holiness, is something qualitatively entirely new in relation to merely natural morality, something that completely surpasses natural morali-ty; but it forms no antithesis to natural morality, but rather fulfills it and transfigures it. And so here. In every natural love, even in the most imperfect, there is, insofar as it is love, a reflection of caritas, a certain image of it, a "seed" that tends to a fulfillment that this natural love can never attain by its own strength but that it nevertheless calls for. This is why it is entirely false to deny any moral value to this purely natural, still unbaptized love and to treat it like a morally neutral instinct. Not only does it possess the high personal values that are proper to every genuine value-response, such as enthusiasm over beauty in nature and in art, it also possesses a certain moral value, though this comes in different degrees.

Of course we have to repeat what was said at the beginning of this chapter: there is, morally speaking, a vast distance between love for God and love of neighbor, on the one hand, and all other natural kinds of love, on the other hand. The love for God includes all of morality, and the love of neighbor is inseparably bonded with morality. The natural categories of love never include all of morality, they never coincide with morality, not even if they have been transformed by the spirit of caritas to the point that they take on a quality that manifests a sublime, supernatural morality and in this way gives glory to God in a special way. But if they have not been so transformed, then the difference between them and the love for God and the love of neighbor is immeasurably great. They do not include all of morality in the way in which the love for God and the love of neighbor do (if only because of the categorial character of these loves); we rather have here a very great difference between the quality of caritas and any purely unbaptized natural love, a difference that, as we saw, does not coincide with any categorial difference. And as we said, this difference stands out clearly when we compare the "baptized" natural categories of love with the "unbaptized" ones.

But even the "unbaptized" natural love is a bearer of moral values, though these may be more or less; even in the most imperfect love there remains, insofar as it is love at all, a moral value. For an essential core of love qua love remains common to eros and agape, in spite of their difference. This may have been what Lacordaire had in mind when he said: "There are not two loves, one of them heavenly and one earthly. There is just one single feeling, with the difference that the one is infinite."

CHAPTER TWELVE

Love and Morality

We have already on various occasions pointed to the manifold relationships between love and morality. The main thing we saw was that love for God is not only the bearer of the highest moral values but that it encompasses morality in its entirety, and that love of neighbor is inseparable from morality. We need not go into this eminent connection between the spirit of caritas and moral goodness. Aside from the fact that this connection is obvious, we have already considered it extensively. Here it is our goal to study the much looser and also much less obvious relationship of all categories of natural love—such as parental and filial love, love between siblings, love between friends, and spousal love—with the sphere of morality. Of this, too, we have already spoken on various occasions. We pointed to the moral value which these kinds of love can possess, and this even prior to their being transformed in Christ and filled with the spirit of caritas. We must now pose the question in its full breadth: what relationships exist between these kinds of natural love and the sphere of morality?

The question of the relationship of natural love in all its various categories to the sphere of morality comprises both a positive and a negative aspect. The question includes the moral dangers which are bound up with these categories of love and, above all, the moral values of the person that are bound up with and generated by love.

Part I: Love and Moral Dangers

We begin with the negative aspect and ask what moral dangers in general lurk in natural love, and for what failures it can be made responsible? In the second part of this chapter we will then go into the relationship between natural love and morality from a positive perspective.

Life as well as literature offer many examples which show that love in the life of a person can play a morally fatal role. In the case of José in Bizet's *Carmen,* which we have frequently drawn on as an example, we must say that his love for Carmen became fatal for him from a moral perspective. Had he not met Carmen and fallen in love with her, he would have remained as he showed himself in the opening scene with Micaela. He would not have become a deserter or a smuggler, he would not lived with Carmen as a concubine, he would not have become unfaithful to Micaela, he would not have become a murderer out of jealousy. Many examples of this kind could be cited. Analogously, even if in any entirely different way, Chevalier des Grieux became involved in many moral wrongs through his love for Manon. Did not Antony get himself into no end of trouble through his love for Cleopatra? Was it not the love for Vronsky which led Anna Karenina to adultery, and was it not above all the love for Faust which led the innocent and kindly Gretchen to become guilty? Almost everyone will have met someone who has experienced something analogous.

One could say that moral dangers are only to be found in the love between man and woman, in the love which is organically tied to sensuality. Yet this would be erroneous. Even if there are particular dangers which only occur in this kind of love, there are also moral dangers in the love toward parents, toward children, toward siblings and toward friends. We have only to think of a love, such as that of Balzac's Pere Goriot toward his daughters, or of the many cases in which an intense loves brings a mother to the point of acquiescing in moral wrong done by a son or daughter. Or there are all the cases in which the love toward a brother or friend drives someone to do morally wrong deeds which he would never have done of his own accord.

The question which concerns us here is the following. In what sense does a particular morally negative stance originate in love *per se* when we say of someone, "This love was his downfall," or at least, "Without this love he would not have done this or that wrong"? What is the connection between such a natural love and moral lapsing? To what extent is it a matter of moral dangers which are really intrinsic to natural love and really an outgrowth of love?

The danger of preferring to commit a wrong rather than to renounce some happiness that is in itself good

Often there is the general danger of human beings preferring to contravene a moral command rather than to forego some good which they intensely long for. As long as we are dealing with goods that particularly satisfy pride and concupiscence, such as power, an influential position, fame, public success, it is just a typical case of the moral drama of human existence: the conflict between the power of attraction of the merely subjectively satisfying and the demand of morally relevant values, which is the conflict between two fundamentally different categories of motivation. Yet a conflict can also arise between the possession of goods capable of bringing deep happiness and the moral imperatives rooted in morally relevant values.

When, for example, a Catholic marries a divorced woman whom he deeply loves, we have not only to do with a conflict between something merely subjectively satisfying and the moral imperative; we have rather to do with the lofty good of marriage with a beloved person, on the one hand, and the religious imperative, on the other hand. We are dealing here with the moral demand to sacrifice the highest earthly joy, one of the noblest forms of happiness. This kind of conflict can arise in the case of many goods. When a great conductor prefers to make compromises with a totalitarian regime, such as the Third Reich or Soviet Russia, rather than to refrain from performing in these countries where he is able to unfold his talent in a unique way, it is a good with real value that prompts him to compromise with evil rather than to sacrifice the good.

Whenever my heart is attached to a good with great intensity, a good which is meant to bring me happiness and which in its capacity to bring happiness is morally altogether unobjectionable, I may be in danger of being unwilling to refrain from it, even if I am morally required to do so. The inner conflict here is not that between pride and concupiscence, on the one hand, and an attitude of reverence, love, and value-response, on the other. It is also not the conflict of something legitimately satisfying and pleasant for me and the demand of morally relevant values. Rather it is a conflict between the possession of a good with high values, which is meant to bring us happiness and which as such is a great gift from God, on the one hand, and the moral requirement to refrain here and now from it for the sake of certain morally relevant values, on the other hand.

It is the danger that our interest in a legitimate good becomes disordered, with the result that we place it above the commandments of God. This danger has often led people to consider it morally safer not to allow one's heart to become attached to a creaturely good so as never to be in danger of offending God by seeking to possess this good under all circumstances, or, if one possesses it, by striving not to lose it. Yet this is surely an erroneous conclusion.[1]

The true conclusion to be drawn from this danger is rather that one is only protected against it if one loves God above all, or, on a purely moral level, if one understands the absolute priority of moral requirements over everything else, even in the face of the greatest happiness, and if one always gives first place to moral requirements. It would be false to believe that indifference toward all high creaturely goods makes us more alert to the world of moral values and more ready to follow them. Equally false is the view that our love for God becomes greater if we become insensitive toward all natural values, which after all also herald the glory of God, and if we refrain from any special love for a human being. Moreover, it must also be emphasized that a true interest in a high good is not somehow weaker if one loves God above all things, for there is no greater love for a good than when it is loved in God. And when people try in this way to avoid the danger of violating God's commandments or

---

1   St. Augustine speaks against this when he says: "Are you supposed to love nothing at all? Certainly not. If you did not love anything you would become inert and dead human beings, contemptible and wretched. Love, but take care what it is that you love." *On the Psalms*, 31, 2. 5.

the requirements of morality, they are liable to another great danger, namely, the danger of becoming cold-hearted, and isolated in their pride.

But this is not our theme at present. We want to point out that the danger of committing a wrong rather than losing the love of a beloved person, the danger of yielding to the beloved even if he would prompt us to something wrong out of fear of him turning away from us, is a particular case of the general danger of preferring to do what is morally wrong rather than to lose a good which is the source of a great joy. One cannot make the *love* for a person, be it spousal love, the love of a mother, or any other love, more responsible for this danger than any deep attachment to a high creaturely good. Rather, we must say that this general danger in man not to follow the moral call because one is not ready to renounce some deep legitimate happiness (or to muster the strength to make this decision), *also* exists in all unbaptized human loves. This danger does not flow from the fact that a love is *too* great, too intense, but because it is disordered, that is, because the general primacy of moral obligation over happiness does not exist in the lover, or expressed religiously, that he does not love God above all things. Not the magnitude of the love but the general moral state of the lover is to blame for the fact that he does what is wrong. We could as well say that even his love reflects his general moral vulnerability. It is not a specific aspect of love, something in its special word and content, which produces this danger, nor is it the intensity of love as such, but rather the general danger of placing one's happiness—one's earthly happiness, to be precise—above the moral law.

However, this general moral danger in man, which is *also* to be found in natural unbaptized love, is at the same time also an offense against love, an infidelity to the genius of love. And this is of great significance, because it shows us that this danger does not derive from love qua love and that when, on the occasion of a love, the disordered desire for happiness and an overall false value hierarchy assert themselves, this is at the same time a betrayal of the genius of love. When one says, "Had this person not loved, he would not have gone astray," one must understand this only to mean, "Had this person not been put to the test, his weak moral stance would not have come to light and would not have led to sinful deeds." The greater the temptation, the greater the danger of falling. A person who is never put into a situation in which there is conflict between moral demands and a good capable of imparting great happiness, may not go astray, but not because of the primacy of moral demands over all other things in him.

It is true that love, like every deep attachment to a good endowed with true values—be it beauty in nature or in art, or truth in philosophy or science—and every deep experience of being moved by a value, makes the one who loves lay aside all mediocre safeguards against making mistakes. Love always has the character of an "adventure." If one makes the absence of danger into an ideal, then the drooling idiot is the ideal. In clinging to mediocre safeguards taken against all possible missteps, one not only removes all greatness from life but all moral greatness from it, indeed one locks oneself into a stance which is by no means morally unobjectionable, even when it appears that a person has in no way gone astray. One holds on to the mediocre safeguards, not because one above all wishes not to offend God, but because one likes the pleasant feeling of a false security, because one wants to avoid reaching for deeper safeguards, for safeguards which originate in the confrontation with God and the love of God. Indeed, one wants to protect oneself precisely against this confrontation.[2]

Influence of the beloved on the one who loves

The second general source of danger in natural love is the bad influence the beloved can exercise on the lover.

Both spousal love and the love of friends, or the love for a child and the love of a child for its parents, opens the lover to the influence of the beloved. It lies in the nature of love to open oneself trustingly to the influence of the beloved person, be it the influence of ideas, perspectives, or principles, be it an influence on our actions, or be it a joyful desire to go along with the beloved person. This influence, which takes on many forms, plays a special role in the love of children toward their parents, since parents, after all, represent a moral and spiritual authority. It belongs to those things which in themselves are good, which are an avenue willed by God to help us and then lead us to the good, but

---

2   We have been speaking of the general danger of violating moral laws so as not to have to lose or to give up some good that confers happiness. But in the various categories of love there are other elements that can contribute to a moral failing. Thus in the love between man and woman there arises sometimes a concupiscent passion that does not belong to love as such. We are not thinking here of the legitimate use of sensuality, that is, of the desire for union that belongs to the meaning and nature of this love and that includes becoming one flesh. And we are not thinking of being enchanted with love and ardently longing for this union. We are rather thinking of a dark passion, a puzzling kind of sensual attraction that gets connected with love, though it only exists next to love and, far from being an organic expression of it, is rather a factor opposed to love. It compromises and pollutes love. It is possible only with a love that is engendered primarily by vital values. This element (more about it later) is in a different way responsible for much immorality, since it is, in contrast to love, itself a dark passion of morally dubious character. Something similar arises in the case of the love of a mother for her child and leads to all kinds of moral disorder: we refer to an animal-like solidarity that is definitely not love but is rather a solidarity with the child who is taken as an extension of the mother's ego. It can thus be something extremely primitive and even have the character of a kind of dark passion. This, too, coexists with love, even if not just in an accidental way; it is not a fruit of love, but rather, on the contrary, something that pollutes love. As we said, we will return to the moral dangers of these factors that coexist with love.

which at the same time can become disastrous when the influence comes from someone who is morally unworthy and dangerous. This holds for every influence, not only for the one that arises out of love. It holds for the influence of the teacher, the master, the role-model in any field—wherever one person has influence on another. It also holds for the influence of a milieu, a tradition, etc. The danger exists whenever the content of the influence is bad; but when it is good in respect of its content, then the influence becomes a blessing. That a person is exposed to influence is something good and belongs to human nature. The moral danger which it can present is a part of the general danger to which fallen man is exposed *in statu viae* (in his earthly existence).

When, then, we are faced with the possibility of bad influence which can pass from a beloved person to the lover, we should not see this as a moral danger rooted in love. The fact that through love one becomes receptive to the influence of a beloved person can as such in no way be described as a moral danger, since this influence can as well be morally beneficial as morally harmful.

There are, however, kinds of influence which in themselves are illegitimate irrespective of whether the content of the influence is good or bad. To these belongs the nearly hypnotic effect that some people have on others. To influence a person in such a way as to bring the person to the level of a depersonalized dependence and to circumvent and assault the spiritual center of freedom in the other person, this is something illegitimate and morally ominous regardless of the direction in which the influence is being used, whether for evil or good. In a similar manner, every kind of brainwashing, every brutal manipulation of the associative mechanisms and imaginative sphere of a person, is an illegitimate influence on the grounds that it is also a depersonalizing influence. And of course the influence exercised by means of terrorism and intimidation is intrinsically wrong, even if one is trying by these means to keep people from immoral behavior.

The question now arises for us: does the influence made possible by love belong to the legitimate forms of influence, or does it contain an illegitimate element? Is the influence which Faust exercised on Gretchen only regrettable in its moral content or is it regrettable in the very form of the influence? The legitimacy of the influence, after all, hinges primarily on whether it addresses the other person as person, whether it takes the other seriously as person. As long as one influences persons in such a way as to convince them or to provide their spirit with nourishment, as long as one opens them to values and helps them truly to grasp values previously unknown to them, one addresses them as persons. The more alert and clear-sighted their minds thereby become, the better for this kind of influence. Similarly, the influence is completely legitimate when one guides them as a legitimate authority, for one here appeals to their free act of submitting, to their free will. Again, when a master authoritatively teaches his disciples, it is a legitimate influence, since the influence, after all, rests on the recognition of the disciple that the master is more capable than he is, at least in a particular field.

When we love someone, his influence acts on us primarily by making him more able to disclose new values to us, to initiate us into new worlds. The revelation of values is in a special way facilitated through the devotion to the beloved person, through the *sursum corda* (lifting one's heart towards higher things) immanent in all love, through the exposure of one's own soul to the beloved, through the radiance which extends from the beloved person to everything he values.

Another thoroughly legitimate influence arises out of love from the fact that, as St. Augustine says, one becomes like the person one loves. This influence grows out of the self-donation that lies in the value-responding character of love and through it the person actualizes himself as person.

Yet is the influence which Faust exercises upon Gretchen not of a different kind? Is it not as a kind of influence that goes beyond the just-mentioned influence? Does not love make Gretchen see right and wrong with less clarity? (We are, of course, prescinding from the breakthrough in the last scene of the first part of *Faust*.) Does not her love make many things seem morally permissible which in reality are not? We are not thinking here of an influence towards something bad, the possibility of which, as we saw, does not represent any moral danger on the part of love qua love, but we are thinking of the reality which Gretchen brings to expression in the words: "*Doch—alles, was mich dazu trieb, Gott! War so gut! ach, war so lieb*" ("And yet everything that drove me to it [yielding to Faust] was so good and, yes, so pleasant").

There are of course many elements in this case which have nothing to do with love as such: the innocence of Gretchen, which goes together with a great naïveté, her way of looking up to Faust as her superior in regard to his intellect, his knowledge, and also his status as lord. All of this constitutes the possibility of an influence that cannot be attributed to love as such. This influence, which rests on an assumed superiority, is a superiority which the naïve person is not really capable of assessing, and it can easily also have the character of a formally illegitimate influence. After all, this kind of influence also exists in cases where there is no love, as in cases where a person impresses another through his real or supposed superiority. As always, we must keep in mind here that love can coexist with many elements which in themselves either have nothing to do with love as such or which sometimes even contradict the genius of love. Never can any influence that emanates from these elements be attributed to love as such; they may be formally illegitimate and thereby give the false impression that formally illegitimate forms of influence are found in love.

A typical form of such influence is an addictive dependence [*Hörigkeit*] on a person, which sometimes goes hand in hand with certain kinds of love. In reality, addictive dependence is by its nature opposed to love. Not only can this dependence exist without love—which, in fact, is typically the case—but in its subpersonal, enigmatic character it is antithetical to specifically personal love. Unlike love an addictive dependence is in no way a source of joy. Though it can coexist with love, it goes without saying that this typically illegitimate form of influence should by no means be considered as something founded in love as such. It also often happens that a husband, a beloved person, a friend, a mother or son is by far the more dynamic and dominant personality and is therefore capable of exercising an influence which is in no way is the result of love. This influence, which merely results from a dynamic predominance of one person over another, can just as well exist without love. It, too, since it is something subpersonal, is thoroughly antithetical to love as such, and yet it can coexist with love.

We want to prescind from all of these "accidental" factors as we start from examples in literature with our work of examining the influence of the beloved person on the one who loves him or her. Our question is: does my love grant the beloved a *formally* illegitimate kind of influence? Without a doubt this must be answered in the negative. In every instance where an illegitimate influence exists between those who love each another, it can be traced to factors which only coexist with love. Naturally, one cannot deny that the legitimate channel of influence brought about by love can become dangerous through the qualitative content of the influence. Yet, as has already been mentioned above, this is rooted is the tragic situation of human beings.

We will now turn to moral dangers which are not only general dangers that can be found, among other places, in love—such as the danger of preferring to do something immoral rather than to sacrifice (or even just to risk losing) the joy that flows from love, as well as the danger of being influenced in a bad direction—but dangers that are specific to love and more closely connected to it.

The danger of a morally illicit relationship in the love between man and woman

To begin with, we must mention the danger that exists in the love between a man and woman, namely, the danger of an illicit physical relationship. We are here thinking neither of the temptations that grow out of a sensuality isolated from love, nor of the temptations in which sensuality attaches itself to a peripheral kind of "being in love." Sensuality in this case is, as it were, the formal principle; and this concupiscent desire lacks all of the essential characteristics of authentic being in love, such as reverently looking up to the other, a value-responding enchantment with the other, a certain humility before the other, and a greater spiritual alertness and gentleness. This temptation to yield to an isolated sensuality, which is the danger of impurity in the proper sense, is banished by every authentic love. Love reveals the true meaning of sensuality—namely the great and profound meaning of bodily union as the fulfillment of a personal union—and so love is the greatest natural protection against these temptations. We are rather thinking here of the danger that exists in a real love—the danger of the lovers being swept away into a bodily union when this is not possible (or not yet possible) in a legitimate and sanctioned way. We have in mind the case in which this bodily union is entirely understood to involve a full commitment and a lasting bond. This danger of being swept away into such a union outside of marriage is admittedly inherent in this kind of love. We are thinking, for example, of Anna Karenina and Vronsky or of Gretchen in *Faust* or of Francesca da Rimini or of Abelard and Heliose or of Chevalier des Grieux in *Manon Lescaut*.

In each of these instances we encounter the desire and longing to belong entirely to the beloved person. It is a desire that grows organically out of this kind of love. This longing can become a great temptation and lead to a moral fall. One is tempted to say that in this case it is the ardor and intensity of this love that is at fault, for here it is not just a coexisting factor that is at fault, nor is it any other general moral danger. To sin out of an isolated sensuality is utterly different from this longing and is different from it in every essential respect. This moral danger arises logically, as it were, from the categorial character of this kind of love whenever—for whatever reason—sexual union is not possible with the sanction of marriage. And yet if one looks closely, one can see that such a fall is also a betrayal of love, that it is something that from the standpoint of love is short-sighted. This is because the mutual sin, rather than bringing about union, brings about separation. In order to be the fulfillment of the longed-for union, the sexual relation must for the Christian be sanctioned by God; and sheltered in this divine sanction it must be sanctioned by the lovers and must not have the character of a unsanctioned state of being swept away. We have dealt with this in extensively in an earlier book, *Purity*.

But there is also an analogous conflict for the non-Christian. If, for example, a person is married and his behavior involves infidelity toward his spouse, then this adulterous union would lack moral sanction and, because of the way in which the couple is carried away, would lose its capacity to constitute a true and real union. Since it is poisoned by a bad conscience, this union even carries within itself an element of separation.

Here it is enough to establish that this fall cannot be attributed to love or its ardor and intensity; instead it has to be attributed to an absence of moral alertness and to the fact that the primacy of the moral sphere above everything else is not sufficiently secured, which in turn undermines the ultimate depth of this love. Also lacking is a full understanding of the mystery of sexual union; this lack is another deficiency of the love. At issue here is a moral danger that arises from the fact that the love between man and woman has not yet reached the full maturity of its genius, has not yet arrived at its full depth. It is therefore impossible to show that a moral fall comes from a tendency rooted in the nature of love as such. The failure is rather rooted in the imperfection of the given case of love, which in turn originates in the moral deficiency of the overall state of the couple.

The danger of love degenerating into passion

It must be pointed out emphatically that yet another general source of danger comes into play here. It is the danger that arises as soon as an affective value-response degenerates into a passion. In our book *The Heart* (Part I, chapter 2), we have discussed the difference between a passion and a value-response in great detail. This deep difference within the affective sphere has for the most part been overlooked; accordingly the notion of passion (*passiones*) has been construed very broadly (this is the case with many Scholastic concepts).

The difference is in no way one of degree. In their dark and irrational character, in their tendency to cloud the mind and to assault the free center of a person, as happens with ambition, avarice, and the desire for revenge, these passions are already distinguished from value-responses by the fact that they are in no way motivated by values but by something merely subjectively satisfying, that is, that they are rooted in pride and concupiscence.

It can also happen that under particular circumstances certain value-responses take on a character that has much in common with real passions. For example, a given case of anger, which as such is aroused by an objective injustice and which represents a value-response—in this case, a value-response to a disvalue—can often reach the point at which one is completely "besides oneself" and no longer knows what one is doing. Though this anger is very different from passions that are by nature dark and destructive and that in their qualitative character cloud the mind and eliminate freedom, and though it is qualitatively good and is justified (as being a right response to certain disvalues), it can nevertheless degenerate into an affective state which in its way of clouding the mind and dethroning freedom is formally similar to the anger that is not a value-response and that is a typical case of a passion. That this goes hand in hand with a particular degree of anger, with the power and intensity of it, should not mislead us into thinking that every affective value-response, if it reaches a particular degree, takes on the traits of a passion. There are many affective value-responses which, even when they reach the highest pitch of intensity, never take on the character of a passion. Thus holy joy may lead to ecstasy, to the true loss of self which is the radical antithesis of being swept away by passion. The most ardent love of God can never take on the traits of a "passion" in the precise sense of that term. Protection against the degeneration into passion is not to be sought in a lesser intensity of the affective value-response but in interior formation of it, in the transformation of it through Christ, as I tried to show in my book *The Heart*.

The danger of a value-response giving way to a passion as long as it is not transformed in Christ, however, depends very much on the character of the value-response. Certain affective value-responses, such as righteous anger, are exposed to this danger much more than a value-responding joy or a value-responding sadness.

Now the love between man and woman also belongs to those affective value-responses which, as long as they are not transformed in Christ, are vulnerable to turning into passion. This love can assume a dark character that creates confusion in the mind of the passionate person, so that he ceases to be his own master. By this I am in no way referring to the true loss of self that love ought to possess, to the way in which one is lifted beyond oneself, and to the character of a certain enchantment which the Song of Songs brings to expression so wonderfully. For all of this belongs to the very nature of the love between man and woman and is not weakened but rather elevated when this love is formed in Christ. We have in mind instead the character of a dark passion. It is an element that greatly varies according to the individual quality of a love. It is more traceable to factors that coexist with love than to love as such. All the same, so long as spousal love remains unbaptized, the danger of giving way to passion cannot be denied; it is primarily the danger of seeking an unsanctioned bodily union. We discussed earlier the danger of an illicit relationship between man and woman that is bound up with this kind of love; to this we must now add that the danger also arises when this love takes on the traits of a passion. But as we have already said, this represents a betrayal of the genius of love.

Jealousy

Jealousy represents an entirely different moral danger which can arise in all categories of natural love and which for the most part finds its most dramatic expression in the love between man and woman. Jealousy as such has the character of a passion and not an affective response. Yet it stands in a deep and meaningful relation to love. We are not thinking here of an unfounded jealousy, a jealousy which has its roots in the character of a particular person. We are rather thinking of the jealousy of a person who, justifiably or unjustifiably, believes that a third person is stealing the heart of one whom he loves, and who therefore feels a hatred for this third person and a desperate anger toward the beloved person. We are thinking here of the jealousy of Othello or Medea, without thereby excluding other forms of jealousy, such as that of a child towards his siblings who, whether in fact or just in his perception, are depriving him of his mother's affection, or the jealousy of a mother toward another person whom her child, whether actually or only in her perception, loves more than her.

In contrast to the pure sorrow over the unfaithfulness of a beloved person, this jealousy, in its bitterness and animosity, is always something dubious. Worse still is the fact that jealousy for its part runs the danger of leading to actions, whether to small ones like acts of unkindness or to major ones like the murder of the beloved person or of the one who deprives me of his love.

That jealousy can lead to immoral actions is obvious. Yet in order to understand that jealousy is in itself something morally negative—though it is very human to feel jealousy, and deeply understandable—we must penetrate more deeply into the nature of jealousy. We will, therefore, now attempt to clarify what jealousy is and to distinguish it from much else with which it can easily be confused. And first of all, jealousy must be clearly distinguished from *envy*.

The envious person is filled with *ressentiment* towards another person because this person possesses certain goods which he does not. The fact that the other may be richer, more influential, more powerful, or more famous, that he may be more intelligent, kinder, or more beautiful, that he may in some respect be happier, awakens in the envious person an enmity and a hatred toward him. The envious person begrudges the other his excellences and happiness, and in fact he takes satisfaction in the other losing his excellences and becoming miserable. The theme of envy is not the appropriation of the goods that make the other happy, but rather the fact that the other possesses them. When the goods in question are such that they could be stolen from the other and taken for oneself, such as wealth or an influential position, envy does not aim at taking them but at their owner losing them. The thief who robs a wealthy man is not driven by envy but by avarice. The envious person is satisfied if the wealthy man goes bankrupt, whereas this in no way satisfies the avaricious person. Someone who is envious of a colleague is satisfied by the colleague's failure, even though this in no way makes him any more famous. The envious person is satisfied when a person of attractive appearance is disfigured through illness. He is filled with malicious joy [*Schadenfreude*] when a virtuous person of whom he is envious has a moral lapse. The satisfaction that he, who gains nothing, takes in the other person losing something is typical for envy and for the moral baseness which makes it worse than all avarice and ambition. The root of envy is pride mixed with concupiscence. Envy has no tie whatsoever to love.

In envy the objective good for the other person also plays a decisive role. In his begrudging spirit the envious person takes aim at what is objectively good for him. This is what he begrudges the other person. The envious person does not so much suffer from the fact that the other is subjectively satisfied but from the fact that the other is in possession of goods which are objectively good for him. He begrudges the beautiful person his beauty, the healthy person his health, the intelligent person his understanding, the famous person his fame, and the virtuous person his virtue. Envy and avarice, then, are distinguished from one another like this: the avaricious person does not know the perspective of the objective good for the person but only that of the subjectively satisfying.

If the envious person knows this perspective, he knows it only in the negative way in which it is known by the person who hates. The hate-filled person wants to inflict objective harm on the hated person, whereas the envious person wishes that the other lose the objective goods that he possesses. The envious person is angered that the other possesses them and takes satisfaction in him losing them. Envy therefore forms a specific antithesis to love, which, as we saw in chapter 7, precisely rejoices at all objective goods for the other and also rejoices "for the other."

Jealousy is both formally and materially entirely different from envy. In the first place, one notices the completely different qualities of envy and jealousy—the entirely different word that is spoken in each of them. In jealousy the anger goes hand in hand with a deep pain; the jealous person is consumed by a fire, and his heart is torn up by despair, anger, sorrow, agitation, love, and hate. The envious person looks at the other with evil, hate-filled eyes; he is not filled with deep pain, nor does his heart bleed like that of the jealous person, nor does he despair. The envious person is indeed dissatisfied and interiorly poisoned, but hatred, a squinting and begrudging spirit, and malicious joy are the most characteristic of the envious spirit. The jealous person awakens our pity, the envious person our antipathy. Above all, in envy there is no element of love. We do not mean that it is impossible under particular circumstances to feel envy towards a person one loves. But in envy qua envy there is no element of love. When love and envy coexist, they just stand side by side. In the case of jealousy, on the other hand, love is always presupposed; indeed, love is always an essential factor in the response of jealousy.

In his despair the jealous person is desperately preoccupied by the real or perceived fact that the person loved by him is turning his heart toward someone else. The jealous person lacerates himself, as it were. Yet enmity toward the rival also plays a decisive role here, a desperate desire to dethrone the rival in the heart of the beloved.

Envy and jealousy are also clearly different in purely formal terms. As we already said, one can be envious of a person because of impersonal goods which he possesses and I do not possess, but jealousy, by contrast, always arises toward a person who is loved by someone whom I myself love. The theme of jealousy is always this: the heart of someone I love belongs to a third person or, at least, more to the other than to myself. In jealousy there are always three people involved: the one who is jealous; the one whom the jealous person loves; and the one who supposedly possesses the heart of the beloved person or is more loved by him or her. Moreover, jealousy has a much more dynamic character than envy; it surges up and can overcome the jealous person. Envy is much more static and, consequently, cooler and more deliberate.

In our context, however, it is more important to distinguish real jealousy from variations of jealousy, than to distinguish it from envy, which both formally and materially is clearly something entirely different from jealousy.

We sometimes say that someone is jealous of another person's influence, fame, and so forth. In such instances, we do not have merely envy in mind. Contrary to envy, here it is necessarily something which I begrudge the other person because I believe myself to have a claim to it and because he is taking something from me which I would possess were it not for him. The envious person is not concerned with the question whether he would possess something if the other did not possess it. The envious person begrudges the other person every good, even when he stands no chance of possessing it in the event that the other were no longer to have it. The envious person is satisfied only if the other person no longer possesses a good, whereas the jealous person is only satisfied if through the other's loss of it he can get it for himself.

Despite this formal similarity with real jealousy, this jealousy over impersonal goods has a completely different character from jealousy in its genuine form. Here jealousy and envy are usually mixed together and there is missing the essential element of love that is present in real jealousy. Likewise, these variations of jealousy do not awaken our pity in the way that real jealousy does, and they lack the tragic element of real jealousy. Authentic jealousy essentially presupposes love and is permeated with an intense love. It is also characterized by a specific mistrust—a painful mistrust, in fact—of the beloved person as well as by being on the alert for evidence of the beloved person's love for a third person. As the jealous person seeks for such evidence, a painful unrest fills him and he begins interpreting everything in the light of his apprehension. He is driven by a despairing restlessness and, curiously enough, love is here not only a driving force but is often reawakened by jealousy. Love is often rekindled in people whose love had begun to slumber, especially when it is a love between man and woman. Put more correctly, the same situation which awakens jealousy also frequently allows love to be enkindled anew.

Before we turn to the question of the moral disvalue of jealousy, we must still distinguish true jealousy from a quasi-jealousy which at first glance resembles jealousy in many ways but which in reality is entirely distinct from it. We mean the quasi-jealousy of a Count Almaviva (a figure in Mozart's opera, *The Marriage of Figaro*) who, although he no longer loves Rosina and is now in love with Susanna, is still jealous of Rosina on account of Cherubino. The Count feels an anger which is based on the fact that someone dares to step too close to a woman he considers his possession. Wounded pride, anger at the intruder, and indignation at being put into the ridiculous role of the cuckold all play a role, yet this is above all a case of an animalistic jealousy originating in the sexual sphere. This jealousy is not permeated by a real sorrow. On the contrary, compared to real jealousy it is something entirely peripheral, lacking any despair and lacking entirely the gesture of a desperate desire to recapture the beloved, as in the case of Medea. This quasi-jealousy is not tragic, it does not awaken our compassion; it is rather something absurd and repulsive.

We need not deal with this quasi-jealousy here since it cannot be seen as a danger intrinsic to love. It does not presuppose love in any way and does not contain any element of love. We will therefore refrain from speaking further about it here.

It is not difficult to see that jealousy taken in the strict and proper sense that we have outlined here represents at the very least an attitude that in itself is morally imperfect, as understandable and deeply human as it may be. The acrimonious attitude toward the beloved and the hostility toward the rival are morally negative. We see this clearly when we compare jealousy with the pure and deep sorrow which the saint would feel at the loss of the love of a friend, of a beloved wife, or of a loved child, a sorrow which in no way goes hand in hand with enmity toward the third person or with bitterness toward the beloved person. It is the deep sorrow over the loss of the great good of love, the bleeding heart in which there is nothing of the restless inner turmoil or lashing out that we find in the jealous person; nothing of being on the alert for new evidence of unfaithfulness, nothing of the despair that wells up. This deep sorrow is morally noble and through the spirit of caritas it possesses a definite moral value. By bringing in for comparison this sorrow that which pulses through the veins of this love and prevents jealousy from arising, we bring clearly to evidence the moral disvalue of jealousy.

Beyond this there is the moral danger of passion which jealousy can give rise to, including being beside oneself and no longer aware of one's actions. Whether we think of the jealousy of Othello, Medea, or Orlando Furioso, we always encounter the moral danger that is inherent in this elementary passion. The full measure of the moral danger inherent in jealousy reveals itself in the actions to which it can lead. We have only to think of the countless duels instigated by jealousy and of the many instances in which jealousy has led to the murder of the rival, as was the case with Medea, or even to the murder of the beloved person, as in the case of Othello.

For us the essential question is this: to what extent is jealousy a danger rooted in natural, unbaptized love? Is this love as such responsible for the emergence of jealousy? We have already seen that a close relationship exists between jealousy and this kind of love. Without love jealousy in its true and authentic form cannot exist. Jealousy is not only a general imperfection that actualizes itself on the occasion of love and manifests itself in love, like the above-mentioned danger of placing some real joy above the moral law; jealousy is an attitude which presupposes love and which can only actualize itself when love exists. It grows out of love and stands in a logical relationship to it. Because I love and yearn for a return of love, and because a third person hinders this return of love, or diverts it away from me, I am jealous.

Here we are dealing with one of the moral dangers that are inherent in the categories of natural love so long as they are not suffused with caritas. If someone who does not possess the spirit of caritas does not become jealous even when he has cause to be, then his behavior is not just devoid of moral merit, not just morally neutral: it is in fact a *disvalue*. It is an indication that something is lacking in his love. This is one of the most interesting cases in which the cessation of something in itself morally negative for bad reasons, represents in turn something negative, even if not necessarily in a moral respect. It is similar to the situation in which a person, whether out of indifference or weakness, allows himself to be treated badly and to be abused without in any way defending himself. A person certainly shows a sublime attitude when, filled with the spirit of caritas and the imitation of Christ, he turns his left cheek after being struck on the right: but the behavior of the one who allows himself to be pushed around and to be used, not only lacks this moral sublimity entirely, but it has disvalue, even if it is not necessarily immoral.

Jealousy is morally bad and ought not to exist, or, more precisely, it should be overcome. Yet only when jealousy is overcome or eradicated through the spirit of caritas does moral value arise. On the other hand, it is morally even more suspect when a lack of understanding for the exclusivity of spousal love prevents jealousy from arising—a specifically modern perversion—than when jealousy exists, provided that the jealousy does not lead to serious immoral deeds, such as revenge, murder, and so forth.

Though we have to say that jealousy is rooted in natural love, it would be completely wrong to believe that the intentio unionis and the desire to have one's love returned could be made responsible for jealousy, or, more precisely, for the moral disvalue of jealousy. Certainly this desire plays a decisive role in jealousy, but it is, as we saw, essentially connected with the theme of these categories of love, and without this desire for requital they would not be possible—they would be ungenuine and perverted. The lack or loss of the return of love should cause deep sorrow to the person who loves; otherwise he would not really have loved. To respond with jealousy rather than with pure sorrow and a bleeding heart is morally wrong and a disvalue, but this disvalue does not originate in the intentio unionis as such but in the absence of the spirit of caritas, and also in the tendency, rooted in certain false sensitivities, to be affected in the wrong way by the injustice which one suffers. Jealousy emerges from the fact of "remaining stuck in oneself," which in general expresses itself in the way one reacts to the objective wrong that one is made to suffer. The bitterness against the beloved, the anger toward him, the tendency toward violence in jealousy as well as the desire to harm the rival are all the result of the "unredeemed" character of fallen human nature. It is not the interest in the union that is morally negative, but the particular form it takes in jealousy.

Jealousy also involves a perversion of love because union with the other takes priority over the happiness of the other. We have already spoken at length about this issue of priority. Again we must say: it is not the interest in the union which is at fault but rather the fact that union takes the first place in my interest, when in fact I ought to be interested first of all in the happiness of the other person. And this perversion comes from a lack of love, from a love that is not sufficiently deep and that is a betrayal of love itself. As we saw, only when natural love in all its forms is permeated by the love of Christ and the spirit of caritas can the genius of these categories of love be brought to full fruition and truly become love. As long as they remain unredeemed and as long as the person who loves is as a whole not transformed in Christ, these natural kinds of love will be capable of producing bad fruit such as jealousy. And so we find here what we found above: love qua love is not responsible for the moral danger, but the unredeemed character of the love is.

The perversion of love which exists in jealousy and which takes benevolence towards a beloved person and turns it into bitter opposition to him, stands in much closer relationship with love than the other moral dangers that may actualize themselves in love. Yet it should be seen neither as a danger rooted in natural love nor as a result of natural love. This would be just as wrong as seeing the tendency to convert other people by force as being rooted in the nature of religious faith. Though the ardent desire that another find the true faith is deeply rooted in the nature of authentic faith and, above all, in authentic love of neighbor, force should never be used as a means to conversion. This danger is deeply rooted in the nature of fallen man as such and not in the nature of true faith, to which it is in fact antithetical. Such behavior, which has unfortunately so often occurred in history and, sad to say, frequently at the hands of Christians, is the result of the capacity for violence which lies deep in human nature and which is capable of creeping into religious faith. It is a danger of fanatically imposing a good on another which by its nature cannot be imposed by force. It is not the typical violent behavior of the egoist but the particular danger of the idealist who believes that he is fulfilling a duty. Even though this use of force crept into the faith of genuinely religious Christians and hence gave the appearance of deriving from their faith, the truth is that this violence was not the result of their faith but of the imperfection of their Christian faith. It was in fact rooted in their fallen human nature and was expressed in their faith. Had their faith been completely pure and authentic, they would have entirely overcome this tendency toward violence or, more precisely, they would have recognized its incompatibility with faith. This is what we see in the case of the saints.

It can of course be said that if these fanatics had no faith whatsoever and if they had not been idealists of any sort, they would not have practiced this kind of idealistic violence. They would not have wanted to force the good or the true on anyone. But this is hardly a reason for claiming that these violent deeds are the fruit of religious faith or even of the Christian faith, nor that they are a danger intrinsic to faith as such. Apart from the fact that these non-idealists for the most part act out violently in pursuit of their egoistic aims, in the naked gratification of their pride and concupiscence, the fact that some act can be the occasion for the actualization of morally negative attitudes in no way justifies making that act responsible for the moral evil. We already said earlier that such an approach would force us to see the drooling idiot as the moral ideal, since he is morally speaking surely the least endangered of anyone. For the same reason we must not make earthly loves as such responsible for possible jealousy but rather fallen human nature, the imperfection of the one who loves, and the unredeemed aspect of his love. This love can become real love only through being redeemed.

We will now turn our attention to another danger of natural love.

The unfaithfulness that comes from letting an existing love be displaced by a new love

One particular danger immanent in these natural loves is that a new love can lead to unfaithfulness toward an earlier one. Unfaithfulness is clearly a moral injustice, and the danger of unfaithfulness is an essential and significant kind of relationship between love and morality. How many tragedies in life are brought about by unfaithfulness, above all by unfaithfulness in matters of love! In considering faithfulness, we touch upon a singularly important relationship between love and morality in both the positive and the negative respect. Faithfulness, which belongs to love essentially and is required by it, has an emphatically moral value, unfaithfulness an emphatically moral disvalue.

We will still consider in detail this dimension of love and morality in its positive aspect in chapter 13. This will necessarily entail that we also consider unfaithfulness. But here we are only considering the unfaithfulness which is brought about by a new love. We encounter here the curious fact that a new love can lead a person to neglect the demand of faithfulness that arises from an earlier love. It appears, at least at first glance, as if there was a tendency of love to become unfaithful to earlier loves and to the ties arising from them.

This danger exists above all in the category of love that exists between man and woman, the category which we have called spousal love. Yet it is not restricted to this category. While it appears here most frequently and most dramatically, it can still be found analogously wherever a new person enters our life and so fills our heart that our interest for the person who previously possessed our heart is diminished or even extinguished. This, for example, is the case when a new baby becomes the favorite of the mother or father and captures the place which the elder child had earlier possessed, or when a new friend causes an old friend to recede into the background.

Clearly there is no such danger in Christian love of neighbor. In this type of love, God does not speak a unique "word" between me and my neighbor, which is why a relationship marked by an exclusive character does not come about. But aside from this, it is actually impossible to withdraw the love of neighbor from someone in order to bestow it upon someone else, since this love by its very nature derives its existence from caritas. Just as it is impossible to be unloving toward one neighbor in order to bestow advantages on another neighbor, as we saw above, so it is impossible that in turning to a new neighbor with love one would cease loving or would love less some neighbor to whom one had previously turned with love. This is because the caritas immanent in Christian love of neighbor is inseparable from the readiness to encounter every neighbor with love, even though this will be done differently according to the theme of the situation. The only possibility is that we encounter a neighbor with authentic love of neighbor at one time and then later abandon this disposition of love and therefore treat another neighbor without love. This means that we have fallen out of the bond with God and that we are no longer filled with caritas, and that the reverent and loving self no longer reigns within us fully but that pride and concupiscence now assert themselves. Yet the love of neighbor can never uproot or even lessen our love for another person. There can never be a conflict between the love we have for two neighbors.

By contrast, a conflict can arise in all other categories of love, where love refers to a particular person. This possible conflict results from the different theme of these kinds of love, that is, of their categorial character, as well as from the fact that unbaptized love does not necessarily involve the actualization of the reverent and loving self. But here we are not thinking of those cases in which the love itself dies and is replaced by a love for another person; we are thinking of those cases in which a new love displaces an old one.

The question which now arises is this: to what extent can the love toward a third person displace an existing love which is still fully alive? Here we must distinguish between two different cases. First of all, there is the case in which a peripheral infatuation brings about a fleeting "unfaithfulness" yet without ever really dethroning the beloved person. This case, which is bound up with the general human susceptibility to drift into the periphery, is not a matter of concern for us at present, since this kind of peripheral infatuation hardly deserves to be called by the name of love. In the second case, we have a love between a man and a woman, yet a love that, though genuine, is far from being the highest love of which this man or woman is capable. Many deeper levels may not yet have been awakened in them, and these levels may be awakened by another person. An entirely new kind of mutual understanding and a much deeper ordering of one to the other may exist between the man or the woman and some third person whom he or she comes to know. Romeo, for example, already loves a girl when he meets Juliet and is gripped by a much deeper love.

In all these cases in which one can say that the "second love" is the more authentic love, that only now does a person find the one for whom he or she is, as it were, predestined, the problem we are raising does not exist. These cannot be presented as examples of a moral danger in love, for if we prescind from bonds of a different kind, especially from marital bonds, entering into this second love in no way involves anything morally wrong; on the contrary, it is right that one would grant the deeper and more valid love the place that it deserves, as in the case of Romeo.

Our question is: is it possible for a deep love that is fully alive to be displaced by another love which is not qualitatively superior to it? Do we not in all these cases have to do with a love which in itself was no longer fully alive, where the person who loves had to a certain extent fallen asleep or where a certain form of disappointment had set in? Can a new love come to be and dethrone one that is alive? Clearly not. If we think of the famous examples in literature of a man or woman withdrawing their heart from someone they had fully loved, we always find that the love had already grown cold. Jason's love for Medea had grown cold when he turned toward another woman. It lies in the nature of this kind of love that it is exclusive and that, as long as it is alive and well, another person cannot awaken such a love in our heart.

We must rather say that my love must have somehow fallen asleep if another person can win my heart away from the one whom I loved. Yet there are here very many degrees and kinds. A general human danger also makes itself felt, namely, the danger that over time I easily cease to appreciate sufficiently a good which I possess, that I becomes insensitive to it, and that therefore something new makes a stronger impression on me than something which I have already possessed for a long time. This danger is not confined to any particular sphere of goods but can arise in the attitude toward any sphere of goods, including marital love. If I love another person with this love I can over time, without ceasing to love the other and without entirely revoking the gift of my heart, lose a lively sense of the being of the beloved person and of the image of this person that once ignited my heart, as well as lose a sense for the gift which the beloved person has become for me. It is at moments like this that a new person can step into my life and conquer my heart.

This danger is found most of all in people who are morally unconscious, who follow the spontaneous inclination of their nature without ever having discovered their capacity for sanction and disavowal.[3] Siegfried in Wagner's *Ring* cycle, Tom Jones in Fielding's novel of the same name, or Ingénu in Voltaire are all such types. (Note that these figures are presented here only as examples of what we call moral unconsciousness, not of unfaithfulness.) But we have to ask whether these types of person can love in the full sense of the term, even if we limit ourselves to "unredeemed" love. To what degree does the lack of moral consciousness that characterizes them decisively impair their ability to give their heart, so that they are prevented from having a full understanding of the bond inherent in this giving?

Here we must mention another circumstance. It is true that in spousal love there is a particular radiance at the moment when, in the first phase of love, the interchange of loving looks takes place, when the two enter into familiarity and unity of heart with each other, when they cross a certain interpersonal space and no longer hold each other at a distance. It is not just a matter of the newness of this love; rather, the discovery of each other is a singular moment

---

3 [These terms "sanction" and "disavowal" have a very definite meaning in the setting of von Hildebrand's moral philosophy; the fullest account that he gives of them is found in his *Ethics*, chapter 25. Trans.]

which engenders great joy. Certainly, it would be completely false to believe that this special joy is as such superior to a deep and lasting state of communion. And yet it has its own particular radiance, and it is much easier to be fully alert at this moment than during a deeply lived unity over time. Indeed, it is impossible not to be alert at the time of a new love. This advantage which the new has over the old in love (which goes entirely beyond the upper hand of the new over the old in general) can also play a role in the dethronement of an existing love through a new one.

In order to exclude all possible misunderstandings, it must stressed emphatically that all forms of unfaithfulness which are motivated by a purely sensual desire are excluded from the present discussion, since it is clear that they are entirely unrelated to dangers which lie *within* love. Rather than being dangers within love, these sensual desires are responsible for causing dangers and threats to love. In the present context we are equally disinterested in the Don Giovanni's passing from one woman to another, because he does not love any of his conquests. We are only concerned with the case in which a genuine love for one person is destroyed or at least diminished by the love for another person. This seems to be possible only under the following circumstances.

First, as we already saw, this can happen when the unfaithfulness consists in a passing superficial infatuation. This danger comes from the general human tendency to glide into the periphery and also from the enigmatic preference for a superficial happiness. No real *sursum corda* (lifting up of one's heart) is required here.

Second, there are all the instances involving qualitatively entirely different kinds of love. In these instances the person who dethrones someone in my heart appeals to entirely different sides of me.

Third, there are the cases in which a person, though he may love someone, finds another person to whom he is ordered in a far deeper way, someone who appeals not only to different but much deeper sides, someone who allows for an encounter in a much deeper sphere of values and to whom he can make a far more thoroughgoing and valid gift of heart.

Fourth, there are all those cases in which for some reason or other the first love has to a certain degree fallen asleep. A new person can therefore win a place in a heart that had formerly belonged to someone else, even though the new love need not be qualitatively different.

Naturally, the situation is entirely different when we are dealing with an unrequited love or a diminished reciprocation of love; it is in this setting that a love for another person is much more understandable. Yet in these cases the causes for the new love are already to be found in the imperfection of the first love.

Thus far, we have only considered the most typical and dramatic case of a new love displacing an already existing love, namely, the case that occurs in spousal love. Yet this can also occur in analogous ways in other categories of love. We encounter in all other categories of natural love this danger of a new love leading to unfaithfulness toward an earlier love, especially when a person who played a central role in someone's life is ousted by a new person. Take the case where a child once stood at the very center of the lives of its parents and was the source of their joy. Now they are given a new child, which takes over the place which the older child had previously occupied. Even though this situation does not involve the exclusivity of spousal love, even though one can love more than one person with this kind of love, that is, with the same category of love—this is of course impossible in spousal love—here in the case of the child it is the first place in the heart of the parent that possesses a certain exclusivity. Naturally, it is not necessary for a child, or for that matter for a friend, to capture this first place in the heart of a person, because in the context of the love for children or for a friend, it is entirely possible (though impossible in spousal love) to love several people with equal intensity, to love them without in any way giving preference to any one of them. Yet a child or friend may be the person one loves most and to whom one has given one's heart entirely. It is then in principle possible that a new child or a new friend will take over the first place in the heart of the parents or of the friend, thereby displacing the one who had previously been first. This cannot of course be compared with the parallel situation in spousal love, for the case of the displaced child usually just results in a lessening rather than a complete loss of love.

We now prescind from all those cases in which the change in love is well founded and entirely legitimate because the one who changes has received the gift of being ordered to another person in an entirely new and deeper manner. Let us focus our attention exclusively on the situation in which one can speak of a culpable unfaithfulness, and let us raise the question whether we can blame love as such for a person becoming unfaithful. Clearly, the cause of the unfaithfulness is a general danger rooted in the unfaithful person, namely, a certain tendency toward discontinuity; one allows oneself to be completely controlled by the theme of a new situation and one unquestioningly follows one's latest impulse.

Above all, the danger here is that of moral unconsciousness. These people do not understand the bond immanent in the word of love that was once spoken. It is therefore the imperfection of the first love rather than the appearance of the new love which is to blame for the unfaithfulness. It is more correct to say that the general inconstancy of a person and the resulting imperfection of his love make it possible for someone whom he loves to be displaced from his heart by a new person. Displacing a person is not a danger intrinsic to love.

We need not address the danger of an egoistic love for a person which comes from unredeemed love, since we have already dealt with this earlier. Perhaps more than any other danger this one is rooted in love as such, at least as long as love is not suffused by the spirit of caritas.

Part II: Love and the Moral Good

Having considered the moral dangers which may go hand in hand with natural love, we will now turn to the positive relationships that exist between natural love and the sphere of morality. Here we can distinguish seven fundamental relationships or, as one could also say, we can particularize our question in seven different directions.

Various positive relationships between love and morality

First of all, we must ask which moral values can arise from the love between friends or from spousal love, as a result of the love being established in a high sphere of value. In *Die Metaphysik der Gemeinschaft* (The Metaphysics of Community) we spoke of the realm of values and of goods in which the encounter between those who love one another takes place, and we emphasized its tremendous influence on the depth and quality of the love. At this point, we are concerned with the fact that the quality as well as the qualitative depth of a love depends on the values which predominate in the loving person's perception of the beloved person, be it moral, intellectual, vital, or other values, and which flow into the overall beauty of the beloved person. Of decisive importance for the quality of a love is not only the realm of values where two people encounter one another, but also that realm in which I find the beloved person, in other words, the values in this person that have kindled my heart. We could also speak of the realm of values in which my love has placed the beloved person, even if he is not yet consciously incorporated into this realm of values. Our question here is the following: which values do we have in mind when we contrast the love of Leonore in Beethoven's *Fidelio* as spiritual, noble, and deep, with the love of Dmitri Karamazov for Grushenka (characters in Dostoevsky's novel, *The Brothers Karamazov*) as primarily vital rather than spiritual, and of lesser depth despite its central role in his life? Undoubtedly the values we have in mind here are moral values: Leonore's love ranks morally much higher than that of Dmitri. But we are not primarily thinking of the moral difference that derives from the overall personality of each of them; in other words, we are not thinking of the elements in their love that are determined entirely by the lovers, but we are also thinking of the difference that comes from the values to which each responds in the beloved person.

This relationship between love, whether the love of friendship or spousal love, and the world of moral values, a relationship which exists analogously in all other categories of natural love, is of eminent significance. It touches precisely on the great hierarchical differences within love, on the qualitative hierarchy, and on the degrees of depth. This is an entirely different way of characterizing the essence of a particular love than when we speak of the category of the love or the degree of the love. Even if the qualitative differences of love that allow us to speak of a higher and a lower, of a more or less noble love, do not pertain exclusively to moral values, these values nevertheless play here a decisive role.

We will therefore investigate more closely this connection between love and morality. We will investigate the relationship to the moral sphere which is proper to love as a value-response and which arises out of its value-responding function. But before beginning with this analysis, we first want to mention the six other dimensions of natural love and morality.

In the second relation between love and morality, we must ask which moral values accrue to a love in virtue of the moral standing of the person who loves. It is obvious that the quality of a value-response is not only influenced by the object of the value-response but also by the personality of the one who gives the value-response. The difference between a deep and sublime joy, and a peripheral and less sublime joy is of course primarily determined through the value of the object to which this joy refers. The joy over the conversion of a beloved person necessarily has a deeper and more sublime character than the joy over the fact that this person has received a pay raise. Yet the personality of the person who is joyful also has an influence on the quality and depth of the joy: his depth, his spiritual alertness, his general moral standing—everything which, so to speak, he has invested in this joy. All of this applies to love in a special way. What the one who loves has invested in his love affects the love greatly. The personality of the one who loves is in a special way a factor that determines the depth and quality of his love and thus also the moral value of his love. It is in this sense that Leonardo da Vinci says: "The greater a man, the greater his love."

This second highly significant factor that influences the moral value of love stands out particularly in the already mentioned situations in which there is a discrepancy between the nobility of a love and the personality of the beloved person. A mother can possess a heroically deep love of an unworthy son or daughter; and the love of someone like the Countess Almaviva has a nobility which is in no way grounded in the corresponding qualities of Count Almaviva (these are characters in Mozart's opera, *The Marriage of Figaro*).

We will therefore also have to investigate what sort of influence the personality of the one who loves has on the moral quality of his love, and which moral values accrue to his love as a result of all that he has invested in it. This relationship of the act of love as such to the moral sphere is extremely manifold, giving rise to many different kinds of questions. One of the important questions concerns which morally valuable elements are invested in love by the one who loves. Here we are still speaking entirely without reference to the "investment" which arises from the transformation in Christ, that is, from being filled with the spirit of caritas. We are here confining ourselves completely to the natural categories of love as they exist prior to their transformation. Even in this relationship between love and morality we find great differences of rank within one and the same category of love. The moral quality of a love will vary according to the personality of the one who loves and according to what and how much he invests in his love.

A third relationship between love and morality is expressed in the effect which love can have upon the entire person. We are not here referring to accidental effects or even to effects in a strictly causal sense. We mean the way in which love irradiates the entire person, his moral standing, we mean the way in which someone is changed when a great love awakens and, assuming the love remains completely alert and awake, endures. We are thinking of the melting of the heart, of the new level of overall alertness, of the new capacity for seeing values, of the increase in a certain humility, and of much else that goes hand in hand with an ardent love. Plato has spoken about all of this in a wonderful way in his *Phaedrus*.

But this source of moral values and moral differences within the love of friendship and within spousal love is not entirely independent of the question which we touched upon in the first fundamental relationship between love and morality. The moral "effect" of love will also very much depend upon the quality and qualitative depth possessed by a given love. When a person experiences a noble, spiritual love, the awakening and uplifting effect proper to love as such will be entirely different from and more significant than in the case of a less deep love.

A fourth relationship to the moral sphere comes to light when we ask whether a natural love is ever morally obligatory. Can we not say that from a moral point of view a mother ought to love her child, at least as long as it is small? Or is it only loving behavior and loving actions toward the child that are required and not the actual love for the child? The same question arises in the case of the love of the child for its parents. Is it morally irrelevant whether or not a child loves its parents? We are here not considering extreme situations in which parents treat a child in such a way that any love toward them is extinguished in the child. Likewise, we will not consider instances of already grown children in which there is no intellectual or cultural affinity, with the result that the parents and the children live in different worlds and have nothing to say to one another.

Our question is this: is it morally irrelevant whether children love parents who are loving and loveable? Does not the moral commandment to honor one's parents also encompass love? And even when love is not morally required (as we saw, the value of another personality does not oblige us to embrace the other with the love of friendship, and even less to love him or her with spousal love), it is still remains an open question whether our refusal to give the response of love and to become involved in love is not morally relevant, provided that we have received the gift of seeing the overall beauty of a person and of taking delight in the person. The love between friends and the love between man and woman, and indeed love of any kind, is not free in the sense in which an act of the will is free. One cannot just posit love like a response of the will, and even less can one command it like an action. But in the case of love between friends and of love between man and woman there is a factor which in a special way highlights its gift character, namely, that there must be a special affinity with another which enables me to see the overall beauty of an individual person so deeply that my heart is taken hold of and moved by his or her unique beauty. In order to receive the gift of such a love toward another person, there must be a special affinity. Yet even if it is true that I cannot freely call these kinds of love into existence, it is nevertheless in my power to refuse responding with love. True though it is that I am not morally required to love someone as a friend or even as a spouse, however high they may stand in my estimation, however much I may respect, admire, or revere them,[4] it still remains a question whether it is morally irrelevant if I refuse to respond with love, provided the disposition exists and I could love them. Is there not here a kind of moral obligation to give this response? If I have seen the overall beauty of a person and been deeply affected by it, then do I not after all owe this person my love? Are we not dealing with a kind of moral obligation, namely the obligation to give the full response to a gift?

The primary issue is why I refuse my love and what obstacles stand in the way of loving. As we will see later in this chapter when we examine more closely the relationship of love to the moral sphere, such a refusal can be motivated by factors of eminent moral relevance. The attitudes that lie at the root of the refusal may have a morally negative character.

In this context we also touch upon the issue of sanctioning the love which, so to speak, is a "gift" that has welled up in my heart.

Of course there are cases in which the refusal to enter a relationship of love is morally *obligatory*, despite the fact that all the preconditions for a love exist. Indeed, one can be morally obliged to resist a growing love with all one's strength. But what is too often not recognized is that the moral character of the refusal can be thoroughly negative if it arises from morally negative attitudes. Even if this moral character lies primarily in the morally negative motivation of the refusal to love, a study of these cases will show that a person in these circumstances should not refuse love but should hand himself over to love.

The fifth relationship between the categories of natural love and morality lies in the duty of faithfulness, which is indeed deeply bound up with love. The eminent moral value of faithfulness is in no need of explanation, since its specifically moral character is obvious. And yet to work out the nature of faithfulness is such a central problem, and the question of faithfulness in the love among friends, in spousal love, and in marriage has so many aspects, that we will dedicate an entire chapter to it.[5]

---

4   A different question is whether a response of love—love simply speaking, which is clearly distinct from love for a friend and prior to every categorial form of love—is not in fact always required in relation to a person whom we revere on account of the moral nobility of his personality. We are thinking here in the text of the love that is emphatically love for a friend.

5   We have already discussed unfaithfulness in part I of this chapter, even if from a different point of view.

The sixth relationship concerns the question of the *ordo amoris* (the order or ranking of loves). While one usually takes love in a more general sense in discussing the ordo amoris, there is a real analogy to this issue even when love is taken in the most proper sense. This holds even for the categories of natural love. The particular issue we encounter here is the problem of loving one person "more than another." Is one's own child entitled to be loved more than the child of other parents? Does a wife have the right to be loved in a way which is not only different in kind but also more than any other person? Does the ordo amoris have moral significance within the sphere of the categories of natural love? Is it morally relevant to abide by this ordo? The question of the ordo amoris will form the subject of chapter 14.

Finally, every kind of natural love which takes root in my soul presents me with an eminently moral task, namely the specifically moral task of suffusing every natural love with the spirit of caritas. Since it coincides with the transformation of natural love through Christ, this task is moral in the sense of Christian morality, which, as we have emphasized in various books, fulfills and crowns natural morality even while vastly transcending it.

As we already emphasized in chapter 11, every natural love is meant to be suffused with the spirit of caritas, and in fact only then can a given natural love, be it the love of a child, the love among friends, or the love between man and woman, fully unfold and flourish in its specific genius. It is in this sense that we must say that while all forms of natural love are a gift which we are not capable of giving to ourselves, all of them contain a requirement which appeals to our free cooperation. We must learn to love in truth, learn to love fully in accord with the genius of love. This task of learning to love in truth is fulfilled when our love is suffused with the spirit of caritas.

There is no need to show that this is a moral task and that here we are here dealing with an eminent relationship between natural love and morality. For the requirement is a moral one, the task is religious and moral, and when the task is fulfilled, even the categories of natural love become bearers of the highest moral values. But we will not delve further into the analysis of this especially important relationship between love and morality, the seventh of these relationships, since we have already dealt with it in chapter 11.

1. Moral values and the value-response of love

We now turn to a careful analysis of the various fundamental relationships between natural love and morality. We begin with the first of these relationships, namely with the question of the moral values that grow out of love as a value-response.

In our *Ethics* we pointed out that in the realm of value-response there is an extraordinarily intelligible connection between the type and rank of the value of a good, on the one hand, and the quality of the response, on the other. The quality as well as the degree of a value-responding joy corresponds to the type and rank of the value motivating the joy. The enthusiasm for Rossini's *The Barber of Seville* is qualitatively entirely different from the enthusiasm for Beethoven's *Ninth Symphony*. The enthusiasm for the *Ninth Symphony* will of necessity be qualitatively more sublime, deeper, and greater, provided that one really grasps the value of each work of art and gives a pure value-response.

The relationship between the content of a response and the value arises by itself necessarily, and at the same time it is something that ought to come about. The good with the higher value will necessarily receive a different response than a lesser good, always presuming, of course, that its value is really understood and that the response is exclusively motivated by the value. It is impossible that someone who understands and gives a value-response to the real values of *The Barber of Seville* and the *Ninth Symphony* of Beethoven will not be incomparably more enthused by the *Ninth Symphony,* impossible that the "word" of his enthusiasm will not in each case be qualitatively entirely different. Yet aside from the necessary dependence of the content of a given value-response on the value of the good to which the response is being given, we are here dealing with a relationship of ought [*Sollensbeziehung*]. To the *Ninth Symphony* is due a different response than to *The Barber of Seville*. Every good with real values is owed an adequate response, and the higher the good, the "more" the response should have as regards enthusiasm, admiration, etc.

In this context the most important thing to see is that the dependence of the quality and degree of a value-response on the value of some good implies that this value has a decisive influence on the moral value of a value-response. In our *Ethics* we showed that the question whether a value-response can be a bearer of moral values depends upon what values in the good actually motivate the response. For moral value to arise in the person he must respond to a special kind of value that we called "morally relevant value" and contrasted with "morally irrelevant value." Moreover, we showed that the rank of the morally relevant value to which the person responds has an important influence on the rank of the moral value of the value-response. Since love is a value-response, we also find this relationship between the "word" uttered in love and the value by which the love is motivated. We prescind, however, from the due relation [*Sollensbeziehung*] and focus instead on the necessary connection between the "word" of love and the values in the beloved person which enkindle the love. Our question is the following: what influence do the values which motivate the love between man and woman have on the moral value of such a love?

Spousal love. We saw that it is not always morally relevant values that motivate the love between man and woman. On the other hand, it cannot be denied, as we have seen, that the moral difference between the love of Leonore for Florestan and the love of Dmitri for Grushenka is affected by the values by which these two loves are motivated. The quality and depth of a love, which after all depends decisively on the values which enkindle the love, also strongly influences the moral value of the love.

The beauty of the individual person as a whole [*Gesamtschönheit der Individualität*] is, as we saw in chapter 3, the value which enkindles a love. Yet we also saw that this beauty of the whole person is nourished by particular kinds of values. The "antiphon"[6] of this overall beauty may be moral, intellectual or other values, and these values that provide the "antiphon" to the beauty of a person as a whole have a decisive influence on the quality and depth of a love and on the degree to which the love has moral value. It is for this reason that the love of Leonore for Florestan, in which the "antiphon" to his overall beauty as person is his moral nobility and greatness of soul, possesses a moral seriousness and nobility that is lacking in Dmitri's love for Gruschenka, in which purely vital values provide the "antiphon" to her overall beauty. It is irrelevant here whether this overall beauty of the whole person is real or imagined; even if someone is mistaken and has an image of the other person which is illusory, his love will be influenced by the values which he believes to nourish the overall beauty of the other person.

In which realm of values is the beloved person situated for the one who loves? To which realm of values is the one who loves transported by loving? All of this has a decisive influence on the quality and depth of his love; and as soon as morally relevant values begin to nourish the overall beauty of a person, they become a source for the moral value of the love.

Every love between man and woman in which moral and/or religious values are the "antiphon" of the beauty of the whole person is definitely the bearer of moral value. In fact, the more sublime the moral values which make up the "antiphon," the higher the love will rank from a moral point of view.

Yet even if moral values are not the "antiphon" of the beauty of the whole person, even if they are not that which first awakens love, as for example in the love of Romeo and Juliet, nonetheless they do play an eminent role as a background. It is impossible to bracket out significant moral values from the image Romeo and Juliet have of one another. Juliet stands resplendent in her purity and goodness before Romeo, even as he stands before her in his moral nobility and faithfulness. Even in this example of a love between man and woman we see that a moral value grows out of the moral values making up the background, even though it is not as high a moral value as in the case in which moral values provide the "antiphon." Romeo and Juliet in their love encounter one another in several different realms of values, yet the sphere of moral values cannot be ignored.

We are dealing with an entirely different circumstance when two people are not incorporated in a primary way in the same realm of values. Here it may be that the one who loves, while conscious that the beloved person is not yet incorporated in the realm of moral or religious values, is still completely filled

---

6   [Von Hildebrand adapts here "antiphon" from its liturgical use and makes it mean something like "that which precedes and 'frames' the beauty of a person." Trans.]

with the desire to introduce the beloved person to this realm of values and to make him or her at home in it. While moral values, which the one person already possesses, are not the "antiphon" of the overall beauty of the beloved person, still the fact that the beloved person is objectively ordered toward this sphere of values plays a decisive role in the love of the one who loves. He still sees the beloved person in the light of these values, which the beloved person is meant to acquire, and he cannot separate his image of the beloved from this ordination. Of course, in this case the relationship of love to moral values is more conditioned by the character of the lover than by that of the beloved. But even if it is in consequence of the moral status of the lover that moral values play such a role in his image of the beloved, they also affect the moral value of his love. This is a case which very often occurs. When a man or woman of great moral stature ardently loves in a spousal way someone who is of lesser stature, it is usually a case such as this. We are about to see that love in such a case not only derives its moral nobility from the kind of response that it is, but also from other sources. And yet a certain moral value accrues to a love even if moral values in the beloved person only play a role for the lover insofar as he does what, as we have seen, is done in every love, namely, insofar as he "draws out" something in the beloved person that is meant to be.

We already mentioned that, when love is kindled by the beauty, the poetry, and the charm of the appearance of a person, the one who loves cannot avoid "extending" the radiance of these values to the entire personality of the beloved. When Miranda sees Ferdinand in Shakespeare's *The Tempest*, she is overwhelmed by his beauty and by the nobility of his appearance, yet in the gesture of love she immediately extends the radiance of these values to the entire personality of the prince. For Miranda, Ferdinand cannot be anything other than noble, good, and elegant.

The role of moral values in the "extension" of particular values to the overall value of the person is also of significance for the moral value of love. Here again we find great differences. All of this must be taken into consideration if we want to do justice to the moral value that emerges from spousal love considered as a response to the other. Even in the case where moral values do not form the "antiphon" of the beauty of the whole person and are not even contained as background in the motivation of the love, nonetheless moral value can accrue to love in its response-function, namely through the role which moral values play in love when the lover "draws out" the value-essence of the beloved person. But of course the moral value, to the extent that it arises from the response-function of love, will be greatest if moral and religious values form the antiphon of the beauty of the whole person and if those who love one another encounter each other in this realm of values. Yet even within those cases in which moral values only play a role in the process of drawing out the value-essence of the beloved person, the moral value of a love varies greatly according to how great this role is.

We say "according to how great this role is," since in every love there is ultimately present, even if only in a vague hoping and wishing way, the act of drawing out the value-essence of the beloved person into the realm of the moral. Consider the love of someone like José, whose love is primarily enkindled by vital values and who is powerfully drawn to Carmen by dark and uncanny passion and by something strangely incomprehensible about her, even though he is conscious of the moral disvalues in her. Even here love somehow draws out the value-essence of the beloved, if only if a very vague way, into the world of moral values. In his love José somehow believes that Carmen is at a fundamental level good and that this goodness will still triumph, that the bewitching power of her personality in all of its wildness is nonetheless ordered toward the good. The word of love, "He or she is fundamentally good," is spoken even here, though with a vague and indeterminate grasp of the good. As paradoxical as it may sound, even in the case of José's love for Carmen, which is kindled by values far removed from morally relevant values, love as it were opens a door for the one who loves, and through this door he somehow grasps the connection between all values of a person and moral values. He has enough of an inkling of the centrality of moral values to believe in and wish for the "goodness" of the other, however concealed it may still be.

Of course, in the case of a love like that of José, the moral value which derives from this love—insofar as the love is considered as a response—is extremely small, especially when measured against the high moral value of a love such as that of Leonore for Florestan. But this already leads us to those moral values which do not arise from love as a response to the beloved person but from the "gift" of love as such, for this drawing out of the value-essence in love is a gesture rooted in the "gift" of love.

Other categories of love. But before we turn to our second question, namely, which moral values are found in the categories of natural love on the basis of sources other than the value-responding character of love, we must still briefly examine the way in which the values responded to affect the moral value of love that is categorially different from spousal love. We dealt first with spousal love because the role of morally relevant values here is harder to show than with the other categories of natural love.

In the case of the love among friends we can easily see the difference in quality and depth that is conditioned by the kind of value that plays a primary role in the motivation of this love. It shows itself especially in the realm of goods and values in which the friends encounter one another, or to put it more precisely, in which the relationship is situated. If it is primarily the realm of moral value, then the love will possess a nobler quality than if it is the realm of intellectual goods and values that plays the primary role.

There are many levels here, ranging from a holy friendship like the one between St. Augustine and St. Paulinus of Nola all the way to a friendship that is social in character or even that is just a kind of comradeship. In between lie many noble spiritual friendships, such as those between Goethe and Schiller or Schubert and Schwind. The higher the realm of values in which friends encounter one another, and the greater the role played by moral and religious values in the motivation of the love among friends, then the higher will be the quality of this love, the deeper the love will be, and the more the love will itself have moral value.

In the noblest friendships love is after all always suffused with definite responses to moral values, responses such as esteem and reverence. Here too we find that even if the moral values of my friend are not the point of entry for a friendship, if they are not the "antiphon" for the beauty of the whole person of my friend, they can still play a role as a background. We also find here that the friendship of the morally more awakened of two friends is permeated by the desire to help the morally less awakened friend to find a home in the moral sphere, even if the moral values already possessed by the friend do not provide the primary motivation for the love and even if the two friends do not encounter each other in the sphere of moral value. For the morally more awakened one will see his friend in the light of the world of moral value, so that the ordination of his friend to moral values will decisively influence the quality of his love.

We must, however, understand that one can speak of authentic love among friends only if the world of moral values plays some role in the relationship, and that this love can never exist between "buddies" who encounter one another at the level of moral disvalue. Aristotle already saw this clearly when at the beginning of Book VIII of his *Nichomachean Ethics* he distinguished three kinds of friendship: the first based on pleasure and amusement, the second on the useful, and the third on the moral good. Only this last one did he acknowledge to be real friendship. This is all the more true in the case of the love among friends.

We need not concern ourselves any further with the love among friends, since everything we already said about the moral values that arise from the response character of the love between man and woman applies *mutatis mutandis* to the love between friends. It is even easier for us to understand that a real love for a friend always includes a response to moral values, or at least to understand that one friend sees another in the light of the world of moral values and as ordered to this world.

It is far more important for us to enter briefly into a consideration of the love of parents for their children, since here the entire situation is different from what is found with the love among friends as well as with the love between man and woman.

The love of parents for a child, particularly when the child is very small, is not primarily motivated by qualitative values but, as we saw, first and foremost by the ontological value which the child possesses by virtue of its human nature, a value, moreover, which the child possesses in an especially touching way. I say in a touching way, because this ontological value stands out here in a particular way: qualitative values do not yet stand in the foreground and the ontological value is not yet "filled out" but is given "naked," while at the same time it is surrounded by the radiance of all the possibilities that are still open. This is intensified by the fact of the child's neediness and dependence on our help. Yet over and above this datum, which after all every child possesses as such, parental love is grounded in a mysterious objective ordination, that is, in the fact that the parents were permitted to collaborate with the coming into existence of this person and that God in a unique way has entrusted this being to them. It is obvious that both of these factors are morally relevant in nature. The ontological value of the spiritual person is eminently morally relevant, and even more so is the relationship to God who has entrusted this being to us.

A further deep motive of parental love comes about in a happy marriage; it is that the child is the fruit of the parents' love and unity, and also that the child is for each spouse the image of the other.

Once the child becomes a fully distinct individual and is endowed with qualitative values and disvalues, parental love is subject, *mutatis mutandis*, to the law that we already examined in the case of the love between man and woman and in the case of the love among friends. Yet even here the just-mentioned factor of the ontological value has its force. One source of the moral value of parental love is that the ontological value of the person, which in the case of the newborn child stands completely front and center, continues in later years to play a special role. We should remember that the ontological value of the person is always ordered to the world of moral values; we can never separate the character of the *imago Dei* from the vocation of the person to be morally good. This is why authentic parental love always retains this sense of the moral values to which the child is ordered, irrespective of how the child may turn out. The special objective ordination after all remains intact, even though the entrustment of the child to its parents by God is modified when the child grows up. We will later see why parents are in fact obliged to have parental love for their children.[7]

As for the love of the child for its parents, the parents stand before a small child not only as persons but as representatives of God, even though the child may not yet know anything about God or, to put it more precisely, may not yet have an intellectual grasp of this representative function of the parents. If we consider the child's sense of being sheltered in the "omnipotence" of the

---

7   The many negative factors that can creep into the parental relation should not obscure for us the fact that real parental love always has moral value. We have discussed these negative factors elsewhere. Let us just make a point of stressing again that any parental attachment in which the child takes on the character of an extended ego of the parent lacks this moral value; in fact, such attachment is not really love.

parents and in their love and kindness, and if we consider the kind of moral authority with which the parents are invested in the eyes of the child as it grows up, then we realize that it is superfluous to say here any more about the role of moral values in the motivation of this love. It is not difficult to see that the love of a child for its parents is a bearer of positive moral values on the basis of its response-character. This moral quality of the child's love is after all expressed in the commandment to honor one's parents, even if the commandment does not speak directly about love.

2. Moral values and the personality of the one who loves

We now turn to the second question, namely, the question of the moral value that arises from natural love in all its categories not only as a result of the value responded to, that is, as a result of the value-responding character of love, but also as a result of the nature of the one who loves. We have once again to underline that the "gift" of love in its moral value also depends upon the character of the one who loves. Moreover, we should also emphasize that the "gift" of love always possesses a certain moral character, despite all the great differences in moral value that we find in the various kinds of natural love, including differences based on what a person invests in his or her love. We have only to think of people who are incapable of any love, who cannot love anyone, and then we see clearly the moral value of love. It is a value rooted in the "word" uttered by the one who loves, rooted in the commitment to the beloved person, in the intentio benevolentiae proper to love—however imperfect the love may still be. We saw at the end of chapter 11 that a faint and distant image of caritas is to be found in every natural love, even if the love has in no way been transformed by the spirit of caritas, indeed, even if it is not a natural love that has been enkindled by moral values, and even if the love in its quality ranks rather low. In every love as such—provided that it really deserves the name of love—there dwells a seed tending toward a goal that can only be reached through the spirit of caritas. Every love somehow longs for the redemption through caritas. The "gift" of love itself always possesses a breath of moral goodness, however modest this may be. "*Rien n'est perdu, tant qu'on aime*" ("Nothing is lost as long as one loves"), as Fr. Troisfontaine, S.J., says in summarizing Gabriel Marcel's philosophy.

We will now, as we said, turn to the second source of moral value in love, the source that originates in the person who loves. When Leonardo da Vinci says, "The greater the human being, the greater will be his love," he is in effect referring to this source of love. In fact, this source in an analogous way plays a great role in all values-responses. However much the quality of the response is formed and molded by the value to which it is a response, the personality of the one making the response is in many respects decisive for the moral value of the response. The personality of the one giving the value-response already strongly influences the grasping and understanding of values, and this influence is even more in evidence with the response to values. It is also true of being affected by the value of a good. The same work of art can move and touch one person more deeply than another, even if both have the same artistic sensibility. The greater potential of the one person, his greater inner fire, is the cause of his being more deeply affected. Of course, the depth of an impression can vary greatly with one and the same person, according to his bodily and spiritual disposition at any given moment. But it is most of all the personality as a whole that is decisive for the depth of an impression.

In the case of love we see with particular clarity this general influence on the value-response that is exercised by the personality giving the response. We already saw that there are cases in which a love possesses a quality, a heroism, and a depth that far surpass the values of the beloved person. In such cases we say of a mother or a wife that the son or husband does not deserve such a love. As problematic as this way of speaking is, it does show a significant discrepancy between the quality of a love and the personality of the beloved. We are only considering these cases to call attention to the fact that the quality of a love, and hence also the moral value of a love, depends upon the personality of the one who loves. We could also say that we are here pointing toward all that the lover invests in his or her love.

The greater a personality, the more he will infuse into his love what is best and most beautiful in himself, provided that his love is really full and deep. We saw earlier that it is an attribute of the love between man and woman that they will mobilize everything good and beautiful they possess so as to give it to the beloved as a gift. This holds analogously in every love where the beloved is granted the central place in the heart of the one who loves. Closely related to this is the question which is here occupying us, namely what the one who loves invests in his love. At the same time, it must clearly be emphasized that this influence of the personality of the lover on the quality of his love and on its moral value can only be found in the case of a person who is truly capable of giving himself or herself, that is, of loving fully and completely. There are doubtless certain rich personalities who are not really capable of a love in which they give themselves completely. Such, for example, seems to have been the case with Goethe. This does not exclude that they are capable of an intense love that exhibits many traits of love, such as the love between man and woman or the love between friends. Yet they never give themselves fully in their loves; other things such as their professional work—whether they are artists or philosophers, scientists or statesmen—play a greater role in their lives. In the case of such people what they invest in their love will not correspond to the greatness and richness of their personality.[8]

---

8   But we prescind here from these cases of a personality which, however great and rich it is, is small and limited in terms of the capacity for love. We will later explore the elements that hinder a full love. We are thinking here only of cases of

The role that love plays in the life of a person is a first important factor manifesting the influence of the personality as a whole on love. Love plays a much greater role for some people than for others. To love stands much more at the center of their lives than other great goods, as for example beauty in nature and in art, the interest in knowledge or politics, and so forth. In the case of productive artists, scientists, philosophers, and statesmen we very often find love more or less giving way to their work. We here prescind from cases in which the role of the love is greater because all other interests are weak. We are not thinking about people in whom the role of love is only relatively great because of the weakness of their relations to all other great goods.

In general, love plays a much greater role in the life of persons than do impersonal things having great value, such as truth or beauty in nature and art. This is especially true of the love between man and woman. Yet this, as already noted, says nothing about how great the role of love in their lives is; it is rather a sign that the lofty non-personal spheres of value play only a slight role. Above all, it is possible that non-personal goods that are not the bearers of high values, indeed that to a large extent are not the bearers of real values at all, can play a great role in their lives, perhaps a greater role than love. For many people, prosperity and wealth mean more than love, for others, it is success and fame that play a much greater role than love, and for still others, it is the gratification of their appetites. These cases we are not considering here, but we are considering those persons who have a great understanding for the high spheres of value and who are capable of a genuine enthusiasm for truth and for beauty in nature and art. It is about such people that we wish to ask: for which of them do non-personal bearers of high values play a greater role than love, and for which of them do persons and the love for persons and being in community with persons play the greater role?

Most of the time playing the greater role is bound up with the potential to give oneself in a particular way. No doubt every value-response encompasses the giving of oneself, yet it is not this potential for self-gift that we here have in mind. Human beings are indeed very different with regard to their potential for this overall capacity to give themselves, and this difference is still incomparably more important[9] for both their overall personality and especially for their moral standing. It is in fact the decisive question. Yet this difference does not just have to do with a natural disposition but also contains a free decision. No doubt the *envergure* (stature) of a personality also plays a role in the degree of this capacity for self-gift, but the free decision of a person is here the main point.

---

love signed by complete self-donation. It is in these cases that the one who loves invests the "treasures" of his personality in his love.

9   [More important, that is, than the self-giving proper to love, discussed immediately below. Trans.]

Love, as we already saw, contains yet another kind of self-giving [*Hingabe*] to persons. This self-giving is contained in every love, even though, within the realm of love toward creatures, it exists in a unique way in the love between man and woman. It engenders a certain kind of dependence on the beloved person, not an illegitimate dependency or falling under the influence of the other, resulting in some kind of lack of independence, but rather a dependence through which the well-being of the beloved person and his stance toward the lover has an influence on the happiness of the lover. We have after all already pointed this out. As soon as I truly love someone, irrespective of the category of love, the happiness of the beloved and his or her stance toward me plays a role in my own happiness; and of course the greater and more intense my love, the more this will be the case. Already the fact that every kind of love other than the love of neighbor aims by nature at requital, the fact that my union of love with another involves a requital of my love by the other, throws light on the difference between the self-gift proper to love and the self-gift proper to every authentic value-response. And if we are here pointing to the differences among people with respect to the capacity for love, or in other words if we are pointing to the role which love as such plays in the life of a person,[10] then it is the special self-gift of love, the special self-gift to another person that we have in mind. This self-gift is not as dependent on free choice as the general self-gift that is proper to every value-response and that is naturally also to be found in love. This general self-gift expresses itself in love above all in the readiness to make sacrifices for the other and to devote oneself to the other. The particular self-gift proper to love, which is bound up with the role of love in the life of a person, is not so entirely within our power and cannot be acquired through a free decision. Yet this kind of self-gift is also not independent of our free overall attitude. This is why it contributes not only to the qualitative greatness of love but also to its moral value.

This self-gift expresses itself especially in how much a person invests into his or her love. In certain people all that is best and most beautiful in them emerges and stands out in their love in a particular way. They are most themselves when they love. They invest all of their spiritual *élan*, their plentitude and, above all, their moral stature in their love. Other people are most themselves in their relation to beauty in nature and art or in their relation to their country or in one or another great task to which they have dedicated themselves. Their human relationships exist "on the side," and while they may be beautiful and noble, it is not in their loves that these persons show their "best."[11]

10	We do not mean to portray the capacity for loving and the role of love in a person's life as being identical factors, though they are closely related.

11	Of course, I prescind in this context from the religious sphere. For it is unmistakably clear that in a religious person who loves Christ and through Christ loves God

If we think of Leonore in Beethoven's *Fidelio* or of Imogene in Shakespeare's *Cymbeline*, then we have typical examples of all the great moral characteristics which are actualized and invested in their love. The heroism, the ultimate commitment that is not deterred by any danger, the unconditional devotion combined with humility—all of this radiates from their love and makes it a thing of great value.

This process of investing is not a deliberate one but takes place by itself; it makes itself consciously felt in the desire to offer the beloved one's best. Beyond the already mentioned capacity for love, the one who loves also invests the stature and the richness of his personality in his love. This investing can endow a love with values that far exceed what arises from the value-response to the beauty of the beloved person. Even if a great personality loves a lesser personality, his love will be suffused by the breath of his being, by his greatness and fullness, and it will emanate a radiance that goes not only far beyond what the other person is in reality but also goes beyond the image the greater personality has of the beloved person. Consider, for example, the love of a person like Keats for Fanny Brown or of the love of Mozart for his wife Constanze.

In this context, however, it is not the high extra-moral values, such as stature of personality, inner plenitude, spiritual contact with morally non-relevant goods, alertness, creative power, the capacity to register differences, which have a bearing on the process of investing. Rather, it is the warmth, the heroism, the moral stature of a person, the moral depth and seriousness, the faithfulness, goodness and purity which are invested in love; these are what endow love with great moral value.

There is naturally a deep connection between the first and second sources of moral values in a natural love, namely the value-responding function of love and the personality of the one who loves (that is, the moral status of the one who loves and all that he invests in his love). We already saw that who a person loves is very characteristic for that person. We already mentioned that someone like Werther could never have loved a person like Carmen, and conversely that José could hardly have loved a Lotte. In order for the heart of a person to be so touched by the high values of another person as to enkindle love, a certain moral status is presupposed.

On the other hand, it is also true that a morally awakened person has many levels and that there is nothing to prevent him from being taken captive by the

---

something incomparably great is actualized, something that in an entirely new sense is that person's "best"; it is something to which he is called in an ultimate way and which he can realize only through the grace of God. Here the primacy and the unique role of love for God are clearly called for and required. But at present we are only speaking, as we have said, of the relation of natural love to the world of morality.

charm of another person who is much less morally conscious and awakened. In the lives of great moral personalities we often see that they are capable of various kinds of loves, that is, of more and less sublime loves. To which level in a person does the beauty of another person appeal? Is this beauty a charm of a vital sort, which appeals to a peripheral level, or is it the radiance of a spiritual and moral nobility which appeals to the deepest and most authentic level? It is for this reason that the sublimity of a love is not in every respect guaranteed by the moral status of a person. The decisive influence of the personality of the one who loves is expressed above all in what they "invest" in their love.

With this we already touch upon the third dimension of the relationship between love and morality, namely, the effect of love on the person. As is so often the case, we have here a reciprocal relationship. On the one hand, a love is deeper and more beautiful to the extent that the one who loves is great and deep. On the other hand, love makes the one who loves greater and more beautiful. When we now turn to the effect of love, we find not only that many important qualities which otherwise would only slumber as potentialities in a person are actualized through loving, but we also find that love in many cases also leads a person to a full awakening and to stances and attitudes of which he would not be capable without this love.[12]

3. Moral values and the "effect" of love

We therefore now turn our attention to the effect of love. When someone who has never before really loved anyone, now loves someone for the first time, be it a friend, a sister or a brother, or be it that a spousal love arises in him, there will always take place in the entire being of that person a certain breakthrough. Naturally, the quality of this breakthrough will depend on the depth and moral stature of the personality of the one who loves as well as on the nature of the beloved person. It is clear that the question who is loved is also of great importance, since, as we already saw earlier, the nature of those values which nourish the overall beauty of the person plays a decisive role in determining the quality and depth of the love. The depth and quality of the love clearly have a decisive influence on the kind of breakthrough.

In every intense and complete love a person undergoes a certain awakening. I begin to live more authentically; a new dimension in my personal existence discloses itself and I am liberated from the captivity of habits, from the bonds of convention, from dependence on the opinions of others, from the social image I have of myself.[13] My true self breaks through in love; by lov-

---

12   In this context we are, as already noted, prescinding from any consideration of religious awakening, from all kinds of conversion and *metanoia*.

13   This is shown in a unique way in Wagner's *Tristan und Isolde* when Tristan in the first act, after his love for Isolde has been fully revealed, sings: "Was träumte mir von Tristans Ehre" ("What fantasies I had about Tristan's honor"). By "Ehre" and "honor" is meant the entire sphere of human fame.

ing and giving myself in love I am able to receive as a gift my better and more authentic self. By loving I become more beautiful, and this precisely through the special commitment and self-gift which is proper to love, and also through a certain humility. In loving, I grow in humility because love is a gift and because I experience myself being "seized" by something that is greater than myself. Before I had relied on my own strength and my ideal had been to live life out of my own power without any dependence on anyone else, but now all of this collapses when I love. I experience my creaturehood, and in a blissful way, for I experience that the incomparably precious thing which I have received is a pure gift. Above all, I approach the person whom I love with a humility that I have not known before. In the presence of the beloved person I am prepared to take off the armor with which I approach all other people, the armor of self-assertion and latent rivalry. We will return to all of this in detail when we study the obstacles that can lead a person to refuse to love or to be loved. Here it suffices to point out that every deep and intense love goes hand in hand with becoming more awakened and with becoming liberated from the many shackles of everyday life. Every great love makes a person both more magnanimous and more humble; and these values are all moral values.

This effect of love is obscured by the fact that there are undoubtedly many dangers in natural love that exist because of fallen human nature, as we saw. Naturally, the magnitude of these dangers depends on the category of the love and on the moral status of the one who loves. Yet we also saw in speaking of the dangers in love (chapter 12, part 1) that one must always distinguish between effects rooted in the nature of love and those effects which may result from fallen human nature, effects which are caused by the intrusion of factors other than love. This of course holds not only in the particular case of love, but in general. Thus great and high-level intellectual work, particularly when it is successful, can make a person proud, conceited, and full of himself, and yet this is not to deny that in itself this work can have an ennobling influence on a person.

Whenever there is a noble, great, and deep love which is not bound up with any dark passion, the effect of this love is liberating and it challenges us to heroism, and does so without any threat of enslavement or any moral danger. One could object: do these examples, such as Leonore in Beethoven's *Fidelio*, really have to do with an effect of love? Is not the nobility and heroism in Leonore's love, the inner freedom which we encounter in her, not clearly a result of Leonore's outstanding moral personality? Is this not a typical case in which a great moral personality invests and actualizes all the moral values of their person in his or her love? Can one really speak of an effect precisely of love?

While this is undoubtedly true, it would nevertheless be wrong to say that all of this greatness and moral freedom, this heroism, would have been actualized in Leonore if she had not come to know Florestan and if she had not received the gift of such a love. While the personality of the one who loves is significant and decisive for the emergence of the moral values of a love, we cannot overlook the fact that the gift of a great natural love in and of itself has a morally relevant effect on the one who loves.

The actualization of many moral powers slumbering in a personality is, after all, an "effect" of love. None of these traits would have developed were it not that this love was given to this person. Yet there is even more to the effect of love. Love is not just an opportunity for the development of moral powers in a person in the way in which the demands of an unusual situation allow for the development of certain powers. Nor does love offer an occasion for development as in the situation where for some reason a person is forced to act in a play and thereby discovers a talent for acting. The liberating "effect" of love is not just an occasion for the unfolding of moral powers; in addition, the gift-character of love has a specifically positive effect on the personality of the person who loves. We can see this most clearly if we consider a person who is neither a great moral personality nor is in any particular moral danger, a person whose love possesses neither the sublime character which we find in the case of Leonore nor the intermingling of dangerous moments which we find in a primarily vital love. Consider a relatively mediocre, conventional, decent person who suddenly falls intensely in love. We can clearly see the liberating "effect" of love: we can see how, if only intermittently, such a person is transported to a higher level of existence, how he becomes generally more conscious of values, how he increasingly discovers the true countenance of the world, how his mediocrity is dissolved, how his soul becomes more beautiful than it was before.

The degree to which all of this happens naturally depends upon the personality of the one who loves and on the quality of the love, which for its part depends on the values in the beloved person that engender the response of love. Yet a certain effect in this general direction is always present as the result of loving. This emerges with particular clarity in the love between man and woman. And yet even if the awakening and the greater consciousness of values possesses a far more definite character in the love between man and woman, still something analogous is to be found in every great love. When a person who has never really loved finds a friend whom he loves deeply and to whom he gives his heart, a great transformation of his entire being begins to take place. This person transcends himself in a way that is otherwise impossible in the natural (as distinct from the supernatural) world. There is no substitute for the self-gift of love; as we already saw, no other value-response, not even one directed toward morally relevant goods, can replace this particular kind of breakthrough and this specific commitment that involves giving one's heart. Of all the value-responses to truth, to beauty in nature and in art, as enriching as they can be, as much as they can enlarge a personality, as inspiring as they can be, none can replace this particular form of commitment and self-gift.

Even if the response to morally relevant goods is far more essential, far more important and morally valuable than one or another natural love, and even if, as we already saw, such a response possesses a unique kind of transcendence that is lacking in natural love, this specifically moral response cannot replace the special kind of breakthrough that is released by love. The new warmth, the new *élan*, the moving way in which the heart melts—all of this is proper only to love. This is in general true of love and of the giving of one's heart—it is true across the different categories of love. Whether it is a mother who loves her son or daughter so much that they become her most important earthly good, or whether it is a brother who loves his sister to this extent, or a sister her brother—as soon as the love involves a complete gift of the heart, as soon as it is no longer one love among others but is the central love, granting the beloved person primacy of place, then we are directly dealing with the effect of love as love.

Let us emphasize once again: the more sublime the quality of a love, the higher the sphere of values in which the love is situated, then the greater will be the moral effect of this love on the person who loves. We already saw the world of difference between the love of Leonore and the love of a Dmitri Karamazov. Even if for a moment we prescind from the disastrous effect of the dark passion which is entwined in Dmitri's love, we cannot fail to see how great the difference is between the effect of these two loves. The love of a Leonore or of someone like Imogene in Shakespeare's *Cymbeline* or of a person like Sonja for Raskolnikov in Dostoevsky's *Crime and Punishment* has a morally ennobling, liberating, and uplifting effect on the basis of the sphere of values in which it is rooted; a love primarily rooted in the sphere of vital values can never have such an effect. The influence which the quality of a love has on the moral effect of a love is also bound up with this fact: the higher the quality of a love, the more incompatible it is with being entangled in morally negative stances. Aspects of dark and blind passion, slavish dependency, and the tendency of being swept away in an unsanctioned way are kept out of the love of a Leonore or an Imogene by the quality of their love. The clear light, the *sursum corda* ("lift up your heart") which is characteristic of the love of an Imogene, prevents these dark forces from slipping in.[14]

We can appreciate the moral significance of the effect of any full love in the sense just explained only if we compare the person who loves with someone who is incapable of loving. If we consider a person who, for whatever reason, is incapable of giving his heart to another, a person for whom there is

---

14   Naturally this should not be misunderstood as if in this sublime love the lovers do not experience "being grasped" by something powerful and "losing themselves." But this "being grasped" by something great has an entirely different character from "being swept away." I have discussed this is my works, *Purity* and *Transformation in Christ*.

some inner resistance to making this commitment, then the moral significance of making this commitment will not escape our notice. The moral significance of giving one's own heart stands out clearly when we think of a person whose heart is too insensitive ever to be affected by another person, a person who is too self-absorbed even to look at another person in such a way as to be struck by the beauty of the other, a person who is too egoistic to become involved with another person to the point of letting his heart be enflamed by the other. The words of Schiller in the final movement of the Ninth Symphony, "*Ja, wer auch nur eine Seele sein nennt auf dem Erdenrund! Und wer's nie gekonnt, der stehle weinend sich aus diesem Bund!*"[15] refer to the poverty of a life lived without a community of love and without being united with a person on the basis of mutual love. In a similar way we can say of the person who is incapable of loving that he or she has not fully lived.

The quality of love is decisive for the moral character of the effect of love in two respects: first, through the radiation of the moral nobility and depth of the love, and second, through the fact that a love is protected by its nobility and depth from the accretion of those elements that can have such morally disastrous consequences as to outweigh by far all the positive moral effects of love. Likewise, the kind of personality found in the one who loves, and the kind of person he was before he began to love, also have a decisive influence on the values of the effect of love.

As we already saw, the capacity for love [*Liebespotential*] varies greatly from one person to another. The greater this capacity, the more ardent and the richer will be the love and, accordingly, the effect of the love will also be entirely different. It is not difficult to see that the effect of love on the person who loves will be deeper and more radical the greater the outpouring of love, which also depends on a person's capacity for love. This difference primarily concerns how great the effect of love is; it concerns the fact that a love which is nourished by a great capacity for love moves a person in an entirely different way, penetrating to the very roots of his being; and yet this difference is also significant from a moral standpoint, for the person capable of greater love also gives himself more fully. Such a person goes much further in casting off

---

15   "Whoever can call just one other person his own [should join in our jubilation]. But let anyone who has never achieved this weep and slink away from our community." Of course, these words from Schiller's *Ode to Joy* cannot in any way be applied to the person whose heart is entirely filled in and through Christ with the love for God as well as with the love of neighbor and who because of a vow does not call any other human being "his own." Indeed, such a person has an incomparably greater capacity for love and through his exclusive commitment to Christ he is lifted above natural love in all its forms. The fire of caritas, the holy love, lives in him or her, and the effect of this love is incomparable with that of any natural love. Of course, such a love is a special charism which not everyone who has chosen consecrated virginity possesses throughout his or her lifetime.

the chains that bind him to laziness, comfort, worldly success and a thousand other peripheral goods.

The greater a person's capacity for love, the more that person shows forth the truth of wonderful words of the Song of Songs: "*Si homo dederit omnem substantiam domus suae pro dilectione, quasi nihil despiciat eam.*"[16]

And so we see clearly how various are the relationships existing between the kinds of natural love and the world of morality. Even if these natural loves per se do not arise from the fundamental moral attitude of a person, even if they do not belong to the typical moral stances of a person, such as the pure value-response to morally relevant goods, and above all even if they are not morally obligatory in the way in which love of neighbor and the love for God are obligatory, they can nevertheless possess great moral value.

4. Moral values and disvalues in the acceptance or refusal of love

Yet even moral obligation can play a certain role within the context of natural love, as we already pointed out. We will now turn to this further relationship between natural love and morality.

We saw that the love for a friend and the love of man and woman are both gifts and that one cannot speak of a moral obligation to love in either of these ways. And yet we said that this does not yet answer the question whether one can speak of a moral obligation to give the right response when I am granted the gift of encountering a person whose being deeply touches my heart. The question which now occupies us has to do with whether it is morally obligatory or not to open myself to love when the gift of friendship or of spousal love is offered by God. We are not asking here whether there is a moral obligation to continue loving someone who has already been my friend; we will address this question when we speak in the next chapter about faithfulness.

Cases in which the refusal of a love is morally obligatory. The moral relevance of the response of being open to the gift of a love will become clearer if we consider the motives one may have for refusing to enter such a love. It can of course happen that I have a moral obligation not to allow myself to become drawn into a spousal love. This is the case when an existing bond precludes such a love. This bond can result either from an already existing love of this kind, in which case it is a requirement of faithfulness not to enter upon any other love of this kind, or it can be a bond that exists because of a vow. It can also happen that I clearly recognize that a person who deeply touches my heart represents a great danger for me, that the other could endanger me morally and influence my faith in an adverse way. Then I am strictly obliged not to become involved in this love. As soon as a person whom I might love represents a danger for my relation with God, I am not permitted to become involved with that person.

---

16 "If a man were to give away all of his personal wealth for the sake of love, he would regard the loss as nothing."

The latter also applies in the case of the love among friends. While the obligation not to become involved in a love of friendship because of an earlier bond does not apply in an analogous way, still the influence of a person that endangers my soul engenders an obligation which is just as strict. We are not permitted to enter into a friendship with a person which in any way draws us away from God.

All these negative obligations are quite easy to understand. The motive for refusing a love in these cases is not only legitimate but involves a clear moral obligation not to become involved in the love.

Yet there are many other illegitimate motives which move persons not to become involved in love. We are of course prescinding here from obstacles to love such as hardheartedness and being completely dominated by pride and concupiscence, since these obstacles prevent a person from reaching the point at which their heart could even be touched. We are thinking here of the motives which could lead a person to refuse a love.

1. *First illegitimate reason for refusing a love: spiritual sluggishness and shrinking away from commitment.* One such motive is a spiritual sluggishness which recoils from all intensity and from every *élan*. The beauty of another person may very well touch the heart of a person who is sluggish in this way, yet he shrinks from the commitment of love, from being possessed by love, and from being torn from a conventional and harmless rhythm of life. This spiritual sluggishness can even be found in hardworking people, for it has nothing to do with the kind of sluggishness which shrinks from all work, which avoids all effort and aims at effortless play or distracting amusement as the ideal. It is a much deeper sluggishness which leads a person to resist every spiritual *élan* and to fear any "losing themselves," to fear every experience of great intensity. It is also a specific sluggishness of the heart, one that is closely bound up with mediocrity. Above all, people who are sluggish in this sense naturally shrink from the great adventure presented by the love between man and woman. Here we see at its greatest the experience of being possessed, being torn from a conventional rhythm of life, in which one oversees everything and yields to the pull of the customary. *"Herz, mein Herz, was soll das geben, welch' ein fremdes neues Leben, ich erkenne Dich nicht mehr."*[17] This is particularly abhorrent to the sluggish, mediocre person. In fact every great love, every deep commitment to another person is repugnant to this type of person.

Now if someone who is motivated in this way refuses to become involved in a great love that has been offered to him as a gift, despite the fact that the

---

17 [Von Hildebrand quotes here by memory some lines from a poem of Goethe that begins with the words, *"Neue Liebe, neues Leben."* "My heart, O my heart, what is going on? What strange new life awakens in me! I hardly know you any more" (my translation). Trans.]

beauty of the other person has touched his heart, then surely this is not moral-ly irrelevant. It is definitely a stance marked by a moral disvalue; it is also a form of egotism; indeed, this sluggishness is a form of concupiscence. It is admittedly not a moral wrong, not a sin, as when one refuses to give a response to a morally relevant good, or when one destroys a morally relevant good, or when one contravenes a moral commandment. The morally negative relevance of such behavior does not have the same central character of a moral wrong that we find in murder, theft, in impurity of any kind, in adultery, deception, betrayal, malicious pleasure, or envy. This moral difference becomes clear when we consider those cases in which someone refuses to give himself to God—whether he has closed himself to faith or to the authentic love for God—because of this mediocrity and sluggishness. Here we are dealing with immorality in the full sense of the term, with a primordial sin. While the refusal to become involved in a human love is not immoral in this way, still it is somehow something that is not morally in order and ought not to be: this sluggishness of heart is by nature morally negative and the refusal to enter into a relationship of love, the unwillingness to accept the gift of love, is also regrettable from a moral point of view and it is above all symptomatic of a cer-tain moral imperfection.

Before turning to the question of the extent to which one can speak of a moral obligation to enter into a relationship of love, we want to consider other sorts of illegitimate motives which can lead to a refusal of love. As we already mentioned, spiritual sluggishness is also bound up with a specific fear of any kind of intensity. One often forgets that the mediocre person shrinks from intense joy as much as from great suffering. The aversion to suffering is char-acteristic of all human beings and is deeply rooted in human nature. It is quite natural, and the fact that a person suffers is a pronounced disvalue. This aver-sion has nothing to do with intensity but rather applies to all suffering, and the greater the suffering, the greater the aversion. The aversion to intensity as such, which is manifested in the fact that a person shrinks from intense happi-ness, intense joy, and all intense positive affectivity, is a sign of a mediocre per-son. Such persons wish to linger with small joys in a state of harmless happi-ness, to remain in a context in which they have a complete overview, in which they feel themselves to be master of the situation, a context to which they are accustomed, lacking any element of surprise or adventure. Such persons avoid any and every great love. They may very well be able to love many people, yet they shrink from the intensity of a great love, from a love in which they would really give their heart. They are afraid of any kind of "being possessed" [*Gehabtwerden*] as well as of the great and intense happiness with which this is bound up. This fear is something morally negative. It is admittedly not the bearer of moral disvalues such as we find in envy, malicious pleasure, or hatred. It does not belong to those attitudes which are flagrantly immoral or sinful. Yet it is not morally neutral in the way in which the lack of interest in chemistry is neutral. It is not morally unobjectionable but is rather something which is really morally negative. From a moral point of view it should not exist in a person. And if this is the attitude behind a person's refusal to enter in to a love, then from a moral point of view the refusal is something deplorable.

2. *Second illegitimate reason for refusing a love: fear of being disappointed.* The fear which may lead a person not to accept the offer of love may be an entirely different kind of fear with roots which do not lie in mediocrity. We have in mind the fear of being disappointed. This kind of fear, which is fear in a more proper sense, is much nobler than the above-mentioned fear related to the spiritual sluggishness of the heart.

Those suffering from this fear are by no means mediocre people. They are in fact capable of giving themselves deeply and they yearn to do so, yet they possess a deep distrust and they fear so greatly the pain of disappointment that they would rather forgo the commitment of love and the joy it brings. These people represent more of a tragic type, whereas the mediocre person, whether primarily sluggish or fearful of all intensity of experience, represents more of a depressing type.

Naturally, this fear is often traceable to disappointments experienced by a person in similar situations. Yet it can also rest upon a general attitude of distrust and is typical of the person who does not believe in the love of God for him. Moreover, such a person often has a certain kind of inferiority complex and so cannot imagine that he could be loved.

This attitude is also not morally unobjectionable, and though it is far less negative than the mediocrity of the heart, nevertheless from a moral point of view a person should not allow it to reign in him but should instead struggle to overcome it.

3. *Third illegitimate reason for refusing a love: the ideal of independence and the "bachelor mentality."* Another typical motive for refusing to enter into a great love is an ideal of independence rooted in pride and concupiscence. We are thinking of persons who are not so egotistical that they would not be ready occasionally to do someone a favor or to stand up for one or another ideal or to make sacrifices in their work: we have in mind those who do not want to bind themselves to another person, who in their hearts want to remain independent. Their ideal of independence, which is capricious through and through, leads them to see the dependence that results from the gift of one's own heart as a bothersome constraint of their freedom. As we have already seen, the problem is not so much the dependence which results from having to care for another, for these people do not regard caring for others as a constraint upon their independence when it comes from their profession. If they are required to care for others as doctors or as welfare officials or as teachers, they will conscientiously fulfill these obligations. After all, they have freely chosen their profession. What they most of all shrink from is not the dependence that results from their obligations, from caring for another, but the dependence that flows from their own love, from the fact that their happiness depends upon the

beloved person, that the happiness and the grief of the beloved becomes their own happiness and grief. It is the independence of their heart, the independence of their own subjectivity [*Eigenleben*], which they do not want to give up. This idol of independence is clearly rooted in pride and in concupiscence and its morally negative character cannot be overlooked.

A particular form of this idol of independence is to be found in a certain "bachelor mentality." We do not mean to say that every bachelor has this attitude. We have in mind the bachelor ideal that we mentioned in chapter 9. This "bachelor" takes pleasure in remaining independent in his subjectivity [*Eigenleben*] and of avoiding the specific kind of commitment which is involved in the love between man and woman and above all in a marriage that is filled by a deep spousal love. Such a person wants to be independent in the sense that no one disturbs his state of being self-enclosed. This person also wants to avoid the unique surrender of his heart and of the entire rhythm of his life. His is an attitude which specifically resists marriage, but also resists any total love in which one gives one's heart. This typical "bachelor" may have many peripheral love affairs. While he shrinks from every "loss of self" in a higher sense, from every "divine madness," from every experience of being absorbed in anything which is greater than himself and elevates him, it does not necessarily follow that the "bachelor" will shrink from the experience of being swept away, provided it does not entail a bond or a commitment of the heart and provided he can withdraw whenever he pleases.

It is interesting to compare this attitude of the "bachelor" with that of the man who enters a marriage without giving away his heart and who perceives his wife as an extended ego. Such a marriage after all contains nothing whatsoever which would conflict with the bachelor ideal. It lacks the commitment, the gift of the heart, and the dependence on the beloved that flows from love. Nevertheless, the bachelor of whom we speak will prefer to have a housekeeper and eventually turn to extra-marital affairs, since he abhors the formal bond that is even involved in a marriage in which the solidarity with the spouse merely has the character of an extended ego rather than of love. The formal bond, the rightful claims of his spouse on him—already this is too much for his ideal of independence. The attitude of seeing in the spouse simply an extended ego presupposes a certain primitive brutality, and this the bachelor need not have. He may be too good-natured, sensitive, and sophisticated to consider as desirable or enjoyable a marriage in which the other is a kind of possession. This explains why the bachelor abhors marriage in any form.

Clearly this attitude is also not morally irrelevant. It is not morally neutral like a special affinity for sports. While there is nothing morally negative in the fact that someone does not feel made for marriage and that he lacks the capacity for spousal love, still there clearly is—just as with each of the above-mentioned obstacles—something morally negative in the attitude of a person who, even when he is deeply touched by another and would be capable of a spousal love, resists entering into this love and the marriage to which it might lead, and does so simply for the sake of not having to give up his splendid "bachelor" independence.

Cases in which the acceptance and reciprocation of love is morally "required." The question now arises: in light of the moral disvalue of these motives for refusing to enter into a deep relationship of love, can we speak of a moral obligation to enter into it when one is in fact presented with the offer of such a love?

While we have thus far spoken primarily about the love between friends and the love between man and woman, we said that our considerations also apply analogously to any love in which one really gives one's heart, whatever the category of the love. Now one could object that surely the question of an obligation to love is entirely different in regard to the love of parents and children and even in regard to the love among siblings, than in regard to the love between friends and between man and woman. Since these loves involve a situation in which the relation to the other person is not brought about by love but results from an objective ordering of persons to one another [*Zuordnung*] that precedes love, the same question of obligation cannot be raised here. This is undoubtedly true, yet it does not rule out the possibility that even within the love of friendship and within spousal love I could refuse a love in which I must surrender my heart, and that the question arises even here whether I am not morally obligated not to refuse the love.

In the love of friendship and in spousal love someone only becomes my friend or my spousally beloved because of the fact that I enter into this love. It is quite true that this situation does not exist in the case of these other categories of love. A child is the child of its parents whether they love the child or not, and in fact this is true not only objectively but also at the level of their conscious experiencing. Independently of love, parents are parents to their children, brothers and sisters are siblings to one another. The bonds of community are not constituted by love here. They are determined by objective factors, so that they are discovered: the other person presents himself or herself to us as already standing within this community and in this way appeals to our love. It would seem, therefore, that the question whether we are obligated to love our parents, our children, our siblings, corresponds to the question whether one is obligated to love one's friend or one's spouse. Yet this is not the question with which we are occupied here. We already mentioned that we will deal with this question in discussing the role of faithfulness in love. We are asking rather whether an obligation exists to enter into a love when the offer of such a love is made to me, an "offer" in the sense that I encounter a person whose beauty touches my heart and whom I could love. In the case of a spousal love, this would be the moment when a bond of community does not yet exist, that is, when the question is whether someone will become my fiancé or my spouse. Indeed, it is the moment in which I receive the first "invitation" to this love. It is the same in the case of the love of friendship. Can one pose this question in regard to the love of parents for their children, the love of children for their parents, or the love of siblings for each other, when independently of my love the other person is already connected with me within a community?

We will see that this question can indeed be posed, but this becomes apparent only after we have made a further differentiation with regard to the concept of "the obligation to love." One can mean by this the obligation to take a loving attitude toward a person that corresponds to the special character of the objective relationship. In the case of the love of the child for its parents, this entails a reverent, obedient, trustful attitude on the part of the child, a sense of solidarity, a spirit of considerateness; put simply, an attitude which lovingly does justice to what is due to parents as parents. The case of the love of parents for their children involves the responsible care for the children, a deep solidarity with them, lovingly entering their world, the readiness to make special sacrifices for the child, and the loving atmosphere in which the child is immersed and in which it feels itself to be sheltered. In the case of the love of siblings, there is the solidarity, the intimacy, the loving support of brother or sister for one another. All of this—and it is a great deal—can be considered under the heading of love when one speaks of an obligation to love.

But love can also be considered as the gift of my heart, the commitment through which the other becomes the center of my own life, this unique delight and pleasure in the other person who becomes at the very least one main source of my earthly joy.

The question of an obligation to love in the first sense cannot be posed in the same way with regard to parental love, filial love, and sibling love as it can be posed with regard to the love between friends and the love between man and woman. This is because of the different relationship that kinds of love have to a particular form of community. In the case of parental, filial, and sibling love, there is doubtless a moral obligation in this first sense. There is a moral obligation to approach the other with the loving attitude called for by the objective character of the community, to behave in such a way as to correspond to the essence of the objective community. As already noted, there is no analogy to this in the case of the love between friends and of the love between man and woman, unless it be an analogy to the form of faithfulness to a love which already exists, for without this love the other person would not have become my friend or my spousally beloved. A certain analogy would only exist in the case of a spouse in a marriage that was not entered out of love.

If, however, we think of love in the second sense, namely, in terms of the gift of one's heart, we can pose the question with respect to every category of love, since an obligation to love in such a way is never rooted in the objective ordering of persons within a community.[18] The offer of this love is always

---

18 Naturally, we are here prescinding from the love of parents for a small child, of which we spoke elsewhere.

rooted in the individual character of the other person, and the question whether it is obligatory to enter such a love can also be posed with regard to parental love, filial love, and the love between siblings. Here, too, someone can refuse to enter into love on the basis of the above-mentioned illegitimate motives. We will certainly have to inquire whether or not the question of the obligation to enter such a love is influenced by the fact of the already existing order of persons in a community. But in any case one need not settle this issue of influence in order to examine the question of the obligation to love in the full and most proper sense.

Since the refusal to enter into a love in the absence of any moral obligation would appear always to result from morally negative motives, one might be tempted to say there is after all a moral obligation to enter into a love, an obligation not to refuse it. Yet before we can answer this question decisively we must first ask whether the following alternative is correct: is it true that if the refusal to love is not morally obligatory, then the refusal necessarily results from morally negative motives?

Are there not cases in which someone declines a love on the basis of motives which do not have the morally negative character of those motives that we examined above? For example, if a great artist believes that a marriage would for him be incompatible with a full commitment to his work and if he therefore does not enter into a burgeoning spousal love, then this motive would not have the morally negative character of the "sluggishness" of the heart or of the idol of bachelor independence. We do not here wish to determine whether in making this choice such an artist does justice to the true hierarchy of values, nor whether a marriage would really be incompatible with his work. It suffices to ascertain that this motive for the refusal does not of itself represent something morally negative. The same also holds true for a daughter who dedicates herself entirely to the care of her ailing parents and therefore believes that she must refrain from marrying. If she does not enter into a relation that could grow into a spousal love, then clearly the motive for her refusal is not something morally negative. To what extent her choice is right depends so much upon individual factors that nothing can be decided about it in general. Thus we can see that—prescinding from cases in which the refusal of love is morally required—it is impossible to say that the person who turns down the gift of a love acts always from morally negative motives.

We can see, however, that in these instances there is a moral call to accept and not to refuse such a gift, a call that is overruled in such people by their conviction concerning a higher call. Regardless of whether their conviction is right, the refusal results because they believe that it is required by their commitment to a good that they place above marriage. Implicitly this shows that there is a call to accept this gift and that only for weighty reasons should the gift be declined. Of course, people in these cases usually perceive themselves as abstaining from a source of happiness and thus do not distinctly perceive the morally relevant call which arises here. Yet in reality a morally relevant call does exist.

We can say quite generally that it is not morally indifferent whether one appreciates a gift one receives, whether one gratefully accepts it, or whether one declines it for the sake of some lesser good. If someone is capable of grasping the value of a particular good, then it is not morally neutral if he sacrifices the possession of this good for a much more peripheral good. The attitude of Esau, who sacrificed his right as firstborn for a bowl of lentil soup, is not morally irrelevant. Even if it is not a serious sin, not a moral wrong in the strict sense, still it is morally bad.

In our context, however, we are dealing with a gift of a special kind, the acceptance of which appeals to many morally positive attitudes. The moral relevance of this gift and of the offer to accept it is thereby enhanced.

The invitation and call to love. We now turn to a consideration of the "offer" of any great and central love, not just the case of a burgeoning spousal love. There is always a morally relevant call to accept the gift of love when the refusal to love results from the above-mentioned morally negative motives. When we speak of a "gift," we do not in this context mean the love of the other person for us but we mean instead the fact that we encounter a person whom we can love—the gift of being able to love. It is clear, however, that this call is not on the same level as the imperative call arising from morally relevant values. Not only does it lack the character of a strict moral obligation, it also differs from the non-obligatory call that arises from morally relevant values. What is different in our case of the gift of a human love is that the moral question is not the direct theme but is only a secondary theme. It is not the moral question which is at stake; we are not dealing with the moral theme.

Rather, we are dealing with a kind of morally relevant call similar to the case of someone who possesses a great artistic or intellectual talent and who does nothing to develop this talent, indeed, who evades all opportunities that would stir up his talent and who does so because of his sluggishness and because he shrinks from the effort and *élan* which the development and application of his talent would demand. Without a doubt there is in this case also a moral call to develop the talent, and while this call is not a moral imperative in the strict sense, it still possesses a morally relevant character. Even though the theme of the situation is not primarily moral, still it is clearly not morally neutral, as when we are presented with the decision whether or not to go to the movies—assuming that no other circumstance exists which should influence my decision from a moral point of view—I go simply because I am interested in movies, because I enjoy them, and because at the moment I feel like going to see a movie.

The case of the gift of love has a certain analogy to the case of a religious vocation. Someone may believe that he is called to the convent or to the priesthood, yet cannot make up his mind to enter religious life because he shrinks from the sacrifices bound up with such a life.

Of course, the case of the vocation is in many respects entirely different. In the first place, a vocation presupposes faith and can only arise within a Christian setting. Yet the moment one sees the whole problem of talents in a religious light, it acquires an entirely new moral significance. As soon as the gift of having some special talent is seen by me in the light of God and I consider it as a "talent" as entrusted to me by God (we read of this in the Gospel), my obligation to develop and use it becomes something entirely different and new, far surpassing the obligation felt by the nonbeliever. All gifts of God contain within themselves a responsibility: I owe it to the divine giver to receive them and "manage them" in the right way.

Thus the call to enter a great love also gains a far more moral character when I realize that this gift comes from God, whom I understand as the God of Christianity. But even if I recognize that the call to love comes from God, there is still with regard to moral relevance a great difference between this call and the call to the priesthood or religious life. Since this latter has to do with a special surrender and devotion to God, it takes on an incomparably greater moral relevance, for it is much closer to the ultimate ground and source of all morality.

The only thing these two cases have in common is that both involve a call which is morally relevant though without the moral element being thematic. Yet the great difference, which is also morally significant, is that the case of a priestly or religious vocation has to do with an eminently religious theme, whereas the case of human love only involves a sublime human theme that is natural (as distinct from supernatural).

If we spoke of a certain analogy between the call to love and a religious vocation, this neither means that they should be placed on the same level nor should it be denied that the moral relevance is of a different order when the theme is religious. The point of analogy is simply this: in both cases the theme is not a moral theme even though a morally relevant call is present.

And so we have seen what manifold relationships exist between natural love and the sphere of morality. These result from love insofar as it is a value-response, from the "gift" of love, and from the moral status of the person who loves. We saw the moral significance of the effect of a great love. And, finally, we saw that, while natural love in the proper sense cannot of itself be commanded (it is a gift which we cannot give to ourselves), one can speak of a morally relevant call to accept the gift of love, a call that one should not decline unless this is required for other reasons.

It now remains for us to investigate the two other fundamental relationships between natural love and the sphere of morality, namely, faithfulness and the ordo amoris. This will be the subject of the following two chapters.

CHAPTER THIRTEEN

Faithfulness

The moral obligation to be faithful

The question of the obligation to love naturally leads us to faithfulness. If, as we saw, we cannot speak of a strict obligation to turn toward someone with a love of friendship, let alone with a spousal love, there is nonetheless a strict moral obligation to be faithful as soon as a friendship or a mutual spousal love has been constituted. This obligation is of an eminently moral nature. Faithfulness is in general a central moral virtue, and the special faithfulness proper to love is clearly a moral value. As we already mentioned, it is certainly the case that unfaithfulness in love is morally bad.

As we said, faithfulness is in general a very important virtue, a fundamental moral attitude. Faithfulness always presupposes continuity, yet not every form of continuity is faithfulness, not even faithfulness in the broad sense. We have written about the nature and significance of continuity in other books.[1] Continuity is something much more general than faithfulness; it is of fundamental importance for the entirety of personal existence and for the whole life of the spiritual person. As we have shown elsewhere, continuity is the presupposition for all spiritual growth, for all development, and for authentic personal life. Continuity also makes itself morally felt in the virtue of perseverance. That we should hold fast to everything which in itself is morally required on the basis of its value, includes continuity, but this imperative of continuity flows from values. Continuity as such is not required here for its own sake but as an element of the superactual value-response.

Faithfulness in the broad sense

Faithfulness in the broad sense is to persevere in the superactual value-response to all goods possessing great values. Thus one says, for example, "Remain faithful to the tenets of morality," "Remain faithful to your religion," "Remain faithful to God," etc. Here it is obviously a matter of the duty of continuity, perseverance, and holding fast to a value-response. Faithfulness in this broad sense is clearly the result of the obligation which also exists when I am

---

1   Cf. my *The Art of Living,* chapter 2, and my *Liturgy and Personality,* chapter 9.

confronted by a morally relevant good for the first time. This is apparent from the fact that I am obligated to cease adhering to something once considered valuable, as soon as I realize that in reality it is an idol or that something I had thought to be true turns out to be false. It is for this reason that the expression "Remain faithful to your religion" is unfortunate, for I ought to adhere to my faith because it is the true religion and not because I once decided for it or because I grew up with it. This would hardly be a reason for staying with it if I were to discover that it is not the true religion. In other words, continuity for the sake of the truth rather than continuity as such is what is valuable here.

Faithfulness in the strict sense

With faithfulness in the narrow sense, by contrast, we are not dealing with perseverance and with an obligation that is objectively there for everyone, but with a distinct source of morality and with a way of relating to a good to which I was not morally required to make a commitment but to which I am morally required to hold fast once I have made the commitment to it. Of course here, too, it is true that I am obligated to break away from a good should I realize that my devotion to it is for some reason false or displeasing to God.

When we consider faithfulness as a specific trait of a person's character, we have in mind something which has to do with his relationship to other people, namely, the fact that over the course of time he abides by the love and loving commitment he once gave to another person, that he neither forgets the "word" of love that he once spoke to someone, nor simply withdraws it for no objective reason.

An unfaithful person is above all someone in whom the love he had given to another person evaporates under the influence of new impressions or of his liking for other persons, or simply by the passing of time. There are of course many things which are closely bound up with faithfulness—things, that is, which faithfulness requires—but which do not constitute the qualitative core of faithfulness. We can see this most clearly when we consider those things that specifically characterize unfaithfulness.

If a friend, moved by fear or by his own interests, hesitates to do what one could legitimately expect of him as a friend, if so to speak he disowns his friendship for such reasons, then, although he is not indeed faithful, his behavior is more an expression of cowardice, egotism, and unreliability than of unfaithfulness. It can be that in his heart my friend is as attached to me as ever, that interiorly he does not disown the friendship, and that he suffers under the fact that he lacks the courage to step in on my behalf, or that he places his own interests above the friendship. Of course, faithfulness in these cases implies a friendship should prove itself, yet the friend fails to prove himself not specifically because of a lack of faithfulness but because of weakness, cowardice, or a limited commitment, which is expressed in the fact that he places his own interests above his friendship.

This shows that the "heart" of faithfulness consists in holding fast to the "word" of love which I have spoken to someone. Speaking this special word of love to this person was not obligatory; it was not of itself a morally required value-response. Yet once I have spoken the word of love, there arises a moral obligation neither to "forget" it nor to let it disappear; and this is the obligation that defines faithfulness.

In this respect faithfulness is like the adherence to a promise that has been made, the adherence to the obligations that have been brought into existence through a social act. The analogy consists in the fact that we are not dealing with an adherence to obligations existing without my cooperation and grounded in the nature of some good and its values, an adherence that is an element of the required superactual response. I was not obligated to make a promise or to enter into a contract, yet once I do so there arises from my voluntary commitment an objective obligation—one that is no longer subject to my arbitrary whim—to remain firm in the commitment and to fulfill the obligations resulting from it.

Yet this analogy should not mislead us about the difference between these cases. The adherence to a commitment freely entered into is not yet the specific reality of faithfulness in the proper sense. Such a commitment mainly involves reliability and conscientiousness. Of course, faithfulness includes these and I expect from faithful friends that they keep their promises toward me. Yet those who are very reliable in all things to which they have committed themselves are not yet specifically "faithful." They are dependable and have in common with the faithful person that one can count on them. But there is a specifically conscientious and absolutely reliable type of bureaucrat whose heart is shriveled up, in whose life love plays no role, and who therefore does not recognize as real and valid the bond that results from the I-Thou encounter of love [*Ineinanderblick der Liebe*]: this person is not specifically faithful in the strict sense of the word.

Yet the following must still be distinguished. To the extent that adherence has to do with the content of a promise, it is above all conscientiousness and not faithfulness that is at issue. But one can speak of faithfulness as soon as one is dealing with a personal bond that has arisen from some other social act, as in the case of the foster father or the vassal to his emperor. In fact, this personal bond need not even result from a social act but can also result from an objective ordering of persons to one another, as in the case of parents toward their children or of children toward their parents. Yet this form of faithfulness is here also not our theme. Our task here is not to investigate the nature of faithfulness in general and all the different kinds of faithfulness but only the faithfulness that has to do with love.

Faithfulness in the proper sense as holding fast to love

The particular faithfulness of which we will speak has to do in the first place only with the relationship to other persons and in the second place within this framework of persons only to a holding fast to *love*. Faithfulness in this sense is a holding fast to the "word" of love, to the solidarity with this word and with everything that lies in the spirit of this relationship. This can also go hand in hand with social acts. After all, the "faithful" servant, assuming that he was not born into service, as happened in earlier times, is usually bound to his master through a social act. Yet his "faithfulness" does not primarily refer to the fulfillment of his obligations—which he does through his dutifulness, conscientiousness, and reliability—but to holding fast to the devotedness, solidarity, and love for the master. It is clear here that the adherence to what is constituted through the social act goes hand in hand with the adherence to the solidarity with the master and to the human relationship toward him.

A particularly exalted example of the faithfulness of a subordinate is Kurwenal in Wagner's opera *Tristan und Isolde*. Here we have the unconditional solidarity that comes from love and reverence, from faith in the beloved master, from the unconditional commitment to him.

A typical example of faithfulness is also to be found in the relationship of a follower or disciple to his or her master. Here we are not thinking of the situation in which the allegiance is as such morally required, as in the case of the disciples of Christ, who owed an unconditional adherence to Him as the epiphany of God. Rather, we are thinking of cases in which the allegiance of disciples or followers, while built upon a value-response, is not morally obligatory. Among the followers of someone like Gaius Gracchus, or the disciples of Socrates, or the disciples of a great artist, whether Goethe, Leonardo da Vinci, Wagner, etc., one can distinguish between the faithful and the unfaithful. Faithful are those who hold fast to the master through all fluctuations in their loyalty and love—*provided* of course that the recognition of the unworthiness of the master or his own defection from his own ideal does not yield a moral obligation for the disciple to leave the master.

One can also speak of faithfulness in the case of the disciples of a saint as long as their resolute discipleship refers to things concerning the particular way of the saint and is not a value-response to his holiness, for this response is morally obligatory.[2]

---

2   The highpoint of unfaithfulness is betrayal. Although there are various other moral disvalues at issue here, as we have already seen, betrayal is at the same time the most extreme antithesis of faithfulness. Naturally we are here dealing with betraying not strangers but friends or people to whom I stand in a special relationship. After all, the word betrayal in each case has a different meaning. I am a traitor in our specific sense when I do something that abuses the trust of a friend, a lord, or master, and thereby grievously offends against the implicit loyalty toward the other.

With strangers or even enemies a betrayal in this sense would not even be possible. A betrayal here would be something like denouncing the other to the police, or luring the other into a trap so as then to inflict some harm on him. This

Continuity as presupposition and essential mark of faithfulness

We will more clearly understand the nature of faithfulness in the narrow sense if we briefly bring to mind the various presuppositions of this virtue. The first is continuity, and we have already pointed out its significance for faithfulness. Persons who are so immersed in the present moment that anything past is more or less forgotten, however important it may be, however much it may appeal to a superactual adherence on their part, are also incapable of faithfulness in this sense. Even if they love someone while they are with that person, even if the beloved person plays a great role in their lives—as soon as they come into a new environment and are assailed by new impressions, the beloved person becomes more or less submerged because the present possesses an illegitimate priority in their lives. Many peripheral impressions also gain the upper hand in the present moment. In these persons the superactual attitudes, indeed the entire superactual realm of the soul, is in a condition of atrophy.

This discontinuity makes them incapable of any kind of faithfulness, including faithfulness in the broad sense. But what interests us at present is that discontinuity also makes a person incapable of faithfulness in his or her relationships to other people. A person lacking in continuity is not so much unfaithful as incapable of faithfulness. He or she behaves like an unfaithful person, yet the reason for this is a formal failure of a general kind, an atrophy of personality, which makes faithfulness impossible and therefore represents more a lack of faithfulness than a typical unfaithfulness. The general formal discontinuity which makes the person incapable of faithfulness does not have a primarily moral character. It is a general atrophy. Nevertheless, this does not mean that a person in no way is responsible for it and is incapable of countering it with his or her free will, even if in a more indirect way. Discontinuity in many people is a result of living at a peripheral level and of letting themselves go. Many people lack continuity because they are spiritually sluggish. They allow themselves to drift and avoid taking any principled stance. They are too sluggish for any real cooperation, they do not live as full selves, and they allow themselves to be driven from one impression to another. Of course, this kind of discontinuity is

---

form of betrayal lies beyond unfaithfulness and has nothing to do with it. Even to abuse the trust which a stranger shows towards me would be a form of betrayal which could not be considered unfaithfulness in the proper sense. Only the betrayal of someone to whom I am bound in a relationship of love, whether as a friend, a master, or a lord, someone who can count on my loyalty and who on the basis of our relationship has given me his or her trust, only this is a specific highpoint of unfaithfulness. [This paragraph ends with a sentence that I cannot unriddle: "Aber er is es auch da nur objektiv." Trans.]

The motive for betrayal need not be precisely unfaithfulness; it can, as we already saw, be cowardice or egoism.

clearly morally culpable; people are fully responsible for this discontinuity. Thus it leads not only to the loss of faithfulness but to unfaithfulness in the most typical sense. These people shut their ears to all requirements which can arise out of an experience and to all demands of values. Thus they live only in the moment because they deliberately withdraw from anything superactual.

This is a source of unfaithfulness. For this reason faithfulness implies that one does not grant the present moment an illegitimate priority, that one clearly understands the requirements of goods that are endowed with high values, that one grasp the bonds which grow out of all deeper human relationships, that one does not flee into the periphery, and that one does not evade every superactual stance.

Whether in the context of a deep friendship or a mutual spousal love, faithfulness always requires that neither the absence of the beloved, nor the attractiveness of new impressions, nor physical distance should lead to the altering of anything in the actuality of the love and especially not to a "forgetting" of the beloved person. The faithful person does not allow himself or herself to be influenced by the immediacy of the present, nor by distance, nor by the prominence of the "new" and the "unusual."

True faithfulness in a special way presupposes depth.[3] Superficial persons, who do not live out of their depth, neither discover the requirement of love to remain faithful nor are they able to hold fast to love in the midst of changing situations. The superactual attitudes play a decisive part in faithfulness, and the superactual life of the person who remains in the periphery is atrophied.

True faithfulness and pseudo-continuity

This becomes even clearer when we make a further distinction between true faithfulness and a certain pseudo-continuity. We mean the "continuity" that arises out of pure habit. It is a way of continuing on that comes from a certain spiritual sluggishness. There are people who are so dominated by habit that they only feel at ease when they are in a setting to which they are accustomed; the question whether something is habitual plays for them a far greater role than its content and its intrinsic merit. Whether something is uplifting or oppressive, beautiful or ugly, interesting or boring is subordinate to the question whether or not they are accustomed to it. These people shrink from anything that is new and unfamiliar. Thus they hold fast to each relationship

---

3   In speaking here of depth we have in mind *structural depth*. This is one of the different kinds or concepts of depth that we distinguished in our earlier work, *Sittlichkeit und ethische Werterkenntnis* (Morality and Ethical Value Knowledge), part III, first published in *Jahrbuch für Philosophie und phänomenologische Forschung* 5 (1922).

they formed in the past, not because they understand its true meaning, its legitimate root, but simply because continuing on is preferable to them in their spiritual sluggishness, because they shrink from anything unknown and untried. This continuing-on is in no way tied to depth; on the contrary, this unfounded, illegitimate role of the habitual actually prevents these people from becoming deep. They live in the periphery just like those who rush from one "new" situation to another and for whom it is novelty rather than value that is decisive.

In true faithfulness there also lies an element of recollection [*sich sammeln*]. Faithful persons recognize that continuing on is required by the nature of true love; they understand how every form of unfaithfulness is a betrayal of love, and they have tasted the deep happiness of love which can only be experienced when a person lives in his or her depth.

Additional essential traits of faithfulness

Faithfulness and remaining uninfluenced. A second essential trait of faithfulness is remaining uninfluenced by the judgments of others and their attitude toward the person we love. Of course, we are here prescinding from those cases in which someone calls my attention to illusions I may have about the person whom I consider my friend or whom I love with a spousal love. As long as someone conveys facts to me about the words and deeds of a beloved person, facts that contradict my image of him or her, the decisive question for me to ask is who the person informing me is, whether he is entirely reliable, and whether he acted out of love. To plug my ears and to ignore this information would not reveal faithfulness and the ability to resist influence but would rather be a policy of burying my head in the sand. Naturally, what we find out about a beloved person should not prompt us to forsake and abandon him or her. But we would have to confront the beloved person and find out how these words and deeds are to be explained, whether they are merely a momentary slip-up or a symptom revealing that we were mistaken about him or her. Of decisive importance in this entire matter is how deeply we know the beloved person, whether our image of him has time and again been confirmed in its beauty, and whether we have had the opportunity really to come to know him with all his positive qualities and his weaknesses. We will still return to this subject shortly.

Here we are concerned with understanding the particular resistance to outside influence that essentially belongs to faithfulness.

There is a kind of person who is too easily influenced; the judgments of others about the beloved person make an impression on him but not because of the reasons given (information about the words or deeds of the beloved person) but because this person in general allows himself to be illegitimately influenced by the judgments of others. This is true above all of the type of person whom we described elsewhere as susceptible to the suggestive power of others.[4] In the extreme case of someone in whom the meaningful motivation by an object is entirely replaced by a purely dynamic resonating with energetic others, one would have to say that such a one is entirely incapable of love; love after all implies a response to the other person, i.e., the meaningful motivation by the being of the other. We are here rather thinking of persons in whom this suggestive dependence is only present to a limited degree. These people allow themselves to be influenced in their love through the judgments of other people simply by the dynamism of the other's words.

Faithfulness and seeing the other "from within." Of special significance is the influence that leads us to consider the beloved person under a false external aspect and that appeals to a tendency in us to see the other "from without." We have spoken in various places about the great danger of "seeing from without."[5] It is the source of a typical misunderstanding of the other person and is radically antithetical to love. Love is by nature a "seeing from within." The temptation to "see from without" dwells in everyone, and the susceptibility to "seeing from without" becomes especially great when a person sinks into the periphery and does not live in his or her depth.

By seeing the beloved person "from without" the humility of that person can come to appear as "servility," his or her purity as a deficiency of sensual life, commitment to principle as pedantry and conventionalism or even as mediocrity, and zeal for truth as arrogance and fanaticism. There is no doubt that one can "drag down" a friend or a beloved person in the eyes of someone by speaking of him or her in such a way that the image of the beloved person becomes distorted or poisoned. This can even happen with regard to values like the external beauty of the beloved person. By joking one can undermine the impression of this beauty, as by saying that the nose of another person is too short or too long, or that the beauty of the other has noticeably faded, or that this beauty is nothing more than the bloom of youth, and so forth.

Faithfulness implies that I be immune to all of these influences, that I do not permit a third person to have any kind of influence on my attitude toward to the beloved person by appealing to a "view from without" (the third person always starts from something which really exists in the beloved, but he then distorts it). This faithfulness is required by love and by the true image of the

---

4   Dietrich von Hildebrand, "Legitime und Illegitime Formen der Beeinflussung," in *Die Menschheit am Scheideweg* (Mankind at the Crossroads).

5   See my essay on authority and also the one, just mentioned, on legitimate and illegitimate influence in my book, *Die Menschheit am Scheideweg*. Goethe wonderfully characterized "seeing from without" when he says of poetry that it is like a stained glass window in a church. From the outside the window looks black, but the entire splendor of the window is revealed to us when we enter into the church. In relation to another person there is an analogous "seeing from without": it is a typical misperceiving of the other, a false interpretation of external aspects that leads to a complete misunderstanding of the other person's essence.

beloved person which has been revealed to us through seeing him or her "from within." This faithfulness has a decidedly moral character and is of luminous beauty.

Faithfulness and the readiness to make sacrifices. A further characteristic of faithfulness is the readiness to make sacrifices. How much am I prepared to take upon myself for my friend or for the person whom I love with a spousal love? At first glance this does not seem to be faithfulness in the proper sense but to be more a sign of the overall ardor of the value-response. To what extent has the value-response triumphed over everything else in a person, what sacrifices is he ready to accept rather than to refuse the required value-response, or to refrain from helping the other person? This is why in the case of the love of neighbor one will not, in considering the heroic deeds of the saints, speak of faithfulness. Yet when in the case of any kind of natural love, above all for a friend or for a person loved with spousal love, for a husband or a wife, this readiness to make sacrifices takes on indeed the character of a sign indicating the greatness and depth of the love. Yet beyond this there is an unmistakable faithfulness in holding fast to the beloved person, however many heavy crosses this may bring. Penelope is a beautiful example of faithfulness. All attempts of her suitors fail because of her love for Odysseus. Despite the utter uncertainty of his return, despite all of the pressure created by the suitors hovering around her, she unflinchingly holds fast to her love for him and to her bond with him.

Leonore in Beethoven's *Fidelio* is of course an example of the heroic power of love; but in holding fast to her love and in being unwilling to give up in her attempts to rescue Florestan and to get him back, there is also a glorious faithfulness. The holding fast, the refusal to give up, the unflinching perseverance in trying to save the beloved and to reestablish the external unity of a love, however difficult it may be, however hopeless it may appear, actualizes a deep faithfulness.

Faithfulness and hope. Here we touch upon another significant characteristic of faithfulness, namely, its relationship to hope. We considered the role of hope in love on various occasions in this book, above all in chapter 3. Yet this hope is also a bearer of faithfulness. In the hope that one will be able to overcome all obstacles in order to restore the longed-for unity with the beloved person, in never ceasing to try to restore it, there also lies a great faithfulness. A friend of mine, who had a very happy marriage, was seriously injured in an automobile accident. For months she lay in a coma. Serious injuries to the brain and complete paralysis presented what seemed a hopeless situation. The doctor told the husband that she would never recover and since she might not die right away, he should make arrangements to have her placed in a home for people in a vegetative state. The husband, however, refused to hear anything of the sort. From the beginning he came to her bedside every day after work for five hours, and he explained that he would by no means give her up, and that as long as she was still alive he would care for her at home. She survived the accident and after eight months returned home, at that time still largely crippled but fully conscious. After further months during which she was lovingly cared for by her husband and her children she has even been able to go back to work.

Even if the conduct of this man is above all an example of the power of love, of selflessness, and of an exceptional moral personality, it is undoubtedly also a moving example of faithfulness. The place of hope in this faithfulness and in unflinchingly holding fast is unmistakable. Of course, this hope presupposes faith in God; the husband was in fact a faithful Christian.

Faithfulness and faith in the beloved person. But faithfulness also has an inner relationship to faith in the beloved person. We spoke about the credit of love in chapter 3. This credit of love implies a faith in the beloved person, a holding fast to the image which has been luminously revealed to us. This faith can reach very far; if a person whose moral greatness and moral nobility have been clearly revealed to me is accused of serious wrong by apparently definitive circumstantial evidence, my faith in him is not necessarily shaken, but I may say: "Never will I be able to believe that this person could have done something like this." By introducing this extraordinary case, which involves not only love but veneration (which is motivated by and grounded in great virtues that have proven themselves in an unmistakable way), we hope to throw more light on how the faithful person holds fast and never gives up on the beloved person.

Pseudo-faithfulness

Yet we must affirm here emphatically that there is also such a thing as false faithfulness. Every kind of adherence, whether to a religion, a principle, a custom, or a person, is a false faithfulness if it is independent of the question whether the religion is true, whether the principle is true, whether the custom is good, or whether the other is a true friend and is as loveable he seems to me. Here the general principle holds that I may never separate an attitude from its object, from the value of the object and from the requirement arising from the value. As soon as I do so the attitude becomes undermined, loses its meaning, and can neither be described as good or bad. It is absurd to praise enthusiasm as long as I do not know to what object the enthusiasm is directed. It is nonsensical to praise unshakeable conviction as long as I do not know whether the conviction is directed to a falsehood or a truth. In the same way it is false to hold fast to a person out of supposed faithfulness after I have clearly recognized that I was mistaken about him, that he is not what I took him for, or even that he is a sham, a traitor, or a base, mean person.[6]

---

6   One cannot object that in the case of the love of neighbor I must hold fast to the other person, whatever kind of person he is, and even if he is an enemy of God and a monster. This is not an objection to what we just said, since, as we saw in chap-

Here we are clearly speaking only of faithfulness in natural loves, especially in friendship and in the love between man and woman. For in these categories love is a value-response to a particular individual, to the overall beauty of this individual. And if this individual reveals itself to be entirely other than I had believed it to be, if I clearly see that I was living in an illusion, then, though I should continue loving such a person in the sense of love of neighbor, I should in no way consider myself obligated to continue loving him with a spousal love or as a friend. I must rather strive to free my heart from this kind of love.

If one cannot bring oneself to do this, then it is either due to a head-in-the-sand policy (because one shrinks from disappointment and the pain bound up with it), which has nothing to do with faithfulness, or one mistakenly imagines that it is a lack of love and an offense against caritas if one does not hold fast to the person. This is a confusion of the situation of love of neighbor with the meaningful basis of all friendships and (even more) of all relationships of spousal love. My conduct in friendship and spousal love is made ungenuine by this confusion. I live in an illusion of a different kind. Neither of these reasons for persisting in a relationship has anything to do with genuine faithfulness.[7]

Having briefly considered the nature of faithfulness in our love toward persons, we now want to enter into a more detailed consideration of the requirements of faithfulness in the various categories of natural love. Since these requirements of faithfulness vary greatly according to the genius of a particular relationship, we must treat of faithfulness as it is found in the

---

ter 11, caritas is of itself the bearer of the highest moral values and does not consist of a value-response to another person but responds to Christ the word incarnate, the infinitely holy one. Moreover, when caritas actualizes itself as the love of neighbor, it is a response to the ontological value of the *imago Dei* which even the greatest sinner cannot completely destroy as long as he lives.

7   We have an entirely different situation, however, when what is at stake is not only a matter of love but also of a formal bond, such as in a marriage. The obligation to hold fast to the bond of marriage, that is, not to marry another person except in the case of an annulment of the first marriage, is of course independent of the conduct and the character of the other spouse. But this is an obligation toward God, in whose hands this marital bond was solemnly placed. This obligation, however, is not faithfulness in loving the other person, for there is no requirement here to continue loving the spouse with a spousal love or even with a love that is not tied to a particular category [*Liebe schlechtweg*]. Indeed, the continuation of living together as husband and wife is in no way morally required when one spouse behaves in such a way that living together becomes unbearable or even morally dangerous for other spouse. A certain degree of immorality, lovelessness, and abuse objectively makes a separation absolutely desirable. Above all, however, continuing to live together as husband and wife even under these circumstances lacks the character of faithfulness.

various categories of love. This will show us more clearly how intimately the requirement of faithfulness is bound up with love; it will also show us how significant is the relationship between love and morality that we encounter here in faithfulness. For it bears repeating that true faithfulness is an eminently moral virtue.

Faithfulness and exclusivity

The question of faithfulness as well as the question of unfaithfulness in love is bound up with the exclusivity of love. Here we must from the outset distinguish between two different kinds of exclusivity. The first only exists in the love between man and woman. We have already on various occasions pointed to this kind of exclusivity. It is impossible for me to love two persons at the same time with this kind of love. The quality of this love prevents it from dwelling in my heart for two different people at the same time. It is also impossible for me to love one person with a greater spousal love and at the same time to love another with a lesser spousal love. Exclusivity in this context does not refer to the degree of the love but to its categorial character.

Not only is this exclusivity something which ought to exist, it is in fact impossible to love two persons at the same time with a spousal love. The obligation of faithfulness, by contrast, means that I should hold fast to my love in the sense that my spousal love should not be replaced by another spousal love without reason.

There is, however, a different kind of exclusivity that is not rooted in the quality of the love but in the degree of the love. It can happen in any of the categories of love that I love a certain other person above everything else. It can be a mother, a father, a daughter, a son, a brother, a sister, or a friend who plays the leading role in my life, whom I love more than all others, indeed, to whom (as far as human beings are concerned) I give my heart completely. The categorial character of the given love plays no role here; it is simply a matter of love reaching a degree where I give this person a unique place in my heart. This incontestable primacy of place in my heart also has a certain exclusivity, but one of an entirely different kind, as is evident. All the same, it is also impossible here to grant two people this unique place in my heart at the same time, even if for entirely different reasons. Here it is the degree of a love—a love considered apart from any categorial determination—which brings about the exclusivity, even though it is entirely possible to love several people to different degrees with a love that is qualitatively the same. There are, of course, people who do not love anyone with this highest degree of love. Apart from spousal love, there is no qualitative exclusivity in the other categories of love. Even the exclusivity of the degree of love only exists in a love of the highest degree. Otherwise, parents can love all of their children equally. The love for one child need not take away anything from the love for another. Likewise, one can love several friends equally.

It is not difficult to see that exclusivity in both dimensions–the qualitative dimension and the dimension of degree of love—has significant consequences for faithfulness as well as unfaithfulness in the various categories of love. What constitutes unfaithfulness in the context of the love between man and woman is not unfaithfulness in the love of friendship, etc.

One more thing must be emphasized before we turn to a consideration of the requirements of faithfulness in the different natural categories of love. Faithfulness always requires only that the love with which I turn to someone, the word of love that I have spoken to someone, not be taken back without an objective reason or even be diminished. But faithfulness does not demand more than I once gave; it does not require an increase in love. To be sure, there are obligations to grow in love, even within the categories of natural love. All deep loves ought to increase and to become richer and deeper over time, but this requirement goes beyond faithfulness.

The treatment of the requirements of faithfulness in the various kinds of natural love unavoidably goes hand in hand with the question of when unfaithfulness exists. The positive here does not entirely allow itself to be separated from the negative. In showing what obligations are placed upon a relationship by faithfulness, we necessarily also show what constitutes unfaithfulness in love of some kind.

There is good reason for concentrating upon faithfulness in the love between man and woman and in friendship. The "home" of faithfulness is these relationships. One speaks of a faithful friend and this epithet is here especially significant. It is much more obvious to refer to a friend as faithful than to speak of a faithful mother, a faithful son, or a faithful sister. It is also obvious in the case of a spouse to raise the question of faithfulness, even if the term "faithful" has here another specific character.

We will, however, prescind from unfaithfulness in marriage, which we already touched upon in part I of chapter 12. We have already dealt with this subject in other books. We will here limit ourselves to the obligations which arise from the interpenetration of souls in the love between man and woman.[8]

Faithfulness in the love between man and woman

The most typical case of unfaithfulness in the love between man and woman is the withdrawal of spousal love and the granting of this love to another person. We saw that it is impossible to love two people in this way at the same time. As soon as I address a second person with this kind of love, I have necessarily withdrawn it from the previously beloved person. I implicitly declare, "I no longer love you," to the previously beloved person when I can say to

---

8   Faithfulness in marriage not only pertains to love and the bonds arising from love but also to the bonds which emerge from the act of marrying and the consummation of the marriage.

another person, "I love you" (in both cases love of course means a spousal love). As soon as I love another person with a spousal love, not only do I love the previously beloved person less, but my spousal love for that person is entirely eliminated.

Indeed, unfaithfulness lies primarily in withdrawing from spousal love, in ceasing in my devotion to a person, which implies a revoking of the word spoken in this love. All of this can happen when for one reason or another a love ceases, even if it is not displaced by a spousal love for another person. Yet the unfaithfulness that is bound up with a "new love," of which we already treated extensively from another perspective in part 1 of chapter 12, goes still further. There is here a still more specific unfaithfulness, a still greater antithesis to the word spoken previously to the beloved person. Naturally, we are only dealing with unfaithfulness when the cessation of the love is one-sided. If love dies out in both persons, neither is guilty of any unfaithfulness toward the other.

We must nevertheless emphatically say that the cessation of a love and the initiation of a new spousal love for another person is only unfaithful if this cessation has no basis whatsoever other than the inconstancy of the person who loves, his discontinuity, his gliding off into the periphery, all of which, as we saw, are largely responsible for abandoning the beloved person for the sake of the awakening spousal love for someone else. If I discover that the beloved is not the person who I thought he or she was, if I clearly recognize that our mutual understanding is not as deep as I assumed, or that the beloved person is so unfaithful or shows such traits of character as to make it impossible for me to desire the marriage which is yearned for in every spousal love, then for me to break off the love is completely legitimate and is anything but unfaithfulness or the lack of faithfulness. Indeed, the obligation to faithfulness is so lacking here that it would be a case of the above-mentioned false faithfulness if I were to hold on compulsively to the love.

As we said, we are here speaking only of the relationship that is constituted through the interpenetration of souls [*Ineinanderblick der Liebe*] that takes place in the love between man and woman. After all, this interpenetration of looks in love [*Ineinanderblick der Liebe*] not only implies that both persons love each another but that they have declared their love to each another.

An engagement brings into existence a new bond. In addition to the mutually declared love, there is in an engagement, after all, a deliberate decision, a "promise," to marry the other person. Of course, the wish to marry the other person is always virtually contained in a fully developed spousal love, even in advance of any declaration or of any certainty that the other person reciprocates my love, and this wish of course attains a new level of actualization in the interpenetration of souls that is reached when love is declared. But there is the additional element of a promise in an engagement, and this is the source of a new bond. We need not emphasize that in the act of marrying and in the consummation of marriage, a community comes into existence, which, as already discussed above, contains completely new commitments and obligations. The obligations of faithfulness, however, that arise in marriage are not our theme here but only those which are situated in the interpenetration of souls in love.

Ending a spousal love and granting this love to another person is, as we said, the most radical case of unfaithfulness (always on the presupposition that the discontinuation is not, as we already emphasized on various occasions, objectively motivated, justified, and even in a certain sense required).

In faithfully loving I not only hold fast to my love at all times (if I have not in any way been mistaken about the beloved person), and I not only do not turn my love to someone else, but I will also avoid anything that is incompatible with faithfulness, such as flirting with other persons, engaging in overly tender actions, attempting to have other people to fall in love me, or enjoying this when this happens by itself. All of this contradicts the genius of mutual spousal love and exhibits a certain unfaithfulness. If it comes to the point that one prefers flirting with others to being together with the beloved person, that one enjoys this "playing" more than being with the beloved, then it is a clear sign that the spousal love for that person is no longer fully alive and that, even if not necessarily dead, it is nonetheless asleep. For none of this is possible in the case of a spousal love that is fully alive.

It is an entirely different kind of "unfaithfulness" against the spousally beloved person when a person succumbs to a purely sensual temptation and engages in sexual relations with someone else. This is usually presented as a typical unfaithfulness only in marriage. This form of adultery, in which the husband need not necessarily cease loving his wife or the wife her husband, is also a typical unfaithfulness, quite apart from the sin of fornication.

But this applies *mutatis mutandis* to our problem, that is, to unfaithfulness in the context of a union of mutual love prior to marriage, indeed, even prior to an engagement. Here we are also prescinding from the serious sin of fornication and the sin of impurity. But even here—and this is often not seen very clearly—to fall out of sheer sensuality, to succumb in a sensuously seductive situation, is to be unfaithful to the beloved person. Of course, even from the standpoint of unfaithfulness it is not nearly as weighty as in the case of married people. But the mystery of bodily union is so deeply and mysteriously bound up with spousal love that even a lapse caused by sheer sensuality is nonetheless intrinsically incompatible with the bond of mutual love and is a "betrayal" of the beloved person.

This is already evident from the fact that every truly loving person perceives this as an apostasy from his love and an injustice against the beloved person, unless he is completely blind for the mystery of the sphere of sensuality and for the true meaning of bodily union and, with it, the sin of impurity. But this person is also incapable of a real spousal love. For really being in love entails an understanding for the depth and mystery of bodily union, for the sphere of sensuality [*der sinnlichen Sphaere*]. While the truly loving person who is not blind to this may fall out of weakness, still he will beg the beloved person for forgiveness, he will perceive his behavior as a betrayal against the beloved person, aside from the fact that he will deeply repent of it as sinful and as an offense against God.

The truly faithful person is the one who not only understands this clearly but also resists all temptations of this kind, primarily out of love for God but also out of love for the person who is loved with spousal love. Here the moral beauty of faithfulness shines before us clearly. No temptation in the world could bring such a person to betray the beloved person.

It is clear that there is moral value in the faithfulness that is proper to the attitude of the person who fully grasps the commitment that lies in the inter-penetration of souls in love; there is moral value in the person whose love is not lessened by insensitivity, habit, or discontinuity, and even less by outside influences.

But at this point we must emphasize the important difference between a person who is generally unfaithful and one who on a single occasion falls into unfaithfulness.

It is, as we already saw, doubtful whether a generally unfaithful person, a person without continuity, or a person who is completely morally unconscious, is even capable of a full spousal love. On the other hand, it is surely impossible to claim that these people are incapable of passionately loving another person for a time and really being in love with them. But upon coming into a new environment or after a long separation, they forget the beloved person and begin to love someone else with the same kind of love. There are countless examples for this type of person. The most extreme case is, for example, Aljoscha in Dostoevsky's *The Insulted and the Injured*. His discontinuity and his moral unconsciousness takes on psychopathic proportions as he insensibly drifts from his love for Natascha to Katja. But even Goethe's remark in *Dichtung und Wahrheit* (*Poetry and Truth*) about how beautiful it is when a new love arises after a previous one has ended tends in the direction of unfaithfulness, even though he was an entire-ly healthy, exceptional person, and not a person distinctly marked by moral unconsciousness. And yet he lacked a central element of continuity.

The mutual love between man and woman, however, not only demands that spousal love not be withdrawn from the beloved person and not be given to another person, but also that the love not abate for any reason. Here we have in mind primarily the case in which someone loves another "more" with a non-spousal love; from the perspective of love in general [*Liebe schlechtweg*: love prior to any categorial determination] he grants the other a place in his heart to which spousal love is entitled and which in fact it possessed before.

Unfaithfulness, which involves only a decline in love, is related in several ways to the problem of the ordo amoris, which we will treat in the next chapter. In the question why I should love one person more than another there is an overlapping of the obligations that result from the ordo amoris and from faithfulness, even if both obligations are in themselves distinct. The obligation of the ordo amoris to love one person more than another centers on the given category of love, or rather on the "word" that was "spoken" between two persons, or on the objective ordering of persons to one another, etc., while the obligation of faithfulness always centers upon the love which has actually come into existence between two persons.

We begin our analysis of the unfaithfulness that lies in the decline of love by turning again to the most pronounced case, namely, the decline that is brought about by the role which another person has begun to play in my life. When, for example, my child suddenly begins to occupy the first place in my heart, displacing my spouse, we have a case of unfaithfulness. There is no unfaithfulness in the fact that a father or mother loves the child more than his or her spouse, but only in the fact that this decreases the love for the spouse, so that the spouse is robbed of something which he or she had possessed before.[9] Again, when a person in a spousal relationship meets someone whom he or she loves as a friend more than anyone else, and who becomes the central figure in his or her life, in other words, who from the standpoint of love as such [*Liebe schlechtweg*] is loved "more" than the spouse, there is unfaithfulness only if the friendship leads the one spouse to love the other less than before, only if the beloved person is deprived of what he or she already possessed (more on this in the next chapter).

But it can also happen that I become so absorbed by an impersonal good, such as professional work, that my love is pushed into the background to the point that, while the love does not cease or die, it does lose its intensity and, above all, displaces the beloved person from the central role he or she had held in my heart and life.

Naturally, it is only in certain cases that one can speak of a love for an impersonal good in the narrow sense of the word love, such as the love for a nation or country. Yet here it not a matter of what is first from the standpoint of love but also of what plays the greatest role in my life, what concerns me above all else, what is most important to me. Goods that are not loved in the true sense of the word, such as the professional work of a bureaucrat or a lawyer, can adversely affect the love for another person by consuming all of a

---

9   It often happens that the children play such a role that the love for a spouse recedes into the background and no longer occupies the first place in the heart of the father or mother. We prescind from the case in which this displacement occurs in both parents in equal measure, for, regrettable as this certainly is, the disvalue in question here is more a matter of an offense against the ordo amoris than of unfaithfulness in the proper sense. One can, nevertheless, speak here of an unfaithfulness of the parents to the God-given gift of their love.

person's attention, thoughts, and worries and, above all, by becoming a person's primary source of happiness. This also can lead to a decline of love, especially of spousal love, which after all demands by its nature that I be fully affected by and concerned with the beloved person.

The rivalry posed to a love by an impersonal good, however, always has a different character than the rivalry posed by a person. When love is withdrawn from me and given to another, a particularly stinging wound is inflicted on me, and I feel betrayed. The inner space that was formed in the I-Thou community of love is, so to speak, burst open. The abandonment of the inner space through the fact that a third person possesses the heart of my beloved is the source of a very particular kind of wound.

This special hurt is absent when love merely diminishes due to impersonal goods or when love dies away, as happens when a person takes his love for granted and becomes insensitive to it. The specific abandonment, the demolition of love are not in evidence here. Yet there is something specifically depressing when prose eliminates all poetry, as one could say, and when a humdrum spirit of taking everything for granted descends like mold on a person's love, more or less suffocating it. A love which expires in this way does so with an especially hopeless note. It is a betrayal of love as such. It is heartbreaking when I consider that the other person once loved me, when I consider what the interpenetration of souls once led me to hope for, and consider how this love by its nature was meant to endure; and now it is no longer possible to reach the other, to reach him or her with the ray of my love—I reach into emptiness. Again, a real unfaithfulness is here in evidence, even if it possesses a different note than in the above-mentioned case.

The person who loves faithfully will not allow this decline in love to take place. This will never happen to the true lover, to the person who is, as it were, the ideal case of one who loves. Yet every person who loves faithfully will at least be conscious of this requirement of love to endure and will consciously resist these tendencies.

This type of "unfaithfulness" usually goes hand in hand with the general danger of a loss of sensitivity in spousal love and of a certain de-actualization of love. This danger exists, as already mentioned, for everyone. It lies in human nature as a general danger in the relationship to all great goods. It shows itself in the commitment to all great tasks, in the appreciation of great gifts, in all natural love, and especially in the love between man and woman—indeed, it even makes itself felt in the spiritual life. In no realm of human existence is it always spring or summer; there are also times of autumn and winter. Holding fast in winter to what was given to us in spring, to what we received effortlessly, is a great and general obligation which permeates the entire spiritual life. *Fides* is holding fast to truth which was given to us, and this involves both holding fast to Tabor [seasons of special grace and light] in times of spiritual aridity as well as holding fast to faithfulness.

In the insensitivity that can lead to a lessening of or even to the extinguishing of the love between man and woman, a sluggishness of a spiritual sort makes itself felt. In the beginning this love comes upon me as a gift and I am transported on high through the *élan* of love; without my cooperation I am drawn into an intensity and alertness of life. But I cannot hold fast to this in the long run because of my spiritual sluggishness. After all, as we saw, this sluggishness often has the effect of holding me back from the "adventure" of love and so from giving myself over to a spousal love. Yet in many cases where this sluggishness is not so extreme, I will enter indeed into a love, but with a sluggishness that prevents me from holding fast to the *élan* of love and to all the spiritual "intensity" involved in it; it also prevents me from really acting out of my free spiritual center, which is indispensable for the continuation and preservation of love. We could say that as soon this love is no longer given to me as a pure gift, as soon as it is no longer, as it were, "imposed" on me, I again fall so far back into a humdrum view of the world that I do not even consider the full alertness and ardor of love as desirable; I am more comfortable in my present state of soul that agrees with my sluggishness.[10]

It is a requirement of the love between man and woman to resist every "forgetting," every relenting in ardor, every succumbing to the power of habit and insensitivity and to being dominated by insensitivity; and the one who

---

10 The danger of becoming insensitive is particularly great for people living together permanently, and it is all the greater the more intimate this living together is. This intimacy, which has a great significance and is desired precisely in spousal love, can, when seen "from without" lead to insensitivity. Even if in our context, as we already noted, we restrict ourselves to the requirements of the love between man and woman and are not considering the new requirements that result from marriage, still it clarifies things to point out the special danger that arises within marriage of becoming insensitive to a spousal love. In addition to this there is the truth contained in the expression that "no man is a hero in the presence of his valet." The intimacy of living together can lead me more and more to lose my glorious image of the beloved person. This, however, is my fault for being so superficial and seeing things so much from the outside that the tribute that we all have to pay to our earthly existence clouds or even obscures the valid image of the beloved person. For it is clearly the fault of the valet if the true hero does not appear to him as a hero; he suffers from a valet-view of the world.

Again, it can happen that I notice small but irritating failings in the other person as a result of the intimacy of living together with him or her, and that I increasingly lose the original image I had of the beloved person. Since I do not see how inessential these traits are in and of themselves, since I fail to realize that these traits do not alter anything in the image that I originally had of the beloved person and that had enkindled my heart, I can gradually allow the image to become increasingly obscured and my love to grow cold. I fail to return each time to the original image and I allow dust to accumulate on the image. All of this, of course, gets worse to the degree that I am morally unawakened.

fulfills this requirement is adorned in a special way by the moving and beautiful virtue of faithfulness.

Faithfulness in friendship

As we already saw, the sphere of friendship is also an area in which faithfulness plays a special role.

Faithfulness as such seems to be even more a part of the essence of friendship. When I praise a friend for the quality of his or her friendship, the epithet "faithful" is the first thing to come out of my mouth, whereas in the love between man and woman, I will first of all speak of the ardor, the depth, and the degree of a person's love. This does not mean that faithfulness in the love between man and woman is any less essential to this love or any less rooted in the nature of this love—by no means. In fact, faithfulness is much more categorically obligatory in the love between man and woman than in friendship, that is, unfaithfulness is much more serious and far worse in spousal love than in friendship.

When I praise a friend as faithful, then I am above all thinking of the fact that I can rely on him or her as soon as I need help, that I can count on my friend's lasting concern for my happiness, that my friend's solidarity with me will not change through the course of time, through other people and influences, through physical separation, etc. We said at the beginning of this chapter that the friend who does not betray me in spite of the danger which may threaten him or her shows moral courage more than faithfulness; and this is true. Yet the kind of faithfulness with which we are concerned here, which is something other than the moral courage shown in these special situations, also plays a role, if not the primary one. This faithfulness is closely bound up with the *testing and proving [Bewährung]* of a friendship.

Thus faithfulness is present when the testing and proving has to do just with the continuation of the friendship over time and not with situations requiring moral courage and the readiness to sacrifice for a friend. Yet the fundamental point is that faithfulness in friendship is less oriented to love as such and to the voice of the heart than it is to solidarity with the friend and to standing up for my friend through my decisions and actions. This kind of faithfulness plays a prominent role in all forms of friendship, even if faithfulness requires different actions and a different kind of commitment to the friend according to the closeness and depth of the friendship.

The faithfulness in question here resembles that of the faithful servant or faithful disciple. It is therefore rather outside of our specific theme here, namely, the faithfulness that refers to love qua love.

In the case of faithfulness in this specific sense, the factors which cause unfaithfulness are similar to those that we identified in the love between man and woman. Here it is only that the obligations of faithfulness, as we already said, vary greatly according to the individual character of the ordering of persons to one another and according to the mutual love.

Yet we must point out a few decisive differences between faithfulness in the love of friendship and faithfulness in the love between man and woman. First of all, a fundamental difference derives from the fact that the love of friendship is not exclusive in the way in which the love between man and woman is exclusive. The most radical form of unfaithfulness in the case of spousal love, as we saw, lies in turning with spousal love to a third person and therefore necessarily withdrawing it from the previously beloved person. In the case of a friend, by contrast, there is no unfaithfulness in also loving a new person since this kind of love can after all be directed to several people at the same time.

It is possible here that two friends can occupy the same place in my heart and that this may even be the first place in terms of love as such [*Liebe schlechtweg*]. It is entirely possible that I could say of two friends: "I love both of these people more than any others, yet they are equally important to me; both rank ahead of all others in my heart." For this reason one cannot speak of unfaithfulness when another new friend comes to be as loved as much as the first friend, as long as the new friend does not displace the previous friend from the first place. As long as the new friend only occupies the same place, then it is not a case of unfaithfulness. This is above all true if the first friend never occupied the place of relative primacy. Then there is also no unfaithfulness when one comes to love another friend more than the existing friend, because the existing friend loses nothing through the new friendship and my love for him or her need not in any way wane. It is only a case of unfaithfulness when there is a waning of my love for a friend and when my love for the new friend pushes the first one into the background. And here we find once again the different degrees of unfaithfulness.

The most radical case occurs when the love for a new friend completely extinguishes my love for the previous friend, when the relationship to the earlier friend sinks to the level of total indifference. The second level of unfaithfulness occurs when the love for my friend weakens because of the new friendship. And the third level is when the friend who had occupied the relative first place in my heart no longer does so but is replaced by another in this first place, yet without my love for him or her weakening in any way.

The waning of my love for a friend because of blunted sensitivity is also a form of unfaithfulness. Yet here the surpassing importance of the specific word spoken by God between two friends comes to the fore. For love so varies according to this word that the question of insensitivity also has an entirely different meaning according to the individual bond of love that is at stake.

But there can be no doubt that in the case of a deep love of friendship I am justified in complaining that I no longer play the role in the life of the other that I once played—assuming of course that the change in this role is not objectively motivated but is the result of insensitivity. This would then also be a matter of unfaithfulness.

The moral virtue of faithfulness in love

Let us summarize as follows.

Faithfulness is deeply bound up with love. It is a specifically moral obligation that arises from a bond with other persons that is brought into existence by love. Faithfulness in the narrow sense always presupposes a bond of an already existing love. It has to do with holding fast to the love for another person. In the first place, faithfulness has to do with love as such [*Liebe schlechtweg*], independently of all categorial differences within love. Every love demands that one adheres unwaveringly to it, and the greater, the more central, and the more intense the love is, the more this demand holds. This is of course all said on the assumption that there is no objective reason for changing a relationship, taking "objective reason" in the sense of a radical transformation in the beloved person or a ceasing of his or her love for me or the discovery that I was living in an illusion about the beloved person. We saw, however, that beyond this faithfulness, which is demanded by love as such in every category of natural love, there are special obligations of faithfulness in the love between man and woman. It should be explicitly emphasized that faithfulness to commitments toward other persons which do not arise from mutual love but through social acts or an objective ordering of persons to each other have *not* been our theme here. These obligations and moral tasks belong to a philosophy of community or to a social ethics, whereas our theme here was only love.

CHAPTER FOURTEEN

Ordo Amoris

The ordo amoris, or order of love, considered in general

One can speak of the ordo amoris in a general sense, in which case one is not considering love in the narrow and proper sense, but only analogously. In speaking in this general way we touch upon the role which something should play in our life, on the degree of importance which something should have for us, on the weight it should possess, and on how much our heart should be attached to it.

Indeed, the ordo amoris encompasses the entire order of preferring one thing to another, and it encompasses the obligation to do justice to the hierarchy of values in our response. In this general sense, it then implies the very general obligation to chose the higher good over the lower good in our actions, in our affective responses—in every kind of relating to things.[1]

---

1   Max Scheler tried to reduce all of morality to the ordo amoris. Moral goodness arises, according to him, whenever one acts in conformity with the ordo amoris, that is, whenever one chooses the higher over the lower good. Moral badness arises whenever one chooses the lower good the higher good. Although it is true that conformity with the ordo amoris (taken in this general sense) plays a great role in morality, it is still a mistake to reduce all of morality to it. I have spoken of this at length in my *Ethics*, especially in chapter 3. At present it suffices to point out the following: a moral value is realized in a value-response to a morally relevant good even if the situation is such that there is no choosing of one good over another. Of course, the morally relevant value must be apprehended in the rank that it occupies in the hierarchy of values, and the value-response must correspond to this rank. But this correspondence belongs to the response as an adequate response and does not necessarily involve consciously placing the morally relevant good above or below any other good. The call to give an adequate value-response issues primarily from the value of the good and not from the relation of the good to other goods. The value responded to is the primary theme and not the relation to other goods. Above all, it is quite wrong to reduce moral badness to choosing the lower over the higher good. As long as a person lives in a pure value-responding attitude it is not possible for him to choose the lower over the higher, or at the most he makes an intellectual mistake about the true ranking of the goods. In most cases the act of choosing the lower over the higher comes either as a result of value

In this most general sense, the ordo amoris encompasses the following spheres. There is an ordo of the will, which primarily bears on the sphere of action and has to do with observing the hierarchy of morally relevant goods. There is also an ordo that has to do with the role which a good should play in our soul; this ordo also encompasses the hierarchy of objective goods for the person. This also includes an ordo of love, taking love in an analogous sense, and it has to do with the degree of happiness that a good bestows on us. This ordo also extends to the experience of being affected, which involves the question of how deeply something ought to move us, as well as to the enthusiasm and admiration with which we ought to respond. Finally, we can speak of an ordo amoris in the particular and proper sense of love, in which case it is always a matter of the love for persons.

The question of the ordo amoris in the general sense is only meaningful in the context of legitimate goods. Once it is a matter of an illegitimate good, that is, of something which only satisfies my pride and concupiscence, that good should not play any role whatsoever for me. Anything which inherently bears a disvalue, even if it is subjectively satisfying, should not just have a minor role in my life but should have none whatsoever. These pseudo-goods should be banned from my life not because of the ordo amoris, but because they are bad in themselves. Thus the ordo amoris in this general sense has to do only with my stance to real and legitimate goods. This general sense of the ordo amoris, however, is not our theme here.

Ordo amoris in the more precise sense

We want only to speak of the ordo amoris in the more precise sense of the hierarchy that exists for love in the proper and strict sense of the word, since love in this sense is after all the theme of this book. The ordo amoris which concerns us here has to do with the question of which persons we should love *more* than others.

This question, however, must be distinguished from the question which occupied us in chapter 12 (part 2), namely, which loves are morally required. As we already saw, the love for God and the love of neighbor are obligatory, whereas spousal love is not obligatory in this sense. Whether I find a person whom I can love with spousal love does not depend upon me, just as little as whether I possess the capacity for such a love. The same is true *mutatis mutandis* for the love between friends. One can only speak in an analogous sense of an obligation to love someone with a spousal love, as we saw in chapter 12 (part 2). The emergence of such a love is a gift and one can only speak of a moral obligation to love once such a gift has been given. The question of which

---

blindness, which is itself culpable, or else from some deficiency in the basic moral attitude of the person. Moral badness lies primarily in the absence of the value-responding attitude and in approaching everything exclusively from the point of view of the merely subjectively satisfying.

kinds of love are required must be distinguished from the question of the ordo amoris, which has to do with the ranking that should be observed with respect to those whom I love.

The question immediately arises whether the ordo amoris has only to do with loves that are obligatory, whether the obligation to love someone "more" is only meaningful when there is already an obligation to love. That this is the case would at first seem obvious. Yet when we look more closely, we discover that the ordo amoris also encompasses those loves which are not in themselves obligatory in the strict sense. I ought to love someone "more" even when the awakening of the love is not obligatory, although once I have received the gift of love I am obliged in the broad sense of the word to accept the love.[2]

Despite the fact that we must distinguish the question of the ordo amoris from the question of which loves are morally obligatory, it does not follow that the ordo amoris does not encompass any aspect of moral obligation. While it is clear that the obligation to love God more than all other persons represents something over and above the obligation simply to love God, the former is of course just as morally obligatory as the latter.

Yet even in those cases in which I am given all the prerequisites for love, so that my response of love is, as we saw, morally relevant in the broad sense, my compliance with the requirement of the ordo amoris to love some "more" than others has a morally relevant character. Of course, it is not morally obligatory, as in the love for God, yet it is nevertheless morally relevant, as we already saw in chapter 12 (part 2).

Factors relevant to determining the ordo amoris

We must now ask which factors are relevant to the ordo amoris, in other words, which factors require me to love one person "more" than another.

1. *The rank of the value of some good—the objective lovability of a person.* In the ordo amoris in the general sense, the first and decisive factor is the rank of the value with which a given good is endowed. For it is a very general

---

2   We must also consider the following. It would be false to think that every ought [*Sollen*] presupposes that something non-necessary happens, something that could be otherwise. The "ought" reaches far beyond obligations or rules; it is not restricted to those cases in which there is a tension between what is not yet real and what has become real. It is also not restricted to what lies in our power to realize, as in the case of an obligation. There is no sense in being obliged to do something which is not in my power or which has already been realized. The ought [*Sollen*], however, has a much further reach. We can say of everything having a value that it not only is so, but that it also ought to be so. As long as something is qualitatively neutral, it simply is so and one cannot say that it ought to be so, that is, the element of the ought is lacking here. When something is marked by qualitative disvalues, then we find a negative ought, that is, it should *not* be so. Thus, for example, it is meaningful to say that the exclusivity of spousal love ought to be, even though this love is by necessity exclusive.

and fundamental law that a response is due to every good having value, a response that in fact corresponds to the rank of the value. And this means that a response to a higher good contains a certain "more" in comparison to a lesser good. Other things being equal, it is clear that I should admire the greater artist more than the lesser one, that I should revere a saint more than a Socrates. This fundamental law of the due response extends to all value-responses and hence also to love. Admittedly, in our love for other persons, there are so many other factors in question that this obligation at first does not seem to apply here. It is completely correct to say that due relation in no way demands that I should love a saint more than my wife, my children, or my closest friend. While it is clear that I should revere the saint "more"—indeed, revere the saint in an entirely new sense of the word—it is not clear that I should love the saint more. I can clearly see that another person exists at a higher moral and religious plane than the one I love, but I do not thereby acquire the obligation to love more the one who stands higher. This is undoubtedly correct, because, as we said, other factors here play a role in the kind and degree of the love. Nevertheless, this fundamental law—that more of a response is due to a higher good—extends also to love. This is clearly expressed in the fact that we should love God above all things, because God stands incomparably above created persons, because He is the embodiment and source of all values, because everything we love in other persons is only a faint reflection of His glory, and because He is infinite beauty, the infinitely holy one. For all of these reasons we must and should not only adore Him alone but also love Him *more* than any creature. Given His incomparable superiority it is completely clear that the obligation to give a due response not only extends to love but requires us to love *more*.

But even in the case of our love for human persons, the question of due response plays a significant role. It is entirely meaningful to say that one person would deserve to be loved more than another person. When, for example, parents have two children and one is a nobler, more gracious, reliable, faithful, and deeper person, the other a superficial egotist, an unreliable scoundrel, then the gracious, noble child clearly *deserves* to be loved more. (This is not true in the case of the love of neighbor.) This is not to deny that parents are challenged to pray for the wayward child and to give extra attention to it, especially in light of the way it is endangered and has deviated from the right path. The child's moral neediness awakens compassion. The task of the parents toward such a child may be especially great. Yet love in the true sense, the joy over the beloved person, the delight in his or her being, the desire to be in his or her presence, the specific value-response of love, all of this is deserved more by the good child. More love is due to this child in the sense of love as such and of the specifically parental love. We rightly say of parents who for one or another reason do not live up to this obligation that their failure is deplorable, that they should love the good child *more*, that the good child deserves it much more. When parents do not do so, we suspect that they do not appreciate the moral and human superiority of their child, that they have not grasped the difference between one child and another, that they live in illusions, that their love is not a pure love but that various illegitimate elements are affecting it.[3]

But the role of the value hierarchy is much clearer in the context of the love between friends. It is not difficult to see that a noble, kind, reliable, faithful person deserves much more to be our friend than a person who is unreliable, lacking in continuity, immoral, and superficial. In reading Dickens' novel, *David Copperfield*, it is impossible not to ask how David could love Steerforth so much and consider him as his great friend, indeed, be drawn to him even more than to the noble and reliable Tommy Traddles. There are people we ought never call friends, never choose as friends, never love with a love of friendship. As much as we should love them with the love of neighbor, it is a mistake to love them as friends. There is even a morally relevant requirement never to form friendships with bad people. This obligation, of course, goes beyond the ordo amoris, for it is no longer a question of preference, or loving *more*; rather, it is the clear obligation not to form friendships with these people. This negative requirement not to love a person as a friend is also a significant relationship between love and morality.

Yet in the context of our discussion of the ordo amoris, we are concerned with the way in which the value hierarchy and the resulting due relation affects the obligation to observe the ordo amoris proper to love. Of course, it would be wrong to consider the objective rank of a person's value a sufficient basis for me loving him or her as a friend, as if other elements, such as affinity, played no role, and it would also be wrong to think that the objective superiority of one person over another (when this is in fact the case) always requires that I must love the superior person as a friend *more* than I love other friends.

A decisive factor for friendship is, after all, that the other reciprocates my love. As long as the other does not take an interest in me, I can admire, respect, revere, and love him or her, but this love is simply a general kind of love [*Liebe*

---

3   At first glance, this could appear to be incompatible with the parable of the prodigal son. In reality, however, this is in no way the case. The prodigal son objectively stands above the more correct yet self-righteous older brother because of the overwhelming moral value and unique significance of his deep repentance. In addition the response of the father, which shows itself in celebrating the return of the lost son, refers to the fact of the *metanoia,* of the moral resurrection of the lost son, which in itself is a great moral and religious event and requires a special response of joy: "For your brother was dead and has come to life again." One could object: even if this is true, in the other parable of the lost sheep Christ does say that one must above all else go after the lost sheep. Yet even this is not incompatible with our thesis, for here it is not a matter of more love but of the greater effort called for by the greater danger, and of being challenged to act out of the concern for saving what was lost and bringing it back.

schlechtweg] and not the love of friendship, in which the consciousness of mutual love plays an important role, along with the reality of the bond between me and the other person, the trust and the feeling of being understood by the other, and much else. As long as the other person does not reciprocate my love, it is at best a potential friendship.[4] We then perhaps say: if only I could be the friend of this person; I would be happy to be able to call him or her a friend. It is not difficult to see what a decisive role the value hierarchy plays in this case of a potential love of friendship. It is, after all, very typical of someone which persons he chooses as friends and above all to whom he feels himself drawn more. The objective value status of the person whom I love as a friend more than others is very characteristic of my own value status. Hence the proverb that says: Tell me who your friends are and I will tell you who you are.

The statement that this person deserves to be more loved than another can have two meanings. On the one hand, "more" refers to "deserving," while on the other hand, it refers to "loving." We can speak of the first even in the context of the love between man and woman. Two women love one man. He returns the love of the one who seems to us to be less deserving, to which we then say that it is too bad that he loves this woman, since the other would have been more deserving of his love. It is not a matter here of the degree of love; rather we are sorry that he has devoted an exclusive spousal love to the first woman rather than the second. It is not the degree but the "decision" for the one rather than the other. The "more" here has to do with deserving: the one woman is more deserving of being loved with this exclusive spousal love than the other. Only this way of being "more deserving" comes into question in spousal love when we are speaking of two or more persons and are comparing them from the point of view of their dignity to be loved with spousal love. For as we have seen, only one person can be loved with this love at the same time. Only in this sense, then, can the objective hierarchical ranking play a role as long as we are talking about the love between man and woman.

In the love of friendship, by contrast, it would be meaningful to say that one friend deserves to be *more loved* than another. Here the "more" has to do with the *degree* of the love; a decision to choose the one rather than the other is not at issue, since this love is not, in virtue of its categorial structure, exclusive. Here the *more* can have to do with the degree of the love.

In the context of the love between man and woman, the factor of an objective ranking is only at issue in the following manner. It is at issue, first of all, insofar as a person, on the basis of the value of his personality, would have been objectively more deserving of being spousally loved than another person who was in fact loved. But this already goes beyond the ordo amoris in the strict sense.

---

4   Naturally, the degree of love which a friend devotes to me plays a role for the ordo amoris. We will still return to this factor and discuss it further. This factor can also modify the obligation emanating from the value hierarchy.

It is also at issue, and in a way that really belongs to the ordo amoris, when a spousally beloved person, such as a husband or wife, deserves to be more loved than he or she is in fact loved. Here the "more" has to do with the degree of love as such, with the intensity and ardor of the love, with the place which the beloved person occupies in my heart, the role which he or she plays in my entire life, or ought to play. Here we are no longer comparing various persons but are considering the obligation, grounded in the value of a person's personality, to love that person to a certain degree. And this obligation also has a moral character.

Finally, the ordo amoris of love as such [*Liebe schlechtweg*] is at issue within spousal love in the following way. As we shall see later, the question of the objective hierarchy of values strongly conditions the ordo amoris of love. Since a spousal love can be compared with respect to its degree with a maternal love, a love of friendship, etc., provided that we compare them from the point of view of love as such [*Liebe schlechtweg*], the ordo amoris also makes itself felt in the context of a spousal love.

Yet it must be stressed emphatically that in the love between man and woman many more factors besides the value of a particular personality (his or her worthiness of being loved) are involved than in the love of friendship. An entirely different type of affinity, a completely new ordering of one person to another is here required. The "worthiness" of being loved can never alone and exclusively be the foundation of this love. After all, we have frequently seen that the overall beauty of the individual personality, which is especially important in this kind of love, can only be revealed, grasped, and understood when two persons are ordered in a special way to each other. And this is above all true for the unique charm of the beloved person, in whose individuality the entire charm of femininity (for the man) and masculinity (for the woman) is embodied. Despite the role of value discussed above, we can never speak of an obligation to love a person with spousal love on the ground that in many respects he or she ranks higher than the person I love spousally, nor can we say that from the point of view of love as such [*Liebe schlechtweg*] I should love the better person more.

This concept of "love as such" [*Liebe schlechtweg*] requires clarification. In *Die Metaphysik der Gemeinschaft* (The Metaphysics of Community) we called *Liebe schlechtweg* a distinct kind of love and we distinguished it from the other categories of love. In that work love as such *does not mean the same thing* that it means in the present work. We now mean the degree of love considered independently of its categorial character. When we ask the question, "Whom do you love more, your mother or your sister?" then we are not concerned with the categorial character of love but only with the degree of the love. The question is, "Who is more dear to you, who plays a greater role in your life, whose presence do you desire more, who has the greater place in your heart, etc.?" The categorial character is so different in the love for a mother and the love for a sister that in posing this question one must prescind from the category of the love. It is love as such which is here thematic. The question, "Whom do you love more?" can after all be asked independently of any categorial character. And here the question about whom you love most of all persons, about who is nearest to your heart, attains its full meaning, independently of all categorial character.

Different again from this question, which only touches upon the difference in degree in comparing loves for other persons, is the question whether in the life of a person there is someone whom he or she loves with an ultimate commitment, who completely possesses his or her heart—prescinding, of course, from the incomparable love for God. While we can address the first question, "Whom do you love the most?" to every person who is at all capable of love, there are countless people who in their lives have never given their heart to another person in the way of this ultimate commitment, whether because they have never encountered a person who could awaken love in this measure, or whether because they are incapable of such an ultimate commitment.

When we speak here of love as such we have in mind love independently of any categorical character. We are aiming at this both in the question of loving "more" as well as in the question of this ultimate commitment with which a particular person is loved above all else.

The entire problem of the ordo amoris has to do, for the most part, with love as such. With the question, "Whom should I love more?" "love" usually means "love as such" and not the categorial character of love. In certain categories of love, "loving more" can refer to the degree of this category of love, whereas in the case of others, by contrast, this is not the case, as we will still see.[5]

2. *The objective ordering of persons one to another.* A second factor which is decisive for the ordo amoris is the objective ordering of persons one to another, of which we were just now speaking and of which we have previously spoken. This ordering of persons to each other is something objective—we find it already existing. This is true in the first place of our being ordered to God, which St. Augustine captures in the words: "*Fecisti nos ad te, Domine*" —"You have made us for yourself, O Lord." But creaturely persons, too, are ordered to each other in an objective way; thus the child is ordered to its parents and the parents to the child.

But persons can be ordered to each other on the basis of the affinity which they have for one another—a "being for one another" or "being suited to one another" that lies in their character, as we already saw. This, however, must not

---

5   [The last four paragraphs of this section form a long footnote in the German. I have taken the liberty of placing them in the main text because they say something very important for understanding the focus of chapter 14. I am thinking especially of this sentence, "The entire problem of the ordo amoris has to do, for the most part, with love as such." Trans.]

be taken in the sense of "birds of a feather flock together." First of all, this adage only applies to a certain kind of similarity. Second—and this is much more important—the ordering of persons to one another is not just a psychological ease in relating to each other, but it is an objective and objectively valid ordering, divinely ordained, and it can only develop in the realm of value.

While this factor of the ordering of persons to one another is something new *vis-à-vis* the rank of a person's value, it nevertheless presupposes the value-response character of love. Two thieves or lechers associating with each other, or even just two foolish persons associating on the basis of their foolishness—this excludes every value-response and has nothing to do with an objective ordering of persons. Now the objective ordering of persons is decisive for the ordo amoris, as one can easily see. It is clear that, other things being equal, a mother should love her child more than a child not her own, or, as we can also say, that her own child has a right to "be loved more." In the ordering of persons in the case of the love of friendship and of spousal love, it is a matter of an affinity which expresses itself in the fact that two persons understand each other much more deeply and that each grasps the beauty of the individuality of the other with far greater clarity than the beauty of other persons. This affinity does not presuppose a similarity in their nature; even very different characters can be friends. It is something far more mysterious. Certain people are granted the ability to see more deeply, to grasp the unique value of another personality in his or her individuality. Similarity only plays a role in this ordering of persons to one another insofar as it refers to the encounter of persons with each other in certain shared spheres of values. The question of which realm of goods and values two people are "incorporated" in is an important aspect of this objective ordering.

Yet this ordering of persons, which rests upon the identity of the individuality of each, can be very different in character. It can be mutual, in which case it is rooted in the special word which God has spoken between two people. On the other hand, it can also have a one-sided character, as is the case when a person has a special love for me and I play a great role in his life but without me for my part feeling the same for him. This ordering of persons can also have the character of something divinely ordained.

Before considering the two kinds of ordering between two people, it should be clearly emphasized that we are not dealing here with the question of the motivation of love, of the value datum that awakens love. We already dealt with this earlier and in great detail. Rather, the issue here is the problem of the ordo amoris, i.e., the factors which explain why I ought to love one person more than another, or rather, what degree of love and what place in my heart another person is entitled to.

The first kind of ordering of persons plays a decisive role in the love between friends and between man and woman; it concerns the "word" which God has "spoken" between two persons. This reveals itself in the fact that the essence of the other person flashes up for me in all its beauty and that the other also has a similar understanding for me. It also reveals itself in the fact that we encounter one another in one or several spheres of goods and values, in the fact that a true interpenetration of souls comes into existence, and that something significant stands between and above us. Claudel has wonderfully expressed this "word" which God has spoken between two people in a deep spousal love when he has Violaine say in the *Annonce faite à Marie*: "*Il y a un grand mystère entre nous*" ("There is a great mystery between us"). Of course, this ordering of persons is inseparably bound up with mutual love. A special word is spoken *between* two people only in the case of mutuality.

Mutuality does not mean that the love of both persons must be equally great or have the same character. It can be the case that someone loves a friend more than the friend loves him, or that someone plays a greater role in the life of a friend than the friend plays in his life. Certainly, this difference is not the ideal in friendship and even less so in spousal love. Yet as long as some mutuality exists, one can still speak of a word uttered by God between two people, a word that becomes a "commission" for both to love each other.[6]

The person who is ordered to me in such a way that God speaks a special word between the two of us has a greater right to my love than others with whom this word has not been spoken. And the fact that someone loves me in a special way and has a special understanding for me gives that person a greater claim on my love than that the claim possessed by one who loves me less. Yet the ordo amoris depends not only on the question whether such a word was spoken but above all what the nature of this word is, what "commission" of love it contains, that is, what kind and what degree of love this "commission" prescribes.

Even a one-sided ordination is not without significance for the ordo amoris. First of all, there can even be a "commission" to love a person in a special way when the person does not reciprocate my love. The overall beauty of the individuality of the other person which has been revealed to me in a special way can also contain a challenge to love him; thus it is not only the case that I will love such a person more than a person whose overall beauty I have not grasped, but it *should* also be so. The one-sided ordering of persons, however, operates in yet another way for the ordo amoris: the love with which someone approaches me contains an appeal to me to turn to them with love.[7]

---

6   This "word" spoken by God between two persons takes on an entirely new meaning in the case of an absolute equality of love, especially in the case of the love between man and woman. At present it suffices to point out this second moment, which is normative for the ordo amoris.

7   The fact that I owe someone gratitude also plays an important role for the ordo amoris. If out of kindness someone has conferred many benefits on me, clearly I

3. *The one-sided ordering of a person to me.* To the rank of a value and to the ordering of persons to one another, we can in fact add this as a third factor in the ordo amoris: the commitment of a person to me is, all other things being equal, a reason to turn toward him or her with more love than toward someone who loves me less.

We are not thinking here of the role which the love of another person can play in enkindling my love for him or her. It often happens, especially in the sphere of spousal love, that the love of one person enkindles the love of the other; a mutual ordering of persons in the above-mentioned sense exists and the love of the one person stirs up the love of the other. This, however, does not refer to the ordo amoris but to the role of the love of the other person as motivation of my love for him or her. We are also not thinking here of the way in which in general the attraction someone feels for me generates my own sympathy for him or her. This does not indeed necessarily happen, but sympathy, enthusiasm, and interest in me on the part of some other usually awakens in me a warmth and devotion toward the other. But at present we are concerned with the question of the extent to which the love of another person for me, even if as a personality the other does not particularly attract me, contains a "call" to turn toward him with love; whether my situation in relation to such a person is not different from the situation in relation to someone who has no real interest in me, and whether this situation does not require me to love the other more. It is the question of the extent to which his love for me grants him a certain "claim" on my love.

In this case we are dealing with the ordo amoris within the context of a particular kind of love which lies beyond both the love between friends and the love between man and woman. I cannot, after all, give myself the love of friendship, and in the event that I am not attracted to another person in this way, no amount of love with which he may approach me can generate love in me, unless of course his love reveals an entirely new aspect of his being which enkindles love in me. Thus in the case in which I am not attracted to someone, it is not a matter of this person having a claim to being loved as a friend; rather, I should turn to him in a loving way, and this will show itself in my concern for him, in owing him deeds of love (though in the absence of the love of friendship that usually lies at the root of these deeds of love), in making more time for him, and being with him more frequently. The fact that someone loves me in a special way means that he has been objectively entrusted to me. And

---

have a moral obligation to be grateful to that person. Of course, gratitude and love are not identical, though in this context it is not possible to go into the relationship between love and gratitude. Yet surely the one to whom I owe great gratitude has a great "claim" to be more loved by me than the person to whom I have no debt of gratitude. Other things being equal, the obligation to thank counts for something in the ordo amoris.

this ordering of persons calls me to show more concern for him than for some-one who does not love me.

The spirit of caritas demands that I not only treat the person who loves me as I am required to treat every neighbor, even the one who hates me, but to do such things as to take more time for him. When the question arises whether I should accept the invitation of this person or the invitation of anoth-er who may be more attractive or interesting to me yet who is far less inter-ested in me, I should take particular account of the one who loves me more and for whom my presence represents a deeper and greater joy and happiness. This always holds only on the assumption of other things being equal. Here we are concerned only with the factors affecting the ordo amoris, and so it suffices to say that the love with which someone approaches me implies an ordering of persons which also affects the ordo amoris, even if it is the actions which I perform out of love that are more at issue here than the experienced response.

It must, however, be added that the factor of how deeply another person loves me and what role I play in his life, also affects the ordo amoris within the mutual ordering of persons to one another and within their mutual love. When one of two friends, both of whom I love equally, loves me much more than the other does, then this is also a factor affecting the ordo amoris. Again, this does not mean that I must therefore love him more as a friend—this is not even within my control—but that in many situations I should give him priority, that I should have the awareness of owing him more love to the extent that this is expressed in actions.

4. *The categorial identity of a love.* A fourth factor which can determine the ordo amoris is closely bound up with the categorial identity of a love. The issue here concerns the role that the categorial identity plays for love as such [*Liebe schlechtweg*] or, better, of the extent to which there is a claim for a cer-tain degree of love as such that is based on the categorial identity of a love. Thus it is clear that, irrespective of the perspective of the hierarchy of values, the love for God, given its categorial character, which includes the absolute-ness of commitment and the gesture of adoration, must also possess an incom-parable excellence in respect to love as such [*Liebe schlechtweg*]. Clearly, the love of God is absolutely exclusive since after all there is only one God. To "love someone more than everything else," to love above all things, clearly refers to love as such. Something similar obtains in the case of the love between man and woman, as we are about to show.

Spousal love and marriage. The categorial identity of spousal love, the element of decision for the other that it contains, its unique commitment to the other, the giving of one's heart—all of this implies that the one who loves should give this love the first place in his heart. It is in fact not just a claim that the other has, but this love formally involves the tendency to occupy the first place. We expect that Romeo will love Juliet more than all other persons. In our context it is important to see that a spousal love, simply on the basis of its categorial identity, has a legitimate claim to occupy the first place—a claim which normally, as long as love is in full bloom, is fulfilled by itself.

When we say that spousal love because of its categorial identity must be first among my loves and when we therefore say that I should love the spousally beloved person most of all, then in speaking of love we obviously mean not spousal love but love as such [*Liebe schlechtweg*]. For as we saw, we can only love one person with spousal love at one and the same time. It would be senseless to lay down as a commandment that I ought have the most spousal love for a certain person. The question of more or less in comparison to other persons cannot be meaningfully posed in the context of this essentially exclusive category of love. Yet it is with good reason that we say that the person who is loved with spousal love has a claim, on the basis of the categorial identity of this love, to be loved the most in the sense of love as such.

When we speak of the ordo amoris we can be thinking about the factors that determine whether I should love one person more than another. But we can also be thinking about the factors that require a person to occupy the highest place and to possess my heart completely. There is no place for this difference in the love for God, the love for the absolute person. Here the priority over all other categories of love is absolute and everything which we have already considered—value rank, categorial identity, the degree and quality of love—all clearly demand that I not only love God more than any creature but also that I grant Him a place in my heart which is incomparable with the place occupied by even the most beloved human person.

Yet there are two questions that arise as soon as we turn our attention to the love for a human person. First, who has a claim to be loved more than another? Whom should I love more? And second, when does a person have the claim to occupy the first place in my heart, that is, not only to be loved more but to be the most beloved person (in the sense of love as such)?[8]

---

8   We can have two different things in mind when we speak of the first place in the heart of a person. I can first of all ask which person I love most of all with love as such. Or I can ask whether this love is the greatest of which I am capable. Many people, as already mentioned, never meet the person who would awaken the greatest love of which they are capable. Yet they can nevertheless love some one person more than anyone else, a person who plays the greatest role in their life. Of course, we mean something entirely different when we compare different people and say that the love of someone like Jonathan for David is still much greater than that of Carlos for Marquis Posa; here we are thinking of the objective greatness and depth of their love, which varies according to the different levels of depth of these persons and according to their capacity for love. The highest love of a person, the highest, greatest of which they are capable, may be much smaller than the love of another person who is much more capable of love and is a much deeper person. There is clearly a difference between the question of the greatest love a certain person is capable of, the love in which he gives his all in love, and the question of the objectively greatest and deepest love in itself.

We now want to go into the question of when there is an obligation to grant another person the uncontested place of primacy in my heart. Thus far we have considered the factors which are normative for the relative ought to love someone more; now we turn to the question of what underlies the obligation to grant someone the first place in my heart.

The question arises whether the obligation to grant a spousally beloved person the first place (in the sense of love as such) exists even when a mother or a brother has previously occupied the first place in my heart. I meet someone with whom I fall in love and whom I want to marry. This person reciprocates my love and we get engaged. My mother or sister had already long before an exceptional place in my heart. The mother or sister was *the* person on whom I depended, who played the greatest role in my life, whom I loved above all. This does not always come to an end because I come to love someone with this entirely different spousal love. The obligation to grant the premier place, which, as we saw, is rooted in spousal love as such, varies greatly according to how perfect the ordering of the bride and groom to each other is, according to how deep and ardent the love for the other is which is granted to me, and also—and this is important—according to how great the love of the other is for me. There are extraordinary situations in which a mother, a daughter, or a son is *the* person in my life, situations in which, because of their extraordinary personality, a value-response by me grants one of them the place of primacy in my subjectivity [*Eigenleben*]. In these cases the mutual relationship is so unique, so deep and so inspiring for both, that it transcends all categorial kinds of love and on the basis of its own depth rightfully claims the first place in the hearts of both persons. While a spousal love is not excluded when such a relationship already exists, there is nevertheless from the start a conflict between the material requirement of the unique relationship toward the mother, the daughter, the sister, the brother, the friend, and the formal requirement of the spousal love. Both legitimately demand the place of primacy in the heart of a person. The conflict is resolved in this case by the depth and sublimity of the relationship. This material consideration that is present in an individual case prevails over the priority rooted in the category of love. Of course, this implies, even if this prevailing is unavoidable, an imperfection in the spousal love, which then falls short of what it ought to be according to its genius.

Needless to say, these unusual situations in which someone is legitimately "*the*" person outside of the context of a spousal love must be clearly distinguished from all cases of illegitimate attachments. There is the mother who is attached to her child through an animalistic bond and in her child sees an extended ego, thereby granting the child a fundamental priority even over her husband. Or there is the son or daughter who is so dominated by the mother that they never arrive at any life of their own but always remain clinging to her skirt. These cases are not deserving of the name of real love; they lack both the value-responding foundation as well as the depth and sublimity of a relationship.

In cases of an extraordinary value datum, cases in which the beloved person is such an unusual personality that here a special value-response coincides with all the other elements of the ordering of persons to each other and the affinity between them, the categorial requirements no longer play a normative role. Whether this most beloved person is a daughter, a male or female friend, or a mother, loses significance in the individual value-response; after all, one does not love this person because he or she is a mother, a daughter, a son, but because the person is this individual, this personality.

There emerge, then, two different hierarchies. The first is exclusively based on the unusual value rank of one or both persons, as well as on the extraordinary affinity, the deep mutual understanding and the encounter of the persons in a high realm of goods and values. When someone is granted such a relationship, then it has a claim to the premier place among human relationships in his or her life; indeed, it legitimately demands this place. This requirement is exclusively rooted in the material or qualitative nature of this love and is therefore dependent upon the special individual nature of a love.

The second is the requirement which arises from the categorial nature of the love between man and woman. It is of a formal nature and is grounded in the general nature of this category of love, in the exclusivity of this love, in the totality of its commitment and the way in which it involves a decision for the other. There is no other relationship, be it to a mother, to a child, or to a friend, in which there is such a formal requirement to occupy the first place. This primacy can, as we saw, legitimately occur on the basis of individual personalities, but it is then in no way a "fulfillment" of what belongs to the category of love. On the contrary, this exceptional place in my heart is entirely beyond the categorial nature of this love.

In the case of spousal love the fulfillment of the formal requirement of this category of love occurs when the spousally beloved person is simply the most important human person for me and occupies the first place in my heart and is loved "more" than any other person. Prescinding from such extraordinary cases in which another love because of its individual nature is justified in receiving the place of primacy, we can therefore say that a spousal love when it has led to the full interpenetration of souls [*Ineinanderblick der Liebe*] should have priority over every other love.

This holds *a fortiori* when this spousal love has led to marriage and has found a unique fulfillment through consent (*consensus*) and bodily union. This is the reason why in the ordo amoris the husband or wife occupies the primary place. This primacy is rooted in the interpenetration of souls proper to spousal love, in the categorial nature of this love, and in the consent and mutual bodily surrender which flows from this love.

Marriage is as such the consequence of the primacy of spousal love, which is grounded in its categorial nature. The fact that I go so far as even to unite my exterior life with the beloved, that I formally bind myself for my entire life, indeed that I desire to become "one flesh" with the beloved, grants this person a unique place in my life. The reality of marrying is the strongest objective expression of the primacy that is grounded in the interpenetration of souls proper to spousal love. When such a love exists and there is no objective obstacle to marrying, then one *ought* to marry.

While marriage is itself the result of the primacy of spousal love, it is at the same time also an intensification of this primacy. Just as the obligation to *faithfulness* becomes much more weighty in marriage, so too the obligation that this person be loved "more" than any other and that he or she occupy the first place in my heart.

The commitment of spousal love with its decision for the beloved clearly takes on a new character through the act of marrying, through the volitional commitment in which I choose once and for all to live *my* life with the other person, and above all through the unique surrender of myself in the consummation of marriage. We in no way wish to underestimate this intensification which is, on the one hand, an intensification and, on the other hand, something entirely new. The two demands for the primary place in my heart are related to each other like a seed is related to its full unfolding. A world separates them, and this is expressed in the fact that marriage is indissoluble and is a sacrament. This, however, does not refer directly to our problem.[9]

---

9   The indissolubility of marriage does not imply that a spouse may not be more attached to another person, such as a child or a parent, than to his or her own spouse. It is precisely this question of the primacy of love, the issue of loving someone "more" than another, which is here our problem. The entirely new situation which is constituted by marriage refers primarily to the indissolubility of marriage, a new kind of obligation to be faithful, etc. And the obligation to let my spouse occupy the first place also undergoes a great intensification. We are only *emphasizing* the primacy which is rooted in spousal love, because it is this which is most often overlooked and because, if it is not understood, the path to understanding the primacy of my spouse in my heart is blocked.

For as we already saw, when spousal love is missing in a marriage or when it only exists in a very rudimentary or imperfect form, marriage will not necessarily bring about this primacy.

The question of the indissolubility of marriage clearly represents something entirely new with regard to the ordo amoris. This is already apparent, as we saw, from the fact that mutual spousal love does not contain any obligation of indissolubility. We saw that when one person ceases to love, or when both cease to love, or when man and woman realize that they are not made for one another, it is entirely legitimate to dissolve the relationship. Not even an engagement creates a bond that cannot be broken in the case of weighty reasons.

And even in the case of a consent which has not yet been followed by consummation, when it is a *matrimonium ratum non consummatum*, the bond is not indissoluble. We already saw this in the chapter on faithfulness. Even the duties which result from the consent and the community formed by marriage do not belong to the ordo amoris in the strict sense.

But it would nevertheless be false to say that the act of marrying and the act of consummating the marriage give rise to the obligation to love my spouse more than any other person *even in the absence of the underlying spousal love.*

We cannot, however, conclude our discussion of the question of the primacy of spousal love without pointing out the strange justification of the primacy of marital love in St. Thomas. It seems to us to contain several weighty errors. St. Thomas says in regard to the love of a husband for his wife that he should love her above all other persons because she is a part of his body.

In the first place, the classical motivation of marriage is here ignored. The other, after all, becomes a part of my body *because* I love him or her. St. Thomas assumes that this primacy of love only begins in marriage; being married to the other person is seen as a *motive* for marital love rather than seeing consent and consummation as *consequences* of the fulfillment of spousal love. According to this conception, there would be no reason to love the other person in a special way before he or she is married to me.[10]

But there is here yet another error in addition to the mistake which lies in failing to understand that a requirement of primacy already lies in spousal love, and also in addition to the mistake which lies in seeing marital love exclusively as a result of consent and bodily union. The error is not *only* the reduction of the priority in the ordo amoris to the consent and consummation, to the act of marrying, while failing to see the obligation which is already rooted in spousal love as such. The bond which arises from the consent and consummation of marriage is, after all, not presented as the reason for love but the fact that the spouse is a "part of my body." It is assumed that the love of my body is extended to the other person, that it is here a matter of an extension of self-love. We already saw earlier how impossible it is to derive the love of other persons from the love of oneself. Yet here the ultimate degree of intimacy with another person, the "becoming one flesh" and the ultimate in *being-close*, is seen as the motive and primacy of this love.

Here the confusion of cause and effect is taken to an extreme. This closeness, this intimacy is after all the fulfillment of an existing love and is in no way its motivation. It is because I love the other with spousal love that I want

---

10 What sometimes underlies this tendency to derive love from unity is the idea that love can only be taken seriously when one is obliged to it. Marital love, for example, is only taken seriously if I am obliged to it on the basis of the act of marrying. The spousal love which precedes marriage, which in truth ought to be the reason for the act of marrying, is not taken seriously by many. Since the idea of obligation predominates, one takes one's cue from cases in which a unity between persons already exists for one or another reason—yet without asking whether this unity was perhaps first constituted through love. Thus it is that one speaks of marital love as a love which is the result of an act of marrying, because it is obligatory in a new way as a result of marrying. In truth, the meaningful motivation for the act of marrying is spousal love, which in its categorial nature as love is identical with marital love.

to be so close to him or her. Being-close would not be a *basis* for loving the other. It is the result of the love and it loses its true, divinely ordained unitive meaning as soon as one sees the other person as an extended ego.

Any kind of attachment which originates in the fact that I view the other as an extended ego is, after all, not a real love but something completely different, as we already saw above.

The love of friendship. Now that we have clarified the true reasons for the premier place that the love for a spouse or for a spousally loved person should have within human love, we turn to the factors that, in the setting of the love of friendship, can make us love one person more than another. In speaking of the love for a friend we designate a particular category of love, but one which extends over a wide range with innumerable nuances, as we have already seen. Although even within spousal love there are many differences based on the quality, depth, sublimity, intensity, and greatness of the love, the categorial character of spousal love is nevertheless unambiguous and is sharply demarcated from the other categories of love. This results from the exclusive character of this love and from the decision for the other that belongs to it.

But with love for a friend there is clearly a great range that touches even the categorial character. The word "friend" can have a very different ring and content in different cases. We can call friends people with whom we have been bound for years in friendly relations and with whom we have had shared certain experiences. But we can also call friends people with whom we are deeply united and who play a fundamental role in our life. In between are found innumerable different relations ranging from slight closeness to great closeness. We can call people friends because we are of one mind with them in certain areas, because we like them, because we are sure of the benevolence we feel for each other and of the warm interest we take in each other. But from such friendship there is a long way to the deep relationship of a David and Jonathan, of a Pylades and Orestes, of a St. Augustine and Alypius. The place which a friend should have in my heart according to the ordo amoris, clearly depends on the nature of the friendship, its intensity, on the degree to which the friends are ordered to each other, and on the particular word spoken by God between them.

The categorial character of love for a friend differs from spousal love, love of children for their parents, love of parents for their children, etc., in that it does not involve any obligation to love one friend more than another one; it does not tell us what place a friend can claim in our heart.

As long as we think only of the categorial character of love for a friend, about which we spoke in our book, *Die Metaphysik der Gemeinschaft* (The Metaphysics of Community), and not of the particular "word" that is spoken between the friends in a particular individual friendship, we can only say that each friend, even the most distant one, can claim more love from us than a mere acquaintance who is not our friend.

We prescind here from love of neighbor and from the obligations that flow from the need and neediness of another. We only want to say that the most distant friend has a claim that I sacrifice a certain amount of time for him and that I take an interest in his well-being, an interest that I do not owe to a mere acquaintance. What would be an unkindness towards a friend is nothing of the kind towards a mere acquaintance—as long as the acquaintance is not in some special predicament which gives rise to some higher claim on my attention that derives from caritas.[11]

The love of parents for their children. A different situation obtains with respect to the ordo amoris in the love of parents for their children. Here the factor that is decisive for the place proper to children in the ordo amoris is the objective ordering of persons to each other, which is prior to all value-response to the individuality of persons.

The factors that motivate this love over and above the objective ordering

---

11 There is a vast space that is filled by people with whom we are more or less famil-iar. In this space are found people whom we do not like or to whom we are indif-ferent, who do not interest us or attract us in any way, but also people whom we do like, whose presence sometimes gives us joy, with whom we are on friendly terms. Of course, for all of them we should have the deep interest and the true kindly attention in Christ that belongs to real love of neighbor. And of course we should avoid all antipathy and indifference in our judgment about these people, in our readiness to help them when they are in need, and in our wish to discover in them all that is best and most beautiful. But all the same it is entirely legitimate if we feel that God has not spoken any particular word between us and that a friend-ship is at present out of the question. This holds even for acquaintances whom we like and find agreeable but with whom there is no basis for a real friendship.

And yet the line that separates the likeable acquaintance whom I appreciate from a real friend—we are thinking here of the lowest level in the realm of friend-ship—is by no means as clear and unambiguous as in the case of spousal love. The question, "Do you love me?" when asked in the setting of spousal love is an unam-biguous question; the difference between spousal love and friendship is, independ-ent of the degrees of depth and intensity, an unambiguous difference. But the ques-tion, "Is this person here an acquaintance or a friend?" is by no means so unam-biguous. All the same, there is a real difference between an acquaintance towards whom I have kindly feelings, whom I like, whom I enjoy meeting in society, and a real friend, even one who is not a close friend. As soon as I call someone a friend I imply that we belong together, that each reaches into the subjectivity [*Eigenleben*] of the other, and I imply that a certain word is spoken between us and that we are concerned for each other. This is why it makes good sense to say, "While I like this person and appreciate him, he is not my friend." Friendship pre-supposes a mutuality of love, and not just an objectively given mutuality but one that is declared. Each friendship must be "entered into"; and even if this does not happen by means of a social act or by means of a one-time explicit declaration, even if it happens by gradually growing into the friendship, it is still the case that both know that they can call each other friends. Aristotle points this out in a won-

will be examined later when we treat of the different kinds of love one by one.[12] There we will examine the value-response to the mere fact that the child is a person, we will also examine the preciousness of a human being, who besides exists in such a touching, helpless, and needy situation. This value cannot be detached from the objective ordering of persons, which after all helps to throw this value into relief. But at present we are not speaking of the motives of the love of parents for their children, but of the question of the ordo amoris. Here we have to distinguish between the small child, up until the age of about 10 or 12, and the grown child. In the case of the small child the love of the parents has a special character from the time the child is still completely unconscious until it has definitely developed a certain personality. Not only is the child dependent on the parents in a unique way, not only does it constantly need the help and care of the parents, but the *love* of the parents responds here to something different. Besides the response to the sheer value of the child as a human being and besides the response that comes later on to the value of the grown-up individuality of the child, this love is a specifically hopeful, anticipatory love. During this period one's own child claims in one respect to rank right behind the love of the spouses for each other.[13] It is the category of parental love that calls for this preferential position for the child, and calls for it independent of the particular character or personality of the child.

---

derful way in saying that I not only have to know that my friend loves me, and my friend not only has to know that I love him, but my friend has to know that I know that he loves me, and I have to know that he knows that I love him. It could after all be that my friend and I both know that each is loved by other, but neither of us would have to know that the other knows that he is loved.

Each friendship must be "entered into," and even if the love for the friend precedes this phase of constituting the friendship, the love receives its full categorial character only through the constituting of the friendship. A bond then exists between me and the friend, a bond that does not exist between me and the one who is a likeable, appreciated, enjoyable acquaintance. This is what makes it possible to say: as soon as someone is a friend, as soon as I can call him a friend, as soon as he is granted this place in my heart, I owe him "more" in the way of love than I owe an acquaintance. He has a claim to be loved "more" and in particular to be treated differently by me, to be given a different kind of concern and interest, a claim to receive deeds of love. This much can be said, even though the measure of the love and of the concern and of the entire way of showing attention depends entirely on the individual "word" spoken between the friends and on the closeness and depth of the friendship.

12 [This is one of the places where von Hildebrand refers to a continuation of the present work; he seems to have planned further chapters that he did not complete. Trans.]

13 We say "in one respect," because different requirements that derive from special individual relations can intersect here, for example, an extraordinary relation to a mother, to a brother or a sister, or to a friend.

It is in respect of loving care, of degree of concern, of giving attention, and performing deeds of love that the categorial character of this love implies that it should be preferred to all other human loves apart from spousal love. In this respect one's own child occupies a very special position. It has this position first of all because it is a child and hence needs care and loving devotion; secondly, because it is *my* child and not someone else's child. The first fact gives the child a priority in comparison with friends, adult siblings and parents, none of whom has the particular neediness of a child. But this priority shows itself only when it is *my* child, when this objective ordering of persons comes into play. And besides, this second factor is all by itself a reason for preferring my own child, as we can see from the fact that my own children have a priority over other people's children in claiming my love.

We should stress that this priority also holds for adopted children. Here, too, we find an objective ordering of persons that is independent of whether the ordering is objectively given as with my own child, or is the result of a social act of adopting performed in a fully responsible way.

It is not hard to understand that one's own child, whether one's own by birth or by adoption, occupies such a privileged place with regard to loving care, concern, being given attention. For the relation to one's child is here bound up with a special responsibility, with a moral duty that would be present even if one's heart were cold and insensitive. This priority is rooted in the objective ordering of persons as well as in the fact of the child "needing" our love and being entrusted to us in its helplessness.

But it would be a great mistake to think that one's own child has only a claim to loving care. It also has a claim to receive love in the sense of the voice of the heart, in the sense of the lived value-response of a very special kind. The child appeals to our love qua love. It appeals to our tender devotion, to the special warmth of love; it should be encompassed by this love and grow up sheltered in it, so that it can thrive and grow in the sun of this love. No act of providing for a child out of duty, however perfect the act, can replace this love. Here the words "*tua res agitur*" hold in an eminent way; it is my concern to love the child; my own child is an "*amandus*," one to be loved.

It could of course happen, as we have said, that an extraordinary relation to a mother or a father or a brother of sister or friend could enable me to love such a person more than I love my own child. But this should never limit the love and devotion to my own child, should never overshadow this love; my child should always receive the full measure of love that it needs. In fact, the special, individual relation to someone other than my child should in a certain sense make me more capable of love in general and should thus empower me to love my child better. In the case of my love for my spouse, this empowerment to love my child is obvious. But this should of course be the case analogously with all great and deep loves.

The preference of beloved persons based on the ordo amoris in constrast with the illegitimate preference of them

In connection with the ordo amoris we want to return to a question that we have already touched upon. On the one hand, there is without a doubt an ordo amoris even within natural love and there is a moral duty to do justice to it. I ought to give preference to a spouse, a bride, my children, my parents, my friends. This refers not so much to the love itself as to its degree, its depth, and also to the benefits (including acts of hindering evil) performed for the beloved person. It refers to the sphere of action and to the primacy of committing oneself to the objective good for the beloved. It is only right to grant to the existing relation of love and to the existing community of love the privilege of being preferred in many situations and in many respects. On the other hand, love of neighbor forbids the egoism for the other that we discussed at length in chapter 11, an attitude to which the just-mentioned preference can easily lead. Where is the line separating the justified and indeed obligatory preference deriving from the ordo amoris from the unjustified preference? We have already referred to this difficult problem.

We said that any preference that takes no account of all other objective requirements is not allowed. It is without a doubt entirely legitimate to try to get my wife a good seat on the train. It is also entirely legitimate and flows from the ordo amoris for this to concern me more than whether some stranger gets a good seat. But as soon as I see that some very elderly person or perhaps a sick or handicapped person is looking for a good seat, I have to give the preference to that person. There are many duties that in certain situations outweigh the requirements of the ordo amoris.

But we want to stress here that the requirements of the ordo amoris objectively exist and are not as such eliminated just because caritas requires us in certain situations to yield to other requirements. Indeed, the ordo amoris is so far from contradicting caritas that caritas in fact requires us to take account of the obligations of the ordo amoris as long as other moral obligations do not outweigh these.

It is after all a general law that the obligation imposed by certain morally relevant goods should in certain situations yield to the obligation of higher morally relevant goods. Other things being equal, I should keep my promise to help a friend in some matter of importance to him or her. But if on the way to my friend I come across someone whose life is endangered, I should at least for the time being set aside the fulfillment of that promise. Or if two people whom I do not know are in great need and I can help only one of them, then obviously I should choose the one with the greater need. This law holds for all situations in which the obligation deriving from the ordo amoris comes into conflict with the obligation of a higher morally relevant good. Here the higher good should predominate.

But caritas precisely obliges us to do justice to the obligations of the ordo amoris. It would be an offense against caritas if in the setting of spousal love one person was not primarily concerned with the details of the well-being of the beloved person, provided of course that the right of some stranger to be considered first did not oblige the lover to yield the first place to that person. But apart from such a circumstance it would be a lack of love, a deficiency of goodness on the part of the lover if he did not take account, down to the last detail, of the primacy that flows from the *logos* of his spousal relation and from the categorial character of his love. The same holds analogously for parents in their relation to their children. My own children have, other things being equal, a claim that I as parent make a primary commitment for their well-being, that I give preference to their well-being over the well-being of other people's children. This is why one has often rightly insisted that caritas has to show itself first of all towards those who are close to myself or with whom I live at home. Whoever ignores the obligations deriving from the ordo amoris also sins against caritas. And this brings us to another important theme in the relation of the ordo amoris and caritas.

Caritas, along with the triumphant goodness that lives in it, also requires from me that in my different relations based on natural love for other persons I act in accord with the genius of these relations, that I do justice to the claim that the other has on my special attention in the setting of our mutual love. What would be unkind in one relation is by no means unkind in another. In a close friendship it would be unkind not to tell the friend about events in my life, events that I would not have to tell some friend who is less close to me. If when separated from a person whom I love spousally I write only once a month, then I offend against the ordo amoris and thus commit an unkindness. But there is no unkindness in writing only once a month to a friend from whom I am separated. And many more such examples could be adduced.

This extends to the sphere of expression, especially the expression of tenderness. For spousal love many things are appropriate that are not appropriate in a relation of friendship. Of course, I prescind here from the one-flesh union that goes far beyond the sphere of tenderness and is allowable and appropriate only within marriage. For example, someone who loves another spousally rightly feels it to be a deficiency of love if the other has no need to kiss him. I speak here of the need, because there may be good moral reasons not to satisfy this need before marriage or at least before an engagement. But something is missing if there is no need.

In conclusion we can say that the ordo amoris conditions all of our behavior towards the beloved person. The spirit of caritas, too, requires the fulfillment of what flows from the ordo amoris. What in the setting of one relation of love would be an unkindness, would not necessarily be so in the setting of another. The factors that condition the inner structure of the relation are, first of all, the categorial character of the love, and then secondly, the quality and degree of the love as love [*Liebe schlechtweg*]—or, as we could also say, the "word" that God has spoken between two persons.[14]

14 Back in chapter 6 we mentioned the difference between the union of persons that comes from membership in the same community and the union that comes from love. In speaking of the intentio unionis and in stressing that personal union can only come from mutual love, we made reference to the objective union, completely different in kind, which for instance results from belonging to the same state or nation and which does not presuppose that the individuals know or (even less) love one another.

In my book, *Die Metaphysik der Gemeinschaft* (The Metaphysics of Community), I explored in some detail the way in which love is involved in these communities which do not originate in love, and the extent to which this already existing union can provide the basis for love, or in other words, to what extent it appeals to love. This varies very much according to the kind of community and the realm of goods that makes up the theme of the community, and also according to whether or not the community is one in which one can become a member without doing anything or knowing about the community.

Needless to say, the fact that someone is a member of the mystical body of Christ, that he or she is a believing Catholic, makes for a special kind of union that cannot be compared with the union of persons within a state or a nation or even within mankind. The appeal to love, too, is also present in an extraordinary way on account of the incomparable depth and closeness of the union.

Here, too, one could speak of an ordo amoris in an analogous sense. First of all, one can raise the question about the ordo of the union and even about the resulting obligation. Which community should establish a deeper union among the members of the community? Which should be more important for us, belonging to the same state, or belonging to the same nation, or belonging to mankind? What closeness and depth of the lived union should be possessed by the consciousness of belonging to the same community? What kind of feeling of solidarity should we have for someone whom we discover to be our countryman or a citizen of the state to which we belong? All of these questions refer to the ordo of union and of the experience of union; indirectly they refer also to the issue of the claim to love that arises from such union. We prescind from all of this here, since our specific subject was the ordo in the setting of love, that is, the ordo amoris in the strict sense of the word amor.

Conclusion

We want to bring this book to a conclusion by pointing out the three kinds of self-donation [*Hingabe*] found in the realm of love.

The first is stepping out of my own world [*Eigenleben*] in the manner proper to love of neighbor. In this kind of self-donation my own world, my subjectivity [*Eigenleben*] is not abandoned, but it keeps silent, so to speak. I leave it behind, as can be seen from the fact that my own happiness is in no way thematic. Such commitment has nothing to do with my happiness: the other is exclusively thematic. But it has to be stressed that my own world, my subjectivity is not thrown away in this love; rather, one steps out of it.

The second kind of self-donation is what we find in the quality of caritas. The flowing goodness—the incomparable manner in which the loving person pours himself out—amounts to a sublime self-donation that is the absolute antithesis to all egoism, to all hardness of heart, and to all indifference. This love goes hand in hand with love of neighbor, which after all lives from the spirit of caritas. But even if love of neighbor is not possible apart from this spirit of caritas, which belongs essentially to this love, the spirit of caritas is nevertheless not in its essential identity linked only to the categorial theme of love of neighbor, for it can also be found in other categories of love, as we saw. Caritas is not only present in the love for God, which as a kind of love is entirely different from love of neighbor, but it can only constitute itself in the love for God. Thus we have to distinguish between the self-donation contained in the spirit of caritas, the self-donation in which the heart of the one who loves is melted in holy goodness and kindness, from the act of stepping out of one's subjectivity. The former self-donation does not involve stepping out of my subjectivity but rather being transfigured in my subjectivity. This is why it is clearly different from the latter kind of self-donation. It is the self-donation of goodness and kindness.

There is finally a third kind of self-donation; it clearly differs from the previous two. This is the donation of the heart, of my subjectivity [*Eigenleben*], in the sense that the beloved person becomes the center of my life and the source of my most personal happiness, for which I depend on the beloved person. This kind of self-donation is found in its highest form in the love for God, but it is also found in spousal love. It is found in some way in every deep and intense natural love. It characterizes any love, whatever its category, in which the beloved person stands at the center of my life. This self-donation cannot be separated from the intentio unionis, which is necessarily included in it.

It is easy to see that this kind of self-donation is incompatible with the first one, which consists in stepping out of my subjectivity. But it is not only compatible with the second kind of self-donation, but it can reach its real fulfillment only when joined to it, only when the spirit of caritas transfigures this third kind of love.

If we want to penetrate the nature of love and the different categories of love, it is all-important to distinguish clearly these three kinds of self-donation. It is above all important to exclude once and for all the error of confusing self-lessness with the categorial character of love of neighbor. We must understand that self-donation and intentio unionis, far from excluding each other, are in fact closely bound together, for the third form of self-donation necessarily includes the intentio unionis.

*   *   *   *

We are perhaps entitled to hope that this book constitutes a decisive step forward in the philosophical exploration of the nature of love. We of course fully realize how far we are from doing full justice to this primordial datum of inexhaustible depth, which is a wonder in the realm of data and fills us with a deep marveling. But who could possibly do full justice to this fundamental reality! Can we not say with St. Augustine: "What can anyone say in speaking of Thee? And yet woe to them who speak not of Thee at all, since they who say most are but dumb" (*Confessions*, I, 4)?

And so we hope that, in spite of all its deficiencies, this book illuminates the nature of love more deeply. Indeed, we even hope that in these investigations something is revealed of the inexhaustible depth and the incomparable glory of this most central of all personal acts. We hope to have brought to light something of what is meant in the Song of Songs when it is said that "love is strong as death." We also hope to have made evident something of the breadth of love that comes from the mysterious *coincidentia oppositorum* (union of apparent opposites) of love: its strength and tenderness, its meekness and audacity. Siegfried Johannes Hamburger speaks magnificently of this when he says: "Let us seek to look into the face and heart of love, this most primordial of all primordial realities, and let us try really to open ourselves for the sublime freedom and greatness that belongs to love in the midst of all its tenderness—and then this essential audacity, this fundamental audacity will shine forth on the face of love."[1]

---

1   Siegfried Johannes Hamburger, "Die Kühnheit der Liebe," in B. Schwarz, ed., *Wahrheit, Wert und Sein* (Regensburg, 1970), 100.

Bibliography of the Philosophical Writings of Dietrich von Hildebrand[1]

The Art of Living (with Alice von Hildebrand). Manchester, NH: Sophia Institute Press, 1994.

Ästhetik [Aesthetics]. Vol. 1. Stuttgart: Kohlhammer, 1977.

Ästhetik [Aesthetics]. Vol. 2. Stuttgart: Kohlhammer, 1984.

"Das Cogito und die Erkenntnis der realen Welt" [The Cogito and our Knowledge of the Real World]. Edited by Josef Seifert. *Aletheia* 6 (1993–1994): 2–27.

Das Wesen der Liebe [The Nature of Love]. Regensburg: Josef Habbel, 1971.

Die Idee der sittlichen Handlung [The Concept of Moral Action]. Darmstadt: Wissenschaftliche Buchgesellschaft, 1969.

Die Menschheit am Scheideweg [Mankind at the Crossroads]. Regensburg: Habbel Verlag, 1955.

Die Metaphysik der Gemeinschaft [The Metaphysics of Community]. Regensburg: Josef Habbel, 1955.

Ethics. Chicago: Franciscan Herald Press, 1972.

Graven Images: Substitutes for True Morality (with Alice Jourdain). New York: David McKay Company, 1957.

The Heart: An Analysis of Divine and Human Affectivity. South Bend, Indiana: St. Augustine's Press, 2007.

Man and Woman. Manchester: Sophia Institute Press, 1992.

Marriage. Manchester: Sophia Institute Press, 1984.

---

1   For a much more extensive list of von Hildebrand's writings, including his religious and political writings, see the bibliography compiled by Adolf Preis, "Hildebrand Bibliographie," in the journal *Aletheia* 5 (1992): 363-430. The Dietrich von Hildebrand Legacy Project will provide for a fuller and constantly updated bibliography on its website, www.hildebrandlegacy.org.

Memoiren und Aufsätze gegen den Nationalsozialismus [Memoirs and Anti-Nazi Writings]. Edited by Ernst Wenisch. Mainz: Matthias Grünewald Verlag, 1994.

Moralia [Ethical Studies]. Regensburg: Josef Habbel, 1980.

Morality and Situation Ethics. Chicago: Franciscan Herald Press, 1966.

The New Tower of Babel. Manchester: Sophia Institute Press, 1994.

Purity. Steubenville, Ohio: Franciscan University Press, 1989.

Sittlichkeit und ethische Werterkenntnis [Morality and Ethical Value Knowledge]. Darmstadt: Wissenschaftliche Buchgesellschaft, 1969.

"The Three Modes of Participation in Value." *International Philosophy Quarterly* 1 (1961): 58–84.

What is Philosophy? New York/London: Routledge, 1990.

About the Author

Dietrich von Hildebrand was a philosopher, religious writer, anti-Nazi activist, and proponent of beauty and culture. Born October 12, 1889 as the son of a famous German sculptor, von Hildebrand grew up in the rich artistic setting of Florence and Munich. He studied philosophy under Edmund Husserl, the founder of phenomenology and a giant of twentieth century philosophy, and under Adolf Reinach, whom he regarded as his primary teacher. He was profoundly influenced by his close friend, German philosopher Max Scheler, who helped to pave the way for his conversion to Catholicism in 1914.

By 1930 von Hildebrand had become an important voice in German Catholicism, perhaps best known for his pioneering work on man and woman and on marriage. One can trace the chapter on marriage in *Gaudium et spes* of Vatican II back to von Hildebrand's writings in the 20's in which he argued that the marital act has not only a procreative meaning but a no less significant unitive meaning.

But it was above all in his ethical writings that von Hildebrand distinguished himself, beginning already in his dissertation on moral action (1914) and then in his foundational philosophical work, *Ethics* (1953), in which he developed the concept of value which underlies his entire work. While at the University of Munich, von Hildebrand wrote his treatise on the nature of community, *Die Metaphysik der Gemeinschaft* (The Metaphysics of Community, 1930), in which he used the resources of phenomenology to rethink fundamental issues of social philosophy and of moral philosophy.

Von Hildebrand had an unusual affinity for beauty which he never considered a mere luxury but a human necessity. Toward the very end of von Hildebrand's life, this lifelong passion came to fruition in the magisterial two-volume study in the philosophy of beauty, the *Ästhetik* (Aesthetics, 1977, 1984).

When Hitler came to power in 1933, von Hildebrand left his native Germany, and dedicated himself to resisting Nazism. He moved to Vienna and founded a journal for combating at the level of philosophical first principles the rising Nazi ideology and for defending the independence of Austria against Germany. With the German occupation of Austria in 1938, von Hildebrand became a political fugitive; fleeing through Czechoslovakia, Switzerland, France, Portugal, and Brazil, he eventually arrived in the United States in 1940.

In addition to his primarily philosophical works, to which *The Nature of Love* should be classified, von Hildebrand also wrote many works unfolding the faith and morals of Catholicism, such as *In Defense of Purity* (1927), *Marriage* (1929), *Liturgy and Personality* (1933), and *Transformation in Christ* (1940), now recognized as a classic of Christian spirituality.

In the United States von Hildebrand taught at Fordham University from 1941 until his retirement in 1960. Many of his most important philosophical works—among them *Ethics* (1953), *Morality and Situation Ethics* (1955), *What is Philosophy?* (1960), *The Heart* (1965), *The Nature of Love* (1971), and *Ästhetik* (1977, 1984)—were completed in the United States. Von Hildebrand died in New Rochelle, New York on January 26, 1977.

About the Dietrich von Hildebrand Legacy Project

The Legacy Project was founded in 2004 to preserve and promote the thought and witness of Dietrich von Hildebrand. For further information, please visit www.hildebrandlegacy.org.

About the Translators

John F. Crosby was born in Washington, D.C., and grew up in Mobile, Alabama. He received his B.A. from Georgetown University in 1966 and his Ph.D. from the University of Salzburg, Austria, in 1970. His teacher in philosophy was Dietrich von Hildebrand. He has taught at the University of Dallas, the University of Salzburg, the Lateran University in Rome, and at the International Academy of Philosophy in Liechtenstein; since 1990 he has been teaching at Franciscan University of Steubenville. He has published extensively on the thought of John Henry Cardinal Newman, as well as on the thought of Karol Wojtyla/Pope John Paul II. His books on personalist philosophy are *The Selfhood of the Human Person* (1996) and *Personalist Papers* (2003). Previous translations from German include works of Dietrich von Hildebrand and of Adolf Reinach. He and his wife, Pia, are the parents of six children.

John Henry Crosby, the eldest of these six, was born in Dallas, Texas. As the son of an Austrian mother, he grew up with German as his first language. He studied philosophy, history, and literature at Franciscan University of Steubenville, Ohio, and violin performance at Carnegie Mellon University. Together with his father, John F. Crosby, he founded in 2004 the Dietrich von Hildebrand Legacy Project, which he continues to direct.

Index

105–106, 112, 117, 126, 148, 192, 222, 301
world of value, xv, 63, 75–78, 81, 165, 217, 225–227, 260
"worthiness" of being loved, 120, 355

yearning: for belonging to the beloved, 282; for closer contact with valuable goods, 112; for eternal salvation, 218; for eternal

union with God, 141, 215; for goods with high value, 31; for happiness, 27, 123; for love, 32–33; for perfection of the self, 123; for redemption through caritas, 307; for the return of love, 57, 132; for truth, 33; for union, 32, 49–51, 133, 144; for value, 36

zeal, 70, 119, 213, 257, 334